Pre-Publication Acclaim for *From Refugee to Consul: An American Adventure*

Since Joseph Pulitzer, through Theodore von Kármán to George Széll and others, Hungarian expatriates in America have contributed mightily to the economy, culture, and safety of their adopted country. Less well known, but also significant were the contributions of John and Helen Mary Szablya, refugees from Communist Hungary of 1956, after the brutal suppression of the popular uprising that year. Helen Szablya's new memoir, *From Refugee to Consul: An American Adventure,* while a sequel to her colorful description of life under Nazi and Communist tyranny (*My Only Choice*) presents us with ample evidence that this highly talented couple belongs to the ranks of most influential Hungarian émigrés in America.

First of all this is a love song from Helen to her late husband John. John is present everywhere, including the pages on which he is not mentioned, as a teacher, a professional, a family man, a lover, a supporter.

Next, Helen's pride in her widespread and diverse family. Hers was a family that embraced diversity long before it became popular in our society.

The expression of the author's deep and abiding faith is on par with the two themes already mentioned. John and Helen retained their allegiance to the Roman Catholic Church; they firmly believed that their good fortune was the product of divine grace.

Over the last twenty years, Helen's professional life and considerable part of John's life revolved around assisting the reawakened Hungarian Republic. They fostered cultural exchanges and through Helen's career as Honorary Consul General they became major supporters of American-Hungarian relations.

It gave me great pleasure to read this book of recollections by one of our prominent compatriots.

Derick P. Pasternak, MD, MBA; Colonel, retired, US Army; International healthcare consultant; Chair, Peacebuilding Committee, Rotary Club of Ballard (Seattle); Hungarian refugee of 1956.

～

In October, 1956, the people of Hungary rose up against the Soviet empire. By the invasion of the Soviet Army on November 4, 1956, the majority of us students from the Sopron University eagerly joined the revolution, but the inevitable subsequent defeat left almost all of us with a dilemma. Should we stay at home and await the reprisals, or set out into the wide world?

This was the time when Canada opened its doors to one of the largest refugee migrations in its history and where we eventually established the Sopron Division at UBC in Vancouver, British Columbia.

You're about to read a classic book about János Szablya, a graduate of the Technical University of Budapest who joined the Sopron Group, and became an associate professor of the Sopron Division at UBC.

His wife Helen wrote this magnificent documentation about their life and family in their adopted country of Canada.

Reading this book opened up stories in me about us Soproners that I've never heard before and for this I am forever grateful.

Kocsis Tibor, BSF 1961, University of British Columbia Sopron Forestry Division; Sopron Alumni Association Coordinator; Holder of the Silver Cross of Merit of Hungary

~

Can you imagine losing everything you own, having to leave your home and loved ones behind with just the shirt on your back and your young children in your arms? Having to start a new life in a strange land thousands of miles away? For many people who are fortunate enough that their country or generation have never experienced occupation, oppression or war first-hand, World War II, Communism, Fascism, revolutions and emigration are merely abstract concepts and they have no idea how those events affected people who lived through them. We are grateful to masterful storytellers like Helen Szablya who put a human face on these historic events and make them relatable through their personal stories, losses and lessons, trials and triumphs. Against many odds the Szablyas thrived and managed to raise a wonderful family, build a successful business and meaningful career in their new home, while still staying devoted to their original homeland. To top it off, Helen is one of the most optimistic, cheerful and positive people I know....a great role model for anyone facing hardships.

Katalin Pearman, Honorary Consul of Hungary for WA and ID, in Seattle.

~

Helen Szablya did not get a consulate for Hungary established in Seattle all by herself, but she unquestionably was the inspiring and guiding force that made it happen. I had the honor of serving on the staff of the Blue Ribbon Commission that helped Hungary make the transition from the East back to the West in the 1990's. That experience opened my eyes to the great potential of Hungary when it once again was free. So I was delighted when I returned to Seattle to find Helen Szablya and her fine family of immigrants and their descendants working to assist Hungary by opening a consulate in the Pacific Northwest. The work they undertook fully justifies their long effort and shows how dramatic and even perilous human stories can sometimes have unexpected and happy futures. That is true for people like Helen and her family and for countries like Hungary and the US. Thank you, Helen, for telling those stories!

Bruce Chapman, Secretary of State, Washington, 1976-81; USA Ambassador to the UN in Vienna 1985-88; President and CEO of Discovery Institute in Seattle

~

After reading *My Only Choice*, the saga of agonizing injustice and devastation perpetrated by both fascists and communists on the loving family of Helen Szablya in Hungary, it is faith affirming to read her autobiographical sequel: *From Refugee to Consul: An American Adventure.*

Through tragedies and triumphs, Helen Szablya keeps her eyes on the stars and her heart anchored in the conviction that God has a plan for her family...a plan that will ultimately bring happiness and fulfillment.

This is a love story. It delves into the depth and breadth of a romance between a great man and equally great woman. It reveals their dedication to the dynamic family they created. It documents their determination to contribute mightily to the nations that welcomed them as refugees; and it explores their unshakeable devotion to their native land, Hungary.

In this book we witness the power of dedication, determination, devotion, hope and hard work to span continents and oceans and to build a lasting legacy of love.

> *Annette Lantos Tillemann-Dick, daughter of the late, only Holocaust and Communism survivor Congressman Tom Lantos, Head of the Foreign Affairs Committee at the time of his death.*

~

Just how do you become a Consul of the same country from which you escaped? Curious? Read Helen M. Szablya's book *From Refugee to Consul: An American Adventure.* It is a wonderful book that takes us on an incredible life journey. If you want to get something done, call on Helen. The little Central European country of Hungary learned that early on. As Secretary of State I was on Bruce Chapman's "Friends of the Hungarian Consulate" Committee he established to accomplish Helen's goal: she was appointed as Honorary Consul General of Hungary for WA, OR and ID, and she made things happen! Her list of accomplishments makes me proud because we worked together on so many issues. With Helen's leadership, Hungary's voice was loudly heard on the American West Coast. I shall forever be indebted to her for her leadership.

> *Ralph Munro, Secretary of State, Washington 1981 - 2001*

FROM REFUGEE TO CONSUL:
An American Adventure

FROM REFUGEE TO CONSUL:
An American Adventure

Helen M. Szablya

Szablya Consultants, Inc.
Seattle, Washington

From Refugee to Consul: An American Adventure

Copyright 2021 by Helen M. Szablya

ISBN: 978-0-578-31351-1

Library of Congress Control Number: 2021921554

First Edition

～

Also by Helen M. Szablya

In English:

> *The Fall of the Red Star* (first prizes from Washington Press Association and National Federation of Press Women)
> *Hungary Remembered* (an oral history drama) George Washington Honor Medal from the Freedoms Foundation and Gold Medal Hungarian Congress, Árpád Academy, Cleveland, Major Grant Washington Commission for the Humanities
> *My Only Choice: Hungary 1942 - 1956*

Translation and collaborator for the English edition:

> Ernest Töttösy's book *Téboly* Hungarian into English: *Mind Twisters*

In Hungarian:

> *A vörös csillag lehull* (grant by Ministry of Hungarian Heritage, Hungary)
> *56-os cserkészcsapat*
> *Emlékezünk* (an oral history drama, as above)
> *Vasfüggöny Kölnivel…Magyarország 1942-1956*
> *Szökevényből konzul, óceánon innen, vasfüggönyön túl*

～

Printed in the United States of America

Cover design and illustration: Zoltán Papp • Book design by Ann Marra

Cover photograph of ship 5478060 © Ivan Cholakov | Dreamstime.com

To the love of my life, my husband John;
and to God's great gifts to us,
the four generations of our family

And to all Hungarians
who have been living the fate of the exiled,
and those who had remained behind:
Only together could we achieve
a free and independent Hungary again.

Preface

"It happened to me!" are the most powerful words in the human language.

From Refugee to Consul: An American Adventure is the true story of what happened to me and my family! Our story begins as refugees following the Hungarian Revolution of 1956, continues as we made our home in Canada, eventually landing in the US and establishing the Hungarian Consulate in the Northwest after the fall of the Soviet Union in 1989.

After all our struggles and efforts while exiled, Hungary once again became a free, democratic country. This was achieved by the concerted efforts of the Hungarians who had left after 1956 and those who had stayed behind.

This book takes off where my previous autobiography, *My Only Choice: Hungary 1942 – 1956* ends. As refugees arriving in Canada, we experienced culture shock that was both educational and laughable! It was humor and trust in God that helped us survive and thrive.

Especially today in 2021 where there is growing displacement in the world, refugees and immigrants desperately trying to find a place to call home, my experience is more relevant than ever before. Immigrants everywhere through hard work and perseverance accomplish tremendous achievements. Mine is one of those stories.

I am proud to say, "I lived it. It happened to me!"

Acknowledgments

There are so many I need to thank, beginning with God for giving us these experiences and letting us live through them, so we can tell others about it. I thank all those who lived the story with me. My wonderful late husband John, (John F. Szablya, PhD., P.E.) who taught me, this sixteen-year-old, how to live a happy life, and was my equal and loving partner all through our 54-year honeymoon. Our love for each other helped us through every challenge coming our way.

I want to thank every one of my children for all the work they put into this book. Not one of them escaped contributing something, but the heroes were my husband John, whose memories are incorporated in this book, Helen A. Szablya, our oldest, whose memories are also incorporated into this book and who read through and edited the book all the way, giving me ideas; Alexandra Szablya, and Niki McKay, my daughters, and Leann Rayfuse, a great and true friend who did the tedious copyediting. A humongous thank you to Ann Marra, who worked tirelessly on shaping the book, the photos and organizing it all so elegantly with her artistic talents.

My thanks go to all those who will be publicizing my book as they publicized the first volume, which includes the Hungarian American Coalition, the American Hungarian Federation. Julia Bika (Nyugati Hírlevél), the American Hungarian Journal in Los Angeles and many more.

The Hungarian American Association of Washington and the Seattle-Pécs Sister City Association are both a delight to work with. I look forward to their launching of the book for local Hungarians and Seattleites.

Thanks to all those who wrote pre-publication reviews: Bruce Chapman, Ralph Munro, Sam Reed, Sheilah Kast, Tibor Kocsis, Derick P. Pasternak, Annette Lantos Tilleman-Dick and Katalin Pearman.

Introduction

Dear Friends, whose lives appear in this book, everything in the book is true. Thank you for living it with me. May you enjoy reliving our lives by reading this book as much as I enjoyed writing it!

Dear Readers, too young to remember any of these historical events, may you receive some insight into what it was like to live, feel and survive when we were young while growing older. What it was like to leave our beloved homeland, as a refugee, starting anew, working on getting our homeland free, then, after the regime change, working on helping it rise from the long decades of extremism and binding strong ties between our native and adopted countries.

Happy reading to All!

Prologue

The all-encompassing waves washed over our five-story 24,000-ton ship in the open sea, as if trying to swallow it, on our way across the Atlantic. It was the first week of January 1957. The rising ship pressed me into the stairs only to fly me up as if on wings on its way back into the valley of the waves.

Are we going to die here, in the middle of the ocean? Are we never going to get to our new home in Canada? Is this going to be the end of our escape to freedom?

People were meandering back and forth in the hallways on their way to the bathrooms, some carrying bags on behalf of those who could not even make it out of their bunks.

I was on my way to the purser's office where the purser and I were preparing the visas for the 500 refugees on the Empress of Britain, on this, her second to her maiden voyage across the Atlantic.

But no, ships do not sink any more like the Titanic! Technology has come such a long way! I tried to console myself, while I finally made it up to the top of the stairs and turned towards the Purser's Office.

Another huge wave almost knocked me off my feet, but before that happened I managed to throw myself onto a chair.

"Let's start!" The purser motioned the first person to the table. "Mrs. Szablya will interpret," she said to Dean Kálmán Roller, who came to get the visas for all six members of his family. The others were too seasick. He sat down as quickly as I had.

Names? Places and times of births? This was a long case.

The purser smiled at me and said "milestone" a word I did not understand. Finally she drew a milestone and said each wave was a milestone.

"OOOPS!" We quickly grabbed the papers that were sliding off the table as the ship took a sharp slant to one side.

Four of us spoke English of the 500 Hungarian refugees, and one of the four, John, my husband, was seasick, so he stayed in the cabin with our three children. The six-week-old Louis was not seasick, but every time the ship played havoc with his crib, he lifted both his trembling little arms and cried out: "YOAOAOAY!"

Nothing teaches you better how to speak a language than exactly such an emergency. I learned English and knew English, but never wanted to speak it because I did not feel I spoke well enough. No one asked now, not even I asked myself how good my English was. I just opened my mouth and the words came.

I had to concentrate now on the visas. I no longer had time to philosophize about whether or not we are going to arrive at our destination.

1

"There is no way left for us to escape!" Yet we were now trying the impossible again. Indeed, we had only "hope against hope." I remember this is what I said to Mother when they brought us back last time we tried. The border seemed so far away and every step an effort, the mud sucking against my boots as if the earth of our homeland was holding me, keeping me from the freedom and peace I so longed for.

Every few minutes a flare could illuminate our hiding place of the dark and only the night protected us from the guns along the border.

I fell again then slipped off the trail and fell again.

Then we were finally beyond the pear trees…the border should be here now. My mind wandered to all that we would leave behind: Mother, Grandfather, Little Grandma, and Grandpa, our friends, our homes, and the country that I love, our native land. The land whose mud pulled hard on my feet begging me to stay…it hurt…it hurt as if I cut the umbilical cord between Hungary and me. I remembered Uncle Charles' words: "Where there is no memory, there is no pain."

I felt something soft under my feet. The realization hit deep within me with a twinge of pain…leaving; "no-man's-land!" The pain of leaving melted away as my heart rejoiced.

I cleared no-man's land as quickly as I could.

In the faint light of the stars I saw John's outstretched arms as he waited for me in the darkness, half crying, half laughing. I fell into his embrace. Looking through my tears in the dark, I could just make out the Austrian flag.

We were free!

"Quickly, we have to run a little farther! A few more steps!"

Suddenly the flares turned the night into day. We were just 30 feet from the Iron Curtain, we were inside Austria. We were safe! They could no longer hurt us! As we were crying and laughing at the same time, our four-year-old Helen embraced our knees and cried. She knew something especially important had happened and something frightening, but she also saw our happiness. Our moods saturated her whole being. The baby was now sound asleep in his basket, as was two-and-a-half-year-old Jancsi in the knapsack my husband, John, carried on his back.

Freedom! What a glorious feeling! What a joy! How I used to dream about being free for what felt like my entire life; in my dreams I felt like a butterfly, flying around a meadow of flowers in the golden sunshine, under a blue sky. Then came the morning and I was back after feeling blissful for a short while. Upon waking, reality's bleakness would break the spell.

The flares from the border lit the path toward the lights of the village ahead.

Shadows appeared from the first houses just shy of the village at the edge of the vineyards. The shadows greeted us with such love! You would have never guessed we crossed the border on the night when the number of refugees surpassed the 130,000-mark.

"You come with me!"

"And you with me!" They surrounded us and each one of us was grabbed by eager helping hands.

The Austrians had just rid themselves of the Soviets and their armies a year and a half before. They knew not only why but what we were running away from.

"You will not go to the Red Cross! You come to our house!" They would say to us.

"OK, one of you can go to enter the names in their book, but come right back!"

Frau Halwax pulled us right into her house. The closest house to the border; full of light, love and hospitality. They did not have running water, yet the kitchen was so well equipped there was no comparison to the last house we hid in, in Hungary.

Frau Halwax invited us over to her table. "Here, have some sausage and wine! You have to taste my cake! I baked it just for you, all seven layers of it, for those, who were going to share our home today."

Herr Halwax sat down with John and me and told us his entire life's story in a Burgenland German dialect, while the wine was flowing. Frau Halwax made beds for us all. Helen slept with her that night, John and I shared a cot, Jancsi slept in the kitchen with us on a makeshift bed. Louis, the baby, had his basket.

We felt so rich; we had each other, our three children, the clothes on our backs and six diapers – and we were free!

Frau Halwax took our shoes and washed them with soap and water, they were so muddy. I thought they would never be shoes again. But by the next morning they were as good as new. Or at least that's the way they seemed to me.

We felt right at home in Austria. Our second "mother-tongue" was German, so there was no barrier between the Austrians and us.

What a glorious morning! The Red Cross bus came around to pick up the refugee crop from the previous evening. They took us to Eisenstadt, our first refugee camp.

We took a last look back towards Hungary. John said to me: "Let us look back one more time, and then let us look just ahead. Our home is where we are together."

2

The camp in Eisenstadt was a former palace, abandoned by the Soviets when they had left Austria. It was in horrible shape when the first Hungarian refugees arrived. They immediately started to clean it up, so by the time we arrived it was better.

"Let me give your baby a bath!" a friendly Red Cross lady volunteered. I was more than happy to comply.

When I got him back, he was in brand new clothes and diapers, which we could add to the eight we had received just after we had crossed the border.

Red Cross ladies were carrying hot chocolate in plastic pails and were handing steaming cups of it to all of us. They let me relax and nurse Louis on a bed.

"Did you hear? There will soon be a Mass at the minibus which the Pope donated to serve as a Chapel for the refugees." The news quickly circulated.

I remembered hearing about this before on the foreign news broadcasts while still in Hungary – and now we are going to see it – firsthand. How exciting!

We scrambled to get there. Indeed there was a minibus, its tailgate folded down and a priest was just beginning Mass. Tears trickled down from the refugees' eyes as they began singing the well known hymn: "Boldogasszony Anyánk," a prayer to Mary, "Our Lady of Hungary." Ever since our first king, Saint Stephen, offered Mary the Hungarian crown, lifting it up to her statue and she surprisingly bent down to accept it, she has been "Our Lady of Hungary." In that moment, none of the refugees imagined ever seeing our homeland again.

After Mass we sent a message to my father's friend, Ignatz Kosztelitz, who lived in Vienna to please come get us and bring us some money. We had barely done this, when – to our great surprise – the camp authorities simply gave us free train tickets to Vienna! We had mentioned to the authorities that John's cousin lived there and so now we were on our way. However, we only knew their address and nothing else.

The train took us through sunlit fields. One of our fellow passengers turned out to be a music teacher, so she immediately started teaching our children a Hungarian nursery rhyme. Pretty soon the children sang along with her as the Lajta River gently waved its way along the railroad tracks.

VIENNA! The "City of my Dreams" according to the song my beloved Governess Elsie taught me before she returned home prior to the siege of Budapest in 1944.

It was dark by the time we arrived. Vienna – now indeed the "city of my dreams" as for years it meant freedom to Hungarians – appeared in all the radiant brilliance of its lights. I remembered 1948, when Vienna was in such terrible shape compared to Budapest! Now, my mouth fell open as I looked from wonder to wonder! Escalator in the railroad station! The red streetcars, cars whizzing by. We walked and walked until we arrived at the Schwarzenberg Palace where John's cousin lived in a small house within the Palace Garden. I am sure they did not expect us to turn up in front of their door on a Sunday evening.

"John, how would you like it, if someone would burst into our house at this time of the evening, hungry, with three small children, to be 'adopted' by them? They have never even seen me." I turned to my husband.

I did not need to worry.

We rang the bell. Three astonished adults looked at us, but they immediately recognized the family.

"What are you doing here? We heard you just had a baby!"

Kurt Lohwag was a good-looking man. The two ladies, his wife Irmgard and his mother Aunt Nellie, immediately asked us in and showed us to the table. But, what are they going to feed us at the end of a weekend, I wondered. They must be out of everything!

Now it was my turn to be astonished as Irmgard opened the refrigerator door. It was packed with a dreamland of food. Slices of ham, salami, butter, cheese and all kinds of cold cuts! Aunt Nellie was slicing the bread.

"You have to eat! You must be hungry!"

"We are indeed hungry. We have not had anything to eat since morning," John admitted.

That food! It was like biting into the past and the future at the same time. That is what food tasted like when we were kids, before the war. From now on we will eat this kind of food again. It tasted like peace and freedom! Fresh, crunchy bread and butter, pink slices of ham, salami slices so thin you could see through them! Buttery Trappist cheese, sliced Ementhaler, spreadable liver sausage and fruit!

"Now you must tell us how you got away? And with such a small baby!" said Irmgard.

While we were eating, we told them how, after twice being captured and returned to Budapest we finally succeeded in escaping. We told them how we forged papers on Technical University letterhead that ordered John to take over the Department of Electrical Engineering at the University in Sopron.

Kurt immediately spoke up: "I heard there are many here from the Sopron University. You know, I teach a course at the British Council too, in addition to being a professor at the Agrarian University. My mother is British, so I have been speaking English since childhood."

"There are?" we asked almost in unison. "Where are they?" It just amazed us that we would meet them after all.

"Where do you intend to go from here?" asked Kurt.

"My father lives in Canada. He is an MD in Winnipeg, Manitoba. He had to leave Hungary in 1949. We have not seen him since."

"I will ask around tomorrow to see about the Sopron people," Kurt decided.

"We have a big room, where you can all sleep, but there is no heat in it," said Kurt after we had our fill.

"Let me bring you some blankets and something to lie on. We will make you comfortable," Irmgard suggested.

Soon we were all settled in the middle of the huge room, huddled together, in our winter coats, and had a well-deserved good night's rest.

In the morning we found Jancsi in the corner of the big room. He was so used to putting his head in the corner of his crib that he kept pushing himself up and up until his head got settled in the corner of that huge room.

Aunt Nellie greeted us with a fantastic breakfast, bursting with news: "Kurt called from the university. You know what? They are here in one group. You know, the people you had talked about yesterday, that university, Sopron, or something. Their Dean asked the Austrians to bring them all into one camp. And – guess what? They are going to Canada, just like you. Isn't this amazing???"

We were flabbergasted.

"Providence is unbelievable. Once again, God sent us just what we needed," John grabbed me and twirled me around in the air. He always did this when he was really happy! He was 6'5" and I was 5'4" so it was easy for him to do this and I loved it!

The kids did not quite understand what this was about, but they must have decided it was something good and they smiled and happily jumped around us.

The telephone rang. Aunt Nellie answered it then handed it to John: "It is Kurt. He wants to talk to you."

It was great fun to watch John's face as his smile became wider and happier.

"Yes! That is great news! We will go right away!"

Kurt had talked to the Canadian Embassy. When they heard that John was a professor and spoke English, they wanted to see him as soon as possible.

Aunt Nellie volunteered to take care of the "Purtzelchen" (an endearing word for "little baby") as she nicknamed Louis. We took the two older ones by the hand and left for the Embassy.

Aunt Nellie told us surprising news: we could go by streetcar for free! All we had to do was show our Hungarian ID-books. The Austrians outdid themselves to show hospitality to their former compatriots in the Austro-Hungarian Monarchy. Having known Soviet occupation themselves, they were well acquainted with the Hell from where we had escaped.

A young man interviewed us, and only much later did we discover that he was the Ambassador himself.

"I heard that you are headed to Canada, you are a professor of electrical engineering and you speak English."

"My father-in-law is an MD in Winnipeg, Manitoba. We would like to join him. We actually have had our Canadian visas for the past five years. They have been well hidden behind a wall in the cellar of one of our friends. The chauffeur of the British Council in Budapest hand delivered them to us because when someone's visa was sent out by mail, that person was arrested. The British Council, acting for the Canadians in Hungary, did not want to take any chances." John said.

"That is frightening. They would do that to someone simply receiving something in an unsolicited mail?" The Ambassador was surprised.

"It was common procedure," John answered.

"I wanted to talk to you about the Sopron Forestry University that is here in Austria. Their Dean, Kálmán Roller, asked the Austrian authorities to gather in one place all the students and faculty who had anything to do with the Sopron University. The University then started to explore possible university affiliations around the world. The University of British Columbia in Vancouver, British Columbia was the foresters' choice," the Ambassador explained.

"Vancouver? In British Columbia? The most beautiful city in the world!" John exclaimed.

"That is where they are going," the Ambassador addressed us, smiling at John's enthusiasm. "Would you like to go with them and act as their interpreters, you and your family? I know your wife also speaks English."

"Would we?" John's eyes shone with happiness. "It was my dream, ever since I was a child to see this legendary city."

"Then come back tomorrow and we will discuss the details."

We shook hands and left full of anticipation for our future lives.

First, we had to get to the Kosztelitzes, my father's friend and his wife, whom we asked to pick us up in Eisenstadt. They used to have a drugstore in Váci utca, in Hungary, almost across the street from one of our branch stores. They specialized in expensive perfumes.

Ignatz was happy to see us.

"You know, we drove to Eisenstadt to pick you up and even brought you some money you asked for."

"I am sorry we left," I said, "but we received free train tickets to go to Vienna, when they found out that John's cousin, Kurt lived there. We did not know when you would be able to come, or even if you would be able… so we just grabbed the opportunity."

"Anyway, here is some money for you and just tell me if you need more. Your father entrusted you to our care. What can we do for you? How can we help?"

We proceeded to tell him and his charming wife about our good luck with the Sopron School of Forestry and the Canadian Embassy.

"Do you know how lucky you are to come at this time? Right after the Revolution?" He went on. "There are some people here from the Second World War, 'deepees' as they call the 'displaced persons.' They still live in camps."

As we were going home to Aunt Nellie, we happened to look up. The name of the street was Rennweg.

"Rennweg!" I mused. "John, Rennweg 2 is where the Sacre Coeur School is in Vienna. You know, like the Sophianum, my school. We were always told that wherever there is a Sacre Coeur School, we will be 'at home.' Let's visit them!"

To be "at home" was the understatement of the year. We rang the bell and told them who we were. "Which was your class?" with Fides Schick?

"Yes."

"Was your father the general or the manufacturer?"

There were several girls with the name Bartha; the general had 13 children I believe. But Dora, who was around my age, was not in the same class as I was.

"The manufacturer."

That was enough ID. We were accepted with open arms. First they brought us some soup for lunch with huge Knödels (dumplings). It felt really good.

"All our rooms are already full of refugees, but we can place you in our convent school in Pressbaum, a mere 12 miles away from here, where we already have the refugee families with several children. Half of your old teachers are here with us. They had left Hungary after the Communists disbanded their order. So, you will find many friends here."

"Thank you, thank you," we could not be grateful enough for this wonderful solution, while waiting for arrangements with the Canadians and the Sopron group.

We received instructions on how to get to Pressbaum. It was really easy. We travelled on the long-distance streetcar that went to the suburbs. It stopped right in front of the Convent School. The building resembled our school in Budapest, but ivy running up the walls completely covered it in green.

Mutter (Mother) Sommer was running to greet us with a smile and Reverend Mother Paradeis, who was now Pressbaum's superior, Mother Skalak…they were all our teachers!

"Did you ever think we will meet again under these circumstances? After we left the convent on that truck singing into the night?"

"We had no idea where or how we would ever meet."

The sentences flew back and forth between us.

The Hungarian Sisters also ran to greet us. (Mothers were the teachers, sisters were the housekeepers in those days. Nowadays they are all sisters.) They were smiling, and laughing and roughhousing with the children as they led us to our new living quarters. It was during the Christmas holidays, so I had the honor to stay in the sick room with our children, but John had to sleep with the priest in the garden in another house. During the day we could be together, but during the night no man was allowed in the Convent. We must remember, all of this was before Vatican II – now, everything is different.

We had our own bathroom beside the sick room, where we could wash the diapers and whatever else needed washing.

During the day we went to Vienna with John and the baby, to take care of business. I was nursing him, so he had to come with us. The other two children stayed at the convent and were entertained by teenage refugees, other families' children, who were also living at the convent. Each family was assigned their own room. There was a Hungarian sister, who "adopted" our family. In our absence she ironed everything we washed, she watched the children and did what she could to make our stay more comfortable.

John, being 6' 5" tall, helped Mutter Sommer with the Christmas decorations. How much fun we had getting to know our teachers as adults, no longer having to discipline us!

Mother Skalak's brother and his family with four children came over the border on Christmas Eve. They had counted on the soldiers celebrating on that national family holiday. And they were right! They came out single file on the railroad tracks at Hegyeshalom.

The Communists could not kill the Christmas spirit in Hungarians. They did try one Christmas when they made the theaters play, the movies run, restaurants serve, and the streetcars had to go according to schedule. Not a soul showed up. The family feast of Christmas Eve could not be erased.

As Christmas neared, the Mothers were asking questions about our needs, trying to figure out what could help us for our future; what the "angels" should bring us on Christmas Eve.

❧

While in Vienna we had many official things to do, buying a few little things for our trip to Canada, but we managed to sneak away for a bit of sightseeing as well. We went to the Museum of Fine Arts, to the "Schatzkammer" (Chamber of Treasures), to the St. Stephansdom.

Louis was keeping company with Aunt Nellie, whose daily job now was to babysit him and scold us, when we arrived back.

"He was hungry, I had to give him sugar-water," she said, but we could see she thoroughly enjoyed her "job." Then she fed us lunch, so we could go on with our errands.

My sister Marietta, and Dénes her fiancé, showed up one day at Kurt's home.

"Our escape was so easy out of Hungary. We showed up at the Ujváris. The guide took us across the border, by the lake. It was dark and I was really afraid, but then…" Marietta said.

Her eyes lit up as she continued: "You know, I could not believe my eyes. Vienna was so incredibly beautiful. Everything was as you and Anyu (Mother) always told us. Freedom really does exist. And…it is wonderful!"

Dénes, who was four years older than I was, just smiled at Marietta's enthusiasm. He already knew, since he had experienced it when he was younger, and he remembered.

"I hear you went to the Convent and are staying there. How lucky for you to find them waiting with open arms," he said.

"I found a place with a nice old lady," Marietta continued.

"I went to the camp," Dénes added. "We will soon be leaving for Canada. We have been in Vienna since the 27th of November."

We told them about our good news with the Sopron Forestry School.

"How wonderful!" Marietta's eyes filled with tears. "You already have a place to go!"

"Of course, we are going to Winnipeg first to see Apu! But, yes, it is miraculous, how Providence leads us."

"You will have to be at our wedding in Winnipeg!"

"Of course, how could we miss that?!"

"And Ilike (little Helen's nickname), you have to be the flower girl! And Jancsi…well, what could Jancsi be?"

"Of course, you will be my best man," Marietta turned to John. According to Hungarian custom, there are two witnesses at the wedding, both male, usually a relative, or best friend.

"Where does that leave me? Who will be mine?" Dénes looked puzzled. "Maybe your father can find you a best man, and I can have John."

It was good to be together again – now in freedom.

⁓

"In the event you were not baptized, I baptize you in the name of the Father and of the Son and of the Holy Spirit," said the priest at Karlskirche, a magnificent old church in the middle of Vienna, as he poured water on Louis's little head. Irmgard held the baby in her arms and Kurt stood right beside her.

Before we had left Hungary, when Louis was nine days old, there was still curfew in the evening. Our neighbor, Juci, a dear friend, came over and held him in her arms, while John, my husband baptized him. Just in case something bad might happen during our trip. However, we needed to have a baptismal certificate. So, it was arranged with the priest and that is how he had an official conditional baptism.

After the baptism we had a delicious lunch with the proud godparents, Irmgard and Kurt Lohwag, a childless couple, who now had someone they could call their own. Even though I had never seen them before we had arrived on their doorstep, they became instant family along with Kurt's dear mother, our jovial Aunt Nellie.

3

We had to make physical contact with the Sopron Forestry University, so we had to travel with the children to Strobl am Wolfgangsee, where the Faculty was gathered at a Teachers' Vacation Hotel. The students were settled in St. Wolfgang.

We finally arrived in Strobl am Wolfgangsee. I will never forget the moment we walked into the hotel where the Faculty was housed. Professor Oscar Sziklai, who eventually became one of our best friends, came haltingly to meet us.

John introduced us: "We are the ones whom the Canadian Embassy sent to be your interpreters and translators during your resettlement in beautiful British Columbia. I am John Szablya, from the Technical University in Budapest, professor of electrical engineering. This is my wife, Helen, who also speaks English and our three little children: Helen (Ilike), John (Jancsi) and Louis (Lajos)."

Oscar's face seemed to say "Now what?" with his eyebrows raised and a brave smile.

"Welcome!" he said. "We desperately need you, but…there is no place in the hotel…except…there is the doorman's room. I guess, it will have to do for tonight."

Many inquiring faces greeted us in the well-lit dining room, where we ate our dinner.

"I am Maria, Oscar's wife," a smiling blonde offered. We have three sons. Of course, they are running around now. Just a little older than yours."

"We are the Adamovich Family," Professor László Adamovich introduced himself, his wife, Ili, and two of the four children, who happened to be sitting and eating.

The families were all welcoming and helped us get settled.

"We have to register here, but then we can return to Vienna," John tried to console the poor man, as Oscar was in charge that day of finding places for everyone to stay.

The doorman's room was adequate, but very drafty. Jancsi woke up with a bad earache the next morning.

"We will find you better accommodations," Oscar said and arranged a room for us at the village pub which had a small hotel.

So, during the day we were able to do our official business of registering, and we still had time to visit St. Wolfgang, the neighboring village with a small, beautiful old church, which had a brilliantly carved wooden altar created by a monk who had made it his life's work. It was inspirational!

Strobl was a storybook Austrian village, complete with a small church, the ringing of bells and romantic, old-fashioned houses. The lake, the surrounding snowy mountains and the frosty trees glittering in the radiant sunshine played their magic.

Our Roman Catholic faith was and is my North Star, so in the morning we went to the Rorate Mass, which was an early morning daily Mass celebrated throughout Advent, while we were expecting the birth of Christ. The snow crunched under our boots as we walked in the dark of the early morning. Everything was so peaceful and beautiful. It was like a dream, but I knew it was my new reality.

~

Our idyllic intermezzo was over. We were on our way back to Vienna.

On the train we met Professor Kowald, a history professor. What a great treat it was to sit with him, because he knew everything about the countryside through which we traveled, told us interesting stories and pointed out the important landmarks.

"Our countries were one at the time of the Austro-Hungarian Monarchy," I started. "My father-in-law told me that in his youth, after 1867, they lived in the golden age of history! If you had an Austro-Hungarian passport, you could travel anywhere in the world without a visa because the other parts of the world knew you would go home."

"We had a perfect economic unit in our country," John added. "We had food, forests, minerals, coal, we could be fully self-sustaining."

"You know," Professor Kowald chimed in, "nowadays Austrians are truly thinking about restoring the economic unit, uniting the countries that were created from the Austro-Hungarian Empire after WWII. And I am all for it!"

"So are we. What a good idea!" We both agreed with him.

The children were standing by the window and listened when the professor pointed out the Abbey of Mertz. The imposing building looked down onto the Danube, our shared river with the Austrians.

We exchanged addresses. We wanted to have friends all over the world. But, we had no address book with us when we had crossed the border, because in the event of capture, the addresses would have betrayed our friends and we couldn't take that risk. Now we had to start from nothing, so we took advantage of our very first new connection.

We were happy to move back to our "home" in the sickroom of the convent. Christmas was getting near and we had no idea how we were going to celebrate, but for the commemoration of Christ's birth we were in the best possible place. The Austrian and Hungarian tradition is that the Baby Jesus brings presents on Christmas Eve...in the evening. A few days before that, one room in the house is off limits to children while the "angels" prepare the room.

We definitely were not disappointed! Each family staying in the convent had their own Christmas tree in a separate room. The "little Baby Jesus" rang the bell and we entered with the children. We were flabbergasted. Tears started rolling down our cheeks.

Under the Christmas tree there were many presents, especially selected for us, brought by the students and their parents. After singing some Christmas carols in Hungarian and in German with our former teachers, who, by now had transformed into friends, we opened the presents.

"Look, what I got," Ilike showed joyfully, "a little basket, just like Louis' with a little baby Jesus in it. And he has a real blanket."

"One of the sisters had been very busy making it especially for her," said Mother Sommer. Among the many practical presents, I received a good pair of lace-up shoes and John a travel manicure set.

The room lit up with Christmas brightness and joy.

"How can we ever thank you?" I asked our hosts.

"You would have done the same, had we showed up on your doorsteps. Our students brought you all of these gifts."

"Remember your last Christmas Mass at the Sophianum?" I asked the mothers and sisters. "How could we forget? So many of you wanted to come! We made sure to let all those participate who had the most sorrow at home, to get the consolation you needed."

"What a unique Mass that was, watched by the Communists, who could spy on us from the nationalized school, yet knowing we did not have much more to lose, drinking in the solace of the Mass the peace and joy radiating from our beloved school."

"In the end we sisters went singing into the night when they came for us in a truck," said Mother Sommer.

"We knew that much," I said, "my classmate Erzsike Pápai lived really close and they saw what happened, but then, we knew nothing more, just rumors, until we met here and now. I am so glad you could get out!"

At midnight Mass we sang Christmas hymns alternating between German and Hungarian, so that everyone should feel at home. After Mass we went upstairs and one of the sisters brought us a tray of hot chocolate, cookies, and a bottle of wine. A white candle decorated with red hearts was the final touch for the perfect romantic mood.

The little Baby Jesus was born into our hearts as we remembered those who could not be with us.

December 27th arrived with the speed of light. We had to be on our way. We said our thank yous and teary good-byes to the mothers and sisters, the fellow refugee families at the convent and of course to Kurt and his Family. Aunt Nellie did not want to let go of her frequent companion, baby Louis. The Kosztelitzes wished us bon voyage. Marietta and Dénes were already on their way to Canada.

We took our leave from Vienna, the "city of our dreams," with its snowy forged iron gates, its Sacher Torte (my favorite), its streets, the Stephansdom, the Graben, the Karlskirche, the Mariahilfestrasse and its Christmas lights. And the Viennese people! They were the kindest to us. When traveling on the streetcars, they stuffed goodies, chocolate and once even a 100 Schilling bill into the baby's basket. Will we ever see Vienna again? In those days Trans-Atlantic travel was awfully expensive. We were refugees, enriched by one suitcase to our name, which we acquired in Vienna, and of course, the knapsack in which little John traveled across the border.

At least we did not have much to pack! We could live the words of the Sermon on the Mount: "do not worry about food and drink for yourself, or about clothes...look at the lilies of the fields..." And so far, we were not disappointed in our belief.

Our next stop was the camp at Wienerneustadt where we reconnected with the Sopron University. In the first room there were several Hungarian doctors administering smallpox shots to everyone.

"Come, I will show you where you can clean up," Manca, Professor Adamovich's sister urged us. The "bathroom" had a trough with taps above it. That is where we could wash our hands, faces and teeth.

In the morning we boarded our special train. The goal was to get us through Europe as quickly as possible so that we could arrive in time for our Trans-Atlantic ocean liner. As ours was a special train, we could only travel when there were no other scheduled trains on the tracks.

We had our own compartment as there were five of us, as did all other large families. There were some interpreters with us from the Red Cross and we also did the best we could. German was a second mother tongue for us. When we spoke to Austrians, they couldn't believe we were refugees, as they thought we were native Austrians!

The train went through Salzburg and I could see the Castle in its full, lit splendor.

"Look kids, remember Salzburg when we traveled to Strobl? Where is Apu? I wish he would be here!" Of course, John was somewhere interpreting, while I was lucky enough to have been nursing Louis, and so had the chance to see the beautiful sight.

The next day, when the train stopped at a station, the doors immediately flung open and an energetic walkyrian woman asked: "How many in this compartment?"

"Five," John said.

In came flying 10 huge sandwiches in bags, European bread with thick sausages and ham, liverwurst, everything that we could desire. It was definitely a sign that we would not starve. Of course, the children were way too little to eat that much, but we did our best.

We asked our Red Cross personnel, riding on the train how long this supply was supposed to last, but they had absolutely no idea.

The train stopped right beside the Dome Church in Köln, which was amazing, because I loved that church so much, I kept a photo of it on my desk all through high school. And now it was right here! It was so close to the train it seemed I could just reach out and touch it. Was it ever beautiful! Wow!

In the afternoon we arrived at the Belgian border in Liège.

A most interesting dinner was cooking for our university. This was the station where American soldiers usually crossed the border when being taken through Europe. The station had a kitchen equipped to feed 500 people with ham and French fries. We were shown their equipment, while they were busy cooking our supper. It was unbelievable! Especially, coming from behind the Iron Curtain, where French fries were not even available.

Of course, the Red Cross ladies, just like at every station and every stop were helping everywhere. Louis received another bath and was outfitted again with new outfits and diapers. The ladies were all smiles to have an opportunity to bathe a little one just a few weeks old.

Between the railroad tracks the resident priest offered Mass in which we all took part, giving thanks to God for all we were given, especially for freedom, and praying for those we left behind; for all those who had died for us, for their families and for our future lives.

From this station our train was speeding through all of Belgium to Ostende. The ferry took off from there to the famous white cliffs of Dover.

The baby got a bath during the ferry trip again, along with new clothes. At one of the stations the ladies helping us told us about all the baby clothes they had. "When we had asked for clothes for the refugees, everyone gave us their no longer used baby clothes. Right now we could dress 90 babies from our supply."

Louis even received a fur coat with fur shoes, and a "muff" hand warmer (that was girl's stuff, so he gave it up for Helen). Not that he had much to say about it.

Finally, we saw Dover. There we transferred to a train. Red Cross ladies galore here too. They helped us into the separate compartments that loaded from the platform. While the German ladies who knew what we had experienced had thrown us hearty sandwiches, these ladies in England never had any experience with the Soviets as their enemies. We laughed when they asked us very sincerely: "Would you care for some tea?" which is all they had to offer in the way of nutrition.

We had to get to Liverpool on the same day to embark in the Empress of Britain cruise ship for its second trip across the Atlantic. It was a brand new Canadian Pacific ship. The Canadian Government paid full fare for all of us. The train truly sped this time through England from Dover to Liverpool in eight hours. We stopped very briefly in the outskirts of London only to take some water for the train. No matter how much we strained our eyes to see something of London, we did not see anything besides a few streetlights.

Three students were our "roommates" in the compartment on this trip from Dover to Liverpool. Tibor Kocsis, who to this day, keeps all Sopron alumni and professors notified by email about all the Sopron happenings: events, news, deaths. By now, those students still alive are mostly all in their 80s.

Another of the student-room mates, László Rétházy, publishes a news-magazine "KAPOCS" (meaning "Connector"). Once or twice a year he brings us the news of the past year or months and bios, memories, obituaries of all professors and alumni and their families of the old Alma Mater, Sopron-UBC.

4

The siren's scream marked midnight. The beginning of not only a new day, but a New Year: 1957. Our daughter, little Helen, was on the middle of the bridge to board the Empress of Britain, while she turned four years old. It was her birthday! What a celebration!

We made it! The train got there just in time for us to embarque. Everything was strange, new and luxurious!

We got a room-size cabin all for our family, with a bunkbed and a small crib for our baby. We tucked in the children and when they were asleep, the two of us went to explore the ship. We watched as the suitcases, trunks, packages were loaded. A huge crane lifted a bundle of our luggage in a house-sized net over the opening that led all the way to the bottom of the ship, under its five stories into the hold. As soon as the net was above the ship it was opened and the packages fell helter-skelter down the abyss. I couldn't help wondering how those suitcases and packages will survive. I have never seen a crane that big or traveled on a ship that size. Others were out and about discovering each nook and cranny of the oceanliner.

I will never forget the last minutes before the ship was launched and as it started out of the port. We were leaving Europe…cutting the umbilical cord with our place of birth. When, if ever, will we see Europe again? We were leaning onto the railing, looking back. Tears welled up in our eyes thinking of all those we had left behind. Parents, grandparents, relatives and friends…the ship slowly moved out as a group of students, standing in a circle intoned the Hungarian National Anthem. We all joined into their farewell song.

Our future was filled with question marks. Where will we end up?

One thing we knew: we were free and we had a choice. May God give us good choices and help us follow the right one, the best one for us.

"Morning!" A steward came into our cabin and locked the portholes shut. That should have given us a clue, but it was our first trip…

Immediately we were wanted. The ship was having an emergency exercise. Half of the passengers were Hungarian, almost none of them spoke English.

So…"here is the text" we were told, implying to translate it.

The water was no longer calm, the ship was rolling in the waves.

"Honey, I cannot do it, I feel really, really sick," said John. The kids did not say anything, they just threw up. "I will take care of the kids, but you have to do the interpreting," said John who knew I never got seasick.

So, here we go!

As I was going up the steps the sea threw me up one instant so it felt like flying, then it pressed me down into the floor so I could barely lift my leg. Finally, I arrived there.

Luckily, no one has ever told me that it was difficult what I was doing, or trying to do. It was there, it needed to be done, so I did it. Whoa! No dictionary, no help. Text in English: read it in Hungarian! I don't know how I did it, but it was done! Later, years later, friends told me when I confessed I was the one: "You did very well. We were wondering who of the ship's crew spoke Hungarian so well."

By the time I got back to the cabin, John was busy translating the news into Hungarian. This was our next task. Every day we had to read the news into the ship's microphone. As the Canadian Government was paying all our expenses, the CPS (Canadian Pacific Steamships) felt we had to get all the services paying passengers received. And we did!

On breaks in interpreting I was taking care of my room full of seasick people. Baby Louis and I were the only ones in the family who did not get seasick. There was one other nursing mother on the ship. She did not get sick either. God knew we needed to keep down the nourishment for our little ones. Baby Louis, every time the waves would throw us upwards, lifted both his arms and went: "YOAOAOAY!"

The next day the lovely purser and I started to process the Canadian visas for everyone. Again, no dictionary. So, whatever word that would not come to my mind, I said it in French and somehow we understood each other. One such word was "fiancé." I said it in French, but did not realize the word meant the same thing in English. Another word I did not understand was "milestone." She tried to explain it to me like this: "The waves are like milestones." In the end she drew it for me and then I understood. Occasionally we were interrupted in our work with the visas because someone needed an interpreter in the sick room. For example, one of the students wanted to tell the nurse not to give him ice cold orange juice. He had pneumonia because he stayed on the deck too long and got a cold (that was of course before the waves tried to swallow our ship). Actually, it was beautiful from the Promenade deck to look right into the turquoise belly of the waves as they tried – and often managed – to scale the entire five stories of the ship. The foam on the top of the waves made the green of the water even deeper.

Anyway, in Hungary whatever a sick person drank had to be hot. In Canada it seemed they subscribed to the ice cold version. So the nurse gave the student something hot instead, although she doubted that was a good idea. The student then asked me to send a male interpreter. I was not ashamed, but apparently he was. So I got John to put on something and waddle over to the sick room to talk with him. It turned out he wanted to call his mother in Hungary. The ship even paid for that. He did and he was very happy. That is Canadian hospitality and love of neighbor!

I decided I wanted to talk with my father too. When the future is uncertain, one has so many questions. Of course the ship called my father collect. I tried to ask him questions about whether to pursue a university job, or an engineering one for John. He was for the university. Of course we did not talk long, but it was giving us some goal to strive for, to make plans for our new lives, even though we knew nothing about what university life was like in Canada. We trusted my father who has been living in Canada already for five years and had passed his Canadian medical credentials exam four years before. We had a solid anchor.

We worked on 500 visas with the purser. Usually, the head (meaning a man in those days) of the family came and registered all family members. They were barely able to mutter their answers and looked really pale. Hungarian is phonetic, so names and city names did not need spelling. This fact Canadians found amazing. The only thing I needed to ask now and then was: "Do you spell this with and 'i' or a 'y.' At the end of last names the sound was the same for these two letters. Later, one of the immigration clerks asked me: "What kind of school did you go to that you know how to spell all the names?" He was amazed when I told him Hungarian was phonetic.

All that wonderful food we received at mealtime went to waste because people could not eat it, or if they did, they could not keep it down. I felt so sorry for them. Two days before we landed, the ship was turning and a wave got it right in the middle. Everything from that beautiful buffet table fell on the floor and our plates were flying as well. The tables were screwed to the floor, so they remained in place.

I was not afraid at all on the ship. I thought nowadays ships did not sink any more. I even enjoyed the ride, like on a roller coaster. Slowly people got used to the waves and went up to the Promenade Deck where they could see natural light and felt better.

In our "free" time John and I visited all the ship's locations. The movie theater, the swimming pool, which of course was not in use at all during the winter. The British immigrants were on a different deck. There were 500 of them as well. We marvelled at their different ways, how they dressed their babies in strong, darker colors, what they liked to eat and what they said about English food. It did not seem very creative: baked and boiled meat, potatoes and vegetables. It sounded boring. Was that true for Canada too?

We had not yet learned the expression "culture shock."

5

"America!" Skyscrapers, the New York skyline, streamlined automobiles and conveyor belts! Beautiful young women and men! Just as seen in magazines! I couldn't wait for my first glimpse of the shore after the stormy midwinter Atlantic crossing, on the 8th of January, 1957!

And what to my wondering eyes did appear? A snow-covered fairyland of colorful deep red, royal blue, hunter green gingerbread houses! We looked at the "skyline" of St. John New Brunswick, Canada.

We arrived. We stood on the deck of the Empress of Britain, with John and our three little children, in the freezing cold, with all our earthly belongings: a suitcase, a diaper bag and a knapsack. The friendly purser lady took a photo of us on the Promenade deck. That photo was on National Canadian TV (CBC) coast-to-coast the next day. It is also on the cover of this book.

We received our first money we earned during the crossing. CPS gave us $37.38 for interpreting on the boat. We did not expect to be paid, but were happy to accept our first income since we had left Hungary.

We were supposed to arrive in Montreal with our dream-like cruise ship in which we crossed the Atlantic, but the port was frozen.

Now what? Port authorities re-routed us to Halifax. That too was frozen.

That is why we finally arrived in St. John, New Brunswick.

As 500 out of the 1000 passengers were Hungarian and only four of us spoke English, we were immediately needed to tell everyone the bad news:

There was a CPR strike (January 1957), so the 500 Hungarians had to stay in the Immigration Building until it was over, which turned out to be 10 days. The building was designed for housing 2-3 people to be deported, but there was a customs long-room and an auditorium with a stage. The Red Cross ladies were there all the time to help us.

Great! Now what are we going to do? At least we spoke English. All the others relied on the four of us who did. There were a few students who spoke a few words, maybe two or three.

There was a divorce lawyer in town, Mr. Perry, who spoke Hungarian. Hurrah! Here was someone who even knew the Canadian customs, not only the language. We became friends fast.

In no time at all the Immigration authorities had bunk beds set up in the long-room for all the students and other stranded passengers.

The Sopron Forestry Faculty professors slept on the stage, the wives and children in the three cells, designed for those who would be deported.

Pretty soon John and I were surrounded by students:

"You have to talk to the people here. They have no bread. That is, they have something they call bread, but it looks and tastes like cotton. How in the world are we going to survive without bread?"

They were right, but John knew that this was what people ate in America. Now what can we do?

Students were recruited to help the American cook and Aunt Paula, the veterinary Professor's wife, who enjoyed cooking for masses, finally took over from the American cook. The poor man had something coming! He just looked and could not believe his eyes! What all these people wanted to eat! And how can you make icing and filling for a cake without a good fistful of salt, with just unsalted butter? To be helpful, he threw in the amount of salt he thought would be just right. Poor Aunt Paula almost fainted!

Salt in butter? What for? Who has ever heard of such a thing?

Despite, or maybe because all of these adventures, we had an absolutely great time!

St. John experienced a record cold that year; 47 below.

One of the students' ears got frozen, so the Red Cross immediately distributed hats with flaps to everyone and they locked the Immigration Building to prevent people from going outside.

We were interpreters, so our Canadian-Hungarian interpreter colleague took us out in the evening in his car to show us what ice-cream sodas and milkshakes were like. I liked the milk shake, but the ice-cream soda was weird. Ice cream into a soft drink? I tasted Coke for the first time in my life in Vienna, after our escape and was not a great fan of it. I preferred beer.

He was teaching us about Canadian customs, like ketchup. I never even heard of it before. He asked us:

"Do you know for what we use ketchup?"

Of course I did not.

"When housewives spoil the dinner, they pour ketchup all over it and nobody will find out," he joked.

He told us how he had acquired his knowledge of Hungarian. He was of Hungarian aristocratic descent. The spelling of his name was changed by a few letters, when his parents settled in Canada. He was in Hungary only once, when he was parachuted into Trans-Danubia during WW2. Sir Winston Churchill had a plan to have British troops advance across Egypt to Hungary and cut the advance of the Soviets. Our friend was dropped into Hungary as a part of that plan. The Army perfected his Hungarian. They were shipped across the Sea in the Queen Elizabeth, 3,000 of them in a space that normally took 1,000 passengers. Every shift could sleep eight hours. The rest of the time they had to stand or else they would not have had space enough on the ship. The captain received his day's sailing orders in a sealed envelope in the morning and had to guide the ship according to that, in order to avoid the Germans and their submarines.

Much later during our stay we heard someone call him Captain Parry. Then he let us in on his secret. He was working for Canadian Intelligence. His work was to separate out the university from the other immigrants. Only the university faculty, students and their immediate families were being transported on the Freedom Train across Canada and greeted in every city. That was the real reason why we had to stay an extra 10 days in St. John, NB. The strike was at the CPR and we were traveling on CNR in the end. So the strike had nothing to do with our group.

In order to entertain the students, the town organized a big party, with beautifully dressed young ladies and a live band!

We received playing cards and little bags with toiletries (toothpaste, soap, comb, etc.) They spoiled my baby to death with new clothes and one of the Red Cross ladies asked if she could please, bathe him. I was overjoyed to say yes. She said she had 12 kids and missed them as they were adults by then. She was Scottish. It was really hard to understand her!

One of the ladies brought me a cocktail dress because I told her my sister was getting married in Winnipeg on January 26th. She got it from a friend who was my size. Even my daughters wore that dress; it was so well made and lovely.

Hurrah for the Canadians!

Phone calls were much more expensive then, practically forbidding, but my father said we should tell the Dean to call anyone he needs and my father will take care of it. So we did and Dean Roller was going to call George Allen the Dean of Forestry in Vancouver, B.C. John was the interpreter. Of course, we were used to Hungarian long distance calls. So John called the operator and asked to make the call to Dean Allen whose number we did not know.

"Do you want to talk with him at home or at work?"

"Wherever he is. And we would like you to charge it to Dr. Louis Kovács in Winnipeg."

"Where do you want to talk with Dr. Kovács?"

"Wherever he is."

Then we hung up. The phone rang right away.

"Do not hang up!" the operator said. "You will be able to speak right away."

She caught up with my father in the operating room. He OK'd the charge and instantly the operator gave us Dean Allen.

It was that simple. Would this have been in Hungary at the time we left, we could have waited even a day or two to get the call through and without a phone number – forget it. We also would have had to tell them what language we would be speaking. If we would have changed the language during the conversation and the person listening in (spying) would not have understood us, we would have been disconnected.

Dean Roller and my father became very good friends, when the Rollers moved to Winnipeg after all the students of the Sopron Forestry School at UBC had graduated.

Other ships arrived and we were called upon to do the visas for them too. I believe we must have assisted with at least 1,000 or more visas.

On the ship a young couple, Miki Kovács and Márta Erdős asked John to arrange with the ship's captain to marry them. The captain had a good laugh and said that went out of fashion a long time ago. He no longer married couples on the ship.

So now, in St. John the two of them approached John again.

This time it worked. The Bishop never performed a wedding for the faithful in town because he was afraid he would be flooded. Now, he volunteered his services for the young new refugee-immigrants.

The first time the young couple went to the parish church one of the Knights of Columbus lead them in. He put the hood of Marta's coat on her head. Marta said: "Thank you, but I am not cold," and removed it. The knight pulled it right back up. We had a learning experience here. In Canada women had to wear something on their head when they entered the church. St. Paul wrote in one of his letters that women should wear a hat because they were competing with their hairdos. It was not the custom in Hungary to do that. There, men were not allowed to wear their hats, but women were allowed to do so. Of course, would St. Paul have written his letter in our days, he would have forbidden for women to wear something on their heads because now they were competing with their hats! We have learned much more about church customs in America later.

But now, back to the wedding. The entire city got involved. How exciting! The Knights of Columbus took care of a hotel for their short "honeymoon," the professors put some money together and bought them a suitcase. That was their desire for a wedding present.

Being Catholics, they had to go to confession. Now, how are we going to do this? We agreed with the parish priest that the confessor would sit in the middle, the priest on one end, John on the other. John would interpret, but would not see their answer, as they could do that with sign-language. In the end, this was solved by using Latin. In those days in Hungary Latin was taught in every high school. This way the couple could communicate with the priest in Latin.

Next was the nuptial Mass. We received the entire text in English and were busy translating it into Hungarian. All was perfect.

The day of the wedding arrived.

The Mass was proceeding beautifully. John was standing by the young couple, answering the questions with them.

During Mass the parish priest was hastily approaching us.

"Here is another prayer that the bishop insists on praying, but I only have the text is Latin." With that he thrust the text into John's hands and went back to the altar.

John had the chance to read it a few times. Then it was time for him to speak up and do the best he could. He did a marvelous job! Everyone told him after the wedding about how beautiful the prayer was. John said he was trying his best, but was not entirely sure he said exactly what was in the Latin text. He made sure though that it sounded perfect for the occasion.

~

Finally the day arrived when we moved on. We all boarded the triumphant Freedom Train with our boxes and makeshift bundles that grew by the day. Our families became richer with a big paper box full of colorful American magazines. Such treasures!

6

The Freedom Train was on its way across Canada to be received and feted in all large cities. A few tiny cities almost got lost in the white, huge expanding spaces. The 16 million Canadians were barely noticeable in the world's second largest country.

On the train we again received a compartment of our own. All the large families were housed close together: the Adamoviches, who had four, the Sziklais who had three, the Rollers who had four and the Medveczkys who had three, joined the Szablyas who had three. We enjoyed that and became life-long friends. The Sopron Forestry Faculty and students became one big extended family.

A special reception waited for us in Montreal, where we spent six hours. The university came to greet us and we were taken by local families on a sightseeing tour. Our host was an engineer and his family. It was the first big city in Canada we had a chance to see. It did not give the impression of the big city it was, being the second most important after Toronto. I liked the French touch in this part of the country, however, when I heard the loudspeaker at the train station I turned to John:

"Couldn't they have found a person who could speak better French than this?"

Well, later we found out why the French sounded so different. The French who came to Canada brought their language with them, but the French in the old country and in the new developed in different ways. Although the root was the same, the spoken language was not.

After the celebrations we sped on to our next stop: Ottawa.

Dean Roller came to tell John and me that we would have to interpret his talk into English and French because the Immigration Minister, Mr. Pickersgill would be greeting us.

We, including Dean Roller, were not even warned that we would have a reception in Ottawa, and we were already in our pajamas. Quickly we put on our winter coats over our nightclothes and slipped our bare feet into our boots, running to meet the dignitaries at 11 p.m.

Dean Roller's words spoke about the whisper in the forests and many other eloquent words. I was trying to rack my brain to find the equivalents in French, while John was repeating Dean Roller's words in English. Well, I would have said something, but before we could get to the French translation, the conductor came and ordered us back onto the train.

Our train trip was comfortable in the sleeping compartment and the dining car had all kinds of wonderful – and for us – totally unusual food.

I remember reading the name of a station, which surprised me at first: "Sioux-St. Marie" was the name. Of course, we had heard of Indians and read stories about them, but to think that here stations are named after them and we might actually meet some...WOW! A European dream-come-true!

The infinite white prairie passed in front of the windows hour after hour with absolutely no one and nothing in sight. Now and then, here and there we saw some houses and some funny big red houses. We later found out they were barns. We also found out that the towering round cement buildings were called silos. The Canadians stored their famous wheat in them. We had never seen anything like those silos, although Hungary was also famous for its crops.

My excitement grew by the day, then by the hour. We were going to see Apu, my dad. I had not seen him since the day he left Hungary in 1949. I was 14 – now I was 22 with a husband and three little ones. What would it be like to get to know him as an adult? We corresponded of course, mostly through the diplomatic mail because mail was censored, but that is not the same as touching and kissing.

WINNIPEG! We arrived at the station and disembarked. We said good-bye to our new Sopron friends to stay for a while with my father.

We stepped off the train, clutching our children and all our earthly possessions. Where is my father? My eyes searched the station. My heart started beating faster.

"That must be my father!" I told John. "But no, it can't be. This one is smoking. My father never smoked. The elegant, gray-coated man in the fashionable grey hat turned around. "It is Father!"

We burst into each other's arms. The children jumped around and John could embrace his father-in-law for the first time since we had gotten married.

"I never thought our dreams would come true! That this would ever happen!" I snuggled into my father's shoulder, just as the reporter of the Winnipeg Free Press snapped our photo for next day's paper.

We could not get enough of looking at each other, kissing, embracing, trying to express all our love compressed for seven long years in our hearts.

"You know how lucky you were to escape right now, during the Revolution? You were able to just come straight to Canada. Many of the refugees from World War II are still waiting in camps as deepees, 'displaced persons.'"

"And Uncle Paul!" I suddenly noticed him standing there with his everlasting smile. He was here too, the one we went to see at the Bishop's Palace where he was hiding in 1944 as one of the monks. Father stayed with him, his mother, and his sister, here in Winnipeg, while he was preparing to validate his medical degree in Canada. Uncle Paul was a constant companion of my life. He was even there when my mother's water broke before I was born. Being a diplomat, he had been saying to us always: "Don't worry as long as you see me, if there will be trouble, you will not see me." And that is how it was. In 1944 he was in hiding, and in 1948, when the Communists finally took over the country, he did not come back from Oslo, from his assignment. He chose to resign along with Prime Minister Ferenc Nagy.

Between the two of them, my dad and Uncle Paul had two cars. That was lucky as there were five of us and the luggage too. We settled in and started to roll towards "home."

Neon signs! And they were moving! Colorful in the dark night, they amazed us. We had not seen them since the beginning of the war; first the blackout, then the ruins.

"How beautiful!" I remarked.

Uncle Paul thought a moment and then said: "During the night it is quite bearable." He did not seem to have a great opinion about the beauty of the prairie city, the center of the world's wheat exchange. I took it with a grain of salt. The next day I agreed with him when I saw everything in the shining sun: the telephone wires, the transmission lines, everything in plain sight and so close to the earth it scared me. Underneath it, snow, piles and piles of it, even snow walls on the side of the streets. The snow ploughs just piled the snow to the sides.

22 Young Street. WE ARRIVED! Father lived on the second floor, which was for us, Europeans, the first floor.

"In America the bottom floor is the first floor or the main floor!" Father explained as he opened the door.

The height of luxury! was all I could think. The light gave a rosy-gold coloring to the whole place: the living room with its dreamy furniture, the pretty doo-dads. And a TV! So far, I had only seen one at an exhibition in Hungary, but that was not like Father's! That was a green globe with a wobbly image on it. This was an elegant cabinet with a screen!

49

He had a bedroom with a double bed! Oh, how we always wanted to have one of those! We used to call them "French beds" in Hungary.

"You will be sleeping here," he turned to me. "Here is a crib I brought home from the hospital for my dear baby Lajos, my little namesake!" He looked at Louis with a proud and happy smile.

"Where will you sleep then?" I asked while I eyed the bed of my dreams.

"I will sleep on the chesterfield (this is what Canadians called the sofa at the time) and we will pull the armchairs together for Ilike and Jancsi.

The bathroom and the kitchen looked so modern and new!

Father poured whiskey into crystal glasses for the men. "And how about Helen?" John looked at him.

"Helen? Oh, ya," he answered, after he looked at me and realized I was no longer a child. Besides, it was he who offered me beer when we started out on the Arlberg express to Paris, when I was a teenager.

My first culture shock. In Canada only adults were allowed to drink. What a change to Hungary, where we even gave tastes of beer to babies!

"This is rye," my father explained. "Rye and ginger ale is the drink preferred by Canadians at the moment."

I was thinking: "Now, what is ginger ale?" I liked the rye. Soon I found out that ginger ale was a yellow, bubbling soft drink. I took a liking to the Canadians' preferred drink.

We slept like babies that night in the nice, warm, comfortable, secure home of my father.

~

The next morning we had to go shopping for food. The sun was shining, the sky was blue, it was warm in the house. Of course, there was snow in the streets, but then, we definitely did not expect what greeted us outside. In an instant we felt the cutting edge of 30 degrees below zero, which greeted us as we stepped out the door. I felt truly blessed in my sheepskin coat. Really grateful I did not throw it away when I felt it too burdensome and hot, while trying to escape across the Hungarian border. Ilike pretty soon cried: "I cannot speak, my mouth does not move." Warm air blew out from the shops enticing the customers to enter.

Paradise on earth! That is what the grocery store was to us. Oranges, bananas, green lettuce, strawberries, every kind of fruit, right in the middle of January. Salad cream (I have never even heard about it), but it was highly recommended by Mrs. Novák, who accompanied us on our first trip to buy food. This version of sour cream became one of our favorite foods in Canada. And fresh squeezed orange juice! We had no orange juice whatsoever in

Hungary and oranges only now and then, like before Christmas. We were allowed to buy only one or two, determined by the state. Tomato juice! We used to can that ourselves, but to get it ready-made in the store! And the prices! They were unbelievably low! We could not stop wondering about all these miracles.

We were so engulfed in the ooh-ing and aah-ing a journalist could not help but notice us. He interviewed us about our experience. To protect the family that was still back in Hungary, we used a false name. We told the reporter how much everything would cost and what it was that we never could get in Hungary out of all the delicious foods we had picked up.

We had lots of fun cooking and discovering those wonderful tastes of freedom. Every time I put something into my mouth that we had not had for many years in Hungary, I thought of all those we had left behind.

Mrs. Novak showed us all the novelties of the Canadian kitchen and where everything was. She reminded me of our janitor in Hungary with her rotund body and blond, curly hair. She was my father's cleaning lady, but also a member of the Hungarian church and society.

I liked the arrangements here, in Canada. You could not tell from people's appearance whether they were millionaires, or janitors. We met the janitor's wife coming out the door. She wore a real Persian lamb coat.

My sister Marietta and Dénes came over in the afternoon. By now they were going by the English names Marietta and Dennis. Marietta stayed with a lady close by and Dennis with the Hungarian Catholic priest, Father Pius, a delightful Franciscan and my father's dear friend. Marietta was going to school with the fourth graders to learn more English and also started a job at the Misericordia Hospital, where our father worked during the morning hours. From the afternoon into the late evening he had his own practice. He was always so busy, we rarely saw him, even though he wanted to see as much of us as possible. Once we did not see him for three days, even though we stayed up until the TV went off the air and Baby Louis woke us up in the morning. He was home sometime during the night because his bed was slept in, but when???

TV! We never had TV before, I did not even know anyone who would have had one in Hungary. In Canada everyone had a TV, although the program only started at 5 p.m. and lasted until midnight. At midnight, the national anthem (then still the British anthem) was played, and the Queen was seen with the Royal Canadian Mounted Police in their characteristic red topped uniform and big hats. There were so many things about TV that I had never experienced. We could see old movies, which were new to us as they had never been played in Hungary. They had cartoons. I was eagerly watching them with the children. Popeye the Sailorman and Olive Oyl, his love. He ate spinach and that made him so strong, he could defeat anyone. I loved the wit and irony behind the characters. The children of course laughed about what they saw. We laughed along, but we could catch the delicious nuances. One such episode was when the couple made fun of American parties, where they made you hold your plate, your cup, your food on the plate, your napkin, then, after both your hands were packed… you were supposed to manage putting something into your mouth. During the entire time they sang: "It's the natural thing to do… it's the natural thing to do."

We had not seen American cartoons during or after the war. No wonder that I looked astonished at John, when in one episode the water was covering the picnicking crowd as it rose, then the crowd was still alive, and the cartoon went on. "But…but that is not possible!" John had a good laugh. "In cartoons everything is possible." He remembered the cartoons from before the war. He was a teenager by then, while I was only four years old and did not frequent movie houses. That was the only place where you could even see cartoons.

Whenever Father came home he was usually starved. We had to have food ready, whenever he arrived. "Come with me to do my house calls," he would say after he ate something – and off we went.

He wanted to give us whatever he could to make up for the deprivations, but he too was a beginner. What we thought of as a "luxurious apartment" as we later found out, was a simple one-bedroom apartment in Canada. At the time I felt we would never live in a luxury like that again, when we were sitting and watching TV, snuggling with John in my brand new pink "baby-doll pajamas." "I must confess I am still afraid of him," I whispered to John. "I never know when he will get angry. I so want his approval. Every time I must give an answer or choose something, I am afraid he may not like it." John caressed my hair and looked me in the eyes: "I understand. It has been seven years of separation. How should you know the way you can please him?"

"But, you know, John, it was always like this. I was always afraid of him and yet I always loved him. He gives us all the good things in life, he spends money on us. It seems to me like he wants to express his love through money. I would so like to sit down with him and just talk freely, without any reservations. If he could just answer normally and not be so unpredictable."

We heard the key turn in the door. Father was home. "Miss Gracey will come and you will go out shopping with her. You need to have some clothes," he said, even though I had assured him I did have a change of clothes.

I needed a patent leather belt; I was aware of that. My dress had no belt, but this was the only one I could fit into, having had Louis just before we had left Hungary. Miss Gracey, a most delightful, serious, beautiful lady, head of the midwives at Misericordia Hospital took me to a department store. We went from one department to the next. I kept telling her I needed a belt. She just smiled: "We will get there, don't worry." It was such a huge thing in Hungary to get one, I could not believe my eyes or ears, when we could buy one for just 90 cents.

We bought blouses, a matching short sleeve sweater and cardigan, two beautiful skirts, a summer skirt and blouse as well as a "house dress." That was the dress we wore inside, a light summer dress (in the middle of winter, but the thermostat was set at 85 degrees Fahrenheit). We used that instead of an apron. We bought a beautiful robe, lingerie, scarves, gloves, hats, boots, "over-boots," shoes. Over-boots were used over high-heeled shoes. But then, we also had over-stockings, over and under every kind of lingerie for protection against the devastating cold. We experienced Winnipeg saying that you had to get dressed for 15 minutes to go out for five.

Culture shock after culture shock! We felt it, even if we did not yet know the expression!

John had to go to father's personal tailor, Mike, who was one of his friends and patients. Mike also belonged to the Hungarian Church. The two beautiful suits he made served John for many years to come. John also had to go to the department store and get whatever else was necessary. Father explained to him that to work you wore white shirts with a tie, but when you were at home, you wore plaid shirts and fun-colored shirts. He bought a plaid flannel shirt for John to look like a real Canadian.

Naturally, the children received everything they needed. Father had serious conversations with them. They loved it. The grandchildren were totally unafraid of their grandfather. They had fun with him, and he enjoyed it. He somehow never got angry at them.

One day I made tomato sauce with potatoes to go with the meat. He said he did not eat anything this good for the past eight years. He praised me! I was so happy!

We had to prepare also for Marietta's wedding which was approaching with the speed of light. Ilike received a beautiful blue madeira dress as a flower girl and Jancsi a navy-blue sailor suit. (Nowadays Jancsi's grandson is wearing that very same suit.) They looked adorable in their outfits!

"Helen, come quick, we have to go to Mrs. W's., the wife of a patient of mine. When she heard about the upcoming wedding, she decided to give you a suitable dress." Even though I had a suitable dress already from the Red Cross lady in St. John, I could not say "no" to such a graceful offer.

"I was the anesthesiologist when her husband had surgery. I went in every day to check on him. And now, she wants to return the kindness." We arrived at a beautiful condominium. The lady was not only apparently rich, but exceedingly kind and outgoing.

"You know, we were refugees from Russia, at the time when all those pogroms were going on in the beginning of the century. I know what it is like. I simply never could get rid of anything I acquired since. When my dresses should have been given away, I put them in storage because you never know…I remembered the days when you could exchange clothing for food…I knew I had to save them. And now – here is the perfect opportunity – YOU! I want to give them all, so you should have a wardrobe. I have the perfect little fur jacket too for the wedding." Her eyes radiated happiness as she was bringing out the clothes. They fit me perfectly. The "lilies of the field" appeared in my mind from the Sermon on the Mount. God will provide in all that we need…could not have been more perfectly demonstrated.

A refugee understanding another refugee, the language of universal love between generations, faiths, and nationalities.

Another day we visited one of my father's colleagues and his wife. I could not believe my eyes how orderly their kitchen was. Everything was wiped down, as if no one had ever eaten in the kitchen. I was very shy and did not dare to put out my hand to greet them. It should be the older one who does that. At least that is what we had been taught.

Dr. Bennett shook my father's hand, but Mrs. Bennett did not extend her hand and remained seated. It took awhile for us to find out that this was the perfect behavior. Ladies did not get up to greet others, but gentlemen did. They shook hands with men, but not with women. Touching each other was not necessarily welcomed. We had to remember, North America's first immigrants were the Puritans. We had to learn a lot!!! Culture shock was the order of the day.

Some of my father's patients came to our house at all hours of the day to visit or to ask for advice and my father offered drinks to them. Usually rye and ginger ale, the trending drink. Not everyone emptied his glass every time. The glasses were left there while my father accompanied them to the door.

One day when he came back, he noticed Jancsi emptying the glasses in his 2 ½ year old stomach. Naturally, we took it away from him, but it was too late! He was in such a happy mood, he made somersaults, jumped around, laughed...and we were due to leave in 90 minutes to an especially important, elegant and charming doctor couple for dinner. What are we going to do?

In a few minutes Jancsi fell sound asleep. Thank God, he slept until we had to leave. When he woke up, he was perfectly normal again. Another lesson. Remove whiskey glasses along with departing guests. They are not safe on the table, even for just a few minutes.

The dinner was a fairytale dream. A grey-haired smiling, elegant lady was our hostess and her husband the perfect gentleman in his tailored suit. The tablecloth's heavy damask shone as brilliantly as the crystal glasses and Rosenthal porcelain. He was the doyen of the doctors in Winnipeg and his household showed he must have been a good one to amass this much riches. Their kindness and good mood showed they felt perfectly at home with their treasures and did not think anything of using them daily. The lady of the house sat at one end of the table, the host on the other. They served the usual Canadian fare, but with a European flair.

When we were all seated, we said grace, then Mrs. S. took a little silver bell into her hand and rang for the maid. Now that was not at all the custom in Canada, it just showed they could afford to have a maid. The maid brought us the meal. First the soup, then the roast and baked potatoes with peas and carrots. Dr. S. cut the roast ceremoniously, while Mrs. S. dished out the vegetables and baked potatoes. They served sour cream and butter to put on the potatoes. The dinner ended with a delicious dessert, served with ice cream. We learned that this way of serving was called "a la mode." Ice cream was available any time and was made with real cream. People ate ice cream year-round. Even in this devastatingly cold country!

I was worried the children might break something, or do something "outrageous," but whatever they did, the lady laughed at them and was happy to have us. I was relieved when we finally made it home without any mishap. Even Jancsi did not step out of line, despite his adventure with the leftover whiskies.

Louis accompanied us everywhere we went in his basket. He was a good baby, he must have felt that we needed him to cope. One evening when little Jancsi was trying to "help" carry him, he spilled out of his basket into the snow. Luckily, nothing happened. The snow must have been at least two feet deep if not more, and acted as a soft pillow.

7

Marietta's wedding, of course, was going to be in our Hungarian Catholic church, named after St. Anthony of Padua.

Father was proud and happy to introduce his family to the parishioners, most of whom were also his patients.

The Kovalszki Family, the Huhn Family, the Kovaleks, the Lábadys, Bencsics Kata and her husband Lajos, and many more curious, smiling faces surrounded us. They tried to be the first to greet the family of Dr. Kovács, or at least that part which made it out of Hungary. His patient-friends knew how lonely he was. He left three teenagers at home. In his new homeland he searched out friends who had teenagers and helped them any way he could.

We have known about some of the good deeds from the people at the Canadian Embassy in Vienna. Before they asked us to join the university, they had made sure who we were. They inquired about my father at Winnipeg Immigration authorities and received glorious praises on how he was the Hungarian medical doctor in Winnipeg. How helpful he was to immigration.

Throughout the years we heard from his many patients about the details of his love for them.

"He found that my toddler son needed heart surgery. We had just arrived as refugees. He took care of our son and we never received a bill, neither from him, nor the heart surgeon, a tall good-looking woman said.

"He came to our home and examined my father. Seeing we had no money, he not only had not charged us, he left us the medicine my father needed," said a young man around thirty.

He also paid for some of the expenses of the church.

When we came out after Mass, he practically had office hours on the stairs of the church. People came and asked for his medical advice and he gave it freely. He loved being a medical doctor. It was his heart's desire since he, a serious three-year-old, looked out the window and saw their doctor come to their home in a beautiful carriage, drawn by four horses. It may have been the four horses that impressed him at the time, but his entire being was created for becoming a doctor. He loved helping people. He was patient with them, but not with us. That was another matter completely. I was still afraid of when he would burst out because of something we did not do in a way he expected. He became angry fast, but never with his patients. Only with those whom he loved and desperately wanted to show them his love. His anger did not last long, then he regretted it and tried to make up for it – with money, or a present. How I wished I could have exchanged that for expressions of love and praise for accomplishments, which almost never came. If they did it was in the form of bragging in front of us to another person about what his daughter had achieved.

One night he took us to the Hungarian church for a ladies' card-night. I was sitting with Mrs. Huhn, watching. She was a nice, well-endowed lady. She had arrived in Canada before WWII with her parents. She remembered that during the war they did not dare to speak Hungarian, or German, lest they would be interned as "friendly enemies." Mrs. Huhn won a beautiful cup and saucer, the first prize. She gave it to me.

"Thank you Mrs. Huhn, this is our first dish in our new homeland," I told her. She was really pleased it made me happy. It remained my favorite cup.

The fun custom in those days was to serve coffee or tea in dainty, elegant cups that did not even try to match. Every one of them was from someone and had its own story. All were exquisite and different, adorned with flowers, birds, gold or silver.

Cards played a big part in having Hungarian churches. Money for the church was raised by the people who wanted to have the church. They organized dances, card parties, bake sales (ladies made cookies and coffee cakes, cakes and cupcakes, then sold it to each other and the money belonged to the church). What I could not understand why they did not simply give the money to the church instead of going through all that trouble?

Well, it turned out they had tremendous fun doing it. These were the opportunities to get together with friends, to share recipes and gossip. It gave them an opportunity to have discussions during which much important information was exchanged. These meetings and events totally acted like what we call nowadays "group therapy." And it was for free! Of course, women did not work outside the home, but boy, did they get things done! Whatever they wanted to achieve: a community swimming pool, the census for the city, a cooperative nursery school. Just let the ladies know! That is how the Hungarian churches came into being, when the Hungarian population has reached a number that could not only raise the money, but also support the church.

Strange customs ruled in Hungarian churches abroad. Culture shock?! In our own churches? Yet that is what happened. For example, I figured out that ladies went into the church, sang and prayed, while men found something important to do in the basement of the church. The basement itself was a new concept for us Europeans. We had cellars and catacombs, but no basements. These were basically an extra floor under the house, where people went down mostly to have fun, or might have the TV there, or a workshop. Some of them were "daylight basements," if they had windows and some even had sliding doors.

What did the men do in the basement? After the sermon you could see them coming up and taking their places. Once I peeked. They were playing cards downstairs. I was shocked, but they must have liked the arrangement because they did it every Sunday.

Of course, here too we had to put on a hat, or ridiculous little doilies on our heads if we had nothing else handy. Even a glove would do – but your head had to be covered. St. Paul's command ruled on the North American continent.

Father Pius was the parish priest, Father's dear friend, where Dénes was staying before the wedding.

The day finally arrived Marietta and Dénes were waiting for: January 26, 1957. The church was packed with Father's friends and colleagues. Father led his daughter down the aisle with great pride and joy. Marietta was the only daughter, whose wedding he was able to attend and where Mother was not present. Dénes expected them at the altar, according to custom.

Marietta was a beautiful girl always, but that day she was glowing. Radiant with happiness and expectations, in her shining white cloud-dress and veil. Father Pius outdid himself conducting the service. His sermon was permeated with love that he had for Father and his family.

John and I were busy keeping the children quiet and happy in their cute outfits.

Mike the tailor had the latest home movie equipment and was happy to show it off while filming the entire ceremony. He had a row of strong lights above his camera, the latest.

Later, we saw on Mike's movie that during communion – to keep Jancsi quiet – Father was giving him his gold watch to play with. Watches were still of great value at the time. Jancsi seriously took it from him and was occupied with his new-found treasure, while the wedding came to an end.

After the church ceremony we headed to a restaurant. Father invited all his colleagues and their spouses to dinner. His best friends were Tony and Barbara Natsuk, a fellow anesthetist and Tom and Marjorie McCarthy, a dentist and his wife. There were many others, but I knew them best because they showed up at the house most often.

Shrimp cocktail was the appetizer. I have never had it before. I loved it! Tiny pink shrimps and a red sauce, just piquant enough to spice the shrimp.

While I loved the shrimp, not so much the steak that came after that. I know steak was the best for all Canadians, non-plus-ultra, but I just could not get a taste for it for at least the first 20 years of our American adventure. Was it ever hard to chew that steak! It seemed like we had to eat shoe soles! Heroically I ate as much as I could, but then I just gave up. Many years later I learned that you did not eat beef steak well done, but medium, or rare in order to get it tender. I found out from a lady, who made excellent steaks. She told me the more expensive and the thicker the steak is, the better it will turn out. I tried…and now I can make as good a steak as anyone. I even learned to love it. It only took a few decades. Until then I tried to avoid it like the plague.

"Come, cut the cake!" the guests started urging the young couple after the toasts and the dinner.

They are going to cut the cake? I watched them with surprise as they followed the directions. They cut it together and then they had to feed the cake to each other. What a sight! Luckily they did not have to cut it for every guest. That task was taken over by professionals.

What a curiosity that wedding cake was! It had three tiers. The cake was a fruit-cake saturated with dried fruit and covered by a layer of hard icing, which would keep it fresh. The bottom layer was for the wedding guests. Everyone received a piece of it. The second tier was for their first anniversary, the third for the baptism of their first child. On the top it was decorated by a miniature bride and groom.

After dinner, the young couple took off on their honeymoon. They did not have to go far. The Hotel Alexander was right in the middle of the city. Winnipeg has a dry climate. Most of the blankets and sheets were full of static electricity as they rubbed against each other. Every time they touched the blanket, or one another, they got an electric shock. Sparks were flying in the dark.

We learned from them how to handle that effect. You have to touch the nose of the person with your finger whom you are going to kiss, caress or engage in any way that involved touching. That grounded the static electricity and made it safe to make love.

Maria, their daughter was born the same year November 24, 1957, right into the hands of her grandfather, our father. Maria was the only grandchild whose birth Father witnessed. His photo was in the Misericordia Hospital's yearbook that year, holding his granddaughter with a radiant smile.

While we were in Winnipeg, we did everything in order to find a job in Vancouver because we had to follow the Sopron university as soon as possible. We could use Father's phone which was a godsend. Phone calls were prohibitively expensive in those days. You did not call long distance. Period.

John spoke with the Head of Department of Electrical Engineering at the University of British Columbia (UBC), Frank Noakes. From him we later learned…the rest of the story.

For the time being he said he had no job opening, but he would talk with John when he will arrive in British Columbia. We knew he had to leave in order to find us the best possible livelihood.

John followed the Sopron university three weeks after we had arrived in Winnipeg. I stayed for another three weeks to be with my father, Marietta and Dénes.

This was difficult for me because we did not like to spend even one night separate from each other. And now, to wait three weeks!

Marietta started cooking Canadian food. She received a great recipe from a friend. It consisted of a slice of salmon, rice and cream of mushroom soup. Individual servings were wrapped in foil and it was cooked for 45 minutes in a 350-degree oven. It was delicious! She calculated how much it cost. It came out to $3.50 for the entire family. She thought this to be expensive, but Father just laughed and said: "In a restaurant you would have to pay this much for one order of the same."

He enjoyed challenging us. One day he brought home a humongous turkey. Of course, in a bachelor's kitchen he had nothing to cook it in. He had a pan which was big enough to squeeze the turkey in, but it was maybe two and one-half inches deep only. So, the entire turkey was towering above the little pan. Mrs. Kovalek, the Hungarian butcher's wife gave us the idea, to put the lard (we used to cook with lard in the '50s) all over the turkey, then cover it with foil and put it in the oven like that for six hours at a low temperature. It will be all done. We should just set the time bake. That was also interesting for us. We never had anything like time-bake! Or temperature settings on the oven! We looked up how to set it, then checked and rechecked it. Everything looked alright.

Well, the timer worked, but by the time we got home, not only the turkey was done, but the entire kitchen floor was covered with lard. We did not put the foil inside the pan, but on the outside, so when the lard melted some was overflowing the oven. Do you know how hard it is to get the melted lard off the floor? We had to use paper first to wipe it up and only then wash the floor with dishwashing detergent. No more turkeys for us, until we buy a turkey roaster!

Dishwashing detergent seemed like magic to us too. You just added it to the dish water and the dishes came out sparkling clean. The fat was dissolved, the dishes were air dried! Dishwashers were not available yet, but even this was so new and infinitely helpful!

And the many thermostats in the house! I remembered my days when I was working at the Technical University in Budapest in the summer while in high school. One of my jobs was to be a living thermostat. We did experiments with viscosity of molasses. The temperature had to be held within two degrees. We achieved that with cold running water, by regulating its flow; some days all day. To think of all the available and affordable thermostats in every household here: the room temperature, the oven, the fridge, the toaster, the iron, and many more things! To think that in Hungary the country's largest technical university had to use a human being to substitute for such a simple gadget.

Valentine's Day! What in the world was that? Our children received nice little envelopes addressed to them from the Kovalek children. The cards in the envelopes had a cute little poem that ended by saying: "Be my Valentine!" What in the world did that mean? Was it love? Courting? Friendship? But they were not love letters. Of course, they could have been, as we later found out. Anybody could be anybody else's Valentine. As a matter of fact, in schools all the children sent it to all their classmates, to their teachers, to parents, grandparents, friends, cousins. It was an excellent opportunity for stores to sell cards, flowers, candies, chocolates, or anything else to express your love for another person. By now Valentine's Day became popular the world over because once the stores in other places found out what it was, they immediately adopted it for another excellent chance to sell their wares.

We received many clothes from Father's many good friends. The Kovalek children were about the same age as ours. One of the precious gifts was a green "gentleman's suit" with a plaid front on the jacket. All our boys had a chance to wear it. It was so cute!

My six weeks in Winnipeg came to an end. We said our teary good-byes at the CNN train station. Father upgraded our ticket, so we had our separate compartment with sleeping accommodation. A very friendly conductor told us about the dining car, about the trip, about the next interesting spots. He was friendly with the children and called Ilike "honey-bunny." I had never heard that expression before, but I quickly added it to my vocabulary.

After the first night we went through unbelievably tall mountains, deep ravines, mighty rivers, and calm lakes. We could not take our eyes off the landscape.

In the afternoon I told Jancsi I am now going to nurse Louis. He answered: "OK, I will guard the river for you in the meantime." He said it with such seriousness it was hilarious.

Calgary – Edmonton – Jasper National Park – Banff – went by like a dream.

8

March, 1957.

Beautiful sunshine greeted us as we stepped off the CNN train in Vancouver, B.C., with the three kids, right into my John's outstretched arms. I nestled in his embrace and said: "I hope we will never leave here!" The tall, snowy mountains, the blooming flowers, and trees after the 30-degree below zero frozen arctic landscape of Winnipeg, Manitoba, took my breath away. "No, we won't!" he whispered back.

The Vámossys picked us up. They were my father's good friends, still from Hungary. At least the husband. We spent the night in their luxury home in the British Properties, a housing development he started. The ancient untouched forest started right behind the new homes.

When we had arrived in Winnipeg, I thought my father's home, a one-bedroom apartment, close to Misericordia Hospital where he worked as an MD, was so modern, luxurious, extravagant. And now, this! I could not believe my eyes. Here in the middle of the wilderness with a view to end all views! The city, the sea, and the mountains! Like Switzerland on the seashore! Oh, if our friends could just see this!

Uncle Laci was explaining his philosophy: "My houses sell like hotcakes because once the wives walk in, they insist on buying this house: the view from the kitchen sink is the same as from the living-dining rooms and the master bedroom."

The sun was setting over the Lions Gate Bridge, painting the sky red, yellow, and that special light green color that – as we have since discovered – was always hidden somewhere in the Pacific Northwest sunsets.

The dinner was ready so fast! Even the tiny potatoes came from a can, already peeled. During the dinner his wife, Jeanne, a widow, whom he married in Canada, told us about her first experiences out West. She, a French Canadian pioneer in Alberta, and her husband were homesteading in the frozen North.

"I had my first baby in the city, staying with a friend. After I went back to the homestead, the baby did not gain any weight. In the end he died. It turned out that the formula the baby received was not right for him.

"What is a formula? Some vitamins?"

"Formula is what the baby eats. Every baby gets his/her own formula."

"Don't you breastfeed the babies?"

"Oh, no! That went out of fashion a long time ago. I guess it was the Puritans who thought women should not bare their breasts. It was immoral, or something. They also figured it was better for the baby."

I just listened. Never heard anything like that! Wasn't mother's milk best for the babies? We did not have any "formula" in Hungary. We helped out each other with mother's milk if one of us did not have enough for their baby.

Jeanne was swallowing her tears, as she continued: "It was so cold, we had to burn a fire for a few days to thaw the ground to dig his grave. Then, I got pregnant again. It was the middle of the winter when the birth started. We went to the doctor's house by sleigh. I had twins. It was 36 degrees below zero. Going home we got into a terrible snow blizzard, so we could not even see where we were going."

"How awful!" I whispered.

"Finally, my husband threw the reins between the horses and they – guided by their animal instinct – took the family home."

"The horses know where to go! How wonderful! I have heard about that before, but I never met anyone, who had actually done that," I said.

All together Jeanne had six children, but only three grew to adulthood. It was a hard life. She missed going to Mass at the homestead, so she decided to build a chapel. A few of the neighbors got together and started building it with their own hands. She remembered pushing wheelbarrows full of bricks to the site. It took quite a while of course, but finally it was all finished. The Bishop came to bless the chapel. What pride and joy! They did it all themselves! No one here waited for the government to do what they desired. If you wanted something, you just had to start doing it. The neighbors joined in – naturally.

They lived on the farm until her husband died. Then the family came into town and she taught French in a school. That is when she met her second husband, my father's Hungarian friend. Her money, proceeds from the farm, made it possible for the newly married couple to start the housing development in British Columbia. Their admiring smiles made obvious their love for each other.

What a different world! How are we going to get used to this? Everyone doing everything themselves. Everyone – we were told – did building, painting, repairing the plumbing, the electricity. They simply looked it up and did it. There were books about all the work that needed to be done around the house. No, the whole thing was mind-boggling! Women did everything in and around the house, children, cleaning, cooking, washing, ironing – but the machines they had! WOW!

There was one tiny little thing wrong with the machines. They were absolutely useless for babysitting at the same time they did their perfect, automatic work. I missed that, and the company of those who helped me around my home in Hungary. The cleaning lady, who scolded us for coming home too soon. She was not ready with the washing yet – at 11 p.m. She was also babysitting the two children sleeping in their cribs. However, I must say: everybody was not so lucky. We had a special arrangement with a neighbor family who were friends, babysitters and cleaning ladies all at the same time.

The next day the Vámossys took us to the airport to take a small plane to our destination: Powell River, B.C.

Powell River! John was telling me some unbelievable things about it.

We are going there! but there is no road? no railroad? you have to take not one, but two ferries to get there? Or you have to fly? What kind of a place is that?

That flight over the blue water and dense green forest as far as the eye could see! No people seemed to live anywhere. Here and there a village with a few houses.

"Those must be the ferry stops," I pointed and turned to John for an answer.

"They are. And, you know what? You can still homestead on the 'Queen's land' in and around this great wilderness. You can claim land and you receive it for free. The only condition is that every year you have to produce $100 worth of income from your claimed land."

"But, how can you do that, if there are no roads? How do you even get to that land?"

"By boat would be the only way. And then, you must fell one tree at least and somehow get it to a populated area to sell it. Those trees are absolutely huge. They form forests where no one has ever been yet. As we say in Hungarian: 'Human hands have not yet put their foot in them.' Anyway, without a jungle knife there is no way to make even a step because of the forbidding undergrowth."

I silently decided not to try to go even near it.

The children could not take their eyes off the beauty of the landscape below us. Louis slept. Then, the homes in Powell River and a huge factory showed up. There was a cluster of small brown barracks.

"This will be our home for the next three months!" John pointed. We arrived at the camp by car. Mel Julson, the electrical engineer of the paper factory came to pick us up. He had already met my husband, the electrical engineer among the many forest engineers and students, who had already settled there.

We finally arrived at our new home. The barracks of the workers, who had just finished the world's – at the time largest – paper machine served now as the camp of the Sopron Forestry University. They were here to learn English from the volunteer teachers.

"The barracks were built of plywood on the outside and cardboard on the inside," John and his friend Mel helpfully explained.

"What? The walls are made of paper?" I could not believe my ears. When I touched them, they did not seem to be paper; they were much harder than I thought paper should be.

"We have three rooms because two people are assigned to a room and there are five of us," John continued.

Now those paper walls had one big advantage we discovered: one could cut a door into the wall any time – as we did – to have access to the children in the next room. We also took out the entire wall between the other two rooms. This way we could see all the children at once and they had a nice big room to play.

There were no kitchens in the barracks. The kitchen and a big dining room were in a separate building. Aunt Paula resumed cooking for all of us, just like in St. John N.B. She was a great cook and there were many students who helped her around the kitchen after classes. We did not have to worry about preparing food, only about interpreting and translating. The teenagers and the other families were happy to take care of our kids, when we needed to go to do our jobs. Negotiations, complaints, permissions, work opportunities, medical appointments, everything came our way sooner or later.

One of the dishes Aunt Paula used to make was gizzard paprikash. We all loved it, but Canadians could not imagine why we would want to eat "animal food." Each immigrant received $90 from the government for a month's keep. Aunt Paula saved us one-third of that money, so everyone was given $30/month for spending money. It worked out beautifully.

The first thing we bought with our money we received was a manual typewriter (no electric ones yet). We always typed everything. We wanted to write long letters to our parents and friends, about the children, about the beautiful surroundings. Translations we had to do would go much faster. What a beautiful typewriter that was! We thoroughly enjoyed the grayish snake-leather imitation color of it. It had the American keyboard, which meant we had no accents, and the "y" and "z" were switched on it, but one could get used to that.

We had one bathroom with showers for the men and one with showers and a bathtub for the ladies in each of the barracks and several sinks and toilets to accommodate us all. I loved going out there every morning bringing with me my wonderful thick terry towel that was so big, when I wrapped it around me, it reached from above my breasts to my knees. I loved the smell of it, the softness. Every day I thanked God for giving us all these wonderful luxuries.

The barracks had furniture, but just the bare minimum: beds, cribs for the little children, tables, chairs, shelves, a closet.

My father gave us a radio. Evenings we listened to the latest hits on "Lucky Lager Dancetime." Every night we sat there with John and listened, while we shared our daily one bottle of…what else? Lucky Lager beer. We danced the time away, while the children slept in the other room. Real American music: swing and rock and roll, our admired, but back in Hungary seldom – if ever – heard American stars.

There was a TV in the dining-room barracks, in a room entirely dedicated to this pastime. There were always quite a lot of people there to watch this – for us – new phenomenon.

In another building there were washing machines with wringers. Another miracle! After the wash we hung out the clothes to dry.

There was also a constant secondhand clothes supply, given by the townspeople, filled with all kinds of clothing; from baby outfits to grandmother outfits. WHAT A TREASURE TROVE! How much fun we had picking things for the children and ourselves! Such an abundance of clothes! Such good materials!

"Look what I found! It will look so good on my daughter Julika!" Ili's eyes were radiant as she admired the dress.

"Three great shirts for my eight-year-old son!" said Maria.

"A robe, just my color! I will look so enchanting when going to take a shower!" grinned one of the older ladies.

Canadians must be the best neighbors in the whole wide world. A few years later we became aware of the why of this phenomenon. Among the definitions we had to learn for our citizenship exam was: Canadians have to be good neighbors.

When any of the young wives came to me and said: "I would like to talk to you in private," I already knew she was pregnant. Naturally, they wanted me to go with them to the doctor. We went to the doctors with anyone who needed it. We still had no dictionaries; we had to circumscribe words we did not know. For instance the word "spleen" came up. I told the doctor, it was like the liver, but on the other side. That is when I heard the word for the first time and immediately started using it.

Whenever we walked on the street, or even within the camp we were just ooh-ing and aah-ing at the beauty of nature around us. The sparkling sea, the pristine forests farther away and, as far as the eye could see, no other city, not even a house, besides our town, Powell River. The river passed right by the camp. A bridge led to town, where the few stores sold their wares. The largest, the department store was called Hudson's Bay.

On a small hill, just opposite the camp a brown bear came out and looked around. Sometimes he stayed all day wandering in the sun. One day a mother bear walked on the sidewalk with her cubs. She toddled into one of the homes and gave a whack to the refrigerator, which opened up to her "friendly greeting." She fed her cubs and herself from what she had found. Then the bear-family returned to the street and resumed their Sunday walk.

Now, we should – and actually could – not forget that we lived on the other side of the fence of the huge MacMillan, Bloedel and Powell River paper factory. An awful boiled wood smell filled our lungs every time the wind blew in our direction. People who worked for the paper factory called it the "smell of money." One of my friends, Edith, wife of Professor Sándor Jablánczy was pregnant with their fourth child. Her oldest was 16 at the time. For Edith it was something awful to smell that disgusting odor almost constantly.

We made lots of new friends, as we lived like one extended family. There were about 200 students and very few girls among them. Most of the girls tied their fate to their sweetheart's in the first few months after they had left Hungary. There were 14 babies born that first year. Two of them were faculty and the rest were students' babies. We used to call them "Pickersgill babies" after the Minister of Immigration because their medical expenses were all paid for by the Canadian Government.

***

March 15th is a Hungarian National Holiday, in remembrance of the 1848 Revolution against the Habsburgs. Of course, we were going to have a great celebration. In anticipation the students decorated the auditorium with flowers of the beautiful dogwood tree. We did not have any in Hungary and they were in full bloom in March.

Mr. Vincent Forbes was our excellent camp manager, responsible for the entire camp. As interpreters, we spent lots of time with him. When he entered the building, he definitely needed us – he almost fainted. Dogwood was a protected plant, and no one was supposed to break off even a tiny branch. And, here he was! Responsible for the camp! I don't know how he did it, but not even the Royal Canadian Mounted Policeman standing at the door said a word. The "Mounties" as they are nicknamed were all tall, good looking young men. Absolutely no women were allowed. The men were not allowed to get married in the first five years of their service. During those years they could be commissioned to the Northern provinces and territories. In their district they were the police force, the judge, and the hangman. All in one person. It was a grueling, difficult job. This was the first live "Mountie" I saw. Police were not usually visible on the streets.

Dean Roller made an official announcement that the Communist Hungarian Government revoked our Hungarian citizenship, therefore we were now stateless. In a way it was sad, on the other hand, we were now totally free. We were "landed immigrants" in Canada. This was the equivalent of having a green card in the USA.

Culture shocks galore greeted us everywhere.

One of the student wives was applying for a job in a pub. She had a baby in her arms. They would not let her enter because the child was not 21 years old yet. This was terribly hard for us to understand. The baby was not capable of ordering a drink and her mother could not leave her outside. But of course, rules are rules. Even if they do not make sense.

One day we went shopping at the Hudson's Bay Company. When we went to the cashier, she asked us: "Cash or charge?" What did she mean by that? How else can you shop if you do not have cash? What exactly does "charge" mean? We were puzzled. The salesman explained that it was possible to have an account and pay it once a month. Of course, they had to fill in the receipt by hand because there were no real credit cards, only a paper card with the account number on it, as identification. How strange! Who will make sure we would pay?

We could walk around in the department store, pick up the merchandise, feel the texture, smell it, try it on, take it after we paid, and return it, if we had some complaint about it. Weren't they afraid someone would steal something? I asked the Julsons about that. Their answer was: "Why would anyone take something that does not belong to them?" I guess Canadians had no answer for that because nothing ever seemed to disappear. Amazing!

I remembered, when in Hungary I wanted to buy a pink sweat suit for our daughter, there were none. For almost a year I was going to the "Pioneer Department Store," the one that offered the most choices, asking for it. A grumpy employee cuffed at me every time: "We don't have any!" You can imagine my joy, when one day they finally produced my heart's desire. I paid fast before they could change their minds.

"Speaking of honesty, let me tell you a true story" said Jean Julson, Mel's wife. "A lady was given back too much change and, having noticed it, quickly returned with it. The cashier started thanking her. The lady got quite upset: 'You do not have to thank me for that. Anyone else would have done it. It is the natural thing to do. This was not my money after all.'"

We met with the Julsons several times. Other families also invited us to their homes, among them the band leader of the high school. I remember him so well because he gave us a blue alcoholic drink. I never had a blue drink before.

Another new experience was the Jell-o salad. The hostess served fruits in a green aspic, which had salad cream on top of it. We were supposed to eat that. Well, it tasted good, but weird. In Hungary we used to have dishes with gelatin, but it was prepared as a thick, well cooked meat stew and it was see-through with chunks of meat in it. We called it "kocsonya."

There were some older Hungarian-Americans in Powell River who came after the turn of the century and were still there. The custom at the time was to go to America, work for a few years, then go back home and buy a house from the proceeds. One of them had a teenage daughter who helped with interpreting. The students told us about a very funny incident. The girl was interpreting in court. The word "swear" can be translated as "making an oath" or "swear." She used the word to swear. The poor student for the world of him, could not quite understand why he should "swear on the Bible."

Again, we found the same with the Canadian-Hungarian language as with that of the Quebec French speakers. Their language developed differently from the language in the home country. A few Hungarians in Canada used some ancient words for cup for example. They called it: "findzsa." Nowadays we call it: "csésze." I recognized the word only because it was given in our Hungarian grammar book in school as an example for the use of the "dzs" letter we have in our alphabet.

What made this place unique were the people. Intelligent, loving people, all in the same boat. Or at least coming from the same boat: the Empress of Britain. We were young, we had children and we enjoyed the natural beauty around us. We had fun with each other as did our children. The students had their own fun evenings besides all the English lessons.

We welcomed a wonderful family to help us with interpreting. The Udvardy's. Miklós was a professor at UBC. He left Hungary earlier than we did. He went to Finland on a scholarship.

"And there he met me," Maud chimed in. "Ours is a real romantic story. We met at a concert. Next time we sat again beside each other, so we started talking. We talked and walked ourselves into real love."

"At the end of the season I popped the question," Miklós added. "She said yes, and took me home for the first time. I could not believe my eyes!"

Maud was the only child of the owner of the largest Finnish paper factory. She said yes because I was asking her to marry me without knowing she had money.

Maud and I became friends fast. She was funny, down-to-earth and delightful. Our three children were about the same age, each of them only one year older than ours. They played together and we became the happy owners of all their hand-me-down clothes, baby carriage and what-have-you. They brought a few things with them to brighten the barracks. They lived right across from us in three rooms just like we did.

"Come ladies," Maud said one afternoon, "I will tell you about life in Canada." Naturally, everyone wanted to hear this. After all, she was talking about our future life as Canadians. She was Swedish-Finnish herself, and spoke both languages, but not Hungarian. So, she spoke English to the Hungarian ladies, but I was there to interpret in case it was needed

"The Canadians live in a happy and free country; the second largest in the world with only 16 million inhabitants. 100 years ago there were only Indian tribes living where now British Columbia is, but no cities or villages anywhere. We need to understand that everything here is new. A 50-year-old chair would be 'antique.' The coastal mountains were so forbidding that only two pioneer parties came across the Frasier Valley. Once there, close to Hell's Gate Canyon, where the Frasier is the narrowest and wildest, we saw a plaque for all the mules that tumbled into the ravine at that point. The rest of the parties of wagon trains came up on the coast through California."

"We still have the pioneering spirit in us. Once you come this far from your extended family, there is no one you can count on, except your neighbors. That is why being a good neighbor and being hospitable to everyone is in the Canadian spirit, given freely. You only have to let your neighborhood know what you need, and someone will help you with it. This attitude developed with the early pioneers. They were single-family groups that arrived into a wilderness. Necessity developed a virtue, which became part of the Canadian character.

"That is what we experienced ourselves in St. John, New Brunswick, when we surprised them by landing there instead of Montreal," Aglaya, Dean Roller's wife interjected. "It seems to me that people here have a great life, every weekday is full and rich, enjoyable, fun, but they do not have any great holidays. Or, rather their holidays do not differ much from their weekdays. In Europe we have the big Feast Days, market days, for which we prepare ahead for weeks or even a month for Christmas or Easter. I found the lack of this exciting anticipation remarkably interesting, and characteristic in North America. Of course, as a European I missed the feast days."

"Social life revolves around the churches and schools. People meet each other at services, at meetings, they have parties, fun together. I would advise you to go to every possible meeting when you are invited and I promise you, you will have lots of fun".

"People here are very natural and very formal at the same time. You will never know which one is the millionaire and which the janitor. They all dress alike and behave alike. If you have a fur coat, or a mink stole, you wear it to church as well as to the grocery store, come rain or shine. You always have to dress like a lady."

"Talking about dressing as a lady! You will be invited to afternoon 'tea parties,' a very British custom followed all over in Canada. They will serve you tea in delicate cups, all different. Apparently they do not believe in having an entire set of one kind. Small sandwiches with ham, cheese, sliced cucumber, egg, and cookies come with the tea. On such occasions you must wear a hat! Do not even think about going without it! It is so important that you can almost go naked, but you have to wear a hat."

Many of us started giggling at the thought of that image.

"Oh, yes, I should not forget: you always have to wear white gloves for afternoon tea."

"You always have to give honest answers to their direct questions. If they offer you a second helping and you would like it, you have to say so, or you will not be asked again. It is not like the Hungarian customs. You do not have to refuse five times before you accept another bite. They will believe your first answer. If they would not, it would be implied that you lied the first time."

"You know, there are so many things that are strange to us Europeans. I cannot even think of all of them, but we just must get used to them. When in America, do as the Americans do," she finished with her characteristic smile and twinkle in her big blue eyes.

Miklós and John became friends fast. Miklós was a professor of ornithology at the University of British Columbia. John told him all about his experience with UBC and that he had to go to meet Dr. Frank Noakes, the Head of Department when he had arrived from Winnipeg. In the morning Dr. Noakes told him there was no opening in the department, but he showed John around, nevertheless. He must have liked their discussions about their subject, electrical power engineering because he suddenly asked: "Do you know Paul Biringer?" It did not ring a bell in a way Dr. Noakes pronounced it, but John asked anyway:

"How do you spell it?"

"B-i-r-i-n-g-e-r."

John's face lit up: "Of course I know him. We were in the same classes, we graduated together." Frank – as he wanted everyone to call him – said: "Did you know he was assistant professor at the University of Toronto?"

"I did not. I only knew he managed to get abroad. I am really happy for him."

"Do you know John Szögyén?"

"Spell it please!" John was not taking any chances. "Of course, I know him. He was in the same classes with Paul and me."

Frank pulled out an application form and told John: "Well, why don't you fill out these application forms, just in case something might turn up." Miklós told him that this is an exceptionally good sign.

John waited for a reply. Miklós proved to be right. One nice day the letter arrived offering John $5,500 a year, which was a huge amount at the time. Engineering professors got much better offers than for example English professors. As we later found out, they only received $3,200 a year. UBC asked us to move to Vancouver and start work on May 1st.

Needless to say, we were overjoyed. God brought us here with a special purpose. When later we became much better acquainted with the Noakes Family, Frank told us the rest of the story:

John's subject, electric machines, was taught by the same professor for the past 29 years. Professor Coulthard had a stroke the year before and was allowed only to take graduate students. When Frank heard that the Dean of Forestry was going to Austria to meet with the Sopron University, he asked Dean Allen to look around to maybe find a replacement among the refugees. John, being the interpreter, met Dean Allen and asked him if there would be a job for him. Dean Allen said to write down his resumé in a few words on a piece of paper. When Dean Allen arrived back to UBC he told Frank: "I found you an electrical engineer, who was teaching the same subject in Hungary – and – he is the only one among them who speaks English." So basically, it was almost all arranged before John arrived. It was just that Frank wanted to be sure he was the right one before he committed himself. He had a chance to check with his friends. In those days in Canada, if you said you were an engineer and could do the job, they would hire you without a diploma. The principle was: if he cannot do the job, we will see that within six weeks anyway, and we will let him go. That was because refugees did not carry around their diplomas. If they were caught with them, they would immediately be labeled escapees and jailed. So, John became an assistant professor without even showing his diploma, or any other kind of papers.

9

The day I stopped ironing sheets.

So, we are off to Vancouver! The most beautiful city in the world! At least that is how John's mother introduced him to Vancouver when he was just a child. She made him promise to at least get to Vancouver someday in his lifetime. And now, we are going to live there!

I couldn't wait to see where. It was student and young faculty housing, we were told. John spoke with Mr. Brown, in charge of this housing project. The rent will be $55 a month. There was a big oil furnace in the middle of the hut…What? Why did he call it "a hut"? Weren't these supposed to be houses, homes?

The street's name was Westbrook Pl. The housing was called "Westbrook Camp." Now, why that strange name?

Mr. Brown was happy to explain:

"These houses were barracks for soldiers during WWII in the Interior, in Eastern British Columbia where they were trained. After the war, these soldiers went to university on VA grants, so they needed housing at the university. Many of them had families by then. So, the Army decided to transport the barracks over the mountains to this place, very close to UBC's buildings to accommodate them. Great solution! There was only one problem. The houses started shifting and having gaps between the ceiling and the walls, as they were settling. Now what? Someone had the bright idea, to bring a cement truck and pour foundations under the houses. So, by now the gaps are not too bad and the houses are stable. If you want to paint your house inside, I can give you the paint for free, but you have to paint it yourselves."

By that time, my head was spinning. Paint the house? Ourselves? What about those gaps?

There was an improvement compared to Powell River. The walls were made out of plywood. Nevertheless, we were told if they catch fire, the time we have to get out is two and one-half minutes.

"John, why are they building such flimsy houses? Don't they have bricks?" I asked.

"I am sure they have, but they have so much wood, they just use it because it was always handy, even for the pioneers, who just cut the trees in the virgin forest. Now, aren't you glad we do not have to build the houses ourselves?" He looked at me with a sarcastic smile.

Well, yes, that was a consideration. We were lucky enough.

The man who had lived in the house came by and we asked him for the keys to the house. He was a student with a lovely family: wife and three children. He graduated and they were about to take off to where he used to work every summer. That company offered him a permanent job.

"Keys?" they asked astounded. "We do not have any keys. What would you need that for?"

"Well, what did you do when you went away for the entire summer for your summer job?"

"We did not lock the house. What for? No one would come in if they knew we were gone."

Another neighbor came and immediately affirmed their statement: "We used to put a broom across our door to signal we are not at home, if we left the door wide open. Like when we washed the floor and wanted it to dry."

OK, so no keys. Nevertheless, the next day we asked Mr. Brown for keys. He had them made for us, although he did not see the need for them.

Betty and Andy Belshaw from New Zealand lived across from us. She came over with some sheets: "I brought you these to put them up on your windows in the evenings, until you can get yourself some drapes."

"You are so thoughtful. Thank you very much." I did not even think of drapes at this point, but as a good neighbor, she did.

Éva Székessy, the sister of one of the Sopron Professors Laci Székessy, came with us when we left for Vancouver. She was now busy watching the kids and washing the linoleum floors, while we went to town to shop for furniture. What a godsend she was!

Ede Brokes, the manager at Royal Bank on Hastings Street, was actually an old alumni of the Sopron School of Forestry. He left Hungary right after the war. He was now in the position to give each of the professors a $1,000 loan through the Royal Bank to buy appliances and furniture. We bought an electric stove, a completely automatic Westinghouse washing machine and a dreamy refrigerator (at least for us it was, after having had to buy ice from a horse-drawn carriage daily for our icebox in Hungary). For the kitchen we bought a kitchen table and six chairs. We bought bedroom furniture: a double bed, our all-time dream, called a "French bed" in Hungary (this was the standard bed in Canada), two dressers, one with a mirror. For the living room we bought a sofa (called "chesterfield" at the time in Canada) and an armchair, as well as a desk, where we could do our work. We could bring the cribs with us from Powell River, so we had those now for the two boys. We bought a single bed for Ilike.

One of several culture shocks was when we saw the advertisement during our buying spree, on the side of a refrigerator: "Great value!" It was on sale. But value? How could a refrigerator be designated as "value"? Value to us was associated with something spiritual, some trait that made you more humane, lovable. Ok, money had value too, as well as houses, or land. But, a refrigerator? A stove? Furniture? Value was friendship, sitting down, having a drink, and discussing your life with someone. People were of value. But everyday things??? It took us a while to get used to it.

Now, back to earth. We had some painting to do. First the gaps between the ceiling and the walls. We bought some strips of dry-wall tape and nailed them over the gaps. That took care of that.

Wait, we are becoming do-it-yourself people as well? Of course, if in Canada, do as the Canadians. So, we started painting with the paint Mr. Brown gave us. It was oil paint. How could we have known that for one dollar extra per can we could have received water-based paint!!! Oil-based only came off with turpentine. Every time I needed to nurse Louis, I had to wash my hands and arms with turpentine, then of course with soap and water. Our hut had only a living room, two bedrooms, a bathroom and a kitchen. I painted, we painted, but after three weeks of that I was ready for a nervous breakdown. Why do we have to do the things we don't know how? Why don't they have specialists for the various professions as in Europe?

Why do I have to do more work than any one of our maids was doing in Hungary? John in the meantime, had to go to work to get ready to teach his subject, but in English. He also painted when he came home, but I tried to do as much as I could. Besides cooking and cleaning, washing, and ironing on top of feeding Louis and looking after the kids.

Then came the nightmares. We dreamed that we were separated; that we were in Hungary. How in the world were we going to get out to Canada? How will we be together again? Our nightmares were so real! When we woke up it seemed like we were dreaming that we were in Canada and the reality was that of being separated; one of us was in Hungary. Or all of us were in Hungary and trying to get out. It was horrible!

I complained to John. At least he had his work at the university which he loved, but my work in Canada was…woman's work. I was getting more and more desperate about having been thrown back into the Middle Ages. Into being a slave, one could say a slave of love, or, as we used to say in Hungary: to have children is like a sweet jail term. They were so sweet, but you were their captive.

John used the best weapon he had if I complained: "I will call your father." Just like a little girl, who is afraid of spanking, I immediately lifted myself out of my self-pity and looked at the bright side.

Some days I went to pick up John with the children at the university. Of course, we had no car (in a country where everything was built around cars and driving), but we had a big baby carriage the Udvardys had passed on to us. Louis was happy in it. Ilike and Jancsi loved to walk along in the beautiful sunshine. After all, it was summer! The entire university still had barracks for some of the departments. We passed the University Hospital, a three-story building on the corner, mostly for sick students. Then we walked to the Law Department, another "hut" and sat down on the lawn. It was breathtaking. Yes, Vancouver was a beautiful town, but…why did the Canadians have such a weird lifestyle?

When we got up from the grass, we walked around the lovely homes. We selected one of them.

"Why would it be impossible for us to own this house? We had so much, then suddenly there was nothing. Why couldn't there be a change, or we could become wealthy, and then we would buy this house." We both liked it. It was not pretentious, but beautiful in a real American tradition. White house, green trim. It had a tennis court, but otherwise, it was just a cozy looking family home. We decided on this one. Why not? We were young, in love and nothing was impossible. Dreaming is allowed…

Finally, the painting was finished. Our home was lovely. We even had some nylon curtains on the windows and under them shades, so I returned the sheets to Betty. She offered: "I am going to Woodward's every two weeks to load up on groceries. I see that you get only to the grocery store on the corner. You don't have a car. Would you like to come with me?"

Would I? I was so happy to be able to go with her and buy the heavy staples for two weeks at a much cheaper price, than at the local grocery store.

We did not have a car, but somehow, we acquired a woman's bicycle. I used that to go do my errands. Sometimes John would use it too, but being as tall as he was and the bicycle being a fairly small women's bike – he looked, as we say in Hungarian: "like a monkey on a knife-sharpening stone." Of course, looks aren't everything, but it was also difficult for him to pedal with his long legs.

The Udvardys lived very close to us, but on the other side of University Boulevard, where the rich houses were. We loved having them within walking distance. We were able to borrow anything from them.

Maud invited me over for tea one day, to meet her lovely friend Mrs. Koerner. The Koerner family came from Czechoslovakia and became timber barons in British Columbia. I had my favorite dress on, which we had bought in Winnipeg at a store called "Sweet Sixteen" back in January. It was navy blue with white dots, but the dots were square shaped. It had a white collar and a huge navy bow under the collar.

The two friends wanted me to tell them about our escape and what it was like to live under Communism. Maud must have told her a lot about us already, so Marianne wanted to hear the whole story. That was the first time I talked about our escape to anyone outside the family. While I was talking, I trembled inside the entire time. I guess my voice must have trembled along with my feelings.

We talked about more fun things too while we had our treats. Maud was volunteering during the war. Of course, everything was scarce, and they were young. So, she told us their secret. In order to be efficient with a bottle of vodka, they poured it on the stone in the sauna. This way the entire company got into a good mood on that one bottle. And – no hangover. The alcohol went straight into their blood through their lungs.

Maud and her mother (her father had already passed away) were rich, but she could not get to her money from Canada. So, they had to invent all kinds of ways to help her and her family enjoy what they had. When they traveled, all their tickets were bought in Finland. Maud's mother came to visit them with a ticket around the world, then exchanged it for a return ticket to Finland and left the money for them. She sent them boxes of chocolates, in which some of the chocolates were replaced with gemstones.

When Maud immigrated to Canada, she was legally allowed to bring out enough money to buy a house, which she did. Then the furniture was transported from Finland by boat and was insured as best they could. During the trip some of the antique chairs and other pieces got damaged. They received enough money from the insurance to buy their Chevrolet which they were still driving. Of course, there was no money left for the repairs, but those could wait.

"Our immigration was also pretty exciting," Maud said with her usual twinkle in her eyes. "Miklós got a job at an American university, but his visa has not arrived yet. In the meantime, I was approaching the ninth month of my first pregnancy. We wanted the baby to be born on the other side of the Atlantic. So, we decided to go to the continent, to Toronto, in Canada. There was no job for Miklós in Canada and our money was limited for that trip. So, he started to look. Nothing. Finally, he saw an ad. A restaurant was looking for a cook. Miklós applied and got the job. He told me he was a scout and they used to cook. Luckily, he never had to cook, thereby avoiding the disaster his cooking would have caused. The University of Toronto had a collection of one-cell animals that needed to be catalogued. 'Do you know anything about them?' they asked Miklós. He gladly accepted the job, even though he was an ornithologist. When he got the job here in Vancouver, B.C., the University of Toronto asked him to take the collection with him and finish the cataloguing. Apparently, they must have been satisfied with the job he did. We decided to stay in Vancouver, B.C. because we loved it here, even though in the meantime Miklós's American visa arrived."

After us, the Rollers were the first ones to come to Vancouver. They got a "hut" in Acadia camp, which was walking distance from Westbrook camp. So, the two families were the stronghold-fortresses for all the students who came to look for summer jobs.

The students slept everywhere in our house. Finally, we had to borrow tents from neighbors and of course, the Udvardys. The students camped on the lawn between the houses. I was conscientiously changing the sheets and bed linens. I washed and ironed them at first; then came the great day when I decided I was no longer ironing sheets. It was impossible to keep up with the daily changing crowds. I never ironed sheets again once I realized the futility of this effort.

We received my Dad's original trunks which he had used when moving to Canada. We used them to bring our stuff from Winnipeg. John had a brilliant idea! Laci Székessy, Éva's brother, a fellow Sopron professor came over to help. I will never forget as Laci was sitting on the shelf they just made in the closet, just the size of the trunk, above the clothes, with my husband. Two big men in that tiny space. Someone was going out to get some beer for the thirsty workers. And we were laughing. What a funny sight. What beautiful days!

Everything was made into alcohol, even the flowers and potatoes at our camp. After all, beer was not free!

In Westbrook camp the huts were scattered on a grassy terrain. It was like a friendly meadow with even friendlier people in it. We were all young, with little children. We had no money, but we enjoyed life. For us it was the first time ever – after five and one-half years of marriage – that we lived in a place we did not have to share with anyone. We were free to do whatever we wanted.

Sidney and Marguerite Mendel were our closest neighbor-friends. They were originally from England. Anna, their daughter was exactly the same age as our Ilike. They became best friends almost instantly. Sidney attended law school in England, but at UBC he was an English professor. Marguerite was a midwife. Sidney was Jewish, Marguerite was Anglican. They instilled all these values in their daughter. I babysat Anna while Marguerite was working. We simply exchanged babysitting. Whenever we wanted to go out, they babysat for us. Anna was like a sister to my children. The Mendels read a lot; so, they knew quite a bit about our problems with Communism. I heard from them for the first time about "Darkness at Noon" Arthur Koestler's book.

The Hungarian professors came one after another to settle in Vancouver, when their stay ended in Powell River. The students found jobs for the summer, most of them in the forest industry. Actually, British Columbia was mapped by the students. We must remember, all forests in B.C. were virgin forests. A helicopter dropped a student on top of a mountain with measuring instruments, a gun in case a grizzly bear stopped by, and a shortwave radio, that being the most modern way of communication in 1957. On top of each of the mountains other students were dropped. During the one day while they were on that mountain top, they did the measurements between the peaks. Photos were taken from a plane simultaneously. Then, during the winter the drawings were made.

About 10% of the students were girls. "Women are not allowed in the forest," was the verdict they heard from everyone. One of the women, Márta Kovács (the wife of the couple who got married in St. John, N.B.) decided she was going to visit her husband in the forest. She wanted to see for herself what was so forbidding about it. She traveled by train, by car, by jeep, on foot and finally arrived at the small house where her husband lived all alone. When she came back, she had no doubt; she told everyone she would not want to go near that forest by herself. It was so easy to get lost once you were inside the forest. The lumber companies were cutting out the trees in a way that left blocks of forests standing. Once you turned the corner and no longer saw your house, all blocks looked exactly alike. It was like a labyrinth.

Many of the students became choker men which was a dangerous job. They had to throw chains around the unbelievably huge logs. When a tree was falling, the woodcutters yelled: "Timber!" If you did not get out of the way the tree could fall on you.

Some of the professors arrived from Powell River in Westbrook Camp. The Jablanczys were the first family to move in. Their daughter, Edith was

81

the oldest at 16, Sanyi was 14, Micu was 8, and Mother Edith was close to giving birth again. Father Sándor was preparing to teach and at the same time decided to do his PhD at UBC. All five of them were beautiful people, but Mother Edith was a beauty. She had red hair and green eyes; her face was as radiant as only expectant mothers' looks can be. She loved to come over to our house every afternoon – to smoke a cigarette. She said her husband did not know she smoked so she did not want to smoke in her own house. That was just OK with me. We could exchange all the news and talk about old times. She loved to complain about all the things she had to leave behind in Sopron: her beautiful crystals in her lovely apartment, the carpets and porcelain. She was complaining, but not with bitterness. She was happy they got out and were free. Her husband was a total gentleman and secretly giggled about Edith coming over to smoke because he knew about it but kept his knowledge secret from her. Games people play!

Baba (Maria) and Oszi (Oscar) Sziklai lived in the house next to and opposite to the Jablanczys with their three sons. Oscar was the one who greeted us at Strobl am Wolfgangsee when we first met with the Sopron foresters. We became lifelong friends. Baba and Oszi were a good-looking couple. Oszi's hair was black, Baba's blonde and curly. Their children inherited their good looks. They were long-time friends with the Rollers. They were always kidding around that they do not get pregnant again because their life's story seemed to follow that of the Rollers' – and the Rollers had four sons.

Right next door to them lived Sopron Professor Frank Tuskó with his wife Mimi and children: Agi 13 and Csaba 9. A student couple Jóska and Imelda Rédey lived in the same block. We had a whole Hungarian colony.

Pretty soon, out of the 33 children in that part of our grassy meadow, 17 were Hungarian, just picking up English. So, we noticed that English-speaking mothers quickly learned: "Nem szabad!" meaning "don't do that!"

The inhabitants of the "huts" often changed as students and professors came and went. One of the young couples had a farewell party when they were leaving to go to Fort Churchill on Hudson's Bay in the Arctic. Their only entertainment was the radio station, which they were running. Their family life, therefore, was quite intense; they averaged one child per year, born in the only hospital around, the military hospital.

The average number of children per family was four in those years. I felt we had to get busy ourselves, after all Canada needed more people! John thought we should wait until we will have our own house. A couple like us, married over five years was supposed to have a house already. We just started a bit late with our six diapers.

10

My father noticed while we were still in Winnipeg that there was a Dr. John Kovach in Vancouver; both of them advertised in the same Canadian-Hungarian newspaper. He called John before we moved to Vancouver. Dr. Kovach and his charming wife, Pauline, became our guardian-angel-friends. They immediately invited us together with their best friends, his colleague Dr. Ian and Mariann Balmer, as well as Grant, a lawyer and Betty Deachman. The three couples became our guiding lights on how to be a true Canadian.

Dr. John Kovach was born in a Hungarian village in Saskatchewan and became a well-known heart surgeon. They had no children, so they loved to borrow our Ilike now and then. Pauline would take her to their beautiful home with a gorgeous view of the ocean and the mountains. Ilike loved their company and being spoiled by them.

Pauline was the first woman whom I ever saw smoking tiny cigars. And, believe it or not – in those days – both of them: John, our doctor and Pauline, a nurse, recommended that I should start smoking if I wanted to lose weight.

They owned a Buick with that year's ornamental ovals on the hood. Physicians had to change their cars every year or every two years, or their patients would have abandoned them, saying: "They must be bad doctors because they cannot afford to buy a new car." So, when they did change their car to a new Buick Le Sabre, Pauline jokingly said: "We had to exchange our car, the ashtray was full."

The Balmers, the Kovachs and the Deachmans used to drop by (a neighborly thing to do between friends at the time) and "shoot the breeze." Nowadays we would say: "hang out." The Deachmans lived very close in a condominium. We loved to discuss international politics with them, the situation in Hungary, and received interesting information in return about the entire British Commonwealth. Grant was running to be a representative in the Parliament. He found a great campaigning idea. What would be a flyer he could distribute that people would keep? His wife had a pecan pie recipe everyone loved. So, Grant stood at the bus stop and distributed the recipes on his campaign flyer.

Dr. Balmer brought us a newsletter published by the Canadian Intelligence Service, which we began to receive regularly. He used to be in the Air Force during WWII. Mariann, his wife, was the daughter of the Prime Minister of Alberta when Ian married her.

Grant was a fundraiser. We had no idea what the word meant, so we went to a meeting to find out. It was a fundraiser for a swimming pool on Dunbar (a district in Vancouver). A community got together to make their dream come true and have their own swimming pool in the district! No one was even thinking of asking the government or the city. They simply took matters in their own hands.

So, this is a fundraiser? He explains, people discuss, then decide and donate. The swimming pool will be built. I could just imagine how this would have worked under the Communist system!

In July there was a polio outbreak in Hungary. Our friends begged us to send them Salk vaccines as they were not available in Hungary yet. How could we say no? We remembered the days when we were trembling and praying during polio epidemics. The first two months we received only $200 a month from Immigration, then finally UBC's first salary came in July. We ended up sending vaccines for 31 children in Hungary. Thanks to our friend Miklós Bán in Switzerland, who mailed it from there, we could buy it at a discount for $140 for the 31 doses.

Of course, we still had to eat. It was John (Dr. Kovach) who arranged with Woodward's (a big department store with the largest supermarket in its basement) to issue us a credit card. That made it possible for us to send the vaccines.

In order to get a credit card, you had to have a credit history, meaning, you had to have a record of asking for a loan, then paying it back in time. No record, no credit. We did not have enough time yet to establish our credit. That is why his guarantee was needed.

Grant dropped in one day and asked us if we had a friend, or someone, who wanted to come to Canada. The last plane of refugees was going to come next week. We just received a letter from John's best childhood friend, Toma Wagner from Austria. We were already talking him into coming to Vancouver. So, we told Grant about him. "Consider it done!" Grant said. That is when we found out that he had many connections to the government and was active in liberal politics.

Toma arrived on that last plane and moved in with us. From then on he slept on Ilike's bed as a roommate to Jancsi, while Ilike occupied the sofa in the living room.

We had lots of fun with Toma. We kidded each other, he helped me with everything, watched the kids for us when we had to go somewhere.

In Hungary, under Communism, there was a movement among the miners. The "hot pickaxe" movement. The miners changed shifts underground, so the pickaxe's handle was still hot when it changed hands. This was to speed up work. Of course, it made mining more dangerous because twice as many people were underground, but who cared in a system that assured us at every step: "Human lives are our greatest value?" It seemed that bottom lines trumped human lives. We instituted a similar system.

Toma was helping with giving the kids a bath. We gave them a shower with a hand-held shower head. John, Toma and I handed one child after another to the next person. One handled the shower, the other the soap, the next one the towel. This became our "hot child" method. Of course, we knew what that meant and laughed every time. The kids heard it. One day, when neighbors told Ilike they are going to have "hot dogs," Ilike told them very seriously: "Interesting. We have 'hot child' at home."

One night son Jancsi had a piece of candy. He gave it to Toma to take care of it for him because it was bedtime. Next day when he asked for his candy Toma gave it to him. He looked at Toma with big eyes and declared: "Toma, you are a good man!" He never expected to get his candy back from him.

John was going to teach and work in his chosen profession. But, what was I going to do in this topsy-turvy dead-end-for-women world? There was absolutely no hope for going back to university. None whatsoever! I was a "housewife" and that was a noble profession, which was the dream of all women. I had the "MRS" degree and on top of that I had three children. "What a challenge!" I was told. "To bring up the children, to see their development, to teach them, to care for them. What else do you want?" I wonder if any of those men had ever tried to do all of that? I doubt it, or they would have known the utter boredom that can be yours when all day you talk baby-talk. Your brain goes to sleep for lack of use.

I was not going to let that happen to me. To me having children was a state of life that had nothing to do with your intellectual pursuits. Besides, we all needed money. I had the advantage of being able to speak the language.

John bought me three books in Hungarian from a Hungarian bookstore somewhere East. I appreciated them, but I decided to go on a reader's strike. I was not going to let anyone tell me that by reading novels, or a cookbook I will become something that I believe worthwhile.

So, what am I going to do? I was thinking of my grandfather, who was a great businessman. "You have to give people what they want, what they need." He went into the drugstore business because he realized that ladies, who do the shopping, sometimes bypass food for beauty products. He made his millions taking the cue from customers.

Now, what do we newly arrived Hungarians need? What are we looking for? The first thing that came to mind was textbooks for the students. Miklós Bán again came to the rescue and connected me with Pannonia Books, who were the representatives for the Hungarian Culture, the state legal entity that was established to distribute books internationally. I started my "bookstore" in the living room of our "hut." I received the list of textbooks from the professors and distributed order forms for them among the students when they came back around the end of August.

As long as Hungarians were coming into my living room to pick up the textbooks, it just made sense to have other books, cookbooks, literature, novels, even joke books.

I arranged to receive the books on consignment from places like Argentina, Spain, Brussels, Italy. The publishing houses trusted me because I had a university professor for a husband.

One thing led to another. What else were my customers asking for? Espresso machines. We were used to drinking strong espressos in Hungary. Vancouver's climate was rainy and gray many of the days. We kept calling each other to keep awake and drinking lots of instant coffee. Hungarians considered Canadian coffee to be sour and watery compared to espresso.

My next line, therefore, was espresso machines, followed by nylon-velour sweaters. They looked like velvet and wore like iron. We all knew this wonder-material from "home" and could not wait to have those tops again. I found a source in Montreal. In the evenings we went around to our Hungarian friends. We did not even have to ask if they wanted an espresso machine. It was enough to ask: "Which one do you prefer?"

We tried in vain to get our Canadian friends to switch to espresso, except for the ones that spent time in Europe, like Douglas and Dorothy Derry, who had lived in France for a while. She spoke perfect French. In France they told her, when she excused herself for her French: "But, you never forget your mother tongue." This was a huge compliment from the French, who consider most strangers as "salle étranger" (dirty stranger). She was the one who introduced me to the Faculty Wives' French Club, which I loved.

September! UBC opened its doors!

John started teaching. He spoke English very well and he knew the technical language, but…when it came to simple words, like "screw" he drew on the board and asked the students what this was called.

He started the year by making a deal with them. If he made a mistake in English, they would correct him. Then he made a mistake on purpose. If no one corrected him, he asked: "Why didn't you correct me?" The students understood then that he truly meant his request.

He asked the students whether they could understand him.

"No problem whatsoever! You should hear some of the professors! It took us a whole year to understand Professor Beddoes! He speaks the most beautiful Queen's English!" they laughed.

The Beddoes Family, Mike and Maureen, became some of our best friends. They spoke real British English. We enjoyed listening to them and to the BBC every morning. We soon understood the saying: "America and England are divided by the same language."

By the end of the school year, we got so used to the Canadian of the Pacific Northwest, the English broadcasts started to sound strange and snobbish.

People in Canada told us they preferred if we did not try to change our accent because if we talk like a German, or a Hungarian, a Russian or a Chinese, they will understand us. However, if we try to imitate any other English (London, Australia, New Zealand, Oxford) it would become more difficult for them to comprehend what we are saying.

When we arrived in Canada, Immigration officials greeted us with "very OK, very OK" thinking we would understand that for sure and gave us a copy of George Mikes's book in Hungarian, titled: "How to be an Alien" (Anglia papucsban). It was a hilarious book, explaining all the strange (for us) customs of the English, who brought their customs to Canada. Mikes states that it does not matter which accent we learn when we are studying the language. People will always tell us we speak the way we do because we are Hungarians. So, don't worry, just speak!

George Mikes had an English wife and worked for BBC in the Hungarian section. During the 1956 Revolution against the Soviets, he came to Hungary and installed an instant radio station in Győr.

Canadians distinguished themselves from the American "melting pot" method by asking all nationalities, to keep their customs, traits, language, and culture besides becoming Canadians because that is how a distinct, independent Canada will develop.

11

My old Hungarian School, the Sophianum Sacré Coeur greeted us in Vancouver, B.C. too. We went to visit the nuns. Of course, I did not forget the obligatory Canadian custom: white gloves and a hat. I kissed Reverend Mother's hand. She was not used to this of course, but she gave in. Our reception was the same as in Pressbaum. We went "home" to the mothers, who opened their arms and their heart.

We told all the Hungarian girls we knew to apply at that school. So, Edit Jablánczy, Móki Gerencsér followed by her sisters, and many others became students of the Sacré Coeur school: Point Grey. One of them, Judit Kováts attended that school as well. Her mother, by her maiden name Lilly Filotás was also a Sacré Coeur student in Budapest, but much before my time. She was a famous radio announcer and had her own magazine in Hungary. When the Communists came, she was deported together with her officer husband into internal exile in 1951. So, they were close to Miskolc, where she started the free radio station during the 1956 Uprising. They were broadcasting until the last minute when they had to escape on all fours. She told me once: "You know what weird things one thinks at times like these. While I was running on all fours, all I could think of was not having my toothbrush with me."

She started the Hungarian radio station in Vancouver, and I advertised on her program, before Christmas and whenever I could afford it.

By that time, I expanded into sending IKKA parcels to Hungary. That basically meant to take the order and the money, then send it on. IKKA parcels were the Hungarian government's only legitimate way to send money to your loved ones who had remained behind in Hungary. I managed to send medicines as well through Switzerland. I had plenty of things to advertise. My "store" was still in my living room. Most of my business was through correspondence. I could do that easily while being with my children.

September was also the start for pre-school. We learned from our neighbors that there was a Westbrook Co-Operative Nursery School, organized by the parents. How in the world did that work? Of course, we wanted to enroll Ilike and Jancsi, so we went to a meeting.

Culture shock! By now it was not surprising, but still something that was out of our experience. We saw it repeatedly how people here did not beg the government or took to the streets to ask for what they wanted, they simply made it happen. We, the parents, established the organization, settled the non-profit status, paid tuition, hired the teachers, collected the money, rented space at an Anglican Church and decided about how to use our money. Everyone contributed their own specialty. We had a two-week schedule to rotate the parent-helpers. The first year we were only members, but later I became treasurer of the organization.

The law mandated that there had to be an adult with every eight children under school age. Therefore, in the two classes, for the three- and four-year-olds, we needed two parents to help every day besides the teacher. At first it was only mother-helpers, but John introduced the parent-helper concept, when he started working as one, showing others that men were able to do that too. Again, I was thankful that my mother-in-law brought him up to be able to do all kinds of "women's work." He was not only able, he liked to do it: to be with the children, to take care of their needs, to teach them.

Hallowe'en caught me entirely by surprise. Neighbor children, dressed in outlandish costumes, knocked on the door and said: "Trick or treat!" I asked them: "What did you say?" They repeated it. I asked them what they meant by that. "Well, you have to give us a treat, or we will play a trick on you." "What kind of trick?" I asked, but the kids were too small to answer that question. I gave them an apple. Pretty soon other little goblins came around. "Oh boy!" I thought. I had to think of something to acquire some treats. I told Ilike to grab a grocery bag and go out "trick or treating" and bring home the bag, so I can hand out something to the children, who kept coming and I was running out of apples.

Ilike gladly complied with my wishes and pretty soon came back with two grocery bags filled with goodies. One kind neighbor helped her carry it home. Now we had our own treasures to hand out...and then some...

The Bowers, the Forsyths and other neighbors of British origin made a huge campfire and burned Guy Fawkes...in effigy. He was the man who burned down the British Parliament. While they were satisfying the British tradition, they distributed to us neighbors rye and ginger ale, Canada's as well as our favorite drinks. I loved every minute of it. What a fun holiday! Next year I was already looking forward to it and manufactured costumes for the children.

In November of 1957 John gave the first of one of our many hundreds of talks about our escape from Hungary to the Faculty Women Auxiliary of UBC. We were wives of professors. We had no male members, as there was no such phenomenon in those days. We met many wonderful and interesting people. The first ones to connect with us, who also became great friends, were the deJongs.

Mrs. deJong heard John telling our story. She brought her husband and children with her and brought a lovely long sleeve T-shirt for Louis, along with a birthday cake to Louis' first birthday. In December they picked up the two older children in their car and took them all over town, to see the Christmas lights. We did not even know what Christmas lights were. We had nothing of the sort in Communist Hungary.

The closer we got to Christmas we noticed more and more lights here and there. We finally went to the drugstore and bought a string of lights. We put it up around the edge of our roof. The fashion then was having big light bulbs in many different colors. We had that string of lights even 50 years later. One of our children gratefully took it because they were in fashion again.

Father sent us $50 for Christmas. We organized our entire gift-list, holiday feast and everything we needed for Christmas, out of that money. Joe Rédey, the student who lived close to us with his wife, worked at a Christmas tree vendor. He brought us an exquisite tree for free. It was not a salable tree because it was made of the bottom of one tree and the top of another. However, he and other students wired it together solidly. It was absolutely beautiful and huge!

Of course, we wanted to do everything for the children as it was done in Hungary. There the little Baby Jesus comes in the afternoon of Christmas Eve with angel helpers. Everything arrives on this day starting with the Christmas tree. We closed our bedroom for the entire day, but we prepared everything the night before. We were up practically all night with Toma. We had to smuggle in the Christmas tree after the children went to sleep, decorate it completely, with make-shift ornaments, self-prepared paper chains, even the children's smaller toys. Then came the gifts. That too was out of our experience that we had to assemble some of the toys, like the doll house we got for Ilike and some of the boys' toys as well.

After our almost sleepless night we had to keep the door of our bedroom closed all day, to have the little Baby Jesus come and bring everything at once, just like in Hungary. The beautiful, illuminated tree with the presents underneath, none of them wrapped. It was an indescribable feeling for us in our childhood, to see that all at once, after the ringing of the angels' bells and we wanted our children to have the same experience we did.

We did it! We managed to keep them out all day and have a wonderful, radiant Christmas Eve in our "hut."

When one of John's students graduated and moved away from Vancouver with his family, wife and three children, we bought their TV. So now, we became proud owners of the second TV on our block. This meant that some of the children now gathered in our living room as well as in that of the Bowers'. It was a fascinating experience to see all those children, 10 to 12 of them, at least, in complete silence, watching the cartoons. What a great babysitter that TV was. No problem of the children getting too much "screen-time" (the concept did not even exist then). Children's TV came on only at 5:00 p.m. and the program was over when the news came on.

∽

1958! What a glorious year! It was British Columbia's Centennial. So, when I went to get my business license at City Hall, I chose the name "Centennial Agencies."

Even the weather was celebrating. For six consecutive weeks we had no rain! The sun was constantly shining.

On January 1st Ilike turned five. She started school that year in September. In those days private schools could accept children if they felt they were mature enough. She was going to be six years old on January 1st.

To say she was "mature" would be an understatement. By that time, she was my greatest help. She was only five, when one Saturday morning we woke up to great silence at 11:00 a.m. We jumped out of bed to see what happened. None of the children woke us up? They were sitting in front of the TV, all dressed up, happily watching it. On Saturday mornings there were cartoons on TV.

"How come you did not wake us up?" John asked.

"Who dressed you?" came my question.

"I did," Ilike said matter of factly.

"Aren't you hungry?" we pursued.

"I fed them," said Ilike.

"What?" We ran into the kitchen, only to find everything in order. Cereal boxes were on the table, but no mess whatsoever.

We could not believe our eyes or ears and could not count our blessings enough. What an angel God gave us in this child!

∽

One day John was sick with a cold and was in bed. A young, slim, good-looking man knocked on our door.

"I am Frank Kollár. I used to teach in Sopron. I went with the mining group to the University of Toronto and did a master's degree. I came here for a PhD. We are just moving in with my wife, Vera, and our daughters, Judit and Zsuzsi. We will be living just around the corner, in the same block."

I invited him in right away. He sat down beside John on a chair and we started to tell each other about our adventures before and after we had left Hungary.

We kept talking and talking and completely forgot about everything. Suddenly I realized it was lunch time. I offered him lunch, but he said: "No, no I have to go home in a few minutes."

Dinner time passed and Frank was still there. We enjoyed each other's company, but he said he did not want dinner because he must go home.

Finally, when it was dark, Vera appeared in her coat thrown on above her nightgown to get him. We got used to Frank's complete lack of time-consciousness and became best friends with them.

With the Kollárs we had a complete circle of friends right in the "camp." Their daughters were about the same age as Ilike and Jancsi. They played together all the time and we had adult fun with the parents.

I learned to drive on everyone's cars, especially on the Morris Minor that belonged to Maureen and Mike Beddoes. John had a driver's license from Hungary from 1942. All men who could be drafted had to have a driver's license. However, he had not used it since. He went downtown to the Department of Licensing with Mike Beddoes. That tiny car had standard transmission as almost all cars at the time. Automatic was brand new, but not perfected yet. Brakes could totally burn out by the time the car got down from a 3,000-foot mountain. The drive to the testing station was all the time John had to practice. The examiner came out to the car. Someone had parked so close to the tiny car, John had to climb in from the other side, over the standard transmission with his 6'5" frame and long legs. The examiner laughed so hard by the time the test started he was very lenient with John. Besides, no examiner would have thought a 33-year-old man would not know how to drive. So, John got his license right away. Mike, our trusting friend made John drive out of the parking lot. In the next block he said goodbye to John and stepped out of the car, instructing him: "You now have your license, I am getting out here. You drive." John told me how scared he was, but, being an engineer, he could do it.

I was not so lucky. I learned on the Beddoes's car, but also on all our neighbors' cars. All of them were different. I went for the exam in a big car, after having practiced on the Morris Minor – I failed. Next time I failed again, and again. I was always driving in a different car. The examiner finally said: "Come back when you have your own car. It will be much easier. You have to drive well because you will be transporting children." And that is what happened.

After our first year in Vancouver, we started to look for a not too old used car. We found a year-old turquoise Dodge station wagon for $2,100. We were so incredibly happy with it. I passed right away with our own car.

In an economy where everything was designed and executed based on people having cars, it was almost impossible to live without it, especially with three children. We commuted by bus. Just to get to church on Sundays, we had to take two buses. One to get out of the university's endowment lands, then transfer to another bus to take us to Our Lady of Perpetual Help Church. We used to stand at the bus station with the three children, waiting. Almost always a driver stopped and asked if we needed a ride. We happily said yes and jumped in the car.

I had a few disputes in the confessional with the priest. Namely, I could not understand why it was possible to go to confession only the day before, on Saturday afternoon. That meant we had to do our trip twice when we wanted to receive the Sacrament of Penance. I told him in Hungary confessions were heard during the entire duration of the Mass. He did not want to believe it and said the Pope did not like that. I could not believe my ears! Was that the same church? If we both wanted to go to confession, it took us the entire afternoon. If the buses did not get us there on time, we could not even make it at all. The same with Masses. One of us had to go to the early Mass to get home in time and the other could barely reach the last Mass. Of course, we could always take the children, which we did most of the time.

Now that we had a car, this did not matter anymore.

I could not know then that someday I would write an article "Is it the same church?" for the "Our Family Magazine," yet, unknown even to myself, I was already gathering material.

I always wanted to be a writer, but in my sixth language? It did not look very promising.

Constant collections for something or other were another trait of the Canadian church we did not like. As soon as we started attending church in Vancouver, the priest said he was going to have a six-week campaign, when he would be talking only about money to raise funds for the church. For those six weeks I simply closed my ears and read my prayer book. Why talk that much about money? And why take two collections during every Mass? The first for donations, the second, after Communion, for your space in the pew.

Then that ridiculous little hat/veil/doily/glove-routine on your head!

Thank God, Father Zsigmond, a Hungarian priest, who was parish priest in Port Moody and taught theology in the seminary, arranged with the German church to have a Hungarian Mass said every Sunday at 1:00 p.m., when they were finished with their Masses. That was genuinely good news! It also meant we started out around 12:30 p.m. and did not get home until nearly 4:00 p.m. Naturally, we immediately were thinking about getting our own church. However, all we could muster from the entire congregation every Sunday was approximately $16, which we gave to Father Zsigmond. His advice to us was "Do whatever you want, stand, sit, kneel at certain parts of the Mass the way you are used to and show the others how it is done." He knew very well these are nothing but customs, changeable anytime, anywhere.

Our car was the first vehicle to transport many of the Hungarians in our block not only to the church, but also to the beach. We loved going to the Spanish Banks. This was a fantastic natural phenomenon. The water was very shallow where the waves and the sand met, we had to walk a mile to get to the water at low tide. Here, the water suddenly became deep. With the arrival of high tide, the water would spill straight out to the beach, meaning you would have to swim a mile to the shore. Of course, we carefully watched the tide table to make sure we went swimming at high tide. While the low tide was ruling, the sun warmed up the sand. It became hot during the six-week sunny summer of 1958. We drove out to our favorite spot at night with the 17 people we could squeeze into our station wagon, put on the headlights to be able to find our way back from the water – and off we went. What a terrific feeling to feel the hot sand on your feet under the cooling waters of the sea!

In Vancouver, the seashore belonged to everyone. It was not developed yet at all. Everywhere logs, which rolled off the logging boats and lots of driftwood lay around on the beach. There were no dressing rooms, no food stands, only unadulterated beach with its velvety soft sand. The skyline of the city was practically non-existent. One building was as tall as 12 stories. The rest were typical northwest style single-dwelling homes. Still, it was quite a sight when you looked at it from the water. I loved swimming towards the city.

The Centennial celebrations included a visit from the USA Navy.

One of our neighbors, Fritz Bowers and his wife Denise, owned a fishing boat. It was large and could sleep eight people. It was cheaper than a pleasure boat and they had three children, so they bought it to tour the nearby islands. One time they even went up to Alaska in it.

Fritz, who was in the same department with John and some others of the professors, including us, decided we would go out to greet the Fleet. Under the Lionsgate Bridge, trying to go against the tide that was just coming in, we had to use the full power of the boat, to just stay in place and not be swept backward.

Finally, we were able to get through and soon the Fleet was getting close. In the meantime, we were drinking beer and jumping off the boat, swimming, then drinking some more beer. Someone suggested a challenge. Jump in with an open bottle, then drink its content. John whispered into my ear to put my finger into the open bottle while I jumped. This way the salt water did not enter the bottle and the beer was still enjoyable. There were only eight people on the boat, but we greeted every one of the boats by shouting: "Hurrah for the Newcastle (or whatever the approaching boat's name was)! We must have made an awful lot of noise because the next day the Vancouver Sun reported that a boat with about 32 people aboard greeted the USA Navy accompanied by a lot of "hurrahs" and frolicking.

That same Navy Fleet helped the local ships provide a wonderful evening of brilliant fireworks for our Centennial Dominion Day (former name of Canada Day). Naturally, we watched it from the beach. We felt like real patriotic Canadians, even though we were not citizens yet. We had a stateless passport, which made it possible for us to travel. It was basically a statement on the part of Canada that we could return to the country.

⁓

That September Ilike went to school for the first time. Edit Jablanczy, who went to the same school, took her by the hand and off they went on the bus, one to 12th grade, another to first.

That made me think of school again. We had another pair of good friends: Dean and Marta Friesen. She was a Hungarian from Chile. He was Dean of Extension. I asked him when I started my business where he would recommend I could learn about the difference between trade in Europe and Canada. He immediately said there was a course organized by UBC's Extension Department and the Vancouver Board of Trade. It was a three-year course that gave a Diploma in Sales and Marketing Management. Marketing was a totally new subject in the late '50s. The course was like what later became known as an Executive MBA. Those who participated had to be owners or managers of businesses. He failed to mention it also helped to be a man. I had to wait for two and one-half years to get in. Every year they admitted one woman and 60 men. My first year was in the 1959/60 school year.

⁓

"We have to visit the Upper Levels Highway today, on its day of opening!" John was enthusiastic, as always, when it was about an engineering feat, especially connected with energy and traffic.

"All right!" and off we went. We piled the children into our new (at least for us) station wagon and started on our long journey. Now, to be completely honest, the highway was only declared open because it was supposed to be finished that day. Of course, it was not yet finished, but it was just about passable, not regarding the fact that the road was an earth road and had many, big potholes.

This did not deter us. We went slowly and carefully. It was beautiful! The sun's brilliant rays lit our way. The sky sparkled in blue and the untouched forests' radiant green kissed the mountains.

At one of the bends, we saw a small island in the middle of the bay with one house on it, dense green forest, and a boat.

"You know," John said "this entire island is for sale for $30,000. The boat is included, as that is the only way to reach the island."

"The entire island?" my mouth dropped.

"It is not that big…" John looked at it critically.

I knew that the most expensive houses in those days ran around $30,000… But, to get an entire island for the same amount?

The state of the road got gradually worse, but it was still possible to navigate it all the way to Horseshoe Bay. That is as far as it went. But it was "open." Horseshoe Bay was the first ferry station towards Powell River. Ferries also went to other islands and to the huge Vancouver Island just across the straight.

"Look, kids" John started to explain to them. "There is a small island in the middle of this bay, that makes the bay look like a horseshoe."

"Let's get out and look around," I suggested. The children rejoiced and ran all over the place. They finally got out after the long, bumpy car trip.

People walked around in the park surrounding the ferry station. There were some motorboats for rent. An old man sat on a bench and enjoyed the sun.

The Upper Levels Highway and Marine Drive on the shore ran parallel to each other. Marine Drive was already covered with trees, but on the Upper Levels Highway, which ran along the middle of the mountain between the shore and the ridge, opened up spectacular views. It was also needed because the population was growing, and traffic was increasing.

North of Horseshoe Bay in the Sechelt area one could still homestead in the original virgin forest that we saw on our way up to Powell River, just in the spring of 1957, which now seemed to be ages ago.

What a beautiful country! The second largest in the world and only 16 million people! Truly, the land of opportunity! No wonder my father wanted to come here!

Still, it was also a bit scary. Such huge parcels of land and no one near or far!

"John, can you imagine comparing these forests with our park-like meadows in Hungary we dare to call 'forests'? Our forests are inviting, while these are forbidding."

"Do you know," John asked, "that if you go for a walk, or I should say rather hike on Mount Seymour, which is within Vancouver city limits, you have to tell the ranger, so he should send a rescue party to find you if you do not return by the time you registered?"

"Really? And within city limits?"

We could see Mount Seymour and all the other mountains, like Mount Grouse and the Sleeping Beauty, when we just stepped out the door of our home. I did this often, to prove to myself what a beautiful part of the world we ended up.

"How I wish we could share this with our friends in Hungary! To show them where we are, what we are able to enjoy!" That we could not do, but to say good-bye to all whom we had left behind, we sent out hundreds of Christmas cards to our family and friends in Hungary, addressing them as we remembered their addresses. We had none with us in order to protect them in case we would be captured. We only signed the card, and we had our address on the envelope.

Who would respond was the question. If they responded it meant they wanted to keep in touch with us. If they did not, it meant that it was better for them not to receive letters from abroad.

We sent them out way ahead of Christmas. Of course, our list included all the nice people we have been meeting ever since we had left Hungary. We noticed that in Canada everyone was sending Christmas cards to everyone they knew, even if they met every day. We never did that in Hungary, we wished them merry Christmas, when we met. That just added more and more people to our list.

The cards started coming our way. To accommodate them we hung them up on the wall on loose strings, so they formed nice half-circles. We had our whole living room decorated. That first year we kept the cards up until June because we had no other decorations on the walls yet.

12

We planned a scenic camping trip with the children to visit my father in Winnipeg, including Yellowstone, the Badlands, going on the USA side, then returning through Banff and Lake Louise, the beauties of the Canadian Rockies and the Coastal Mountains.

Just before we started out, we got a phone call from Father.

"When are you arriving?" he asked.

"On the 27th," I answered.

"Then don't even come!" he answered in a gruff tone, then he added: "Your mother is coming on the 25th from Hungary!"

"What? How come?" I was stupefied. She could not get out of the country, although she had continued trying ever since we had left. At first she applied for "family unification." She was told she cannot do that if she was married to Uncle Charles. So, she divorced him and applied again. We have not heard about her latest attempt, or this sudden permission. When Father left, my mother was told they would give her a passport in 10 years. But, who believed the Communists, whatever they said? It was exactly 10 years.

"Come as fast as you can," Father continued.

"Of course, we will. We will be there, one way or another. We will change our plans and will come back through the USA, we will now go through Canada, that should be faster."

We had a day to change all our plans, but we had to make it. I was still in complete denial. I could not believe we would see Mother again.

The next day we started out and reached Hope, B.C. The road was two lanes, but good. Of course, it was a mountain road, so we had to drive carefully. No seat belts at the time. The children were sitting and playing in the back of the station wagon. We took with us a AAA guide, in order to avoid the recommended motels. They were way too expensive for us. We took our camping gear, but the weather did not cooperate, and we had to hurry.

We set out the next day on the brand new, but far from ready, Trans-Canada Highway. We drove from early morning til late at night and made 180 miles all day. At one point the sign said: "Safe speed 10 miles per hour." Even that was the understatement of the year. It was supposed to be a two-way road, but it only had one lane; if you could call it a "lane." There was no railing on the edge of the road. On one side there was the mountain that would have kept you safe, but on the other – nothing. The road itself was dust, pebbles, and potholes, with occasional rocks. Whenever something came from the other way, we had to inch our way to avoid each other. The weather was getting worse all the time. We slept at a motel, which was a log cabin. Between the logs the wind blew in and through the house. Jancsi got an earache again from the wind, just like on that one night in Austria, in the drafty room. When we finally arrived in Alberta, the Trans-Canada Highway was already in its intended glory. It was a two-way highway, but on both sides the shoulder was as wide as a lane. We enjoyed driving as fast as we could.

We arrived in Calgary where we walked right into a friend, Professor Ferenc Vecsey, who belonged with the mining group of the Sopron University and now worked as a mining engineer in Calgary. We slept in their basement. Just before we fell asleep we heard a big truck go by the house.

Next day when we were about to leave our friend called from work and said there was an earthquake somewhere; the company's seismograph showed it. So that is what sounded like a big truck.

We drove all day against a 55-mile headwind. When we stopped at the gas stations, we could barely open the doors, the wind was so strong. We had no radio in our car, we heard no news. Just the day before we arrived in Winnipeg, we stopped at a rest area to eat lunch.

"What a terrible earthquake!" we heard a man say at the next table. "A lake was created by it!" his wife added.

"The water flooded the entire campsite. Can you imagine those poor people?" This was the man again.

"Where was this and when?" John asked them.

"Where were you man? You did not hear the news? It was August 17th, in Yellowstone Park, in the middle of the night." (The 1959 Hebgen Lake earthquake also known as the 1959 Yellowstone earthquake occurred on August 17 at 11:37 p.m. (MST) in southwestern Montana, United States.)

We realized that, according to plan we should have been at that exact campsite that was flooded. We would no longer be among the living.

God saved us again by sending Mother at the exact time for us to avoid certain death. No way of knowing why things happen the way they do.

"John, we sent your parents the entire itinerary and, knowing your father, they know about the earthquake. He listens to all the newscasts."

"We need to send them a telegram as soon as we can," John replied. From the next village we sent the telegram. It turned out they knew exactly what happened and knew we had to be at the exact same spot for the past days.

To telephone to Hungary to his parents would have taken much-much longer. We would have had to get an international connection to a country that was nine hours ahead of us, with a post office of a small village, at the time when it was open and let them know we would make a phone call at a mutually agreed upon date. They would go to John's parents' home and let them know. Then, on the date, they would have to sit at the post office maybe an entire day and wait for the connection. We spoke with John's parents only now and then; it was that difficult.

Now we understood where all that wind came from and did everything in its power to keep us from arriving at our destination.

⁓

Finally we arrived in Winnipeg.

"Thank God, you are here in time," said Father when he saw our station wagon stop in front of the house. He rented a motel room for us because once Mother and Grandfather (we just heard that he was coming too) will have arrived, there is no way we could fit in his one-bedroom apartment. Marietta and her daughter Maria arrived too.

It was a windy and terribly rainy day when Mother and Grandfather arrived. The rain was so bad in the normally extremely dry Winnipeg that John's trousers were wet enough to have to wring the water from them.

Then the seemingly impossible happened. We met again! Not even the horrible weather could stop our happiness and joy.

Marietta and I could not wait to show Mother all the wonders of Winnipeg, while she was full of stories and kept missing Elizabeth and her daughter Rita.

Although Mother was used to riches when she was young, she became overwhelmed now with the choices at the department store. After a while she said she had a headache, so we took her to the restaurant of the Hudson's Bay for: what else in Canada? a cup of tea. She enjoyed that because she loved everything British and spoke English very well.

We visited the Sisters who owned Misericordia Hospital at their residence. Mother was brilliant and radiant in her yellow dress and big straw hat speaking English and French with equal ease to the Sisters, who could not have enough of her. They surrounded Mother and questioned her about life in Hungary. They told her how much Father had missed her and all of us.

On Mother's first night in Winnipeg, Louis started coughing and could not stop. The more he coughed, the more he cried. It was just a vicious circle. In the end we went over to my parents to see if Father had some remedy for him.

We found them in the middle of giggling and love-making. (They already had their first argument by then. It was all my fault. I told Mother to tell Father piecemeal how much money had to be paid and to whom in Hungary still. It was a bad idea. He wanted to know all at once. I should not have said anything.)

Father advised us to let the shower run hot and sit with Louis right beside the shower. That worked. I also found another excellent remedy. Louis, who was almost three years old by then, was intelligent. So, when he was coughing, I started to tell him: "Peter Piper picked a peck of pickled peppers, a pack of pickled peppers…" I made a mistake on purpose. Louis stopped coughing, then corrected me and forgot about crying to make his cough worse.

13

Naturally, our trip home did not lead us through Yellowstone Park, we went on the fastest route, but this time, having learned from our former trip through the Trans-Canada Highway, we came home through the USA on excellent roads.

We were barely out of Winnipeg, when our car broke down. We had to come back to Winnipeg to have it fixed.

Marie's daughter Maria was the happiest girl alive when she saw us returning. She ran and hugged our knees with an overjoyed smile and a big thank you in her eyes. We brought back the kids with whom she so loved to play. She also loved to take a walk with us because we let her off the "child-leash" as soon as we reached the park and she could run around to her heart's desire.

Finally the next day we set out on our journey home.

Drive carefully! Mountain pass! That was still strange to me. The roads were very good, but it never hurts to remind people that in some places it might be quite dangerous to drive too fast or pass, especially when the road was curving.

We went through Stevens Pass. We read one of the signs that told us about an avalanche during a horrible time in 1910 when two trains were swept down 150 feet into the valley by a 14-foot high snow wall; the most deadly avalanche ever in the USA until then: 96 people died.

We were happy when we arrived home safely.

~

This was the year when I was finally admitted to start my three years of the Diploma in Sales and Marketing Management course. I was so excited! I could study again!

Oh boy, was it ever interesting! So, here we were 60 men and one woman. Those men were managers at LaFarge Cement, Johnson & Johnson, Hudson's Bay, many great companies. And here was I, owner of my own (one-person) business. The way we learned was we had to use our company's experiences, structure, and management as an example. We had to write our assignments on these kinds of subjects. I simply used our nationalized Hungarian business' experiences and described our organizational chart.

We learned about sales, management, organizing, advertising, but first and foremost marketing, which was a new concept. When we were marketing, "we were delivering a certain standard of living" to our clients. We learned about hiring, firing, setting quotas, rewards, premiums, accounting and law.

Law was most interesting because in Canada and the USA, except for Quebec and Louisiana, "case law" was followed, while in Europe the "Code Napoleon." In case law the judge had to follow the tradition of previous judgments, decrees and sentences, while in Europe the judge had to follow the law and decide for him or herself.

The contracts here were much longer because every word had to be defined, while under the Code Napoleon one word would describe a concept and there was no reason to explain it in further detail.

Here you can take a deposition and know what the defendant or witness would say in court, if you tried to do that in Europe they would arrest you. To have a last-minute surprise evidence may tip the case in your favor in Europe, while here this is not allowed.

It was fascinating! I enjoyed every minute of it. We got together only once a week, but the assignments kept us busy during the week.

The men were all dressed in suits and ties, just as they came from work. They chatted with each other, joked, and shared news. They did not even dare to speak to me. The entire year.

I ranked second in my class, when we took our exam. I could not believe it!

At the end of the second year I was pregnant with Steve. The final exam would have been on his due date. I asked if I could take the exam before the others. I had to promise not to tell anyone about the questions. The second year the male students decided to talk to me sometimes, yet this was not a hard promise to make, as I was not going to see any of them.

I was alone in the room and wrote the exam. We did not get any ranks that year. John was still curious and asked the leading professor again and again. Finally he pulled John aside and told him: "Now, you cannot tell this to anyone, but the law professor did not keep himself to the agreement and looked at Helen's exam ahead of time. When he saw how good it was, he did not check how she did last year, but instead made the exam much harder. He thought 'if a woman could do it this well, the exam was too easy.' He made the exam difficult enough for the entire class to get a D. So there was no ranking last year."

John was so proud! I just loved it when he appreciated my work.

During the third year the class accepted me as a human being and we actually talked to each other. At the end of the year we had a lovely graduation ceremony at one of the downtown hotels. As we were handed the diplomas and I went out to get mine the guys whistled with delight. I wore a black cocktail dress with a pink tulle egg over it. The latest fashion. The dress was the one I received from the Red Cross and the tulle egg was made by a friend of mine, one of the Sopron professors' wives, Aunt Ági Fodor, everyone's darling "Ági néni." John loved extravagant things and Ági néni loved to make extravagant things for me because her husband never let her make them for herself when they were young. She enjoyed making dresses for all of the professors' families, and charged very little, so we should be able afford it.

Before we got to the end of the three years many wonderful events happened to us.

In 1960 we received a letter from John's parents announcing they were given passports to come after us. This came like "lightning from a blue sky" as we say in Hungary. We knew they applied for a passport and a visa, but the usual timeline was that it was rejected the first five times. The sixth application might be successful. In between the applications there needed to be six months. So we were counting on three to four years.

We later learned that a man, Gyula Tóth, met my father-in-law in the street. John's father used to be Gyula's legal guardian after Gyula's father had died in Ábrahámhegy. While chatting, he asked: "You would like to see your son, my childhood friend and neighbor, John, don't you?" Of course my father-in-law affirmed that he would. Being a talkative man he told Gyula that they handed in their application for a passport.

Gyula said: "I think I can help you." Lo and behold, he was really able to do it. They received the passport at the time of the first application.

Our joy was dampened only by our financial distress. Whew!

We asked the university for a three-bedroom "hut." They rejected our petition because the Housing Department claimed this would result in "slum conditions." I suppose they were right, but that meant we had to buy a house. In Vancouver at the time, there were only about 20 apartment houses that would take children, but only under two, or above 12 years old. Renting a house did not make much sense at the time because for renting or buying the monthly payments were about the same amount. However, there was the down payment, which was not high, but at least $1,500. We had no down payment, the house had to be big enough, and preferably not too far from the university. We started looking at houses, hoping for the impossible.

Impossible? Why, that was just up our alley! Didn't we love to do the impossible? That thought perked us up. With the help of one of the Faculty wives, who was a realtor, we looked and looked. In the meantime, Father told us he would help us with the down payment. We should borrow $1,500 from the bank and he would send us $50 a month to repay it. We had the down payment!

We could get the credit from the bank. We had already "established credit" because we paid back the $1,000 we borrowed for the furniture and the appliances in a year.

We found our home! 3391 West 39th Street. One and a half blocks away from Dunbar and two blocks away from 41st Street, a main thoroughfare going straight into Marine Drive and UBC. The house had four bedrooms on two floors, two bathrooms, two kitchens, and a family room in the basement. It sat on a big lot. From the upstairs it had some view towards the Fraser River. We managed to have the two former owners hold the mortgage on it, still, our payments went up from the university housing's $55 a month to $160 a month, plus insurance and taxes. John's salary thankfully went up by then to $8,000 a year, and of course, we had some income from my business.

John sat out to change the wiring in our home, while I started painting. John painted the ceiling and the top of the walls, while I did as far as I could reach. Our friends came to help as best they could. We were not used to doing our remodeling in Europe, but what the heck! I remember Professor Adamovich, our beloved friend Laci, was trying to remove wallpaper with a scout's shovel and was succeeding too! Being a forester, his help with the garden was much more efficient. The Sopron ladies came and helped with cleaning and watching the children. Young people were moving our furniture over from the camp in three days so we had to "remodel" the entire downstairs.

The same day we moved in the morning, we invited the Head of Department Frank and Mrs. Noakes over for tea in the afternoon. We did it!

The impossible was beaten again. We were so happy with our first house. Our own! The house was grey, covered with permanent siding, white window sills and doors, but the porch stairs were the trendy vivid red color. Inside we still had our same furniture; we just had to add more to it slowly, when friends moved away, or when we could get something inexpensive at a "rummage sale."

14

Culture shock! When we had first found out about rummage sales, we did not know whether it was acceptable for us (according to the university) to go shopping there. Churches usually had them once a year for fundraising. Everyone brought their things they no longer wanted and sold it to others who thought they found treasure.

Then, as we went to our first rummage sale, who comes out the door, but Mrs. Noakes, with a broad smile on her face: "Look at the great jacket I just found for Frank!" No more questions about acceptability.

We had to find out because it was a tricky question. For example: for Faculty wives it would have been unacceptable to work as a cleaning lady. Working as a realtor was OK, but not as a cosmetician, or beautician. The Faculty at any university was considered to be like aristocracy in Europe. They were the highest-ranking people in society. Thank God rummage sales were OK! After all they were fundraisers for churches and charities.

We, the Hungarian professors' wives, had great fun parading in front of each other in the fashion show we held evenings after every rummage sale we attended, showing off our treasures. And treasures they were! We watched carefully when churches in the richest districts had their rummage sales. Once I got a full-length black velvet coat for $1.00 and a once worn white rabbit-fur jacket for $5.00. Shirts for son Jancsi were eight for a dollar. Unbelievable!

We found many other ways to save money and told each other about our latest finds. One was a German sausage factory, where they sold the broken pieces for a bargain. Pretty soon we named the store: "second hand sausage place." They knew how to please their customers. If they did not have any more broken pieces, they simply broke up a few of them to satisfy the demand.

Our days at Westbrook and Acadia camps were wonderful, beautiful days because we were young! We had parties, especially on our "namesdays." In Hungary we celebrated our patron saint's feast day instead of birthdays. This had two great advantages: you did not get older on your namesday, and everyone knew when it was because florists posted it in their shop windows in Hungary: "Don't forget Maria Day, Helen Day, Andrew Day...!"

So, we ladies got together in the afternoon and celebrated. We pooled our money, each of us contributing $1.00 and one of us would buy a present on the money collected, which the lady of the house secretly wished for. The hostess, who was the celebrated recipient of the gift, organized the party and made everything at home, from scratch. They were fantastic desserts and of course a cake, without candles.

Other interesting ways to acquire what we did not have were buying the kind of wash powder that had in it a towel, a washcloth, another promotional "must have" for your household. The same went for cereals. What gift came in the box determined which brand we were going to buy.

Talking of brands, for years the refugees were buying Palmolive soap, Colgate toothpaste and whatever the brand names were in that first bag containing our toiletries, which we had received when we entered the country. To this day I have this bag. Later I kept my mending materials in it. Some of the ladies used the cloth of the bags as doilies to cover their shelves. While most refugees did not know the word "soap," or "toothpaste," they recognized the brand. So, it proved excellent business for the companies supplying the merchandise.

After we had moved into our new house, we had to prepare the upstairs for John's parents. I had a fantastic laugh watching our dear friend, Toma, and John trying to wallpaper the upstairs. Of course, we could not afford to buy the easy, "just apply water" wallpaper. So, we had to cut the wallpaper and put the glue on it ourselves. When the men got as far as putting the glue on all over the surface, then, knowing the glue will dry in a minute they lifted their arms and put the wallpaper on the wall any odd way they could. It ended up diagonally. We all laughed so hard, it makes me even laugh today when I think of it; we learned by trial and error until we got the hang of it.

We received a table and two armchairs from our dear friends, Dr. Ian and Mariann Balmer. By now he was our doctor because John and Pauline Kovach had moved away. John was wanted on the East Coast for his heart surgery skills, so we said a teary good-bye to them.

We put a phone upstairs, so John's parents could answer it up there as well. There were two bedrooms upstairs. One we prepared for the grandparents, the other for Ilike.

Maureen and Mike Beddoes brought us two blankets they bought especially for John's parents. By then the Beddoes family had their own house too, not far from where we lived, on 49th and Collingwood. They had a baby while still in camp, Andrew, and an eight-year-old, Michael.

The Bohns, also from the Department of Electrical Engineering, Eric and Jenny, came from Frisia. We spoke German with them. They bought a house close to where we did just a little before us. Their daughter Ilene was one of Ilike's friends. Just like we had two boys after Ilike, so did they after Ilene.

John's parents arrived. They stepped off the plane radiant with happiness to see their only son again after four years. Their beautiful white hair was glowing in the sunshine.

We were so happy to be able to bring them home into their – by then completely decorated – new place. We were proud to tell them they had a phone and a radio; they had their own kitchen and bathroom, and even a little view from their bedroom.

They brought many of our things with them including the beautiful family paintings and porcelain. Having spent all their lives in the arts community, they knew the art experts. So, it was much easier for them to bring out the paintings than it was for my mother. The art would follow them aboard a ship across the Panama Canal. We had to pay for 1,000 cubic feet, even though their stuff only required 10 cubic feet of space. It was not expensive, but that was the rule.

My mother had to pay in gold for bringing out silver. The Hungarian authorities declared one of the paintings protected, therefore it could not be taken from the country. They took her gold watch from her before she boarded the plane and brought her back beyond the "no-man's land" where visitors could no longer enter, so she could hand the watch to my sister Elizabeth.

John's parents brought out many of our books. "Where there is no memory, there is no pain!" We remembered Uncle Charles' words. We adhered to that. It worked wonders in our new homeland. Now, we could swear we did not own many of those books, yet, when we opened them, they had inscriptions on the day we gave them to each other. Uncle Charles was right.

Mother, Father and Grandfather finally moved to a house in Winnipeg. Mother was walking around in the neighborhood to find a house that had everything they needed. 917 Palmerstone was a beautiful house on a corner lot, close to the river, with a huge screened-in sunporch, where Grandfather would sit during the summer. There were two bedrooms downstairs and two upstairs. There was a nice bathroom, a kitchen with a breakfast nook that would seat four, with blue seat coverings in the white kitchen. They had a dining room right next to the kitchen and a much larger living room.

They planted many flowers in the large garden of the corner lot. We gave Father's address to our guides who took us across the border when we escaped. Well, guess who called Father soon after our departure from Hungary, but our guides. They arrived in Winnipeg. From then on Victor Baricza was my parents' gardener. He did a great job! Father said he gave him and his family $50 when they arrived, and they started their life anew.

Mother truly enjoyed having her own house again, decorating it according to their taste and having enough space for Grandfather.

Mother passed her driver's test, realizing how important that was in Canada. Life was based on everyone having a car and being able to drive. Father's patients all loved her and soon she was elected President of the Altar Society at the Hungarian church. She became the center of Hungarian social life in Winnipeg. Boy, could she organize! She called everyone before an event to make sure they took part in it. Her radiant smile bewitched them all.

She also decided to start our old business, Molnár & Moser, again. She started making our face creams in the basement with a kitchen mixer. She had a devoted cleaning lady, Ica. Ica's husband became Mother's helper in making and delivering creams to her customers. Once someone tried the cream, they were sold on it. Beauty salons were selling her creams. She then started to make eau de colognes too. We had representatives in Romania and Slovakia before we were nationalized in Hungary. She made connections with them again. They lived now in Australia and Israel. They started to pay her license fees. Mother registered our trademark in Canada. Marie and I started to sell her products too, in Toronto and in Vancouver, respectively. It was all very exciting!

15

The tension was growing in our home. Two women in the same household would be difficult at any rate, but even though I loved my mother-in-law and thought of her as a strong and beautiful woman, admired by everyone (at least I thought so), she was also stubborn and everything had to be exactly as she wanted it, otherwise it was not good. I was so much younger than her and my self-confidence crumbled when she told me how to do things.

My mother listened to my complaints over the phone, when she called from Winnipeg and offered to host them in Winnipeg. I could not accept that of course. I felt wonderful that she wanted to help, but that is not why we brought them out of Hungary. The purpose was to be with their only son and family. I heard breathing while we talked. I realized it must have been my father-in-law on the line, upstairs. So he had heard our conversation. Luckily I did not accept the offer. He knew my problem anyway. He thought we were both angels, my mother-in-law and myself, we just could not get along well together. Of course he also saw both of us were trying to hide that and were nice to each other.

I was looking for work – in vain. At the same time there were all those bindingly "unacceptable jobs" so defined by the University. So my mother-in-law started to look for work too. She took on anything, cleaning, babysitting, and cooking.

I felt miserable. Money was so scarce for a while, I had to delay payment for all our bills, until one of the creditors came to the door to collect. I smiled and said I already mailed it yesterday. Then, when he had left, I quickly mailed a check.

In the meantime, I started feeling out of sorts. I thought it must be the stress. Then I started to throw up. I knew I had to be pregnant. I almost never threw up. Well, we always said we wanted our next baby after we had bought a house. We did. Now this tiny life was growing in me. The fourth! What joy! But, I have never felt this nauseous before with any of my kids. It could have been my nerves trying to cope with our state of misery. I knew God was going to help us through this, but at the moment it felt like too much. What are we going to do?

I wrote a letter to my parents about our situation:

It was awfully difficult the first time and we hope to arrange somehow that we should not have to live together. I could not write about it before because I was so bitter and depressed about our life. I was pestering John for a while that we should have another baby, but now, when it happened and I felt so miserable, I did not know what to feel. I felt the grandparents wanted it and that made me feel I didn't. I could not recognize myself in this feeling. I felt like God had abandoned me. I could not hope, I could not trust in God, I felt the end of everything was here. When I was downtown looking for work I felt I wanted to end it all by stepping off the curb in front of a car. Then I thought of John, how he would receive the news. Thank God, I could not do it.

Simply, this is what happened. For years we were so happy with John we felt in Seventh Heaven. We were so happy I wanted to embrace the entire world and make everyone happy. That is why, and that is the only reason why, I invited them in a letter, to give them a chance to see their only son again. I remembered my father-in-law before we started our escape, how sad his eyes were when he told me: 'We will never see you again!' I looked him in the eye and told him: 'Yes you will. We will see each other again.' Naturally they accepted the invitation. They came. You cannot imagine how much love we had in preparation for their arrival. We prepared the upstairs in the best possible way. It could not have been better. After their arrival, I felt that they were taking away from me everything in succession that was beautiful, that was good, that made my life happy, that was worth living for.

Is this why I gave up everything, including my youth? By the time we will have paid for all the expenses we incurred I will be 30 years old, or even more. It is in vain that we have babysitters now in their persons because we cannot travel anywhere with John, I probably will not even be able to buy a dress before we will have repaid everything.

I even discussed with John that I will go to visit you with the children and will not come back until they have left. He discouraged me. He told me it was all about having enough money. If I leave that would be $500 for my ticket and then his. He would obviously come after me. Our debts would be that much more. He persuaded me of the *futility and craziness of my escaping all for what we had worked and to just run away from the problem. He loved me more than ever.*

Please, understand that I am an adult and I had fought so hard with life to become one in order to be able to feel that I was an adult. I wanted to keep knowing and feeling that I had free will and that I am the one who decides about my affairs. I just did not want to acquiesce playing the child again in our own house vis-a-vis those who came to us to be our dependents. I expected them to accept our way of life and not want to rule over us. I did not want them to constantly breathe down our neck, no matter what we were doing. Simply, it was unbearable.

The same day when your letter finally came, John's mother got a job and John talked with his father that they should try to remain upstairs. It worked for a few days, and then they relapsed. But now it is much better that she is away most of the day. I prayed to God so hard to not let this happen to me, but there was no answer. And then, it happened. With this job for my mother-in-law everything changed. I felt God's grace spread all over me. I was myself again, my strength came back, I felt it was my home again. Thank God, I got over these horrible months, I can trust again, trust in God that he will help us and we will be able to handle our terrible financial problems and also to live separately from my parents-in-law. I would have gladly moved back to the camp if we could have just been alone.

Please, don't let anyone see this letter, but I am happy I had the strength to write it all to you.

The children are all in school now. Louis is in Kindergarten. He leaves every morning with a radiant smile and returns the same way. He is so proud to be in Kindergarten. The other two look very elegant in their school uniforms.

With all my love, your daughter, Helen

My father-in-law was a sweetheart and wanted to help in every way he could. He loved to send out ads for my business, hand addressing envelopes and mailing them out. He went through the phonebook to find Hungarian names to which we could send flyers. He loved to walk, but he knew absolutely nothing about keeping house. He was good at keeping the children entertained, however. He told them long stories and whistled classical music to them even when they were babies. Ilike reacted very well to that when she was little. She kicked to the rhythm of Beethoven's violin concerto, when she was only six months old.

Now the grandparents bribed Ilike to keep her room tidy. They gave her a few pennies for every drawer she kept in order. She adored both of them.

Jancsi and Louis stayed together in the "boys' bedroom." Jancsi did not care about keeping his side in order, but Louis organized everything to the T. Of course they were despising how the other one kept his side of the room, but all in all they loved and protected each other.

They played a lot in the street with the Fanning boys, who lived in the house right across from us. Side streets in those days were practically playgrounds. When it was time to eat mothers would call the kids, whistled, or rang a bell and the children came running.

Louis was four years old by that time and decided to teach me baseball. He pitched me a plastic toy baseball; I hit it with the big plastic bat. I held it like a tennis racquet. Then he said: "Now, run!" I told him: "That is impossible! That cannot be the rules!" He ran into the house and brought out a few sweaters. He threw them down on the ground and instructed me that I had to run around those sweaters. By now I truly thought one of us had to be insane. The neighbors came out to witness the spectacle and told me rolling with laughter, how mistaken I was and that this, indeed, was how you played baseball.

God helped us again, just like I knew He would. John's parents finally got a wonderful job, which they both liked. She became the housekeeper-boss of an elegant retirement home and did the cooking for them, which she loved. The home was a magnificent old home, furnished with antique furniture, with only a few inhabitants, mainly old ladies. The lady of the house owned an antique store, so she had to be there all day. That is why she needed someone to look after the house, as if it would have been hers. The house was much like the house that John's parents used to own, not in style, but in elegance, so my mother-in-law felt truly "at home" there. They both received room and board at the retirement home and got paid $200 a month, the salary of an accountant in those days.

John's parents found a great movie theater on Arbutus and 16th, which played German movies once a week. We met with them there, we took them to church every Sunday, and then we went to Queen Elizabeth Park, and watched the Ed Sullivan Show together. We enjoyed each other's company.

Thank God, our finances started to settle into their usual rhythm and pretty soon I did not have to dodge creditors, such as water, electricity, telephone. We rented the upstairs mainly to Australian citizens, who came with the P&O Cruise ships and got off in Vancouver, B.C. As Australian citizens they were also British subjects, members of the British Commonwealth, therefore they were immediately allowed to work. If they resided in the country longer than six weeks they were also allowed to vote in the Canadian elections. This way many chose to go from one country of the British Commonwealth to the other. They worked in each of the countries where they stayed. That made it possible for Australian, or any citizens of the British Commonwealth to travel around the world. We developed lifelong friendships with some of our tenants.

We had a most interesting and disturbing case. Someone called inquiring about our rental. After I answered, he asked in a timid voice: "I am black, do you still want me to rent your place?" I reassured him that we had nothing against any kind of people. Vernon was a delightful tenant and stayed for quite a while. He was a medical student from Trinidad and Tobago. He was welcomed by everyone in the neighborhood.

~

I was so happy! Mother was coming to help with the new baby. I could hardly wait to show her everything we loved so much about Vancouver; to talk with her all day, to see her enjoy the children. She was staying for three weeks!

She stepped off the plane, her smiling self, joy in her eyes and happiness beaming from her all over.

She came three days before Steve was born, actually on his due date, just after my second-year exam at the sales and marketing course. The university let me take the exam early because it would have been on my due date March 12th. John and I were keeping our fingers crossed that the baby should be born on March 15th, a great Hungarian National Holiday. A friend of ours was hoping for the 17th, the 1,000th St. Patrick's Day. I could not imagine why he was not born yet. All the others were early – 3 to 10 days early.

While in Winnipeg the sun was always shining, here it rained. After the three weeks, when Mother went home, she said that while she was here, the sun only came out three times and each time we jumped in the car and took her to look at the sunset. Nevertheless, we enjoyed ourselves.

I drove her all over town, I showed her the children's schools, and we went to stores. One afternoon I anticipated that a phone call would be long, so I made myself comfortable on the floor. Mother was fretting: "What if the baby will come early if you are not careful?" I laughed so hard: "The baby is already overdue!"

Then finally, while watching TV one evening, I felt labor starting, but I did not say anything yet. Sometime during the night John and I set out for the hospital. There was a tradition among expectant mothers in Vancouver at the time. Both General Hospital and Grace were close to Queen Elizabeth Park. It was a beautiful place which replaced an old quarry. There was a top viewpoint from where you could see Vancouver in all its beauty. The custom was to drive up there before going to the hospital and look at the gorgeous view. We parked and kissed. Then we took off to the hospital.

According to the custom of the day John went home. He had to go to work. I waited while my back was hurting. A midwife came and gave me something to take away the edge of the pain. Indeed it felt better after that. In the morning Dr. Balmer appeared. I was happy to see him because I knew the doctor is called around the end of the birth. At one point they put anesthetic over my head. I rejoiced. Now, finally, everything will be over. But, lo and behold, the pain was still there when I woke up and the doctors who were there before decided they were going to get some coffee. They had to wait until the baby's head was in the right position. I was so mad! Every time I had pain, the anesthetic was put over my head. Well, I knew I did not want any of that again. Next time I give birth I do not want them to put gas over my head and then the pain would come right back. I had heard of how wonderful these new ways were now, but I think this new way was for the birds! Dr.Balmer reappeared and then Stephen John Patrick was born. After the first girl, we now had the third boy in a row. John always wanted to have at least two girls because he had always wanted to have a sister, but we wanted to have many children, so we were glad he was healthy and a delightful addition to our family.

Stephen and I were so lucky; I got a bed in the "Sunroom" of the Vancouver General Hospital. This was a veranda with only four beds in it. The sun was shining and all was well with the world. Next to us was a huge room with 16 beds. We had much fun with the other three mothers.

In Canada a British therapist came and did the same exercises with us as Queen Elizabeth did after she had her children.

When we went home we received a big bag full of baby things from the hospital: lotion, cream, powder, shampoo, food and baby formula samples, a lovely certificate and a beautiful poem about babies. It was helpful, practical and a clever advertisement for the companies donating the samples.

Mother and Father bought us a beautiful baby carriage which could be used in six different ways: as a full size baby carriage, as a stroller, which could be in a sitting or a lying position, as a baby carrying basket, it had a hood against sun and rain, a full cover for rain. It was just the best! And it was blue! We set up his crib in our bedroom, but he spent time in his baby carriage as well because we could push that into any room where we were, even the porch.

Mother decided that it would be a great idea to take Ilike with her back to Winnipeg. What an adventure that would be for eight-year-old Ilike and she was eager to go!

It was awfully hard to say goodbye to Mother. Father always wanted her to stay with him in Winnipeg. When am I going to see her again? We didn't have any money to fly over and to drive with four children in the car, one of them a baby!?

We waved as long as we could see the plane. In those days we were allowed to go all the way to the gate, so we could see passengers if they waved right at a window with a white handkerchief. Both Mother and Ilike waved wildly.

Ilike had the time of her life with my mother and father. My mother introduced her to all of her friends, the church and her new business. The two weeks that Ilike spent with her grandmother solidified their relationship forever. And, on the plane ride home, Ilike, who is prone to motion sickness, threw up into the bag that is supplied by airlines. Afterward, she surprised the airline attendants by consuming 16 quarters of four sandwiches before landing in Vancouver.

16

I finished the three-year course and received my Diploma in Sales and Marketing Management. I was swimming in happiness and enjoyed being whistled at by my classmates (all men) during the graduation ceremony.

Then we got a letter from Mother:

My dear Helen and John!

This will come as a great surprise to you, but I waited until you finished your exams. That was excitement enough for you.

On March 22nd at 10:00 a.m. I went through a serious surgery. My womb, my ovaries and ducts were removed as well as three tumors. One of them was twisted onto the right kidney duct. I had great pains already in Toronto when I was there in February, visiting Marietta. The pains kept increasing. I had bad pain at Christmas time, then it started again on the first of February.

I went to Marietta's Ob-Gyn, Dr. Luthor. He determined that my womb was large, and three tumors were attached to it on the right side. He said I should stay in Toronto and he will immediately operate. I would have wanted to do that, but Father said I should come home to Winnipeg to have it done. So, I came home after two weeks. We had to wait until after my period. Mrs. Grace, the lady who could take care of Grandfather, was busy, so we had to wait after my second period, which was a week late. Then it came furiously, and I felt awful. Every day I had cramps for about five hours, it felt like in the first two hours of giving birth. I had to take pain killers, but I kept working — you know me. Two days before the surgery I ran around doing errands for five hours without any food or drink. It hurt something awful, but I felt it was better that way.

The surgery lasted three and one-half hours. Father was beside himself, he kept kissing my hands. Now I see how much he loves me. He runs in to see me day and night. The Sister Superior herself is looking after me. They treat me like a queen. The next day, on the 23rd, I got up twice. Today I will get up three times.

She wrote this letter on the 27th, five days after her surgery.

I sat down right away and wrote her what I felt in my heart after having read her letter:

My dear Mother,

Thank you for writing down everything in detail. Please, keep doing so. How I wish I could be there with you and kiss you every instant of every day.

I was so happy you wrote that Father kept kissing your hands.

You know, it is so interesting. I am sure you felt that too when we started to grow up. Just in the last couple of days I was thinking of how Ilike might think about me. I started to see myself with her eyes, and then I realized that for her I am probably the same as you were for me. 'The' everything, the out-of-this-world being, absolute beauty and goodness. I remember sometimes at school, I stood beside the register of the central heating during the entire recess and I would see you in front of me in your pink night-jacket, the way you slept in the dark bedroom when I came in to kiss you. As I was thinking of you, I could feel the scent of your face cream. You were you and no one else, an impossible to determine, sweet being. Only now, when I was thinking about Ilike in this sense, did you start to exist for me as a separate person, a human being, who is not only my mother. That you too have thoughts of which I know nothing. Maybe you too thought: 'How I wish little Ilike would go to sleep. She is sweet, but I would love to be alone, I am so tired' or something similar. I was never thinking about why you did what you did because everything came so naturally. I think you know what I mean to say, when I repeat what older people say, namely that you get your own children back so much more once they have children too. I am almost shocked when Ilike looks at me with admiring eyes: 'You are so exquisite; I think you are the most beautiful Mommy in the whole wide world!' It seems I am hearing the same words I used to tell you and all of this is so weird because I am still convinced that You and only You are the most beautiful Mommy in the whole wide world.

118

She must have answered me right away, when she was eight days after her surgery on the 29th.

My dear Helen!

Thank you for your darling letter. We cried with Father when we read it.

You were always the dearest for me. I was never bored with you. You were always an adult and mature. You understood me as no one else. You were my best friend. My dear little Everything, my darling child.

I feel fine, I can wash myself and I walk around. Marietta is coming next week.

Choking on my tears, it took some time before I got back to my senses. I was alone at home, but maybe it was for the best. The story of our lives passed in front of me. The light and the luxury, my mother, the cosmopolitan lady, who was the center of attraction wherever she appeared. The splendid woman who was waving to me from the terrace of our villa on Svábhegy, which was surrounded by roses. The skating and shopping trips together, the cascading pearls of her laughter, the eternal joy of life in her voice. Then came the destruction and misery, the constant fear for our lives and even in the midst of monstrosities my strong, determined, always full of joy Mother, whom neither the Russians, nor the AVO could break. Who took it in stride for her to become an electrician, when this was the only way for her to earn money for us, and clenching her teeth she led us as an example of survival even in the wildest of Communist times. She could remain human even in the midst of war, saving members of the family and strangers, poor and rich, teaching us to respect and love every human being, be they servants, or high ranking authorities, being immovable in her faith in God and in her love of my Father, even when circumstances forced her to marry someone else because her life and all of ours were at risk.

I saw the woman who did not have the word "impossible" in her vocabulary, who lived through letting almost all of her family go, while knowing she may never see them again. She could resign herself to staying alone in Hungary, if she would only know we were safe. The woman, who survived what the Communists dealt her, who lost everything apart from her family for which they had worked hard with Father, but could leave her interrogators behind the Iron Curtain with a raised head. She was my Mother whom I adored.

119

17

Then it was my turn to come visit. I wrote to Mother that I was coming with little Stephen.

Little Stephen was one year old on March 15th. The three other children woke up early and woke him at 7:00 a.m. by singing "Happy Birthday to you…"

They just loved him to pieces. Whatever he did could only be "extraordinary." Nothing less would do. We celebrated all day. Mother sent him a little red sweater and hat. When I looked at the watch and saw it was exactly the time, when he was born, I gave him the present. He was so happy with it. He screamed with happiness.

Maybe there was something extraordinary about him. When he was eight months old, standing in his crib I heard him imitating the "chipmunk song" from the TV ads. He was actually singing it. Whenever we started to hum it, he immediately jumped in and took over. Before he could speak, he could sing about 25 nursery rhymes, without the words, just the melody. Amazing little guy!

So, he was coming with me to Winnipeg on May 7th! What an adventure! We booked the flight on a jet plane. For the very first time we were going to fly on a real jet! We were so lucky to find a return ticket for $95 for me. Stephen could still fly free.

Mother read the good news to Grandfather that his little namesake will visit him. He answered: "Oh, how wonderful! That will be so great!"

Those were his last words. He collapsed in his chair and started to slide down. Mother was trying to hold him up and call my father all at once. They could not find him. He was not in the hospital, not in his office, he must have been on a house call. There were no cell phones, texts, or email, twitter or any other way than trying to find a person by phone.

He arrived too late, but immediately tried to revive Grandfather. He kept doing it, for another hour and a half – in vain. Grandfather had a stroke, even though all his life he has had low blood pressure. He was 86 years old.

Mother was only three months after her horrible surgery, and she was using all her strength to hold him up.

My grandfather, István Bartha had a majestic funeral. His former business partners from England sent money to pay for it. They still wanted to express their gratitude for having been an honorable businessman and paying his bills even after WWII broke out and there was no possibility to send money. He smuggled out the funds across enemy lines to pay his business partners.

Father bought three plots in the St. Mary Cemetery, side by side: for Grandfather, Mother and himself.

Unfortunately, we could not be there for the funeral yet, but on the 7th, we arrived in Winnipeg. We should not forget about our great trip during which I found out how you can "walk" to Winnipeg in two hours. Stephen could not stay put for very long. We walked up and down, up and down, up and down the aisle for a while. Then he decided it was even more interesting to climb on all fours, under the seats all around the airplane. The jovial passengers kept informing me: "He is here now!" "He is heading towards the back!" "Now he turned around!" He kept us all entertained with a happy, mischievous smile on his face.

In his white coat he looked like a little blue-eyed angel, apart from behaving like a little devil. He was not crying; he was just having fun.

Finally, we arrived and could get off the plane. I was expecting Mother to be sick, I was surprised to see her step out of the crowd smiling and radiant as ever, coming to greet us. Her words, however, talked about something else: "I am dying!" she said with a smile. I smiled back at her: "All my dying friends looked just like you!" She looked as beautiful as ever.

Then we just were happy to see each other and did not talk about this again until later. We arrived at their delightful home, surrounded by lovely flowers in full bloom, and silky grass around the flowerbeds.

When we entered the house, we saw that Mother defied all the Canadian customs and exchanged the furniture between the dining and living rooms. For us Hungarians, food always came first. So, she had to have the big table with the dining room set in the much larger living room and exiled the living room furniture to the dining room. I loved the little breakfast nook in the kitchen. There were telephones everywhere in the house. Both Father and Mother regarded the telephone as their favorite and most important tool. Just about everything could be settled over the telephone! And this was what kept them in touch with their children and grandchildren!

Father's patients called him at any time of the day or night. Sometimes he was angry when the phone rang, but by the time he answered it his voice was compassionate. He was always ready for his patients. He felt it imperative to go immediately when he was needed. Once, when Mother was close to dying, he confessed to me: "I told this client of mine, who just called, to take two aspirins and call me in the morning…for the first time in my life. Was it wrong?" I assured him it was the normal thing to do and urged him to do it more often.

In those days doctors did not tell cancer patients that they had cancer. The patients were fed lies in order to give them hope. I was not supposed to even talk about cancer. In the evening Father took me on his house calls, just as he used to. He told me as if talking to himself: "The cancer was wrapped around the kidney duct and was already grown onto the pelvic bone. My colleagues wanted to do cobalt treatments. It is the latest. I don't think it will work, but I cannot prevent them doing whatever they think is best. They want to try everything. Mother does not know. She has somewhere between two and five years left to live, if all goes well and the treatment works. We have to keep the hope alive in her."

I was speechless. We drove along in silence, while a heavy stone settled in our soul.

Stephen, Mother and I had great fun, while Mother was taking care of her business as well as of the Altar Society and the household. She had help with that, but still, she was constantly running around, and I was trying to help her, as was little Stephen. What a help he was!!! I bet everyone has a good idea about how a 14-month-old active little boy can help in the above-mentioned activities. Mother's happiness and laughter was a big reward not only for Stephen, but also for me. Of course, Grandmother could find nothing wrong with him, no matter what he did.

Stephen found a good friend in the gardener, Mr. Baricza. His fascination with the lawn mower made him take his first steps by himself as he was walking after it with his own little lawn mower. He had the greatest smile being proud of himself that he too was doing something very useful.

"Come, let's go shopping!" Mother said. "I think we should have matching suits. You definitely need a suit. I can see you did not bring one." We went shopping as we always did. Father said we should do this, any color, but black. Mother was still in mourning for Grandfather, but this was not the custom in Canada. People did not wear black while mourning. So, we picked a soft blue wool material and had the suits made for both of us. We looked smashing!

One evening we went out to Tom and Jerry's and had a "Pink Lady" cocktail, Mother's favorite. She even danced with Father. It was so good to see them together!

In the morning, the phone rang. It was John. He told me: "I was promoted to Associate Professor today and that means somewhat more money too."

"Really? Wow! How wonderful! I am so very happy! Congratulations! It could not have happened at a better time. You know what? My period is late by a week and I can feel my breasts. I know I am pregnant again. Remember, when you told me with so much anticipation: 'Let's make a little girl!' and we went straight to bed to do something about it? It worked!"

God gave us this wonderful news to compensate us for the three weeks spent apart. During that time, John took care of the children and his mother came over on Sundays and cooked for them. The children were in school during the day. John's lectures were over around the same time the children came home. Professors only needed to be in the classroom when they had to give a lecture; otherwise, no one cared where they worked, as long as they performed.

"You know, Ilike is really something special," John continued. "If she arrives home before I do, she is already putting away the vacuum cleaner, or finishing with cleaning the bathroom, just like you did. We warm up the dinner or she cooks something. You know how much she likes cooking," John could not stop praising our nine-year-old Ilike.

I did not want to be left out from praising her, so I said: "She was always like that. Remember, I used to say: she was born an adult. I don't think she even remembers a day when she did not have someone to look after. She was 17 months old when Jancsi was born."

After I put down the receiver Mother and I celebrated with Stephen all the good news. Of course, Mother already knew about my part of the secret, as we were thinking about it now for a week. But, what a great day! My darling John and I both had an extraordinary secret to tell each other.

In the mornings Mother was ready to do anything. In the afternoon, she got the cobalt treatment and from then on, she felt miserable. She was nauseous and just wanted to sleep. She told me how they compared symptoms with the other patients waiting for treatment. She was comparing herself to Grandmother when she was having cancer. Mother kept telling me she felt she had cancer, but no one would tell her.

Then she started coughing. I told Father, who brought her antibiotics and also arranged for an X-ray. The Sister doing the X-ray came to visit Mother, who asked her what she thought about the X-ray. The Sister said she could not tell us anything, she was only taking the X-ray and from then on it was the MD's job to evaluate it.

Father and I were desperate because we knew the sarcoma spread to her lungs. She suspected the same, but she was not told. She kept taking the useless antibiotics for a while. Then, every day she had the superfluous cobalt treatments that made her feel so sick.

One day she went to the hospital overnight for a blood transfusion. She felt wonderful after it and looked so gorgeous! The doctors put her in the most exquisite room, usually reserved for the Bishop, with a beautiful view on the river. They spoiled her. Coming out of the room those same doctor-friends broke down in tears in the hallway. Every one of Father's friends loved her so much. While inside the room with her they were gentle and joking. I was so frustrated that no one would tell her anything.

My parents danced together at home in the evening. Father did everything in his might to make her feel happy and comfortable. I came closer and closer to my departure date. We were all hesitant about my leaving, until Mother said: "If I am going to die, then stay, if not, then go home to your children and husband, who must miss you very much!" When Father heard this, he said: "If this is what she said, you must go. We cannot make her think there was no hope."

Father brought home a half Indian (now First Nation) half Eskimo young girl. She was at Misericordia Hospital because she got pregnant. She was one of 15 children. She worked in the Air Force. She was naïve and had no idea she was pregnant until she was in the fifth month of her pregnancy. She gave birth to the baby and her mother adopted the little one. She was a good-natured woman with great humor and very helpful. It was a delight to talk with her. I asked her to, please, treat my mother as she would treat her own. She promised.

It felt terrible to leave my mother, but I had to go. Will I see her again?

18

On June 28, 1962, 55 years ago, Mother died. She was with me today, as I felt her presence while reading our correspondence from a long time ago, just before she passed away from that horrible, fast-killing sarcoma.

I returned on June 26, 1962 with the entire family, as did Marietta and Dennis with their daughter, Maria.

She spoke to us. She asked if we were all there. I knew she meant Elizabeth, whom the Communists would not allow to come. But I felt that Elizabeth was with us too in spirit and Mother wanted her to be there. I assured her that we were all there. She must have believed me, even though she did not hear Elizabeth's voice. Our voices were so much alike that even my husband mixed us up over the telephone.

We spent what felt like eternity that passed in a minute in that room with her. I remember its darkness and hopelessness. We came immediately when Father called us, but it seemed like we came almost too late. A month ago, she was still playing with little Stephen and going out shopping with me. And now!

The next day I was just stepping into the bathtub, when a phone call came from the hospital: "Come immediately!"

We went as fast as possible, but she had already died. Father was with her in the morning, but he went out to get the doctor because he felt she was doing worse. By the time he got back, she was no longer responding. We stood around her and kissed her cooling face. Her departing soul must have smiled at us surrounding her.

That night we sat together, all of us, in the veranda Mother liked so much and talked about her, about our memories. Father said Mother did not take morphine until the last three days when she did not know they were giving it to her. She only took aspirin because she did not want to become like her mother when she was taking morphine, cursing and swearing, although she had never done that before. It was a beautiful summer night. We felt so at home, she was there with us, her presence lived in our souls. Her love permeated us and our unborn babies. Both Marietta and I were pregnant, and she knew about her forthcoming grandchildren.

When we went to bed, John and I decided to make love in her honor because we felt this was what she – love personified – would have wanted us to do.

19

Mother's funeral was conducted on July 1st, Dominion Day (Canada Day since 1982). Mother and Father were together again for only two and a half short years. As soon as Mother arrived from Hungary, they celebrated their 25th wedding anniversary although it was actually their 26th anniversary.

During those two and a half years Mother became the center of social life among the Hungarians and the darling of their friends among the Canadian MDs. Her life was like a whirlwind. She practically flew from place to place like a butterfly and brought smiles to everyone's faces whom she had a chance to meet. There was something eternally charming in her manner, her body language, her optimism, and joy.

The Funeral Mass was held at the Cathedral. The entire church was packed with mourners. The nursing school, the doctors with their families from Misericordia Hospital, Hungarian and Canadian friends, the Sisters from Misericordia and, of course, Father's patients. Most of them were in denial. They simply could not imagine how this young, ever-smiling, healthy-looking woman could just die. The insurance company did not want to believe it either. When she arrived from Hungary my parents bought a life insurance policy for her. She was examined from head-to-toe as you can imagine an insurance company would require from someone of her age. They claimed she was so healthy; she could not have possibly died. She was 48 years old.

Our entire family wore black, of course, as it was the custom in Hungary. The women did not only have hats on, but veils too. The grandchildren wore white. We sat in the first row and unabashedly cried. It was not just a custom, but a requirement in Hungary to cry at a funeral.

After Mass all who were at church wanted to shake our hands and speak words of consolation, in many languages: Hungarian, German, Ukrainian, English. Father's patients came from many different nationalities. Canada encouraged all minorities to keep their languages and culture.

I believe I counted to 250. After that everything was a blur. Finally the waves of people stopped. We sat with my Father in the car of the Funeral Director. The hearse and all the rest of the cars started their pilgrimage to St. Mary's Cemetery. As the chain of 150 cars was approaching the Cemetery the cannons sounded for Dominion Day. Father said: "This is for you, my darling Baba (Mother's nickname), the cannons are shooting for you this year!" I told Father and Marietta: "She is with us! Can't you feel her presence? She is always with us now."

We had reached the cemetery, yet, the last of the cars had not taken off from the Cathedral. Fr. Szerén Szabó, the Hungarian parish priest, was saying a few words and blessed the coffin. Then, according to Hungarian custom, the coffin was lowered, and we all threw a handful of dirt on the coffin, starting with Father.

The night before the funeral Father spent the entire night with Mother at the Funeral Home, praying for her, talking to her, loving her. I am sure he also asked her for forgiveness for the many times he was rude, when he really wanted to be loving, for anything in what he wronged her.

Mother felt just the same way before she died. She confided in me and asked me about the story of Mary Magdalene, who felt sorry for her sins, how Jesus forgave her. I heard that when she saw the priest in her room praying the rosary, she took it away from him and held on to it. That was a few days before she died.

The evening found us on the family porch again, reminiscing in a quiet, enchanted way, feeling her presence in the warm, quiet, starry Winnipeg night.

20

While all of this was going on, just after John's parents had arrived, the Hungarians elected John President of the Holy Name Society along with a co-president, István Lázár. This basically meant they were in charge of trying to find a church for the Hungarians. The two of them went to Archbishop Duke several times to make this dream possible. The Archbishop was known as the "Iron Duke." When he became the archbishop the church finances were in such bad shape, the creditors stood at the back of the church and immediately took the money from the ushers to pay the interest and hopefully some of the capital the church owed on real estate. Now the Duke was old and the Church could not have been in a better shape than it actually was. It was the Archbishop who had turned everything around. However, poor Archbishop Duke became very forgetful. Every time John and István visited him, he blessed the co-presidents and agreed with whatever they said. As soon as they left his office, he promptly forgot.

Finally, it came to the point that István and John decided, if all else fails, they would buy a house in their own names and create a place of worship there.

In the end, Archbishop Duke assigned the job to take care of the Hungarians, to Bishop Johnson, who was his Auxiliary Bishop. This happened when John and István told the Archbishop that 120 Hungarian families joined the Jehovah's Witnesses because they happened to have material in Hungarian.

"Thank God for Bishop Johnson!" is all we could say.

Collections at Hungarian masses on Sundays still brought in just around $16. So, we started a vigorous campaign. The men went from house to house to all Catholic Hungarians to discuss with them how much they could contribute. In the meantime they also looked for churches.

The one we settled on was close to the corner of King's Way and Main Street. It was a Methodist Church that was for sale. The lot was huge. Besides the lovely church there was a great building with a gym, a stage, and a full basement with classrooms. Also on the lot was a four-bedroom house. The selling price was $40,000.

$16 a week income? A $40,000 property? The Archbishop asked Father Géza Henye, a Hungarian priest assigned to us from the Eastern provinces, who lived at Rosary Cathedral downtown: "So, how much do you need for the $5,000 down payment?"

Father Henye answered: "We do not need any money. The Hungarians already raised enough for the down payment and we have pledges of work to remodel the church for our needs."

Archbishop Duke and Bishop Johnson did not know yet what Hungarians were like. Their astonishment had no boundaries. We Hungarians customarily acted like straw-fire. When we saw the goal, we became enthusiastic and made it happen. Now, we just had to keep that straw fire burning!

A Hungarian steak-house owner paid for the remodeling of the altar, while his mother volunteered to paint Our Lady of Hungary, the painting to hang above the new altar. Behind the picture there were royal blue velvet drapes. John's father, being a great expert in art, advised the artist how to paint the Madonna and the child Jesus to resemble the Eszterházy Madonna, a famous painting by Raphael in the Hungarian Museum of Fine Arts.

The men of the Holy Name Society painted the gym and the ladies of the Altar Society cooked a fantastic dinner for the Blessing of the Church on July 8, 1962. We even had silver medals made in Italy bearing the altar picture's likeness. On the other side of the medal we had the date of the Church's Blessing.

We barely made it back from Mother's funeral for the festivities. Son Jancsi (eight) was the youngest donor to the church. He gave all of his collected pocket money: $8.00 for buying the church. That is why he had the honor of being the altar boy to carry the cross in front of the Bishop. He was happy and proud, as were his parents and grandparents.

We had our own church! I was so proud of my husband's and István's achievement! By now we had been here for five years thinking and dreaming about this. It was, for us local Hungarians, a dream come true! Every week we had Hungarian Mass from then on and people could go to confession in Hungarian whenever they liked.

~

Five years also meant we could now become Canadian citizens. Until now we were stateless, so we had applied on the first possible date, which was four years and nine months after our arrival.

We studied for the exam, learned a lot about Canadian government, rights and responsibilities. We asked the Deachmans to be our sponsors. By then Grant was a member of Parliament.

I will never forget that beautiful day. The sun was shining in Vancouver as we drove to the Court House for the oath. The children were young enough to become citizens through us; they did not have to take the exam. Stephen was our first Canadian-born.

It was a touching ceremony. We made the oath on our own Bible, given to us by the ladies who organized the event. We were so very happy to finally have citizenship in a country that was free! And, it was a country we all loved and appreciated for its morals, its values, its way of life.

After the oath we applied for our Canadian passports. Then we were entertained with refreshments, music and a very interesting documentary that showed us Canada's tremendous size.

The documentary was about a medical doctor, whose area had an incredible 2,000 mile radius. He was sitting by a microphone and had radio communication with his patients through small (maybe 10 beds) hospitals with nurses or midwives in charge. If the patient was extremely ill there was a helicopter parked right by his "office" and he could go to the patient, or the patient could be brought in. However, because of the forbidding distances and weather, that was not always possible. Some of the patients were brought on dog-sleds and always with their entire family. If the patient had TB for instance, he had to remain in the hospital. During that time his family would live right near the hospital until he got better.

We already thought Canada was special, but the more we heard, the more interesting it became. We also saw a documentary about the Royal Canadian Mounted Police. Normally they would ride a horse, but when they went as bodyguards for the Queen, they rode motorcycles. They drove them right into the belly of the airplane.

We admired the "Mounties" as Canadians call them. They were all tall, good looking young men, in red tops and black pants. Their khaki hats with their wide brim were indeed extraordinary.

The Mounties were in charge of the University Endowment Lands, where our university housing was when we first arrived. Across the street from us there were virgin forest and fraternity houses. Side by side. The undergrowth was such that one could advance only with the help of a jungle knife. If a child was missing for any length of time, the Mounties would come to help look for the child, just in case the child somehow managed to crawl into the undergrowth.

The University was on a peninsula. If you were speeding and a police car wanted to catch you, once you entered the University grounds the police could not pursue you. If you speeded within the University grounds and wanted to dispute the ticket, you had to go to the Court in Victoria, on Vancouver Island. So you were really careful.

Leo Koerner, a Czech timber baron and his wife Thea, a beautiful Austro-Hungarian operetta singer, built an extraordinary Faculty Club and added a two million dollar west wing to the library at UBC.

The Faculty Club, John's and my favorite place ever since it was opened, was heavily subsidized to offer the best for the Faculty, their families and guests. The design was the most modern imaginable. The view was panoramic through the picture windows, from the tip of the peninsula, where the University was located. The bar was separated from the dining area by a waving wall built of bricks. Right by the entrance there was a large fireplace, sofas and armchairs, each individually selected for the club. The two walls of the entrance facing each other were built by two masons. One came from Ireland, the other from Scotland. Each was given a pile of rocks and they had to build the wall according to their whim. Needless to say the walls turned out to be very different and interesting.

One of the Sopron students became a bartender at the Faculty Club. He invented the Maple Leaf cocktail, which I loved best of all.

We took all our favorite people there. We celebrated birthdays, namesdays, and anniversaries there. Naturally, when my mother was there we took her too.

We had the most extraordinary balls there for the Faculty. Our beloved Ági néni made me a beautiful golden rayon dress with blue velvet trim and a stole that was gold on one side and blue on the other. John in his tuxedo and I in my beautiful dress had a night I always called our black and gold night! Oh, how romantic it was!

We loved dancing together and won the dance contest whenever we entered one. John's tall, strong body could easily lift me and twirl me around and around, flying over the crowd. We danced up and down stairs, let go of each other and he led me with his eyes from across the room. I was 26 at the time.

Our happiness knew no boundaries, "Our cup runneth over with love..." there actually was a song at the time by that name.

~

Now John became an associate professor and I was pregnant with our fifth child.

My sister Elizabeth wrote from Hungary that she was summoned to the police and they asked her: "Now that your mother is dead, do you want to go and see her grave?" Just how cruel could they get? She begged them to let her go to see Mother again, but they would not let her do that. They now decided to "rub it in."

Of course she accepted the offer. At least she would be able to see all the rest of us.

Father met her in Rome. They were there when John the XXIII was elected Pope.

Elizabeth arrived at our house in Vancouver on the day our dear friend, Steve's godfather, John's first graduate student at UBC, Ken Julien from Trinidad and Tobago, received his PhD. We went to the ceremony together and then to the Faculty Club for lunch.

Elizabeth told us not to give her any shellfish, or crab, any sea monsters to eat. We agreed. Then John asked her:

"Do you like potato soup?" She said yes, so we ordered clam chowder.

"This is the best potato soup I ever had!" was Elizabeth's reaction. She never made the above request ever again. I am glad to say she loved all the subsequent "sea monsters."

The day before her arrival, Elizabeth called us from one of the stations. An Australian girl was babysitting our children, who were fast asleep. She could not understand Elizabeth, who in turn could not understand her. The Hungarian and Australian accents did not cooperate. So the babysitter tried to wake Ilike. She tried and tried, but could not. Once our children fell asleep, not even cannon fire would wake them. I always tell people: it is guaranteed, it has been tested during the 1956 Hungarian Uprising. So her phone call did not achieve anything constructive, but she arrived anyway.

My sister and I enjoyed her visit so very much. We had not seen each other since 1956. We talked and talked, day and night, catching up on each other's news.

She told us how the Communist authorities kept rejecting her pleas to come and see our mother alive, then the satanic: "Now, you can go to see her grave!" This was but deliberate torture, the will to hurt the "class enemy" who was a young child when they took over, her irreplaceable engineer husband and two children, born under Communist rule.

Her son and my Steve were about the same age. We bought baby things for each other at a lovely baby store in Kerrisdale.

Elizabeth wanted to see an Elvis Presley movie, so we went – with Steve. Steve and I spent the entire movie walking up and down the stairs in the cinema. That is where he learned to do it. We had fun! In those days I still could not stand the look of Elvis. I liked to listen to him, but he looked so hoity-toity and his movements were so annoying. He looked like a skinny teenager and not like a grown man. At the same time the teenage girls adored him, screaming and scratching each other for joy of seeing and listening to him in person. I was still not used to the expressions of love in this weird way.

We had a huge party for Elizabeth with all our Sopron and Canadian friends. Luckily the weather was good because some of them had to entertain each other on the front porch for lack of space in the house. The mood was super-fantastic!

We took Elizabeth to the USA border, then, through Point Roberts she was able to enter the USA. The 49th parallel cuts off the end of a peninsula in a way that leaves space to have excellent dancing places and summer cottages on the USA side. Anyone could enter there because there was no other way to reach the real shores of the USA. We took a photo of her standing with one leg in Canada and the other in the USA.

This place was also special because here, the USA laws governed, therefore we could order beer and wine and dance in the very same restaurant! In B.C., at the time, we could not order drinks in the restaurants, we had to BYOB (bring your own booze). When the police came to enforce the Canadian law, they called the restaurant owner, who warned us and we hid the booze under the table.

We also had beer parlors in Canada, but they were segregated. "Gentlemen" and "Ladies and Escorts." When a Hungarian first saw this, he would comment on what nice toilets they had in Canada. We had a good laugh explaining to them that these were not restrooms, but that is where you could drink beer. A man could not enter alone to "Ladies and Escorts," only in the company of a lady. For example a couple could not meet there because the man would not be able to enter. In the worst case, he had to ask a complete stranger: "May I come in with you to meet my wife?" Children could not enter at all, only adults above 21 years of age. "Nice protection" for the ladies, or was it "discrimination"?

When Elizabeth left we were only hoping against hope, but not sure at all that we will see each other again in this life.

21

The Greenfields, Gene and Louise, came into our lives at the American Association of Electrical Engineers (AIEE) Summer Power Meeting in Seattle, Washington.

This happened to be the meeting when the AIEE's name was changed to the Institute of Electrical and Electronics Engineers (IEEE). One of the comments came from my husband, John, during the discussion. He jumped up and told the meeting he was a proud member of AIEE, but he was a Hungarian-Canadian and therefore was very much for changing the name to be more inclusive. Gene Greenfield took note of him. At another session the topic was university and research. Again, Gene loved the enforcement of his proposal that university and research should go hand-in-hand. Universities should be engaged with research. He was the Director of Research and Development at Washington State University (WSU). Gene and John spent much of the day together. In the evening John said: "I met this wonderful man, who thinks just the way I do. We will meet them tonight."

"You know what?" I answered. "I met this lovely lady who took us under her wings and ferried us around all day in her light blue Cadillac. We had the same interests. We went to the Museum of Fine Arts…"

"And here comes Gene, my new friend," John motioned.

"And that is my new friend, Louise," I added.

It turned out that our new friends were married to each other. We went into the banquet room then danced the night away. They loved to dance as well.

Our friendship developed. We found out what else we had in common. We both loved classical music. Gene and Louise also played in a Chamber Quartet in Pullman. Both our fathers were MDs. Louise's father came from the Austro-Hungarian Monarchy.

Louise and Gene came to Vancouver on business the following year. I took Louise to the newly opened Queen Elizabeth Theater. We talked about freedom. I mentioned that Canada was becoming quite "pink." For instance, it was hard for me to see Soviet uniforms at the Faculty Club, when the Soviet Army's Choir was invited. It was hard to see how lenient the government was with the Sons of Freedom Dukhabors. They were exploding transmission towers and railroad tracks and because they were such pacifists, they did not want history to be taught to their children. They claimed history was merely a history of wars. They protested against their children being taken to a boarding school to educate them. One example of a demonstration of theirs was when the Prime Minister came to address them, the women showed up naked, but only the old and the ugly. Authorities considered all of that freedom of speech, of opinion. Finally, when the sect blew up the railroad tracks just before Princess Margaret's train was scheduled there, authorities decided to put the men in jail. As a protest, all families migrated into the middle of Vancouver and camped out in front of the Court.

Louise said that maybe we would like it better in the USA, where people were less tolerant with Communism. It made me think.

I believe, as a result of our little talk, and after Mother's death, in 1962 we received a letter of invitation from Washington State University, from Dr. A.L. Betts, Head of the Department of Electrical Engineering. They offered John a job, which sounded absolutely perfect. Except, we would have to leave Vancouver, B.C., which we considered our hometown since we had left Hungary.

What weighed the heaviest among the many pros and cons was John's subject and main interest: power engineering. The dams on the Columbia River, among them Grand Coulee Dam, the largest in the world at the time, was in Washington State. WSU wanted to build a laboratory there that could use the entire power coming from Grand Coulee for research. John was asked to join the Committee that was working to make it a reality, while also teaching his subject; a great combination of teaching and research.

We asked our good friends, the Udvardys, what Pullman was like. That was the university which invited them when they had left Finland. Miklós said: "It is like Szekszárd in Hungary." Well, we took his description and went to see for ourselves in December, 1962. When we arrived back we told Miklós: "Now we know what Szekszárd looks like." He answered: "Interesting, I have never been to Szekszárd either." We had a good laugh. We both learned in school that Szekszárd was among rolling hills and had vineyards. Pullman had the rolling hills, without the added interest of vineyards. By now this fault has been remedied and WSU has a department dedicated to vineyards and wine.

I was in the last month of pregnancy when we left. Louise was so excited! We flew to Pullman. First stop was Seattle. Then, from there we flew into Pullman's tiny airport. A small house and a short runway was all. The propeller plane landed in front of the building where Louise expected us.

She drove us to their lovely family home, just three houses down from the President's house, across from Greek Row (fraternities and sororities). The Greenfields' house was like coming home. Everything reminded us of the homes where we grew up, but with an American flair. In the bathroom she had matching towel sets. I thought in those days it was the height of luxury to have matching towels and décor in the bathroom.

Louise wanted to make us feel at home and happy in Pullman, as did Gene. They invited over people they thought would give us good vibes about – they were hoping – our future home.

Gail Gladwell, a former Vancouverite came over. As it turned out she used to teach in Powell River, when we were there and remembered her Hungarian students in the high school. We were both young mothers with babies.

The Austins, Helen and George, made their case to lure us to Pullman. They spent quite a lot of time in India and told us about their experiences. He was an external examiner (British for accreditation) for a university in India. Kashmir was one of their favorite places. We became very good friends with them. They came to Pullman in 1948 and had lived there ever since. There were many good things in Pullman: concerts, talks, balls, get-togethers, above all PEOPLE who were friendly, cooperative and helpful in everything.

Louise took me to the only restaurant in the region where we could have lunch. It was a typical 60s diner with a bar, named the Office. Excellent excuse: "I was at the Office!" if anyone asked. The standard fare: hamburgers, chicken fried steaks, chips with everything, mixed salad with Thousand Island dressing, various sandwiches and pies. The food was excellent.

We visited the Compton Union Building (CUB) for students. We learned about the fact that freshmen had to stay in dorms, no apartments until their sophomore year. Students had to be in by 10:30 p.m., or they were locked out and had to ring the bell. If they did not have written permission they were in trouble. Student parties were chaperoned by volunteer faculty couples.

During our stay, Louise packed towels in the car, just to make sure, in case I would deliver my baby. It did not happen during our stay, but it was fun to watch her excitement.

We left Pullman still undecided, although it definitely raised my interest and awakened my imagination. The Christmas decorations on Main Street, looking old fashioned even in the 60s, put up by the Rotarians, made me think of the lovely old home Louise showed us, right across the street from Sacred Heart Church. I could quite happily think of something like that to call our home with our bunch of children in front of the fireplace reading "The night before Christmas…"

22

We had tickets to the movie "Rosenkavalier" with Elizabeth Schwarzkopf for January 11, 1963. We had seen it once a few years back, and liked it so much, we wanted to see it again. I especially liked the aria about hope.

On the 10th, at night while we were watching TV with John, the pains started coming. So much for the movie! We called John's parents to say that they should go instead of us.

By the time we decided to leave for the hospital it was getting light outside. Of course, we made the trip again to Queen Elizabeth Park to look at the view before heading to General Hospital. What a mesmerizing, beautiful city!

Mother had long predicted that doctors may not be able to make it on time. She said they always called in the last minute for Father. She assured me though that childbirth is something which happens all on its own too, even if the doctor does not quite make it. I was thinking of that when the intern decided it would take quite a while and had not called the doctor. However, the midwife, who had five children of her own said I should go straight to the labor room. She had way more experience than the young intern doctor. However, no one called the doctor. There was a student nurse with me. I felt Mother's spiritual presence. "I am here with you," I heard her whisper.

I felt like pushing, so I told the nurse, who gave me some oxygen and promptly panicked. She called the intern as fast as she could and also called a registered nurse. She did not dare be left alone for the birth. The intern came as fast as his legs could carry him and they also called the doctor. This was the only time I gave natural birth to one of my children, without any interference from anesthesia, spinal, or gas they used to administer in Hungary. My doctor arrived to tell me from the door: "It's a girl!" I felt Mother's love and radiance move into my little girl.

"Please, call home and tell them!" I asked Dr. Balmer. Ilike answered the phone. Our second girl! John's heart's deepest desire just got fulfilled. But he did not know it yet. He was in class, teaching.

He told me that his heart was bursting, when he heard the news, which came in a whisper from the lab technician. He went on with the lecture, but a few weeks later one of the students came to him to explain what his notes meant. John just looked and said: "This does not make any sense." He asked the other students to check their notes. They all had the same nonsense. Then he realized it was the day, when our second daughter was born. He told the students, and they all had a good laugh. Then he corrected their notes.

John handed out cigars (which was the custom in those days) to everyone, including the garbage man who happened to be coming that day. He could not contain his joy. We had been waiting for this event for the past ten years.

Ilike was overjoyed to finally have a little sister after the three boys she had to "boss around" at least according to the boys' claims. We now had two cribs in the house. Stephen's had blue sheets and Sandy's had pink. I felt so spoiled and happy. I had the baby carriage of my dreams and my children wore and had the colors that matched their sex.

I remembered the days when our oldest, Ilike, had to sit on the potty while I was mending her clothes to put them back on her. Most of her clothing had been worn already by seven or eight children. I was the first who wore those clothes, then my sisters, our cousins, second cousins and finally it came back to the second Ilike, my daughter. No wonder they were falling apart. Yet, I felt blessed then too. My mother told me that it did not matter at all what the children were wearing as long as they were healthy. My mother said that with a smile. When I was born, my mother was the only heiress of our fortune, which was nationalized by the Communists by then. She never bothered about money, her firm belief was: "The best things in life are free." That was her way of thinking, despite the fact that she was the only heiress of a millionaire (a billionaire in today's money). She was constantly aware of the fact and repeated it to us many times: "The best things in life are free..." She did not only pay lip service to this saying, she lived it. Her joy of life was not altered by nationalization, losing all we had, or even persecution. And I knew her spirit lived on in my little pink bundle of joy!

When our little daughter was one week old we went with our best friends to the Faculty Club and celebrated with pink champagne. The whole family rejoiced. We had our second girl! John's mother now finally had her namesake. John always wanted to have a sister named Alexandra, after his mother. We agreed on having many children, but John always added, we had to have at least two girls. Alexandra (or Sandy as we called her) was baptized in our new Hungarian Catholic Church. She was a good girl.

We loved to sit with her in our lap, watch TV and sing to her: "Here she goes, Miss America!" She loved lying on her tummy in her Daddy's lap and watching TV when she was a little older.

In the meantime, in February we got a telegram from the President of Washington State University, Dr. Clement French. WSU asked us to please make up our minds whether we are coming or not. We waited with the answer. It was so hard to decide.

John travelled to Pullman for house-hunting and to visit Immigration in Spokane.

"I hope you did not give up your job at UBC," the officer greeted him. "We filed the wrong papers and we have to start everything all over."

That did not seem very hopeful, but John went on to Pullman and found a great place for us. An apartment block just started leasing, though not quite finished yet. It would be ready by the time we arrived. The owners, Mr. and Mrs. Anderson, built the Statesman Apartments especially for faculty families with children, who were coming into town. Everything was built to be child-friendly. John chose the perfect place for us with three bedrooms on the ground floor, 1600 square feet. There would be a swimming pool, washer-dryer in the apartment, dishwasher, wall-to-wall carpeting, ceramic tile on the floor of the hallway, one and one-half bathrooms, and in the kitchen a stainless steel sink, everything the latest, floor to ceiling, with 38 linear feet of closet space.

We never said "yes," but we could not say "no" to the offer, so we sent the telegram and accepted.

Now to get ready! Of course I had to take care of my fledgling business. I left part of the business to my mother-in-law, and my books to a Hungarian bookstore that opened downtown and was already selling my books on commission.

What does the future hold for me, personally??? My secret Voice told me I should not worry, I will have my special mission, as always. The Voice asked: "Did I ever disappoint you?" That gave me the courage to wait eagerly for what would come next.

John's parents took it all in stride. They would see us less often, but we were only moving to the neighboring state, not like when we had escaped when the Iron Curtain's forbidding presence would probably never let us meet again.

Album

1957 – 1963

Molnár and Moser flagstore, Christmas, 1940s.

Mother at the Lake Balaton, 1947.

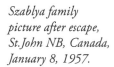

Szablya family picture after escape, St.John NB, Canada, January 8, 1957.

Anna Mendel and Ilike, 1957.

Powell River, Paula néni cooking with student volunteers, 1957.

Fun times in Vancouver, BC at Spanish Banks beach, 1958.

On Spanish Banks with best friends, 1958.

Children in Vancouver, BC. Christmas at church, 1958.

Ilike 5 years old feeding her brothers.

John working at University of British Columbia.

149

*John's favorite photo of
Louis and me, 1958.*

*John painted on ivory by
his Aunt Ernestine Lohwag,
1929.*

Our first house, 3391 W 39th Ave, Vancouver, BC, 1960.

Our first car, a 1957 Dodge station wagon, 1958. In the background our "hut" in Westbrook Camp. We lived in the left half.

Mother's funeral, Winnepeg, 1962.

Our Lady of Hungary Church, Vancouver, BC, 1962.

Three Hungarian Scouts, 1962.

John's favorite photo of me. At Lapwai Indian rezervation, 1966.

23

It was 6 o'clock in the evening and 106°F in the shade.

Is this what they call hell??? The heat, though overwhelming, did not quite feel like 106, but after the cool Vancouver, B.C. days for the past six and a half years it certainly felt like hell.

We were in the middle of the dry desert in Vantage, Washington, on September 6, 1963. My 29th birthday.

John was filling up the car, while I was busy with our five children in the back of the station wagon.

"Let's hurry to reach Pullman before midnight. I do not want you to be homeless on your birthday," John said.

I definitely did not feel homeless, there was a lovely apartment waiting for us and the desert was completely fascinating with its orange-lilac-sand-green colors playing a lightshow on the basalt mountains.

Coming from Vancouver we longed for our evergreen plant life but being young and happy we could not get enough of our new, curious surroundings.

We crossed the bridge over the Columbia River at Vantage.

"This is one of the sites where we plan to have our lab for EPRDC, the "Energy and Power Research and Development Center," John pointed in the direction of the planned lab.

"Is this where we are going to end up?" I thought, trying to hide my mixed feelings. I reminded myself about how I loved the impossible, about the pilgrims, about new opportunities, but somehow I did not yet feel I wanted to live where rattlesnakes could show up on our doorstep at any time of the day or night.

During the past two months we had moved four times with the children.

John was invited to Washington State University (WSU) with an irresistible offer: being part of designing and implementing, then doing research in the world's most powerful laboratory, EPRDC. It also involved a 50-percent pay raise. Our hearts were bleeding for all we had to leave behind, as we made our decision.

Coming with first priority meant that Congress had to pass a consent to let us immigrate, naming each of us by name. We were all Canadian citizens, but we happened to be born in Hungary. John's position ended at UBC on June 30th and started on July 1st at WSU.

As Canadian citizens, we could have entered the country any time, do there anything we wanted, even start a revolution… but we could not work. So John started working for WSU at the Department of Electrical Engineering at UBC, in Canada, on July 1st, until the Hungarian quota would let us enter, right after Labor Day.

To make the picture even more interesting, the USA Consul General in Vancouver, B.C. was a Hungarian-American with whom we spoke Hungarian, while he was issuing our visas.

I decided to write a letter to President John F. Kennedy, describing this crazy situation. When we finally entered the consulate for our immigration visas, the letter was in front of the Consul General, on his table, and the immigration laws were changed. I am sure it was not my letter, but it could have been the last straw that broke the camel's back.

Here we were on our way to our new home…Pullman. Not long after we had crossed the bridge we reached the part of the highway where the road turned to Pullman. We read the conspicuously placed sign: "Gravel road for the next 150 miles." That was the only road to Pullman. Soon, two and one-half-year-old Steve decided he could not stand this any longer and started to cry. Sandy, our youngest at the time, was eight months old, but she was not bothered by the trip at all. The other children tried to quiet Steve to no avail.

The car was bumping ahead on the gravel in the total darkness in which the stars can be seen so beautifully.

"If Steve just would stop crying," I did everything I could think of to make him happy. He just cried and cried. His cries echoed in our souls. We were mourning the beauty we left behind, the Faculty Club, the international, cosmopolitan city of Vancouver with its snowy mountains, the warm sea and above all John's parents, the friendships we built up since we had left Hungary and our pride and joy, the Hungarian Catholic Church.

Yet, there was some joy and freedom connected with our leaving Vancouver. We were facing new challenges. Those have been important for the Szablyas. Life without challenges would be pretty boring!

Othello! Finally there was a place with a store in it where we could stop. Steve was still crying and crying.

"Come, Steve, let's go into the store! Maybe you will find something you will really like." We climbed out of the car and stretched our aching limbs.

Steve fell in love with a plastic blue princess telephone. We bought it for him to keep him quiet. I really have no idea what was so magic about that phone, but there was not a peep out of Steve after that. He quietly played with the telephone all the way to Pullman.

There was still a long drive ahead of us, through the desert with nothing but sagebrush. No traffic, no car lights coming towards us, or behind us; nothing, just the dark desert with the starry sky. Even Colfax, the Whitman County seat with its population of 3,000 was in a deep sleep.

We managed to arrive before midnight. John was happy to give me a home for my birthday.

Our furniture had already been delivered with all our boxes in our new apartment home with three bedrooms, but they were all piled high in the living room. We had to start by setting up the beds. Ilike (10 ½), Jancsi (9) and Louis (6 ½) did the best they could to help us and before the morning hours we could all settle into our beds, the only furniture we set up for the night.

We arrived into a dust-nest!

The next day when we woke up and looked out the window, we saw that behind us someone had just finished harvesting the day before. On the other side the builders were starting to dig the swimming pool and the earth moving equipment came all the way up to our windows. I wanted to cry. Our apartment had a sliding door just out onto the construction ground in the front, in the back it had a back patio about five stairs down from the parking lot, where the children could play, protected by a retaining wall. When I looked out the corner back window, I could see the rolling hills. Whenever sadness overcame me, I stepped to that window. I remembered how I wanted sometime in my youth to be a farmer's wife with six children. The view of the wheat fields gave me that impression. So I lived one of my fantasies, while the veil of dust in the front brought me back to reality. Every time.

On Sunday we went to church, duly dressed for the occasion, with all five of our children in tow and sat down in the annex, where all the families with numerous small children were sitting. John whispered into my ear: "Let us give thanks to God for guiding us so lovingly and ask God to continue to do so!" We got to know our neighbors in the pews and registered in the parish. We felt at home with all the children swarming around us. It was easy to identify with the parents. We were all in the same boat.

When we went home I felt better about our life. Optimism started to fill me. I decided to go to all the possible meetings and places for which we were eligible to go, or invited and we will find friends. We already had a few we met besides the Greenfields, the Gladwells, the Austins. As the saying goes: "Strangers are friends we have not yet met."

⁓

We registered the children in Jefferson School on Military Hill. Ilike was in 6th grade, Jancsi in 4th, Louis in 2nd and we joined the PTA. To reach the school the children just had to go up a grassy hill and down the other side.

As in Vancouver, the faculty wives also had their own group. As was customary the spouses were women. At the first meeting, President French welcomed us and told us how important we were, how much depended on us for the university. He asked us to please, make a happy, warm home for our husbands, so they should want to stay in Pullman and enjoy teaching as well as research. Many of the wives were highly educated, so it was important to appreciate them giving up opportunities in order to follow their husbands. The wives used their creativity and talents to enrich the community culturally, educationally, musically, artistically and went ahead to make it happen, what they missed from their old lives. There was always a chance to get another university degree, start a business, or immerse yourself in volunteer work, raising money for the common good through the service clubs.

State universities were land grant universities, meaning they had received 100,000 acres from the government and had to make do with whatever they could raise from that land. State universities were for the applied sciences: agriculture, engineering, veterinarians and nurses. The liberal arts then joined the other subjects to round out their education. The "universities of" Washington, Idaho, etc., were for the liberal sciences, MDs, lawyers. They ended up adding natural sciences in order to be able to offer the general requirements, and then developed them further from there.

We listened to the local radio station. The owner and operator, Bill Whipple, his wife Norine and son, Dan, lived in the apartment right above us. Dan was the same age as Steve. We became good friends. The station had a special program every day in the morning where they would advertise anything one of the listeners wanted to sell, was looking for, or had to advertise. It was very useful, as many people came to Pullman for only a few years to graduate and then leave. I liked listening to it. Naturally everything cost much less than in the stores.

⁓

On Columbus Day, which happened to be on our wedding anniversary, October 12th in 1963, there was a children's parade downtown. I decided to make Hungarian costumes for all our children and let them parade down Main Street. I had to carry the youngest, Sandy, in my arms because she was only 10 months old. She too wore a Hungarian outfit.

The Szablya Family won first prize. The judges decided we would deserve it just for having five children, let alone having Hungarian costumes for all of them. There were other families, who had more, but they were not in the parade.

We were overjoyed and it was a holiday. So we went home and while the little ones took their naps John and I disappeared into our bedroom. We decided to celebrate and have sex in the middle of the day, on the wall-to-wall carpet…

Six weeks later I was pregnant. It was a bit risky when we had sex because we were trying the rhythm method and this was a questionable day, but love and desire do not know boundaries with the Szablyas and we always thought how romantic it would be to have a baby conceived on our wedding anniversary. Our children think that a Szablya merely has to think of becoming pregnant and they do.

We went to the only OB/GYN not just in town, but in the region, including Lewiston and Clarkston 30 miles away. Dr. Devlin was a delightful fellow parishioner and friend. He had five children: four girls and one boy. He was excellent and funny. He knew we wanted to have another girl, so he always told us it was going to be a boy. Of course, in those days gender could not be determined without birth. No ultrasound yet.

He said I should go to the lab downtown to get my blood type verified. The next month when I went to see him, I still did not have a chance to go downtown. We had one car. John took that in the morning. I did not even discover the first year what kind of stores we had downtown on Main and Grand Streets.

Grocery shopping happened in the evening. I quickly learned the custom of locals who waited for the *Pullman Herald* to come out in the middle of the week. We wrote down from the grocery ads what was on sale in which store and that is what the family ate. We visited both big stores, Dissmore's IGA and Safeway, one after the other and met our friends in both.

Pullman produces a different weather pattern every year. According to the Austins, who had lived there since 1948, there is a 20-year cycle, but people do not stay in Pullman long enough, or forget that there actually was a year like that in Pullman. Our first year there was no snow (totally unusual) and the coldest that year was 27 degrees Fahrenheit around Christmas.

We joined the Lyons Club and the Lady Lyons, respectively. John's meetings were Monday evenings. The rest of the days he was away a lot on EPRDC business, often out of town, so I decided to make a pruszlik (Hungarian festive vest) for myself during those lonely evenings. Ilike was learning to sew in school and we bought a sewing machine in Moscow, Idaho, the neighboring town, where Pullmanites did most of their shopping. It was only eight miles away and there was no sales tax in Idaho.

Ilike sewed the vest and I did the embroidery. We did the design together. Even the boys helped, braiding the golden strands. I loved my pruszlik and wore it on festive occasions for many years to come.

We had balls for the faculty occasionally in the Compton Union Building (CUB). The Christmas Ball was the most elegant and best. It was a black tie event. I got to wear my golden ball gown Ági néni made for me in Vancouver. I put on the "pruszlik" over it and added the ermine cape I inherited from my mother. As we were going up the steps with John, one of our friends, Terry Raff said: "Here comes Hungary!" It was a glorious evening with lots of dancing and fun.

At balls in the CUB no alcohol could be served. Therefore we got nice punch, without any mood-altering additive in it. Another friend stood by the bowl, disappointed. I asked him whether he was going to have some. "I am sorry, but I never touch the stuff" (meaning without alcohol), he said with a sad smile.

We have learned through the years that friends got together before these balls at each others' homes and had a before-the-ball cocktail party to lift their moods. Next year we joined the Bogyos at theirs.

The Bogyo family, one nice evening, dropped by our home and introduced themselves as Hungarians with five kids. That cemented our friendship. They became our best friends besides the Greenfields.

They came to Pullman from South Africa, having left Hungary not long after WWII. Tamás worked for the BBC's Hungarian section at first, Linda was 19. South Africa seemed like a promising opportunity for them. Tamás had a good job.

They had to leave South Africa because they lived in a rural environment. Next door to them lived a veterinarian. He had to enforce the disinfection of the cattle by driving them across a lake, which had the disinfectant dissolved in it. The next day, he and his entire family were murdered by the locals. The Bogyos did not want to take any chances with their children.

By the time we met, Tamás had a PhD in Math and another in Genetics. That is how they came to the USA, for the second of his PhDs. In Hungary he used to attend the Academy of Music as well, and graduated in the same class with John Starker, the world famous cellist.

The Bogyos brought us together with many new friends they had gathered during their years in Pullman.

24

"Helen, the IEEE Transactions accepted my paper. I will have to give my presentation in February in New York!" John brought home the great news one day. "I want to take you with me."

"New York! How I always wanted to see New York. But, how can we afford it?" I asked.

"Remember? We will have some insurance money coming to us for our long-play records and the mixer that got 'lost' while moving to Pullman."

"Oh, how wonderful, of course!" I kissed him with passion and joy.

"We have to ask your parents if they would come to stay with the kids while we are gone. Just how long will that be?"

"About a week. Let's call them, right now!" John started dialing.

They were so happy for us. Of course, they agreed to come.

The next weeks were filled with preparations. I was writing down everything they will need to know about the children. I was explaining everything to Ilike, who was 11 years old by then. There was so much to do.

Ooops! I just remembered that we only had our old Hungarian winter coats, in which we had escaped. Mine was even mended a bit, where the barbed wire got caught in it. Who needs a winter coat in Vancouver? We certainly did not. We wore our coats in Pullman again. No one cares in Pullman what you wear. They simply think it is something you feel comfortable in, you like it, have memories about it and that is why you wear it. The students, when they saw John approaching in his attire said: "Here comes 'the coat.' " We all laughed about that. His coat was so long, and he was so tall! But now we were going to a prestigious meeting in New York! We should get new ones, but…Finally, I decided it was better to go in our coats that looked quite ridiculous in New York, than to stay at home on account of that. I had a few clothes that used to belong to my mother that I took for evenings. As I was pregnant, her clothes fitted me perfectly because our bodies were built somewhat differently otherwise.

John's parents arrived in time for us to explain to them whatever they needed to know and – we were on our way.

We stayed at the Stadtler-Hilton at Pennsylvania Station, which was cheaper than the convention hotel, but was still close. A dear friend of ours, Laci Szepesváry, picked us up at the airport and took us to the hotel. He lived in New Jersey and was truly helpful showing us around in his car.

John was very proud about the fact that on his last trip to New York, in 1959, when he went alone, he could totally get around without a map. He remembered everything so well from 1939, when he was there with his parents at the New York World's Fair. His father organized the Hungarian Pavilion.

We went to the opening reception of the IEEE Winter Power Meeting in 1964 and met our friends from previous IEEE meetings, like Professor Alger, one of the leading electrical engineers in those days. John's classmates at the Technical University of Budapest, Paul Biringer and John Szőgyén, were there. They were the ones who gave references about John to his first boss in Vancouver. Of course, the Greenfields were there. Wives accompanied their husbands to these meetings whenever they could. They were fun and educational. The wives did excellent networking while they had their own programs during the day. In the evenings, the programs were together with spouses.

Whenever we could we went to discover New York with John. He was still at home in the city and was so proud of the sights as if he would have built them himself. We went to Times Square in the evening. I was in awe as I stood there among the many moving neon signs, big billboards, and brilliant lights. It seemed like a dream. During the day we found espresso cups in one of the little shops on Times Square. We bought six of them, two of each color.

One day Paul, John's friend, took us to a kosher deli and ordered pastrami sandwiches. I remember the taste to this day; they were so delicious!

The old Metropolitan Operahouse's "golden horseshoe" surrounded us when we saw Lohengrin there. The sight and the voices overwhelmed me, despite my having been such an opera fan for decades.

We went wandering around on the streets of New York, even at 2 o'clock in the morning. You could still do that in 1962, although we were warned against pickpockets and it was not advisable to wear an expensive necklace. However, with John by my side, with his towering six feet five inches no one even came close to us.

The Metropolitan Museum and the Guggenheim, the Empire State Building and the Rockettes. We crammed it all into our days there and even took in a Broadway show.

John's parents heroically survived the days with the children. Of course, they enjoyed them, but they were no longer young at 84 and 71. One day they even called the school, to please send Ilike home – they needed help dealing with the younger ones.

Ilike – as always – saved the day. She always knew what the others needed and how to deal with them. Even when she was 17 months old and could not speak much, she could interpret to us what the baby just wanted; why he was crying.

25

My dear Grandmother and Grandfather! I miss you so much! The visiting hours are right now and through the glass wall I can see other grandparents smiling at their grandbabies.

Something about me: I love to eat and sleep. My mom says I have the same dimples as Jancsi does, my hair is brown and my eyes are blue.

My birth went well and fast. We came into the hospital just before midnight and it was 1:32 a.m., when I found myself in front of a mirror. My mom saw me enter the world in the same mirror. I think it must have been rather interesting for her too.

I see my dad every day, even more than once. I hope I will meet my brothers and sisters, as well as you because I am really curious.

Until then I send you millions of hugs and kisses:

Your newborn granddaughter: Rita

This is how it happened, in her own words. Dr. Devlin told us when the hospital got in touch with him: "It is going to be a girl. I am in Lewiston at a party and there is a thunderstorm. Only girls can cause that much trouble." This was the first time he did not say it was going to be a boy.

Rita was born with the first spinal I ever had. It was unbelievable to see the birth and not feel when the pains were coming. The nurse put her hand on my stomach and told me when to push.

Then I saw the baby's strong shoulders.

"A football player!" someone said.

Then: "It's a girl!"

The first thing I noticed were her dimples! She was so cute! I loved dimples! And it was a girl! So, we now had a perfect balance in our family; as many boys, as girls. Yaaay! We made it!

Men were not allowed in the delivery rooms at the time. They had to wait outside. A contemporary joke was: "It is easy for her inside, but I, out here…" When John was told we had a girl, he blurted: "Did you check it properly?"

The nurse turned around and brought out Rita, saying angrily: "See it for yourself!"

John felt so embarrassed, but at the same time overwhelmingly happy, he did not know what to say. He asked this only because he felt he could not take it if later he would be told it was a boy. He so wanted to have equilibrium in the family.

Almost twenty years later Rita worked at a copier place in Pullman. An old lady came in and was telling a story to someone: "You know, I could not believe what a male chauvinist pig a man can be." She told the exact same story. Rita started laughing and told the lady: "To the contrary! He so wanted me to be a girl that he could not believe his dream came true and now he had three girls and three boys." So, finally the truth came out and the lady was shocked and pleased by it.

Before Rita was born, in about the second trimester, Mrs. Caine entered our family's life. She was Louise's cleaning lady and I could really use some help once a week. So Mrs. Caine became our cleaning lady and in a few weeks our babysitter, then in some years our adopted grandmother and trusted friend for life. She regarded Rita from the beginning as her "own."

Rita, in our three times hand-me-down baby clothes did not seem to have much color. Mrs. Caine even called her "homely," but her sunny, ever-present dimpled smile, and radiant blue eyes proved every time we looked at her what a beauty she would become.

She was supposed to be born in July, but she made her entrance into this world on June 27, 1964, two days after her dad turned 40. Sandy was 17 months old.

For three weeks Ilike insisted on cooking for the family. She loved cooking and it was such a great help. I appreciated her love so much. Of course, I was right close by for any kind of help she needed.

～

By the time Rita was six weeks old, the swimming pool was ready in our desert-sand covered yard. Rita usually woke at six a.m. We went swimming right after I had fed her, also a few times during the day, and finally after the last feeding, sometimes close to two a.m. They were short swims, but just right to be followed by giving John and I to each other.

Our older boys, both Jancsi and Louis, went through the life-guard course with the scouts. It was so important for us because of the swimming pool. All adults were authorized to spank any one of the children who tried to climb across the fence to the swimming pool.

Rita's Hungarian godparents were the former Dean of the Sopron University, Kálmán Roller and his wife Aglaya (who by that time moved away from Vancouver, B.C.). The stand-ins were Bill and Norine Whipple, who lived right above us, owners of the radio station. Our children who were not born in Hungary all had two sets of godparents: one in Hungary, one who stood in for them. All four were listed in the parish registry.

At the time, my little grandmother from Cegléd was in Winnipeg, visiting my father. She came over to help for 10 days. We went to Spokane to get her at the airport. It was amazing to hold her in my arms. My real, live grandmother that I had thought I would never see again when we had escaped. Pullmanites decided I looked like her.

She loved handling baby Rita, her great-granddaughter. She showed me many tricks of Hungarian cooking. For instance she made strudel from scratch, pulling the dough paper thin, stretching it all over our big table.

One day I asked her how she made that beautiful pink icing for the Hungarian "punch cake" I loved so much. She said: "Go to Safeway and buy the icing, then follow the directions."

"But Grandmother, you certainly did not have a Safeway close-by when you made that fantastic cake?"

"But, if we would have had icing in a box then, I would have used it." She sanctioned all the shortcuts one could take in cooking.

We wanted to show her everything. We traveled around in our desert-land. We took her down to Lewiston on the famous serpentine road, on the many hairpin curves that could be clearly seen from the top of the grade. In a few places there were runoffs built for semis, for being able to stop in case they lost their brakes.

We went to see a logging festival. Lumberjacks had competitions, like log-rolling. There was outdoor food and lots of fun. Lapwai was close by, which was an Indian Reservation. A friend lived right there in a trailer. She was studying their ways and became a part of them. She told us the most interesting things about their customs and way of life. She was the one who initiated the Museum in Lewiston.

Among the many treasures in the Museum, of all things, there was a grand piano brought over the pass on mule-back. There was a guest book from the time when Meriweather Lewis was in the Wild West. The curator kept the book open on various pages day by day. On the pages of the guest book beside the names of men were the prostitutes favored by them. There were few women in those days in the Wild West and usually the prostitutes got married and they became the matrons in town as they grew older. Naturally their families did not want these inscriptions shown, so if a name turned up that was recognized, they asked the curator to please turn the page. Here, in the "Wild West" we were that close to the "ancient" past.

26

Mrs. Caine, who came into our lives while I was pregnant with Rita and loved her as her own grandchild, was left in charge of her and the rest of the children after school.

Today we took the day off. John and I headed to Lake Coeur d'Alene, which was about 60 miles from Pullman, in Idaho State.

We wound our way on the two-lane highway. At Tensed we passed an old convent of which Mrs. Caine told us many tales. It was close to an Indian reservation. Now the Lake was getting close. At one point we could see a glimpse of the water. Trees surrounded the road, and then we arrived.

"Look, there are some lots for sale. A good place to take a swim," said John.

"We can always say we want to see the lot if they will notice us," I added. "Let's!"

We followed the private road and stopped at a place where we could drive close to the water.

"The water is delightful!" John tempted me to follow him.

I proceeded carefully. The surface was warm, but as soon as you advanced a few steps the bottom was colder. The farther you went, the colder it got. So, I decided to start swimming in the top lukewarm slice of the water.

"Oh, how heavenly!" I cried out, enjoying the float in the waves, the movement of my arms and legs in the sun-warmed top layer of the lake.

"I wonder for how much they are selling these lots?" John's eyes sparkled. He spent every summer in his youth at Lake Balaton, in Ábrahámhegy.

"It is probably way beyond our means," I said, thinking we do not even have a house yet in Pullman, how could we even think of buying a lot this far from where we lived and worked.

"Let's just inquire," John did not let go that easily.

The tall emerald green ponderosa pines on the hills that surrounded the lake, the blue water, the sunshine's golden rays lured us. I closed my eyes. "Wouldn't it be wonderful?"

We inquired. It turned out it was $50 for each foot of beach line, up to the road.

"Wouldn't it be wonderful to find a lot that would go up from the beach and would become wider as it went up the hill?" I asked shrewdly.

"You mean like a pie-shape?" said John.

We were full of anticipation when we finally met the owner. He showed us the map of his family's property. Lo and behold! There was a lot that was shaped just like the slice of a pie. Our hearts beat with excitement. We looked at each other.

"How much is this one?" we asked Mr. Bennion, who was the son of the original homesteaders of the estate.

"This one is $6,500, but you can pay in $50 installments a month because my mother would like to have a regular income from the lots sold."

"$50 a month!" Even we could afford that. We looked at each other. We could not believe our ears. We were grinning ear-to-ear.

"Let's shake hands on the deal!" Mr. Bennion suggested.

John put out his hand. It was a big decision, but it looked like it was the right one.

I was secretly plotting that this might lead us to buy a house. We had a bedroom for the three boys and one for the two girls, the baby slept with us. The apartment was still large enough, but if we had another one???

By this time, our home was a little paradise with the swimming pool, the beautiful big lawn, our patio right outside our sliding doors. In the back we had a little place where the storage was, which was separated from the parking lot by a retaining wall. A few steps led down to this safe place for our toddlers to use the tricycles and play ball.

John was all full of plans. The "handshake" in those days was good enough to seal the contract. We had a formal one within six months, outlining the Bennion properties' rules. The lots were supposed to remain large; it was a neighborhood with a private road, trying to protect the natural habitat.

John started to design a house for our lake property practically on the way home. Big picture windows towards the lake…

I was thinking of how we are going to get down to the lake with the children. I looked with enthusiasm at John's drawings, but I knew it was a long way from becoming a reality.

We loved our lot on the lake. Right now, of course, there was no water, or electricity, or even a toilet. We are going to come out here with six children. We should have had our heads examined to think about this as relaxation.

Nevertheless, the children could not wait to come to see "our lake." We packed up our good old, trusty two-tone turquoise station wagon with the huge top carrier that John made from a four-by-eight piece of plywood with sides. Frank Noakes helped him with advice. The only way at the time was the do-it-yourself, so John stumbled through the difficulties of living such a different life. The students affectionately called our car with the top "the Hungarian tank." We had a huge green canvas to cover it; we tied it down with ropes pulled through grommets in the canvas.

We loaded the kids into the station wagon and started out to show them our treasure.

"Are we there yet?" was their constant question.

"Not yet, but look hard, and let me know when you can see the lake."

In Tensed we pointed out the convent, where Mrs. Caine used to come on horseback to retreat when she was little, with her brother, during summer vacations.

We stopped at the well that was the last one before we reached our lot and filled up two 10-gallon plastic water tanks with water, then we were on our way again.

"I can see the water," Jancsi yelled with joy. "I am first to see the lake."

"I am next," chimed in Sandy, our three-year old.

(From then on, every time one of the children proclaimed: "First to see the lake," Sandy added her: "and I am next." Once, in the several years we went to the lake weekly, Sandy managed to utter: "First to see the lake!" So, Steve said: "And I am next!" Sandy immediately started crying: "But I am next!" Every one of us laughed our heads off.)

As soon as we arrived:

"Can we go into the water, now?"

"Right now?"

"Yes, of course, but first we have to get down to the water. The hill to the lake was 100 feet. There was no road. We started out and carefully worked our way down, constantly watching out for the six children. They had great fun sliding and stumbling their way down. The last 10 feet were the most difficult because there were bushes and the sand was slippery, giving way under our feet, but we finally made it.

The older ones jumped in helter-skelter, but we held the two little ones tight.

The beach was rocky and under the water some of the rocks were big. As we carefully advanced, Ilike, Jancsi, Louis were already swimming and spraying each other with water. Steve stayed close to us. Rita happily splashed the water with her hands, delighted with the sparkles of the drops. Sandy, in her little blue bathing suit, wanted to swim like the others.

By the time we climbed up the slope the children were dirtier than when we started out to the water. The sandy slope left their mark on them.

Around this time John's department had decided to redo the lab. John gladly threw himself into the job. He had designed the new lab for the Special Electrical Machines Department at the Technical University in Budapest, Hungary, just before we had our chance to escape. All he saw of the lab he had dreamed up was the first breaker. Then in Vancouver, B.C., at UBC he again had designed the new lab just before he left. This was his third lab to design.

While the lab was being redone, the machines that had been the teaching tools originating from the time of the First World War were replaced. To say they were a bit outdated would be the understatement of the year. They all stood on beautiful hardwood platforms. John noticed that the Department was going to throw out the platforms, so he asked for them from Dr. Betts, the Head of the Department, who gladly agreed for him to take the "useless things."

We took the platforms out to the lake and put them side by side on the ground, then fastened them so they should not move. We received much appreciated help from John's students.

"I ordered a tent," John said. "It is nine by twelve feet. I think that should be big enough for all eight of us."

Well, yes, it should have been, and it ultimately was. However, Rita, our then youngest, insisted on sleeping "fenced in" as she was used to doing at home. We had to put up the travel playpen in the middle of the tent for her to go to sleep. We put everyone else's inflatable mattresses and sleeping bags on the platform-turned floor. There was not a square inch left in the tent.

After the kids went to sleep, John and I sat on our folding armchairs and shared a bottle of beer. The stars, millions of them, sparkled in the sky, undisturbed by any artificial light. Oh, how beautiful! The beer relaxed us, even though it was only a half a bottle for each of us. We could not afford any more. Even this counted as a luxury.

During the day, the blazing sun drenched us with sunlight and high temperatures. None of which agrees with me. In addition, we had to do all the chores we did at home, only under much more difficult circumstances.

We had no water at all, only what we brought from the fountain that was about a mile and a half away. Luckily, we could drive there. We had two 10-gallon tanks, which we filled to the brim. We invented a genius way to keep them tilted, on the table and we placed our baby-tub under it. In no time at all we had "running" water. There was just one problem: the water was hot. The sun warmed it immediately. We had to cool drinking water in the cooler, which we stocked with ice before we left for our weekly escape to the lake.

Naturally, we had to solve the problem of the toilet. We bought a chemical toilet and put it farther up the hill from where the tent was. Then we hammered down some fence posts and fastened to them a few yards of white flannel we happened to have at home. Now we could say that we had the toilet with the most beautiful view.

We used a camp stove and a pressure cooker to make cooking time short.

"Look, Helen, I am reading here in the paper that we could have electricity connected to our lot."

"Great! And where would the cable lead? To the tree?"

"Yes! to the tree."

"Are you crazy?" I looked at my electrical engineer husband. "How can you do that?"

"You will see," John was brainstorming by himself and soon we actually had electricity connected to the only place we had on the lot – a tree.

"We have an outlet on the tree!" I said. "I can't believe you managed that."

"I took a piece of plywood and fastened the outlets on that. The plywood was fastened to the tree and the wires came straight to the outlets from the poles."

"This is amazing." Now, we had a hotplate to cook on. We also had a huge camping lantern for after dark. We did not have to use that much because in the summer it was pretty late when we no longer had daylight.

We did not bring good clothes, or anything valuable, to the camp, but we decided to leave the tent up all summer. Our thinking was that when people would see the tent, they would think we are somewhere near. The Bennions, who turned out to be genuinely nice people, told us they never locked their door, even during the winter. The worst thing that could happen was that a hunter would come in and make some coffee for himself.

We never missed any of our things.

In Pullman, summer vacation was on, which meant that John could work during the weekends instead of during the week. We went out to the lot when other people worked, during the weekdays. While we were home during the weekend, I washed our clothes, unpacked and repacked everything, naturally with the help of the children, but still. Having the nice memories of the lake for our children changed our lives. I so wished I could at least close my eyes on the lakeshore, but it was impossible because of the little ones. Every time I tried, John fell asleep as well. We did not know it at the time, but he had sleep apnea, so he fell asleep anytime, anywhere, sometimes just for a minute, but that would have been enough for the little ones to drown. We knew that toddlers, when they fall into water, just go down like an axe. They do not yet move their limbs, like older children. They simply breathe in the water.

John could not stop planning about how we will get water from the lake, what kind of house we will build. On our way to the lake, we looked at log cabins and pre-fab houses to see if we could make life more comfortable.

Oscar Sziklai, our dear friend from Vancouver, the professor who greeted us when we had arrived from Vienna to the Sopron University group for the first time, came to visit our lot. I used the opportunity to ask him how to build a road down to the water. He advised us to cut into the hillside with a shovel and then straighten out the ground to make a trail.

I immediately recruited the older ones to help me do it. We worked in the blazing sun trying to build the road down to the lake, cutting into the dry ground. Have you ever tried that? I guess in that case I don't have to emphasize its difficulty. It seemed like an unending task.

Just work, work, work – but then, when we swam in the lake and looked at the yellow-orange-red colors of the setting sun, with an occasional blue and green mixed into it, when we shared our beer in the evening it all was worth it.

One day we went into Coeur d'Alene; a lovely little town with sandy beaches. At that time the city was still small with many old-fashioned romantic houses. We had to get to town to buy groceries, there was nothing closer.

We wandered around the boats at the marina and looked at the old-fashioned fishing boats as well as the latest model yachts.

"Let's look at sailboats!" John loved sailboats. He had had one which his Uncle, Feripapa, bought for him when he was old enough. He won first prize in a competition, a wooden owl, which of course we had left behind in Hungary, but John's parents brought it out for us.

He won because he was the only one who finished the competition in his class of boat in the stormy Balaton. We had a chance once in Hungary to sail that boat before it was sold.

We now looked at similar size boats at the lot where they were sold. We dreamed about owning one someday. John's eyes were sparkling with happiness just to look at them.

I was still hoping to get a house before we did that. I always said I would like to sail too, but I had no experience and all I saw was how much the women had to work, where the family owned a sailboat.

Thanks to the place where we lived, our toddlers learned to swim fast. The swimming pool was securely fenced in and the door could only be opened with our own keys.

The mothers did the teaching, standing in the swimming pool. We held on to our toddlers' bathing suits and egged them on: "Dig and kick, dig and kick." We did not want them to drown in case they would fall in. It was a few days before Rita's third birthday when I decided to become pro-active:

"Rita, I am going to let go of you and unless you dig and kick, you will go under." I let go and I heard myself scream happily: "She is swimming! She is doing it!" Rita was digging and kicking with all her might, aiming at the side of the pool, where she emerged, grabbing the edge of the pool with a triumphant smile, wiping the water off her face. In a few days she could swim the length of the pool without turning her head to breathe.

By that time Sandy swam like a little fish. She swam above and under the water, she jumped in, she was not in the least afraid. After all, she had already reached the ripe old age of four and a half years.

The two lifeguard sons, Jancsi and Louis were godsends for us parents. When Rita and Sandy were three and four Jancsi was able to swim holding both girls in his arms. We could let them go out to the swimming pool and down to the lake with their brothers.

Naturally, all this took years to accomplish. In the meantime, at home in Pullman…

27

Ilike turned 13 in January and started high school in September. A few months into her studies a senior, Dan Brewer, asked her out on a date.

Oh my, oh my, oh my! What are we going to do now? We were not familiar with American customs. We went to the school and asked the teachers. We got particularly good information from the gym teacher:

"You can let her go with Dan. He is a responsible, honest boy. No harm will come to her with him."

Still: no chaperone? How does that work? We were puzzled and we worried our heads off. Finally, we said they could go out, but he should pick her up at the house (so we could see him) and after the dance they should come in for an ice cream – which they did.

The four of us sat there with the ice cream – and had a great conversation. Dan was intelligent, cultured, well educated, had a good head on his shoulders. He played the piano. We were joyfully surprised.

Dan Brewer was a blessing in disguise. Ilike was at the age when one does not have the greatest admiration for one's parents, one is somewhat rebellious. Dan, who was adopted by loving parents, told Ilike what a wonderful thing it is to have parents and how grateful you must be for them.

Ilike always told the younger ones how lucky they were because she was the first one and she fought for their rights too, when she was the trailblazer educating us how to be an American parent. One date led to another. Dan graduated from high school that year.

I will never forget that exceptional event. It was, for us, the first American high school graduation we had seen. All the students wore black flowing graduation gowns and the square hats with the golden tassel, which was switched from one side of the hat to the other immediately after having received their diplomas. Pomp and Circumstance, the music played at all graduations.

To see all those enthusiastic young faces, the choir singing "Glory, glory, Hallelujah" the Battle Hymn of the Republic, was exhilarating. The principal's talk and the valedictorian's words spoke about their future lives, starting with today. Patriotism and freedom, spirit and knowledge, their own and their country's Future with a capital F, were the topics. My tears were rolling, but I saw others were similarly engaged, lifting their tissues to their eyes.

Summer Palace moved into our lives with Dan Brewer.

Who said there was no culture in Pullman? We experienced what active, as compared to passive, culture was like.

A university town presented challenge after challenge for the inhabitants. There were so many spouses who in those days did not work; we had several symphony orchestras, chamber orchestras, as well as theater.

Professor Dr. Paul Wadleigh, Chairman of the Theater Department's Summer Palace idea, made Pullman famous in the 60s. Summer Palace was authentic American theater, as produced in the 19th century. Everything had to be done exactly as it was done at the time of the touring theaters. Students came from all over the United States to learn this art.

"Dan said I should come to the tryouts. Maybe I can sell some popcorn or do something. He will be working all the time, playing the piano for them," Ilike came home one day from school excited and happy.

"Of course, you may try out," John answered.

Well, it so happened that Wadleigh's son was there at the auditions and threw a book to Helen to indeed "try out." That first year Ilike became a moaning black slave with unbelievably blue eyes. All she did was a-moaning, and a-moaning on the stage, but Mrs. Wadleigh, who did the costumes, "tried out" some of the people too. She immediately picked out Ilike and let her work on one of the sewing machines at Summer Palace. She was the only one who was allowed besides Mrs. Wadleigh. Ilike had a lot of experience. Ever since we had bought our Singer sewing machine, she had been sewing darling dresses and nightgowns for her little sisters. She even sewed her own prom dress with great skill and wore that dress two years in a row. She just changed the top for the next year. One year there was a maroon velvet ribbon around the empire waist and a white thick lace top, next year it was a black glittery lace cover over the white satin top.

This is when our long-time involvement with Summer Palace started. In the coming years it kept us occupied from April on.

"What?" I asked. "You will start summer theater in April?"

"We have to shovel out the manure first from the livestock arena, then build the entire inside in the custom of the 19th century," Ilike was all enthused.

Paul Wadleigh shoveled the manure right along with them. Occasionally they stopped to have breathing and speech exercises, practicing in anticipation of the upcoming plays.

Hammering, sawing, sewing, and wiring, wallpapering and building the scenery all went on day and night during the – sometimes three weeks long – "hell week."

The grandstand in the livestock arena served as seating for the audience. Everything else was made by the students and Professor Paul Wadleigh.

Publicity was well served by the parades through downtown Pullman, where the can-can girls (Ilike being one of them) were distributing the flyers for the coming attractions. They jumped off the parade and stood in the middle of the roads, at the intersection. Even big semi trucks received their invitations.

A marching band was formed by Pullman citizens owning antique instruments. During the publicity marches John and I were dancing to their music in the streets, showing people how to dance the polka. Our children, of course, were embarrassed, as is the custom of children when their parents are "showing off" or just plain having fun.

The audience was preparing for the plays as well. We were all encouraged to come dressed in period clothing, long skirts, whatever we could drum up. Our role was also to boo the villains, and cheer the heroes, just as in the 19th century.

Auditions went on not only for the plays, but also for the variety show. These auditions were continuous throughout the summer season. The acts were needed during intermission and after the plays.

In the second year, Ilike got a role in Lady Audley's Secret. The lead was played by Cheryl Eskelson.

From the third year on, Ilike was playing leads. The first one was in "Under the Gaslight." The heroine is locked into a wooden house, right by the tracks. The hero is tied to the tracks and the cardboard engine, pushed from the back by three people, with one girl running a steaming kettle beside them is dangerously approaching.

Ilike had to save the hero, but for that she had to break out of the wooden house. Luckily, she had an axe to do it. The first day, no matter how much she tried, the door would not want to open. It was supposed to "break away" when she hit it with the axe! So, to hit it harder, she had to hold the wooden structure with one hand, so it should not fall over, while breaking down the door with the other. In the meantime, the young man who carried the engine was whispering: "Hurry up with that door, or the engine will run him over!" totally forgetting he was the engine. Finally, she managed a small crack in the door and pushed through with her hand…there is a scar on her finger to this day! For all future performances, the door was built less sturdily!

As this was a 19th century theater no sound effects could be used. An orchestra played them. The train was played by most unusual instruments, among them gravelly dust ground between bricks.

We had so much fun with this theater! The entire town got more and more involved. Before the show the can-can girls and actors danced round dances with whoever wanted to join them. In the meantime, a booth was selling popcorn, peanuts and pink lemonade.

As years rolled by our entire family got involved in Summer Palace. Steve and Sandy were street urchins in "Under the Gaslight." Every night they were involved in a mud fight on stage. They were made up with mud colored grease paint. Naturally, every night we had to either be there for the entire show or pick them up after that scene to take them home and straight into the bathtub. One day I got caught right in the middle of the orchestra playing the sounds of the train. It was quite an all-body resounding experience!

The variety show featured a barbershop quartet led by Bob Small. Naturally, our full of songs, harmonizing street urchins, picked up their songs and a few days after they auditioned with Paul Wadleigh. We surprised the barbershop quartet with the urchins coming out and listening to them, walking around. When the barbershop stopped the two little ones started to sing harmonizing with each other. They brought down the house!

In another year Rita joined them and they became a trio. By that time, the girls wore the same size clothes. They looked and acted like twins. Rita, when she was one and a half years old, knocked over Sandy and sat on her, pointing at her older sister: "Baby!" Rita decided that from then on Sandy should be the baby because they were the same size.

In Summer Palace the two of them wore matching outfits, navy blue skirts covered in flowers, white ruffled blouses, and enormous straw hats. By that time, they were five and six years old. One day Wadleigh was vexed with the students and told them: "You have to take care of the booth. It seems that Rita Szablya (age 5) is in charge of the food." Indeed, Rita was standing there with her forever smiling face, her blonde curls under her big hat, her laughing blue eyes looking at the customers: "Popcorn, peanuts and pink lemonade!" Then: "Please, take your own change; I don't know yet how to do that." Needless to say, no one cheated her, but "Rita's in charge of the food stand" became a standing tease.

Their repertoire got larger with songs they heard from the others. Ilike and the hero had a duet: "I am wild about Harry and Harry is wild about me." The street urchins "stole" their song too and came out right after them.

Then, just as Ilike's beau grabbed her in his arms and carried her off the stage, Steve did the same with Sandy.

The actors often came home with us. We had a kegger for those old enough. They sat on the floor and improvised. We still lived in our apartment, but… we were constantly watching the housing market in Pullman.

28

1967 marked the Centennial of Canada. Celebrations abounded in our entire new homeland. We were still proud Canadian citizens.

July 1st, Dominion Day, was Canada's National Holiday. We knew there must be many Canadians at the university, so we invited all the Canadians to come together at the Statesman apartment's beautiful green grass "backyard" of many acres, for a potluck picnic at our home. Our sliding door opened straight onto our patio and the nice green lawn. Usually the entire apartment block participated in the outdoor parties.

Many people gathered from all over Pullman. It was fun to see how many university people and students were actually from Canada.

The folding tables could barely hold the food. Every lady wanted to outdo the other. They brought their best specialties to the potluck. We had a huge sheet cake made with decorations congratulating Canada on its 100th birthday. Everyone wanted to get a piece.

Women rarely worked outside the home in those days. We stayed home with the children. We held coffee klatches, which would be called "group therapy" sessions nowadays. One could learn so much at those parties! We told each other true stories about people that warned us against dangers, troubles, gave us advice on what to do in emergencies, without us realizing what was happening. Happy thoughts were shared too, how to celebrate and prepare ornaments, what the latest "Heloise" advice was or who read what in "Dear Abby." For those who have no clue who Heloise or Abby were, let me explain. Heloise had a household advice column. She was an army wife in Hawaii when she started writing it. She gave excellent advice on how you could use almost everything we are recycling today. "Dear Abby" was a column that gave advice about family, love, any kind of crisis or problem the readers sent. They both gave good, down-to-earth advice.

I remember my mother saying how it was a necessity in Hungary to get together with her friends. At the end of their conversations they all went home happy that all they had to carry was their own cross.

People were open with each other and helped their neighbors. We were told that in America, if you needed something done, all you had to do was let your neighbors know and you could be sure that help was on its way.

"That is Hungarian music!"

"It's coming from the TV!"

"Come, come everybody! They are dancing too!"

"In Hungarian costumes!"

"But where is it?"

"Who are they?" the entire family looked at the TV excitedly.

"This is the Gödöllő Subcamp of the Farragut State Park World Jamboree," came the announcement.

"But scouting is not allowed in Communist Hungary," I said.

"And the Hungarian Scouts in Exterris, (Hungarian Scouts Abroad) who are all over the world cannot be members of the World Jamboree as the scouts are a territorial organization and the Hungarian Scouts of the world just go by ethnicity," John added. "That is so exciting. As a cub scout I was in Gödöllő when the World Jamboree was there. Lord Baden Powell came to visit. He liked the gate made from two white stags so much he asked to take them home with him."

"We just have to go and see it for ourselves, who these people are singing in Hungarian and dancing our dances." I said.

Mrs. Caine was mobilized to stay with Rita while the rest of the family took off to Farragut State Park in Idaho. It was the 8th of August, a beautiful sunshiny day in 1967.

When we arrived, we immediately wanted to see the people who lived in the Gödöllő Subcamp. Each of the Subcamps was named after a former World Jamboree location.

Lo and behold! We reached the subcamp and there were two wooden white stags forming a gate. Not just that. A live white stag was blaring at us from his cage.

"There is such a thing as a white stag?" Steve asked with wide open eyes.

"Yes, of course there is. It is rare, but…Listen, I will tell you the tale of the white stag on our way home. Right now, I just must see this wonderful replica of the exact gate I told you about at home, the one Lord Baden Powell asked for and was given at that Jamboree."

"Green Bar Bill" the famous columnist of *Boys' Life* magazine stepped up to us and told John: "I too was at that camp. Now I am the one in charge of this subcamp. Isn't that amazing to meet under these circumstances?"

We told him about how we had found them through the TV.

"I am so glad you could make it. Those dancing and singing were all American Boy Scouts. We learned the Hungarian songs and dances, exactly how they were done in Hungary."

"You certainly did a good job. We would have sworn they were actually Hungarians. The puzzle for us was that we knew scouting was outlawed in Hungary," said John.

"That is exactly why we were trying to do our best to be there for them too."

"Thank you, Bill. You did a marvelous job!" John answered.

"Tomorrow will be the last day of the camp. If you come back then, you can have the two white stags."

"What? You would really, actually, truly give us the white stags of this World Jamboree? Just like you gave it to Lord Baden Powell in Hungary?" John was overjoyed by the surprise of his offer.

"Of course, we will come back, we cannot miss such an opportunity."

"Lady Baden Powell will give the Farewell address at the last ceremony. If you could stay for that it will be spectacular."

Naturally we were going to stay. Now, for our overnight place to sleep. We went back to Spokane for the night and negotiated with the hotel. They gave us a conference room to place all seven of us. Next day we took off again to visit the scouts.

The children made friends with many scouts from all over the world. Ilike helped Nigerian scouts sew their badges, they thanked her with a necklace made of glass beads which she still has today. They corresponded with each other for several years. We went into the various tents, asked, and answered many questions. In the afternoon, when the white stags were taken down, we had to hand-carry them to the car because we could not come all the way to where the Gödöllő subcamp was. Those white stags were made of plywood and they were pretty heavy. Two adults had to carry each. Luckily, scouts are always ready to help.

Slowly the sun was setting over the camp.

In anticipation of the closing ceremony we went to the amphitheater in Farragut State Park and chose a good place from where to observe the event. We made ourselves comfortable on the grass. The sunset painted the surroundings with gorgeous colors as the evening was unfolding.

The most important event was Lady Baden Powell's speech. She appeared in her usual scout uniform and talked about scouting, leadership, goodwill and peace, freedom and democracy.

My thoughts traveled to my native land where scouting was prohibited. In 1948 the scouts were disbanded and outlawed. Yet, my sisters and I knew the leaders who disobeyed the law and kept on with their own troops. They met at homes, but they kept burning the flame of the love of God and freedom, of patriotism and truth. I used to dance with the leaders, my youngest sister with the scouts.

Lady Baden Powell was talking now about the entire world's scouts, she was talking about those Hungarian scouts too, no matter that they were illegal. Scout leaders who became refugees around the world rekindled scouting abroad and Hungarian Scouts in Exterris (Abroad) were born in the USA, in Canada, in South America, in Australia, everywhere in the world, but in Hungary and nations behind the Iron Curtain. Those American-Hungarian Scouts taught their members to read and write in Hungarian, the history of Hungary and about the scouts who no longer existed in Hungary.

At the end of the talk, Lady Baden-Powell started passing around a flame that went from hand to hand and ignited everyone's candle. The amphitheater was filled with scouts, visitors and onlookers. The light of those thousands and thousands of flames in the dark night was a spectacle to behold! It lifted the spirits and we all felt one under the sky full of stars. Our candle lights united with the stars. Heaven and earth sparkled with enthusiasm and joy. We were mesmerized. I was so glad we stayed for this final, forever memorable event.

The white stags traveled home with us. The next year on July 1st, at the time still called Dominion Day, the White Stags were erected again as a gate in front of our home, right on our patio. The local weekly had a big picture of the entire family, standing under the White Stags with a short version of the story.

29

John traveled an awful lot in those days. There were times when he went to Chicago more than once a week. The EPRDC (Electric Power Research and Development Center, a.k.a. the big lab) had meetings at the airport, then flew back home right after the meeting.

Before one of his longer trips I took him to the airport in Spokane. We went to the lake first, to visit our lot.

Our love overflowed and we went down to the shore to our "nest" in the bushes, opening straight onto the lake. John made that for us to have a place to snuggle during one of the summers.

"We always wanted to have a baby conceived on our lot, on the lake," I said.

We were trying the rhythm method once more. I knew we were on a dangerous day that could maybe end up in pregnancy.

John's eyes radiated. We snuggled. It was too cold to get undressed.

"Come, let's go to the Davenport Hotel in Spokane before driving to the airport."

My shining eyes and lifting my eyebrows with a wink gave him the answer.

~

At the Davenport we took a room for six hours and headed straight for the bed. We melted into each other and thought of the song fashionable in those days: "My cup runneth over with love."

Before we started out to the airport, we noticed a paisley tie with blues, light yellows and greys in the shop window at the Davenport. We bought it in remembrance of the day.

~

It turned out we not only had something, but also someone, by whom we could remember that day. Soon I was happy to find out that I did not feel so well because of a little life growing in me.

We sat in the living room with our children and watched a funny film with Doris Day, in which she helped someone deliver a baby in the middle of rush hour traffic, in a car.

When we switched off the TV we said to the children:

"You know what? You are going to have another little brother or sister in November."

"What?"

"Another Szablya?"

"I was just going to tell you" Ilike, our 16 year old said "if you are going to have another one, then let's have the baby now. Otherwise I will not be able to get to know the little one. I am going to university next year. That gives me only four years with my little brother or sister."

"I guess we timed it just right," I said. "How sweet of you to think of it that way and to try to encourage us."

"But, of course."

"We all do."

"Can't wait to see if it is a girl or a boy!"

"Whichever it is, welcome!" Jancsi the baby-lover exclaimed.

"I will be a big sister!" Rita jumped around with a huge smile.

"I guess we will need a bunk bed in the girls' room," Sandy seriously decided.

"I guess we should look for a house." John thought it was time, despite all the comforts of our apartment.

"Actually, we have been looking for a long time," I said, "but last year that house, you know the one on Sunnyside Hill we loved so much, was sold, bought sight unseen by someone who was going to come only for a year."

"You are right, it is about time we asked them and put in a bid. I don't want it to be sold again before we have a chance to get it."

"We can't let it go on the market, even though there are a lot of things that will need fixing," I continued.

"Well, of course, it was built in 1902. It was the original farmhouse for the orchard on Sunnyside Hill," John started explaining.

Jancsi and Louis got excited about the project of remodeling.

"Are we going to have more room?" Ilike wanted to know.

"You will get your own room finally. It is about time." John said.

"First things first! Let's talk to the people who own the house now," I said.

We started bargaining right in March, knowing they will be leaving in July. The house never went to market. We bought it. It was a house we always imagined would be perfect in which to bring up our kids. It had a huge lot and a sweet reminder from the time it was an orchard: seven plum trees. In Hungarian the poor noblemen were called those, who had only seven plum trees. We had lots of laughs about our "social status" with Hungarian friends. Those were not the only trees we had. Tall Douglas firs blanketed their shade on the house during the hot summers, providing us with natural air conditioning.

The house had a lovely glassed-in porch with a door to the huge, long living room that reached all the way through the middle of the house with windows on both sides. A wood burning fireplace was in the middle of the room. The big dining room was separate, one large window facing the rising sun, another the glassed-in porch. Adjoining the dining room we had a sunny kitchen and pantry, with a door to the back yard.

The master bedroom, a corner room with windows on both sides, was on the main floor, right beside the living room. The only bathroom of the house opened from the bedroom and to a den on the other side. Another half-bathroom opened onto the den. A big family room was added to the original house on the side with a lovely porch and a door leading to it. We called it jokingly the "West Wing." It also contained the washing machine and the dryer. The garage opened from that room. This became the two little girls' dominion.

Ilike got her own nice big corner bedroom upstairs with windows on two sides. A tall Douglas fir peaked in through the front window. The boys had a fun bedroom upstairs fashioned after a ship's cabin. The wallpaper, the built-in bunk bed and the drawers built in throughout the room, all had a nautical style, as did the short, royal blue curtains on the window.

Many years later the original owners of the house stopped by and told us about the days when they had no bathroom at all in the house, but they had a well in the yard. One of their sisters was born and died in today's dining room, which was their parents' bedroom. The master bedroom was added later, as was the bathroom and the family room. The boys' room was built for the two brothers, who were telling us the story.

The lilac bush still standing in the same spot in our yard, used to grow all the way up to their window. When they went on a date they just cut some lilacs off the bush through the window.

They used every bit of wood and material they could lay their hands on. That was recycling at its best. The drawers in the boys' room were made from orange and apple crates, all kinds of scrap wood. Of course, there was much to do on the old house. During one of our remodeling ventures our son Louis said: "There is not one corner in this house that would be perpendicular and straight, or a real square." But the house was traditionally romantic and just what we wanted.

Another small upstairs bedroom we destined for Steve at first, so the two teenage boys could have a little privacy without Steve bothering them.

Under the entire old house there was a rock cellar, an old-fashioned, real cellar, except for the huge oil furnace for the central heating and the 22-gallon boiler, which we soon discovered, was way too small for the needs of eight, then soon nine people. We made an agreement with the children that the boys shower in the morning and the girls in the evening. Often we put the three youngest together into the bathtub, one person shaved; another was putting on makeup thereby making the number of people in our minuscule bathroom five.

Old fashioned plumbing meant that if someone started to run water anywhere the shower turned respectively cold or very hot. When our then youngest daughter, Rita, once took a shower the hot water ran out. So she yelled at the top of her voice: "Please, someone flush the toilet, the shower is way too cold."

There was a back porch at the living room's back window. From there a real, old fashioned trap door and stairs led down to the cellar. That was the way coal was delivered before the oil furnace was installed. A very rudimentary "workshop" was also in the cellar, which the boys later turned into a dark room to develop photos.

As a matter of fact we found out later that this cellar was the perfect fallout shelter. It was embedded into granite rocks, we stored some food downstairs, and the boiler had clean water in it that was not subjected to radioactivity. Thank God we never had to try it!

⟿

We were going to move into our new home as soon as the old owners left it. September 1, 1968. Between the two homes we decided to visit my father in Winnipeg as, of course, nothing was ready in time for our move.

We still lived in the Statesman Apartments, when one of the children got the chickenpox. All the children used to play together all the time, so I started calculating. Three weeks between each case. By the time our children will be through with it…no, wait. We will be leaving for Winnipeg when the last one will get it. And that is how it happened. Louis was the last one to get it. He got sick the day we left on our trip to my father's house.

⟿

We managed to make the trip that we wanted to do in 1959. We went on the scenic route and saw Yellowstone Park, the Badlands, the Devil's Rock, Deadwood. John planned our trip and reserved all the motels ahead of time. Otherwise we could have risked sleeping in the car, which was already filled to the brim with the eight of us. On top we had our trusty top carrier that John constructed while we were still in Vancouver, B.C.

The first night we stayed in a motel on the shore of a little stream. The sun was setting by the time we were wading in the water springing over the small rocks and big pebbles. The trees were glistening in the sunshine.

Whenever we could we found a motel with a swimming pool because it was relaxing and made the children happy, it drained their bursting energy, the result of having been cooped up in the car all day long. We stopped for lunch as a big meal because lunches were cheaper and had our breakfast and dinner in our room. We ate food we bought at grocery stores. In those days, like during our first trip to Winnipeg, we got the AAA guidebook to see which motels to avoid because they were usually the more expensive ones, therefore unaffordable for a family of eight.

We stopped at the historic and nature sights and views. I loved the Badlands as they changed colors in the setting and the rising sun. There just never was a dull moment. In one of the caves we visited, at a certain point there was a sign warning the elderly and pregnant women not to proceed because ahead it will be more difficult to get through. Well, the boys just would not leave their pregnant mother behind. They pushed and pulled me through all to the very end.

Before Deadwood we encountered a group of "Black Angels" heading right into town for a convention. Hundreds of motorbikes swooshed by our car. Downtown Deadwood we saw the entire group parked wherever they could.

The trial of the murder of Jesse James was advertised all over town. We hurried to see how this will develop. In the tourist season the murder of Jesse James was repeated every day. The murder took place right on Main Street, and then we proceeded to the "Court" (theater). The jury was chosen from the audience. John volunteered to be one of the jurors. There were some hilarious moments during the mock trial, like when John was asked what happened to his pants, why he was wearing shorts. John answered very seriously that while coming to Court he was attacked by a wild buffalo that tore off the rest of his pants.

This was a fantastic and truly American experience. I have to say it again: Art here is not a spectator sport. People take things in their own hands and create their own entertainment. Calamity Jane had been playing her part for

10 years. Next day we saw the graves of both the real Jesse James and the real pistol-toting Calamity Jane.

Then the endless prairie rolled by. Cornfield after cornfield after cornfield and the Corn Palace in Mitchell SD, an amazing structure dedicated to corn. About 500,000 tourists come from around the nation each year to see exclusive corn murals, glass pillars filled with corn. The city's first Corn Palace was built as a way to prove to the world that South Dakota had a healthy agricultural climate. I didn't think it was as good for me as it was for the corn because the temperature was in the hundreds. Well, we were going to Winnipeg and it was not going to be any better there. However, in the winter the temperatures make up for it, staying in 30 to 70 below zero with the wind chill.

30

The closer we got to Winnipeg the more memories kept coming back from our previous stays. The last time we were there was Christmas 1965 to spend the holidays together with my sister, Elizabeth, her husband, Balázs and their three children: Rita, Paul and Edith; for the first time after 10 years we celebrated Christmas together. They had finally managed to escape through the "straightest way as the crow flies" from Hungary to Canada "through (where else?) Ethiopia." Boy, that crow must have been tipsy!

In 1964 we received a letter from Father, informing us that Elizabeth and Family are going to Ethiopia for three years. Could we please, find out what their goal is? Do they want to leave Hungary and come to Canada? Or do they plan on going back?

Now, this was a tricky question. Hungarian authorities kept very strict surveillance on all correspondence between Hungarians, even within the country, let alone when they were abroad. As there was no Hungarian Embassy or even a Consulate in Ethiopia at the time, their letters were supposed to arrive through the Czech Consulate that just barely opened.

We remembered the coded language we had used with Father when Elizabeth was only eleven, so we tried and wrote a letter in this code. Elizabeth immediately answered in the code. What a brain!

Providence provided us with the next step. On the day, November 23, 1964, when Elizabeth and family were traveling to Addis Ababa, an Italian air plane crashed on its way to Ethiopia. There were no survivors. We heard that on the news. I was on my way to a newcomers' party, while John called Father to ask whether they were on that flight. Thank God, they were not. However, I was already at the party, so John called the hostess and told her that my sister and family traveled through Athens to Ethiopia and not Italy. The hostess gave me the happy news. Harriett Brains, the Dean of Education's wife, joyfully said she was going to Ethiopia with her husband to a higher education conference.

She agreed to take a letter to my sister and even learned the code herself so in case she would have to eat the letter to make it disappear, she should still be able to tell the content to my sister.

"Your sister Elizabeth turned out to be our Guardian Angel, while we were there. She helped me go to the Indian Embassy to get our visas; she took me around in her car. She knew how to drive when the car was surrounded by begging children and other onlookers. I would never have had the nerve! And hers was the only place where I could eat something that did not smell of goat!" Harriet reported happily on their return. The new code was set.

Harriet filled us in with many details she learned from Elizabeth. The Hungarian government, in need of hard currency, started to hire out Hungarian engineers and musicians to jobs in other countries. The government received the salaries and then gave back to the person who did the job as much as the authorities thought they needed to make a living. This gave them the first opportunity to leave Hungary as a family and not leave behind a hostage. The phone call came to Balázs's office. An engineer with 10 years experience, fluent in English and have at least two children was needed in Addis Ababa to design the sewer system for the capital city. The answer was needed in one hour. Luckily Balázs's mother knew another Hungarian, the MD, who was head of the Haile Selassie Hospital in Addis Ababa. After a fast phone call to him the family decided it would be safe for them to go with a five-, three-, and one-year old. They accepted the offer. Seven months passed before they left for Ethiopia.

When they finally arrived through Egypt, Elizabeth just sat down and started crying. She sat among their suitcases, after an exhausting trip, in a house where the water had to be boiled and filtered before it was potable, vegetables had to be cooked and suddenly she was supposed to feed the family. Like – now! And the little one, who wanted to put everything in her mouth! Poor Elizabeth! She finally clenched her teeth and started to boil and filter and cope with whatever was coming.

They also received servants, along with the house. Everyone was prescribed the number of servants they needed to keep. It was for their own security. If you did not hire the sufficient number of servants and a night guard, then your house was burglarized.

Their message to us was clear: they left Hungary with Canada as their goal. This was the only way the Hungarian government would let the entire family out of the country. The job was for three years, but they were aiming at leaving after the first year. At that time they would have vacation, but they could only travel within Ethiopia. After a second year they could go to Hungary. After the third year they could travel anywhere in the world for their vacations.

They did not intend to ask for asylum in Ethiopia because another Hungarian already did that recently. They needed visas to Canada for all of them and they could not tell where they would need them and whether it should be an immigrant or a visitor's visa. They were asking for the impossible. Impossible? Well, that was just up our alley!

We called our dear friend and our sponsor for Canadian citizenship, Grant Deachman, who happened to be the Whip of the Canadian Parliament by then. We asked him the impossible. Now, he was the man who worked on the new Canadian flag and the new National Anthem, which at that time was still the Union Jack and the British Anthem. The Minister of Immigration at the time, Mr. Pickersgill, was a good friend of his. They talked. And the impossible happened. God's ways are indeed mysterious. Why was it that Father got us together with Dr. John Kovach in Vancouver, who got us together with the Balmers and the Deachmans? How did we become such good friends? Why do things happen, generally speaking?

Father could not believe his ears when we told him that the visas are ready anywhere in the world, either visitor's or immigrant visas.

Now, how will they get out of Ethiopia? An exit visa was required.

We received the coded messages from Elizabeth, but we could not make heads or tails out of the one we received one day until…until we got her next letter. Putting the two together finally made sense. We called Father right away: "They are saying they will ask asylum after all. How? Why?" We did not understand.

"Everything is OK. I just wrote out the check for the five tickets and they will be on the plane to Paris."

"Thank God. What happened? How did they get away?"

"I have no idea," Father answered. "We will have to ask them when they get here."

Once we had a chance to talk with them we learned a lot of things about Ethiopia and they told us about the Representative of the United Nations accepting them as refugees and giving them refugee status. They were on good terms with the man in the Ethiopian Ministry, who issued the exit visas. Balázs finished the design of the sewer system for Addis Ababa and put it down on his desk. They asked him for the exit visas and he granted their request.

Now, they just had to safely get out of the country. They had permission from the Hungarian Government to go on vacation, but only inside the country. They were under the surveillance of the Czech Consulate.

And – who should embark on the plane with them, but the Czech Consul. They chatted. He asked them where they were going. Elizabeth said they were leaving for Eritrea (which at the time was still a part of Ethiopia).

Then in Khartoum, Soviet soldiers surrounded the plane. Elizabeth was in terror. "Now they are going to take us for sure." The soldiers though could not have cared less about them. The whole bunch was headed for another plane waiting for them nearby. What a relief!

Elizabeth and family were still scared to death the Czech Consul would arrest them once the plane left Ethiopian air space, as the plane was not even landing in Eritrea. Then, the plane landed in Paris and they all got off without a problem. The Czech Consul either did not care, or wanted to help them. We will never know.

Gisèle Bouteiller, who had stayed with us in 1948, and with whose family my father had stayed after he escaped from Hungary, expected them at the airport and took them home with her. Elizabeth was a bundle of nerves, she was so afraid of the Soviets finding them, she wanted to leave for Canada as soon as possible.

Once the family got settled, Balázs called the Canadian Embassy. They knew nothing about any kind of visas and said that was impossible. As indeed it was. Yet in about an hour they called back and apologized. The visas are ready to be picked up.

When does the next plane leave for Canada? God's mystery continues. The plane was full, but Paul Bouteiller, Gisèle's brother, happened to be the Chef de Protocol of then President Charles de Gaulle. The Air France plane did not take off until the family was on it. When they boarded the plane, a Hungarian couple (the husband was one of the Sopron students) asked them: "Who are you? Someone came in and would not let the plane leave until five people got off and you came on board!" It was October 1, 1965.

"Helen, are you daydreaming?" I heard John bring me back to reality. Not for long. Other memories floated into my mind.

My mother-in-law was with us last time we were in Winnipeg during that memorable Christmas.

She and my father-in-law came to visit us during the summer. They always arrived by train, so our children have named them the grandparents "coming by train." They brought tasty sandwiches for the kids. We had to pick them up in Spokane, so the children were hungrily waiting for the treats. Spokane was 80 miles from Pullman, about an hour and a half.

We spent a lovely time together with them. We took them out to our lake lot; we swam there and in our pool. The children could not get enough of their grandparents. My father-in-law told them many stories and they listened with glowing eyes.

We were so grateful for having had that time together because that same fall my father-in-law started to get sick. He went to the hospital in

November. The doctors said his brain did not get enough oxygen which was very possible, as he had only one lung. The other calcified when he had TB in his twenties. He was 86 years old. Until then he walked a lot and was up to everything that was interesting. He read and wrote a lot of letters to his friends in Hungary.

On November 19th, my mother-in-law's birthday, we received the call. He died in the hospital. Just before he got his citizenship for which he was so well prepared and which he so badly wanted to achieve. He always wanted to be a "British subject."

He was buried from the Our Lady of Hungary church. We had a celebration of life for him, which was a pretty new concept at the time. The priest wore white vestments with Hungarian embroidery down the middle. The church filled up with his many friends and those of the family, the Sopron Forestry professors and students. Everyone loved his smile, his stories, his explanations of life and politics.

That is why we went to Winnipeg with John's mother to celebrate together that Christmas. We went by train with the six children and 13 bags, including diaper bags and purses. Can you imagine what it was like to transfer in Fargo, ND in 30 below temperatures, in the middle of the night?

Other than that, the trip was a white winter dream through the Rockies and the prairies. There was an observation deck above the train car. We spent many hours watching the sparkling, pristine landscape as it whooshed by.

Those first hugs! We held each other tight and for a long time, but not as long as we wanted to because all the children wanted to have part in the general merriment and embraces.

Father's house became a busy beehive. Elizabeth and family, Father, my little Grandma who was still here from Hungary and Mrs. Sassour the housekeeper all stayed in Father's house. We stayed in the neighbor's house of Father's good friend, judge McDonald and his charming wife. They were on vacation, so we ruled their entire home. We just had to go from one door to the other through the side yard. Just a few steps.

And out came the stories about Elizabeth and family's stay in beautiful Ethiopia. They even learned a little Aramaic. So they had a "secret" language between them when they were traveling on the bus.

One of their stories:

Balázs had to go on a field trip for work. He had to clean out a well that plugged up in the countryside. He was collected by several helpers in a jeep. They all wore the local white burnus. Balázs settled among them. As soon as they had left the city limits, the helpers quickly got rid of their white clothing. Underneath they wore uniforms and had submachine guns. They sat on the four corners of the jeep pointing their guns toward the desert. They were there for protection. One of them explained to Balázs that some tribes that lived in the desert had a strange custom. When the father of the would-be-groom was going to ask for a girl in marriage, he had to wear a penis on a chain around his neck. A few months before Balázs's trip to the well some Czech engineers went out into the desert and spent the night. When they woke up they had a part of them missing. Since then guards were going out with all the expats (foreign experts) working in the country. No wonder Elizabeth decided: no more "field trips" for Balázs.

They talked about excursions the family took to the countryside. They showed inviting pictures of lakes where no one was allowed to swim because of the danger of getting terminally ill infected by the bacteria in the water.

In Ethiopia the water everywhere contained a certain amoeba, which rendered those who drank it totally melancholic. When they were presented with a problem, or handed an assignment, their usual answer was: "OK, tomorrow." There were only a few people who had escaped that fate. In order to avoid it you had to filter and boil the water. Even in the Hilton's bar Balázs went behind the counter and made sure the water for the ice was filtered and boiled.

What a job that was with all the little ones! To make sure nothing got into their mouth that was harmful.

Of course it was hot and the roads were bad. There were goats roaming around. People ate a lot of goat meat, which can be delicious when handled just right. We loved it during our stay in Trinidad.

The days were tumultuous running around; doing all the errands before Christmas with nine of Father's grandchildren present for Christmas Eve, a Hungarian celebration of the Nativity. I remember the frantic distribution of presents. The latest-type of speaking, drinking and wetting dolls for all the girls, building sets for the boys. All of us adults grabbed a bunch of presents and dropped them into the neat piles arranged around the tree. Presents are not wrapped in Hungary. So all presents were arranged under the tree in full sight.

And then came THE moment! The Angels rang the bell and it was time for all the children to be let into the room previously forbidden to enter that day!

"The Angels are here!" "Baby Jesus is done with the presents!" The children's shouts, the brilliance in their eyes as the lights on the Christmas tree reflected in them, was simply indescribable. What it must have meant for

Father who has not had the children and grandchildren in his house ever at Christmas time since he had left Hungary! This was actually the only time when it happened. Otherwise he was the one that traveled to our homes. He was happy! And time stood still for a moment as we all thanked God for his graces, for helping us to be together again after all these years.

31

The heat was unbearable outside, especially for me who could not stand the sun at all; even as a child I would escape from it. We finally made it to Winnipeg. It was 1968 and Elizabeth no longer lived in Winnipeg with her family.

After our indescribably wonderful 1965 Christmas with my sister and her family, where we had managed to slip away, just the four of us Elizabeth and I with our husbands to a beer garden. It was wonderful when the families were all together, but oh, how great it was to freely talk, just the four adults after so many years!

Balázs had a job in Winnipeg, but all five of them lived in one bedroom upstairs, with Father and Erzsébet's son, Pali, sleeping in the big double bed downstairs. Rita was sent to a mid-city Catholic school because Father did not want her to go anywhere else. Elizabeth was told by the other parents and friends that her daughter stuck out there as a sore thumb. There was a school much closer to their house. Grandmother and Mrs. Sassour ruled over their family in Father's home. They desperately needed to move out from the house. There was only one bathroom with the only toilet in the home.

However, Father always told his Canadian friends that extended families should live together and therefore would not hear of them moving out. That situation became more and more unbearable.

Brainstorming, we decided to rent a place for them and simply tell Father that they would move on the 1st. We managed to find an apartment while we were there and Balázs put a deposit on it. We announced it to Father.

Did you guess? Of course, all hell broke loose!

As a result, Marietta and her husband Dennis, who lived in Toronto, found Balázs a good job in Toronto. Now they had an excuse, acceptable to Father. Elizabeth and her family moved to Toronto to the same neighborhood, where Marietta and her family lived.

Back to our arrival in Winnipeg, for our vacation in 1968 we moved into the same room, where Elizabeth and family used to live, but we also had the adjacent room that was Mrs. Sassour's. She went home to her son in the evenings while we were there. Little Grandma was here again from Hungary. One of our sons slept with Father, as Pali did before.

This time we decided to enjoy every minute of our vacation. Father was more relaxed too. We went to house calls with him, which gave us time in the car to talk. I was pleased that he liked how we were doing, but I only found this out by listening to his bragging about us to other people. I was always trying so hard to deserve his praises, but he never did it face-to-face. It was difficult that we never knew when he was going to "explode."

When we were there at Christmastime in 1965 with John's mother, he confessed to her that he so wants to show his love, but he does not know how. He said he had never learned how to do it. This again was a roundabout way of telling us, but I was glad for it.

That summer we found out that Winnipeg had a "beach." There was a manmade lake not far from the city called Oasis. We went out there with the children and walked around in the sand, swam in the warm water and I could show off my new rainbow-colored maternity swimsuit. Father really liked that and even complimented me on it.

One day we traveled all the way to Lake Winnipeg, a sea-size lake up north: home of the famous delicious white fish. We visited one of Father's doctor friends, Dr. Tony Natsuk and his family, in their summer cabin.

As always, we did a lot of shopping. Father wanted to show his love through buying us clothes and whatever we needed, or he thought that we needed. A trip to the drugstore ended up, as was usual, with several bags full of medicines we may need for our home, Lidecomb, a cream which combined three kinds of antibiotics. This was not available in the States. He bought us things from pantyhose to toothbrush, antibiotics to perfumes, whatever the drugstore had to offer.

His favorite was, however, buying us clothes. He took us to Holt Renfrew, a fine clothing shop, and department stores. He sent us to wholesale places and to the leather coat factory. We had one problem with the dresses we bought in Winnipeg every time we went. They were excellent for Winnipeg and probably Toronto, but in our "wild west" everything was oh, so much more casual. Our Winnipeg wardrobe we could use only if we went to a wedding, or a funeral.

We visited our favorite people and places in Winnipeg and enjoyed the International Week at all the ethnic churches. Every year they staged open houses for an entire week. What a tremendous dedication! Father volunteered as bartender, as were many other men, but the ladies cooked Hungarian specialties every day to sell to people who came to sample Hungarian cooking. There were exhibits in each church showing off the art and culture of their respective countries. Visitors would buy a passport. When they came to a church, they received a stamp in their passport to prove they had been there. The goal was to collect as many stamps as possible. We wandered from church to church with the children and tasted the wonderful food offered everywhere. When I say food, I mean the specialties from all the ethnic groups, not casseroles and salads. Of course, we spent the most time at St. Anthony of Padua Hungarian Franciscan Church. Chicken paprikás, gulyás, stuffed cabbage, breaded cutlets, Hungarian cakes and pastries. The entire community played as a team to keep the tables full. Food played a big role in Winnipeg, just as it used to be in Cegléd, from where my Father stemmed. He often said he liked Winnipeg because it was just like Cegléd, only bigger. Well, it was just as flat, for sure.

We enjoyed the daylight that was still on at 10:30 p.m. in the night. One day at 11:00 p.m. I woke the children: "Come quick, get up! There are Northern Lights dancing all around the house!" I did not have to say it twice. We were north enough to see a colorful, strong variety of the lights, changing their waves and formations, turning from red to green to grayish-blue. We could not get enough of it and refused to go to bed while it lasted.

Little Grandma and Mrs. Sassour tried to overstuff us with everything that was prepared with so much love. We just could not refuse to take seconds, and thirds… as a result I gained six pounds. (After all, I had to eat for two!) Six pounds in one month!

(As an aside: My obstetrician almost fainted. You cannot do that! He gave me a diet book and diuretics. I thought: "I will show you!" I lost eight pounds in 10 days. After that I continued to eat according to that diet book. As a result, on the last day of my pregnancy I was 131 pounds. I weighed 127 when I became pregnant. Boy, did that dieting make me nervous! However, I wanted to show him I was no wimp! Across the street from us was Sunnyside School and the buzzer that marked the end of the classes went on every hour on the hour, even during the night. I woke up every time it buzzed.

Usually, when I had a baby, the first time I stepped on the scale a few days after birth, I was the same weight as when I got pregnant. This time, I could not believe my eyes, when I stepped on the scale and after having delivered a seven pound three ounce baby, I only lost four pounds. I was the same weight when I became pregnant. Now, explain that!)

We made our way back through Canada, just as we planned, and admired the Canadian landscape. The Trans-Canada highway was finished by this time and was truly enjoyable. Manitoba first merged into Saskatchewan, without any change in landscape, endless prairies and wheat fields everywhere. This province seemed much poorer than Manitoba and much emptier as well. Then came Alberta, rich in oil; the foothills of the mountains climbing ever higher and into the Rockies.

In the mountain region of British Columbia, we looked at Hell's Gate Canyon where the Fraser River runs through the tightest part of the cliffs. A frightening power of water tumbling in green and white foam under the bridge, forced into that small opening.

This Canyon had to be crossed to reach the West Coast. Only two groups of pioneers were brave (or ignorant) enough to choose this route. I am sure the first group had no idea. Why the other group tried, God only knows. We stopped at a historic site, which was a plaque to remember all the mules that lost their lives, falling off the trail into the ravine. Word must have spread about their adventures because the rest of the homesteaders arrived by ship or land from California. The mountain passes were much kinder along that route. What a feeling it must have been to see all those empty spaces and proceed towards the unknown West!

Our smaller children of course knew about the Wild West and constantly demanded to see it. In vain we tried to explain to them that Vancouver, where we were living before, was pretty much the most western part of the American Continent. Suddenly, we saw a herd of cows and cowboys with them: "There, you see?" they happily exclaimed. "Now we are in the Wild West."

When we arrived in Pullman we finally moved into our new home.

32

In September we moved into our new house on Sunnyside Hill, across the street from Sunnyside grade school, close to Pullman High School, where Ilike and Jancsi went, Louis attended Lincoln Middle School by school bus, Steve just had to walk across the street to Sunnyside School, Sandy went by school bus to kindergarten and Rita with a carpool to pre-school. This was the year when we belonged to all levels of PTA in Pullman. Nothing was far in Pullman, but downtown got much closer to us now.

We were feverishly working on the house and in the garden, to have less work after the baby arrived. We also tried to enjoy our lives with only six children before the seventh arrived.

In Winnipeg all the adult size family members received leather coats from Father. He had many patients in the leather factory where the coats were made, and he could receive them at $30 apiece. We looked like a million dollars when we all went to church bedecked in our festive coats, but we were only dressed the way God takes care of the lilies of the field. We had received them free, from Father's goodness of heart and the helpful patients of his.

The leaves turned and fell off the trees. We all diligently raked them. The kids had great fun jumping in the piles! Then we burned the leaves in barrels. Their lovely scent announced the arrival of autumn. People stopped by from the newly built developments and asked if they could take some of the splendid-colored leaves. There were no trees planted in their subdivision yet.

"Of course, you can take them; take them all if you want," we even helped them load their station wagon.

November came and with it the cold weather. Is it going to be a girl or a boy? The children were guessing. It moved around a lot, that I could tell.

The last time I went to the obstetrician and friend, Dr. Devlin, he had an X-ray taken. He was right. The baby was in breech position, bottom first. I remember how cute it looked in the X-ray, sucking its thumb. "Don't worry, my dear baby," I whispered. "Whatever it takes, I will go through it for you."

One day it seemed that I started spotting. So, we went to the hospital in the morning. "It is not the real thing yet," Dr. Devlin said "I think you may as well go home. What seems like spotting is probably the baby's bowel movement coming out in spots, as the bottom is down." He was endowed with good humor, so he added: "Besides, I just had a breech birth. I don't want to have two in one day."

We went home, but I knew it was not a false alarm. That baby would come soon. It was not time for it yet, but all of my children were born sooner than their allotted birth date, except Stephen, who was three days late. I suppose he wanted to be born on March 15th, Hungary's Independence Day. My prediction as a mother giving birth for the seventh time was accurate.

John went back to the University in the afternoon to get some work done. The children kept a close eye on me. The pains started coming in the afternoon. The two teenage boys took charge of the situation. They were so sweet! Jancsi, the older one, sat by me and every time I wanted to get up, he pushed me back onto the bed. I just laughed and said I had to go to the bathroom. OK, so he allowed me to do that. In the meantime, Louis, the 12-year-old, ran around with a big alarm clock in his hand and timed the pains. At one point he asked me whether I would be able to wait until his birthday, on the 15th. I enlightened him of the impossibility of his desire.

The boys were trying to reach John's office but could not. So, finally, when he drove up the driveway, Louis ran out with the alarm clock and cried out: "Where were you? The pains are getting closer to each other, we tried to reach you!" John rushed in, but saw I was just laughing.

Indeed, just as I predicted, we were back in the hospital before midnight. Everybody there was concerned because an "older woman" was giving birth. I was 34. The doctor did not worry. He said I was giving birth all the time; I did not stop, so that will not be a problem. It would be different if I was having my first baby. Nowadays, it is hard to believe that people are having their first babies not only at 34, but way into their 40s and 50s. They also wonder why it is more difficult to get pregnant now. What if they would try to get their babies when their body is at the perfect time and shape to accept them?

This was the day of presidential elections. Our obstetrician friend was extremely excited. He was a big Republican, a Nixon-fan, and kept a close eye on the results that kept coming in as the night progressed.

In the meantime, the baby simply did not slide down. I encouraged Dr. Andy Devlin to break the water. Another one of my children was born right after the water was broken. He did, but the baby did not budge from its position. So, he decided to go and look at the X-ray again. Lo and behold!

As soon as he had left the room, I had the urge to push. Someone called him back fast. He still wanted to give me a spinal, which was the fashion then. He did, but it took a few trials before the needle found the proper place. He claimed it is easier for a breech birth when he can direct how hard to push. The mirror was in place for me to see how the baby is going to be born, but fathers were not allowed in the delivery room in those days. It was way early in the morning, no one was around, so Andy let John stand at the door and view the birth from there, but only because he knew John was not going to faint. So there, for the first time after six other children's birth, John saw how our babies were born. The baby came bottom first, then one leg, then the other and finally we knew it was a girl. Then she was born, and I saw Dr. Devlin open and close his mouth a few times: "My Goodness! She has a double knot on her umbilical cord! For that she had to make two somersaults inside!"

I heard her cry, so I knew she was OK. "No wonder I felt her moving all the time!" I said.

"She was born just at the nick of time, or she may have choked herself, if she would have pulled harder on that knot."

"Thank God, she was born now and not later," John said from the door. He was so happy to have seen her being born.

We had a dear professor friend in Pullman, Dr. Aretta Stevens – Sister Mary Dominique. We already decided on the names before our children were born because in Hungary, once the child was born you immediately had to give a name. Whatever you told the midwife in that first moment of their being that would be registered as the baby's name. We named her Dominique Mary and Aretta became her godmother.

Dominique was born on Tuesday morning and Saturday evening we went to our dinner-dance club. People could not believe their ears, when we told them the baby was born on Tuesday. I must confess, we did not dance too many of the dances, but we were there and enjoyed ourselves.

We could leave because son Jancsi took Dominique on his shoulder and that is where she grew up. He simply adored his little sister. Some days he took her out of her crib and took her upstairs in his bed early in the morning if she was fussing. He has always loved children, including his siblings, his children, and by now, his grandchildren.

I had some problem with the other five too. They loved their new little sister so much, no matter when they came home, they took her out of her crib and played with her. How am I ever going to keep a schedule with her? Every day I kept calculating, yet I could not get a working timetable. It did not seem possible. Too many people wanted to spoil her.

One day Ilike's friend, Susan Waterman, came over with her boyfriend. They were playing with the baby and her boyfriend decided she needed a nickname. He tried the version: "Dom-dom," which of course sounded and turned into "dumb-dumb" within a few seconds.

"We have to find her another name," the family decided and so we came up with Niki. "Dominique, nique, nique s'en allait tout simplement, routier pauvre et chantant…" went the fashionable song, written by a Dominican sister. We loved that song. Everyone was singing it on radio, TV, and in the streets. She was the "singing nun" who wrote and played it on the record.

Those were the exciting days after Vatican II (the Second Vatican Council). Aretta, Niki's godmother, was among the first to be sent out into the "world" in civilian clothes, to become a professor of English at Washington State University. She told us how she just had cut her own hair with scissors, not even paying any attention, as she has not anticipated anyone to see it under her habit. She said she looked as if a mouse would have eaten her hair, when she suddenly received her assignment. She was mortified, but she had to go. These were just the first experiments to see what the problems would be and how they could be remedied with sisters living in the outside world. The development was slow. As a result, many sisters left their order, including Aretta, because the two vocations could not be lived simultaneously as it was set up at the time. She left with permission and remained a third order Dominican. The problem was the convent received her salary. She received as much as she needed to live on – but just barely. A professor, who had to travel and do research had to spend money that would not be in a sister's budget. She received an offer for the use of a car from her mother because Pullman had steep hills and she had to carry the groceries up a steep hill. She was not allowed to receive the car. The order allowed her only a simple bicycle. She was 40 years old.

The order's regulations were being changed, as the experiments showed what needed to be different.

My father and grandmother came over for Niki's baptism from Winnipeg. Sandy, at the ripe old age of almost six, happily announced to Father Skok, when he came over for the celebration after the baptism, that Niki is the first of the next six children. Father laughed as he told us the prediction of our wise daughter.

This was the day when we first used the guest book that finally arrived from Hungary. When John's uncle, Feripapa died, his godson, Imre Gundel who took care of him, inherited his paintings and other belongings. He asked John what he would like to have. John asked for the guestbook that was started when John was two years old. His Christmas was commemorated by a watercolor, painted by his aunt, Ernestine Lohwag. It is still in the guestbook on a separate sheet of paper.

Imre tried to smuggle out the guestbook for years. It took him five years to succeed. In the end a Canadian took it out to Toronto. No Hungarian in his right mind dared to take it because of the names in it. Starting with the royal family members, Governor Miklós Horthy's wife, members of the aristocracy, and giants of artistic life in Hungary, filled the pages. The inscriptions represented many languages, including Asian ones. And now it was ours – and we started adding to it on the day of Niki's baptism.

I thoroughly enjoyed my great, late gift from God, our little daughter, Niki. In the mornings, when she woke up for the first feeding, she was all mine, the house was quiet. The dining room window let in the first rays of sunshine. It was mesmerizing and I felt I was the queen of the house. Everyone else was still asleep when I sat down with little Niki in my arms in the living room. Contentment and happiness overwhelmed me as Niki's little mouth sucked the life-giving milk from my breast.

This is a quote from a book I wrote to each of my children separately for Christmas of 2017.

"I remember Niki…

God's gift to us late in life – is how I thought of my seventh, born when I was 34. Four and a half years after our last baby, Rita. I used to nurse you and hold you up on my shoulder, your soft little face nestling in the cavity of my collarbone, right against my neck and cheek — and I felt in seventh heaven.

The children all went off to school and "you and I, you and I" "Te meg én", "Te meg én" waved goodbye to them from the window.

You started walking earlier than any of my kids because you saw everybody walking around you. You were 11 months, and you crossed the room on your first try. I remember all the kids standing around and egging you on: 'You can do it!' 'You can do it!' And you did! In your little flannel nightgown with the hearts on it, it must have been one that Helen made for her younger sisters: Sandy? Rita?"

Christmas came and with it the coldest winter of Pullman's history. Stephen played Tiny Tim in the Christmas play at church. He had to go to rehearsal. John had a horrible flu. He felt so weak he could not even sign the Christmas letters that waited to be sent out in great piles. (There was only snail-mail at the time.) Ilike was turning 16 on January 1st. She wanted to pass her driver's test as soon as possible after New Year. I had trouble with my sinuses and really did not feel up to it, but I had to drive with Ilike, on the road covered with sheer ice, taking Stephen to the rehearsal.

Niki was born on the 5th of November, so she was still quite young. She was such a good child she slept through anything. This was a real benefit for us. On Christmas Eve the children all went for a "walk." Ilike took them down to the restaurant on the bottom of the hill and got them French fries while the "angels," namely John and I, prepared everything and put out the presents. When we were done, the kids were not back yet. How we waited for these few moments of peace and quiet in our home all sparkling and decorated for the holidays! We sat down thanked God for our children, for all God's gifts to us and toasted with a glass of champagne, our Christmas ritual.

Ilike called and we watched out for them. They came in through the kitchen to the dining room and lo and behold! The angels must have been ready too because the little bells were ringing. The glorious moment arrived when they could open the presents. The Christmas tree's sparkles were mirrored in the children's glowing eyes. Every year Ilike sewed a dress or nightgown for her little sisters for Christmas. We limited their presents from us to $10 per child, but they all had presents from the many relatives, cousins, aunts and uncles, godparents, friends. The room was full of gifts for the nine of us. When we unwrapped them, we carefully folded the gift-wrap that could be saved, and put them in a box, along with the bows and ribbons, to store them for next time when we could reuse them. (And people think we did not recycle!!!) I almost never see anyone doing this nowadays.

We had our usual Christmas Eve dinner: salmon with mushroom sauce and rice, then "bejgli," Hungarian Christmas cake with walnuts and poppy seeds, sent by Grandmother from Vancouver, B.C.

Much later, after dinner, we went to Midnight Mass, which in those days actually started at midnight. Between the two, having had our festive dinner, we had to prepare the room and dishes for the party we arranged for friends after Midnight Mass.

Niki slept in her little crib that John made for her. It consisted of the famous basket in which Louis traveled, when we had escaped. The basket was fastened to an elevated table. All the guests admired her good nature. When she outgrew the basket, she slept in a crib, right in the living room. I remember once telling a guest. "The baby in the corner is asleep." She answered: "Is there a baby here?" I had to show her where the crib stood. We placed the sofas in a way that the crib was almost invisible. Niki very conveniently figured out that when the vacuum was going, or when I was typing, she had to go to sleep. She must have felt the same way about noisy company. Something quite ordinary; no reason to wake up.

The night of the 30th of December, John and I were awakened by the cold in the house. We were freezing.

"What is happening?" I asked.

"Did the furnace go off?" John wondered.

We looked at the room thermometer. It showed 65 degrees. We opened the basement door and heard the furnace working full blast. John went down to look at it more closely. "There is nothing wrong with it," he decided.

Then we glanced out the window to our outdoor thermometer.

"It is 47 degrees below!!!" John exclaimed. "It seems our furnace cannot take more than a 100-degree difference. That explains why we are freezing."

"But what are we going to do?"

"Let's put the children in their snowsuits and put more covering on them."

We fastened an old mattress onto the kitchen door to keep out the cold. We put on our winter coats too and put masking tape around all the window frames to stop the air from coming in.

The next day we found out it was a record low in the history of Pullman. In some lower places it even went down to 52 degrees below.

A record amount of snow fell that year also. A photo in the *Pullman Herald* showed the principal of a school standing beside the snow piled onto the side of the road. It dwarfed the tall man. The university was closed for a week. Even ambulances could not make it up the hills in places. One of the students who fell and got injured was carried by his friends on a stretcher to the hospital because the ambulance could not make it to the dorm.

Obviously, we had a lot of work ahead of us getting this house in shape.

33

Since I had to part with my business when we had left Vancouver, I started to write in earnest as a freelance writer, whenever I had a moment. My very first article was published in 1967, in *Our Sunday Visitor,* a Catholic weekly with a circulation of 500,000 entitled "To my husband - on Father's Day." I got paid $50 for it. My editor wrote a little note with the check: "Have a nice dinner on it with your husband." This was a lot of money at the time, when John's yearly salary was around $15,000. I MADE IT! I was so very happy! I was now a published writer.

TO MY HUSBAND • ON FATHER'S DAY
By HELEN M. SZABLYA

You'll learn much about Helen Szablya when you read this letter to her husband. They live now in Pullman, Washington.

MY DEAR: We were parents in spirit before we ever got married. Do you remember that beautiful, sunny August afternoon when we took a hike and I asked you how many children you wanted to have when we got married? Do you remember what your answer was? Well, we had your desire, we had a girl as our first child and have had five since. We may have others ....What really matters is that we remained parents in spirit, even after we have become parents by flesh.

Remember when we started praying for our children on our honeymoon? You suggested it. We talked about them before they ever came into being as of the living seeds who were already planted within us since we came into this world. Or maybe before that, in our parents, in our ancestors ....

Busy - and happy, after nearly 16 years of marriage I realize many things, which I did not quite understand when you married me. You were

26, already teaching at the university, you were a grown man and I had always looked up to you. Still, I have never felt as if I would not be your equal. I am sure that my thoughts about life must have been pretty immature compared to yours, but your patience let me work out my problems at my own pace. You never forced your ideas on your bride.

When our first baby was born, you were a most loving father and you taught me many things. Remember, you knew how to give the baby a bath, because you had enough foresight to learn it before our baby was born. You knew how to teach me to become a mother, when I was not much more than a child myself. Your stability and kindness helped us through our marriage, and gave the children their always-smiling father.

Our life was never too easy, but - like you promised when you asked me to marry you - it was always happy. I am sure that you remember all the difficulties we went through living behind the Iron Curtain and finally our escape with the ten-day-old baby; the old priest friend of ours, who reminded us of the escape of the Holy Family. I am sure that you were whole-heartedly trying to imitate St. Joseph on those trips (on the first, when we were captured and on the second one, when we almost did not dare to try again). But with God's help we have made it. We had only six diapers and a few medicines besides our three children. We had to start all over. But we were free, we were happy, and you landed your first job, teaching at the University, just like in the old country.

By now you are full professor and you still have time to play with our babies, help with the homework, give rides to the prom, dry up the little ones' tears ... How many times have you told me that if it had not been for us you would have quit? But a father cannot quit, a father has to go on ... Yes, you still bring us happiness, love, tenderness, though sometimes you are tired and your hair is getting gray. You always have time for us, for our problems, no matter how trivial they are, and you always helped me to become myself, to develop fully as a person .... Thank you ...

Our Sunday Visitor June 18, 1967

Later it appeared in other publications and in the Cor Unum annual of the Pressbaum Sacre Coeur (where we found our asylum as refugees), translated into German. What I am describing is how the ideal marriage was in the fifties in the United States. We happened to be the lucky ones blessed with our happy marriage in true life. I can thank my mother-in-law for this because she was determined to bring up her son in a way that her daughter-in-law should thank her for it. She always told us that the hand that rocks the cradle governs the future of the world; it is the person who brings up the next generation and instills in them the right attitude. As her husband – although a darling gentleman – was not able to do any housework, she taught her son to be able to do it all.

That is one of the reasons I had the possibility to add writing to my way of life. Whenever I felt strongly about something, I simply had to sit at my desk and write until it was all on paper. Then send it out, wait for the rejections, and an occasional SUCCESS! I did not know it then, but it has been like that with most writers, including Hemmingway and a very successful TV series "MASH," which had 33 rejections, before it became an all-time favorite.

Niki was not born yet when I saw a competition advertised in *Boys' Life*, the magazine of the boy scouts. It was for a story about the life of scouts. I knew then and there I had to write a book about the courageous scout leaders who kept up scouting in people's homes and kept the boys together to continue teaching them about freedom and democracy. Some of the leaders paid for this with two to three years in prison. I had first-hand experience and a ready-made story. In three months, I wrote my first book. I sent it in. Then I waited.

That year the prize was not awarded. I got a beautiful letter from *Boys' Life* indicating they would have loved to publish it, but they felt the leaders of the illegal scouts already had quite a bit of trouble without them publishing the book.

The book was published first in 1986 by the Hungarian-American Scouts in Exterris (Abroad). Once outside Hungary, the scouts organized and by then there were Hungarian Scouts everywhere in the world except Hungary and the Soviet Bloc.

The book was originally written in English, but the Scouts decided they wanted to publish it in Hungarian for the 30th anniversary of the 1956 Hungarian Uprising. So, in three months I translated it, while leading the work on the *Hungary Remembered* project, also for the 30th anniversary.

This became my first published book. *Az 56-os cserkészcsapat. The Scout Troop of 1956.* It was used as a textbook for the national Hungarian-American scout camp in the USA, the summer of 1986. The scouts had to write skits from it. One of the scout leaders, Gábor Szórád wrote a script for the scouts to "live the book." I talked to some of today's scout leaders who remembered having been woken up in the middle of the night: "The Soviets are coming, the Soviets are coming!" They had to jump out of their sleeping bags and act according to the script.

The evening when the first copy of the published book arrived my dear husband took me out to dinner at the Keg, our then favorite restaurant. He surprised me with a big bouquet of red roses to celebrate this big milestone.

Many of my articles (op-ed pieces and features) were published in Catholic magazines and newspapers, but also *The Seattle Times* and *The Lewiston Morning Tribune, The Pullman Herald,* a weekly. Regional or university newspapers often reprinted the articles.

My clients multiplied as the years went by: The (USA) National Catholic News Service, *Our Sunday Visitor, Ave Maria, Crisis, Our Family* (a Canadian Catholic magazine, frequent contributor), *The Catholic Answer* (frequent contributor), *The Inland Register* (frequent contributor), *The NW Catholic Progress,* and the *Journal American.*

John basked in the glory of being the husband. At one of the IEEE Conferences someone looked at his name tag and asked him: "Are you the husband of Helen Szablya?"

The other day, my daughter told me about a beautiful spider web she had seen. That reminded me of another beautiful spider web I encountered, while writing.

Once Niki was in school, I wrote another one of my important books, our own true story *My Only Choice: Hungary 1942-1956,* I started writing as soon as all the children left for school and I wrote until they returned. I touched nothing in the house until they arrived back in the afternoon. Housework can be done with the children around.

I lived in another world. If someone rang the doorbell, I had to first get to my senses to realize where I was.

While I wrote there was also a spider making a big net on the window. The winter became very cold and the web shone with the many snow crystals frozen on it. The sun was shining through the winter wonder. I cannot forget the beauty of that spider web with the spider in the middle.

34

Gabriel was here today; a breath of fresh air from our past in Pullman. Of the many happy days in the heat of the summer and the freeze of the winter, the leaves turning colors during the long Indian Summer and the short springs which sometimes lasted only a day.

We loved our Pullman home. We lived our happy and busy family lives. Gabriel was the youngest daughter of our dear friends, the Barnsleys, aka Fieldings.

"You must meet them. You will be best friends," Ilike told us when she came home from a lecture Gabriel Fielding (Dr. Alan Barnsley M.D.) gave at the university. He was there for a year as "artist in residence" from England, where he was a famous author in the circle of friends of Graham Greene and Iris Murdoch.

We still lived in the Statesman Apartments at the time. We had our beautiful and convenient swimming pool at our disposal. When we met the Barnsleys at a faculty event, we invited them over to swim. They came – and the rest is history.

Ilike was so right. We became best friends. The Barnsleys: Dina (Edwina) and Alan and their five delightful children and the Szablyas and their – at the time – only six. Michael, the oldest Barnsley, was already studying at Oxford. Jonty (Jonathan) attended WSU, Simon and Jancsi became best friends in high school and the two girls, (Fissy) Felicity and (Gagu) Gabriel made friends with our Rita and Sandy. I remember how Gabriel clung to my neck in the swimming pool because she did not know how to swim yet and the water was too deep for her to stand. She was so cute with her curly red hair and blue eyes, holding on for dear life with an ever-present smile.

Michael, who spent the summer at home, practiced "cannonballs" in the swimming pool, splashing half of the water out of the pool with his forceful jump. The kids played "Marco Polo" in the pool and "Hercules unchained."

Dr. Alan Barnsley was offered a professorship in the English Department at WSU after his first year there. The family stayed in Pullman and bought a house on University Hill. The day they moved in, we invited them for dinner, so they would not have to cook, and we took care of the younger children all day. Well, the family came over around lunchtime and they were just sitting on the sofa, showing no signs of going home to move their belongings to the new house.

"When will you be coming back for dinner?" I inquired.

"Dinner?" they asked.

That is when we found out they thought they were invited for lunch. We quickly gave them something to eat and informed them with great laughter that we still expected them back for "dinner" which we usually ate around 6:00 p.m..

Another day they invited us for "high tea." Having lived in Canada, we knew something about British teatime, so we did not expect to be fed much. They prepared a feast. As it turned out, they called a full dinner "high tea."

In the fall, when catechism classes started, we picked up their children, delivered all our children to church, and then we returned to the parents and basically spent the entire day with them. First, only the adults, then the kids joined us after catechism. We ate, drank, talked and talked. We had so much to say to each other, to discuss, to laugh about the customs in America and play games. "In the manner of the word" was one game Gabriel remembered, when she came today. We divided the company in two. One group went out. The others decided on an adverb, like "angrily," "happily," "lazily." Of course, we found harder and harder words for the competing team to guess. The other group came back. The first group then had to perform a task "in the manner of the word," until the second group found out what the word was.

We played Charades, and other games, and then we had dinner/high tea before we called it a night.

Excursions to the Snake River, to Kamiak Butte, and to Steptoe Butte, were always fun events.

I can feel the sun on my skin when I just think of the Snake River. The road there led through sandy desert-like hills with just enough grass for the cattle to range freely in their fenced off area. Big rocks and sagebrush ruled the countryside. The wildflowers were beautiful in the spring and had a lovely scent, which caused my eyes and nose to itch and I was sneezing and "crying" all the way home in the car, but it was well worth it. We swam in the river, although it was colder than our pool, but I love swimming in nature, when there are no limits, you can just look up to the sky and follow your instinct, wherever it leads you. The road to the river was a rural road and there was nothing and usually no one else on the beach. A hundred years ago no pilgrims had trodden this region yet. Further down on the river there were a few settlements, sheep farms. A ship steamed down the river weekly carrying their mail. There were no other roads to those communities. We always planned on taking the trip, but it would have been too expensive for the entire family to go.

John taught a course Engineering 101. It was for all students, to find out whether the subject interested them. He was still teaching them how to use the slide rule. Ilike, wanting to take a course from her father, took the course one year. That same year, two Wang calculators were purchased by the Engineering department which cost $5,000 each and the students signed up for 30 minutes at a time to use them.

One of John's students, a veteran, received a new-fangled Texas Instruments "calculator" from his parents for Christmas. It cost $400.00. All the students gathered around that calculator, wishing they could have one. No one else in the class could afford one. Neither could we. Slide rules had to suffice.

Professors were discussing whether students should be allowed to use them during tests. As there were only a very few, at that time they could not allow it yet. It would have given too much advantage to those who could afford one.

However, the following year, the calculators' price had come down to $200 and it was determined that it was a reasonable expense for the students. Years went by, the calculators continued to get better, but still a far cry from even the smartphones of today. When Louis, our third child, enrolled in electrical engineering, we finally decided that the two of them, father (the professor) and son (the student) would share a Texas Instruments (TI) 59. In just a few short years it was practically required for students to have one.

The Barnsleys decided to buy one for their oldest son, Michael.

After his first year at Oxford, Michael was talking with John about career choices. He was wondering whether he should become an author, like his father (he was good at it) or go into sciences. John talked him into choosing sciences and to keep writing as a hobby.

Alan and John discussed which calculator would be best for Michael and John recommended to buy a TI 59. It was on this calculator that Dr. Michael Fielding Barnsley started his life's greatest discovery in a new science "fractal geometry"; how to compress fractals and the Fractal Fourier Analysis. It was such an important discovery that he was provided with bodyguards in Europe that no one should kidnap him with his secrets. Michael was forever grateful to John and has been thanking him for his advice and the calculator ever since. How little things can add up to become unbelievable achievements!

Our fun days continued year in and year out. The parties were especially delightful at the Barnsleys. The English Department usually had many representatives there with their wives, as did neighbors, and – always – the Szablyas.

Alan greeted us one day: "I made a Mikulashka for you!"

"You made what?" I asked him.

"A drink. Champagne and cognac."

We loved it.

Dina made the best English and French foods for these exciting events.

By that time Gabriel was around 10 years old. She came to me and asked: "What would you like to drink?"

"Whiskey and water" I said.

She came back soon with a glass that was the color of whiskey. I tasted it and almost spat it out.

"What is this?" I asked Gabriel.

She answered with an honestly innocent smile: "What you asked for: whiskey and vodka."

I told her mother, and we had a good laugh, but I was not offered another drink, so I just drank it very slowly. It lasted me the entire evening.

We also had a very scientific-literary experiment. We started by repeating little poems in different languages whether you have to drink wine or beer first in order not to get a hangover.

It seemed like the various languages and even within one language, some of the versions could not agree which was better. So we divided the company in two. One half drank beer, then wine, the other half wine on beer. I am glad to report that no one got sick, except one person who sacrificed herself on the altar of science and mixed the two in one glass! (I was not the one). That just did not work.

December 26th was Boxing Day. We usually spent the entire day with the Barnsleys and all the friends who came to the open house, as is customary in England. We got used to this in Canada and cherished the custom.

As many artists, Alan was occasionally depressed. In these cases, Dina went in and taught his class. They loved each other and knew everything about the other, so she could easily do it. She used to try it out on us on the Saturdays that we spent together, while the kids were at catechism.

Our relationship continued throughout the years, now, from the oldest generation, I am the only one still alive as I am writing this chapter. The friendship, however, keeps flourishing between our children. Gabriel's visit is living proof of that.

Pullman was a perfect place to raise our seven children starting with the fact that everyone was watching everybody's kids. If they happened to be somewhere, they were not supposed to be, we would be the first ones to know from a kindly neighbor or friend. Seven children were not out of the ordinary in those days in Pullman. There were some with 10. The average number of children all over the USA was four at the time.

The University was right in town, so children could live at home while attending university. The schools were excellent because the parents were mostly professors, people connected to the university, or professionals who worked with them. If the parents did not approve of something, they came out in numbers. At one of the PTA meetings 900 of us showed up. The principal wanted to make Mathematics and English into subjects in which the children would go at their own speed, and both would have been pass/fail courses.

Entertainment in Pullman competed with the big cities. There were several symphonic orchestras, chamber orchestras between the many artists living in the community who were married to a spouse working for the university. There were theatrical and operatic performances, some free, some at a nominal price when compared to those in Seattle. The Lecture Artist series brought the most interesting speakers. We met and chatted with Mitterand, who was at the time the leader of the Opposition in France, but later President and with the brother of the Dalai Lama, who was a professor and talked about their escape with the Dalai Lama from Tibet. The author of the book "Black Like Me," John Griffith, was a sensation. The book was a bestseller at the time. This man took a medicine to darken his skin color, until he actually turned black. He wanted to write a book about what it was like to be black. The same church that he attended as a white man would not let him enter as a black man. When he looked in the mirror and saw his own face, he felt discrimination against himself. It was all hard to believe, especially with our Hungarian background. We had never had any trouble with black people in Europe. When I was little, I was so happy to see a black gentleman, whom I met occasionally when going to school. He was the only one in Hungary. I felt lucky to see him. What possible difference could there be between people of different color? I simply could not understand. One of the black people with whom we had a serious connection with was John's first PhD student at UBC, who was one of the brightest and sweetest men I have ever met. I admired him. He was from Trinidad and Tobago and had a marvelous community of friends all of whom we embraced.

John and I had a mission to let Americans know that extreme Left was equally as horrific as extreme Right. We took our mission seriously. Once my sister Elizabeth was out of Hungary, we sped up this activity. We gave talk after talk about our escape. We went to schools, libraries, universities, service clubs and churches. Teachers were always very thankful that we came and impressed on people how important teaching history was. In those days you could graduate from high school in the USA learning history either until the French Revolution, or starting with the French Revolution.

Would that prepare anyone to vote in the elections of a country that was the leader of the Free World? Another interesting subject was: Twentieth Century Problems. Now, how could you possibly understand those, without having a proper background?

35

As Pullman was a university town, what would have been simpler, than taking courses, in order to have papers to prove what I already knew?

I decided to start inquiring. I brought all my credits from Hungary and UBC and put them into the hands of the Registrar, telling the university, to take their time and give me as many credits as possible because I wanted to graduate majoring in foreign languages. For example, I went to the Head of the English Department, John Elwood, who was a friend from the parties at the Barnsleys. I presented him with 17 published articles and asked him if he would waive the compulsory English 101. He opened his mouth a few times, then closed it and said: "I suppose there is no problem whatsoever, it just has never happened before."

The graduation requirements were 120 semester credits. The decision of the Registrar was that I can be a junior. I had two years ahead of me. Tuition in those days, for a part-time student (six credits maximum), was $60, for a full-time student it was $240. Professors' families did not get free tuition. I could never afford to go full time. I also had my seven children at home. So, I took four credits and decided to "challenge" as many courses as possible. A challenge meant you had to ask permission from the Head of Department, in this case Dr. Seigneuret, to sign permission for you to take the exam from the professor of that subject.

"So, what makes you think you can do the exams?" Dr. Seigneuret asked.

"You know, how it was in Europe. I came from a family where we had German and French governesses and learned the language as children. English was my fourth language and I was attending an American university. We had to learn Russian at school, and I am taking Russian now from Dr. Kosin here at WSU; I have studied Latin for six years…"

He signed the first application. I went to the German professor, who asked me to read Herman Hesse's Siddhartha in German and then we will discuss it. And we did. He gave me an A. Another professor asked me to write five essays in German, which I did.

"I can give you credit for these and even for the next course, which is a graduate course. "

I had a minor in German.

Next time I went to Dr. Seigneuret and he saw I was writing another application, he just took it from me and signed it. Did not even look. He knew if I said I could do it, I could.

I wrote five French essays too. I got As in every exam. I had a minor in French, without ever attending any French class, based on my exams.

That semester I took four credits, but I received another 32 credits for a year's worth of credits. John swelled with pride and bragged happily about his wife's achievement.

This is how it happened that in the history of WSU there were two Helen Szablyas who were seniors at WSU. Ilike was 20, I was 38. No wonder they mixed up our credits and we had to sort it out who attended which class. There was a Shakespeare class we both took, though not together and the administration mixed up our credits.

Ilike graduated in 1973, the same year, however, I graduated in February of 1976 because we went to Germany for a sabbatical year which postponed my progress!

"Would you teach the Russian class until we get another Russian professor?" Geneticist Dr. Igor Kosin was asked. Twenty years later he was asking himself why in the world he was still teaching Russian as well as genetics.

The Kosins were friends from our dinner-dance club. One day I asked him while we were dancing whether it was true he taught Russian literature in Russian. He said it was true. So, I asked to audit his class. I did and I loved it. That was the last push I needed to go back to university. I was going to major in German, as that was the language I spoke best, it was my second mother tongue. We spoke German at home all the time for practice when I was a little girl. However, it turned out that I was taking class after class of Russian because I could not resist his way of teaching. So, I ended up majoring in Russian.

As he was a scientist, he taught grammar in a very original way. One semester it was semantics, the next was syntax. Did you know a verb can be a direct object? As in "I learned to swim." In another class "Teaching German to English speakers," I told that to the professor and she did not want to believe it. Next time we had a class she told the students I was right.

Anyway, it was so much fun, when professors regarded you as one of their friends and an adult. I usually read the same books as they had, had the same kind of experiences, and could give input to the class in many ways. Being a mother of seven, as well as a published writer, and going to class, having gone through so much in your life already, is so different than being a student straight out of high school.

I truly enjoyed being many things at once: a wife, a mother, a writer and a student. I tried to immerse myself fully in everything I did.

～

"You know, John, no one ever carded me in my life. Not when I was a teenager and we went to night clubs in Switzerland, to the Folies Bergere in Paris with my parents, not when I went to a bar by myself in Hungary when I was 16, but married, no one ever questioned my age."

"How curious," he said with a mischievous smile on his face.

A friend, Michelle, a French lady, was a waitress at Rico's, a popular pub in town. He conspired with Michelle and the next time we went to Rico's she carded me. So, I lost my claim to this fame.

Many of the streets were so steep the police closed them when there was too much snow and ice. Some you could still drive, but the other cars always waited till the first car got to the top before it started on its way up. You never knew when the car would decide to slide back down sideways. Of course, after a while you did become an expert in driving in the snow, but at first... Besides, sometimes it was not your fault at all, it was just an ice patch, or something.

One night there was lots of snow, so we decided to go down to Rico's on foot. Walking home there were quite a few of us. Around the lamp posts the air was sparkling with ice crystals. The enchanting whiteness of the snow, the radiance of the frozen air and the beauty of that night is still with me as we marched in the deep snow and laughed arm-in-arm, up the hill, all the way home. Cold can be magic, but it still does not change the fact that it is COLD.

～

For a change from all that cold, I will warm you up and I will tell you about our first few trips to Trinidad and Tobago.

How in the world did we get there? Do you remember when I wrote about our fun times in Vancouver, B.C., with John's first PhD student, Ken Julien, and the Trinidadian community? Well, by now Ken had become the Dean, then acting Vice Chancellor of the University of the West Indies St. Augustine Campus, in Trinidad. The accreditation system in the British Commonwealth was to have three "External Examiners." John was asked by Ken to be one of them. Every year one of the three engineering professors had to come to Trinidad in person to talk to all the graduating engineers. Beforehand they had to approve the exam questions, and then look through all the written exams. Of course, John gladly accepted.

The University of the West Indies (UWI) is situated on several islands. The administration building of the entire university is in Jamaica, meaning a thousand miles away from the engineering and agricultural departments in Trinidad.

The first time John went I could not go with him because Niki was still nursing in June of 1969. However the next year I joined him when he was asked to go again.

Our first stop was in Barbados because one of the students had to be interviewed there. He had already started working in his job.

A hot wall hit my face when I stepped into this wonderland.

"Boy! Is it hot!" I stood stupefied.

"What did you expect in the tropics?" asked John with a great grin on his face. He adored the heat.

"I don't know. I knew it was hot, but I have never experienced this kind of heat before hitting you straight in the face."

A taxi expected us and took us straight to Hemmingway's favorite hotel, the Oceanview. We stayed there only one unforgettable day. The hotel had its own bay on the seashore separated by a small coral reef from the ocean. The old building was furnished with antique furniture and crystal chandeliers, as well as Persian rugs on the wooden floors. Our room looked right onto the sea.

Employees there averaged 26 years working at the hotel. The bartender had his tasty specialties.

At dinner we were given a long menu. We tried to make a selection, but the waiter assured us: "This is the menu. You will get it all. It is not something to choose from."

One dish was better than the next. Each was special in its tropical way. Seafood appetizers, curried chicken and delightful desserts with tropical fruits that tasted so sweet, I never imagined what their taste was supposed to be like when you eat it ripe and fresh from the tree.

Love was in the air and the sand, the quiet night and the stars. We quickly slipped into bed, naked and desiring. What a night it was! What enforcement of our love for each other!

In the morning we went down for a swim. Just as we were leaving, we were given a menu for breakfast. We said we did not usually eat breakfast. They insisted we had to have something. In the end we agreed on a big plate of tropical fruit.

The student duly showed up and John had his interview with him. Then it was off to Trinidad!

I was so very excited to finally see Ken Julien's homeland and their home he had built with Pat, his beautiful wife.

"Passengers returning to Trinidad use the left aisle, please. Tourists and foreign citizens use the right aisle." The language was plain English, yet the setting was different, the mood was comfortable and jovial as we arrived in this country during its "state of emergency."

By the time of our arrival, the "state of emergency" had been in effect for almost two months. It had been declared by the Government of Trinidad and Tobago on April 21, 1970. It was a sequel to unrest and demonstrations fanned mainly by Black Power activists, a movement which has only a vague resemblance to the one with the same name in the U.S. By the middle of June curfew was relaxed to between midnight and five in the morning. The university examinations rolled by as usual.

All around the airport palm trees stretched and tropical plants breathed their scent into the air. The most welcome sight was Ken's beaming face as he ushered us fast through customs and into his car.

"Welcome to Trinidad! Pat is waiting for us already at home with Stephen, our wise two-year-old. Even he is excited waiting for you."

The car veered to the left side of the road. I almost opened my mouth, when I remembered what Ken told us about the first time he had moved back home from Canada. "I started driving and all these cars were coming straight at me. I pulled over to the side of the road and buried my face in my hands. Left, left, left – I kept repeating. In the British countries we drive on the left. Then I slowly reoriented my brain and followed the traffic signs. It was hard to get used to it again."

On the side of the highway, fish, fruit and vegetable vendors offered their fresh wares. Fish that had just arrived from the sea, was smothered in ice; the fruits and vegetables were growing right behind their stalls. A big horse-pulled cart was loaded with coconuts. A man with an East Indian look stood beside the cart in light, white, loose shorts and shirt carrying a huge machete.

"Here, you have to try that," Ken slowed down, turned to the man and asked him for some coconut water.

The big machete moved and the coconut fell apart. We tasted the refreshing coconut water as fresh as nature produced it.

"Heavenly," it felt so good in that horrible heat. "I have never had anything like this before."

The guys contentedly looked at each other with a smile.

"You will have many 'firsts' here I think," John winked at me.

The car was winding up Mount Benedict, the mountain where they lived. I closed my eyes now and again because the driving was just too scary for me on those tight roads, where oncoming traffic was invisible. On top of all that – on the left side.

Pat was all smiles in their beautiful home on the hill with a lovely view of the surrounding hills and mountains, right under the Abbey of St. Benedict on the mountaintop.

Pat fed us all kinds of tropical wonders and offered us Trinidadian Rum, the very best the island produced.

"Cane is an important product for us. Rum is the brandy made from cane. Of course, we make sugar from it too, but there is no home in the country that would not have rum as a staple in the cupboard or on the table," explained Pat.

Stephen looked at us with his great big eyes and recorded our presence in his little mind.

Ken showed us our room downstairs, with air conditioning; bless his soul!

"We have natural air conditioning upstairs," he said. "Have you noticed that our bricks are all manufactured with holes in them and the house is built in the direction of the trade winds? The breeze dances straight through the house all the time."

"Thank God for that!" I muttered. The sweat poured down on John's face: I felt I was going to faint if I didn't become a little cooler. I could never, never stand the sun as a child.

As soon as we unpacked, six o'clock was approaching.

"Come, let's go up, we don't want to miss the sunset," John coaxed me.

I found out he was not kidding. We sat in the direction of the tropical sun setting in all its glory. The pink-orange-blue-yellow sky suddenly radiated a greenish light, so typical for sunsets there.

"The last time I was here I went in to get my camera," John said to me, "and by the time I got back the sun was gone."

As he was saying that the sun sank behind the horizon and suddenly it was pitch dark. We were four degrees from the Equator. The entire sunset only lasted five exhilarating minutes – then it was over. Only the stars twinkled high up in the sky.

After a few helpings of great callaloo soup, curried goat and homemade ice cream we were discussing the coming days with Ken.

"I wanted to explain a bit to you about our 'state of emergency'" Ken said. "Black Power activists came to our country from the USA and spread the word 'Black is Beautiful.' This was appreciated and it was good for those who still remembered the tales of slave grandparents. They could now be proud of their ancestry. The problem was much more economical here than about race. 95% of the population is colored here. Black unemployment though was a heavy burden. There were plenty of jobs if they would have taken what they considered 'slave labor', like masonry."

John asked Ken: "What is your opinion of all that?"

"Let me show you an article I wrote for the local newspaper, *Express*, about that topic." He brought out the article and gave it to us.

Here are some excerpts from it:

"Do I support the Black Power movement? Can I, as a black man, dare to condemn it?...

"If Black Power has, as a symptom, full dignity of the black man, then I welcome it. If Black Power shows itself in arrogance and disdain for others, then I reject it...

"If Black Power preys on the feelings of the unemployed and unemployable for the purposes which will bring them no benefit, then it should be stopped...

"If Black Power forces awareness on the public at large of discriminatory practices within our society, then it would have done what no commission of inquiry could have achieved. If Black Power creates fear, anger, frustration and suffering among the public, then unwelcome hardening of attitudes will rapidly develop...

"If Black Power binds together the majority of our people, then it should be encouraged. If Black Power by design or by accident leads to a racial confrontation, then I regard it as highly dangerous...

"If Black Power gives added meaning to beauty and makes our present queen contests fairer, then many of us will be happy. If Black Power says that ONLY black is beautiful, then it will lose my respect...

"If Black Power believes that opinions, even from black people, should be heard and considered, then let it be heard. If Black Power refuses dialogue, then it cannot be heard...

"If Black Power wishes to remove the word 'nigger' and 'collie' from our vocabulary, I welcome it. If Black Power wishes to add the word 'whitey' to our vocabulary nothing will be gained..."

"WOW! Ken, this is an article worthy of you. This is how we have always known you," said John.

"Would it be possible to have an interview with Eric Williams, the Prime Minister?" I knew Ken was his favorite and they were on very good terms.

Ken looked doubtful. "I am not sure that would be possible, but I can get you one with Archbishop Anthony Pantin."

"We will go to see many places together," continued Ken. "While John is busy working you can come and walk around the university, take photos. Also, the driver will take you around town."

The next day our busy stay in Trinidad and Tobago started in earnest.

36

Ken took both of us to the University campus. I was walking around, feeling rather foolish with my two cameras, looking just as American tourists are portrayed in every comedy. The first photo I took was of the unbelievable (for me) Samaan tree. Its shade covered about a quarter of an acre, or so it seemed. When I sat down underneath and looked up, there was an entire zoo of insects, birds, spiders, plants, flowers living in the crown of the tree.

One of Ken's colleagues, Professor St. Claire King, told me of his disappointment when he first went to England to study. He was looking for the tree mentioned in the nursery rhyme "under the spready chestnut tree." When he asked about it and was shown a chestnut tree, his first reaction was: "What a puny tree? How can they call that 'spready' compared to the Samaan tree?" The only probable explanation seemed to me that the originator of the nursery rhyme had never seen a Samaan tree.

I saw the offices of Ken and John. The buildings on campus were also built with natural air conditioning. Real air conditioning was reserved for equipment, just as in British Columbia, except of course… we were not in B.C. – we were in the tropics.

When the early evening came we went out on a boat into the Caroni swamp, to watch the scarlet ibis – turkey-sized birds – flying home from their daily hunting trips, to nestle into the trees. The unbelievably beautiful coral-colored ibis were floating in the sunset. Soon all the trees "bloomed" with the colorful birds.

We walked around in the small zoo with all the native animals of the islands, like the crocodile, the alligator, the monkeys, the snakes, the parakeets, the bats.

We went to the famous Trinidad Hilton, built into the side of a hill, close to the zoo. The lobby and the swimming pool, open to the public were on the top floor, as was the restaurant with its "Maxi lunch for a mini price." For 4.95 TT (Trinidad and Tobago) dollars you could eat to your heart's content, go back many times to choose from the buffet that offered all kinds of foods imaginable; extravagant (for us) seafood, meats, cold cuts and hot entrées, salads and tropical fruits. We tried it several times while we were there. The Hilton was in a very convenient place. All the Hilton chefs from around the world were trained in Trinidad. Their cuisine was colorful and oh, so tasty!

There were also boutiques in the Hilton. I glanced at a dream of a dress in the shop window. The blouse's deep décolletage, a narrow waist, the sleeves and the skirt were created from white cotton lace tiers decorated with thin black ribbons.

"John! Look at that dress! It has everything that looks good on me," I looked longingly at the apparition.

"Let's go in!" John's eyes lit up, even though we knew it must have been very expensive, being in the Hilton.

We went in and asked to try on the dress. The lady was reluctant to take it in from the window. She really doubted it was worth it. She just finished setting it up. We asked. It was the perfect size. The price was not so much: it was 180 TT dollars.

"Try it on!" John said daringly.

The lady finally took it down and I slipped into the slip that went under the dress; embroidered with black on the white background. Then came the blouse and the skirt.

"It looks like it was made for you, Helen! We cannot pass this up!"

"But, John, we cannot afford such luxuries, even though I love it, love it, love it!" I danced around in it and the skirt flew in the air around me.

John went to pay for the dress. The most beautiful dress I have ever had or will have. It served me well for balls, dinner dances and several of our children's weddings. Now it belongs to my daughter. When I first put it on at the dinner dance club, a friend told me: "Helen, we do not own these kinds of dresses, they are just to be photographed in!" It was.

Our kiss expressed not only my gratefulness for the dress, but our undying love for each other; although it sometimes made us more generous to each other than we could afford.

One day, in the evening, we came back to enjoy the Hilton's great performance of local customs. It was basically for the tourists, but Ken thought we had to see this summary of TT customs. The steel band played by the swimming pool. Steel bands started during WWII. There were empty oil barrels all around and people started drumming on them, and then chisel them so their sounds should differ. Some barrels were taller, others quite short. The local people were so incredibly talented, they made those oil barrels take on all the instruments. Some like an organ, some like a violin, or a harp, a xylophone, or a piano. You name it; they had the sound for it. Even classical music sounded fantastic, when played by a steel band.

227

Only the conductor read music. He went to the players and hummed their part to them. The players immediately took up the tune. I have loved steel band music ever since.

We sat around the band at tables and enjoyed our rum punches and planter's punches with tropical fruits in them. The performers danced in their native costumes, sang calypsos, walked on bright red coals, and tried to fit under the limbo rod with great success. Then it was our turn to start trying. Needless to say, we did not even come close to their amazing feats, but we had lots of laughs. Dancing the Limbo became an international craze in the 60s!

The Juliens invited friends to their house to meet with us. One of them, Erika Hawkins, became the happiest person in the world when we met.

"Pat told me I will meet some of her friends, but you bought that dress..."

It turned out Erika owned that boutique and when she saw the name, she knew we must be Hungarians. Erika happened to be a Hungarian from Rumania.

"First, I looked in the Hilton register, then I called all the ships in the port, all the other hotels, but no one seemed to know about you. I did not even think to ask Pat who her friends will be. And then you turn up, just like that, when I gave up on you."

"Erika, how wonderful to meet you and find out you are Hungarian," I said.

"You know what?" Erika said, "Now you must come to my house, too. My mother is here from Israel because I want my little daughter, Francesca, to learn Hungarian."

Erika was a genius when it came to languages. They lived in Rumania, but her parents spoke Hungarian, when they did not want her to understand them. So, she just decided to learn it on her own. She even wrote perfectly in Hungarian. Her French was equally as good. She switched from one language to another without any difficulty. Her husband worked at the British Embassy in Rumania. That is where they met. She married him, therefore Don had to leave the Embassy. He went to work for Shell. After a while they were transferred to Trinidad and Tobago. Erika absolutely loved the place. She loved that it was an island and she was safe there. After 17 years of marriage they finally had a delightful little girl, Francesca.

We became very good friends with Erika and Don; a lifelong friendship.

Finally, the day arrived when we went to visit Archbishop Anthony Pantin. He was the first and the youngest ever Trinidad-born Archbishop. He was 38 when he became "Your Grace" as we were supposed to address him. He lived in the Archbishop's Palace on the Queen's Park Savannah in Port-of-Spain, the capital city. Ken's driver took us there. We were in awe, until we started talking with the tall, brown, reddish haired figure in a white cassock. He was so casual and alive, smiling, his eyes clinging on the person with whom he was talking. We sat down for a long interview. After some small talk, he said, almost apologetically:

"I tried to sell the palace, but I let the people decide. The vote was NO. They did not want me to sell the palace, but I sold my bishop's ring and we disposed of everything that was unnecessary to help the poor."

He explained that Trinidad and Tobago was 42 percent East Indian and 43 percent black. The rest were mixed.

"Do people intermarry?"

"Actually," the Archbishop said, "they do not."

"Why is that?" I asked.

"Because of their religion. The East Indians had to change so many of their customs when they arrived, they were not really prepared to change religion for marriage."

"Then how come there are so many multiracial people I heard called 'callalu'?"

"Good question. Many of the men have what they call "wifies." Their race does not matter. Of course, there are some who do get married from a different race, but very few. Trinidad's motto is: 'Together we aspire, together we achieve.' That works out pretty well. All religions try to work together. Race does not make a difference in daily life, but…they still think their own race is the real thing. They only want to marry their own kind when it comes down to it. There are only about four percent white people and some of them are ex-patriots, meaning foreigners who come to work here for a while as consultants. They stand out. Everyone knows where they are."

When they call people 'callalu' that simply means they have several kinds of blood in them. Like the callalu soup that has everything in it.

"How do religions work together?" I asked.

"Slaves were emancipated here in 1832. From then on the former slaves did not want to do 'slave labor.' That went on from the beginning and is still that way. The plantations needed workers from a country with a similar climate. East Indians were brought in as indentured laborers. For five years they had to work for the expenses of the trip. Then they could go about their own business. The East Indians were clever business-people. Right away they started small gardens and sold their produce on the side of the road. They also lent money to those who needed it and charged big interest rates. Indians became wealthy fast. So somehow it developed that the black people had the official jobs and Indians had the money. Black people still did not want to do any slave labor. On Mt. St. Benedikt we started a trade school, so they should be able to make money if they did not continue their education after the 'eleven plus exam.' That was highly successful. We now have 600 students. They choose all kinds of trades, but for instance, only two of the 600 chose construction. Some trades are still considered 'slave labor' as is working on plantations. So, we decided, as the religious leaders of Trinidad's various churches, and business leaders of all religions, to buy a lot in the middle of downtown. Then we ourselves went down to work on that lot. We planted sugar cane and did 'slave labor' ourselves. We showed that necessary work was not only the work of slaves, but all people.

"All religions are taken very seriously. We wish each other the very best on every religious holiday, be it Muslim, Christian, Buddhist, Hindu or any other religion, and all are considered government holidays."

"Your Grace," I asked him, "in America we have the Protestant work ethic and diligently work all the time, we organize, and we are admired by other countries for our achievements. How is it here?"

"Maybe we just do not want to follow the WASPs (White, Anglo-Saxon-Protestants)," he smiled with a twinkle in his eye. "Why should we? We do not need to work that hard. Our lives are easier. Our values are different. We enjoy family, the people, the sun, and the sea. We pick the vegetables and plants that grow here like weeds. I don't know if you noticed, but if you eat an avocado and put the seed back in the ground, or just a slice of a cassava, it grows into a tree and you can pick its fruit, when the time comes."

"If you sit under the right banana tree," John chimed in "you do not even have to get up all your life. Banana trees flower and can be harvested at the same time. You can just reach up and eat. The lukewarm rain showers give you enough water to keep yourself clean. The weather is wonderful; you do not need to heat."

"I completely agree," answered the Archbishop. "However, I must tell you, before Christmas and before Carnival everyone works feverishly because whatever you spend on gifts and costumes, you have to earn."

This was our first meeting with Archbishop Pantin. In the end we became really good friends. We met whenever we could and led a meaningful correspondence with him. Unfortunately, he passed away at 70 years of age of a heart attack while working in his office. The process has since started for his canonization.

I wrote several articles about him, about Trinidad, and the many wonders we saw there.

We flew over to Tobago for a short visit. The island paradise of beaches greeted us with waves rolling in soft sounds in the dark. We sat on a rock fence beside the restaurant after dinner and listened. Suddenly an old hit from our youth came back to me and I sang it softly to John:

"I know a song that constantly returns, a house where the quiet softly sings, an old garden under the cypresses, where happy butterflies play in the radiance, a stone built fence from where your eyes see infinity in the dreaming sea at your feet, sending her continuous waves. And there is nothing else, but the song of love, come with me…come with me…"

⌒

We returned to the islands of Trinidad and Tobago again in 1972, this time with our son Steve who was Ken's godson. He was 11 years old; his last year to fly half price. This time all the others stayed with daughter Ilike and Barry Meiners, who was her fiancée. By now, the entire family performed in Summer Palace except for Niki, the youngest. Ilike took care of them all with the help of Mrs. Caine, our good old babysitter. Ilike also played leads in the plays along with Barry. They both majored in speech/acting. Their whole lives were centered in theater.

On this trip to Trinidad we became godparents of Pat and Ken's second son, Philip Alan. Ken's mother was the proud "Porteuse," the one who carried the baby to church. When the baptism started, she handed me the baby and I held him above the baptismal font. We were the only ones present when the priest poured the water over the little one's head: "Philip Alan, I baptize you in the name of the Father and the Son and the Holy Spirit. Amen."

We got to know Pat's family: parents and six brothers and sisters. Pat's maiden name was McCommie. Her grandfather was Scottish, but married and stayed in Trinidad. Everybody looked different in Pat's family. They were all so good looking. One of them, Katherine, became a Dominican Sister. Pat, the oldest, was the most important stewardess with the British West Indies Airlines. She was beautiful. She handled all the dignitaries and accompanied them during their stay on the island. One was the member of Queen Elizabeth's family, Princess Alice, then the Ethiopian Emperor, Hailé Selassié, and many other notable people. She quit being a stewardess when she married Ken. She often joked with a twinkle in her eyes: "You know what BWIA stands for?" She had two answers to that: "But Will It Arrive?" and "Best Women in the Air."

"Once we were struck by lightning," she reminisced. "The plane got a direct hit and was well shaken up."

While we were talking, she was cooking. She was a gourmet cook and loved to treat her guests by finding the best recipes for the specialties of the island.

"What did you do?" I asked her.

"We served free drinks to the frightened passengers," she laughed. "We were also truly grateful that nothing happened besides being thoroughly shaken up."

Steve had the time of his life. Everyone was striving to entertain him. We were invited to friends to the Hilton, where we saw the show with him again. Steve met Erika and Don Hawkins's daughter, Francesca. They loved playing and speaking Hungarian together.

We also visited the island of Tobago with Steve. We stayed at the Turtle Beach hotel, right on the ocean. The entire island abounds in the loveliest sand beaches where you can walk right into the crystal clean turquoise water. One such beach was Pigeon Point. The water there was completely calm. At our hotel, in the breeze, the tiny white foaming waves kept bringing us the messages of the infinite ocean.

Steve had a Kodak Brownie box camera, the simplest in those days. He took photos of everything, but one day he took a photo of the sunset in an approaching storm. It got published in the *Lewiston Morning Tribune* along with my article. He even received a payment of $10 for the photo. He was so proud and happy!

"The coconut has three eyes. Two of them are for seeing, and one is for deciding whether it should fall before or after you pass the tree, so as to miss your head," explained Cecil Lyons (THE man who knows Tobago) to Steve, who first believed him before he burst out laughing.

We stopped at a lime tree. Cecil picked a lime and encouraged us to pick our own. Then he rubbed his hand on it and let us smell the delicious aroma of the fruit.

Next came the cacao bean. He picked a ripe fruit, then opened it and let us suck on the raw cacao bean. It had a piquant-sweet taste. However, he warned us: "Do not bite it, because it is bitter inside. Just like cocoa is bitter. The soft pulp around the cacao bean is used for making vinegar, while the cacao beans are put into a 'sweat-box' and fermented there for a week, after which they go to a drying floor. There they are protected by a cover on wheels from the rain. After having been dried they are ground and ready to enjoy. The cacao plant does not like the sun and therefore is kept in the shade by immortal trees which are planted among the cacao plants."

While Cecil was talking, he led us to an abandoned sugar mill. The big wheel and the steam engine were rusty from the humid climate of the tropics, but we could still make out the inscription: W. and A. McOmie Glasgow, 1857, England. Tropical plants and flowers were growing all over the machinery. It was interesting to recall the visit at a sugar factory just a few days before in Trinidad, where sugar was produced the modern way.

There they crushed the cane to extract even more juice from them. Crushed canes were used as fuel. In a well-operated sugar factory this fuel should be sufficient to supply the total fuel requirement for the steam plant. The leftover "abasse" is used to make hardboard or can be used for animal feed. Maybe it was only our imagination, but the sugar tasted sweeter than it did at home. This overgrown sugar mill however, had little resemblance to the sugar factory.

Cecil was leading us already through a coconut plantation on a road that only the workers were allowed to use as a rule, but to him all roads were open in Tobago. He explained that only small plantation owners picked green coconuts to sell them while green. Owners of large plantations wait until the coconuts fall by themselves. They do not pick them for immediate consumption but process them first.

Next Cecil took us to a boat ride to Bucco Reef which is a coral reef a few miles off shore.

We took a glass-bottom boat to the coral reef. We wondered at the beauty of sea life under the glass bottom, but when we arrived at the reef all we saw through the glass bottom seemed like nothing compared to the brilliance of our next sight. We stepped out into water that was about waist high and received masks and snorkels from our guide. He then led us by the hand as we floated on top of the world's most wonderful aquarium. Tropical fishes of indescribable colors swam through our fingers in "schools," sea stars, corals, snails, crabs, and large fish came into view as we walked around in the water. One wonder appeared after another. We did not want to leave this wonderland, but our next stop was nearly as nice. Right there, way out in the Caribbean Sea, we stopped at the "Nylon Pool," a perfectly calm mirror of water where the surface breaks under our strokes while swimming.

The flora and fauna is entirely different in Trinidad and in Tobago. A very long time ago Trinidad was a part of Venezuela, until a rift took it out into the sea. Now Venezuela is nine miles away. Trinidad was basically a part of the continent, while Tobago was a coral island.

Even the people looked different because of the different foods they were eating. The vegetables were rich in starch in Tobago and that affected the look of people. In Trinidad, people were wirier, more active, and skinnier. There were more of the East-Indians. In Tobago people were darker, sturdier, larger, very quiet and peaceful. They thought Trinidadians were way too busy.

The movie "Swiss Family Robinson" was filmed in Tobago and our charming guide, Cecil Lyons, also took part in this film as one of the chiefs of the native warriors. He told us about one of his friends who could catch sharks on command. He tamed the shark for this film and whenever they needed the shark, he would let it out, then catch it again.

The four days flew by fast. It was time to return to Trinidad. We said farewell to Cecil, but promised to come to see him again, when in Tobago. We kept our promise.

37

In 1970, after our first trip to Trinidad came to an end, we had to hurry to Toronto, to pick up our kids we had left with my sister Elizabeth, then to Winnipeg to gather Sandy. Jancsi (16) who was staying with her in Winnipeg at Father's house, was not coming home. He flew straight to the Hungarian Scout Camp in Sík Sándor Cserkész (Hungarian-American Scout) Park, where they gathered from everywhere in the nation and spoke Hungarian for the two weeks they stayed there. We sent him to learn, but he ended up teaching the second graders. He had the time of his life with the scout leaders, who accepted him as one of them. He was included in their evening campfires, after the others' bedtime.

After the two weeks he was asked by "Ubul Bá" the Hungarian Priest who was also the Scout leader of the camp, to stay with him in the camp to rebuild the roof. As a reward he took our Jancsi with him to the World Jamboree of Hungarian Scouts in Exterris ("abroad," as in Hungary, it was illegal to be a scout) of that year in Raccoon State Park. Needless to say, he was thrilled with the experience.

During our time in Trinidad, Ilike was the only one left in Pullman. She was 17 years old and played leads in Summer Palace. She had also decided she did not like the food that was cooked the year before for the 27 out-of-state students who took part in this summer adventure. So, she volunteered to cook for them, which she did for the entire time. She loved cooking, especially because she loved the taste of good food. Yet, she never gained weight because she was so active. How could she not be, while being a can-can girl, dancing her way down main street and in restaurants to advertise Summer Palace? I admired and appreciated my talented daughter.

She started going out with Barry Meiners who was also studying theater. They played leads together, even Romeo and Juliet in the traveling Shakespeare Company of WSU. In the winter, the players traveled in station wagons to schools around the state to present abbreviated Shakespearean plays, lugging with them scenery and costumes. Dr. Paul Wadleigh, the Director and Head of Department initiated all these excellent opportunities for his students. Summer Palace, the revival of 19th century traveling theaters in the USA, became so famous that not only did students come from all over the country, Dr. Wadleigh even gave a lecture at a conference in London, England about how to create and run such a theater.

The actors often ended up in our house and improvised at after-play parties, or just parties we organized for them. The young men and women felt very much at home with us. We were the only parents whom they did not mind having around. Every one of the plays were taped during performances, then played back to the actors, criticized by themselves and the others in order to learn from them. That was the only modern equipment allowed besides the electric lights in the livestock arena, where the plays were held.

Ilike and Barry soon became an "item" (meaning they were going out together). One day, when Ilike was a junior, Barry asked her out for dinner to the newest, then most fashionable restaurant in Pullman. We were all very excited because we all four of us knew what was going to happen at the restaurant. Barry asked Ilike to marry him and she said "yes." Then they came home, made the announcement and we started to talk about the wedding that would take place next year, right after Ilike graduated from WSU. Barry had already graduated two years prior and lived in San Francisco for one year before returning to Pullman.

Barry's family was a conservative farming family, one of the first settlers in Johnson, a nearby village. His father was a mechanical engineer, but as the only son, he had to take over the farm. We never met him. He died at 49. His mother was Ann Meiners (Hooper) the descendent of one of the signers of the Declaration of Independence. They lived on a farm close to Pullman. It was at her house where I first experienced what an American Thanksgiving was truly like.

Being faculty in Pullman also meant introducing the 10 percent of foreign students to American customs. Good luck for me! I would experience it for the first time along with them. True, I was in Canada before, but there Thanksgiving was in October instead of November and I was improvising in Canada too. The children learned in school about the Pilgrims and the Indians celebrating together. I was aware of a turkey that had to be involved in the festivities. Cranberry was another foodstuff I knew about and I learned that all foreign students would eat rice. So that is what I served for Thanksgiving. Plus, I made a pumpkin pie (with great disgust even thinking of sweet pumpkin) from a canned filling and I bought a mincemeat pie, having no idea what was actually in it. We set the table festively and some foreign students who stayed on campus were invited. That is what those poor students found out about our strange customs, along with me.

236

They should have instead been invited to the Meiners. Wow! First of all, we started with alcoholic eggnog. That in itself would have made everything else taste marvelous, especially after a few cups of the sweet, foamy punch. Appetizers galore. Then came the turkey with all the stuffing, the yams, the mashed potatoes, the salad, the orange-cranberry sauce made happier with a little brandy. Dessert after dessert…I felt so sorry for those poor foreign students who had to experience my "American Thanksgiving."

❧

"Pali and Keri will be coming! It's all settled. They will come for a semester!" John came home with a big, happy smile.

"Are they really?" From the name combination I knew he was talking about all time's most beloved boss, his first boss at the Technical University in Budapest, Dr. Pál K. Kovács and his darling wife, Keri.

"You know after the Revolution he was demoted for having been such a wonderful boss. From being the Head of Department and a member of the Academy, he was assigned to a factory as an assistant engineer. All that, just because he was no longer trusted after the Revolution.

"Remember how he used to get us outside consulting work? One-third went to the person who did the actual work, one-third to the department and one-third to the University. He made sure every member of the department received proportionally from each of the jobs thereby making sure secretaries and the janitor also were included. Now, the Department of Marxism-Leninism, for instance, could not get any outside work and they were jealous of the engineers. That was their main reason for persecuting him.

"Later they rehabilitated him and gave him back his membership in the Academy. Soon after he retired, and since then all his former colleagues and students living abroad, who benefitted from his leadership, invited him and his wife for a semester here, another there. He is just finishing up in Toronto where he was invited by Dr. Paul Biringer, my former classmate at the Technical University. Now it was my turn. They accepted and WSU approved it."

"I can't wait to see them again," I was all smiles with expectation for the good times we will have with that delightful couple.

They arrived in the middle of winter. Both of them were such happy people! They always smiled, laughed, and made jokes. We were very good friends in Hungary, too. They rented an apartment. We spent every afternoon together from then on.

Our favorite pastime was to go over to their home. I took the small children with me. The older ones were self-sufficient by that time. Then we sat and talked, and talked, and talked about all those years that passed since we had left. She told us about their ordeals after the Revolution in 1956. Their oldest son was only one year younger than I was, yet, I never felt that she was older than I. She always treated me as an equal, even when we met and I was 17, but I was the wife of a professor.

"They left us our villa because it had only six rooms. It was nice to remain in our home, but I had to do everything myself. For example, we had the big terrace. I had to wash that terrace every day, while I also worked as a physical therapist. I just could not look at the dirty floor. Once you get used to certain things, you keep on doing them, even if it is difficult."

"I know what you mean," I answered. "When we first arrived and we had to hand wash the few diapers we had to do everything ourselves, it was very difficult.

I could not understand why Americans could not do the same as we were doing in Europe. Everyone did his or her own job, whatever they specialized in and all of us got paid for our work."

"Of course," said Keri. "what I noticed is that people's labor is highly appreciated here and therefore much more expensive than in Europe, where material is more expensive. I think that is why people are trying to do everything by themselves."

While we were talking, we fixed ourselves Irish coffees (with real whisky) and lots of whipped cream and were sipping that. Right after work our husbands would join us. Then we had even more fun. The kids entertained themselves. Keri loved to talk with them. She said she was learning a lot of English by watching Sesame Street. She did speak English, but she always found something new and special.

Steve had just started cub scouts. They were trying to find a name for their troop. Keri suggested "Gulyás" (goulache) and made a flag for them. You can imagine how happy and proud it made both of them, Keri as well as Steve.

Pali and Keri brought us a magnetic tape of the 1972 New Year's Eve celebration on Hungarian radio. We laughed so hard, especially about the comic who pretended to be an Austrian learning Hungarian. The puns were strikingly witty. Every time we listened to it, we were laughing just as hard, as we did the first time around.

One night we sat together with them and Pali became very serious: "We wanted to discuss something with you, asking for your help."

"Of course, Pali, we will do anything for you," John immediately answered.

"All of our sons have become engineers. Feri, our oldest one, accepted a job in Africa. He went with his wife and two children: Tom and Anita. While abroad the children went to French schools. After a few years Feri became ill. It turned out to be an incurable lung disease. He passed away very young. We would like to get the children out to the USA. When the time comes, I would like to ask you to take them under your wings. First Tom will come, then Anita will come to visit with her mother."

"Of course, we will do all we can," I said.

"You can rely on us," John assured them.

Pali's eyes lit up: "I knew you would help. Thank you very much."

Keri added: "Our second son, Gyuri is coming to a conference. He will arrive before Ilike's wedding."

"I am glad our children will meet, so our friendship will continue into their generation," John said.

Occasionally we went up to Spokane to shop for the upcoming wedding. Naturally, the focus was on Ilike. On one occasion, the younger girls were complaining to me on the down escalator, why Ilike is getting all the new things and the attention. Ilike was just passing us on the up escalator. As we were talking, suddenly her voice came booming from above: "Because I am the one getting married." The customers who heard it were laughing out loud. Even the girls loved it.

In Spokane we usually ended up at the Black Angus, where we could watch Spokane Falls tumbling over the rocks, spraying water around. Here and there birds looked for seeds among the rocks. When Niki was a year and a half she looked down where the birds usually jumped around. She saw a rat. Happily, she reported to us: "Bird!"

The night before the wedding, Ilike asked that all the family should come to the living room. We sat down, all nine of us. No one else. She started crying and said: "This is the last time our family will be here together like that. Just the nine of us."

We all realized she was right. That started a long line of memories popping up from different sides of the long living room.

"Let us thank God for these wonderful years and all the happy times we had," John said. "We will always remain one family. Love is what ties us together and God is Love. He will be with us and help us to get together as often as possible."

"We will always love you the same way," I reassured Ilike.

"I will miss you so much," Ilike sobbed. "It just struck me that I will not be getting up here in the morning after my wedding, we will not watch 'Love Boat' together after Mass on Saturdays at the roaring fire Steve started for us." Her eyes glistened with her tears that rolled down her cheeks like as many crystals.

"But you will be happy with Barry, starting your new lives, your new family together," I said, while suddenly realizing I had the same thoughts on our honeymoon with John, when we came home from Mass at the Cathedral in Pécs. The lights went out and the whole big church was lit by candles only. It was romantic, but it aroused an uncanny feeling in me. When we were tucked into our bed, I confessed to John. He, being the wise old man of 27, told me with a bit of laughter: "Don't worry, you are just afraid of the future, of life, of what it will bring. That is the uncanny feeling." Yes, I realized Ilike was only 20 and graduated from university the same week as she was getting married.

I hugged her close to me. John came and hugged both of us. Suddenly the entire family joined in a great family hug, which ended up in a happy laughter. We were ready for the wedding ceremony the next day.

Ilike and Barry did a wonderful job organizing their wedding. We gave them a budget of $1,500 and they managed to pay for everything from that, including the 200 bottles of champagne, at the time around $1.20 a bottle.

The entire family got involved in the preparations. Ilike ordered Bride Magazine. That fascinated Rita, who was nine years old at the time. She started planning her wedding right then and there.

The boys were busy tying cans and noisemakers onto a long string, to be dragged by the bride and groom's car when they would leave on their honeymoon. They ran up and down the street with it to see if it made the right sound effects.

John's mother had written to our mutual friend in Hungary, Kata Benedek, an artist who had painted Ilike's portrait when she was six months old. My mother-in-law had asked the artist to buy Hungarian Kalocsai embroidery for Ilike's wedding dress. A dear Hungarian friend in our vicinity, Ági Csizinszky, designed and sewed the dress for her. We searched far and wide until we could find an exact match for the white cotton from which the vest and six little girls' half-aprons were made of that we received from Hungary.

The motif was carried over into all phases of the wedding. The delightful carrot cake made by our dear friend Loretta Smith, was decorated with the same design, as was Ilike's bouquet. Her three little sisters acted as flower girls. Their dresses were made from a light blue eyelet lace and a pale blue under layer. The two older ones' dresses were tea-length and Niki's was short.

Father Caffrey officiated. He was a good friend and Chaplain at the Newman Center, the student church of WSU. The students and the entire town adored Fr. Caffrey, who, encouraged by Vatican II, did "outrageous" innovations. For example he wanted to have a Midnight Mass for the students, but at Christmas they all went home. So, he "transposed" Christmas to December 12th and had a Midnight Mass on that day for them. One year he lit the entire church with candles only for that event, placed in strategic locations all over the church. The church was so packed, about 500 students had to be turned away because there simply was no more place in the church. We were one of the faculty who attended that Mass because we were on very good terms with Fr. Caffrey. He often came over for dinner to our house at the spur of the moment. Especially every time I prepared chicken liver. I just had to call him when I was making it.

When he entered the church on that Midnight Mass, he announced: "If you see fire, do not yell 'fire.' Put it out!" His sermons were always crowd-pleasers and his folk group musicians headed by Bob Small were groundbreaking at the time. The church was exploding with the happy sounds of young voices, guitars and other suitable instruments.

A local chamber quartet (made up of artists, who were faculty spouses) played music at the wedding. John and I went in together, Barry's mother was accompanied by Brian, Barry's little brother. This was the first wedding I attended in my beautiful lace dress we bought in Trinidad.

Ilike and Barry entered together after the flower girls, the Maid of Honor Nora Chester, and Bridesmaids with their escorts.

Father and Uncle Paul both came from Winnipeg. Uncle Paul drove all the way from there, but Father could not take so much time from his medical practice. He had to fly.

Ilike went up to Vancouver, B.C. for her grandmother and brought her to Pullman on the same day (that was about a 12-hour drive). Grandmother had a beautiful blue satin dress made for the occasion, which she had designed.

Ilike and Barry's surprise was the crucifix, which her grandmother designed and made for her and grandfather's wedding. This is the story we told our children about the crucifix that was now going to become Ilike and Barry's after they had said their wedding vows on the same crucifix:

THE CRUCIFIX

The house Tárnok utca 2, Dísz tér 8 and Úri utca 1 was a six-story, ugly, reinforced concrete apartment building behind the Statue of the Freedom Fighter of 1848-1849.

Today a two-story nondescript building stands in its place.

Dr. John F. Szablya (your dad) and his parents lived there from the time he graduated from high school and started university (1942). At that time, it had four apartments on each floor. Their apartment was on the second floor above the stores, on the corner of Dísz tér and Úri utca. This is where

241

they "entertained" Hitler's personal bodyguards, who were searching the apartments for Jews, on the morning of October 16, 1944. They told stories in cold blood how they were shooting the Jews into the Danube: "Puck, puck, puck!" and whoever tried to swim to the shore they shot again. They thought this to be great fun. We can only imagine what the Szablya's three Jewish friends must have felt listening to this from the closet in the next room.

On January 16, 1945, big German trucks loaded with barrels of gasoline stood in front of the house. Soviet planes shot into the barrels with submachine guns and threw down incendiary projectiles to ignite it. In no time at all the curtains started burning through the broken second story windows. The reinforced concrete house burned down!!! during the Siege of Budapest. They watched the fire from the doorway of Dísz tér 10. The burning gas started to flow into the cellar air raid shelter through the emergency exit, where they lived. They tried to put some of the drinking water on it and sandbags, but finally the steel beams became hotter and hotter and forced them into the caves and tunnels under the Várhegy (Castle Hill). If you walk on Úri utca two or three blocks farther, you can enter the caves, where many of the inhabitants of Várhegy survived the 50-day Siege in 1945. This portion is now neatly restored, but it was dirty, rough and wet in 1945, and, of course, no electricity, gas, water, or sewer, only latrines in corners. The Szablyas moved back into their air raid shelter a few days after the fire, but the beams were still glowing red.

Those of us, who lived in 1945 and went through the Siege, measured time by the Siege from then on. Something happened either "before the Siege" or "after the Siege."

When people came up from the cellars after the Siege was over, they took stock of what was left. The Szablyas had nothing besides the clothes they wore and whatever happened to be in the air raid shelter. Nothing… nothing. The heat of the fire was so intense that porcelain and glass melted into one blob.

A friend of theirs came up from town to see them and suggested they should look for something, maybe there was something after all. They told him there was nothing. No use to look. Their friend nevertheless started to rummage around and suddenly he raised his hand – and in it was the corpus from a crucifix!

The only thing they ever recovered from their former apartment was the corpus from the crucifix, which John's mother, Alexandra Huszár-Szablya sculpted for her wedding with János Szablya Sr.

John and his Uncle, Ferenc Szablya-Frischauf (whom we affectionately called Feripapa) a little later conspired and hid the corpus. Then, for the Szablya parents' 25th wedding anniversary they surprised them with a beautiful new wooden cross, designed by Feripapa, and the corpus on it.

When Dr. John F. Szablya and Ilona Bartha-Kovács got married on October 12, 1951 they made their marriage vows on the same crucifix, which the Szablya parents used. Helen Alexandra Szablya, their oldest daughter, received the original crucifix, when she got married.

As the Szablyas had seven children, they commissioned a graduate student in Fine Arts at Washington State University, to make copies of the crucifix. They ordered 12 copies at first. So now each of the children has one and a very special couple, Mel and Virginia Julson, received one. Mel Julson was the electrical engineer at the Powell River Company and Virginia taught high school there when the Sopron group arrived. They became very good friends with the Szablyas, as John was also an electrical engineer.

On the back of the crucifixes there is a metal plate, on which the first date is the marriage of the Szablya-Huszár couple, then the date when the house burnt down, the next date is that of the Szablya-Bartha-Kovács wedding, then, the date of the wedding of whoever used the crucifix next.

Subsequently, while living in Baltimore in the early 2000s, Ilike found an artist who was able to make another set of copies of the corpus and cross. She did this because my grandchildren were growing older and she wanted the next generation to have a crucifix of their own. Now, each of my grandchildren have one, too.

The tradition goes on with God's help, and of course, wherever you see one of these crucifixes, you will know a Szablya cannot be far away. You will also know, if you are a Szablya by blood or by marriage, and you have one of the crucifixes in the family, you have to be related to the other person owning the same kind of crucifix.

As they were both actors, they pronounced their vows beautifully looking in each others' eyes. The church was full. Clarisse McCartan, wife of the Dean of Students, who also had seven children told me: "You can see how much Pullman has accepted you by all the love that comes into your direction." There were 200 people invited to the reception. It was in one of the fraternity houses, because alcohol was not allowed in the church hall. The price of the rental? We had to clean it before and after the reception. This was quite a job after all those students had left for the summer. We could reap the rewards for having taught our children all the household jobs. The two older boys were opening champagne bottles all night. You can imagine how fast it went among all the young and old alike. There was a rehearsal going on at the time in Bryan Hall. The actors came over and took a few of the bottles to those poor souls who had to miss the reception.

John and I felt that it was the crown of our lives until then. The first one got married. We were all happy. Even Grandmother was dancing, despite her 80 years. She enjoyed it, although she had not danced while her sister-in-law Ernestine Lohwag (Tinti Mama) was alive because Ernestine was in a wheelchair. Though she liked to dance, she wanted to show her empathy.

Steve's girlfriend at the time was "babysitting" Niki at the reception. That is, she was following the four-year-old, who kept getting sips of champagne from a few of the people and became rather happy. Finally Maida came and told us: "I can't follow Niki any more, she is so fast and happy." But there was no problem as everyone pitched in watching the happy little girl.

Then, time came for the couple to leave. Ilike did not throw her full bouquet because between church and the reception she and Barry visited Barry's father's grave and left her large bouquet there – they took a large vase of flowers to Barry's grandmother in the nursing home and gave it to her. This was done while the guests arrived at the reception and were able to have fun and avoided a "reception line" that both Ilike and Barry wanted to avoid. Barry's Grandmother Hooper and his Aunt Marguerite were there at the wedding.

The car was ready with the "Just married" sign and all the clanking cans behind it. However, Ilike and Barry were made so "happy" by the champagne that Jancsi drove them to the motel, where they stayed for the night. He dropped them off, then parked the car for them. When he got out of the car in his tux, people congratulated him, thinking he just got married. He just muttered, truly embarrassed: "I didn't really get married." "Oh, we are so sorry," the same people were commiserating until he explained the situation. He was only in the wedding and that is why he was wearing a tux.

Album

1964 – 1973

Family Picture in Pullman, 1964.

Christmas in Winnipeg, 1965.

Christmas, 1968.

Christmas, 1972.

*Energy and Power Research and Development Center (EPRDC)
Steering Committee planning lab, 1966.*

Camping at Lake Coeur D'Alene with friend Thomas Wagner, 1967.

Ilike at 17 with her Grandfather and Gisele in Paris, 1970.

Newspaper clippings from Pullman's Summer Palace Theatre.

Ilike and the two little ones Sandy and Steve, 1970.

Singing and dancing. Ilike far left, 1969.

Ilike as can-can girl, 1968.

Rita in charge of concession stand, 1970.

Under the Gaslight" with Ilike in the lead saving the hero, 1969.

My father with Cardinal Mindszenty in Winnipeg, 1973.

Family at the border of East Germany, 1973.

38

"You know what?" John came home one day with good news. "We will have a sabbatical coming up and it seems like Dr. Paul K. Kovács, our dear friend, who often taught in Braunschweig as a guest professor can arrange for me to go to Germany to teach for a year at the Technische Universität (TU) there.

"A sabbatical?" I reacted. I was not quite sure yet whether that should make me happy.

"It means we have been here six years and now for the seventh we can go, with our University's approval for a half a year with full salary or a year with half salary to do something that would further our professional knowledge and career. Isn't this marvelous?"

"We would all go?" I asked.

"Yes, of course, the whole family" John answered. "Just imagine what a wonderful opportunity this would be for the children, to go to German schools and we could live like Europeans do."

This made me all enthusiastic for the sabbatical: "You mean we would go to the Opera and theaters, go shopping for European food, fantastic books...?"

John caught me up in his arms and we kissed, imbued with happiness, thinking of how good all this will be: living in Europe again after 17 long years. Even if it was not Hungary, maybe we could just take the children to the border to see with their own eyes the Iron Curtain and a bird's eye view of their "homeland," which four of them have never even seen.

As we had chosen to write and lecture about Hungary, freedom and democracy and we had stated over and over again that the system of extreme Left was as bad as extreme Right, we could not even think of visiting Hungary. In those days Hungarian refugees of 1956 could return to visit because their dollars were wanted by the State, and friends encouraged us to come, but when we had told them carefully why we could not, they asked "what are you writing?" "The truth," I answered. They immediately said: "Then don't come."

Some writers who did go back for a visit – if they were issued visas – were kept in isolation until they signed a document stating that they would write only good things about the Communists and Hungary onward. Usually, to simplify matters, they did not grant them visas. So, we did not even ask.

We started to get ready for our next year. First, we needed to calculate how to make this possible financially. Half a salary, but the German University would also pay John a salary. Of course, no one was supposed to benefit financially from a sabbatical, but we had to make sure we broke even. So, we were preparing our home for renting it to someone for the next year. Can you imagine the amount of work to put everything into the garage that we did not want others to use? We also had to empty closets and make room for the renters.

The children, of course, were very excited. A young German graduate student and his wife spent the year on a Karl Duisberg scholarship at WSU. John was the adviser for all Duisberg students. Suzanne, Peter's wife, came over often to teach the children some German before they would get immersed into the German public school. Louis, the oldest who was coming with us, finished all the credits he needed to graduate from high school and took the German immersion course at WSU during the summer. Jancsi was attending university in Pullman and did not want to miss the first semester. Ilike was already happily married and both she and her husband, Barry Meiners, were in graduate school at the University of Iowa, and would soon become Rockefeller Fellows at the Center of New Performing Arts there.

Finally, the day arrived. We were on our way to Europe; back again for the first time since we had left on the Empress of Britain on January 1, 1957.

This time we flew. Our journey went through JFK Airport in New York on Labor Day weekend. Some friends from New York and New Jersey, Maria Csema and Laci Szepesváry came to chat with us between our flights. Back then anyone could come with you all the way to the gate from where the airplane left.

We also had to cross all the way across JFK to the building of the other airline. To make us get there faster Laci decided to deliver us over by car. After 45 minutes of crawling, we had to say good-bye to him and walk because we did not want to be late for the plane. I never ever thought an airport could be this big! Or that it could have that much traffic!

How we enjoyed traveling in the 70s! Airlines were competing to give us the best seats, food, drinks, tablecloths and real silverware, choices from the menu and perfect service by the lovely stewardesses. Pillow and blanket for every passenger. Especially on international flights! The children were old enough to have a wonderful time. They got their own "wings" to pin on their clothes for flying in the plane; they received all kinds of coloring books and games, entertainment for the long trip across the Atlantic. We used to dress up in our Sunday best clothes for an airplane trip. After all, you wanted to be presentable when you arrived.

We transferred in Frankfurt; another airport of dizzying size. We were taken by bus from one plane to the other, driving all the way through the airport, taking corners at a dizzying speed, to the plane that would take us to Hannover, our ultimate goal.

While waiting to board, we went to the bathroom with the kids. I was appalled when I saw we had to pay separately for each of us to use the toilet, the soap, the hand towel. How can we live in a country that is so expensive? What next? Will we have to pay for the air we breathe too?

We did not have much time to consider that as our plane was leaving.

It was already dark in the evening when we arrived. Professor Dr. Dieter Kind and his wife, Waldtraut, were waiting for us with their oldest child, Christine. It was our first meeting with the dark haired, tall professor and his blonde, blue-eyed sturdy wife. Christina was a blonde, blue eyed beauty. She was 14 years old.

"Willkommen! Welcome to Germany!" they greeted us with happy smiling faces.

"You must be hungry. We will first take you to a restaurant and then to your home," said Waldtraut Kind, the always caring homemaker.

And then: BRAUNSCHWEIG. We held our breath to find out what our home for a year would be like.

We piled into the two waiting cars. The second was Haro Lührmann's, a PhD candidate, also the Chief Engineer at the Department, who immediately took us under his wings.

It was evening, dark but not quite nine o'clock by the time we arrived in Braunschweig. The entire town was asleep. We wound through the empty streets and the main square in the middle of town. We ended up in an elegant restaurant with the mood of an old hunting castle. We were wined and dined to our heart's content, while we got a lot of good advice. My head was in a daze. After the long trip with the children and the nine hours' jetlag, I was just hoping we will be able to remember it all – or at least some of it.

We need not have worried. The next morning when we woke, Haro was already in our kitchen preparing coffee for us on the Melitta coffee maker. I had never seen one of those before, but the coffee was delicious.

"Last night, when we brought you home and you dropped into your beds, I did not think you would be able to wake up," Haro laughed. His smile was contagious, "so I just came in and started the coffee."

"Thank you so much," John and I could not express our gratitude enough. The kitchen was prepared for our arrival. The Department supplied butter, jam, bread – everything for our first "continental breakfast" in the morning.

"Now, get ready and we will go to register you at City Hall," he coaxed us. "Please, bear with me when I will call you 'Professor' all the time and make it clear to everyone who you are."

"Is that necessary?" John asked.

"Well, let me explain something to you," Haro had a mischievous smile on his face, "or, better yet – you will see why."

We clambered into Haro's car and he drove us straight to City Hall.

The city looked quite different in the sunshine than during the night. As we were approaching by plane, we saw the towns below. They were surrounded by walls, or at least they were built in that manner a long, long time ago. The suburbs spread all around the city wall, but one could definitely see how every town used to be a fortress in the feudal era.

Our home where we were brought the night before was on the outskirts of the city, separate houses with gardens around them. The further we went into the city the closer the houses got to each other. Of course, there were new and a little older apartment houses.

"During the war Braunschweig was heavily bombed as it was very near the place where Hitler built the V1, the V2 flying bombs and produced heavy water to make an atomic bomb," explained Haro. "That is why we do not have as many old houses, as some of the neighboring little towns. You have to be sure to visit Celle."

We listened carefully and watched his driving. It was different than in the USA. As soon as he put on his signal, he immediately drove into the other lane. On the streets the signs called for: "einordnen" meaning "get in your target lane" if you want to turn, or stop at a store. The signs were also different, but easily understandable, especially after you learned what they meant.

We arrived at City Hall. Haro led the way and told the receptionist: "Professor Szablya and his family want to register for this year. He will be here as a guest professor. So please, let the clerk know that Professor Szablya would like to see him."

There were quite a few people waiting to go in, but the receptionist immediately took us to a side door and motioned for us to sit down.

A smiling clerk showed up and started to register us immediately. When he finished registering the family, he apologetically said: "Professor, I am so sorry, but the family will have to be checked by the medical doctor to see you are all healthy. Of course, we know you are; it is just a technicality."

The medical doctor greeted the "Professor's family," after we had been ushered into his room through a side door again.

"Professor, we know you are all healthy, but I need to examine at least one member of the family,"

"No problem" we tried to put him at ease.

Sandy volunteered to be examined. It was done in a matter of minutes.

"Welcome to Braunschweig" the doctor said. "I see you are all healthy and well." With that he ushered us out the door.

Next we went to the schools, to register the children. In Europe, high school begins in 5th grade, so Steve and Louis went to the same school. Our experience was with the Hungarian children and students in 1956 that the best results came from placing the children in the class they had just finished, so the only new thing for them would be the language. Louis was enrolled in 11th grade and had no problems. Steve went to 7th grade that he had just finished at home, Sandy in 4th grade and Rita in 3rd. Sandy was the luckiest because her teacher "did not speak any English," although his wife was Australian. Rita's teacher happily chatted with her in English. Niki was enrolled in kindergarten administered by the Lutheran Church. Of course, the four-year-old, going on five in November, had no problems whatsoever, to absorb the language as a thirsty sponge. In a few weeks, when asked if she spoke German, she answered: "Natürlich," "but, of course, how could you even ask?"

The children were not allowed to speak English, only Hungarian or German. If someone spoke English they had to pay a fine, which we placed in a box. That was the money we used to go to the (German) movies.

After all those registrations and being ushered around as "Professor," John understood the method and put it into words: "In Germany first comes God, then a little bit under that is "Professor," then for a long time... nothing. Finally, the ordinary people start from there."

It was wonderful for us to utter the word that became for us the equivalent to "Open Sesame." The magic word opened all doors. We never had to wait in doctor's offices anymore. When it actually happened once, by mistake, that we didn't say "professor," the doctor could not stop apologizing and explained it to us that we have to say immediately "private" and "Professor." How could the receptionist be so rude to make us wait? He was desperate, but finally we were able to put him at ease.

We picked up our new, shining blue, nine-seat Volkswagen bus. We left the bank for the afternoon. We arrived at the door and the bank was closed. On a weekday? Closed? What happened? Did the Deutsche Bank go out of business? We looked at the hours posted on the door and discovered: Wednesday afternoon all the banks were closed in Germany.

We had to come back the next day and establish our account. We asked for checks. Now, we discovered the Deutsche Bank did not know about any kind of checks.

"What is a credit card?" inquired the manager.

I explained, but he replied: "No, we have something, but it is different. We give you what we call checks, but you have to have enough money in the bank to pay for it when you buy them. Then you can use them at the store." It was more like a glorified debit card, which we did not have yet at the time in the USA.

"I will order them for you now that you have an account."

So, we had to have enough cash with us at all times to pay for whatever we were buying at the moment. Good to know.

John's first day at work arrived. He was supposed to be there at 8:00 a.m. after having dropped the girls at their school. The boys took the bus. That meant we had to get up at 6:00 a.m.; a most unusual time for us who were night owls.

Nevertheless, "when in Rome do as the Romans do" applied to Germany too. So, we learned to "grin and bear it." It was not easy, when your entire body was revolting.

Niki had to arrive at the kindergarten at 9:00 a.m. Right after the car left, we got ready and I walked her to school. It was a nice 15-minute walk through the "Gartengebiet," the garden district, where people had small lots to grow vegetables. Some lots had sheds on them to house the tools.

We walked hand-in-hand enjoying the morning. Niki made remarks about the surroundings, asked questions, like: "What is that?" I told her it was the hen cackling. It meant she had laid an egg. "And she lets you know?" Niki asked. "Well she must be awfully proud of herself," I told her. "Is she bragging?" Niki wondered.

After that she used to pull me to go faster. "Let's hurry! I want to hear the egg-song."

She loved kindergarten. I was happy to walk home and do some writing. I must confess, some days I went straight back to bed and slept some more, listening to the birds chirping under the window. Getting up that early was truly for the birds.

After a few weeks in Germany, I decided to write a book about my frustrations in old Europe. So, come with me into my life:

Before you start reading this book, I would like you to know that we had a most beautiful year in Germany. The hospitality of the German people

260

overwhelmed us and even though I will be writing on the child-hostile attitude of the Germans, our children also had a good time, most of the people in our surrounding and many others we have seen, the store where we shopped were extremely courteous and understanding with our unheard-of large family of six children. The seventh, our oldest being married by then. These letters were written to her.

I only dare to write about our lovely hosts in this way because I have heard a true joke from them:

A little boy from America, whose parents were German, came back from a long visit with his grandparents in Germany. When asked about his impressions of his stay, he declared:

"Germany is a land where 'Omas' (grandmothers) live."

Tourists, even if they stay there for a year, get the strangest impressions of a country. By the time they live there for a while, they get used to it and they find out the reasons for the many, at first unexplainable, customs. My book is about these first misconceptions, without the explanations – just as they struck us at the time.

If one of our charming hosts, or anybody from Germany reads this book, I hope they will be able to laugh about themselves and maybe, next time they see a funny sign, something that looks strange in other people's eyes, they too will do it with a twinkle in their eyes and see the humor in it.

Our dear Ilike and Barry!

Finally, I have some time to write to you about our first adventures in good old Germany with my usual dry humor. So, here we go!

We have finally arrived at our destination with five kids, 21 suitcases and bags. We were hoping to meet our VW minibus, which we had ordered ahead of time. The minibus was somewhat late because after our arrival to Hannover we learned that the factory had closed at 3:00 p.m., while our plane did not arrive until 5:00 p.m. Therefore, we had to finish the last leg of our journey with someone else's car, or rather two someone's cars as a European car would be absolutely outraged at the thought of accommodating seven people and their luggage. We saw only a few cars in the ditch on the Autobahn (freeway) due to the racing wind and rainstorm, which did not keep the good Germans from driving at their accustomed 140 mph.

We have a "huge" four room apartment, plus kitchen, bathroom and entryway. Counting all the square inches it might amount to half the size of our house at home. It also has a garden which abounds in lovely stinging nettle, rotten fruit and loads of over ripened vegetables. It seems to be a retired workers' district, interspersed with factories, the only place that would take Americans with six kids, and other weirdos like us. The style of the furniture is average tasteless 40s with a jungle growing in every window.

When we moved into our "luxurious" apartment we felt that we immediately had to move out also to give room to the houseplants, which (or who?) occupied about half the space. The Germans believe that it is important to have them everywhere in order to keep the air from drying out, as the natural humidity in our region hardly went above 96% and they did not believe that would be enough to keep the desired level of mould and mildew growing on everything you forgot to clean every day. Or, to keep the clothes from drying (outside it rained constantly). The presence of plants had other good side effects: the woman of the house was kept busy watering them and caring for them, in case she had finished all her chores for the day, or right before she had started them, so to keep her from nurturing ideas on women's lib. It was also a good child-substitute in more ways than one. Not only did the woman automatically have an outlet for her outbursts of motherly love, she did not have to be bothered to think of a baby, as the apartment was already so crowded with plants, there was no room for a crib. We settled down quite cheerfully with our jungle, though our 10-year-old objected slightly to the fact that she had to share half her bed with a huge cactus. She claimed that it occasionally pricked her at night, which just shows you that in a German apartment you should not have any children.

You also should not have them in stores, on the street, in theaters, in kindergartens (Germany is in dire need of 2 million kindergarten places), preferably not even in schools, if you ask the teachers. The easiest solution is not to have them at all. Unfortunately, I am not making this up. I learned much more about the problem of "child-hatred" from Germany's leading magazines and parents as well. I also sent my articles to the USA about the unusual phenomenon.

Children need to know early enough that they are burdens. They therefore should be treated as follows: push them out of your way, shirk away from them in the bus or streetcar by pulling your coats tight around you. You would not want them to touch you with their dirty clothes. Needless to say, you could not discover any mud on them with a magnifying glass. If you see they intend to cross the street, do not stop, in case you are driving. It is fun to see them jump away, or get scared. If you are an employee at a department store look terribly angry just at the sight of children. If they stop at your counter, even before they utter their intention to buy something, say a few grumpy words to them. If they, God forbid, touch some of your merchandise, which each adult close by handles to their hearts' content, yell at them at the top of your lungs, frowning: "You cannot do that, you know!" When a child wants to pay, take every adult in sight, before you take the child's money, especially if she seems to be in a hurry, as everybody knows that adults have less time than children. Who cares if this little girl is the babysitter while her father works full time and her mother died? You know that adults come first. Then, when you finally take her money, grumble aloud if she does not have the correct change and speak your opinion about these "good-for-nothings," namely children.

If a mother has more than one child with her, especially if they look like they are related to one another, stare at her, like at a natural wonder.

Then, go home and start watering your plants.

39

My letter to Ilike and Barry continues.

We actually have a washing machine! I heard that from our well-meaning friends who had picked us up at the airport. My mind started working at the thought of it: "In a country with the technology of Germany – I indeed underestimated our potentials here – there is a washing machine – maybe even better than mine at home." I saw myself with my usual pile of laundry and a glorious smile on my face – a washing machine.

And indeed, it was a washing machine.

Last year we ordered Montgomery Ward's very first catalogue from the past century as a curiosity. Immediately upon my arrival home I shall look for the price of one such washing machine, which I found in this "completely furnished $300-a-month apartment in an industrial town of Germany, well suited to accommodate university professors," who, according to Germans, are superhuman. They naturally are supposed to enjoy perfect comfort.

Now, back to the washing machine. In the presence of our friends the landlady promised to ask her neighbor to show us how it works, as she too had one such museum piece.

The next day came and the next again. After I have washed our clothes by hand, finally, the day of her "Kaffee Kräntzchen" (coffee clutch) arrived. Her friend appeared. Both stood with great expectation around the washing machine and so did I. With a simple little operation she disassembled the tap on the kitchen sink, then, knowingly, pushed a rubber hose in place of the removed tap. She plugged in the washing machine, then turned it to the desired position of the water temperature (the washing machine heats its own water, but seems to be working at only boiling, or completely cold temperatures. She adjusted the time. The washing machine was supposed to start now. And it started – to pump out the water. Amazing feat – however, when it stopped it would not let in any water. The two ladies pushed their heads together and chatted in an excited, colorful German dialect. The consultation resulted in the amazing discovery that they had forgotten to turn on the water. However, after this too was fixed, the washing machine still did not start to work. The water did not run into the machine. Now what? They both decided, in the same colorful and loud, but completely un-understandable dialect, that there must be something wrong with the washing machine.

New hopes should be coming from a "junger man" (young man), who was supposed to show up at night, or the next day. This "junger man," who turned out to be a 42-year-old wrestler type heavy equipment operator turned up too late however. Louis, our 17-year old, without any colorful talk, but with some powerful sucking on the rubber hose cleared the passage from the dirt that plugged the way of the water. The washing machine then started away happily on its endless rounds. Later on I wanted to show our honorable landlady how her washing machine (which she had owned already for 10 years) worked. She stood there for a minute waiting for this utterly useless demonstration, then ran busily away to wash her clothes by hand in the "Waschküche" (wash kitchen/laundry room), then boil them in a huge kettle, fueled by the paper garbage of her tenants.

She also owned another washing machine, which contrary to ours, would also wring the clothes. She paid 500 marks for it used, yet did not use it, as the "junger man," the only authority she consults, examined it and decided that something was missing from it.

Do not be mistaken, our landlady, Frau Marta Zerza is a delightful person, but her understanding of life and ours are a tiny bit different. We are on very good terms. German being both John's and my second mother tongue we had no problem with language, only with "ways of thinking."

You may be happy to hear that though we might contact rheumatism, arthritis, pneumonia and other fun sicknesses, we shall save oodles of money from the graces of our landlady, who is so concerned for our finances that it is impossible to get her to turn on the furnace because she wants to save money for us. Needless to say, we pay for the heat.

In a few days it turned out why she could not turn on the heat. There was no oil in the big underground tank. "How should I know you will want to heat the house?" Frau Zerza confessed the truth. Unfortunately, the oil prices just quadrupled in the 1973 energy crisis. Now, how in the world she was thinking that we would not want heat? I guess, her thinking was rather that she had to wait for us to fill the tank and pay for it, instead of paying piecemeal.

One of the rooms, where the three little girls sleep, is a "Wintergarten" where, besides the flower-like trees and the girls, there is nothing else but picture windows, luckily double windows, well insulated.

Do you still remember the story of Noah's Ark? We would strongly consider building one, if we could afford it. The constant, gray rain is pouring. There is hardly a day when one can hang out clothes, straight out from the wringer-less washing machine, wrung out solely by my poor old hands. Being permanent press, they remain dripping wet. The "silver lining" is that our bathroom floor is nice and clean, as we constantly have to wipe up after them.

At that moment sounds came in from the neighbor's window: "I am the happiest girl in the whole USA!" How I wished I was in the USA.

One good thing: there is still no charge for the air we breathe, in contrast with the cold water, for which there is. It is very expensive, but still not as high as the electricity. Therefore we can still afford to give the children water to drink now and then, instead of the customary beer.

Another good thing is that professors are considered "honorable supermen." Women's lib being far behind ours, he is the one who gets all the advantages of this, though I (Frau Professor) too get the same honors, if present. Most of the time I am present at the washing machine though, instead of at honorable meetings.

You might wonder why I speak like the Japanese do, in – of all places – Germany? It is because the upstairs is rented to a lovely Japanese couple with a daughter Niki's age. The mother speaks Japanese to her daughter, who speaks German to our daughter, who speaks Hungarian to me and I busily and helpfully translate to everybody into the language they do not understand, being unable to remember who speaks what in that cacophony. I do not speak Japanese, so there we are relying on the four-year-old daughter's German. Luckily, our oldest here, again comes to the rescue. He signals to me that I may take up my usual place in the kitchen and beside the washing machine, where women are supposed to be anyway. He is assuring me that he will take care of everything; which he does.

After the other mother goes back to her hand washing (she does not even have a before-the-flood type washing machine), the screaming becomes absolutely international and the children understand each other remarkably well.

I am happy to say the children are settling down in school very well. We had to get used to their system first, which is that the teachers are at school because they like the convenient hours, from morning til noon, and frequently have "meetings"' because they are not allowed to strike (by law). These meetings take place during school hours, which makes it possible for them to send children home at any hour of the day, without notifying parents. The teachers are also there to collect their salaries, which they do not find enough (other occasions for meetings). Rita's teacher was sick for three weeks, therefore the third grade children were sent home every day for these three weeks, unless they had arts and crafts, P.E. or religion classes, which were taught by other teachers. The principal enlightened me of the fact that they had only four teachers for the four classes, therefore, if one was missing, the children had to be sent "home."

The teachers found the idea of a substitute teacher a fascinating American invention. Especially, when I told it to the principal of the kindergarten, our littlest one attended. The principal was cooking for the children because the cook was sick, she also was substituting for two teachers who were sick and all non-working mothers were asked at arrival to take their children home in order to lighten her load. That is all the mothers they noticed when they had entered the kindergarten as people did not own telephones in Germany in 1973 as a rule, therefore, to notify parents by telephone does not even cross their minds.

The telephone company is your friendly post office, where people are so economically minded that they do not plan on putting in more telephone lines, until 95% of the lines are fully occupied. The planning and the putting in of the new phone lines takes them about two years, during which time phones cannot be given out, not even in dire emergencies, e.g., a physician opens a new office in town. People, who go about asking for a telephone legally might have to wait the full two years, like a friend of ours, who was not enterprising enough. He moved only within the house. The people with whom he exchanged apartments, simply pulled out the telephone from the wall and plugged it in upstairs. Instant service, the telephone company still does not know that they moved. However, the other person wanted to do it legally and during our one-year stay he has never received his telephone.

Like our son, Louis wrote to his friend, the houses here are separated by fences, therefore, if you would like to talk to your neighbor, you would have to unlock the door of your house, then the gate of your garden, go next door, ring the bell, which would trigger the same unlocking actions by your neighbor – until you could finally meet. A natural thing to shorten this would be to use your phone. However, for this you would have to walk a block or two to find a public phone booth. As soon as you got there, you would promptly remember that your neighbor does not have a phone either.

I am sure in the knowledge of the above you could easily understand that all you know about your neighbors is what you hear about them during the ritual of the coffee clutch (Kaffee Kräntzchen) for which all the housewives invited gather equipped with the juiciest gossips of their week. They do not only drink coffee, they heap whipping cream on it and onto their rich cakes. It does not bother them one bit that their party usually takes place right between their main meal of the day, lunch, and their less elaborate dinner. Most of the ladies are in desperate need of dieting and therefore the progressive ones do not put sugar in their coffee, to be found somewhere right under the whipping cream. However, this is not an afternoon to worry about calories (as none of the days are, why should this one be an exception) and spoil their gossiping. After such a newsgathering afternoon my landlady (a real character) came up to me and asked who the young lady was with whom the new tenant upstairs had apparently slept, two days after he had arrived from America. "It could not have been you," she said very tactfully "because it was supposed to be a beautiful woman in a pink nightgown" according to the neighbors. Frau Zerza knew it was not her, though her neighbor very diplomatically asked her if she had slept with him. Needless to say, I was the beautiful appearance in my white, flowered robe, my hair in total disarray, without my glasses, trying to rush the children off to school.

Our new neighbor, the poor devil, started out to work without a car, without an umbrella in the pouring rain and racing wind, he decided to come back and ask me for an umbrella. I told him to wait for my husband who was going to give him a ride. This was a too simple, down-to-earth explanation and Frau Zerza seemed disappointed, as she was expecting a much juicier story.

Another time she noticed a police ambulance across the street and declared she was not going to move from the window now until she found out what happened. She was terribly curious, but it has not even crossed her mind to go over and offer her help, which would also be a friendly and easy way of finding out what happened. To her great chagrin, not much happened. Her neighbor, whom she thought dead already – commenting under her breath that dead people should be picked up by a hearse, not an ambulance – accompanied the policeman to the door. (Maybe he dropped in for a cup of coffee.) However, she had one consolation: she saw that the husband also came home for some reason. Now she had the story all solved; he must have had an accident on the highway. That seemed to comfort her and satisfy her craving for news. Her solution was, if not sensational, as at first she thought it would be, at least out of the ordinary.

I have not received my transcripts yet, but no problem. There is no chance for me to attend university here. Several times in my life I was privileged to travel back to the Middle Ages. This was one of them.

The concept of a babysitter has not been born yet in people's minds. If a child is tactless enough to be born, it will have to suffer the consequences and so will the parents. The mother will have to remain glued to the child (or the child to the mother?) as long as the child will be old enough to be left alone. Meaning, until about the age of two months. From then on, the home and the kitchen will be locked, unless a merciful grandparent happens to live close enough.

When the door is locked it is impossible to go into or out of the house without a key, of which they have only one. The neighbors do not know about the child left alone. The lucky ones have a five-year old babysitter (a sibling) in complete charge. The other alternative is that father resumes his bachelor life, until the child gets old enough, whenever this is considered to be. Mothers take their babies everywhere with them even on buses and streetcars in huge baby carriages that take at least two people to lift onto the respective vehicle.

269

Even though people have only one or two children, baby clothes and toys are made of indestructible materials and they cost accordingly. Nobody can afford them…but they will last…and last…and last… outlast even the children's children and their offspring…if…if in the meantime they do not become delightful delicatessen for the mice and moths and other such natural helpers of deterioration.

I shall leave you now to do my daily rounds of the neighborhood's friendly grocery "supermaket" about which I am going to write you soon.

—

Have I written to you about our kitchen yet? It is rather nice in more ways than one. It is sunny, it has an electric stove (dated a few years after Noah's Ark) and running hot and cold water. I am much luckier than the lady upstairs, who found out that her oven does not work. There was a brand new stove standing in her hallway, used as a table to put her toiletries on under a lovely mirror. Seeing this, she inquired from our landlady about the possibility of using it as a stove. However, Frau Zerza explained to her (how, I will never know as they did not speak any mutual language) that she was keeping the stove for herself, for sometime in the immediate utopia, when she was going to occupy that same apartment. (The lady who wanted to use the stove had a one-year lease). Our landlady did not even have a $100 income, other than the rent. The apartment's heating alone would cost that much in a cold month. She then explained in deed rather than words that our upstairs neighbor should use our stove, in case she had the urge to bake. She pulled the lady down to our apartment, pointed to our stove and in "perfect sign-language," she has solved the problem without having to spend a penny, or having to "give up" her new stove, which served as a toilet-table.

We also have a refrigerator, which, no matter how much we tried, could not even produce one ice cube because of the size of the freezer compartment. We can, however, store enough food for our family for a day or two, if we first remove all the drawers, shelves and other inconveniences from the fridge. Therefore, you may imagine what a frequent customer I am in the neighborhood grocery store, owned by the same family for the past 80 years. In the very first days I found out that prices decrease with each block, as you move away from the suburbs and towards downtown. In the middle of town prices may be even as much as 50% less. After all, we have to pay for the 10 employees, who keep getting in our way, whenever we want to lift something off the shelf and into our cart. They immediately have to replace the item, in order to keep the shelves stocked in the tiny store. They also have to ask about our desires and then personally slice and weigh everything, even though one can get the same thing prepackaged from the refrigerator, for emergencies, like when a customer, God forbid, has to hurry and wants to get something done. The ceremony of shopping for food every day should not be neglected. Besides the "Kaffee-Kräntzchens" this is our only opportunity (if we don't count church) to gather information about our neighbors. Whether the information is true or false does not make much of a difference, as long as it makes our fantasy work.

I'll never forget the day when I first came to this store. That is, the first time I could ever get inside it. It was a 15-minute walk from our home. When I first got there, I noticed it was closed. I remembered I saw something on the door "Closed from 1-3 p.m." I went home and came back at 3:00 p.m. only to see the sign "Closed on Wednesday afternoons." The next day, remembering all that, I went again. Lo and behold! The door gave way, when I tried it.

I walked around the store and looked at the prices. Then I went out the door. "I can't afford to buy anything!" I fretted. Then I thought I had to feed my family, no matter what and I went back in. I started to put things in the cart. Everything looked so good in the deli section, just as it was in Hungary when I was little.

The grocer's entire family was a gem. They all worked in their store. I ended up with a full cart. The deli meat and cheese was cut personally by the grandmother, the sweetest, smiliest lady who talked all the time and asked questions.

I had a huge order; I had to get the supplies to start a household for eight people. I asked for it to be delivered. The owner noted it, but never asked for my address.

"Do you need my address?" I asked.

"No, thank you. I know who you are," came his smiling reply. "I know where you live."

He most courteously and promptly delivered everything personally, straight into my kitchen.

I should have guessed something, when the lovely grandmother behind the counter told me: "You must be the 'Ungarin aus Amerika' (the Hungarian lady from America).

The whole neighborhood was apparently alerted, but the others truly kept it a secret. Nobody addressed us. We passed each other on the streets, later I even smiled at the ones we saw daily, but not even the children would dare to take notice of us.

The gossip machine was in operation already weeks before we came and everybody looked forward to seeing us. I did not know then why our neighbors did not try to enter into conversation with us, why they did not even seem to notice us, when we met face-to-face. It dawned on me one day that maybe it was because we hadn't been officially introduced…

I became quite accustomed to this pre-occupation with gossip. I even gave out information about the new families who moved into the upstairs apartment. There were three families during the year. Our landlady liked to rent the place to foreigners because they only stayed for a while. A German family may have wanted to stay all their lives and maybe even their children and grandchildren would occupy the same rooms as they did.

40

In the first few weeks our homesickness for America was really bad; with the passing of time we grew to love our life in Braunschweig as we got to know it. The daily shopping that first seemed like a burden, became a familiar and agreeable daily entertainment, which I missed if I had to leave it out.

One day, sitting at my typewriter I noticed myself writing about this feeling:

ONLY GUESTS...

Netzeweg 53.

W. Germany.

The grey houses blend in perfectly with the uninterrupted rain. The gusts of wind pick up the muddy leaves and scatter them over the remainder of the inevitable vegetable gardens, standing side by side in a long row. Old people bend over their spades to do the last necessary work before the winter.

The noise of the "washing machine" reminds me of the clothes, which have to be wrung out by hand in the absence of anything better. Permanent press is impossible to wring...it has to drip...drip...drip...for about a day and a half before it can be declared dry, filling the whole house with a dampness one can cut and the mold collects on the window sill.

Why am I so happy then? Why do I shine with joy like I haven't done for years?

The blonde hair of my nine-year-old replaces the sun, her smile reminds me of the golden Palouse and the azure skies of our home reflect in her blue eyes. The long brown hair of my 10-year-old sweeps away the wind and her rosy cheeks bring back the memories of hard Washington apples as she asks for advice on her knitting. And I have time for her...we sit down, and I show her the stitches, her fingers cleverly follow the instructions as one of my sons asks about an English problem he is busily preparing for the school back home...where we shall be again next year.

The five-year-old just woke up, from her nap and I enjoy the funny warmth of a baby which still lingers on around the littlest one in the family. She hugs me with both her arms and blinks around sleepily. The 17-year-old comes in the door dripping) wet, yet he enjoys the rain and even the wind. It is different when one has to walk...The little things one misses when the car whizzes by them get new meaning, even when one gets soaking wet.

On my first trip to accompany the little one to kindergarten. I thought that it would be tedious to do that route every day twice, to come and go among the row of grey houses and vegetable gardens. But already the first morning my daughter and I heard the "egg-song." Though in Pullman we live close to farms, which practically surround our community, Niki has actually never heard something, which she has affectionately named the "egg- song": the happy sounds of a chicken, who has just laid an egg. She stood enchanted by the iron gate painted vivid blue and pressed her ear against it, so she could hear it better.

"What is it?"

The answer made her happy and every day she hurried especially not to miss the "egg-song." She stopped again and again to see from how far she could hear it. The grip of her warm little hand accompanies me everywhere. We ride on the bus together downtown, to buy her shoes, to meet Daddy, or just to look around.

There are so many things to see, when one is "only a guest."

The city comes alive – the grey houses sparkle with new wonders when you learn to know those who live in them, when you get to watch the flowers grow as you pass the gates, when you talk to an old man, who raises homing pigeons. One gets to know the landmarks:

"This is the house with the red and white rose."

Niki will stop and stare:

"They cut the asters yesterday."

Some parts of the inner city were built even before America was discovered. The children walk around bewildered with joy.

"Let's go and stroll a bit after the movie," Sandy suggests, and we admire the floodlit wonder of old churches, guild houses and just plain houses, where some people lived centuries ago, yet, others are still living in them.

One day an older lady, whom we helped catch her blouse as the wind blew it out of her hand and perched it on top of a high fence, showed us her lovely old house from the inside.

It was small and precious like a gem. Antique furniture, which meant family furniture to her. Her home was a very narrow house, the apartment divided into three stories. She herself looked like somebody in a story book, when she waved us good-bye from behind the fine lace curtains on her flowered window. The bathroom and kitchen. were completely modernized, as well as the heating, otherwise, everything could have felt at home in past centuries, including the diminutive enclosed garden.

The wonders open up as we look for them, as we open our eyes and see…

So what if the washing machine acts up, if the furniture is not exactly what we dreamed about, if we have to live in a poor district in four rooms with five children? We are "only guests," we are here to enjoy, to see what is different, to see what is beautiful. And…one cannot capture a smile and hold it, put it away for later, one cannot keep the joy of fresh bread, the laughter of the children, the merry sound of the ringing bells for sometimes in the future. The little hands will be bigger and mine not powerful enough to give them what they need, the children will grow up and we shall remain with the memories, which we enjoy now. The happiness of today will warm us then, the love and time we give our children today will be what they will partly return, but, even more importantly, pass on to their children then and we shall greet again the joy and radiance we once smiled, in our grandchildren's laughing eyes, in the fulfilment of the coming generation.

"Sicut umbra fugit vita" – "Life escapes like a shadow" – is carved in stone on one of the old sundials here.

It can be over, just like a row of grey houses, the rain can cover up our sunshine , the wind can sweep away the smiles, unless – we notice the red-white roses and the asters, the "egg-song" and the flood-lit old houses and churches, the insides of old ladies homes and the shine in a child's eye.

And why should it pass as a row of duties, when we are here to enjoy… when, on this earth, we are "only guests"?

Yes, our complaints turned into a love affair.

One night we had lukewarm rain on a lukewarm night. Both John and I wanted to go out walking, even though it was dark, but we drove to the city to enjoy our walk among the lights and in the dark side streets. It was so romantic. My love! How I enjoyed life with him – always.

One day Rita came home from school with a painting of a crow. The wing of the crow was lifted in a friendly wave. Even the crow looked happy. My dear little Rita, your little crow, waiving with its wing on my pantry door brightened my day in the constant gray rain.

After the first few days, when Sandy was crying before going to school and once even threw up, she happily came home with two boys, with whom she had struck up a friendship. They were very polite and well-behaved. By Christmas, Sandy was the first of our children to receive a regular report card.

Everyone learned English in Germany. In Steve's class, 7th grade, all the children learned and spoke English. Steve turned to his neighbor and asked: "Do you speak English?" The boy did not answer. So Steve asked: "Beszélsz magyarul?" Ah, now he struck a chord. The boy was the son of a Hungarian musician, who worked for the Staatstheater (State Theater) Braunschweig. They became inseparable friends.

Louis also got a friend immediately, who was originally from the USA, but had been living in Braunschweig for a while with his family. In 11th grade Louis' class was reading "A Clockwork Orange." In the book the gang of boys used Russian words as their slang. So, Louis, while reading it, occasionally came to me and asked whether a certain word was in Russian, or in German. Which dictionary should he use?

Louis begged us to let him drive. He was 17, so obviously, being American he had his driver's license. However, in Germany the age was 18. We just told him to go ahead and ask the police; which he did. He was told he had to go and have his driver's license translated by the equivalent of the AAA, the ADAC. So off he went and got it done. He came home with an ear-to-ear grin: "I am allowed to drive in Germany." Yay! We did not expect that, but we looked at the silver lining. Now we could drink at parties and he would drive us home. He liked driving more than drinking apparently.

Although we lived really close to Wolfburg, where VWs are manufactured and we even took our car to the factory, we could not figure out what was wrong. The car only started from second gear, then later from third gear. I don't know how many of you drive stick-shift, but if you do, can you imagine what it was like to start from third gear straight onto the Autobahn?

Finally, after five months of driving the VW minibus, we once again took it back to the factory. Then, someone figured out the problem. The transmission was not connected properly between the front and the back. After that we had no more problems.

Our church, St. Marien in Querum, was extraordinary. Father Bartl became a great friend. He came over quite often. We spent many nice evenings talking with him.

There was also a chaplain there who took excellent care of the youth group. He took them on excursions, they had fantastic meetings, and they bicycled together. There was so much life in and around that church. The faithful who went there experienced an exquisite lifestyle the basis of which was their church. We genuinely enjoyed belonging to the community. Our four younger ones sang in the church children's choir. There was also a female Eucharistic Minister, who worked at the parish full time. She was the first woman we had ever seen distributing communion.

One afternoon someone knocked at the door. It was Father László Nádor, who was the Hungarian priest in Braunschweig, in charge of a German parish. Needless to say, we became inseparable friends with him, too.

In the spring he told us that Cardinal Mindszenty would be in Essen to confirm children and recommended we have the children confirmed. Niki was the only one who got left out because she was not yet old enough. Steve, Sandy and Rita immediately started to prepare from a German book, partially in Hungarian-English, but the exam they had to pass was in Hungarian. Father Laci did not speak English. We managed.

Naturally, the children would need sponsors.

One day, quite early in the year, we called my second cousin Alec and his wife Sophie who lived in Frankfurt. We started to talk in Hungarian and let them guess who called them. They could not do it. They could not even imagine we would be in Germany. Shortly after that we took a trip to Frankfurt and spent the weekend with them. They came out of Hungary and became German citizens immediately because of their ancestry. Alec was chief engineer at the Hoechst factory, Sophie worked at the Public Library. Her second mother tongue was French, after Hungarian. They showed us the photo of their only son who was born and lived for a few days. She was Rh negative and her blood was mixed up with someone else's in the lab. So, they did not change the blood of the otherwise healthy baby. He died. Sophie was pregnant six times and always miscarried.

We asked them to become sponsors of Sandy. Another relative living in Lugano, Mrs. Ragnar Lundmark (Baba Zupka), was asked for Rita, and Steve's was Father Laci. In the end Baba could not be there, so Alec stood in for her. (Readers of my previous book, *My Only Choice* will recognize these names as they were important characters in our life.)

We all went to Essen for the great event. When I was 14, I too was confirmed by Cardinal Mindszenty, in Hungary, in 1948, along with my sister Marietta. Soon after that he was arrested by the Communists and was freed during the 1956 Uprising against the Soviets. Then he escaped to and lived at the American Embassy in Hungary for 15 years. After Pope Paul VI's agreement with the Hungarian Government he moved to Vienna.

Later, during our stay in Germany, when we went to Vienna in 1974, and there met with my sisters, who arrived there from Canada with their children, we had an unforgettable private audience with Cardinal Mindszenty. When the Cardinal shook the hands of our teenage boys (by that time Jancsi joined us in Europe), they saw it from the twinkle in his eyes, he totally understood how awkward they felt. That made the boys feel at ease. From then on, they became fans of the Cardinal. He truly valued all mothers. He gave us each a rosary from Fatima. We talked and talked. He asked the boys to give back to Hungary if and when the possibility arose. Stephen told me that when Hungary became free in 1990. He still remembered it and did his best, as did the others. In the back of the room some priests started to come in and out. Finally, one came and told the Cardinal the Paris "Match" magazine has been waiting for him outside. He smiled and said: "Let them wait! I have too much fun with these Hungarian families."

Even though Hitler initiated them, both the Autobahn and the Volkswagen were great ideas. They took us to many places. We were discovering the neighboring cities on weekends, the Harz Mountains, and a good part of Europe on our most significant vacation in the spring.

The Netherlands was the first foreign country where we traveled. As we had a Zoll Nummer (customs number, meaning we did not have to pay the value added tax) we had to take the car out of the country within the first six months of our stay in Germany. So, off we went to Amsterdam. At the practically non-existent border we had to find someone to get proof that we indeed took the car out of the country. As soon as we had crossed the border we went and bought a case of Heineken. We managed to get a reasonably priced family hotel. We received rooms on the fifth floor. There was no elevator, so we got our exercise even within the hotel. The family who operated this place was very friendly. They served good breakfasts, with sliced meats, cheese, eggs, all included in the price. Our two problems were with the 5th floor and the constant rain. Before we left for Europe, we bought matching long, synthetic, furry coats for all three of the girls, not even thinking that they would stand out in Europe as a sore thumb. One person asked what kind of costume this was? A certain folk's traditional garb? We did not know what to say. Then we blurted out: "Canadian Eskimo." That made him happy. Of course, it must be that.

Have you ever tried to walk with five children in the streets of Amsterdam, or any other big European city's busy downtown? It was almost impossible to keep them all together as we had to walk single file among the many pedestrians.

We went into one of the famous chocolate shops. The owner looked at us menacingly, when he saw all the children trotting in with us. He did not want them in the store. He was convinced they would do some harm to his precious merchandise.

Most of the Dutch people denied speaking either English or German, but especially German. However, when addressed in any of the two, they would answer.

As we were walking through the romantic streets with their canals and tall, old houses, suddenly we found ourselves in the red-light district. When first John said: "Look!" I did not know what he meant, but it soon dawned on me. Women were standing in doors, trying to lure in the gentlemen and ladies alike. I especially remember a young woman in jeans, eating an apple, standing in a doorway, lit up from behind. They even tried to get us to go in, but not very aggressively. We started to hurry to get out of there with the children. They never asked any questions, so they probably did not notice. Louis, the oldest must have guessed, but he did not say anything in front of the younger ones.

We visited a beautiful little church, hidden in a house, where Catholics met, when they were persecuted. It was very touching. I wrote an article about it later.

Of course, we went to see Ann Frank's house. It was shocking for the children. Especially after we told them that Ann, had she survived, would be my age now, actually a few years older. Had she lived and would she have gone through Communism she would have experienced both the extreme Left and extreme Right as equally horrific.

41

"Lanterne, Lanterne" the kids went down the street on the night of "Lanternenfest" (holiday of the lanterns). This feast is similar to our Halloween, but without the candies. The kids are just parading around the neighborhood with the lanterns. Of course, we went with them and enjoyed the evening watching their enthusiastic, smiling faces, radiant in the light of the lanterns. We love when they are singing and harmonizing with each other.

Surprise, surprise! The school just comes up with the most interesting causes to have vacation. "Potato harvest vacation" to let the children help their parents with the potato harvest. Really? In the middle of town? Nevertheless, the children loved every minute of the extra vacation days.

We went to town and walked around, looked at the Gewerbehaus (the Guild House), a beautiful old building that was not bombed during the war. The main square with the statue of Richard the Lionhearted and the Lion was the home of a lovely old church and other old buildings. The cobblestones made the image perfect.

Karstadt was one of our favorite department stores, and Der Grüne Löwe is where we got our hardware.

Oktoberfest permeated the city with anticipation. On corners stood "gemütliche" (fun-loving) cardboard jolly men in "Lederhosen" (short leather pants) advertising the beer houses and restaurants, the special beers made for that occasion.

In the evening, John joined us for our pizza place dinner in the middle of town, where, whenever it was open, a skillful man stood right in the window and was making one pizza after another throwing them in the air, while making them taste exquisite. We loved going there. That was the only restaurant we could afford. Cokes and sweet vermouth as well as a cup of coffee cost the exact same price. Guess which one John and I chose? We sipped our vermouth while the children slurped their Cokes through a straw. Louis, of course could drink if he wanted, except if he preferred to drive.

Alcohol and driving was totally out in Germany. If caught, you would have to leave your car and walk home from that place, your license would be taken away. Therefore, most of the time wives drank orange juice, so their husbands could drink beer, chased by a vodka, brandy, or any little "Stampel" (shot glass) drink of your choice.

I found it remarkable that although you were not supposed to drink and drive (strictly enforced by roadblocks, especially at holiday time) every gas station was selling the tiny bottles you can get on airplanes. Just in case… if you ran out of drinks!

There were lovely automats too for people invited to parties for last minute assistance. If invited somewhere you had to take a bottle of wine for the host and a bouquet to the hostess. These automats were selling such "necessities" day and night. And did they come in handy!

Louis and his friends were bicycling to their meetings at church, where they played ping-pong, or listened to a lecture, while also drinking a beer from the automat provided. Then they could bicycle home. There was no drinking age for the young. Those meetings were something wonderful. The young chaplain who worked with them was loved by the students.

I was truly impressed when I went to one of the meetings that was for the entire church and saw how much these young men and women knew about Marxism, for instance. They studied it (on their own) because they had it hanging over their heads like Damocles' sword in the Greek stories. Germany was still divided. The fear of Communism as alive as ever. The border with East Germany was only 25 kilometers away. Forty percent of Braunschweig's population were refugees from East Germany. What they were discussing was not at all just hearsay, solid knowledge stood behind those young people's words.

We went out several times with the children to the border to show them the Iron Curtain, the no-man's-land's empty, raked soil. They saw how on the Western side farmers were working their land all the way up to the border, while on the Eastern side no person was visible at all.

The newspaper wrote about all fresh escapes, rarely with a happy-ending, mostly the horrible fate of those who tried to scale the electrified barbed wire fence.

⌁

The magic of Weihnachten – Christmas in Germany.

It was so much fun to re-discover and re-experience Europe after having been gone for 17 years!

The angels of our childhood Christmases returned with the atmosphere of Advent. This was not the time for parties, except for coffee-clutches with Advent wreaths. We bought one in 1973, made of wrought iron and dressed it every year again with pine branches. The Braunschweig wreaths were especially interesting because they had four pins for apples besides the four candleholders. We have that wreath to this day. Daughter Sandy dresses it now every Christmas. Frau Schultz, the secretary at the grade school in Kralenriede, where the girls attended classes, and her husband who worked in Wolfsburg at the VW factory invited us for our first Advent coffee-clutch. The air breathed Christmas everywhere, even more so in their home. It was cozy and warm. They asked us how we had escaped from Hungary. As we were telling the story, Mrs. Schultz's tears were running down her cheeks. Finally, she said: "We know what it's like to escape. We too came from there. Actually, 40 percent of Braunschweig's population are refugees," she said. Many of them were those deported from other countries after the war, who had "population exchanges" meaning they deported the people into the country of their origin allowing them to take only one suitcase. It was a cruel experience.

She served delightful café au lait and wonderful Stollen, the German Christmas cake. She even gave me the recipe. That is a rare treasure. People do not give each other recipes and to ask for it, or what the ingredients are, is impolite. These recipes were supposed to be family secrets. We ate the cake at the light of the Advent wreath and candles. It was a magical afternoon that was followed by other magical coffee clutches with other friends.

A beautiful starry night twinkled over Braunschweig, but the radiant stars were outshone by the brilliance in the stars of the children's eyes when we drifted with the crowd into the magic wonderland of the Weihnachtsmarkt in the center of the city, on the main square surrounded by the age-old houses and the Lutheran cathedral. At five o'clock the old bells started ringing and kept on going for 15 minutes.

Our eyes thirstily drank in the many gourmet offerings, the Lebkuchen dolls and hearts, the fruit-kabobs generously sugar-coated, the myriad arts and crafts especially prepared for Christmas. Rita's eyes were fixed on a fruit-kabob:

"May I please have one of those with the lovely oranges and figs and dates," Sandy was busy with the booth selling chocolates. Steve was looking for the bratwurst with a roll, we were admiring our children. Our eyes caught the stars in their eyes as we tried to fulfill all their wishes.

We returned to the Weihnachtsmarkt several times to the great joy of our children.

We also used to come downtown in the middle of the day to have a nice drink, just the two of us, at Mr. Drink. It was a fun bar, where we could discuss what we bought for the kids after our secret Christmas shopping.

In those days all we had was a manual typewriter; no one had anything else. We did not write our usual Christmas letter. We sent only postcards to our hundreds of friends all over the world telling them how much we enjoyed the views, the sounds, the smells, and tastes of Europe and wished them Merry Christmas.

We chose a beautiful noble fir (Edeltanne) Christmas tree. In Hungary we called it "silver fir." It was expensive, but: "We are here only once," said John, "we have to have the tree of our childhood Christmases." Our tree was true to its "noble" name. We kept it up way into February and when we took it out of the house, not one needle fell off the tree, not even in transit, in the staircase – it was still so fresh.

We went to the Midnight Mass at St. Marien. The flowers in German churches were people sized arrangements in huge vases, on both sides of the altar. The church lights in the dark winter night shone with God's love for us, as Jesus came to us in the manger and into our hearts.

—◆—

Sylvester evening – what we call it in Europe – meaning New Year's Eve, we watched TV with the children until – we heard the fireworks. We knew people were going to shoot off some fireworks at midnight, but we did not run outside with the children, thinking it would be just a few small candles or sparklers. However, it did not stop, and the kids came running in: "You have to come out and see this!" So, we got ourselves to the door – and indeed – this was something worth getting up for from the sofa. The entire neighborhood was flooded with fireworks in the sky. Every house was trying to outdo the other. It went on and on… it was quite an experience!

Fasching! It started in Germany on January 11th at 11:00 a.m. and went on till midnight on Mardi Gras, in other words Carnival, the day before Ash Wednesday. The equivalent of the American Christmas party celebrations, but at a much more sensible time – after Christmas. Party followed party… followed by party everywhere. We went to a costume party at the neighbors of the Kinds. John and I dressed in our Trinidad shirtjacks (shirts shaped and worn instead of jackets in the tropics) and we wore posters, advertising rum as a substitute for other energy sources. This was the year of the great energy crunch. Everyone was looking for substitute resources, so we had great success. The parties lasted 'til the wee hours of the morning. They ended with a good amount of coffee, although Mrs. Kind enlightened us that coffee really did not sober you up, it just transformed you into an awake drunk.

One of the highlights was the University Ball. Four orchestras played in four different places, different kinds of music. They usually took over from each other. Between them stood the beautiful German flower arrangements which went all the way up to the ceiling. We danced, and danced, and danced. German gentlemen all know ballroom dancing. They are even taught dancing in the P.E. classes, just like they teach square dancing in America. Every one of the men made me fly across the dance floor with the greatest of ease. One man, with whom I danced, had only one leg from the knee down. He was an exceptionally good friend, he worked with John. He danced like an angel. I would have never known about his handicap had we not been once to their swimming pool. When he went swimming, he simply took off his fake leg. Then he put it back on after he came out of the water. He lost his leg on the last day of the war, in Vienna, at age 16.

Naturally, even there, John was the best among all the dancers. After all, he was my sweetheart! We all wore evening gowns, and the men wore tuxedos, the walls breathed festivity. The chandeliers were radiant, and the mood was fantastic. We drank to our hearts' content and appreciated the hospitality of our German hosts.

We were beginning to feel it would be fun to live in Europe again. Of course, we couldn't, but it was nice to dream…

42

We liked to go to German movies. Our children also loved Sesame Street from the very beginning of our stay. It turned out to be a great tool to learn a language. The stories they had already seen in English, so it was easy for them to follow the storyline and repeat the words, when they needed them in a similar situation.

Steve's friend's musician father worked at the Staatstheater Braunschweig that also staged operatic performances. We were so looking forward to going to the Opera and concerts while we were leaving for Europe, and we used every opportunity once we arrived. Hannover was not far so we frequented the Hannover Opera, where the conductor was Hungarian, as well as one of the singers. Our priest friend, Laci Nádor, took us to meet the family of Gábor von Gaál and we discovered that his wife Amanda Török was a childhood friend. Her mother Erzsók also lived with them. When we first met, we were overwhelmed with joy to meet again. We completely lost track of each other in the fury of the war. Every time we went to Hannover from that time on, we ended up or started at their home.

The first opera we saw in Braunschweig, was my favorite of all time, ever since I had first heard it in the Budapest Opera with Maria Gyurkovits: Lucia di Lammermoor. The production was fabulous, as were the singers. The director chose to start with the last scene, when the hero is taking his own life. Then the story returned to the official beginning, the meeting of the two lovers. Donizetti's masterpiece was truly harmonious and light, the coloratura's areas and the sextet unforgettable. The scenery was projected onto cheese cloth. Changes were made mainly by the lights to make the cheesecloth transparent, followed by another projected image.

During the year we visited many Opera Houses around Europe.

John's task, among others, was to visit all the largest high-power research labs in Europe. That took us to many interesting, fabulous cities, like Paris and Milan, with their famous Opera house.

Braunschweig had its own high-power attractions. Quoting from John's professional report:

The Institute is located in two buildings. A somewhat smaller operation, headed by Professor Salge, is in Hallendorf, some 12 miles Southwest of Braunschweig. It was a high voltage direct current (HYDC) transmission laboratory of Professor Marx (inventor of the Marx generator) during WWII. The Institute is well equipped with several high voltage transformers, surge generators, modern measuring equipment, etc. Their large Marx generator is rated 2 million Volt (50 Joule) and is a triggered type...They have steady access to 6 MVA short circuit capacity, hence are the only university in Germany, if not in Western Europe, capable of doing high power research work. Their pioneering HVDC (high voltage direct current) circuit breaker is well known even in the USA.

From the 60 people that work at the Institute 20 are "assistants" who are all working towards their doctor's degree (equivalent to our student research or teaching assistants).

The duties of the assistants are manifold. Besides their main occupation of carrying out research, they help with developing lectures, gathering material, preparing slides and equipment. There is always at least one assistant attending the lectures taking notes. Colored chalk is used very extensively in lectures and all students carry multi-colored mechanical pencils…

It was a real experience to lecture, while the attending assistant was doing all the chores, including erasing, professionally with a wet cloth, the sections of the chalkboard no longer needed. Not once did I have to touch an eraser during lectures (except when correcting errors) or do anything outside of presenting the material. At the end of the class period the assistant was holding the soap and clean towel to wash hands at the washbasin provided in all lecture rooms.

Assistants are appointed for only a three-year term forcing them to finish. Yet many of them need four or even five years to complete their research and dissertation. They are paid mostly out of slush funds for the balance of their time. It is important to stress that there is *no course work* involved in obtaining the doctor's degree and candidates are not enrolled. Handing in and defending the dissertation is the only legal requirement to become a doctor.

The above makes it possible for engineers working at industrial laboratories or research institutes to present dissertations without actual, as we call it, "residence requirement."

There are two customs at the Institute worth mentioning. Hardly a week goes by without a celebration: buying a new car, submitting a research report, promotion, etc., all call for beer and soft drink drinking, of which a considerable amount is stored in the refrigerator of the workshop. Birthdays are celebrated in the Institute's Library with cake and drinking coffee and spirits. (Factories have the same custom as experienced by our son at Siemens when doing an internship there.)

The biggest celebration is the 'Doktor Feier' (doctor's celebration) on the evening of the oral examination. Everyone in the Institute, friends and their wives are invited. It is held in one of the laboratories, rearranged for the occasion. The partying goes on from 6 p.m. to well past midnight with beer, soft drinks, spirits, and sandwiches. The new doctor is presented with the doctor's hat on which the events of his career at the university are displayed. Cost of the hat material is borne by the colleagues (about 40 cents/person) and is designed and put together by one of the assistants. Cost of the Doctor Feier is taken care of by the new doctor.

John and I were lucky enough to celebrate our Braunschweig "guardian angel" and dear friend Dr. Haro Lührmann's doctorate with him and get acquainted with this lovely celebration.

Back to John's report:

One of the saddest and most disturbing facets of our stay was the confrontation with many misconceptions about the United States…while relating that my salary goes directly to my bank account I was always asked: 'How do you get hold of cash?' 'Well I go to the bank and pick it up.' To which came the frequent reaction 'And you dare to enter a bank? Are you not afraid of being killed?'…This came not only from simple folks, but from many well-meaning, educated people…The day following a bank holdup in Hamburg where two bystanders, a policeman and the holdup man, were killed, I was asked several times 'Feeling at home?' Most people visualize the average American as unfriendly, selfish, money grabbing. Because my wife and I speak German fluently and because of our Hungarian origin, people felt less inhibited to speak to us about America and the Americans.

My wife and I filled the Institute's Library three times with students and their wives. We talked about the U.S. in a relaxed atmosphere with refreshments, from 8 p.m. until well after midnight; and everyone stayed until the very end.

The West Germans are very much afraid of the USSR, particularly since the Ostpolitik did not bring any easing in East-West German relations. They are worried that the U.S. will pull out and leave them virtually defenseless. If one sees the Iron Curtain with its electric fences, mine fields, automatic weapons, watchtower, and military preparedness on the East German side, contrary to the open and unprepared West Germany, one gets a better understanding of the problems.

Our letting down of South Vietnam and our handling of the Mid East situation did not help improve our image. Neither has Watergate. We made a conscientious effort to talk to people and inform them about the U.S. and the Americans. They believed us because they considered us "Europeans" and by speaking in German they felt at ease. It was most interesting to see people's surprise, when we told them that in the U.S. neighbors visit each other, that if one runs out of sugar, one sends the children over to borrow some (a practice we introduced in Germany) that neighbors would help each other, etc…and from there the conversation would go on for hours.

Whoever visited the U.S., or had a closer contact with Americans, is enthusiastic about our country. For example, Professor Kind is very fond of the U.S., has been here many times, has many friends and business contacts. His final analysis of Watergate was: see how a big country's constitution can and does work? I suggest we bring him over for a lecture tour to convey the spirit of appreciation of our country to our own young people.

In the past few years many young Germans took advantage of the high value of the German Mark and toured the United States. Without exception they loved it here and were thrilled with the friendliness of the people: 'You know, one can go into a restaurant in any small place and ask for a cup of coffee, and they are friendly and, when they find out that you are a foreigner, they immediately ask what they could do to help. Wow, they even refill your cup every time it is empty without charging and they give you iced water.' A two-cup size coffee carafe costs $1.00 in Germany, and if ordered by itself, it draws unbelievable unfriendliness in most cases. Most of those Germans who visited the U.S. never met an American family or been invited into an American home, yet they still loved what they had seen.

We made many acquaintances and left many new friends behind. We hope that they will visit us in Pullman to get some true American experience.

John gave numerous lectures on various topics, but the most memorable was, quoting his report again "the presentation of a paper at the prestigious biennial conference EUROCON 1974 which was organized by IEEE (Institute of Electrical and Electronic Engineers, USA), IEE (Institute of Electrical Engineers, U.K.) and all Western European national electrical engineering institutes. Prince Klaus, the highly regarded husband of the Crown Princess of Holland, opened the Conference, which was held in Amsterdam on March 21 through 24. I was fortunate to have as co-author a W.S.U. undergraduate in foreign languages. The lecture, "Energy and Culture" by John F. and Helen M. Szablya, was very successful, drew many personal compliments and was published in abridged form in the EUROCON '74 Conference Digest."

Our presentation was the first multi-media presentation at such a meeting (we used an electric drill, slides and movies) and we took turns speaking while delivering the lecture. Several participants found this a great idea and decided to follow the example themselves. Not only the multimedia presentation, but the fact that the alternating two voices kept the attention of the audience.

Going to many research establishments gave us opportunities to travel to extremely interesting places.

Back to John's report:

> Siemens Central Laboratories in Erlangen, where some 1200 researchers are engaged in advanced industrial research. Invited by Kraftwerk Union (arranged by Karl Deckart, a WSU Fall 1972 Karl Duisberg exchange student). On February 11, 1974, I had the unique opportunity to be guided through many laboratories and to talk to some researchers at that fabulous place. Among others, I saw the new experimental, high speed, magnetically suspended vehicle in the last stages of construction.

> At the CESI (Central Electrical Research Institute) in Milan, Italy, I received the red-carpet treatment from its director, Dr. Giorgio Catenacci, who offered his wholehearted support and cooperation for our planned laboratory (EPRDC). The success of CESI hinges on the fact that their 350 people (30 engineers and 120 highly educated technical professionals) are also doing contract research for customers all over the world, not just testing and development. This makes research not only a profitable undertaking, but also generates testing contracts.

This naturally gave us the perfect opportunity to make a tour of Italy all the way down to Rome and visit La Scala in Milan. Their "The Walkyres" was beautifully sung, but the setting was disappointing, to say the least. The Opera just started doing modern scenery. This resulted in Brünnhilde instead of lying down on a woodpile, was climbing up onto a banquet table in a conference room, while wearing her appropriate costume, meaning armament.

Driving south on our Italian journey took us into spring all the way down from Braunschweig through Italy and then back again as we went North. The pink and white blooming trees, the ancient castles on top of the hills, with the surrounding little towns, their cobblestone covered narrow streets with their inviting little houses felt like wandering through a fairyland.

Assissi! The little town on the top of the mountain. We entered the beautiful church. The priest, celebrating Mass just turned towards the people and greeted us with: "Peace be with you!" Our arrival could not have been more perfect. After Mass we stood at a stone wall and watched the sunset discussing peace with son Jancsi and John. Jancsi's shape reflected on the red-orange-yellow of the setting sun.

We then walked down the cobblestone streets to the restaurant that served food from St. Francis of Assisi's time in the way inns served their food then. It looked cave-like with an open fire burning in the fireplace. We all loved it.

My favorite city in Italy was Florence. The blue green Arno river flowing under the delicate bridges, the Ponte Vecchio's busy small shops and boutiques, the museums, and the most beautiful basilica! We approached it from a side street and when it suddenly appeared as we turned, "my feet took root in the ground," as we say in Hungary. I just stopped and my mouth fell open. It was such a magnificent and unexpected sight!

Italy was a dream to remember forever.

As was Italian traffic, though more of a nightmare. The tiny cars zoomed around, as well as the scooters. The Italians were good drivers, but Heaven protect the pedestrians! The cars were so small, they were not towed, they were lifted on top of a truck if parked in the wrong place and "towed" that way.

We left Milan on the feast of St. Joseph. Who would have thought it would be an official holiday? And who would have remembered that the rule was "no driving except for tourists, on any holiday." Our car was parked in a garage for the night. When we went to get it, the garage was closed for the day. It took a while to find out why, then another while to find the garage's owner, who finally arrived with the key. He released our car amid apologies, accompanied by fast movements of his hands, as Italians do, explaining the unusual situation.

Finally, we were on our way. To our greatest surprise and good luck, we had the entire autostrada to ourselves. You know how wonderful it feels to drive on an empty super-highway? While the beauty of the Italian landscape swishes by?

When we had arrived in Florence, John asked a man for directions: "Dove Plaza Michelangelo?" It was in Italian, so the good Italian started to explain with the speed of lightning. We could understand as much as right and left, straight and the street names. So, we remembered the first two instructions, then stopped again to ask for further directions. The kids were all questions: "What did he say?" John improvised: "He said to go left and then right at the second street." So, we repeated the process. When the children asked again, we said the nice woman told us to go straight then turn right at the fifth street and there…" The children chimed in: "and there will be another nice person from whom we can ask directions…" They figured it all out.

The most interesting such experience we had in Rome. We were coming from the Villa D'Este with its beautiful 900 fountains run by gravity alone. We drove by the Colosseum and saw two policemen there. We asked them directions to the Spanish Stairs. We lived in a beautiful convent formerly used by pilgrims, renting rooms from the sisters while we were there.

The two policemen looked at each other and started to discuss the difficult question. They gesticulated busily, while giving suggestions to each other, then explaining why that turn cannot be made, noticing there was road construction, and a one-way street…bringing up all the obstacles. Finally they turned to us and said: "You cannot get from here to there…" Noticing themselves what they had just told us, they started laughing, then beginning the route planning again, until finally they decided there was only one way: we had to go in the wrong direction in a one-way street in the final block just before we reached the convent. Following their instructions that is what we did from then on, whenever we were going home. Not once did anyone stop us.

The Italian mail deserves special mention. If anyone wanted to make sure their mail would arrive, they would have to mail it from Vatican City. The Vatican mail, besides having exquisite stamps, took the mail out of Italy with a helicopter to Switzerland to forward it. While still in Germany, we saw a photo in the newspaper of Italian mailmen recycling the mail into the river before/instead of delivering it. The sisters where we lived in the shadow of the Vatican, right outside the wall, sent us the confirmation for our registration with someone who was traveling to Germany.

It was these same sisters who gave us instructions about beggars who were really pickpockets. They warned us to never catch a baby if someone throws it at us. Those are dolls. The purpose of the pitch is to rob you while your hands are busy with the "baby."

A retired American colonel tourist, who was also living at the convent, wore a fanny-pack on his waist. While he was expecting his daughter at the railway station someone ran at him, bumped into him and with one slit relieved him of his fanny-pack. Now he was there without his documents and money.

One early morning I happened to be in the corridor. A nice sister beckoned me up to the roof. We were looking out over the rooftops of Rome. All the bells suddenly started ringing to greet the morning. I just stood there mesmerized.

We had a colorful cavalcade of adventures with the children in Rome and other parts of Italy. We rode in horse-drawn carriages, limousines, all kinds of vehicles, including gondolas in Venice, while looking at the sights, visiting museums, dropping coins into the Fontana Trevi.

Needless to say, everywhere we chose inexpensive, but acceptable lodgings. In Venice it was a "Trattoria." The street leading there looked like a dark almost scary alleyway, but when the gate was opened a white marble staircase greeted us. Upstairs our rooms looked at the Canale Grande, the furniture was all antique, the food wonderful. Yet, this was a 4th class accommodation according to the tour book. The owners were kind and friendly. We had a wonderful time. The water instead of streets was quite an experience. The pigeons on St. Mark's Square especially loved Niki. She fed them and they came by the droves, trying to settle on Niki's head, shoulders and arms. She looked adorable. The pizza, an inexpensive food in Italy, was exquisite everywhere. The Italians loved "bambinos". We never had any problems there with the kids. They were surrounded by love and hospitality.

On our way home we stopped by Radio Free Europe in Munich where we were the guests of Zoltán Kovács and his family. He visited us in Pullman one time when he was recording there with Professor Valkó, who was a specialist in agricultural cooperatives and just came back from Israel where he visited the kibutzes. He had a lot of new information from the Hungarians in those kibutzes. He wanted to share it with the Associated Press (AP). To his greatest surprise he could not because it did not fit with their editorial guidelines. How can a news service have "editorial guidelines"? Aren't they just supposed to report the news, the facts, without any opinion? Well, Radio Free Europe reported it.

RFE interviewed us several times. The various editors spoke to John, me and our oldest son Jancsi. He gave them an interview about ultralight planes. That was his great hobby at the time. Guess what! The most questions to RFE came regarding Jancsi's interview. Every inquirer wanted to know how to build an airplane like that. What an excellent way to plan an escape!

Our younger children, Stephen, Sandy, and Rita, sang songs in three-part-harmony in three different languages. Their recorded singing was used several times by the station. It opened the Bicentennial Program of the RFE. While we were still in Braunschweig we received a card from Hungary from a relative who heard us speak on the radio. She wrote it on an open postcard. Those worked the best. No one censored postcards. What for? Obviously, no one would write anything objectionable on an open card. We were so happy to hear that people approved of our interviews.

When we got back to Braunschweig, Prof. Dr. Brinkman, whose room John occupied during our sabbatical, invited us to Siemensstadt in West Berlin. He was the Head of Siemens in West Berlin; that is why John could use his room. He was very seldom at the TU, where he gave occasional lectures.

"You have to come and see our establishment in Berlin."

"We would love to come, but we cannot drive over. The road goes through East Germany and we cannot risk being caught," said John.

The East German police played games with travelers who were at their mercy. They could arrest them just for stopping on the highway. Even if it was because the car broke down. Other times they would stop a car and make the person wait there in the blazing sun for hours in the closed car. Our name was for the Communists like a red cape for a bull.

"Ah, but that should not be a problem. We'll fly you in," Professor Dr. Brinkman volunteered right away.

He took care of everything and flew us straight into the middle of the city of Berlin. A car was waiting for us. We were housed in a beautiful hotel and then the tour of the magnificent West Berlin began.

The unbelievable difference between the two parts of the city amazed us. West Berlin was more luxurious than any of the other European cities. He took us for dinner to his yacht club on a beautiful lake, within city limits. Berlin was so big that when we asked the waiter at a restaurant where the Wall was, even though he was born in Berlin, he said: "I have never been to the Wall, I don't know how to get there." The West was pumping money into the city to emphasize the difference between the two systems.

Our hosts took us to the Wall. We looked at it from a viewpoint where we could look way into East Berlin. We saw the boarded-up houses near the wall, the "no-man's-land" left completely empty, while on the Western side life was bustling all the way to the Wall. The same was true everywhere where the two Germanies met. In East Berlin there was a huge water tower. On that tower the sun was constantly reflected as a cross. People called it the "Pope's revenge."

Siemensstadt in Berlin was so impressive, no wonder Prof. Dr. Brinkman wanted to show it to us. We spent an entire day there. Engineers took John all over the factory, to their high power and high voltage testing laboratories, where he had the opportunity to meet Dr. Slamecka, a well-known authority in high power testing. I was taken to other parts, like the nursery school. Siemensstadt had churches, grade schools and high schools, every kind of business and facility you would expect to have in a town. It was a fascinating experience. What I noticed in the nursery school was that out of the 210 children, only 70 were German, the others were children of "Gastarbeiters", many among them Turks. I wrote several articles about that problem at the time (1974) for the American press.

What kind of population did Germany expect for the 21st century? The number of children dwindled among the German population. I wrote much about the attitude towards children and the fact that they wanted to have all their worldly desires fulfilled and every one of their goals accomplished before having children.

Now (21st century), the world has arrived at the great problem. Now journalists write about it. It was entirely visible already at that time what the future held.

In our days, Americans, but even more Europeans, are repeating the same attitude towards children. As a result, immigrants are needed, no matter how much people protest. Only a few countries stand up for children and have programs where large families are supported. Hungary is one of the leaders.

43

John's report continues.

Next in line was the High Power and High Voltage Laboratories at Les Renardières, 50 miles South of Paris, the showplace of the Electricité de France (EdF), which we visited on June 5, 1974. The high voltage hall is the tallest (150 feet high) and largest in Europe. When it is finished the high-power laboratory will be beyond anything now available.

Naturally this good luck led us to Paris and to our old friends, Gisèle and her husband, Konrad Lieberman, MD. They arranged a hotel for us, close to the Opera, the Louvre, and most of the sights. Konrad and his parents came as Polish refugees before WWII. Konrad and his mother became Paris history enthusiasts. It was a true adventure to travel around Paris with Konrad as he explained the beauties and intricacies of Paris. Going to the restaurants with them was a gourmet's dream.

We drove to the Liebermans straight from Les Renardières and got really lost. When we finally arrived for dinner, we told Konrad: "The signs were so misleading." Konrad, indicating his understanding, said: "You have actually seen some signs?" We had a good laugh. Both Gisèle and Konrad spoke excellent English. Konrad not only had a great sense of humor, when it came to drawing, he was a true artist.

Gisèle and I went to the Opera a lot in Budapest when she visited us for three months in 1948. It was only natural we should get to the Opera together again. While at the Opera, Konrad drew sketches of all our children who were there.

We represented an unusual phenomenon again with our many children, all dressed alike in the clothes they wore for Ilike's wedding. During intermission, a young man stepped to us: "The Szablyas?" he asked. When we affirmed we were indeed the Szablyas, he said: "My mother said you were coming and when I saw all the children…I knew it must be you. I am Andrew, son of Matyi Gundel, who is your second cousin, John, and Dóczi

Deér. We actually met in Hungary, when I was 16 years old. Now, I myself have four children." We joyfully embraced. We remembered meeting him, but needless to say none of us looked the same anymore. "I was in Paris on business, but I was late for my plane, so I decided to come to the Opera." What a lucky coincidence!

Paris enchanted us with its extraordinary beauty. The diamonds of car windshields on the Champs Elysées radiated as bright as ever in the June sunshine.

We had a chance to get together with other dear friends Maria Jary (Aczél) and her French family. My husband John and Maria used to dance together as teenagers. Her husband was an engineering professor, too. She was kind enough to volunteer to remote babysit our small fry while we went on a night tour of Paris with Jancsi (19), our oldest son, who by this time had joined us. Steve was 13 and he was in charge, the youngest, Niki was five. How do you babysit remotely? Steve and Sandy could take care of everything, but they did not speak French. We arranged with the hotel personnel, in case they wanted to talk to the children, they should call Maria and she would interpret over the phone.

The first attraction on Montmartre were the apache dancers clothed entirely in black. I liked their performance the best of all the night's presentations. Their style, the wildly smooth moves and agility was mesmerizing. Last on the tour was the Lido, where the star of the show arrived on stage by a real helicopter.

These shows were definitely not pornography, but artistically sexy and witty. All three of us enjoyed them.

Just in case you thought that we no longer were interested in each other, John and I lived our love four times that day and night. That was always a part of our lives. Of course, we had to wait for the children to be asleep, or away somewhere, but our love remained the same as it was on our honeymoon.

After Paris we went to Brussels. Boy, can I speak French, when I am mad! Our hotel was something else! We went up to our room. I am not kidding, the toilet was just a few feet away from our bed, without any separation in between. I told the manager I thought they were a civilized people! "Belgium… civilized?" was his answer. I got a bit more of their "civilization" when in the tumult going to the Grande Place a guy stole my wallet from my purse. You can imagine my consternation and problem. In it I had credit cards and my ID, my green card…Now what? We went to the police, who simply asked: "Was he a 'Mediterranean' looking guy?" After we confirmed it, they were practically assuring us that we should not even expect to see any of it.

The Grande Place was romantic with its lace-like buildings. We sat there in a street-side coffee, having a few drinks, watching life late into the night, along with the children, who enjoyed all new places and adventures. They loved being immersed in European culture, various atmospheres. Later, when they had kids of their own, they all tried to give them the same kind of opportunities. Niki, who was the youngest at the time, took her children to Europe for an entire month in order to experience "living" in a place, as opposed to spending time there.

The next day we went to the USA Embassy, to let them know that my "green card" was in my wallet. A room full of people were waiting their turn to ask for visas, passports, etc. I decided that we were not going to wait there all day, which was first suggested by the personnel. I went to the door when I saw someone and said I wanted to report that my green card was stolen. I did what any USA salesman would have done, I put my foot in the door saying: "We are doing this so you should know and watch out that someone should not use it to smuggle drugs or commit a similar crime." The lady looked at me and said in a very impertinent voice: "You will still need your green card to get back into the USA. How else would you want to return?" I said: "Actually, we only came to let you know. I can get back with my Canadian passport." The lady suddenly turned apologetic and nice. I don't think any American would approve of the way their Embassy personnel behaves with other people than Americans. Yet, we are the ones who pay their salaries!

Then, we were off home to Braunschweig. On the last day we drove 800 km to get home on time for John to go back to work.

⁓

We visited Ansbach, where John's grandmother was born in the original Gundel House with a bakery on the street level. Although they were John's second cousins, we had never met before. It was an unbelievable experience. We just dropped in from the street – and they received us with such joy! All Gundels from town congregated to meet with us. Frau Trudel Gundel went out immediately to buy some pork chops to fix us a big dinner, Herr Rudolf Gundel showed us around the bakery. Their two sons came later. They were university students. Two more Gundel sisters showed up. Gerlinde took out an album and showed us John's father's photo in it. They had his entire story recorded until he left Hungary to join us in America. We updated them and gave them a newer photo. They in turn gave a photo of John's father as a young man. How amazing that they have been keeping track through all these years of all the Gundels they could contact. And there are many of them! We sent them our Christmas letters from then on, so they have been kept well informed about our branch of the family.

Another great trip took us to Vienna. "Wien, Wien, nur Du allein, Du sollst die Stadt meiner Träume sein…" (Vienna, Vienna, you alone are the city of my dreams…) was what my governess Elsie sang to me often and I learned it from her, along with the desire to go to Vienna.

Where else would we have stayed then but in the Convent of the Sacré Coeur in Pressbaum, where they greeted us with such warmth as refugees in 1956. Some of my old teachers were still there, actually Mère Lomoschitz was the head of the Convent at the time, who had "adopted" us after my favorite teacher Mère Haraszthy died. Until then she considered herself our "Mother."

I wrote and asked if we could stay and they immediately responded and offered that we can stay for just the price of what the extra food would cost them. We received an entire dorm room with more than enough beds for the entire family. The bathroom was down the corridor. During the hours when it was dark, we took flashlights and marched all together to the bathroom.

"You know, you would have to be home by the time we close the gates, before 10:30 pm."

"Sometimes we will have to be later, when we go to concerts, or…"

"We'll show you how to get in then, but you will have to let us know which day you want us to leave the beam off the door," with that Mère Lomoschitz took us to the cellar and showed us the back door. "We had to put a beam across the gate because one night someone broke in. So, you will have to put up the beam after you are inside." She handed us a key to the back door with a smile. They made the rules, but they also told us how to break them.

John was allowed to sleep in the Convent with us. It was now after the Council of Vatican II and rules were relaxed in the Church. The sisters could drive; while we were taught it was a mortal sin to miss Mass even one Sunday, meaning we would go to Hell if we died without having gone to confession, now Mère Lomoschitz explained that it would only count as a mortal sin if we have been missing Mass on 5 or 6 Sundays and have decided not to go to Mass ever again. In order to commit a mortal sin, you have to do it on purpose, in order to hurt God and it had to be something big. That was always the case, but what a difference this reinterpretation of the rules meant! Changes, whose time has come.

We connected with Irmgard Lohwag, Louis' godmother. Her husband Kurt had died by that time. Irmgard joined us several times while we were in Vienna and enjoyed her godson, who by then was a teenager with the long hair customary in those days. Louis went back to Pullman to graduate with his class, but had rejoined us since. He missed our trip to Italy because just before we had left, he called from Pullman. "May I stay for another two weeks? I have just met the woman whom I will marry." (He actually did.) We told him: "Stay, just put down the receiver." It turned out that he and his best friend, in whose parents' house he was staying while in Pullman, went to the prom together. They both had dates, but by the end of the evening each boy had a different girl. They exchanged their dates. And the rest is history...

We took the children to the exact spot on the border, where we crossed into Austria and into freedom in 1956. We went as close as we dared to the Iron Curtain. The same phenomenon we experienced at the East German and the East Berlin borders between the East and the West. Barbed wire fences, with no-man's-land on the Hungarian side and the up-to-the-border farming on the Austrian side. Jancsi and Louis stood side by side to cover us and we took a photo of the watchtower with the guard and the fence. We did not even dare to show we had a camera near the border. We showed the children exactly where we came across, but we kept our distance.

"Look, the cornfield is still there, where we had to take a turn and go straight," John pointed.

We stopped by in the village Mörbisch am See (Fertőmeggyes) where we had arrived on the night of our escape, at Frau Halwax's house. She brought out the Christmas letters we had sent them every year. She had all the news about us. Her son was now an adult. Frau Halwax's wrinkled face under her kerchief radiated with joy to see us again after that winter night in 1956.

My sisters and I decided we were going to meet in Vienna. Between us we had 12 children, and all would meet except Ilike who was married. We could not figure out for a while where we could actually get together with that many children in tow. Finally, we decided on the Burggarten. We sat on a bench together, the three of us and John, while the kids roamed all around the park.

"Do you want an Irish Coffee?" we asked Marietta and Elizabeth, who hardly ever drink. Both said "Yes!" with the sound of someone dying of thirst.

John and I went in search of a coffee house, but we could not find anything close by. That is when John and I put our heads together and invented "instant Irish Coffee," meaning a caffeine pill swallowed with whiskey we always carried around in a cough medicine bottle. My sisters gladly took the offered delicacy. So now it was more bearable to have that many children in a European park.

Dr. Paul K. Kovács and his wife Keri, who were back from the USA, came visiting from Hungary. This was one way to meet with Hungarians. Unfortunately, letters discussing any meeting very often did not arrive, or arrived a few months after the planned meeting. Pali and Keri introduced us to Grinzing, where we sat in a little pub among the vineyards and drank excellent wine, grown by the owners of the pub. Sitting there with them in the sunset we could discuss many things we would not have been able otherwise, like the escape of two of their grandchildren one by one and their future.

Some friends wrote to us that they would go on vacation to the mountains close to the border and walk around. If we would walk around at the same time, maybe we could see each other. Their letter arrived a long time after we were in Vienna. In Hungary even the letters within the country were censored. My father-in-law, while still in Hungary wrote a letter to his brother, also in Hungary. What his brother received was a letter written by a woman to her sister in the countryside. The envelope did not show any sign of having been opened.

We were so close to Hungary, yet light-years away.

44

We were ready to board the plane, looking forward to an indescribable mess checking in with six children and 23 packages that should all conform to the rules. The clerk who checked us in found it so funny he did not even weigh everything separately, just practically "waived us through."

At the time we were still Canadian citizens. We had to be back in the USA within 364 days of our departure. We stopped in Ottawa at the Kollar's, but we crossed the border at Niagara Falls to keep our green cards up to date.

We celebrated John's 50th birthday in Braunschweig, but for my 40th we went to Iowa City, where Ilike and Barry were in graduate school. They were awarded Rockefeller Fellowships at the University of Iowa's Center for Performing Arts where they became a part of the "Iowa Theater Lab" an alternative theater company doing interesting, innovative work. They had just returned from a successful tour of New York-Philadelphia-Baltimore-Pittsburgh. For my birthday the group gave a special performance only for our family. Then Barry made a fantastic Sacher cake as a birthday present.

Before settling into our normal life, we visited John's mother for a wonderful week in Vancouver.

All the kids were now in school as Niki had started first grade. She did not turn six until November 5, but the principal knew her as she was always hanging around there with her sisters. He appreciated that Niki had spent the year in Germany in Kindergarten and she spoke Hungarian, German and English equally well.

At Christmas time the whole family was together again. Ilike and Barry came to visit, Jancsi came home from Youngstown, Ohio, where he was living with the Franciscans, going to university there for a year. The little ones put all their pennies together to get their brother the ticket to join us. We thoroughly enjoyed being together again. Jancsi brought some contemporary Hungarian records from Ohio and the fun dancing began. Everyone got into the Christmas spirit. At Midnight Mass we were there again in full force.

The Iowa Theater Lab was invited to Baltimore for a residency at The Theatre Project. Ilike and Barry moved with them to Baltimore, but left after nine months to return to the Northwest to begin a family and create their own theater.

On their return they started their own alternative theater adventure and named it: "Eclectic Union Theater."

The children were all doing many interesting things. Louis's girlfriend, Kate, went to New Zealand with her parents for half a year for a sabbatical in 1975. Louis was invited and took the opportunity to get acquainted with New Zealand in three weeks. During that time, they visited both islands. Through Louis' photos we got to enjoy his trip too.

Steve also took great photos. He even sold some of them to newspapers. He started a school radio station at his school in Junior High, then again in High School. They organized dances to raise the money for records (there were no CDs yet).

All the children sang in the folk mass. The whole town knew from Summer Palace that our children were good at singing. One day we got a phone call: "The Bishop is coming to the 5:00 p.m. Mass and there is no choir. Could your children sing?" From then on, Louis took his guitar and they became the group for the 5:00 p.m. Mass on Saturdays.

Jancsi came home from Youngstown by bus with a month-long ticket. He visited our friends all across the country and stayed with them. He had a great cross-country experience.

In the Summer of 1975 Maria and Rita, my two sisters' oldest daughters, both 17 years old, came to visit us. We took them all over the Pacific Northwest, including Seattle and Vancouver. We spent time with them at the lake.

This was the time when our dear Vietnamese friends, our extended family, the Mungs arrived from Saigon.

On April 30, 1975 Saigon fell.

Now we must go back in time and tell you how we met Mung.

"I took a trip in the time machine," was the title of my article in the Daily Evergreen, WSU's student newspaper. Demonstrators about Vietnam wore red armbands with the peace sign on it in a white circle. I recalled how Hitler's Nazis wore red armbands, as did the Communists. The students changed the armband's color to blue.

Soon I got a letter. The sender was Vietnamese. I hardly dared to open it, but my fear was in vain. It was a thank you to me for writing the article. The sender was telling me that the North Vietnamese had a peasant uprising at the time of the Hungarian Revolution in 1956. He even mentioned Paul Maleter's name who led the military during the Uprising. We were so impressed with a student who expressed such knowledge of world affairs, we invited him for dinner.

A youngish looking (17- 18-year-old) student, Nguyen Van Mung came in the door. That instant, our Sandy, who was lying on the sofa because she did not feel well, started throwing up. Mung ran to her and held her head. We tried to keep him away: "Don't do it, you may catch it!" we told him, knowing how Asians were getting sicker from our infections.

"But she reminds me so much of my daughter!" he said.

"What? You have a daughter?" we could not believe our ears.

It turned out he not only had a daughter, but five children. He was on an International Atomic Energy Grant as a visiting scientist. He had great international experience, but he was also working on his PhD in agricultural engineering.

That cemented our friendship. Mung and his wife Quyt met in the USA when they were both studying in Illinois. Mung was studying plant breeding at the University of Illinois, Urbana-Champaign and Quyt was getting her Masters in English at Loyola University. They fell in love and became Catholics before they went home and got married. On their honeymoon they went to build a hospital in the Mekong Delta, wearing black pajamas, as the poor people. If the people would have found out they were intellectuals, they would have been killed.

Quyt became the principal of a school. One day the two of them, with several friends, were discussing what they could do to help their suffering country. They decided on educating the children orphaned by the war. So, what was it they would need for their school? They were aware that learning can take place anywhere, even under a tree if there was a teacher and someone wanting to learn. Quyt offered the lunchroom of her school for those hours when the school did not need it. There were 50 such places.

The group put an ad on the radio to find the orphans. At the appointed time 350 children showed up. At the end they started the school with 150 children they somehow were able to accommodate.

What does one need for a school? The friends put together $10.00 from their own money and that was the budget for the year. Mung said they "stole" a green cardboard, which they used as the blackboard. They started teaching. They themselves were the teachers in their free hours (they all worked full time, but nevertheless managed somehow).

The school developed in leaps and bounds. The Jesuit university gave them a carport, which they managed to transplant to an empty lot. The American Embassy gave them a cement brick-making machine. One man, or three children, could make it work. The oldest was a 13-year-old girl. After they were trained to use the machine one adult came there in the morning and put the work into motion. Then the adult went to work. Occasionally, whoever had the time of the original group of intellectuals, came by to see how the children were doing. Once again, it turned out that miracles do happen. The children managed to make enough bricks to transform the carport into a schoolroom. Every year they added children and classrooms. When people saw how well they are doing, even getting accreditation from the government, the donations started coming. One company gave them sewing machines. The goal was to give the children a profession with which they would be able to make a living. Being a seamstress or tailor was one of them. Following their example other such schools started to operate.

Mung was the kind of person who, if he had two shirts, gave one away.

While he was in Pullman, he received $1,000 for the whole year. He lived for free in a dorm and cooked himself rice and a chicken each week. He managed to send money home to his family.

Mung became a member of our family. We went out together a lot and fed him when we could. He loved the snow and the excursions. Then came the bombing of Danang. Mung's family lived in Dalat, which was close to Danang. He had to go home.

Mung became the Head of Agricultural Research in South Vietnam. The family moved to Saigon. The war went on and Saigon was under siege.

Knowing the Communists first-hand we did not think Mung and his family had much future if they took over. Mung was a person who always asked questions and protected the weak. We knew deep down in our hearts that Mung would not last even a day before he would be arrested. They were in grave danger. We begged him to leave the country with his family. We were not the only ones. The USAID counterpart of Mung, a Mr. Rice, tried to persuade him too. Mr. Rice stayed in Vietnam for another 10 days after his family was evacuated just in order to get Mung out of there. Mung said he could not leave without his people, the employees under him.

We called the Embassy and talked to Mr. Rice several times. We even managed to talk to Mung once. That month our phone bill was $400. Finally, Mr. Rice had to leave, but we kept talking to him in Thailand. He went back to Vietnam once more to get Mung and his family out, and was planning on going back again on the day when Saigon fell.

In the meantime we worked feverishly in Pullman to get them out. David and Saralou Seamans had many political connections.

Previously I had written a letter to Pearl S. Buck (Nobel prize winning author of the book *The Good Earth*) about the Mungs and asked her if she would write a story about them. She wrote me back and suggested I should write it because she does not write a story someone else suggests to her. She signed the letter of course. I took that letter with me and we ran all over town asking people to sign the petition to the Embassy to get them on the list. Eighty people signed it that one evening and the Seamans' forwarded it to the right place. Then we watched the television as they were evacuating people through the roof of the Embassy.

We were hoping to see them there.

Oh, what a great day it was when Mung called from Guam!!!

45

Many years later I wrote all this to the Mung family and to our children that they too should have the memories of those days. They had regular email correspondences between them, I just occasionally chimed in. I ended my email with:

> "I love you all! It was a great pleasure to share this with all of you!
>
> Mom/Helen/Sister (between our two families we called each other as Mom and Dad, Sister and Brother)

Mung's son Loc, shared with us the story of their escape, which he recently wrote for his family and the future generations. This story is digested from the 12 pages that Loc sent us.

THE BOAT OF DESTINY

April 30, 2010, marked 35 years of South Vietnam falling to the North Vietnamese Communists, and 35 years of my family's escape from Vietnam in a panic. I was 14 years old at that time. I still remember much about the last horrifying days of Saigon and my family's escape by sea. For a long time, I wanted to write about this sad journey for my family to keep for the later generation, and over the past year, I have been searching from my parents, old newspapers, and the internet for more information about those dark days to supplement the story. One day, while poring over the internet, I found the picture below of a boat named TOURANE 3 (Tourane was the name of the port city of Danang during the French colonialism); the boat that had brought my family out of Vietnam, the boat of our destiny. This picture had been taken by a sailor on a US Navy destroyer named The USS COCHRANE DDG-21, as it was approaching the TOURANE 3 to give assistance. That day was May 2, 1975. We had been on the ocean for two days and were less than 200 kilometers from the Vietnamese coast, but serious problems had begun to pile up.

As North Vietnamese forces tightened their stranglehold around Saigon, they increased their rocket attacks on the city and the airport, and by early dawn of April 29th, the airport had to be closed because the shelling was too intense. One hundred thousand communist troops now encircled Saigon. Over 3 million people were trapped inside the city with no way out.

Both my parents were educated people. My mother was principal of a high school. My father was Head of the Agricultural Research, working for the South Vietnamese Department of Agriculture. They fiercely opposed communism, and at the time wrote articles criticizing this ideology. Histories of the communist countries, including North Vietnam, made them understand the ruthless and deceitful policies of these regimes, which were meant to oppress and deprive people. They understood the communist's hatred of the educated people, and their brutality in trying to eliminate or shut down the intellectuals. Images of mass graves of innocent people massacred by communist forces in the city of Hue during Tet of 1968 (Vietnamese New Year) were still vivid in their minds. News leaked out from Cambodia about the brutal and inhumane policies to create a classless society by the Khmer Rouge after they had taken over this country a few weeks before, was latest evidence of communism's ruthlessness. Therefore, my parents were very worried about their fate and those of their children's. However, they had no money to buy their way out of Vietnam, nor connections to find an escape route. My father had several American friends, including one who was living in Washington State at the time, and another who was a US Department of Agriculture liaison working in Saigon. They had helped get my father and family on the US Government evacuation list; however, the number of Vietnamese with higher priority than my father was in the thousands, thus this option had gone nowhere.

Our family ran in the middle of the bombs and fighting from one relative's house to another depending on where it was safest. We rushed to my aunt's house at around 6 o'clock in the evening. That night, her small house had about 30 people, consisting of her family and relatives taking refuge from other places. People crowded in the house, lying all over the place, on beds, tables, and the floor. Throughout the night, Saigon was heavily shelled by communist forces. Rockets repeatedly fell indiscriminately far and near, all around us. The frail brick house was rattled violently by the explosions, as if it was about to break apart. Outside the window, the sky was lit up by burning fires. We lay awake all night, frightened.

The next morning, on April 29th, my family returned to our home because my aunt's house was too crowded, and the rockets had fallen too close to the house the night before. The U.S. Government had begun Operation Frequent Wind, to evacuate Americans and at-risk Vietnamese by helicopters to the US Navy Seventh Fleet waiting offshore. Forty-five CH-53 and CH-46 helicopters were used to transport people under the escort of Cobra attack helicopters. Rooftops of the U.S. embassy and other buildings were turned into landing zones for the helicopters to pick up people.

Around noon, a colleague of my dad informed him about an escape plan by sea and gave him the address of a ship captain to contact. When we reached the captain after an excruciating journey, he could not find any crew to run the ship. Disappointed, we started home. However, Father suggested to go to the Saigon river because he heard there were some boats there too. After a lot of shoving and pushing we got onto the boat, which however, showed no signs of any intention to move. Finally, we got off the ship and drove on the coast up the river. We were almost ready to give up when we saw a boy, aged about 10 running after our car and waving frantically. We stopped. He told us there was a boat if we continued driving up beside the river that had many people on it. If we wanted to leave, we should try to get on it.

We drove on following his advice, and sure enough, found a big boat, full of people, anchored on the other side of the river. Not too far in front of it, a bridge crossed over the river. On this side of the river, a small taxi boat was anchored beside the bank. We paid the taxi boat owner to take us across the river to the big boat. All of us, except my father, huddled under the roof of the taxi boat; my father stood outside by its nose. As we came close to the boat, a big man, wearing dark sunglasses, hands holding a gun, chased us away. My father begged him to let us on board, but he became angry and threatened to shoot if we did not go away.

In despair, my father told the owner of the taxi boat to turn it around and head back. As we were pulling away, we heard someone from the big boat calling my father: "Mung! Mung! Is that you? Don't go yet! Wait there!" That person was a brother of a friend of my parents. At the time, he was standing on the deck of the big boat. Upon hearing the commotion, he looked down and saw my father. After telling us to wait, he rushed to the big man with the gun and asked him to let my family on board. He told the man: "This is Mr. Mung and Mrs. Quyt. I know them well, please let them on." Upon hearing my parents' names, the big man hastily threw down the gun and rushed to the side of the boat, crying: "Oh heavens! Mung and Quyt? I did not recognize you, Mung! Where is Quyt? Poor you, I almost did you harm! Come up! Come up!" He hurriedly pulled us up onto the boat. We were puzzled, but quickly climbed on, fearing that he would change his mind. After getting on board, we realized that this big mean man was my mother's cousin, whom I called Uncle Kinh.

When Uncle Kinh had been a small boy, his family had gone through hard times, and my grandparents had given them a hand providing them shelter and food. Growing up, he had joined the military and rarely came home. My parents had not seen him for a long time, and therefore, earlier he and my father had not recognized each other.

Uncle Kinh explained to us that he was one of the 3 owners of the boat, The TOURANE 3. The TOURANE 3 had been a commerce boat, transporting goods on the Mekong River between Saigon and Phnom Penh, the Cambodian capital. A few weeks earlier, uncle Kinh had planned an escape by sea. He and two other families had bought the TOURANE 3, fixed it up, and stocked it with fuel and supplies, then sold spaces to families who had wanted to leave the country. When we arrived, the boat had about 320 people and was very crowded. Most of the people stayed under deck, stacking up on each other in a hot, suffocating atmosphere filled with the smells of burning engine oil and vomit. There was one bathroom on the deck by the control room. Only men were allowed to stay on deck. Women and children could go up only to use the bathroom.

Uncle Kinh had picked this location to anchor the boat and wait for the right time to escape to sea because it had been in a remote area with very few people passing by. By night time, uncle Kinh and several other people negotiated with the guards, and finally convinced them to let us go, with the condition that we had to wait another two hours for the tide to recede low enough so that the boat could pass through underneath the bridge, and that we would stop near Nha Be River, a main river leading out to the sea. Overly anxious and concerned about the fast deteriorating conditions and the guards changing their mind, the owners decided to depart before the two hours were up. The boat headed down the river and slowly passed under the bridge. However, the tide was still high, and the boat did not clear the bridge completely. Its roof scraped the bottom of the bridge hard and shook it violently. Panic, the guards on the bridge opened fire at our boat. Rounds and rounds of bullets hit the boat and flew overhead and all around us. Onboard, everyone was terrified. We lay flat on the floor, yelling, crying, praying. I thought either we were going to be killed or arrested. Luckily, as the boat cleared the bridge, the guards stopped shooting. We continued down river. By then, it was dark.

We were going for a distance, when suddenly, bright light lit up the river; a voice blasted over a loudspeaker ordering us to stop the boat. Ahead of us, a South Vietnamese Navy river patrol boat, lights glaring, was fast approaching, and stopped in front of our boat, blocking its way. Its machine guns were aiming directly at our boat, ready to shoot if we didn't obey the order. We turned off the engine and dropped the anchor. However, because of our crew's inexperience, the anchor was not dropped correctly, and therefore, the boat did not stop and slowly drifted down stream and rammed into the patrol boat. Thinking that they were being attacked, the soldiers on the patrol boat opened fire, sending everyone screaming, crying, and begging. The screaming and crying mixing with the deafening sounds of machine guns, created an atmosphere full of madness and chaos. I thought we would be killed this time for sure. Suddenly, the shooting stopped. Everyone became silent, listening. After searching our boat, the soldiers let us go and advised us to stop for the night after we passed the Nha Be area because the situation was too dangerous. We did what we were told and stopped after passing Nha Be. We anchored the boat in the middle of the river, for fear that people would climb onto the boat during the night. All through the night, U.S. Marine helicopters continued to ferry people out to the fleet. In a distance, the Saigon sky lit up every time a rocket hit the ground and exploded.

At dawn the next day, April 30th, I woke up to the sounds of panic and anxiety on the boat. There were problems with the boat engine, and the shootings the night before blew some holes on one side of the boat, causing water to leak in and tilted the boat to one side. After fixing the engine and pumping out the water, we pulled anchor and continued our journey toward the ocean. Because of engine trouble, the boat ran at a maximum speed of only three knots. At about 10:30 that morning, South Vietnamese President Duong Van Minh surrendered unconditionally to the communist forces and ordered all South Vietnamese soldiers to lay down their arms and let whoever wanted to leave the country leave. Shortly afterward, boats of all sizes, packed with people, rushed out to the main rivers, and headed toward the ocean. Many South Vietnamese soldiers, who had just retreated from the battlefields, commandeered small boats, and chased after the bigger ones and climbed on. Because our boat was slow, it was easily caught up by them. By the time we reached the river mouth, we had over 500 people on board. The deck was crammed with soldiers and littered with guns and munitions. After a while, the boat listed to one side because too much water had leaked in, and we had to turn on the pump to pump out the water. By late afternoon, we could no longer see the shore of Vietnam.

The boat ran all day and night, and occasionally, we had to stop to check the engine. All the big and small boats that had been with us on the river, had left us far behind and disappeared on the horizon. We were all alone on the vast open sea, with nothing else in sight besides the shadow of the boat gliding on the water surface, and no other sound besides the tiresome knocking of the engine. After two days, we started to run out of food. Each of us received a fistful of rice and some salt for the day. Water was also limited. As for fuel, there was not enough for us to reach any place. We were worried and began to lose hope. On the morning of May 2nd, disagreement broke out among the soldiers; one group wanted to turn the boat around and go back to Vietnam, and another wanted to continue going east, hoping to be found and rescued by the U.S. Navy. The two groups of soldiers were ready to fight with each other, when suddenly, a U.S. Navy search helicopter flew over high above the sky, then circled down closer to our boat to observe and flew away. We cheered in happiness but turned into despair not long afterward when we did not see the helicopter return. The soldiers suspected that the owners had refused the U.S. help and brought them out to interrogate. Luckily, among the servicemen, there were two South Vietnamese Air Force helicopter pilots who had been observing the situation and trying to find ways to diffuse the tension. They reasoned with the two groups of soldiers and convinced them to drop their guns. We were not sure what was going to happen to us next, when out in a distance, a U.S. Navy destroyer was speeding toward us. It was the USS COCHRANE. Apparently, the search helicopter had called it to come to our aid. I stood watching in awe, as the giant war ship was approaching, like an angel suddenly appeared on the open sea.

After pulling aside our boat, the crew of the COCHRANE passed over to us water and milk in large plastic bags. They gave us the location of a holding area to go to, so that we could be picked up by a larger ship. Then the COCHRANE sped up and fast disappeared on the horizon.

The holding area, about 200 kilometers from the Vietnamese shore, was where the US Navy 7th Fleet assembled to prepare for transporting people, who had escaped Saigon, to the Philippines. Hundreds of boats and ships of all sizes, among them the South Vietnamese Navy fleet, had been directed by the U.S. Navy to come there. Seaworthy ships were ordered to pick up people on overcrowded boats which were in no shape for the high sea. It was in the evening when we arrived at the holding area. Lights from boats and ships lit up the area like a floating city on the ocean. Around midnight, we were picked up by a South Vietnamese Navy ship named HQ-16 Ly Thuong Kiet.

In the afternoon of the next day, May 3rd, after being checked and supplied by US Navy ships, the rag tag fleet, including 29 South Vietnamese Navy ships carrying over 30,000 refugees and 10 U.S. transport and merchant ships carrying over 40,000 refugees, departed. Two rows of ships, stretching for miles, slowly headed for the Philippines under the escort of U.S. Navy ships. On board the HQ-502 were 5,000 people. We reached the Philippines on May 8th and were transferred to a merchant ship named SS Green Forest along with 3,000 other people and taken to Guam Island. By midnight on May 13th, we reached Guam. My family stayed in a refugee camp on Guam Island for about a month, then were sponsored by my dad's friend in Washington State and settled down there.

> Digested from the original written by Loc Khac Nguyen, April 2010. To Mom, Dad, Quy, Bao, Trang, and Thu (Loc's two brothers and two sisters)

The following is a flood of emails that went back and forth between the Mung and Szablya children (by then middle aged people) as a reaction to Loc's story.

I am letting our son Louis tell you the continuation of our side of the story:

Sent: Saturday, June 05, 2010 6:32 p.m.

Subject: RE: Escape Vietnam in 1975

Loc,

Thank you so much for sharing this with us.

I remember the day that your dad called our house in Pullman from Guam. I was the only one home and took the call.

We had been worried sick about you and your family. I had taken calls from your friend from the U.S. Department of Agriculture letting us know that you were on the list and that you should go to the embassy. He let us know in case you called us and to encourage us to make any calls to help push your family up on the priority list. I was on pins and needles waiting to hear anything from your dad.

When I got the call, it seemed surreal. I couldn't believe that it was Mung on the phone. I had to ask him a couple of times because we had failed in our attempt to help him out of Viet Nam.

When I really understood that it was Mung on the phone my eyes filled with tears of joy that your family was safe – I couldn't wait to tell my parents.

I waited for them to come home and for some reason they parked at the bottom of the stairs of the Shirley Street house. When I saw that they were there I ran outside to the top of the stairs and yelled "Mung called, Mung called." I don't think that they believed me because they too thought that your family had not been able to get out. When I told them what had happened they were so excited. We all shed tears of joy and then immediately tried to figure out how we could grease the skids and get you to Pullman.

It turns out that it was our family that was blessed when your family came to Pullman. The deep friendship and fun times are something that I will always treasure. I am a better person for having known you and your entire family.

Thank you and I love you, Louis

Ilike wrote this:

Dear Nguyen Family,

I came across a letter that my mother wrote to me in April 1975. I've scanned it. The last paragraph reads:

"We are desperately trying to get Mung and his family out from Vietnam. As it stands now, it would have been $12,000 to get him out, because the exit visas are $1,000 per person and then the fare. We are trying to get some loan through the bishop and at the same time we wrote to the Ambassador of the United States in Saigon, to do his best, including getting the exit visas for him. Please, pray for him that all should go as is best for everybody concerned. We love you all and think of you a lot. Hugs and kisses: Anyukatok"

As we know, this effort didn't work, but they were always trying!! We are so very glad that you are with us!

Love, Helen (Ilike)

Loc's answer (Mung's third boy, was Head of the office of IBM in Taiwan, married, two boys):

Woa, this is so sweet and touching...thanks for sharing, Helen (Ilike). A few years ago, I received a package from my mom that had been given to her by Helen, your mom. The package contained many letters and postcards exchanged between my parents and yours in the early 70s, and all the letters and cables back and forth between your parents and their American contacts in Vietnam in a desperate effort to get us out of VN. I read them all on the evening that I received the package with teary eyes. I have scanned them into my computer but have not figured out the best way to sort them out so that they could be shared. If anyone is interested, perhaps, I can send them on CDs.

Loc wrote this email to me:

Dear Helen,

Yes, my dad sent me all the correspondence from the earlier years of your friendship and during the frantic last days of South Vietnam, and they are a real treasure. Thanks for saving them!!! Uncle John told us about the novena at a dinner at Janos' house in Seattle when we visited you a few years back. Every time we talk about the events that what happened during our escape, we can't help but think that someone was indeed watching out for us the whole way.

Love, Loc

I wrote back to Loc:

Great Idea!

Thank you, Loc, for writing down your memories. They are so well written and exciting!

Great is the power of prayer! We were about halfway through the novena, when your phone call arrived. You can't imagine our happiness!

We were so glad because we ourselves knew what it was like to escape and finally make it!

Thank you for always giving us so much of yourselves and for being our brothers and sisters, thank you for becoming our true family.

Love you all, Helen (Mother)

From Bao K Nguyen:

Hello everyone from Vietnam.

Yes, I am trampling out and about in Vietnam again. I'm getting the country ready for Rita :)

> *[Author's note: our daughter Rita was working as an environmental scientist in countries nearby.]*

Didn't have much access to the Internet for periods at a time and missed out on the early conversation.

But..but...but John and Helen "forced" us to eat chicken the first day or so of us getting to Pullman. WHOLE pieces of thighs, legs, breasts! "With your hands!" he boomed when he saw Quy, Loc and I trying to show off our newly acquired fork-and-knife skills on the chicken pieces :) We'd never eaten so much chicken in our lives prior! And Steve nearly choked me to death not telling me "chewing tobacco" didn't REALLY mean "chew" at the Boy Scout's camp Grizzly!

Through your love, and of the Seamans' whom Loc and I lived with for a while, we knew of the beautiful America. Hey...no wise-ass comments about the kind of American I turned out to be, LOL.

> *[Author's comment: Bao became a chemical engineer at the Air Force Academy and a jet pilot. Later he worked for NASA before he retired from the Air Force. This was the time when he went to Vietnam to help with environmental cleanup. He is married and has three children].*

John has passed on and all of us are all over the world at any given time. For one reason or the other we failed to keep everyone in close, regular contact. But the gratitude and love from us to all of the Szablya's will always be.

We love you, Bao

P.S. I know that there will be many stories and memories to tell of the families and the "personalities" LOL. Since it's difficult to organize get-togethers and group emails tend to be buried, what does everyone think about setting up a "members-only" Facebook page where we all can come, check in, share stories, memories, and gossip? I can volunteer to do that :)

From Nguyen-Jahiel, Kim Thu (youngest girl, has a PhD in education, as does her husband. They adopted two children from Ethiopia).

Dearest Szablya family,

I share Loc's sentiments 100%! I was a wee girl of just eight years old, too young to understand the magnitude of our experiences. But I know that we seven Nguyen members owe our second lives to all of you. The roof that you put over our heads was just the beginning, just a shelter from the climate. It is the unselfish love, support, patience (I wonder how many toys and outfits Niki had to share with me!), and support from each of you that gave us footing for our new life!

As a little girl, I felt many hands extended to us to give us a new start in life. This is the reason that I went into education...to see whether I can help someone else, as you all have helped us. Unfortunately, I must report to you that I'm not doing much good, according to all the reports on public education (hahaha!).

Much love and with great gratitude, Kim-Thu

46

The Mungs arrived and with that a unique and beautiful relationship started between the two families.

The Seamans family, our co-sponsors took Bao and Loc, the 2nd and 3rd boys, to their home, while all the girls decided to sleep in Ilike's room, which was now Sandy and Rita's room, upstairs. That meant not only our girls and those of the Mungs, but the two cousins who came from Toronto to visit us. Quy, the first boy, slept with our boys. The seven girls arranged themselves in sleeping bags all around the room. Now, if you would have wanted to take even one step – that was at your own risk! The Luedekings, our dear neighbors, who had five girls of their own, offered to have some of the girls come over to them, but they wanted to stay together and giggle. Not that they would have had a language in common, but they learned fast by "show and tell." What do I mean by that? For example, Niki would throw a ball to Kim Thu and say "catch," or "run" while demonstrating. Everyone picked another of the same age and off they went. Of course, the older boys had already studied English at school. Steve organized them and the four of them formed a "company." They went to our friends' homes and offered to mow their lawn, do their weeding, or any other kind of work they were able to do. Pretty soon they had quite a lot of work and were making money.

Quy and Louis became good friends. We could not believe our eyes what all Quy could do. He could do push-ups by using only one finger of one hand to lean on. He had a stick on a chain and did fantastic tricks with it. When Louis tried to imitate just the simplest swing, he uttered: "Are you trying to kill me?" while they both laughed. Louis gave up on that one.

I was on the phone most of the time organizing the start of their new lives, while Mung and Quyt cooked for our little "army" the yummiest Vietnamese food.

Mung visited his old department and established himself as a PhD student. He was now entitled to university housing. They arrived at the right time, in the summer, when all the housing traded inhabitants. In two weeks time – during which we had the time of our lives living together –

they acquired their own "hut" in university housing, as we had done when we had arrived in Vancouver, B.C.

In the meantime, more Vietnamese families kept arriving and Quyt took it on herself to visit all of them. She walked all over town and gave the newcomers encouraging words, helping them with everything they needed, and interpreting for them.

A neighboring town adopted a family with seven children. Their mother was alone with them. The father was missing, so the oldest boy became the head of the family. The well-to-do little town with about 1,000 inhabitants or less provided them with everything: they received a home, appliances, food, clothes, everything they possibly needed. Mung and Quyt were not only informed of every new family, they were their advisers. So, Mung came to us and said: "These people have everything, but there is something they need." "What is it?" John asked. "They need work," Mung answered.

Now the town had a problem. What in the world should they give them for work? This was a farming town. Here farms are not quite handled the same way as in Vietnam at the time. One person could easily take care of several hundred acres with all the machines they had. It was not even harvest time yet. They could not yet communicate very well. After racking their brains, they came up with a temporary solution: they asked the family to sweep the school yard, keep the school clean. So, this hard problem got settled.

In the meantime, Quyt confided in me that she was bleeding rather heavily when her time of the month came. Our dear friend, Dr. Devlin stepped right in. It turned out she already had this condition for a while. So, Dr. Devlin performed a hysterectomy, and no one accepted any money for the hospital, or the treatment.

The Spokane Archdiocese was getting more and more Vietnamese families. Mung told us that very many of them turned to the Catholics for help because they had known them from home. Our two families: the Nguyens and the Szablyas, became the official advisors to the Archdiocese on refugees.

The children started school in September and did extremely well. Mung and Quyt took education very seriously and the discipline was great in their home. They had to study hard. We advised all Vietnamese parents to put their children in those classes they had just finished in Vietnam, the way we did it in Germany. This way they had to study only the English language because they had already learned the material of that grade.

One day I told Quyt about a bargain at the grocery store. Sometimes they sold big turkeys at 29 cents a pound. They cut the frozen turkey in half with a saw. One half was just right for our family. She said they actually thought chicken was better for them because they cooked it in a pressure cooker.

The chicken was so well cooked they could eat the bones, which they could not do with the turkey.

Quyt started working in the library. In those days there were so many faculty spouses around town at any given time that they would only pay the minimum wage of two dollars per hour for a librarian. Quyt, however, managed to get more. She persuaded them that having a Masters from Loyola, she deserved more. I was amazed that they conceded and gave her more.

In the coming years our lives were entirely intertwined. We enjoyed each others' company and the children loved being together.

1976! That magical year! Besides it being the bicentennial of the United States, we had our own news, surprises, mourning and happiness.

That was the year when our first grandchild, Anna Ili (Ili was my nickname from Ilona), was born. I always said she was a "Daughter of the Revolution" in more ways than one. Not only was she constantly active and moving around, but she was also a direct descendant of William Hooper, one of the signers of the Declaration of Independence. It was hard to believe she was the "daughter of refugees" too.

In February I finally graduated with a 4.00 GPA. I was overjoyed!

Then everything seemed so empty. Suddenly all the pressure and studying was over and I started to feel like I did not know what to do with myself. I was quite depressed coming home from church one Saturday afternoon. When we arrived home a great surprise party awaited me. John arranged it with my professors, the Head of Department, and friends. He bought me a beautiful nightgown and robe that I have been eyeing for quite a while. I was surrounded by love and laughter. We had such a great time! All our guests appreciated me, the person I was, my graduation, but above all my family. My family of course were the greatest! They were all "in" on it. I understood what a treasure I had, as I was drinking in all their appreciation.

I had been writing all along while I was studying, but now, I realized: my opportunity was here to write the "book of my life," the great novel to end all novels, the true story of our lives. Suddenly my personal life again had a purpose. One goal was achieved, and now I started another great adventure.

In June I went through graduation. For that occasion John decided he was going to sit with the faculty and got himself a gown for the occasion. Pomp and circumstance… what lovely sounds I was longing to hear; played for me.

Father could not come, he asked John to buy beautiful flowers for me. John bought a big bouquet of red roses in a nice big green vase that I have to this day. Father was still working full time as a medical doctor, but it was still a disappointment for both of us.

Before graduation, I had a complete hysterectomy. Father told us that as soon as we experience any difficulty with our female organs we should get it all out. He said that because of our mother's untimely death at the age of 48 from sarcoma of the uterus, which killed her in six months. I listened to him. I could have no more kids, but I also had my first grandchild that year.

John's mother fell again and broke her hip. The first time she fell she broke her collarbone. She nicely recovered from that, but when she fell again... John was talking with the doctor on the phone who said he will not operate because she would die on the operating table. She was still so weak from the first fall. However, if he does not, she will get pneumonia and will die from that. John agreed with the doctor that he would keep her comfortable. She was 83 years old.

Just to defy death, the phone call came from Barry that Anna Ili was born. We immediately took off to Seattle, where they lived at the time. They were home from the hospital in less than 24 hours, so I stayed with her and John went on to see his mother in Vancouver, B.C.

John's mother had bad osteoporosis, but she lived to welcome into the world her first great-granddaughter. She was overjoyed before she closed her eyes forever.

None of us had much money at the time. Ilike and Barry worked hard to establish their theater company, while Barry worked as a night janitor in The Olympic Hotel and Ilike worked as a waitress. We had five of the children still at home. While I was taking care of Ilike and Anna we were trying to figure out how many different ways we can manage to make omelettes, the cheapest protein. Whenever Anna started to cry and I wanted the parents to have some rest, I took her in my arms and told her: "Come on, let's boil some water!" While the water was boiling, I walked around with her and talked to her. By the time the water was ready for her, she stopped crying.

Seattle was the headquarters for Boeing. One day when I was looking up into the sky, a huge plane stood there in the air, or at least it looked like it stood there. This was impossible, so I looked some more. It was the first 747 jumbo jet I had ever seen. It was brand new at the time. Those huge planes indeed looked like they were standing, while moving full speed ahead.

After a week I had to go back to my family. Ilike drove me to the airport. We kissed good-bye and she went straight for the escalator. She told me much later: "I just could not turn around. If I would have turned around, I would have broken down crying. I wanted so much for you to stay, but I knew you had to go. I knew I had to do it on my own from now on. It was only a week! I had to go back to work very soon, or... but I was also happy of course with my newborn. Just everything felt so difficult." Which was all so very understandable.

As soon as I got home, we got word that our best-loved relatives of ours, Józsi and Ilonka Schmaltz, my godfather and his wife, arrived from Hungary. They were the ones who had adopted my sister at the time I got married, at the time the Hungarian "Capitalists" people who did not agree with the Communists were deported in Hungary, in 1951.

In 1976 this was a once in a lifetime opportunity. We have not seen them since we had left Hungary and did not know whether we would be able to see each other again. We were supposed to meet in Osoyoos, British Columbia. That meant we had to delay John's mother's funeral by a week.

The golden sunshine, the shallow, warm water of the lake, made our holidays joyous. We could not talk enough about everything in Hungary, there in the wide-open nature, where no one could spy on us. It meant we could discuss everything openly. Józsi had fantastic humor. We were laughing our way through the days spent together. What we didn't know was that it was the last time we would see them alive.

After this memorable meeting we went to Vancouver, B.C. where the funeral of John's mother took place at – where else? but in the Our Lady of Hungary Church, for which all of us had worked so hard. In those days it was an exception, but we had a celebration of her life, her Birthday into Heaven. Our dear Hungarian priest friend, the Jesuit Fr. Horányi, wore the colorful "kalocsai" embroidered vestments and gave a beautiful sermon. The church was full of people who loved her and were good friends. At the cemetery we stood at the grave that she picked out and where her husband was already buried. The view of the city from there is spectacular. That is why she decided on this gravesite. Right there we took a family picture with two-week-old Anna in my arms. That was the photo we used for our Christmas letter in 1976, but we told no one where and when it was taken. Louis brought along Kate, who was going to become his wife. He had already taken Kate to see his grandmother while she was well. After the funeral we went to our favorite Chinese place with John's mother's closest friends and exchanged happy stories about her.

When we got back to Pullman, Kinga Székessy, our good friends' daughter, came for three weeks from Bogota, Colombia. She was just between our daughters Sandy and Rita in age. Until that time we spoke Hungarian one week and German the next with the kids. We did not want them to forget. However, Kinga spoke only Spanish, English and Hungarian. We had to speak Hungarian when she was present. They had such a good time with the kids, I told her: "Why don't you stay for the entire year?" She loved the idea and discussed it with her parents. It was settled. She would stay for the year.

In the fall, Professor Kind's daughter, Christine arrived. She was 19 years old at the time. She only spoke English and German. This determined the only language shared by everyone: English. Nevertheless, we tried to speak Hungarian and German, depending on who was in the room. You know how difficult it is to keep track? In the end though, it became automatic to switch to the right language. For the second semester, Louis's sweetheart Kate, and Christine, moved into an apartment together, so the only guest left was Kinga. She did not seem like a guest at all. In order to have her go to public school, we had to become her legal guardians, which her parents signed without objection. We were good friends with the Székessy family and Kinga quickly became like another daughter to us.

When she returned to Colombia, Rita and Niki joined her for six weeks, where they had a delightful time. On their way there they visited a family in California. When they were boarding the plane to Bogota, as they stood in line, Kinga understood what was spoken in Spanish and quickly told the other girls that the people in front of them bribed the clerk, who put them on the plane and dumped the girls. They were stuck in Los Angeles for the night. Our travel agent immediately called the airline and made a great fuss. She talked with the VP and kept repeating: "But children? Traveling alone? You can dump children?" Finally, it dawned on the airline what terrible mistake they had made. (Luckily, our son Jancsi was at the airport and they could sleep at his place, but the airline did not know about that.) The next day Avianca took the children to Colombia in First Class; and the other airline arranged the trip for them, as they had no empty seats on their plane.

When we had left everything behind us in Hungary, we knew that what people cannot take away from you are your love for one another, your knowledge, and your memories. That is why we tried to give our children every possible education and experience whatever we could, even if it was practically beyond our means.

47

For our 25th wedding anniversary Jancsi brought his sweetheart, Marcey Painter. One nice summer day, while they were rehearsing for a Summer Palace show, Jancsi noticed himself saying: "Would you marry me?" Both of them majored in theater. In one of the plays, "Bad Seed" Jancsi played Leroy. He did such a great job that a friend of ours admired the actor, who played Leroy, but did not recognize him.

Another great theatrical adventure was when they were filming Lewis and Clark's story. Jancsi played their French Canadian guide. This entailed having to jump into the frozen river. The director was so concerned, he stood there with a warm coat, to wrap him right into it. For this he was admitted into the Actor's Guild, without which you cannot get a part in films, but that required to have already had seven minutes of film experience. Go, figure!

Jancsi and Marcey were married in Longview where Marcey's parents lived. There was a nice little church that was Marcey's favorite and Fr. Skok, our parish priest, came down with us to marry them. All four of our girls were bridesmaids. My father came from Winnipeg for the occasion.

During the wedding Louis and Kate decided that they just had to follow their example, which they did the following year. To their wedding not only Father, but my two sisters came from Toronto and brought Elizabeth's two daughters, Rita and Edith, with them. We had a marvelous time together.

Driving them home from Spokane to Pullman suddenly the Northern Lights appeared in the sky. We stopped the car and wondered at the beauty of them for a long time. The lights were an intense red and green and danced through the sky radiating their magic. It is rare for the Northern Lights to come that far south, but they do sometimes and then they outdo themselves in splendor.

On the wedding day, in the morning, just when all of us wanted to take a shower, the drains became clogged. Mrs. Eddie, our dear neighbor, came to our rescue. She let all of us take a shower at her house, while Richard Ellsworth, a plumber friend discovered the cause. The roots of our trees had grown into the pipes. He had to dig up the whole yard along the pipe to fix the problem, which he did. On the same day.

Needless to say, that did not spoil our mood and we proceeded to the beautiful wedding ceremony.

Louis and Kate married in Sacred Heart Church where they led the Saturday afternoon Folk Mass choir, with our children forming most of it. Louis was away as an intern in another town before they got married and decided he wanted to embroider Kate's wedding dress with a Kalocsai pattern. Kate in turn made Louis' shirt.

Louis still had a year to go before graduation in electrical engineering. Kate had just started university. They moved into student housing and lived their happy newlywed life. Before Louis' graduation they already knew that they were pregnant. On September 24th Nadine was born. By then they were living in Spokane. Louis got a job with the Washington Water Power Company. As a part of his job, he became the engineer who computerized the utility. Boeing was the manufacturer and Louis helped them test every part of the computer for the Skada project. The project made the cover of WWP's annual report. Louis always loved new projects. Once the work was finished, he looked for something else that was just the latest trend and chose to work on that.

Steve had been working at White Drugs as the manager of the photo department since he was 16. For his High School graduation, he put together a fabulous slide show with the photos blending into each other, which was a very avant-garde method at the time.

After a cavalcade of graduations, marriages, and our new granddaughter Nadine, Steve started WSU just as the time for our second sabbatical arrived.

This time we went only with the three youngest girls: Sandy 19, Rita 17, and Niki 12. We were guests of the University of the West Indies (UWI), where John was going to teach for a year and the electric utility company with which he was doing consulting. It was of course the Juliens, who invited us and they reserved an apartment for our arrival. They happened to be off the island, so they sent charming people, the head of personnel at the electric company and his wife Ken and Kim Bailey, to help us settle into our new life.

On our way to Trinidad the plane glided over green and blue landscapes on the islands, interrupted by golden, sandy beaches and small towns. Suddenly I noticed something I thought was impossible. Under our plane the water was divided into royal blue and the beautiful turquoise of the Caribbean.

"Look!" I pointed to John and the kids. "There is a straight line in the middle of the water!"

"This is where the Atlantic Ocean and the Caribbean Sea meet," John said.

"But, how can it be so straight? As if it was two pools that meet. Unbelievable!" I have never seen anything like it before, or ever after.

We needed our sense of humor to find the way to cope with our new reality. Just how this happened I want to illustrate through the letter we wrote to our daughter Ilike and her husband Barry. We finally sent it to all our friends. The date was October 9th, when we finally settled into our new apartment.

Dear Friends,

I washed the spinach today! What an achievement! Water behaved very erratically and came on, just like that, in the kitchen, not in the middle of the living room, at 8:30 in the morning. So, I used the opportunity. I longed to wash that spinach before it went completely bad, but every time when we yearned for food, water was non-existent. Of course, we have some stored in one of our bathtubs. As an exercise in futility, we have more water-using equipment than at any time during our married years. After all, what more can one ask for? Who needs a river if one has a bridge above the desert?

As soon as we got here to Piarco International Airport, we spotted our boxes right beside the back wall, under some broken windows. Alas! it was not for us to approach them. First, immigration.

"Where are your visas?" We did not know we needed them. Although it seemed that we would have to take advantage of our Baltimore hosts' hospitality again, when we happened to mention that Dr. St. Claire King from the university was there, besides the piles and piles of luggage. The man was somewhat pacified, uttering an "oh!" then proceeded to fish out applications for our visas and promptly issued them for a 100 and odd TT dollars (Trinidad and Tobago dollars). Lucky that we had exchanged some money at the Miami Airport. Then we all loaded into three cars: Dr. King's and two taxis. (As an explanation: Dr. King was an old friend, a former Head of Department. The Juliens were off the island, therefore he came to pick us up.) We were told that in the meantime our house somehow got relocated and was no longer in Port-of-Spain, but in St. Augustine, and was not yet ready. Therefore, they are going to put us up in the Holiday Inn. This "luxury" hotel was built eight years ago. (We later found out "luxury" meant running water! Just kidding!) It had the only revolving restaurant in the Caribbean at the time. Maria, my sister Marietta's daughter and her brand-new husband, Bob Barnes, arrived two days later. They were on their honeymoon. We had dinner with them at the fabulous restaurant and then again in the Hilton.

The first day we walked all over downtown, using the opportunity to see as much as we could. Frederick Street, the busiest shopping street with its colorful crowd enchanted us. We went to see the Cathedral and, on our way back from there, the tropical rain showed us it's torrential downpour. We were totally drenched, but to our greatest surprise in five minutes our clothes were dry again. The rain was a lukewarm delight.

Then we had lunch with St. Claire and his wife, Mary (St. Claire is pitch black, while Mary is Irish blonde, blue eyed and milky white). They have three beautiful boys. Whenever we met we had more fun with them 'than a barrel of monkeys.'

We were taken everywhere to settle our problems. One of the first places was the university where the man who was supposed to dish out the salaries recognized very cordially that we existed. However, he did not keep it a secret that he had no record whatsoever of our existence. The secretary was on vacation but seeing the overwhelming evidence of our presence he sent someone to fetch the file from wherever it was to be found. In five minutes, they had a file as thick as my arm. While walking from office to office in a perpetual daze, with the speed of a zombie, I found many funny, sweet posters and jokes pasted all over filing cabinets, desks, whatsoever. Any place where it was possible to find an empty square inch. One of them I kept repeating to myself ever since, and not only to myself, we tease each other with its wisdom: 'Everything cometh to the one who waiteth, especially if he worketh like hell while he waiteth.' And that is the secret of existence in Trinidad. Thank God that we had been before. Otherwise I would not have stayed a day. In possession of this wisdom, we simply enjoyed the Holiday Inn. It took the girls exactly three days to realize why it was awful to have money, to be 'rich.' They felt it was boring, scary, and extremely restrictive. They wanted to work, to study, to do something.

"No problem," we were assured that soon the apartment would be ready. We went on hearing that for the next 10 days, but we had no complaints. We had a luxury life in the hotel. The beautiful swimming pool had bar stools in the water. The bartender stood right there in front of the well-stocked bar. The food was delicious. The girls started to get acquainted with tropical foods. We loved all of them. The deep fried "flying fish" from Tobago was my favorite.

The apartment as well as the university was in St. Augustine, which was quite a distance from town. We needed to arrange for the girls to go to school. The schools that had their records since the spring, made them wait two weeks to get in and that was unbelievably fast in the conditions here. The Minister of Education had to sign their application personally and that only happened because St. Claire King had a good friend in charge of this in the ministry.

We wanted Sandy to go to the University of the West Indies (UWI), but it was hard to get in because the places were needed for those coming from the Caribbean region. They did not want to take her because, though she had finished high school in the States, she did not have the equivalent of the Canadian 13th grade, called 'A-levels' here. They did not seem to understand that this is one thing she never had or intended to have. In the end a marvelous solution was reached. She got into all the specifically Trinidadian subjects: history of the West Indies and Caribbean English.

After 10 days we finally moved into our place in St. Augustine. We were shown the townhouse, located on three stories. When we got to the bathroom on the third level it had about 10 inches of construction debris in the bathtub and not a drop of water coming out of any of the faucets. The toilet could not be flushed either. At this point I wanted to cry. Is this what a "perfectly ready luxury" apartment was like?

At this point John, as well as Kim and Ken Bailey who were there to help us move in decided they would take me shopping for the essentials and John said:

"Just leave this to me and the girls!"

So, off we went into the grocery store and started shopping for everything. That is everything that was available. For instance, there was no salt available anywhere on the island until the next shipment would arrive on a ship. What can I use instead??? I was looking and looking and finally found a salt mixture with spices and bought some of that. I bought wonderful tropical fruits and vegetables, cereal, flour, sugar, rum of course, and the only available soft drink at the moment, which happened to be ginger ale. I bought some cheese, which we really liked. I later asked an American friend what kind of cheese it was. She looked at me with a matter-of-fact expression: "It is cheese." It was the only available cheese at the time on the island and it would be until a French cheese shop opened as the year went by. There was no butter available. When the ship comes in…

By the time we got home John and the girls did a miracle job with the bathtub. At least there was no more debris in it. No water either, but that would have been too much of a miracle. There was a "standpipe" in front of the townhouse and when the water pressure did not come all the way up to the third floor you could always bring water from there. The water was potable, at least we drank it all the time without boiling it and never got sick. Sometimes there was some red earth in it, but only a few traces and not always.

People are the greatest redeeming value in the island. They are friendly and wonderful. First of all St. Claire King and Mary, as well as Kim and Ken Bailey with their daughter Marcia, were always more than helpful. All our neighbors in the condominium complex were exceptional, especially an East Indian lady, Zilda Ramdin, a widow, who was general manager at the newest branch of an old department store on the island, Kirpalani's.

Naturally, we had a joyous reunion with the Juliens as soon as they got back onto the island from their trip. We went to their home and they came to ours, we went to exhibitions, big island events, concerts, and performances, to the Hilton show and of course, they stood behind all the good things we received in Trinidad. Ken was Chairman and Head of almost everything, among them T&TEC and the UWI. Pat was just as wonderful being his wife. They could achieve practically everything, but even they said as soon as we had met: "You can ask for anything except for a telephone. Not even we can get you one."

Of course, by now everyone has cell phones, but that was then, and this is now.

Next big adventure was driving on the island. This gave me the idea of writing an article "A tribute to traffic in Trinidad" to illustrate my driving the girls to school and driving to other necessary and unavoidable places.

We were given a car by T&TEC. Driving was much better here than we expected. It is confusing and impossible, but that we expected. We found a cartoon here with six identical cartoons under each other of a man driving with his hand hanging out the window. The explanations of the identical hand signals are as follows: "I want to turn right," "I want to turn left," "It is safe to pass," "Unsafe to pass," "I am slowing down," "I am stopping."

When we first arrived in Trinidad a friend said: "If you want to take a picture you only need a pinhole camera. Nothing ever moves in Trinidad."

However, as soon as I started to commute on the roads and finally, driving a car myself (on the left side of the road), I had quite the opposite opinion. Everything moves all the time. I mean, even if you only want to tell something to a friend on the other end of town, you throw yourself into a car, or into a taxi and carry the message yourself. It is quicker than using the phone, even if you happen to have one.

Besides, Trinidad drivers are courteous and make your trip great fun.

Where else in the world could you say that if you get yourself into a jam you will be accommodated? Like the time when I tried to make a right turn (equivalent to our left turn) onto Eastern Main Road, coming out from the University Campus' Main Gate and simply inched my way into the intersection. Instantly someone would stop and wave me by, while the other, oncoming driver would also stop. All they expect is a friendly smile and a "thank you" wave. Or, when I wanted to make a U turn in the middle of another major road? Both lines of traffic stopped until I finished my maneuver.

The taxi drivers are especially helpful. They halt at the smallest hand signal given by a pedestrian and not noticed by any of the other drivers. The taxi drivers risk their lives to stop and let out their fares as soon as one of them as much as touches their shoulder. It is really not their fault if someone is following them so closely that he has to slam on his brakes and send the passengers flying against the windshield or he has to swerve into the oncoming traffic. After all, we all should have known better and have gone into the third lane of the two-lane street. As my 17-year-old daughter, who had a driver's license remarked after having watched my driving for a month: "That third lane is always there! Only sometimes there are no cars in it."

The ingenuity of Trinidadian drivers is endless. I have now seen two lane streets that were used as four lane ones with the result that when one turns into the streets it seems that they are one-way with three lanes of traffic coming at you. That is right at the fourth lane…in a two-lane street.

The pedestrians are very careful and circumspect indeed. Children in uniform walk along the "dual carriageway" (divided highway) and spread into the non-existent "third lane," but mothers of younger ones make sure that their children get across safely. They walk them to the middle of the highway holding them tight and even stop oncoming traffic by lifting their hands, then watch as the children scramble across. Stately old ladies with umbrellas also lift their arms as policemen do in order to stop the speeding cars and the drivers manage to slow down from 100 km/hr to zero speed before they hit the ladies, donkey carts, men driving animals, such as horses, goats, pigs, geese, live chickens and dead dogs. They don't even hit other cars that decide to stop at one of the vendors that line both sides of the "dual carriageway" selling everything from "sweet drinks" (soft drinks) to vegetables to shrimp and fish.

But wait! There must be an accident there! No, the pile-up is simply to accommodate friends who met and now one of them is standing in the wrong lane, in the opposite direction, "liming" (chatting in a leisurely manner) with the passengers of the other car. I believe they are talking over the preparations for a wedding. "No problem!" The cars avoid them, go around them, and barely miss another unfortunate person, whose axle happened to break in the middle of the "dual carriageway." In order that he should not lose time he spread a plastic sheet under the car and started to change axles right there in the right (our left) turn lane of Valpark (one of the largest shopping centers in Trinidad). The other cars docilely went around and felt sorry for the poor guy. I guess they must have given him instructions as they heatedly yelled at him through their rolled down windows. They even have given some of the hand signals. Funny! I could not recognize any of them, although we had to memorize them all for the exam. Would we have missed more than one of the signals in the written test we would not be the proud owners of Trinidad and Tobago Driver's Permits. We passed, yet…What was that he said now? A clenched fist! Did that mean anything? I was racking my brain to remember all the signals, but all that came to mind was that comic strip I quoted above.

However, in real life there are many more signals. Like that man there. It looks like he is explaining trigonometry to his son sitting beside him.

How about this line? It must be a road construction maybe? One where the sign reads: "Go Dead Slow?" It looks like the other end of it must be a few miles from here. I can hardly wait to get there to see the reason. Forty-five minutes and 10 blocks later I am astonished, but grateful when the line simply dissolves into free-flowing traffic and I discover that instead of an ugly accident the delay was caused by…nothing. Nothing "at'all, at'all." (Repetition of word(s) is used to express superlatives).

Further down, after a quick few miles, another pile-up. What can the reason be? Afternoon, an important junction, but then in the morning when I was passing through everybody quietly took their turn. The two lanes formed a disciplined four lanes and only an occasional fifth laner broke the monotony of turning and inching our way through the maze of cars. But now, something must be wrong. Soon I discover that a policeman, or is it two?...are directing traffic with a choreography that would put the Royal Ballet to shame. The drivers are entranced by their movements and forget to drive efficiently. Anyway, the performance is worth it.

A few blocks down a smaller traffic problem develops as a young man in a long white robe with braided hair tries to give a good imitation of the policemen's performance. He dances to the rhythm of an oriental melody unheard by the motorists who have their radios tuned to a fashionable calypso and therefore cannot appreciate the doubtless value of this human creation. Or is the man simply drunk? Did he smoke "ganja?" (marijuana)

I guess I'll never know because most cars simply drive around him.

The next thing to avoid is a pothole all the way across the road. We are no longer on the "dual carriageway" and therefore we have to assume if a car comes at us from the wrong direction, like the right hand side of the road, then he is either a pitiful American tourist, who doesn't know how to drive, or a wise Trini, who knows better than to break his axle on a "slight irregularity" in the road.

Wait! Something fishy is going on around here, but I must be courteous. I slow down and look with amazement. Now, why didn't I think of that? But, of course, this car wants to go up onto the sidewalk on the wrong side of the road in the opposite direction.

As I was following the car with my eyes, I noticed the familiar pregnant goat that always grazes on my side of the road. Only this time she was standing in front of the jeweler's shop window quite amazed by the glitters she saw. Was she contemplating a gift for her soon-to-be-born kid, or thinking of a belated wedding ring?

A honk! Oh, thank you for reminding me. I nearly wandered over into the oncoming third lane while I was admiring the goat. I must watch myself and never forget the rule, "whoever passes has the right-of-way."

I guess whoever backs has the right of way too. This taxi is just backing, and I heard or even read in the Drivers' Manual that whoever hits you from behind is always at fault. He should have kept the distance! So, let the driver beware! However, it flashes through my mind that it would be interesting to look up some of the court decisions. When a car is backing, is the back the front and the front the back, or is the back the back and the front the front going in the wrong direction? Should I back up now to "keep the distance" from the car in front of me, still backing, or try to go forward to avoid the bumper of the car behind me, still trying to advance with the speed limit?

Swoosh! a motor bike just passed me driving straight on the dividing line.

Was that the white-haired Benedictine Father who told me that he would never be able to drive a car, it was too dangerous? The helmet makes him look like a young boy. My husband once wondered aloud: "I could never figure out what would happen, if two motorcycles would meet, on this, their sacred space?"

But lo and behold! We have a picturesque demonstration here of what happens when two goats meet at the happy amazement of schoolchildren. The uniformed little girls forget all about school as they watch our mother goat's two rival suitors fight out their paternity suit right in front of our car.

Today we have a special treat. A police car goes in front of us on the winding Western Main Road coming from Chaguramas. His blue lights are flashing. He must be speeding to an emergency. But why does he go 20 km/hr? Does he want to tell us something? He moves slowly, but he moves. He does not stop, or turn, or give any sign of reason for his actions. He only drives – slowly – on and on until finally we lose him to one of the turns. Maybe he was going home, maybe he forgot to turn off his lights, maybe he did not realize that to pass him would be impossible. Maybe he just wanted to slow down the traffic. Another mystery we'll never solve.

Could be that he wanted to prevent us from running into pedestrians, dressed in dark clothes, darting out in front of unsuspecting cars, or the bicycles that do their Sunday outings in groups of four or five side by side. They are doing us a great favor by teaching us patience.

Naturally, these things did not happen all in one day. I am merely reminiscing about my driving days in Trinidad and trying to figure out why there are still traffic jams despite the obvious friendliness of the drivers and the policemen, who, without fail, have always helped me perform any kind of irregularity if I was in need?

Could it be that traffic jams are caused by people like me, who are sitting in the middle of a right turn in Curepe Junction (the "Grand Central Station" for cars in Trinidad), writing this article?

48

Back to the letter I was writing home:

One day we decided to have another, that is five other sets of keys made for our cage downstairs. All the apartments are separately caged in. Each is three stories high. On the first floor we have the laundry room and a little bathroom, also a big caged-in storage room. On the second floor are the entertaining quarters: living room, dining room, family room and kitchen. On the third floor are three bedrooms, two are air-conditioned and two bathrooms with bathtub shower combination.

As miracles never cease to happen, I trust that the shower and the water will keep up the good work and will not stop on us more than is absolutely necessary. To ensure this I kept telling every engineer who happened by at our place about the strange phenomenon in our house. There was a 4,000-gallon water tank buried right in front of our apartment. The pump was working occasionally, meaning it was pumping the water to our bathrooms. However, there was never any water upstairs as a result. Occasionally, in the middle of the night like 3:30 a.m., when the water pressure would come on on its own, we noticed there was water. So quickly I took a shower, woke up the second person, who took a shower and so on. The time is a bit inconvenient, but we are in Trinidad, so 'no problem!'

Finally, after six weeks of me 'vexing' them as they say in Trinidad, they looked deeper into the matter and found out that the pump was working, but pumped the water right back into the 4,000-gallon storage tank. Maybe if I would not have kept on with my 'vexing' the water would still be pumped back into the storage tank. There were people living in the condos for nine months already and it had not yet occurred to anyone to look into the problem. I had to think of the saying I found at the university, when we first went there: 'Everything cometh to the one that waiteth if he worketh like hell while he waiteth.' I applied it and it worked.

Anyway, I started by saying we went downtown to get the keys. We were also trying to get our drivers' licenses. Therefore, a nice employee of T&TEC took our keys to their locksmith. We were told the keys would be ready by 3:00 p.m., so we proceeded to the License Bureau and with the help of a security person (360 pounds with a huge smile, taller than Apu, who is six foot, five inches) a retired policeman, we barely had to stand in line here and there. We were told to come back in the afternoon to do the written test, luckily the only one we had to take. We went to eat lunch, then returned at 3:08; we passed our test. We had to pay $45 TT (local currency) per person. However, the cashier closed at 3:00 p.m., so we had to come back the next day to pay our fees and have our photos taken. It also meant we still had to be taken home and could not get our car. Then tomorrow someone had to drive to St. Augustine to pick us up. Our American driver's license would have been good for three months, but not to drive a company car! in the left hand drive! Anyway, we realized there was no way to open the cashier that day (not even our retired policeman-security-person-friend could do anything). I am sure glad he was on our side, I would have fainted had I met him in the dark somewhere just at the sight of him.

We went back to get our keys that should have been waiting for us. Instead we found a desperate Ken Bailey. The locksmith apparently decided to leave by the time our good man Antoine went to get the keys, and left a note on his shop door: "Gone fishing." He was so relieved, when instead of getting mad we started laughing our heads off.

Here we were, in Port-of-Spain, without keys to our house. After a few phone calls things started to look up. The wife of Leo Martin the General Manager of T&TEC, herself an optometrist, Jennifer Martin, drove over to our house and tried to find the owner's son. You see, one has to work with people who have telephones. Those who don't you have to visit to tell them something. Jennifer had a phone, so could be reached and was kind enough to drive over to our house. She also happened to have a car and was driving her children to piano lessons that way. So far, so good. Needless to say, the owner's son was not on the premises. There was no manager for the house and the owner was reluctant to give his phone number, claiming it did not work anyway (which was true for most phones, most of the time. That is why 'established' people had two phone lines. Just in case…). As he caved in in the end and gave us both his phone numbers, we gave them to Ken Bailey, who called him. He promised us a key if we picked it up. We got the keys he thought were our keys, but he knew for sure one of them would open the back door. The back door could be reached if one climbed over a six-foot wall. With three keys in our possession we set out to conquer our house. Leo personally drove us out in his air-conditioned car. Although we all kept our fingers crossed, we could not come in through the front door, or gate I should say. Luckily, we located a makeshift ladder that the construction workers used and lugged it over to the wall. By that time Rita was across with the help of Leo and gave a jubilant cry when she could open the back gate. One after another we plopped over the wall onto a dining room chair that Rita brought down. We were all inside. It was about 7:30. Jennifer Martin arrived during this operation and brought us a casserole to eat. She felt so bad about us being locked out.

After we finished dinner and were watching our color TV there was a honk outside. There are no doorbells on our cages. St. Clair and Mary were at the gate. We explained that we would love to invite them in, but we had no key. They roared with laughter and decided if we all came in over the wall, so could they. And across they came. Mary in her semi-formal evening dress dangling into St. Clair's arms. Around midnight, after three good drinks and in an even happier mood they climbed back across. When Mary got on top of the wall she just sat there as if on a horse and laughed and laughed and said she could not go any further. St. Clair got himself over and she finally landed in his arms.

The next day the owner of the condo came with the right key that opened the front door.

Later on during the day we went downtown and finally received our driver's license, along with an "executive size" car, the size of our Duster (medium sized in the USA) automatic transmission, no power steering, but power brakes, with about 100,000 miles on it. The odometer stopped at 85,000. The steering wheel was oval and the car was about a foot wider than all the others on the road. Of course, it was hard to follow a normal size car in traffic because we constantly had to watch our left side to see it did not bump into something, like a "for hire" car (community taxi), which was every fourth car and stopped, when anyone waived it down, a pothole, at least the size of half the tire, or the third lane of traffic, which materialized according to need at any time. This car was not the one intended for us. There was one last week, but we did not have our driver's licenses yet, so it went to someone else, naturally.

Every kind of merchandise stays in the stores only long enough to change hands. Even in the grocery stores one has to watch constantly for the employees bringing in new merchandise and grab it out of their cart, before they even put it out on the shelf.

There are so many things to write about I don't even know where to start and I am awfully rusty because: 1) I have not written for months, 2) I am in a British culture, at least that is the basis of the language and that is taught in schools, 3) the local dialect that sounds as foreign at first as a completely foreign language, yet is English and nothing else, with a very different pronunciation and melody that resembles the French. Another reason might be that we speak Hungarian at home, finally again.

For those to whom it might be of interest I have only learned one thing about multinational corporations from the American newspapers. A university professor in America claimed that they created needs in order to sell their products. My question is: what would the view be of multinationals if they would withhold the products for which there was an obvious demand. (I have seen that demand when I was here eight years ago and the same goods were not sold in Trinidad, only those people had it who travelled and studied abroad and brought it back with them.) Would they then be accused of holding back progress? Nestlés was <u>not</u> accused of anything here and to anybody who boycotts them I wish that they should try to live in a tropical climate without the benefit of Nestlé. They manufacture everything that is drinkable and can be kept without refrigeration until opened. Here they do not even make baby food. Many other brands of baby food are sold.

I will write about this later much more. Right now, I am trying to find out as much about the Island as possible. I had wonderful luck. The very first person I met when we went to the Chaplaincy at the University, to ask about Mass times was Sister Marie Thérèse.

She greeted us and said: " I am Marie Thérèse Rétout, and I am a journalist."
I laughed and said: "I am Helen Szablya and I am also a journalist." We
became instant friends. She wrote full time for the Catholic News and also
contributed to PEOPLE (Caribbean) magazine. She supplied me with
copies of both. She complained about problems with printing and told me
there was a lady here who wrote for the English Catholic Press and said we
would get together. I was looking forward to that.

Although it is only October 9th here, we are all preparing already for a
"Sunshine Christmas" especially because packages to England, the USA
and other parts of the world will have to be shipped during the month of
October to get there by Christmas.

I have another letter from October 30th I wrote to our parish priest,
Father Wesbrook, who was a dear friend. When we were in Pullman, he
spent every Sunday lunch with us and often stayed late into the afternoon.

*I am enclosing for you a copy of the local PEOPLE magazine with
an article in it about Nestlé. There is also an ad on TV for Nestlé
that states: 'Breast feeding is the best for your baby, but when
your baby gets old enough you can start him on Nestum,' which is
something like Pablum in the States. When I asked several people,
learned ones and primitive ones, about Nestlé, they had told me
that Nestlé was not one of the 'multinationals.' They talked proudly
and gratefully about the only factory that provides them with milk.
When one of the well-educated ladies heard me talk about Nestlé in
Hungary and in the States, she said: 'Maybe Nestlé is multinational,
but we do not consider it as one of them. The multinationals are
mostly oil companies, who come here to get rich. They would be like
AMOCO. Multinationals are typically owned 49% by our state.
They are here to set up different industries and we need them. We
have no capital, equipment, or know-how to do it on our own. We
want them here until they give us what we need. Then we buy their
share of the company and they can leave. The problem is that while
they are here, they are juggling the books and we do not get 49% of
the profits as they are trying to get rich on us. Their people need better
accommodations than what we can give our own, otherwise they
don't come. Yet, I would say they are a necessary evil.' Interesting isn't
it? One can understand the multinationals also. If they know they
have to leave, they must make profits while they are here if they want
to survive.*

Everything seems to be very slow and inefficient. Yet, in this heat and under these conditions it is a miracle to achieve anything.

The so-called "ex-patriots'" or employees of corporations from overseas, are supposed to be here typically for three years. They are supposed to teach Trinidadians or 'nationals' as they call themselves how to run things and to consult. They are not supposed to – or allowed to – do the job themselves. Trade Unions work, or more often than not, stop work here. There are strikes and slow-downs all the time. Most of the time the 'ex-pats' are frustrated to tears because their advice is not taken, their attempts to do anything bumps into red tape, non-operational xerox machines, telephones, telexes, cars, even water. The population gives them all the luxury that exists on this island, and yet, they are not satisfied. Why? Because they come here to do a job and most of them want to go ahead with it instead of sipping rum punch because they cannot go ahead with whatever they are here for. This results of course in unending delays in their schedules for going home, etc. Another terrible frustration for them is that their wives are not allowed to do any kind of work. They are condemned to live in luxury, when they are active, interested people, psychologists, teachers, doctors, what-have-you. The papers are full of ads, desperately looking for these kinds of people (but they should be nationals, even if they are recruited from Canada or the U.S., where most of their nationals prefer to stay because they claim to have a preference for houses with running water and electricity.) That tremendous work force (and I am talking now about hundreds of people) already on the island, the wives of ex-pats, most of them with university education will not get a work permit. Therefore, instead of becoming part of the solution they become more and more part of the problem as their talents are not used to correct but to criticize.

Later during our stay, I had a once-in-a-lifetime opportunity to interview the head of the World Health Organization (WHO) committee that discussed the topics of Nestle, breastfeeding, multinationals – a British lady, Elisabeth Quamina, MD, married to a Trinidadian medical doctor, Head of the General Hospital in Port-of-Spain. I asked her to sign the article I wrote after our conversation, which she graciously did. She was very frustrated with the American activists who came to the conferences because it was impossible to discuss anything with them. They could only repeat like parakeets what they had to say, but had no medical or any other scientific knowledge to come to a conclusion or agreement with the medical doctors.

I also had the opportunity to talk with Nestle's employees and leaders. One told me that when she was nursing, Nestle did everything to make it possible for her to be able to nurse her baby. At the time when protests were going on in the USA, the employees were going to take down Nestle posters at clinics. The nurses were fighting with them to leave it there. They had no other posters that were teaching mothers on how to care for their babies. The posters stated that mother's milk was the best for their babies.

I asked our maid what they would feed their babies if Nestle would not be available. She said they would mix arrowroot into their water. Activists did not want mothers to use water that may be contaminated. However, the mothers would use the same water for whatever they fed their babies if they did not have enough milk.

These letters were written in October. Another journal-like letter from the end of February makes two big announcements. To Marcey and Jancsi: Genevieve Marie Josephine (Gennie) was born on January 24th and to Kathy and Louis: Stephen Louis was born on February 7th.

These big events took place while our son Stephen and two of his friends, Karl Pool (now daughter Rita's husband) and Kristy Tenwick (now Stephen's wife), were on the plane to and from Trinidad. They spent here 12 days and we had a marvelous time showing them the sights and enjoying Trinidad and Tobago to the fullest.

We are having a great time in Trinidad. John enjoys his work, my articles are read weekly by more and more people. As we go to the Carnival "jump-ups," "fetes," and other delightful pastimes and strangers greet me as an old friend. It is a wonderful feeling to know that they not only print, but even read my articles.

Sandy is doing very well at the University. She introduced a custom that was never heard of before. She started lending her books to other students and asked them to let her borrow theirs. The dean said that this had never yet happened in the history of the university that somebody publicly announced her willingness to share her books of knowledge. The spirit is very competitive between the students and the academic structure is very rigid. Another of Sandy's firsts at the University was that she dared to ask the professor questions which were greatly solicited by him.

Rita's class invited us to talk to their whole school, from 13 years up to the graduating class and the teachers, about Communism, religion and Marxism, generally speaking about our experiences with extremist systems, planned vs. free enterprise economy. We never had a better audience. The whole hall filled up and we got a standing ovation that was initiated by the children, not the teachers. They made us feel really welcome. The teachers are satisfied with Rita and she was elected prefect of her class for this term. The school also juggled the dates, so that she should be able to sing in her class' concert before she would leave Trinidad.

Yesterday I was asked to go to talk on abortion and life in general in a San Fernando High school. Their teacher read my articles in Catholic News and felt that I could contribute to their studies.

Niki is becoming a wizard at languages. Especially Spanish appeals to her. She is one of the best three in her class, even though she started a month late and started two languages simultaneously: Spanish and French. Both she and Rita have many friends and we have a dog. 'Kutyus' (puppy in Hungarian) who had wandered into our lives on Christmas Eve while we were singing carols. She looked as if she hadn't eaten in days so we fed her. She stayed.

As soon as she sees any of us she lies on her back and expects to be scratched. We like her, even though she behaves like a two-year-old toddler, dragging everything into our doorway that she can lay her paws and teeth on.

Robberies, prowlers, catburglars, pickpockets, what-have-yous are more than common. Between the 13th and 14th of February, the night after John left for New York for a conference, my handbag was stolen from careless me. Now, why would I be so careless as to leave my purse right beside my bed, about a foot from my head while I am asleep in the bed beside it? Niki slept right next to me. The open window was on the third floor of the townhouse in which we live. All other windows were securely closed, and the gate downstairs was locked with a lock and chain. The police said that it was very common for catburglers to climb the walls, then fish out a purse with an actual fishing pole. The scary thing was only that both Niki and I were sound asleep, and they could go through with their plan even though the purse was about 12 feet from the window. Some people claim that thieves use chloroform and spray it into the room so that people should not wake up. In a way I am glad and thank God for not waking up. Who knows what the thief would have done, especially to Niki? According to Trinidad's own PEOPLE magazine, the youngest known case of rape in Trinidad was six months, the oldest victim was 93 years old. One must be very, very careful. This is a pity because the tropical nights are so enticing with their gentle breeze. It would be nice to take a walk after the heat of the day is over, but…the price might be a bit higher than one bargained for. This is not because we are white, or affluent, the same danger applies to anybody who walks, as we heard, even regardless of gender. Especially when there is no man around. Unless one belongs to one certain man one is fair prey to all men regardless of color, race, or creed.

The same night, two other townhouses were broken into, or rather burglarized, right in our compound and four cars. Apparently the thief did not want to or could not drive because although he had my car keys from the purse and went through the car, he threw the keys on the hood and left them there. Maybe he was disgusted that the lock key was not on the key chain and he could not come into the house. He also threw my handbag away. Two weeks later we found it in the flower planters in the next door empty apartment's balcony.

Naturally they stole my driver's license, citizenship paper and credit cards, so it took about a week to get all of this straightened out. To get a duplicate driver's license took only a day because the nice gentleman (six-foot, twelve-inch, 360-pound retired policeman) again came to our help. Few dared to stand in his way. Another half a day was spent trying to telephone American Express after we had sent a telegram and they needed more information. Thank God, we had insurance with them before we left home and registered all our credit cards. Now American Express was taking care of replacing all the cards and stopping them. It was such a relief to know that this was taken care of. The police were very helpful and polite, but basically did not do a thing. They were realists.

Unfortunately, we do not have a telephone and probably will not have a telephone as long as we are going to be here, so there is not much we can do, except all the neighbors are watching each other all the time in order to help if necessary. Burglars usually run when they are disturbed or if they are afraid to be found out. They just want money and jewelry. One lady was robbed only of her gold jewelry. The burglar did not even bother with the silver. My burglar must have been truly disappointed. I had no money in my wallet. However, I was happy because knowing the custom of burglars, and, as I always carried a paperback book in my purse, I had my $100 TT bills in my paperback. When we found my discarded purse, the paperback still had all the money in it. My credit cards came back to me also because there was no way known to the burglar that he could have made any use of them.

One day before this episode, one of the neighborhood schizophrenics wanted to dine with my daughters, believing that one of them was married to him. He even brought a pizza to share with them. Thank God, our neighbor boys took care of him and he did not come back for a while, then he appeared again. The boys: Navaal, Anil and Veeran, our dear neighbor Zilda Ramdin's sons took care of him again.

Navaal met Sandy and suddenly he changed his job location from Tobago to Trinidad and came back home to live. Sandy and Navaal now could look right into each other's homes through the yard. He took it upon himself to show the girls the island. The first time he took them out was almost the last because when they got back Sandy had enough rum to hang her head right out the car window as they were driving home, which was not exactly the safest way to travel. He was very apologetic and came over later in the evening, suggesting to give her lime. Lime seemed to be the antidote for everything in Trinidad.

From then on Navaal was on his best behavior. He even came to church with us on Sundays. We went together to Tobago, the paradise island and to another resort in Trinidad. One day Navaal speared us a fish before breakfast so we could eat our freshest fish ever. He guided us through the coral reef in Tobago and later in Barbados, when he accompanied us up there on our way home to the U.S.

Maybe it should not come as a surprise that when Sandy went to visit Navaal in Trinidad in February, she came back married to him in a civil ceremony about which they told no one. Not even Zilda was told, at whose home they lived while she visited. But, Trinidad, being Trinidad…By the time they entered the house, she said: "So, you got married?!"

Zilda's friend was secretary at an adjoining office in the Red House, the capitol of the island, where they got married and immediately called her. So much for "eloping" on an island.

49

Of course, we cannot say good-bye to Trinidad without talking about their most important event of the year: Carnival.

The Carnival cult is unbelievable here. Since Christmas (the preparation for that already started in October) there was no let down from the preparation for the "Greatest Show on Earth": parties and fun events, but as we get closer to Carnival everything seems to speed up and become more intense, so that finally, everybody who can stand on their feet "jumps up" and I mean literally, we "jump up." It is not only the drinks, it is the whole atmosphere and the wild beat of the calypsos, steel drums, the music in the air, the explosion of colors, and fragrances of the flowers, the palm trees and the moon with the stars in the dark tropical sky. The parties (fêtes) are held outdoors in the most delightful temperature, just right for "jumping up" all over town, in parking lots and in empty tennis courts, wherever there is enough space to "jump up." This is more than understandable if you think of dancing all day in the hot sun once Carnival arrives. People have to practice, and practice, and practice, as do the steel bands. Not the most welcome sound if one wants to sleep, when the practice goes on 'til 2:00 a.m. and one happens to be a Dominican sister right across the street at the Chaplaincy and the university. Every night until the Carnival.

People go to "tents" where the latest calypsos are heard and compete for the greatest popularity.

The Island is becoming a busy beehive of "bands" for the preparation of the Carnival March. Each band consists of 3,000 to 4,000 people but some have as little as only 200 to 300 people. The Carnival and the bands have a theme and everyone's costumes are made according to that theme at big workshops that do nothing else, but that. Some of the costumes cost up to several hundred dollars and very ordinary people buy them. The costumes of "kings" and "queens" cost around $10,000 each. A band has only one of those and I do not think the person wearing it pays for it. (This is 1981 dollars.)

It is a matter of honor in Trinidad and Tobago to pay for the costumes. That is the time of the year when it is easiest to find labor for ironing, housekeeping, cooking, gardening, what-have-you.

In 1981 Sandy and Navaal joined the "Jungle" band and jumped up with them. (https://www.youtube.com/watch?v=ZYjMtJFfrrc)

The winning marching song was ETHEL. (https://www.youtube.com/watch?v=1t4A5w5t498)

Another well-liked calypso was "Tiger-Tiger Burning Bright."

Carnival starts with the big contests of the calypsos, marching songs, kings and queens of Carnival, Junior Carnival kings and queens during the weekend, culminating in Sunday evening when all the final winners are announced and are marching around in Queen Park Savannah. The kings and queens wear costumes that are so spectacular and heavy that they are supported by wheels because it would not be possible to carry the costumes by the people wearing them. The costumes have moving parts sparkling, radiating, turning, while the person wearing it is moving and dancing. They are like mountains of diamonds, decorated with feathers and peacock rainbows beguiling the audience as the kings and queens are competing for the big title.

On Monday morning Jouvé starts Carnival. This is an old-fashioned Carnival, the way it started when people made their own costumes and came individually, or in small groups. After that comes the Junior Carnival organized by the schools. They have the same kind of competition and fabulous costumes with their own kings and queens. The costumes are not nearly as "revealing" as the adult costumes.

Some married couples have the motto "what happens during Carnival, remains in Carnival" giving each other free hand at anything. That anything might happen even without their consent. Our family doctor gave "the pill" for all our daughters to take during that time. While Carnival is a fabulous entertainment, it is always preceded by the papers asking people to behave responsibly. This becomes kind of difficult for many while dancing for 9 hours in the blazing son almost naked, while sipping hard liquor on shredded ice.

We took part in the Sunday evening event and then, on Tuesday, in the very real Carnival. You have to park outside of the city and walk all the way because there is no parking closer to the event. We were so lucky – the Bailey's who lived in the middle of town – invited us to stay with them during this Carnival. Their children and our children, including Navaal of course, went out to jump up for a much, much longer time than we actually did. You know how tiring it is just to watch the march and do a bit of dancing along the way? Especially when one, like I, cannot stand the heat. We were happy to have the Bailey's home as a safe adobe.

However, even Sandy, who adores the heat came into the Bailey's to crash for an hour or so. She slept during that time, like a log, collapsing onto a mattress on the floor.

The events got more and more heated until midnight. Then, with the arrival of Ash Wednesday, the beginning of Lent, everything ended. By morning, the city looked cleaner and more orderly than we have seen it ever before. I could not believe my eyes on our way home. Not a loud noise, no leftover anything. Just peace and quiet all around.

~

We often drove to the Trinidad Yachting Association. We bought a "Kingfish" (glorified board and sail). When we left, we sold it. All of us took a sailing course during the Christmas vacation. The first question was: "What is the first thing you do, when you capsize?" Our teacher, a 14-year-old boy, gave us the answer: "You enjoy the water!" Not something we could say about the Pacific Ocean in Seattle. We enjoyed the water every time we could get away from home. During the course we learned how to upright the boat if it capsized. John, who was an expert sailor, took the course with us. He gave me tips on how to do it. He showed me how to hold on to the cord and pull it using the weight of your body to tip the boat back into upright position. Of course, our boats were dinghys, the "Volkswagen beetles" among the yachts.

~

While we were in Trinidad, we had our 30th wedding anniversary of our June wedding. The Abbot of Mt. St. Benedikt Abbey said Mass for us in the afternoon. After this we had a wonderful party at our home. Many of our friends came. The invitations went out in the usual fashion. You called a friend who had a phone and asked them to tell their friends who lived close by to come to the party. A joke in the newspaper proposed sending out invitations by hiring an airplane that would pull a sign over all the island: "There will be a party at Joe's on Saturday 5:00 p.m." which could mean 5 or 6 or 7 according to "Trinidad time" as we nicknamed it. You gratefully acknowledged those who came, but there was no way of knowing who would not come because of the lack of phones and the arbitrariness of the post office. One friend did not show up for example. It was months later when we found out that he had a bad accident. He was a volunteer dentist for Servol and had just arrived from Canada and forgot about driving on the left.

~

What we liked most about Trinidad was the people and the natural beauty. There were shortages of water, telephone, electricity, and certain food items, but this was all part of Trinidad's sudden growth and industrialization of the country.

~

Our year was unforgettably beautiful. We met with many old friends and made new ones we will cherish as long as we live.

We were sad when our year was up, but we were all excited to see the new grandchildren born during our absence.

On our way home we stopped in Barbados and in Puerto Rico, visiting friends in both places, who treated us royally. In Barbados we stayed at the Ocean View Hotel, which was Hemingway's favorite, with turn-of-the-century charm and all the comforts of the 80s. We spent a week there with the children, swimming in the hotel's own private ocean bay, separated by a coral reef and sitting on the old-fashioned breezy veranda, with the sea under us enjoying each other and reading. In Puerto Rico we enjoyed our foretaste of home when we could drink fresh milk again after a year and receive other American conveniences. There we enjoyed the last beautiful beaches in the Caribbean and its delightful Old San Juan.

50

The sabbatical was over. We found ourselves back in Pullman, in our good old home.

On our way home from Trinidad we visited Jancsi and Marcey who were now living in Seattle. We met Genevieve, their lovely baby girl, who was born on January 24, 1981. She observed us with all seriousness, when Jancsi gave her to me and ran to take care of our luggage. She did not cry, she only looked curious. She must have decided I was OK because she continued to look at me in a fascinated gaze. Soon we became good friends.

Louis now worked in Spokane, for Washington Water Power. They bought an old home and enjoyed their two-year-old chatterbox Nadine, and Stephen, who was born two weeks after Gennie, February 7, 1981.

Son Stephen was the only one who stayed home in Pullman as a sophomore, now a junior in electrical engineering. He also worked at White Drugs, managing the photo department.

That year we all went to the Sopron Homecoming Ball in Vancouver, B.C., where Stephen and Kristy – in the middle of the ball – announced their plans to get married; their long-range plan for when Stephen would graduate.

Ten days after we arrived back from our sabbatical, I left for Baltimore, where Ilike was having her second child. Niki stayed with her on our way back from Trinidad until I arrived. Then we waited, and waited, and waited... finally granddaughter Anna and I decided to leave for Philadelphia to see friends we met in Trinidad. Well, of course, Alexander Philip arrived on the night when we were gone, September 13, 1981. Anna and I hurried home to meet the new arrival. He turned out to be the best baby. He ate, he slept, he was happy. Anna loved him and we all had a great time.

Ilike and Barry had a wonderful opportunity with the "Theater Project" in Baltimore that made it possible to take Alex with them to work. They were also co-directors of the "Baltimore Voices" company. They used 7,000 pages of oral histories taken in six of Baltimore's various neighborhoods collected by the University of Baltimore, creating a new genre, the "oral history drama" for the National Endowment for the Humanities. It was very important to them that they used the exact words of the people. They not only wrote it, but also performed in it and directed it. It had many versions: 20-, 40-, 60- and 90-minute versions. They also learned how to improvise if needed in the manner of the interviewed people.

"Baltimore Voices" was taped for the Public Broadcasting Service (PBS) in Maryland and aired in the spring.

It felt wonderful to be home! The children went back to school, Sandy started at WSU. Rita was a senior in High School and Niki was in 8th grade.

And I was jumping into my car to go and tell…wait…we have a telephone…and it is working…I jumped back out of my car and ran back into the house. Then I lifted the phone. And there was a line…I dialed… and my friend's voice was right there. On the other line. What joy!

And the water, and the electricity – all reliable. WOW! We are home!

As I have mentioned before, Szablyas need a challenge. There was none left! Now what???

We did not need to think for long. John's very good friend Dr. George Karády who happened to be the Director of the Electrical Section of Ebasco, an engineering consulting firm, invited him to be the electrical engineer in charge of opening the Seattle branch of Ebasco. The salary offered was double what he made in Pullman. So, he asked for a "leave of absence" from the university and come Thanksgiving he moved to Seattle.

Now, it is not the easiest to move out of a house where we had brought up our seven children and where we had lived for 15 years, the longest so far from all our homes.

Yes, Pullman lacked the challenges now. We had reached as far as we could go. But oh, the friends, the memories…the house into which we put so much love and work…

A friend arrived with great news. An opportunity arose and we could early-retire. Washington State had a State of Emergency. Whenever Boeing is not doing well for some reason, the State declares an emergency. As a result, everyone who had been working for the university for more than 15 years and was over 58, could take early retirement. These professors were replaced with assistant professors, for a trial period of one year. Their salaries, of course, were much less. The State also hoped that many professors would stay in Pullman and come back to teach a few classes. Once you retired from the State you could get paid for only 40% of the time, but work as much as you wanted. Retirement was better than anything else for us right then. We could remain in the University's health insurance! 100 professors took advantage of it. Unfortunately, this also meant that houses were not sellable because the temporary assistant professors were not going to buy anything for a year at least.

While John started work in Bellevue, a suburb of Seattle, I had my work cut out for me. Rita was going to graduate from high school and Niki from junior high, so I was going to join John only after graduation. In the meantime, we were trying to sell our beloved home, while also trying to find housing in Seattle. The prices in Seattle were higher than in Pullman. Normally our home was one that would sell without even being advertised. It was THE old farmhouse of the original big orchard on Sunnyside Hill, built in 1902, but this time…Pullman had 100 more houses to sell than normally around the end of the school year.

We packed and said good-bye all year. The house was for sale starting in June.

John started work on the Thanksgiving weekend. However, his true start was in January.

For Christmas, our tree was from our own backyard. When our good friend, Frank Brands received 250 saplings to plant from the State of Idaho, he gave us 50. We planted them in our yard. Those baby pine trees became big enough to serve as Christmas trees not only for us, but also for Louis' family in Spokane.

During Spring break Sandy went to visit Navaal in Trinidad. That is when the famous phone call came. Can I marry Navaal today? Needless to say, we were a bit surprised at the question and we said "Of course not," but then we asked them to let us think. While we were thinking for five minutes, we called the former Ambassador to Trinidad who by then was back in Washington DC and discussed with him the legal consequences. Then we called back and gave them the green light. Sandy was on her way home the next day. They planned a church wedding for later.

While we were trying to sell our home, John drove back every weekend on Friday afternoon and drove back Sunday. Every third weekend I went to Seattle to be with him and usually stayed a few days in order to try to find a job. Only two of the children would be coming with us: Sandy and Niki.

Rita was the happiest girl when she graduated from high school, beaming with her sunshine smile as she accepted her diploma. She decided to stay in Pullman and wait for Karl's graduation, then marry him. She did not want to go to university, even though she could have gotten quite a scholarship. We did not want her to stay, but she was so happy just at the thought of it…she stayed, working at various jobs. I can never forget her radiant smile when she went out of our house for the last time, in her red dress. She was beaming with happiness.

The house did not sell, so we rented it to a student couple with several children and left Stephen and Kristy in charge.

It was so hard to leave, but the day finally came when we left in our car, following the huge semi truck full of our furniture, art, clothes, all kinds of things we had. People warned us that professional movers would even wrap our garbage. We were trying to prevent it, but when we did not notice they managed to wrap that too. Our move was paid for by Ebasco.

We stopped on our way to Seattle. Sandy and Niki got out of the car and picked a few sheaves of wheat to remember our lives, our happy days in Pullman. I still have a few bits left over in a tiny vase. We were very emotional about leaving behind basically our child-raising years along with our cherished home and our forever friends. Still, at least we did not have to cross the Iron Curtain, only Snowqualmie Pass, and part of the family was still in Pullman.

—————

Naturally, we could not buy a home in Seattle for a while, so we decided to rent. We had looked all summer to buy, but now we could not afford that. We found a bungalow with four bedrooms and a big family room, where we put our dining room furniture with our legendary "big table"and my grandparents' huge portraits which my mother had brought out from Hungary, when she joined us in 1959. After Mother's death we brought the portraits on top of our "Hungarian tank" namely our station wagon with the top carrier. Luckily, the portraits made it all the way from Winnipeg to Pullman.

One of the bedrooms became my office, where I wrote articles, my column, made translations and edited a newsletter. Sandy and Niki each had a bedroom and we had the nice big master bedroom with a lovely bathroom. Another bathroom belonged to the girls, the kitchen was nice and big as was the living room. Under the entire living room there was a big room in the basement where the washer and dryer also found their place.

During the summer Niki had been looking at Catholic schools. She chose Seattle Prep, the Jesuit high school with its excellent Matteo Ricci program. Seattle Prep used to be an all boys' school, but a few years before our arrival it went co-ed. The program consisted of six years. Three years at Seattle Prep and three years at Seattle University (also Jesuit). The entire class was taking the same rigorous subjects with almost no electables. At the end of the six years they graduated from the university with a B.A. in Liberal Arts. Any university would admit them to a Masters program with this degree. If they chose to stay for another year, they received a second diploma in whatever they wanted to specialize in.

We had barely moved into our house when time for the Sopron Ball arrived and we were going to Vancouver, B.C. for it. The same day Sandy got a letter from Navaal that she should go to the airport on that same day because she will receive a surprise from Navaal. A friend was going to arrive and bring it.

The surprise was Navaal himself! He came to stay!

Well, that was a surprise for all of us. What are we going to do? As far as we were concerned, they were only "engaged" through their civil wedding. So, what could we do? We let Navaal move in downstairs into the big room and left for the ball.

John and I were wondering about what Navaal wanted to do here to make some money.

"I always wanted to design airplanes," said Navaal. "I did my Chemical Engineering Technology degree only because my father was a chemical engineer and he died when I was nine. I wanted to walk in his footsteps. But now, being an adult, I want to follow my heart's desire."

It seemed that we had acquired another child. As a matter of fact, we deducted him and Stephen as dependents because they were full time students. We encountered big financial difficulties. Not only did we have this many dependents, but the Pullman house had to be repainted. Ilike and Barry lived in Baltimore. We owned the house jointly with them where they used to live. The tenant moved out and left them without paying rent for the last six months. The house needed to be repainted. Navaal and I were the "designated crew." Navaal was an excellent worker with great skills. Stephen and Kristy were working on the Pullman house.

Navaal planted a vegetable garden at our rented house. He had a lucky green thumb with everything he grew. There were so many tomatoes, we could not eat them fast enough.

Niki received a work-study job at Seattle Prep to help with the tuition. She was doing odd jobs, like cleaning the parking lot after school. She used to get up at 5:30 a.m. to get to the bus to school. That bus took her to the university where she transferred to a bus that took her to her school. We chose this bus route for her because it was safer than to transfer downtown.

The Journal American, the local (Bellevue and Eastside) newspaper offered free ads for high school students for summer vacation jobs. Through this great ad both Sandy and Niki got excellent cleaning jobs in just a few days. Sandy bought herself a used car at the end of the summer from her savings to become more self-sufficient. They kept the best of the jobs for the entire year, some even until graduation.

The Journal American was a great place to submit my articles. The editor told me about the Washington Press Association. He advised me to meet with them. It turned out to be an excellent match. They had just recently changed their name from Washington Press Women and started admitting male journalists too.

The original goal of the National Federation of Press Women (NFPW) of which Washington Press Association (aka Women) was a branch, was to fight for equal treatment and pay for women journalists, then after print also radio, TV, then digital media. The following year I was on the Board.

As a non-profit organization, we were most always short of cash. At one of the Board meetings the Board members put together $10 each in order to keep our office working. That same meeting we looked at each other: "What is it that we could do that would bring in money, but would not cost us anything?"

"Come on now, we are journalists, writers, we make publicity…"

"PUBLICITY!" Sharon shouted suddenly. "This is it!"

"Why are we constantly inundated with press releases?" Arlene André, our President chimed in.

"And how bad some of them are…" Barbara sighed.

"We should show them how to make publicity! How we want them to write their press releases," it was Sharon's turn again.

"We can do it ourselves, better than anybody. We know what and how we want to receive it."

"We need the money and we can do it ourselves!"

"We will get The Seattle Times auditorium! No charge."

Ideas flew around in the air. We asked the best of our editors from each of the media and advertised the panel. Invitations went out to all sorts of professional associations, among them the fundraisers. We ourselves took care of registration. We had 200+ members. Many hands make easy work.

The very first night sold out immediately. We made $1,600.00.

The next year we not only had to separate the print and the electronic media, we had to repeat both sessions. We had most people come from the fundraising and publicity organizations.

We had our "guaranteed" income, besides membership fees and our competition entrance fees.

The very first time I entered I won a prize with my article I wrote for *The Seattle Times* about the invasion of Grenada by the USA. What we knew for certain was that the former Communist police state was very repressive. A good Trinidadian friend, who always sailed around the islands brought us back a copy of the law declaring that everyone could be arrested who was thinking of doing or writing something, or could be suspected of a deed or word against the government. RETROACTIVELY.

I was so excited about the article. In those days, my weekly articles in the Catholic News of Trinidad and Tobago were also delivered to subscribers in Grenada. As there was a press blackout in the USA, I called my editor in Trinidad and asked her about what was happening.

Sister Marie Thérèse told me how grateful they were to the Americans for occupying the island. In People's Law Number 18 of 1981 Maurice Bishop, the Prime Minister of Grenada, simply outlawed freedom of the press. The Cubans were building a second airport on the island in order to "boost tourism." However the airport was built as a military airport in this strategic location. The island was definitely under the influence of Cuba and becoming a Communist state in every other respect. The seven Caribbean leeward islands formed the Organization of Eastern Caribbean States (OECS) to protect each other's independence, but three of those island-states did not have an army at all, so without American help the independence of the island could not have been defended. All the islands were afraid of becoming themselves the target of the Cubans one by one.

In the coming years I have received many more prizes, even national first prizes. The year I was the President in 1987/88 it was my privilege to sign all 300 prizes of that year.

John was so proud of me; he was so happy his wife had become the President of the Washington Press Association, even though English was her sixth language when we had arrived in North America. I enjoyed watching him brag to friends and whoever would listen.

The National Convention was in Williamsburg that year. From Washington State I was nominated for the National Communicator of Achievement award. Each State's representative had to walk across the stage, accompanied by the President of the State Branch. As I happened to be the President that year it became John's privilege to lead me across the stage.

This was the 75th anniversary of the National Federation of Press Women (NFPW) and the Convention was held in beautiful surroundings in the lovely old town that breathed tradition everywhere. John, as a result of his many miles accumulated by his travels, managed to get us first class tickets for free. We told the stewardess where we are going and she kept us in champagne all the way across the country. She even gave us an extra bottle to take with us to the hotel.

51

John's career was rising equally well. He was made Fellow of IEEE when we were still in Pullman. That is a prestigious award received by a very few every year. Out of the 300,000 members world-wide about 180 are awarded this title every year.

He was also admitted to the Professional Engineers (P.E.) the first year we had arrived in Vancouver, B.C. and received the iron ring with his first graduating class, based on his publications. He became a member of P.E. in five states in the U.S. and two Canadian provinces. The most interesting of these was the one to become a P.E. in Alaska. For that all engineers have to do an exam because it is "arctic engineering," an extremely interesting subject. For instance, the bases of transmission line poles have to be refrigerated, otherwise they may move or fall over in case of a thaw of the permafrost.

During John's lifetime he published more than 140 technical papers. His students would ask me to please tell them the name of the book he used, even if it was in Hungarian because he never used a book during his coursework. He never used any book, but rewrote his lectures every year to teach them the most up to date information. Yet, he still had time for us.

Now he was in a totally different environment at Ebasco. It was an eight to five job, not like university teaching. As soon as we arrived in Seattle, his colleagues at the University of Washington were overjoyed about his retired status. They immediately asked him to teach for them as long as he was in the area. The first year he arrived he waited to teach in order to get used to his new job, but the second year he did and continued to do so whenever they needed him. He was still on the faculty when he died. One year he also helped out at Seattle University, when the professor of electrical engineering, a friend named Father Wood, went on a sabbatical.

So, you can see we were not bored one bit.

As soon as we set up home in Seattle, we received a bilingual English-Hungarian newsletter, the HIREK. Its founders, Marta Boros Horváth and Sue Isely, were the founders of the Hungarian folk dancing group in Seattle. The curiosity was that Sue was actually American. They went through the Seattle phone book and sent out the newsletter to every person with a

Hungarian sounding name. That was the founding of the first Hungarian society ever in Seattle in 1982. It was named the "Hungarian American Association of Washington" and by 1984 they were registered as a non-profit.

A friend of ours from Pullman, Sr. Mariann Redinger, also moved to Seattle to help her seriously ill friend, Veronica (Bonnie) Beacom Dreves with her excellent program, Beginning Families. According to Bonnie being a baby is serious business. Her organization dealt with children from the moment of their conception until six years of age. She spoke not only as a professional, but also as the mother of six, one every year. Her organization was helping parents and teachers to develop each child human being both spiritually as well as physically from the start. Children treated with love in their first years were shown to become better prepared for life.

We were all in the same parish: St. Louise in Bellevue, Washington (Bellevue is a suburb of Seattle on the Eastside of Lake Washington). When Mariann mentioned Beginning Families wanted to start a newsletter I volunteered to be the editor. I, in turn recruited Kate, my daughter-in-law, Louis's wife, to do the layout for us. We made a good team for several years to come and even sent the newsletters to Hungary to people who knew English, such as parents, teachers and pediatricians who were in a position to spread the word.

Our first wedding after our move was back in Pullman. Steve and Kristy married at Sacred Heart Church in Pullman. During the Wedding Mass they were the Eucharistic Ministers. They moved into the parish house, into the basement and became youth ministers. Fr. Westbrook, the parish priest "adopted" them. He was our good friend who had been spending every Sunday afternoon with our family until we moved. Steve stayed for another year to do his MBA, while Kristy finished her special education degree. The next year we had three more graduations before Rita and Karl got married.

Between the two weddings we had another granddaughter. Louis and Kate had Mary on May 27th. We immediately went to see them and were lucky enough to celebrate Mary's zero birthday the hospital organized for the family. Mary was the youngest guest at Rita and Karl's wedding on June 16, 1984.

Rita practically lived to be a bride. She was preparing for her dream-wedding ever since Helen got married and she inherited her Modern Bride magazines. I can still see her sitting down in that cloud-like skirt with the little children around her when she tried on the dress and at the wedding.

She was always searching for ways to have her wedding "just so." She asked WSU President Glenn Terrell when Aretta's wedding was at his house and Rita was the flower girl in her long hot pink dress adorned with lace: "When I get married, can I have my wedding at your house?" He laughingly promised it to her, and she took him by his word. He lent Rita his yard and she got married right by the fishpond. Afterwards we had to go to a sorority because she was only 19 and minors could not drink at the President's House of WSU.

She was the happiest bride who had the wedding of her dreams.

My father came to all his grandchildren's weddings and danced with his grand- and great-grandchildren. John also made a point of dancing with all our grandchildren. Champagne was flowing! People were dancing and life was wonderful.

We reached the end of having immediate ties with Pullman.

By then, Mrs. Caine was old and in a wheelchair. While Rita and Karl were still in Pullman, they continued to visit her. I know she taught them much about life and took good care of them, just as they cared about her. To her, Rita was always like a real granddaughter and she became for us a real grandmother. After Rita and Karl left Pullman, she too left and joined her children at Williams Lake. She was a wonderful woman and a great friend!

This was also the year our house was finally sold! We went to Pullman, signed the papers, and had the down payment in our hands to be able to buy a house in Seattle. When we arrived back at our home in Bellevue, we saw a note on the refrigerator. "Carol Atkinson found THE house for you!" Although it was past 11:00 at night, we jumped back into our car and went to see the place. From what we could see in the moonlight, it looked perfect. Carol, by then an old friend, was one of the parents at Seattle Prep who was a realtor. The school brought us together and she helped us for two and a half years to find a house. God's ways are...by now you know our thoughts about that topic. The money and the house showed up at the very same hour.

The next day we could barely wait for Carol to take us to the house. We went through it and every room had something we loved. The green velvet-brocade wallpaper in the master bedroom, the walk-in-shower. the other two bedrooms... another bathroom, then we reached the kitchen. It had a Kitchen Aid dishwasher, the best brand of those days! As I looked up towards the picture window I wanted to scream for joy: "It even has a view!" The view of the Olympic Mountains, the lake, the cities of Seattle and Bellevue opened up in front of our eyes. Across the street were some lovely silver firs in our neighbor's garden. This house's garden was planned so that flowers should bloom one after another. Something would always beautify "our" garden. The living room and the huge family room had wall to wall picture windows, and a glass sliding door to the backyard patio. There was a rock garden that bloomed all the way to the neighbor's fence. The huge family room became our dining room with the big table and our huge cupboard my father bought us when we were still in Pullman. From that dining room opened an office, which became my office. We could barely talk.

"Yes Carol, this is it. That is THE house!"

"Thank you for finding it!"

"It just went on the market!" said Carol.

"Let's put in our offer!"

"We just have to have this house."

Carol started to work feverishly and in one day she bargained with the owners to get it for us at the exact prize we could afford.

Today I saw Somerset, across the lake from the University Club while sipping my wine during a Hawaiian Luau barbeque.

The Somerset swimming pool appeared in my mind. I felt the water caress me while looking through the glass wall at the marvelous view from the mountain looking at Seattle, Mercer Island, Lake Washington and in the distance the sea and the Olympic Mountains.

A cavalcade of memories flooded my mind. Those were arguably the most beautiful and fruitful years of our lives.

We moved there with our youngest daughter. The rest had already left home as adults, several were married and had children. Our late gift of God, Niki shared these special years with us as we enjoyed being still young enough to love our lives, while growing older.

I never imagined we could ever have our dream house.

Today we went out with Niki. We compared our DNA on the computer through the "23 and Me" website after we came home from dinner. Then we happened to look at each other. Our eyes locked. Her beautiful brown eyes caressed me, radiating her love right into mine. Our relationship was truly special, when she alone moved with us, she became an only child. God's late gift to us still keeps giving even now when she is 50 years old and both her children are adults and graduated from university in June 2018.

We moved into our dream house on August 1, 1984. While we were still in Pullman, Beate the daughter of a friend from Braunschweig, came to stay with us for the summer. This year it was her sister, Mani, who was our

357

visitor and a great helper with our move. She even surprised us with a big bowl full of blackberries she picked that grew wild on the side of the road leading up to our home.

Our children, colleagues and friends came with trucks, cars, whatever they had or could borrow and helped us move everything over from one house to another. Navaal single-handedly moved one of our refrigerators from the basement to the truck. He was a weightlifter who could lift and push 450 pounds.

In the coming few days he also built us bookshelves in the garage, on both sidewalls. There was a small workshop in the garage and over the garage we had a complete attic crawl space for our extra boxes. Once I complained to a friend about the many boxes. She said: "If you have seven children and each saves only three boxes that will make 21 boxes for your attic." Put it this way it did not sound much, but in the end, when you tried to straighten them out in a space, where you could not stand up…

After my 50th birthday, which we managed to have in our new home, I declared to the children that I would no longer go up in the attic. They can store their stuff there, but they have to put it up and manage it themselves.

My 50th birthday happened to be a month after we moved in. We invited our friends and organized a happy gathering. Our old piano from Pullman days got a place in our large family kitchen. We could even dance right by the piano. The kitchen was so inviting, the view was so spectacular from the kitchen counter, everyone stayed in the kitchen until it was so full, it overflowed. Then finally the bravest ones spilled into the big bright living room and the equally big festive dining room with equally spectacular views.

We did not know it yet, but that house became the scene for many memorable, even historical events. God always gave us what we needed. We did not know yet how much Hungary will need us, starting immediately! We also did not know we needed the house for that; exactly that house.

The dignitaries started trickling in. *The Seattle Times* wrote about the Jalowiecki couple from Poland, from where he was exiled because he was one of the leaders of Solidarity. He was a university professor. We contacted the paper and became good friends with Stanislaw Jalowiecki and his family. They even helped us move with their VW bus, filling it to the brim.

We heard that Tibor Tollas, THE poet of the Hungarian Uprising in 1956 was on his way to America. The HAAW, although it has been in existence, did not want to deal with anything that could be called politics or religion in order to prevent all disagreements and protect those who have been going to Hungary to visit old parents.

Well, the Szablyas are always ready for a challenge. We recognized that our greatest contribution to the HAAW is maintaining and nurturing the international aspects of Hungarian life in Seattle. For this reason, neither my husband John, nor I accepted positions on the HAAW Board, aware that there were many fine, competent people for these positions. We needed all our time, money, and energy to nurture the international connections. These ties eventually placed Hungarians on the map of Seattle and Seattle on the map of Hungarians.

This was the reason we invited Tibor Tollas! He stayed with us, we had a reception for him and organized a meeting where he could speak. With that, we became a part of a circle of people who passed Tibor and speakers in this vein from hand-to-hand around the USA and Canada. Every year he traveled for three months of the year in order to go from one place to another, from one country to another, from one continent to another to keep the Hungarians together and raise the necessary funds for his work. His newspaper, *Nemzetőr,* the *National Guardian,* appeared for the first time in Vienna, December 1, 1956. Soon it went to 96 countries in four languages.

And Tibor arrived!

It would be hard to imagine a more charming, enthusiastic, all heart gentleman who burst into our lives in his person. He could only sparkle, not letting off for a minute. One can truly get to know and befriend a person when being with him day and night during all of his stay, taking him places, discussing topics way into the night at our kitchen island-counter, where most of our guests liked to stay, while having breakfast, dinner or helping him communicate with the world through our computer.

He decided that all our daughters were world-beauties. We had only seven children, four girls and three boys, but he kept talking about our "nine beautiful daughters."

He told us about his life during those intimate hours we spent with him:

"When I finished high school, my father said I could become a priest or a soldier because those two were professions where you could study without having to pay. I did not think I could live without women, so I chose to be an officer. But God punished me for that because when I was arrested by the Communists, I spent seven years in prison and there were no women there either."

"Is that where you wrote your beautiful poems?" I asked.

"Not only I. We all wrote poems in our heads and learned each others' poetry in order to publish them some day when one of us may get out of prison."

"They walled up every window tight with tin…" I said.

"Yes, I had a chance to recite that on the corner of Kossuth Lajos utca and Múzeum körút, right by the Astoria Hotel in 1956 to the demonstrating crowd. I was let out of prison during the political thaw in 1956, a few months before the Uprising and worked at the Astoria feeding the furnace.

"It was a horribly memorable occasion I wanted to eternalize with my words. It happened right after Stalin's death. We were all hoping things would become easier, more relaxed. That is what we were expecting, when we heard trucks drive into the yard. You can imagine our disappointment when instead of easements, the people from the trucks were covering our tiny window tight with tin. That was the only light coming into our cell where 22 of us lived together."

"I love how your poem juxtaposes the prison conditions with that of the rest of the world, the ballrooms of London and the comfort of the West, then ends with the warning: 'Beware! Beware! or through the entire world they'll wall up every window tight with tin!' " said John.

My wonderful husband stood by my side all the way, his good humor and perfect diplomatic sense, his ability to talk with everyone, his deep knowledge of so many subjects, of history and politics, philosophy and psychology while being a man of science charmed everyone. Being close in age they really hit it off well, he and Tibor.

Once Tibor was here everyone wanted to see him, talk to him, be with him.

We got space from our church at St. Louise in Bellevue.

Tibor Tollas had an overwhelming success, people bought his books and those of others he published in Munich, where he was always close to the latest news.

The Hungarian Radio Free Europe was located in Munich. RFE prided itself in the fact that they listened to all the Hungarian broadcasts and by the time the talk of one of the leading Communists was finished their broadcasting started already airing the criticism of the talk. The talks were also immediately translated and transmitted to the USA. Their service went both ways. If a person was sent out for any reason from Hungary for a trip, RFE acquired and kept all the data about him or her; their background was right at hand if needed.

During his talk Tibor mentioned that he got his newspapers into Hungary as well, with the help of the good old Danube. The papers were wrapped in plastic and thrown into the Danube. In Hungary people who were watching for them fished out the newspapers.

Whenever a Chinese, Russian, Rumanian, or any nation's delegation came from behind the Iron Curtain, the paper was translated into their respective languages and put into the delegation's mailboxes in their hotel.

Tibor sent his poem "They walled up every window tight with tin" to President Reagan and received a glowing answer: "Thank you for your letter and especially for sharing with me your eloquent and moving poem...I have always thought that a lasting peace can only be based on truth, which includes an accurate understanding of the goals and methods of our adversaries...I wish that more would pay close attention to your witness and understand the nature of the challenge we face. I think that the enthusiasm with which our soldiers were greeted by the citizens of Grenada, who obviously did not want to live under Communism has opened a lot of eyes...Thank you again for writing and God bless you. Sincerely, Ronald Reagan."

After Tibor left Hungary in 1956, he married his sweetheart.

Throughout the years they had three children. Dr. Maria (Maya) Kecskési, his heroic wife, worked and became the Director of the Museum of Folkart, specializing in African Art in Munich. Tibor loved his children, wrote poems to them and his wife. He took care of the children too, when at home. However, during his annual three-month travel times that made it possible for Tibor to keep up the newspaper financially, Maya was alone with the children.

Tibor had excellent PR, without even having heard the name of the concept. While he was on route from one city to another, he wrote meaningful, lovely postcards on the plane to everyone who had done something for him.

One of the Hungarian ladies could not stay to meet him after having helped to prepare the room for his lecture. Tibor made a point of visiting her the next day.

From 1984 on, the Szablyas were part of the speaker-circle and Tibor became an annual visitor.

~~

We also worked together with Holt Ruffin, Head of the "World Without War Council." Soon our work for freedom made us known in the International community. Our home became a place for their foreign visitors, dissident leaders, to deliver a lecture, to mingle with our friends and theirs.

Tibor's circle also supplied us with speakers. Our goal was to let people know about the true face of Communism, to help the captive nations become free.

I had no problems providing publicity for the speakers. All those Washington Press Association experiences together with friends and acquaintances were ready to help me. Their stories were published through my writings and theirs, in *The Seattle Times* and in national publications.

361

We were just one link in the chain of hearts and minds embracing the world; just a little piece in the world-wide net of the fighters for the freedom of Hungary, of all captive nations. What a tremendous force there is in knowing we can rely on and trust each other! That together we can achieve!

Tibor Tollas's burning eyes, his enthusiasm, his excellence when reciting his poetry, or bring us up to date about the actions to free our native land, all helped to make him unforgettable for everyone concerned.

Just as an example of his constant overheated enthusiasm I quote a few lines from one of his letters some years later: "Every time I read your letter, I get a fever of 104 degrees because no one's words are as kind as yours, or expressing so much in a short and meaningful way as John does: 'We can hardly wait for you to get here!!!' But, of course, I am coming! If necessary, I would walk across the sea! How I wish I could stretch the hours I am spending with you, when I have the opportunity to absorb as much power as an empty car battery!"

Many members of the Hungarian Association joined with us in our effort to do everything in our power to help Hungary become free.

The Tibor Tollas event on October 27, 1984 brought many Hungarians into our magic circle. Those who remembered Tibor came to help with all our efforts. The Dibuz, Vadász, Monostory and Csepreghy families and Imre Takáts.

I remember, when Ilona Rittler, a well-known painter and art teacher came to one of such parties and was chatting with Eva Vadász, a very good friend who lived close to us. While they were talking, it turned out they were cell mates in a Hungarian prison. They were captured trying to leave the country in the early '50s. Thirty years later – no wonder they had to talk to discover their identities.

Klára and László Monostory were enthusiastic supporters of our cause. László was an officer in the Hungarian Army. He graduated from the Agricultural University in Hungary. There were 1,000 animals the Hungarian Army "evacuated" from Hungary. Among them were the famous Lipiczaner horses. It was his job to bring them all out of the country. He and his family were in a carriage like the pioneers in America, when their fourth child was born on the way to Austria. He still managed to bring all the animals across the border and place them on farms and in zoos. Much later, after Hungary became free he was decorated in Bábolna – the homeland of these horses – for saving the Lipiczaner breed.

A most beautiful period of our life started overflowing with activities. We woke every morning with an overwhelming incentive to start working, moving ahead. The will to help is a wonderful driving force. We wanted to give our all now that we had the opportunity.

In 1985 Tibor Tollas told us great news. He always worried about what would happen to his efforts to keep the ideas about freedom alive for Hungary once he will no longer be around.

After 1956 and the following horrible revenge a tacit agreement developed between the intelligencia and the government. Young people, who have not yet experienced the atrocities of the ruling class, started to voice democratic opposition. Sándor Lezsák (as I am writing this, he is the VP of the Hungarian Parliament) and his friends at first started the József Attila Young Writers' Circle in Lakitelek. Hundreds of young writers appeared at the first meeting. However, the Circle was outlawed, Sándor was dismissed from his job as a teacher and now he, his wife and his three children were at the mercy of the government. Tibor started an SOS movement for them to gather money to keep them alive. Word went around and we all sent money to Tibor to get it to them.

Soon other news was coming. The same young writers "published" handwritten "samizdat" literature. Tibor again came to the rescue. He started a Book Foundation for the "Forbidden Hungarian Literature" and published the works of the Hungarian writers himself in Munich, distributing them world-wide. We joined in his work as a matter of course. We did not have much money, but when Hungary needed us – we were there. We were obsessed by the possibilities that began opening.

At one point, a few years later, Lezsák and his friends visited Tibor in Munich. Tibor was overjoyed. He could personally hand them his legacy of continuing his work.

One of the speakers Tibor sent was László Gábor Hajnal, an author and journalist, originally from Hungary. In the '80s young people started to become fearless because their generation was no longer treated as harshly as their parents' generation. He told us that in 1968 when Czechoslovakia rose up against the Soviets, they wanted to take the Hungarian Army, in which he served as an officer at the time – against the freedom fighters – all the officers resisted. They told the authorities; their military oath was only for the defense of their homeland in case of an attack. Authorities relented and did not use their services.

László found out the hard way about Communist "liberalism." He decided to take some flowers to lot 301 in the Kerepesi Cemetery, where Imre Nagy, the Prime Minister during the Uprising and the freedom fighters who were executed in prison were buried in unmarked graves. As he was placing the flowers on the ground, he found his hands clapped into handcuffs. He spent some time in prison.

When he got out, he opted to find a way to the West and leave the country.

From then on he wrote as a freelance journalist and author. His wife worked for Radio Free Europe. They lived in Munich with their two children.

He arrived at our home and stayed for a week, during which time we interviewed each other constantly, in our kitchen at the kitchen island-counter, everyone's favorite place. We were writing articles about each other. This turned out to be really lucky. He spoke only a little English but understood much more. We arranged for a TV interview. He and I were on the show together. I was supposed to be the interpreter as he did not want to speak English. In the end I was speaking for him because there was no time for interpreting. I had to turn to him only a couple of times, and then only a fast "yes" or "no" answer.

We invited people to our home for dinner to meet with him. I was the cook, the maid, the interpreter, and the hostess at the same time, along with John. If he could not be home, I had to do all of the above at once. Interpreting while running in and out of the kitchen, cooking, while working with the guest who was staying with us. Yet, I did not feel it because adrenalin was driving us.

Our daughter Niki, the only one who was still living with us, helped us wholeheartedly, while going to school and working 30 hours a week at Nordstrom.

Then came 1986 – the 30th anniversary of the Hungarian Uprising in 1956.

52

The 30th anniversary of the 1956 Hungarian Uprising! Our enthusiasm mounted to its summit.

The Hungarian American Association of Washington (HAAW) wanted to mark this year with a very special event. I thought of the new genre, the oral history drama. Why couldn't we write one from our stories? My daughter-in-law, son János's wife, Marcey Painter Szablya, agreed. I presented the idea to the Board. After some deliberation about whether it would be possible to do it, HAAW gave us the green light and $500 seed money to write the grant to the Washington Commission for the Humanities (WCH), our state branch of the National Endowment for the Humanities (NEH). The genre was originally created by our daughter Ilike, and son-in-law Barry Meiners, for the NEH.

Our hopes were great to receive a major grant. As luck would have it the President of the WCH happened to be the retired Chair of the Department of English at WSU, John Elwood, also a friend. I talked with him. His only problem with the project was: "How can you show the 'other side' of a story like the Hungarian Uprising?" We managed to solve that difficult question, by giving voice to an AVO (security policeman), a Western professor who went to Hungary as a tourist, the Communist Party Secretary, and others.

Marcey and I had 11 months to achieve our goal: the complete performance researched, written, and produced; advertising for interview subjects; auditioning the actors, and doing the rehearsals.

We started writing the grant. We needed supporting letters. Tibor Tollas was immediately "on it." He gathered letters from the Hungarian Freedom Fighters Association, the Hungarian Scouts in Exterris, his own newspaper, the Association of Captive Nations in Europe, the Tibor-Circle's members. He supplied supporting letters from at least 17 places that we could add to our supporting letters of the HAAW, the Washington Press Association and many others.

Have you ever written a grant? It is one of the most frustrating experiences when it comes to proving everything. The most important questions: Why should this project be done and supported? Why should it be done by this group/person?

The Seattle Times and *Journal American* published our request for people to be interviewed, as well as many local and regional newspapers and newsletters. The calls started coming and we began our research. Some interviews were in English, some in Hungarian. Only I could do the Hungarian interviews because Marcey did not speak Hungarian. She learned to read Hungarian (its phonetic, once you know all the sounds of the alphabet), which proved useful, when she could read letters to me over the phone and I could tell her what they meant. Dr. Piroska Magassy gave me a book which proved to be a Godsend: Endre Marton's "The Forbidden Sky." Endre Marton and his wife Ilona were respectively the AP and UPI correspondents during the Hungarian Uprising. Previously that used to be their job until they got imprisoned. Luckily, they were released during a thaw just before the Uprising. After their escape he taught journalism at Georgetown and they received an award for "Journalism under Extenuating Circumstances." Kati Marton, a well-known author, is their daughter.

Doug Margeson, an excellent reporter at the *Journal American*, wanted to be interviewed. He said he was a teenager at the time and remembered thinking for the first time while watching the Uprising on TV, that his country's government was wrong.

One lady, who was not only interviewed, but cooperated with us, was the wife of an American officer stationed in Italy at the time with his family. He was ready to go. They had expected to get their orders any day. Helen, his wife, also wanted him to go.

I interviewed József Kővágó by phone, who used to be Budapest's Mayor after 1945, then again in 1956. The in-between-time he spent in jail. He was one of the few Hungarian leaders who testified at the UN about the Hungarian Uprising. He lived in New York, with his wife in 1986. They were friends with my parents. He was going to be our keynote speaker, but simply could not get away on October 23rd because of so many engagements for this 30th anniversary. He wrote a book about having been the mayor of Budapest after the war, then again in 1956: "You Are All Alone," is the title.

Tibor Tollas was interviewed also by phone, by me. He was in Florida at the time. He became a part of our program, which was developing into a Freedom Month.

Remember, in an oral history drama every word had to be spoken by some of the people interviewed, or had to have actually happened.

The questions were: "What did you do at the time?" "Where were you at the time?" "How did you feel at the time?" They were questions that prompted a longer reply, the interviewees could not answer with a "yes" or "no."

Marcey and I started writing. If I wrote as much as half a page, Marcey started objecting: "This is already the length of a monologue." She was a playwright and an excellent editor.

Rob Bulkley, János and Marcey's friend, agreed to be the director. He worked in theater and had a bluegrass band.

Quite a few actors and actresses came to audition. We needed six excellent actors as they had to assume the characters of all the people whose words were being repeated, sometimes without leaving the stage.

We found the six actors we needed for *Hungary Remembered*. In alphabetical order: Sam Barker playing the Professor, Zoe Klemens Kelly playing Zsuzsa, Paul Killiam playing János, David Klein playing Tibor, Lynda Woodson playing Erzsi, Diane Manning playing Marie, and Carole Dempsey as understudy for all female roles.

Excerpts from the original program:

CAST OF CHARACTERS

The actors in *Hungary Remembered* will play people as they remember themselves. They will be required to change the people they are portraying sometimes from line to line. They must draw the character from the content within the lines, depicting that person in that moment and move on. The actors were given "'names'" only for convenience and could as easily be called 1, 2, or 3. However, as certain people have similar characteristics, those with similar personalities will be played by the same actor.

So, *in general,* the people portrayed by:

MARIE:	are strong, motivated, intelligent, serious, sometimes angry fighters.
ZSUZSA:	are more frivolous, willing to be led, impetuous, younger.
ERZSI:	are cautious, older, staid, careful, the "home bodies."
TIBOR:	are angry, intelligent, the poet, politician, prisoner.
JANOS:	are active, blue collar, "peasant," swift to act.
PROF:	are soldiers, Soviets, sure-of-themselves, self-righteous.

The Seattle University Choir will perform two songs, both in Hungarian, under the baton of Roupen Sharkarian.

The words for the first were sent from Hungary in a handwritten note. The Anonymous writer (at the time we could not name him, but he was the conductor of the choir at St. László church in Hungary, the brother of a friend in Winnipeg, Anikó Bencsics) wrote it to the tune of Beethoven's "Ode To Joy" to commemorate the 1956 Hungarian Uprising.

Zengjen a bátrak országában	Let the ancient festive songs
Ünnepi ének, hősi dal	Resound in the home of braves.
Fogjon össze minden lélek	Hungarians be united
Hadd legyen újra egy a magyar	Joining souls over the globe.
Hős elesettek áldozatának	Sacrifices, blood of heroes
Vére kiontott drága bér	Should be dear to all of us
Néma társak, bús halottak	The spirits of the grieving dead
Szelleme mindég visszatér.	Will return forevermore.

The second piece performed by the choir is the Hungarian National Anthem.
Words by Ferenc Kölcsey (1826), melody by Ferenc Erkel (1874)
Translated by Dr. John F. Szablya

Isten áldd meg a Magyart	God bless the Hungarian
Jó kedvvel bőséggel.	With happiness and plenty.
Nyújts feléje védő kart	Reach him a protective arm
Ha küzd ellenséggel.	When fending off enemies.
Balsors akit régen tép	Bad times are his fate always
Hozz reá víg esztendőt,	Grant him oh happier days
Megbűnhődte már e nép a	These people have suffered for
Multat s jövendőt.	Past and future alike.

Hungary Remembered is written for ensemble playing. The atmosphere should be that of friends getting together to talk over old times, the audience being one of the friends. In general, the actors remain on stage, enacting a memory of a character or as supportive listeners.

COSTUMES should be simple grays, black and whites because the photos were black and white in those days, '40s style suits and dresses. Some accessories can be used for character changes – scarves, shawls, coats, hats, vests, etc.

Some of the clothes used were the actual clothes in which we had escaped, and our baby's basket was also featured, including all the clothes he wore.

The Seattle University Choir was taught the Hungarian words by our daughter Niki (Dominique) who was a member of the Choir as a student at S.U. in 1986.

The actors and actresses also took part in the creation of the play. They poured through poems about the Hungarian Uprising and chose texts by E.E. Cummings, Antal Lökös, Anonymous (a freedom fighter) and Gregory Nagy that somehow perfectly described a situation in the play.

Sándor Petőfi, was a natural, as the Uprising started with the reciting of his famous poem, written for the Revolution against the Habsburgs in 1848 "Hungarians Rise!"

The translated poems of Tibor Tollas were included in the selection and several were chosen. "They Walled Up Every Window Tight With Tin" was quoted throughout the play, one verse at a time as the story progressed.

The first three verses:

> Only this much light was left from our life.
> The stars in the sky and a fistful of sunshine.
> We watched for this day after day from the depths
> of the dim walls, every evening and every afternoon.
> But they stole that too, that handful of sun:
> They walled up every window tight with tin.
> Ten of us lay smothering in a narrow hole.
> Our ten mouths starved for air,
> Gaping mute as the gills of fish
> Driven to the shore. We lack the heart to breathe in,
> Along with the stink, life giving air
> They've walled up every window tight with tin.
> At London dances, in their silken dresses,
> Girls are gliding over the beautiful floors.
> The bright down of their gentle hair
> Blows in the graceful arcs of antique furniture.
> The West is dancing. Have they sold us then?
> And they've walled up every window tight with tin.

Tibor wrote poems for one of the guards' wife, who in turn brought him food now and then. He smuggled in pieces of paper in bread and smuggled out Tibor's poems.

One day he "brought us twenty fresh cherries, God they were so good!" as Tibor was telling his story, then started reciting the poem this event prompted:

One of us got twenty cherries
and his heart was light. He started
to pass them around…
as though his pulse
had tasted the freedom and love
shut off for ten years. And he passed them so
not one of his treasures got lost:
as they wound along, prisoner to prisoner,
we drank them with thirsty eyes –
and on and on, as though some password
had been announced in fruit.
For the cell was flowering with cherries,
Our hearts were fuller
than when Christ, standing at the lake's edge, passed
loaves and fishes to the hungry, hand to hand.
He walked among us on a road of cherries,
and while we gathered all those blossoms
piece by piece, as in a basket,
the light kept pouring.

On stage, the actors were reciting the poem alternating verse by verse, while passing the handful of cherries around between them. Not one of them was missing while it made full circle.

Naturally, we needed to find a space for our project, which snowballed. I happened to sit at the Pacific NW Writers Conference beside Helen Lou Ross. While we chatted, I told her about the project. Her eyes lit up as she said:

"You have to contact my relative, Bob Harmon, professor of history at Seattle University."

She gave me his phone number and I called. Bob was the sweetest person. He immediately said YES! with capital letters in his voice and sent a letter that arrived the next day, adopting the project to be hosted by Seattle University.

He suggested having lectures in the library, by university professors, a few weeks before the oral history drama would be produced, in order to make the subject clear to the proposed audiences. We organized the lecturers and the topics. In alphabetical order: Imre Boba (UW professor of history), Henry Grosshans (WSU Director of publishing and author of several historical books, Colonel, member of lend-lease action during WWII), Bob Harmon (SU professor of history and D-Day participant), Dr. Zoltán Kramár (CWU professor of history) and his wife, Maria Kramár (actual freedom fighter), Dr. John Szablya (Professor WSU and UW, participant in Uprising) together with his wife, Helen M. Szablya. We ended up with 24 lectures before and after the performances of the oral history drama. I gave 12 of these lectures that were held all over the state. The World Without War Council, Holt Ruffin organized a panel after the performance with the participation of the lecturers. The last lecturer was Tibor Tollas. He arrived on November 4th, and, true to his gentlemanly customs, he visited the Choir that sang during the performances and presented each of the members with a single red rose. By the time he arrived, I translated the play into Hungarian. He put the accents on the original Hungarian script. We had no accents on keyboards yet.

We received the major grant of $6,000 from the Washington Commission for the Humanities. The grant we wrote was 167 pages with all the supporting letters, budget, and other "goodies" to be supplied. We diligently kept records of all the "in-kind" donations we received getting signed proof from the people who had offered their work for free. This even included the professional actors, who rehearsed every night for five weeks without receiving any remuneration (none of them was even Hungarian). The Freedoms Foundations at Valley Forge awarded Marcey Painter Szablya, Helen M. Szablya and Professor Robert (Bob) Harmon the "George Washington Honor Medal for the drama and associated lecture series." The Freedoms Foundation at Valley Forge is a non-partisan, independent, not-for-profit organization, which was founded in 1949 with the objective to foster the ideals surrounding the founding of the American Nation and to make it relevant to contemporary life. Its prizes are given to those who forward these ideals.

The support of the Hungarian American Association of Washington was an important contributing factor. Although the Association had only 550 names on its roster, the realization of the project was possible here in Seattle. This should serve as evidence to the generosity and the hard work of the Hungarian community.

Voice of America reported the events in Seattle in a special broadcast and forwarded its report about *Hungary Remembered* to all the world's news agencies in 42 languages. I did the interview with Voice of America at Bellevue Community College. They generously lent their studio and equipment to do the overseas interview for the project.

Hungary Remembered was awarded the gold medal of the Arpad Academy and the Pro Libertate Revolutio Hungariae medal of the Guardian of Liberty (Nemzetőr).

As a continuation of the program, I lectured statewide in Washington during the years 1987 to 1989 as an Inquiring Mind Lecturer of the Washington Commission for the Humanities. Subjects were: "Growing up in Hungary, The Anatomy of a Revolution," and "Women in Marxist Countries."

We held an eight-hour interactive seminar about how to do an oral history drama, the fundraising, the PR, the how, why and when, with the originators of the genre, daughter Ilike and Barry Meiners, as well as Marcey and me. It was videotaped and is now on DVD. The seminar was a pre-conference addition to the ATA annual conference in Washington DC.

To live through it all was an exquisite experience. To listen to the actors say the words you have created through your work and that of many others, was life-changing. We had achieved the almost impossible. Every day was an adventure: to hear all the life stories, to interact with the actors, to acquire all we needed for the oral history drama, write the grant and do the PR work with the media…Life was hectic, busy, almost unbearable – beautiful.

53

While the events of 1986 were going on, Tibor Tollas told me about an intriguing book I undertook to translate. The book was Ernest Töttösy's book: *Mind Twisters* (Hungarian title: *Téboly*). The book is his – an international lawyer's – autobiography of those months when in a Communist prison he was made schizophrenic with the help of a truth serum. What was remarkable is that he was then brought back from schizophrenia. What is amazing in his description is that he remembered everything that had happened to him during that period. The normal reaction is to forget everything that happened during the time of the "treatment." An MD's exact description of how the drug should act shows he indeed remembered. This drug was used during show trials. I did not read the book ahead of time, I just learned the whole story while translating it. The work was fascinating and horrible at the same time. I had to totally immerse myself in the book, to "live it" with him in order to present the story faithfully. I did substantial editing as it was very long in the original. That book came out in March 1987. The author told me he liked my version of the book better than his own. Needless to say, I was very pleased to hear that. Marcey was a great help in editing the book.

We thoroughly enjoyed living in our beautiful dream home. I must tell you: it was OUR dream home. For many it would not have been, as it was "old fashioned" in some ways. But that is exactly what we liked about it because it was like the house we had dreamed about for a long time.

All three of us living in it were extremely busy. John often left at 5:00 a.m. to be able to call their office in New York when they opened. It did not mean he came home earlier. I started interpreting in hospitals, courts and jails in addition to doing translations.

Niki studied and worked. She was now an office helper at Seattle University for the Dean of the Matteo Ricci program.

The TV started a mini-series titled AMERIKA (with a K). I was invited with other media people to preview the series and write an article about it. The topic was what America would be like 10 years after being occupied by the Soviets. That year I won national first prize with this article from the

Washington Press Association (WPA) and the National Federation of Press Women (NFPW).

The Conference was in Little Rock, Arkansas. The President of the local chapter, Charlotte Schexnayder, also happened to be a Senator in Arkansas. So, she arranged with the then Governor of Arkansas, Bill Clinton, to have a reception for our conference. Having been on the Board, we were taken first to the mansion. There were just about four of us chatting with him while the others arrived. Hillary arrived later with two stuffed briefcases, coming from work. I later mentioned this to her and she said: "Yeah, I was always the working woman!"

The NFPW Conference decided to have a 21st Century Planning Committee of which I became one of the members, hand-picked by Charlotte Schexnayder, who was asked to be the President of the Committee. The Committee met twice within a year. Once in Chicago, IL at the O'Hare Hilton Hotel, situated right in the airport September 12 to 13, 1987, and once in Dallas, TX January 1988 in the Executive Inn. We flew in just for the meetings. O'Hare Airport was huge. Planes took off every two minutes. Luckily, the conference rooms were soundproof. There was so much to discover while living IN the airport, like the chapel, where you could go to Mass on Sundays, the businesses on the grounds, and the restaurants.

While we worked on the Committee, we also had lots of fun. To save money, four of us stayed in a room with two queen beds. Of course, we only had one bathroom and lots of giggling went on while getting ready to work. I used to get up earlier to have the bathroom all to myself. While showering I boiled water. Then I made instant coffee for all of us, which was welcomed by all. We needed it for work during our day.

We made many important decisions about the strategies and opportunities for our future at NFPW.

As a journalist, one's bread and butter includes many interviews, so I always looked out for interesting people.

Fr. Flavian, an amazing man, and I became friends when he was deacon at St. Louise Parish in Bellevue, WA. I interviewed him one day. His story was such an important déja vu proof of the horrors of Communism.

THE UNFINISHED MASS

Young Flavian could not believe his eyes. This white man, this European had no big car, no fancy clothes – and – he was barefoot! Flavian asked before he thought: "How come you are barefoot?"

"Why not?" the man smiled. "Are you wearing stockings?"

"But you are a white man."

"I prefer it this way."

"You work, along with the other people, not in some plush office," Flavian continued. "Why do you do it?"

"I do it for Jesus," the French speaking Christian Brother answered.

"Who is he?"

"Come to my classes and listen. You will learn about him. "

Flavian's life commitment to Christ started that day. The young Buddhist was enchanted by what he heard, but even more by what he saw.

A year later Flavian surprised his teacher: "If you can do that for Christ, I want to do the same thing. I want to become a brother like you." This began the conversion of all of Flavian's family.

Flavian became a brother, attended Cambridge University in England, then obtained his M.A. and Ph.D. in psychology from Loyola University, Chicago. He did his post doctoral studies at the Alfred Adler Institute, Chicago and received his M.D. in psychotherapy at the Dr. Carl Rogers La Jolla Institute in California. He spent his life educating young people around the world. In Sri Lanka he became President of St. Benedict's College, then provincial superior of the Christian Brothers in Sri Lanka, India and Pakistan. As such he had an opportunity to work with Mother Teresa taking care of unwanted children in orphanages and leper colonies.

His personality radiates warmth, simplicity and love. No wonder he was elected to two UN commissions: Human Rights and Justice. In this role he went with a UN group to China to fulfill one of his duties.

His first eye-opener was in a prison. A tiny old man had already served 23 years. He received a bowl of rice to eat every noon. In the evening it was "soup" consisting of water and a few grains of boiled rice. "What have you done to deserve this treatment?" The prisoner answered: "I told people not to go along with Atheism, but to keep on praying." He turned out to be Dominic Tang, a bishop. For 23 years the only book he was allowed to read was the Communist Manifesto. He asked Fr. Flavian for his rosary, the first one he had seen since his imprisonment. (Later Fr. Flavian managed to free him through the efforts of the United Nations.)

Fr. Flavian was asked by the bishop to visit his parishioners in Hunan. It took five days by train to arrive there. People there had only three Masses all together in 23 years. An American citizen of Chinese birth received

375

permission to say Mass at his mother's grave. 400 people showed up and begged him to say Mass again the next day. Then 700 came. They kept begging him and he could not resist, so he said Mass again. This time 1,000 came. Along with the people the soldiers came as well and told him to never say Mass again. He continued saying the words of the Mass. Just before consecration the soldiers handcuffed him. Brother Flavian pulled out his diplomatic passport and protested against the arrest of an American citizen. "I am here as a witness. In two weeks the UN will discuss this matter."

The soldiers took the priest anyway: "You cannot start assemblies here. He will be deported to America." Brother Flavian was left alone standing at the improvised altar.

1,000 people were begging him to continue the half-said Mass. He said: "I cannot. I am not a priest." 1,000 people gave him a mandate, crying out to him again: "Go, become a priest and come back to us!"

Two weeks after his return from China, Brother Flavian entered the seminary and at age 62 he became an ordained priest. In 1983 he asked to go back to the people who sent him on his mission. In 1987 he was still waiting to be allowed to return to China as a Catholic priest, able to finish the half-said Mass in Hunan.

This prize-winning article, my interview with Fr. Flavian, was published in *Our Family* magazine November, 1987.

There were many others, for example the 19-part article about George Orwell's *1984*, illustrating how Marxism is lived around the world today, about women in Marxist countries, which was also the topic of one of my talks given for two years all over Washington State. "How the Eucharist Came to Prison," a homily by a Sister just released from a Rumanian prison through an agreement with the Vatican, on a beautiful Corpus Christi day in Vancouver, B.C. Many articles about the encyclicals of John Paul II. I felt we, who lived through what he had experienced, could explain why he said what he did.

President Reagan's words: "Mr. Gorbachov, tear down this wall," and the Summit between the two world leaders brought developments here in Seattle as well. The Seattle Peace and Freedom Coalition formed in April 1987 to promote human rights principles of the 1975 Helsinki Accord. The Moscow counterpart of the group, Press Club Glasnost, organized a four-day seminar on human rights. As a part of that event 20 of us from the Seattle group initiated a conference call with four Soviet activists on December 11th. The seminar took place in apartments, as they had no permission to get a meeting place in Moscow. This conference call via satellite was set up to discuss and test the extent of the Soviet government's "glasnost" meaning openness.

The first one to speak was Lev Timofeyev, whose excellent book I had just finished reading. He spoke English. Four of the seminar participants were arrested, but he deemed it a progress that they were able to organize the seminar. He himself was in prison for two years. "We have semi-glasnost" he said. The persons we talked to spoke cautiously and worded their message "just right." Zulfaya Tockchukova spoke on the phone with Russian speakers and interpreted their words. Another Soviet activist Gennady Krochick, a co-founder with Timofeyev of the Trust Group, said he was not aware of Seattle having a sister city in the Soviet Union (Tashkent), as in the Soviet Union these relationships were still conducted by government officials rather than – as originally intended – by regular people. Keith Axelson believed in the Trust Group – the Seattle Peace and Freedom Coalition had found a kindred spirit. It was a successful people-to-people exchange by phone, yet one of the persons we called was not willing to speak. He obviously had his reasons.

54

In the meantime, exciting things started happening in Hungary. The first truly political visitor to arrive was Sándor Rácz. Maybe so many came because we treated them like family from the very first minute they arrived. The "Szablya Hotel" as it was soon nicknamed, received more and more visitors as the 1980s were closing in on 1990.

Sándor Rácz played an important role during the Uprising in 1956. Though only 23 years old, he was elected to be the President of the National Revolutionary Committee of the Workers. He did not leave the country but was a leader until he was jailed and sentenced. After 1963 the revenge of the system died down somewhat and the pressure of the Western Workers Unions pushed for his freedom. He was pardoned and returned to Izsák, his native village. He married his sweetheart in the Coronation Church on Castle Hill. The church was filled to the rafters at his wedding. He was a great favorite of the people. Slowly, very slowly the opposition started resistance, but almost invisibly. They started a Yurta theater, where they could produce plays that were comparable to the samizdat of the writers.

In 1989 the AFL-CIO achieved permission for him to take a trip to North America. The same group that handed Tibor Tollas around in a circle started working. Sándor Rácz arrived on March 1st to Seattle. He came to our house. We could not pick him up at the airport because – totally unbelievably – so much snow fell on March 1st in Seattle that only a good friend of ours, Béla Vadász, who had a four-wheel-drive could make his way to the airport and bring him to our home.

We were practically "snowed in" the entire time while he was staying at our home March 1st through 7th, but we still managed to have the talk for the public. He was our March 15th Hungarian National Day speaker.

While he was here, we talked and talked and talked. He brought us up to date about everything happening in Hungary, about his life, his family.

We heard from him about Szárszó, where intellectuals met in Hungary to discuss mutual concerns. This was a generation that no longer grew up in constant fear for their lives, for loss of their parents, their homes. These things no longer were part of their experience. Everything was already taken from the previous generation. That made them much braver than those who had survived the crushed Uprising in 1956 and the Stalinist years before that. Basically, there was an old generation, a new one, and one in-between.

In Szárszó the participants decided to become the Parliament for the Hungarian people until a free Parliament would be elected. They said: "Today we have to paint our future on the sky."

The discussion was about the importance to divide the land again, give it back to the farmers instead of keeping the land in cooperatives and in huge state land estates.

Communications, the news had not reported the events properly and honestly. This needed to be changed.

Defense costs in percentage were so high that Hungary ranked in the first fifth highest among the countries; it was two to three times higher than reported to the people. Instead Hungary should pay the country's debts.

In suicides and alcoholism, Hungary was one of the leaders.

The Soviet Union won the war but lost the peace. Socialism was weakening by the day. Glasnost and Perestroika showed that socialism became the cemetery of those countries that had adopted it.

In 40 years, Hungary's population was dwindling, and some managed to leave the country.

The group discussed the importance of the Hungarian diaspora in the surrounding countries. Wherever the boundaries are now, the minorities should get autonomy to acknowledge the union of all Hungarians living in the diaspora.

Transylvanian human rights of Hungarians and other minorities should be tied to and fought for along the universal human rights. The right to sing the Transylvanian anthem.

Political pluralism, the establishment of other parties besides the Communist party.

As the Soviet Union was falling to pieces it became continuously more important for the Central and Eastern European countries to form a unit to help each other when the Soviet Union no longer delivered. At the time, for example, there was a shortage of paper in Hungary.

Cooperation with the West as a continuation of how it used to be previously.

Some talked about the former church schools, the ways students were forming circles to educate themselves.

Five talks of global importance covered all those topics. According to Sándor, László Németh, a famous Hungarian author, could have been Voltaire, conditions permitting. Németh emphasized that they should put their common interests before their personal interests, the importance of moral renewal and democracy.

A new Marshall Plan was discussed. The entire region under Soviet influence must integrate again into the Western European community.

We could not believe our ears. People were actually (at least) talking about changing their future.

The meeting discussed that the present situation in Hungary is not socialism. Foreigners were also present: Americans looking for dissidents, Western representatives, but from the East only a few Polish organizations besides the Hungarians.

They decided it was important to accept principles, not only to react "ad hoc." In the past 40 years there was no opportunity to develop new world views or political culture.

Minorities, like gypsies, colored foreign students, Transylvanian refugees, and Rumanians were important.

The seeds of FIDESZ (Fiatal Demokraták Szövetsége), the present ruling party (2019) were planted at that meeting. The name means: Young Democrats' Association.

Let's organize an opposition party! Some still opposed it because they were afraid the Communist Party would forbid it, so they should not even try. The Party already gave birth to its opposition, no need to organize.

After a public religious service and "táncház" popular folk dancing event, the discussion about a new party continued.

When discussing 1956 with Sándor, this is what he said: "If our hearts beat for the same goal, there is no conflict between us, we can become as one! I am happy that I survived that bitter instant in the history of our nation, which was also so phenomenal and radiant!"

Although we enjoyed our talks, Sándor simply needed to move around sometime. He volunteered to shovel our driveway, which he did – absolutely perfectly. He also noticed that our kitchen tap was dripping.

"May I fix it?" he asked.

We were more than happy to let him help us.

He was a charming man. He kept sending us news. He sent us the program of the reburial of Imre Nagy, the Prime Minister of Hungary during the Revolution, who was buried in an unmarked grave after his execution. It was at this reburial, where the crowd was tumultuous, where Victor Orbán the present Prime Minister of Hungary, then a young man demanded, echoing everyone's wish: "The Soviets should leave our country!" It took tremendous courage to declare this publicly at the time. The "velvet revolution" started. No blood was shed, but the changing of the regimes had started.

Later, when we were able to return to Hungary after 1990, we met him again. At one point we helped him from the USA to campaign when he ran for President of Hungary. We developed a friendship with Sándor that lasted until his death.

Tibor Tollas told us about Sándor Lezsák and people meeting in his backyard. Those people started a "Roundtable Conference" that developed into a Party "Magyar Demokrata Forum." Their elected President became József Antall, a beloved history professor and later librarian at the National Museum. This little group of Lakitelek, the small place where Sándor Lezsák was a teacher – who could only afford a bicycle for transportation – formed the Party that won the first free elections. If only it would have gone as quickly as the time it took to write down this paragraph!

The group of young writers published their own works (samizdat) and sent them to Tibor Tollas in Munich. He published them professionally and we all helped him distribute the works all over the world.

I am convinced Hungary needed both the Hungarians inside Hungary and the ones in the diaspora to return the country's freedom.

If those who had experienced "socialism" would not have spread the truth about it all over the Western world, maybe the Allies would still think about Soviets as their allies, who could not have done any harm to anyone. They needed us to tell them: the Allies sold us from one dictatorship (the Nazis) to an equally horrific dictatorship (the Communists).

Don't forget, it was the Americans who supplied practically all the equipment to the Soviet Union through the lend-lease agreement. Henry Grosshans, a speaker of the *Hungary Remembered* project, a dear friend from Pullman was one of the colonels taking the equipment to the Soviet Union. He was also the author of several books on Europe. From him we had first-hand knowledge about these events.

To persuade the Americans took thousands of us to spread the word; until they saw it for themselves, when the Soviet Union collapsed.

55

Meanwhile on the home front:

Sandy and Navaal both graduated from the University of Washington and decided to finally get married in the church in 1988.

The wedding took place in Blessed Sacrament Church, a beautiful old church in Seattle. All her siblings got so excited they outdid each other to make it the most beautiful wedding ever. The seated dinner after the wedding for about 100 people took place at our home. Guests came from all over the world, Trinidad, England, Australia, Canada. My father and Navaal's mother Zilda Ramdin came already before. Zilda arranged for the Trinidadian part of the catering, we took care of the American-Hungarian part. There was enough food for an army. Champagne and all drinks were abundant for everyone. Sandy's siblings rented the tables, the chairs, the dance floor, which we put on top of the wall-to-wall carpet. We rented glasses and china. Son Steve decorated our garden with many strings of Christmas lights and lanterns.

John and I walked all around the neighborhood and talked to the neighbors, telling them about the coming event, asking them not to complain to the police if we would be too loud, but rather come over and enjoy the party with us.

We found a beautiful dress for Sandy and she wore my mother's three-meter-long veil made of Brussels lace. She wore it sari-like, wrapped around her body.

The siblings rented a limousine for the newly married couple that brought them to the wedding and also took them to the reception on a scenic route.

May 13, 1988. Everything was set. The ceremony was ready to start, when Father Wesbrook, our beloved Pullman parish priest – with whom we called each other brother and sister – arrived from Eastern Washington. He decided he just had to marry Sandy whom he had known since she was a little girl. It was a happy surprise for all of us.

They pronounced their wedding vows on the family crucifix and received their own copy of it.

It was a totally wonderful experience. Everything sparkled and resounded with happiness, as after the dinner the dance started on the make-shift dance floor as well as outside on the patio. The music was as international as the company. Some of the guests I met for the first time only at the wedding party. Navaal was a great cricket player and of course the Seattle cricket players originated from all over the former British Commonwealth.

My father from Winnipeg and Zilda from Trinidad had the best time together flirting. We loved watching them, as my father followed her everywhere she went.

Ilike and Barry with their daughter Anna and son Alex could not come from Maryland, but they created a tape singing: "I am going to the chapel, I am going to get married…" a hit song in those days. We played the tape in the middle of the party and heard their good wishes for the newly married couple afterwards.

Kristy and Steve had their second child, Adam, just two weeks before the wedding, on May 1st. Father Wesbrook, in whose basement the young couple had lived during the first year of their marriage, was in town. What would have been more natural than having Adam baptized the next day? Father celebrated Mass in our home and baptized Adam.

Kristy and Steve bought a house by that time in Newport Hills, about five minutes by car from our house, so we saw them often. After the baptism we had brunch at our house.

Rita was pregnant at the time of the wedding with their first child, Krystal, who was born later in the year, November 28th. Rita and Karl lived in the Tri-Cities, in Eastern Washington. Karl worked at Battelle National Laboratories at Hanford as a nuclear chemist. His father, a former professor at WSU, also worked there as a chemist. That was about a four-hour drive away from Bellevue.

So off I went to Rita and Karl's house in Richland, a nice old house with an age-old tree in the backyard with all the charms of an old gnarled tree, emerging like from a fairy tale. During WWII the first nuclear bomb was built in Richland, on the Hanford site. The building of the nuclear bomb was achieved by dividing the project into several phases. The second phase was being researched as if the first phase would have been solved already. The third phase as if both phases were already solved. That speeded up the process considerably. Scientists were brought from all over the country together with their families and culture followed them. The house in which Rita and Karl lived was built in those days, for those scientists and workers.

During one of my lecture tours I gave a talk in Sunnyside. There a lady told me she was the wife of one of those scientists and they had decided to stay in the area and bought land there. She was the one who told me how they had even Broadway shows brought to Richland at the time to keep the population entertained and liking their lives there enough to stay.

We had a fun time with Rita and Karl, and of course our wonderful little new granddaughter, Krystal. John joined us over the weekend and Krystal was baptized before we went home.

Rita and Karl tried our method with babies. When our first one was born our pediatrician told us it was as important for the baby to sleep during the night as it was for the parents. His advice was not to feed anything nourishing to the baby during the night. Change her diapers and give her boiled water to drink by the teaspoon. Then let them cry if they have to. Of course it is hard for the first couple of days, but the babies easily and fast get used to the regimen: no nourishment during the night.

At first people thought Rita and Karl were such abusive parents, but when they saw the children obey their parents and behave so nicely, they had to ask: how do you do it? The secret was discipline, which started by that first act of getting them used to not nursing during the night.

Then, the same people who had criticized them suddenly appreciated their methods. Her scientist husband realized right away, when I told him how the system worked: "just like Pavlov's dogs."

If the child gets used to loving, fair treatment as a human being, it is easy to let them know how to behave and what is good for them. Letting them have their way is not the kindest treatment because that is not what they will face when life happens. A child learns easily. Much more difficult for an adult.

It is good for the children to have limits. Now, there is another secret. Allow them always one step less than what you are comfortable with because they will always try to see how far they can go, meaning at least one step beyond their limit. Parents should discuss their feelings and attitudes before they set the limits – then they will always be "on the same page." The children will not be able to play one parent against the other. Like saying to Dad "Mommy already agreed I can do that" when they had not even asked her yet.

Rita wrote me a delightful card with a Mama Rabbit in a big hat leaning on an umbrella. Her card read: "To the Mom who taught me how to be a Mom! You did great! I love you, Rita, & Karl, & Krystal too!

We loved having many children. As John used to explain: "The hardest is to jump from one to two because that is a 100% increase, the third one is only 30%, the fourth 25%..." The older ones take care of the younger ones. Their example show the little ones how to behave, what to do in certain circumstances.

In the summer of 1988, on July 9th a very special gathering took place at our house. John's 1978 graduating class decided to have their 10th anniversary class reunion at our house. We felt so honored to feel their obvious love for us. An excellent party developed from all their planning. There was plenty of food, drinks, fun, excitement in the radiant sunshine, ordered especially for them. All had great jobs and families, children, and those who already had children as students, in Pullman, their children were in their teens. The Hardy family lived in Troy, close to the nuclear energy plant where he worked. They had a nice old house with a stream running through their garden. Steve Muchlinski and Merryl were happily married with children. The McSherrys lived in California, the Fries lived in Arizona, the stories were all deliciously different and happy. This class was really special. Many of them were at the university with the GI bill. They were the ones with whom we have been having the wonderful Rico's nights on Fridays, when we all were just "a tiny bit" younger. To this day I have the list of all their names, addresses, phone numbers from those days. By now they are either retired or in a leading position in their industry.

In September I decided to try working at a corporation. I was accepted at Envirosphere, the environmental branch of Ebasco, where John worked. I was still also doing the "Inquiring Mind" lecture series traveling around Washington State lecturing for the Washington Commission for the Humanities. I have never worked before in an 8 to 5 setting. I was excited and had no idea what to expect. Apparently neither did my boss, Katie. She took me around, then gave me something to do. I did it and then went to ask for something more to do. We were "community relations specialists," meaning we had to explain to the population what the company was doing in certain locations and why. Whether it was dangerous, what the dangers were that we were trying to prevent, etc. It was fun to meet up with our friends, now colleagues, not at parties, but at work. I tried to find something meaningful to do, but did not have much luck. Dr. Ellen Hall, a delightful engineer friend, gave me some assignments. She was working on an environmental impact statement for NASA, for which we all got a reward because it was done before the deadline and under budget. I have a beautiful framed award to prove it. I always felt it was rather funny for me to have an award like this, as I was not really working with sciences, but popularizing, explaining them. I was surprised and happy.

Based on my marketing knowledge I felt that the company was sliding into an abyss. They had the order from the powers that be (headquarters) that they had to observe the bottom line; do only what was in the scope of the job and not an inch more, not doing any marketing, not investing in anything in the long term.

Another basic mistake in the eyes of all the employees was we had to do our work in 1988 (!) without the use of computers. The engineers had computers, but the word processing program was removed from their computers. "You should not waste your time writing on the computers." They had to write everything longhand, then give it to the typing pool, then correct their typing and approve it. Then it could be finalized. We, whose job was to produce written material, had to follow the same ritual, but we had no computers at all. The secretaries did.

The engineers did put an end to this nonsense. They simply put back the word processing program on their computers as soon as it felt safe to do so. (When management was busy with something else.)

I practically had to slow down compared to my working speed, when I worked at home. I tried to explain all of the above to management, but to no avail.

I liked to be with John during our breaks, getting a regular salary, going out more for dinner with him after work, but I missed the hours at home, when I could do my writing while I was also washing, cooking, doing dishes, telephoning, writing letters, even gardening. Now there was only the evening to do all these chores and keep doing my freelance activities.

I was working part time because of my commitments to travel around the State for the Inquiring Mind lectures. John and I made a big mistake. I had no experience with 8 to 5 work, and he wanted me so much to get the job, he told me to ask for $14 an hour. The minimum I was getting at the time was $25, which is what I wanted to write in. I went with the $14 and was enlightened that they would give me $15 because that was the lowest they paid anybody. I later noticed that the others got $25 an hour. After six months we discussed my situation and agreed on continuing part time because I still had my lecture obligations. Going back to my office, my boss said they could have given me full time if I had insisted on it. It was water under the bridge by then. Besides, they still did not give me any meaningful work. At least I would not call "meaningful work," alphabetizing 1,500 names, editing a bibliography for a project, tidying up someone's files because the labels were coming off, and the like.

There was one case in the eight months when I had to do a translation from German into English. Finally something where I could use my knowledge. I told one of the department heads he should put out a note that I would be happy to translate articles for any of the engineers. He (although he was a friend) said: "What for?"

One nice day, when I could not stand corporate life and its shenanigans any more, I told my immediate boss, Katie: "I am going home now. Let me know if there is something meaningful I can do and then I will come back."

I felt like a liberated bird. I could work to my full capabilities and put all my energies into it – again. I did not have a regular salary, but I was – free.

This must have been Providence speaking in my inner Voice, the Voice that was always within me from the time I was a child. If we would have put down $25 minimum, if they would have made me full time, I would now be a retired clerk from Envirosphere.

What am I talking about? We employees saw it better where the company was headed. Both Ebasco and Envirosphere were sold, no longer as one company, but two to two other corporations. They did fall into the abyss as a result of their great strategies.

Would I have stayed with them, who would have done all the work that John and I did for Hungary, starting in the very near future?

Son János and Marcey moved from Eugene, Oregon to San José California, where János became the Operations Manager of the Clint Center, the performance halls at Cupertino College.

Niki, in her fourth year at Seattle University, continued working 30 hours a week at Nordstrom, a nationwide family-owned business. She became "Employee of the Month" in June, while also getting high grades at the university.

That was the year when Professor Bob Harmon, Marcey and I received the "George Washington Honor Medal from the Freedoms Foundation at Valley Forge" for the *Hungary Remembered* project.

In November I was invited to give a talk in Los Angeles. Luckily John had to go there at the same time. We stayed a week. We met old friends and made many new ones. We stayed with my classmate Judit Pfeiffer Neszlény, a well known pianist and composer. She was the one who had organized my talk in Pasadena at a museum.

The talk would have been "Women in Marxist Countries" one of my Inquiring Mind topics. We went to the Museum in the morning to look at the setup and orient ourselves. An agitated director of the Museum met us and told us: "You have to cancel the talk. You cannot have this topic at our Museum. This Museum is for poetry, music, art, not politics." We tried to explain that it was a talk that the Washington Commission for the Humanities was sponsoring, to no avail.

So Judit and I assured him that this will be only about poetry.

We went home and re-did the entire talk into a talk about how we wrote *Hungary Remembered* illustrating the show with videos from the performance. John was the one who forwarded the videos to the places we thought would work well with the talk. I was rewriting everything and Judit was helping all of us. We became friends with Éva Szörényi already earlier by correspondence and telephone, but that week we finally met in person. I asked her to come and recite the poem by Tibor Tollas: "They Have Walled Up Every Window Tight With Tin." Éva Szörényi was the Queen of Hungarian theater in Hungary as well as in Los Angeles. She was the President of the Actors Revolutionary Committee during the 1956 Hungarian Uprising; she and her family had to escape. She was the President of the Hungarian Freedom Fighters Association, then she became Honorary President for life. She said that she never did anything without having rehearsed it for several days, but for me she would do it. She was in her 70s by then. Our overwhelming love for Freedom, our feelings towards each other, and our similarities made us soul mates.

In one afternoon we transformed the planned talk into something totally different and had to confront the audience with the change of title, topic, but not our original intent of promoting freedom. It just turned out in a different format. I spoke in English as I was asked to do. In the end someone asked something in Hungarian and I answered. Suddenly the audience inquired: "You speak Hungarian. Then, why did you lecture in English?" I explained that I was asked to do it for the sake of those who did not speak Hungarian, only English.

The director who threatened us that he would be there and stop the lecture if I talked about my original topic, did not even bother to show up. The photographs outside the hall formed an exhibition about poverty in America. Apparently that was not political…

Éva Szörényi was fabulous as she recited the poem so close to both our hearts. This was the poem I quoted earlier as winding its way through the entire oral history drama *Hungary Remembered*. The oral history drama ended with the words of its final conclusion:

> From Vác to Peking hear the prisoners moan.
> If we are not careful throughout the world
> They will wall up all the windows tight with tin.

At the time of the 30th anniversary of the Revolution this was still the situation, unfortunately it still is in many countries.

56

1989. We were going to the Cleveland Ball! And what a year that was!

Our youngest daughter and oldest granddaughter were both debutantes at the Hungarian Ball.

Cleveland was the second largest Hungarian-speaking city in the world. It had more than a 100,000 Hungarians living there. Cleveland ranked even before Szeged, Hungary 's second largest city. Now there are several larger cities in Hungary, but it certainly was a curiosity for us, grade schoolers in Hungary in the 1940s.

Hungarians were coming in waves to the New World. Some came around the turn of the century, another wave during the Great Depression. The next wave were refugees escaping from the Soviets. The 1956ers were the new refugees who were granted asylum.

The Hungarian Days in Cleveland was started by the Nádas siblings and this became a huge enterprise by 1989. Hungarians from all over the world came to the Hungarian Days, organized on the weekend of Thanksgiving in the USA, around the end of November at a beautiful hotel, which was very inexpensive for that weekend. The Americans considered Thanksgiving a weekend when people celebrated with their loved ones and not at a restaurant or hotel. This was a win-win situation for both the hotel and the Hungarians.

The Árpád Academy was born in Cleveland. It was formed in the likeness of the Hungarian Scientific Academy. Hungarian Professionals coming to the Hungarian Days held lectures in their own subject, according to the theme of that year's Conference in Hungarian to Hungarians. Occasionally someone would give their talk in English. Today, many of the talks are in English, to lure the younger audiences.

The Árpád Academy gave out gold and silver medals for outstanding work, recommended by the membership. I received the Gold Medal from the Árpád Academy for the project of *Hungary Remembered*, at the recommendation of Tibor Tollas. John received a Gold Medal a little later for his lifetime engineering work in the field of power. Every year it was an exhilarating event. Of course, we could not go every year. The year when we became the "Hungarian Family of the Year" we could not go. To buy tickets for the family and pay for the event would have been around $10,000. That used to be a lot of money in the "Good Old Days." Not something a family of nine could afford on a professor's salary.

Associated with the Hungarian Days there was also a Ball. A real, old fashioned Hungarian Ball, organized by Rózsa Nádas, the one female sibling of the Nádas Trio who had started this Hungarian event. She was very strict, keeping everything "just so."

The girls were true debutantes every year. The boys were sometimes first attendees, but more often Cleveland boys who knew the opening dance. The boys wore tuxedos. The girls were supposed to wear snow white dresses, shoes and gloves. They entered on the arms of the boys, were introduced by name and then opened the ball with their dance.

Niki and Anna both entered in their shining white dresses. Ilike, the happy mother, and we, the overjoyed parents of one and grandparents of the other, beamed.

During those happy hours, the Hungarians were abuzz with what happened in Hungary on October 23rd. Hungary declared they were no longer a People's Republic, but the Republic of Hungary.

"No longer a People's Republic?" We could not believe our ears. "How could that be? And they were not arrested, shot, executed?"

"Something is in the air. Free elections? It can't be."

But it could and it was. Hungary: really?

It came as a shock. So suddenly, so surprisingly! Our friends: Sándor Rácz, Sándor Lezsák, Éva Mikes and Zoltán Trombitás, so full of hope, actually were able to achieve something? Peacefully? No blood on the streets?

Tibor Tollas's actions achieved their goal? The freedom of Hungary was near. Was here? What did all this mean?

"What do you think?" I turned to John. "Is it time for us to go to see what is happening? If there will be something…?"

"Let's wait and see what will happen before we do anything rash," John answered.

"Yes," I agreed. "We have to be careful because of our activities here of which the Communists are keeping good records, I am sure. Otherwise, why would they have sent me a survey for Hungarian writers about my topics."

"Remember, we even told our children not to go behind the Iron Curtain because they couldn't prove they were not a Szablya. Adding, that if something happened to them, there was no way we could help them."

"Knowing their methods, other writers were detained and forced to sign a document proclaiming they would no longer write anything bad about Communism, but only good."

"It is really easy to simply 'disappear.' Remember that person in 1956? When he was asked where he would like to go as a refugee he answered: 'I just want to go home. I am an American citizen, who visited Hungary and disappeared without leaving any traces. I am finally free'."

All of Ilike's family came from Maryland to celebrate New Year's Eve. Ilike's birthday is on January 1st so it was a huge party. In these celebrations we included Sandy's birthday celebration too, as she was born on the 11th. Our home was brightly lit with Christmas lights, the tree was still standing in the big dining room, good food was abundant, and the house was loud with our children's and grandchildren's merry voices. The brilliant view of Seattle sparkled in the dark from afar. Life was good.

An old friend of John's, Éva Deák and her husband Pál Veress, came to visit us from Hungary. Their news about Hungary revealed the transformation that was taking place slowly, but surely in Hungary. I took them to Mount Rainier and during the long trip we had time to get better acquainted. I found out that Éva and Pál were both writers. While Éva wrote children's books, Pál was a journalist with HVG (World Economy Weekly), the magazine that was the most daring in criticizing the government. I heard about the samizdats, the 168 óra (168 hours) magazine, the Élet és Irodalom (Life and Literature) magazine that were trying the limits of tolerance. Pál talked about their weekly meetings at HVG. They talked over how far they dared to go this week before the new number was published.

After they went home, Éva sent us these magazines regularly.

One friend after another became interested in investing and/or doing business with the newly liberated countries, among them Hungary. I thought about all the good friends in Hungary who could use this kind of help. I got increasingly excited and interested.

I had a business license for translation and also re-established Molnar & Moser, my family's cosmetic company established by my grandfather in Hungary. I registered the trademark in the USA. Now, I added "trade consulting" to my business profile.

I went to all possible international business meetings and conferences in Seattle, became a member of the World Affairs Council, the Trade Development Alliance, the Chamber of Commerce. I looked into the favorable laws Hungary had in place beginning in 1988 to lure foreign investment.

There was an important conference in Seattle on international business, where the newly liberated countries had a definite role. By that time, I was truly excited about maybe getting back our business, starting over our manufacturing under our traditional trademark that was 100 years old in 1989. I attended all international meetings as a journalist. The press could go to all events for free. One of the scheduled lectures, a panel discussion was about Hungary and Poland, the newly "beginning to be free" countries. We had absolutely nothing to do with the Embassy during the days of Communism. This was the first time I found myself talking to the Hungarian Commercial Attachée Dr. István Mohácsi and to Dr. Péter Komáromi, an excellent lawyer, who was just beginning to serve at the Commercial Representation of Hungary in New York City. Péter readily remembered with awe our outstanding old business in Hungary.

It so happened that the Polish representative did not show up to give his talk. Péter Komáromi, having just arrived from Hungary could not give an improvised talk in English yet.

I decided I could easily do it and said so to the moderator. When I finished talking, the moderator asked me if I could come back again tomorrow to give the same talk. I gladly agreed.

John and I then grabbed these two gentlemen and brought them home with us for a salmon dinner for which we had to buy the salmon on our way home. We then baked the salmon and ate it with them while we were drinking and joking. The Komáromis became some of our best Hungarian friends. When in Hungary they usually let us use their office as our office. Péter to this day helps me with everything I need.

At the conference, the panel moderator and I talked about a Conference to be organized in New York: "Discover Hungary 1990." The fee was $600. I knew I could not afford that, but I told him I would try to go there as "Press."

I did not have to think long. I asked Pál Veress at the HVG. He connected me with Zoltán Horváth who made me their correspondent for the exhibition.

Discover Hungary 1990 in New York City. Here I come!

I made many important connections at the fair. We saw each other again with Péter Komáromi who took me under his wing. I met the Hungarian Ambassador Peter Zwack. He bought back his business with the help of investors in 1988. We used to sell their products; the best known was Zwack: Unicum an herb liqueur, which was world famous. When under German rule they were not allowed to buy the ingredients for their products because of their Jewish origin; we used to order it for them. He was now the Ambassador of Hungary.

The Hungarian-American Chamber of Commerce in Budapest was also represented. Executive Director: Péter Fáth. I just knew: it must be. He must be the son of one the Fáth twins: Péter and Pál, our dancing partners when we were teenagers. They too had a business downtown that was nationalized. I asked and he said of course it was him. We started an ongoing relationship with the Chamber of Commerce from that memorable day on when we connected.

Also, from the Chamber of Commerce, David Hughes, the USA Commercial Attaché was supposed to be there, and I talked with him, not realizing that he was actually represented by Andy Anderson who came from Budapest and was American. He was connected to the American Embassy through his wife, Ruth Anderson, who was the American Military Attaché to Hungary. We are very good friends to this day with both the Hughes and Anderson couples, who now took up residence in our neighborhood and retired. They have been very helpful here in Seattle with Hungarian affairs.

Béla Kádár was the Minister of International Commerce and gave an excellent talk. Hungary had all the laws to facilitate business with Hungary and investment into the country.

Many exhibitors showed us their ware. A fantastic display was organized by Judith Folklore. She was an artist who has been collecting original Hungarian folk art, embroideries, antiques for a long time. Her beautiful daughter wore the loveliest Hungarian costumes during the exhibition.

By the end of the exhibition I acquired some of the folk art to serve as samples for investors.

Around this time a friend of ours, Béla Vadász, was asked by Paul Kraabel, President of the City Council of Seattle, to find a sister city in Hungary for Seattle. He gave the same task to the other newly liberated countries as well.

We jumped on the opportunity and suggested Pécs, as we already had our connections in the persons of Éva Mikes and Zoltán Trombitás.

The free elections took place in Hungary in March. The National Democratic Forum (MDF) won the elections and József Antall, history professor became the first Prime Minister. The Communists had no future. FIDESZ and SZDSZ, two young parties also did well.

"It's time," I told John. "We have to go back to Hungary to see what is happening. Will the State give back some of the things that were taken away? Do we need to start our business again? Are we already late?"

"I can't go yet, I don't have any vacation time left right now. Remember we went to the Ball and Los Angeles? But you go and see what you can do."

Album

1974 – 1989

Going to the Opera in
Braunschweig, 1974.

Visiting historical sights in and around
Braunschweig, 1974.

The lantern festival in Braunschweig, October 1973.

IEEE-EUROCON, joint lecture "Energy and Culture," 1974.

Szablya family Christmas, back in Pullman, 1974.

Apu with his mother, 1975.

Family photo at Szablya grandmother's funeral, 1976.

Anyu graduation, June 5, 1976.

Bringing communion to Mrs. Caine in Pullman WA, 1978.

Szablya ChaCha, 1979.

Washington State University Electrical Engineering students graduate, 1978.

WSU-EE graduates of 1978, 10-year reunion at Szablya's home, 1988.

In front of our Trinidad home with our car and the entire family, 1980.

*New Year's Eve in
Trinidad, 1980.*

Christmas time with the Baileys, 1980.

At a fabulous party with Pat and Ken Julien in Trinidad, 1981.

30th wedding anniversary in Trinidad, 1981.

"Baltimore Voices," the first oral history drama, a new genre created by daughter Helen and husband Barry, 1982.

Ilike with Anna and Alex, Baltimore, 1983.

Tertáks with Ilike, Anna and Alex in Columbia, MD, 1986.

Grandfather Dr. Louis Kovács and Rita at her wedding, 1984.

Sandy Szablya and Navaal Ramdin church wedding, 1988.

*Éva Szörényi, Queen of Hungarian actresses visiting
Seattle with the author and daughter Niki, 1989.*

*Two debutantes, youngest daughter Niki and oldest granddaughter Anna with Helen,
John and Ilike, Anna's mother, 1989.*

57

The Hungarian MALEV airplane was slowly descending into Ferihegy airport. My heart raced. As if the city wanted to hide its face from me until I felt the ground with my feet; I could not see it from the plane. After 34 years I was in Hungary again. The country was free. But it was a Velvet Revolution. The transition moved slowly. I still did not know how open I could be with people. I dressed as an ordinary Hungarian, nothing showed that I came from America. I behaved as if I would belong, have never stopped belonging. I carefully avoided using English words when talking. I must have succeeded because no one showed any suspicion. The food was abundant and delicious on the plane, exactly how it should be on anything remotely Hungarian.

I did not know what to expect.

I was back again…after 34 years. I felt I was dreaming and kissing the soil of the land where I was born.

The reality was much more prosaic. We were herded into a bus that took us to the main building, then through customs and immigration. No problem.

My friend, Mária Terták, and I sobbed as we embraced for the first time after all those years. We had a close relationship. She did not have enough milk when her son was born and having had a baby at the same time, I gave her some of my milk every day. My husband John, an only child, and Mária, grew up as brother and sister. Our families were friends for several generations.

Mária and I held each other close on the long way to the city. I eagerly looked out the window; just had to see everything! I had to find out what happened to all I knew and loved.

Üllői út's dark grey buildings stood as bodyguards on both sides. We passed the Killian Barracks. The center of fighting during the 1956 Revolution; Paul Maléter the Minister of Defense and Chief of Staff during the Revolution defended these barracks. Memories, memories…

But the car sped on, leaving behind the bloody remembrances. The School of Art came into view, the beautiful secessionist building also housing the Museum of Art in Industry. John used to come here weekly when his Uncle, also known as Feripapa, moved there when he became the Director of the School. During his 10-year tenure, the School became a University. Many great achievements were tied to his name Ferenc Szablya Frischauf. Good memories surrounded me until we reached the vicinity of my old school belonging to the Sisters of the Sacred Heart. I remember the year the school was nationalized – and then a sombre night the sisters were taken. They disappeared into the dark, singing to their beloved Jesus. It will now be returned to them, but first a place will have to be found for the Piarist priests who were moved there by the Communists because their building was needed for the Lenin Institute.

The soot-covered walls of the buildings made my heart bleed. The air was so dirty from the many uncontrolled diesel-fuel spouting emissions from the old rackety cars and the filterless chimneys of factories you could cut it with a knife.

Elmer, my friend's husband, was just released from the hospital in time for my visit because his asthma flared up breathing that air. I was so thankful for our clean air in America. The average lifespan was 10 years longer there than in Hungary.

As I drank in the sights with my eyes, I could not help but think of where Hungary would be now if progress from the end of the war up to 1948 would have gone on uninterrupted by the Communist takeover. In those days we thought we were now finally free from Nazi occupation and would be able to rebuild the country for ourselves.

I recalled our business trip with my parents to Western Europe. To my greatest astonishment, the luxurious centers of art and culture, the dream of travelers came nothing close to the Budapest of 1948. Vienna lay in shambles as left after the World War; in Paris people had practically nothing to eat. Hungary had a bustling economy by then, rebuilding went full steam ahead.

Then, as soon as nationalizations by the Soviets took place after our return in 1948, Hungary's developments fell way behind, while the other cities boomed under market economy.

As we moved through grey street after sooty boulevard, an icy fist crumpled my heart. What would this city be like today if progress had not stopped 40 years ago? What if it had the chance to use its citizens' initiative, their incentive, to become all it had the potential to become?

Street after street rolled by the window, without any colorful stores. The shops with the sooty signs had nothing in their windows to awaken my interest.

Finally, we reached downtown. The tourist attractions were beautifully renovated, at night they were floodlit. The tourist boutiques displayed lovely Hungarian folk art in all colors of the rainbow. The price for a small tablecloth was between 8,000 to 13,000 Forints.

Mária said her pension was 6,000 Forints a month. Just enough for food and rent – and nothing else. Yet, they now treasured their newly found freedom.

We arrived at their house. After 40 years of zero maintenance, we stepped into their former condominium, which was nationalized, so they had to pay rent. We entered a dirty staircase that reeked of garbage stored in three containers. Right across stood the barely serviceable mailboxes. The stairs were worn down. There was an elevator that had to be opened by a key. It moved slowly to the second floor with hardly enough place for two people, or one and luggage. When we stepped out of it, Mária made sure the doors were hermetically closed. If one of them was left even half an inch open, the elevator would not move from that floor, until someone came around with a key and could remedy the situation. This was good as in most of the houses – I found out during my two weeks there – was no working elevator.

Inside I felt at home immediately. The furniture was all there, the carpets, Elmer's figure skating trophies, the artful pictures. The hosts our good old friends.

The 40 years of non-maintenance ruled inside too. The walls were sooty way up high as was the crystal chandelier, the bathtub had a huge rust-stain in the middle, the toilet flushed like a Niagara in all directions and the mirror was cracked. The hot water heater only worked during the night, therefore during the day we had to watch how much hot water we used so we should not run out.

Nowadays there are some who are nostalgic about the "good old days." I wish for them to go back for just one day to 1990 and experience them. Yes, everyone was equally poor, except for those who were "more equal."

Most women wore a plain skirt and blouse, or pants and blouse. Nothing fancy. I saw nothing in any of the stores I would have wanted to buy. This was good because all I brought with me was $400. We could not afford to spare more for my trip during which I was supposed to find out what can be done, what should be done, what is still there from our former possessions. More and more I was trying to figure out how to help Hungary to get out of this situation.

As our then Prime Minister József Antall said: there were thousands of books written about how to go from Capitalism into Communism, but none how to do it in reverse, from Communism into Capitalism. That had to be written with the lives of people. It was not easy blazing the trail. The same József Antall predicted that the Magyar Demokrata Fórum (MDF) (Hungarian Democratic Forum) was not going to win the next elections because whatever they do is not going to be satisfactory for many, no matter how much they would try.

Mária set the table in the dining room with her old china and silver, she brought out the wine and chicken soup, meat and salad, dessert, everything good she had in order to welcome me.

We could not stop talking about the years when we did not dare to correspond honestly. Mária could not travel because she worked for the East German Cultural Center. The East Germans were not allowed to travel therefore she was not allowed to go anywhere West. She could go to the Eastern countries under Communist rule. Elmer, on the other hand, was an Olympic and world figure skating championship judge. He traveled all over the world. We even met with him now and then, when possible. Of course, the Communists were trying to prevent this as much as they could.

On the day before we took our long trip to Italy from Braunschweig in 1974, we got a phone call from Munich. It was Elmer inquiring when we would come to see him there. We were devastated. We knew nothing about his coming. He said he did let us know. Three months later his letter arrived telling us about that date.

Whoever wanted to meet with us during our stay in Braunschweig could not do so because the correspondence was censored away. Only the surprise visits, or German postcards mailed from the Lake Balaton were successful.

We talked and talked, cutting into each others' words through the meal and beyond.

Then came the night and the nine-hour jet lag.

Mária showed me from my window the TV transmitter right across from us on the Naphegy hillside. It was not there when we had left. There was no public TV at the time.

Now that looming tower looked at me personifying "Big Brother."

We were in the middle of the Velvet Revolution's slow-moving transformation of the country. I fell asleep fast; tiredness took over in no time. But then, during the night I woke up – and there was no going back to sleep.

I had two weeks to find out about the future of our former business empire, make connections for my brand new trade consulting business, explore the possibility of a Seattle-Pécs Sister City arrangement, make connections with old friends and enjoy each others' company.

It was an emotional and merciless job, chasing myself while being horrified of what I will be saying at meetings with those who had power now over all they "nationalized" meaning "stole" from us. I was trying to do what was best for the whole family, what we could save from our fortune and simultaneously help rebuild Hungary now that it was free.

I prayed and mulled it over and over in my head what I would say, tried to imagine their reactions, the developing dialogue. I took out the description of our business, the history of "nationalization" of what our proposal would be.

I tried to set up an appointment with the CEO before I came, but my phone message and two follow-up faxes were not answered. I had to reach out to the Head of Privatization István Tömpe in order to get through to the CEO of the "Azur" company. Their colors were the same as our former company's: blue and silver, hence the "Azur" name. The difference was they owned only our drugstores, they did not manufacture products as we did.

I wrote him the letter in the name of my father, Dr. Lajos Bartha-Kovács, the last family CEO of the business and my own, Mrs. John Szablya, née Ilona Bartha-Kovács, who at the time of nationalization had already started working with him on our business at age 14. I attached a description of our business in a book published in Hungary, in 1986 entitled: "Chronicle of Old Businesses." My grandfather's name was so well known that when the Communists published a book on old stores, an entire chapter was written about him. His name is also mentioned as the founder of the vocation "druggist." He was well known and well liked.

My grandfather, István Bartha bought the Molnár & Moser company, a drugstore, with seven employees after WWI, from the previous owners who founded it in 1889.

He was a pharmacist with an excellent sense of smell. He developed an entire line of perfumes, cosmetics, household and other products under the trade names Molnár & Moser, Molmos, M&M, M.M., La Russe. He registered his trademark in Geneva, Switzerland in 1929.

His principle was to give excellent merchandise at affordable prices.

The store grew into a business empire complete with its own factory. We had our own chain of drugstores and, in addition, owned many more under different names. We represented Elizabeth Arden, Geigy and many others. My grandfather did business with practically all the major firms in the world who sold products related to our line of business. Following WWII we rebuilt our businesses, starting from nothing.

In 1948 we were ready to build a cosmetic house in Budapest, like Elizabeth Arden's on Place Vendome in Paris, the first of its kind in Europe. Geigy's first shipment, with which we would have started a factory, was already in Hungary when, in January of 1949, everything was nationalized without any compensation. "Everything" included 6,500 kilograms of perfume oil and an inventory of almost $1 million, which is more than $10 million in 2020. Many choice properties in Budapest were also confiscated.

My family represented the drugstore industry in the public eye. Our products were sold in all drugstores, groceries, and even general stores in the countryside. We were doing business in Rumania and Czechoslovakia as well.

My letter to Mr. Tömpe continued: "I was happy to hear that there are opportunities now to re-establish relationships between former owners and their companies. This could make it possible to develop great export – using the original recipes and trademarks of the Molnár & Moser company. Maybe even our numerous family members could add their professional knowledge to the renewal of the Hungarian economy.

"I will be there the first week of June to discuss this matter."

And now I was here. One night after another I could not sleep while waiting for the date when I could finally present my proposal.

58

My first meeting was with Mr. Tibor Benke. I insisted on talking with the CEO, Mr. Peter Locke. So, we agreed on another date when all three of the leaders would be present: Peter Locke, Tibor Benke and Peter Veresegyházi.

The mild June sunshine gave me hope as for the second meeting the three of us Ádám Terták, my friend Mária's son, Managing Partner of Ernst and Young Bonitas, my lawyer Dr. István Retteghy, and I, approached the Azur Headquarters in the former Károlyi Mihály Street, now renamed Ferenczy István Street. The building was diagonally across from the house where I used to live for the first 20 years of my life. The house was built by my grandfather, still bearing the original company "Molnár & Moser" name on it. Everything was nationalized, but no one could remove the inscription from the granite of the house's foundation. This was the company I wanted to discuss with their present leaders, renamed Azur after our original colors of blue and silver.

It suddenly struck me: I am going to negotiate with the "fences" of our company? They were the ones who now possessed the stolen goods.

The company had recently been transformed into three shareholding companies. The shareholders were listed as several government companies, plus three individuals. Who could they be?

Three gentlemen were sitting in the room when we were ushered in. The windows looked down on the park where I used to play as a child. This was my territory. Like in all offices in those days they offered us espresso coffee and pálinka (Hungarian brandy) before we started talking.

My first question to them was: "Who are those 'three individuals' indicated as shareholders?" Mr. Tibor Benke looked at me, astonished, as if I would not be quite with it. "Well, the three of us, of course." (Later, when I told that to the Head of Privatization in the Parliament, he turned pale and said: "We have to nationalize them again, then reprivatize." Of course, that did not happen.)

I found it rather interesting that according to the present laws spontaneous privatization was encouraged, so by simply writing their name among the owners they became the owners.

I started negotiating with them, but even before I started Mr. Benke again chimed in: "We are not going to give up the Neruda of course, that is for certain." That was the only store that was still called "Drogéria" by then. It was one of our stores, but it did not even occur to me to talk about that store. Apparently, it was the most important for them.

I suggested that we could forge a relationship where we would provide the company with the former recipes that no one, only our family, knew and in return we would get sufficient shares to make it worthwhile for us.

Peter Locke who was the CEO and I talked about the business and how my grandfather established the druggist school which no longer existed. He said he also was trying to help the employees. We agreed how important that was.

His only suggestion was that we should start manufacturing our products and if they would like them, they would sell them in the store, which is very probable.

I found that rather arrogant considering the fact that the store was selling La Russe Cologne, just one of our products, under our company name, but it was a total fake.

I confronted Mr. Locke with the fact that they, at the moment, were selling Molnár & Moser products and it might be a thought to legalize this act. By that time, I had an original case of "Eau de Cologne Russe M.M." manufactured by Caola. I managed to buy some from various batches from various stores as well. I showed them photos of the product being sold in their stores; on the shelves, in the hand of an employee, and a photo from the outside of the store. When I asked for "Russe," I was told they did not have it. I showed her the bottles on the shelf. Then the seller said, "Why didn't you say you were looking for Molnár & Moser orosz kölni?" The trademark and the design on the bottle were registered in Geneva in 1929 by my grandfather. In those days, that registration counted as worldwide and forever. When I showed the same bottle to any of our old employees, they said in disgust: "This is not Russe."

Locke admitted they were selling it, "but the label is not exactly the same." I told him that neither was the content the same quality or color. It even varied case by case, bottle by bottle. How can this be allowed? He suggested that we should start manufacturing it in Hungary, then ask Caola to stop manufacturing it. He did these pronouncements in front of two witnesses, our lawyer, Dr. Retteghy and Ádám Terták whose company, Ernst & Young, Bonitas was doing Azur's audit. This was how much Azur and the likes cared about intellectual property rights.

415

We agreed on us exploring possibilities of manufacturing, while Locke would send us the new prospectuses about the company, indicating how to buy stocks. By the way, the stock exchange opened officially on the 21st of June (the day after I left Hungary).

I was not the only one who came back to negotiate with our old companies. So did the Zsolnay and the Pick families and countless others.

When we stepped out from there, I suggested that we should give the proposal to Azur in writing, but the Hungarians who were with me did not find this possible.

We must remember, this was a Velvet Revolution, no fighting, therefore no knowing how to proceed. I guess mine would have been a normal Western solution, but they had not dared to be as bold yet. We should not forget they had more than 40 years in a very different social and economic system and the European legal system is totally different than in the USA. They have the Napoleonic Code, while all the English-speaking nations have case law, except for Quebec and Louisiana which were first settled by the French.

In the meantime, by contacting several former employees I discovered that they still considered themselves as one big family and had annual reunions of the former Molnár & Moser employees. It was always scheduled for the time when the one who lived in South America was coming back for his annual vacation. He had a furniture factory there and he financed the entire dinner in a garden restaurant. This year, I, too, was invited. It would be in a few days.

Did I say "invited?" I was the celebrated hero, the "long lost family matriarch" (I may have been the youngest there, but still) of the party! I was showered with huge bouquets of flowers and spoiled with the best of everything.

Our former employees' leader was István Szőke, who used to be my grandfather's right hand. I remember, as a young man he lived with us for a while because he was sick and had to get special medicine, which my father managed to get for him from abroad. When he got married, he chose his wife from the employees of Molnár & Moser, Kata Cséfalvy. He proudly showed me his new, small drugstore. On the shop window he displayed "M.M. Magazine" to remind his customers of our company. His daughter worked with her parents. They were doing very well because they were following my grandfather's principles. Give the consumers what they want. The customer is always right.

The first of the employees I was able to contact was Kata Tóth who has been corresponding with my father. Father gave me her last letter, so I had her address and visited her. Her delight was amazing! She was so happy to see me! We talked about the "good old times." She immediately showed me and actually gave me her work book ID and showed me that the employees were still employees of the Molnár & Moser Company, when on June 8th 1949 the law was passed, according to which our company was nationalized on January 12, 1949. Six months after our business was taken. At the May 1, 1949 compulsory demonstration that took place regularly every year, they were still carrying the sign "Employees of Molnár & Moser."

She gave me the addresses of all the other employees with whom she had contact. All of them were helpful and gave me much information, among others the inventory of our stores on the day of the nationalization, which we had never seen before, old medicine jars from the stores. From then on, whenever I came to town they had a reunion even if it did not coincide with the annual gathering.

One of the first of the relatives and friends I met was my godson and cousin József Schmaltz of the third generation. The oldest József was my grandmother's brother. This József was a teenager when we left in 1956. Now, he was a grown man, big and tall in size, like his father used to be. My first words to him were: "You are so big!" Then we both laughed and hugged. Being an engineer, he helped assemble my electric equipment and use the transformer to adjust for use in Hungary. We tried with Mária before without any success. We only succeeded in blowing the fuse. So, we were more than grateful for his help.

József's sister Ildikó had to cancel an event because she wanted to meet with me. Her excuse was: "I have this cousin who drops in every 34 years…"

My other favorite cousin, Katalin Fábry, now Mrs. Géza Benedek, worked right at the corner bank, where Mária was also banking. I visited her and her family in the Royal Castle District. Her mother Duci néni was still alive. When Katalin and Family were deported from Szolnok and their house was taken, they found refuge at her grandmother's (my grandfather's sister) two room (not two bedroom) apartment. They all lived together there, even after her son was born. Then her grandmother and her father died. So now there were "only" four of them living there together. She is the smiliest person you can imagine. We remembered our beautiful childhood and discussed all the things we could not, while we were separated.

I met my two first cousins and my father's sister in Vecsés, where my cousin, Dr. Miklós Jóos, was district doctor. His younger brother, Lajos, was an engineer and my aunt-godmother, whom I called "Kembi," was with them for the occasion. We spent the siege of Budapest together in 1944-45.

At the time I got married in 1951, due to the Communist deportations, they were deported to Újfehértó because my uncle was a military officer before the war. They were deported, despite his service even after the war, until he retired, coaching the 1948 Olympic gold-medal-winning Pentathlon team. I had not seen them since the time we left. The boys, meaning the M.D. and the engineer, were teenagers at the time. Now they too had children.

Another among the first childhood friends was Dr. János Zlinszky, who was now a Constitutional Judge. It was an exciting reunion. I did not write to him on purpose during the entire 34 years. I knew he was among those who were drafted into a labor camp, his parents deported. We knew about each other because I kept up correspondence with his Aunt Biczu, Mrs. O'svath, who was also my good friend's Magdi's mother.

We discussed so many things about the past 34 years; the unbelievable efforts on part of the Hungarians who remained in Hungary, to gain freedom, and the effort it took us in the diaspora to make the other half of the world understand: extreme right and extreme left are EQUALLY horrific. Naturally, the Allies did not want to recognize the fact that they sold out these countries to the Soviets, an equally cruel system, mainly because of the lack of Foreign Affairs know-how and Stalin's cunning. We Hungarians had to act from both in- and outside the country together to free Hungary again. We instinctively moved in the right direction.

We used to spend a lot of time together growing up with János during our summer holidays on Svábhegy as we used to call it then. Now it was renamed Szabadsághegy (Freedom Mountain), but known under both names. We decided I would go back there for the first time with him. When we approached our former home, he stopped the taxi, and we went on foot to the house. Just like when we were children.

The building was still there. It was in horrible shape, inhabited by many people, divided into apartments, but still there in almost the same form. Except someone had built something that looked like a Tyrolean house in the attic space. It truly looked awful, as did the driveway and the garden, with the overgrown lone pine tree left of our beautiful silver firs. What will the villa's fate be?

My first visit to our old home in Magyar utca 26, built by my grandfather, was easy. The door was open. I stepped inside and saw that everything was in the exact shape as when it was when new. This was the quality of material my grandfather routinely used.

I rang the doorbell at István Boros', our most trusted old employee's apartment. He has lived there since 1944. The apartment was built from one of the spaces of the former laboratory. He married and had a daughter in that apartment. His daughter, Livia opened the door. The joy of her father could easily be seen in his face, despite the stroke that made his speech hard to understand. He jumped up and wanted to show me everything, tell me everything that had happened ever since my mother left the house in 1959. We walked all over the house. With the help of Livia, I could understand that the elevator was no longer there because a Party Secretary liked it and "nationalized" it over to his apartment house. Since then they had no elevator, even though the attic space was made into an apartment too.

We had a joyous reunion. Livia told me that they had bought the apartment from the State. I told her it would have been so much better if they would have returned the house to us, we would have let them have it for free. István knew all our hiding places, every nook and cranny of the house. He brought my father's briefcase home as his own, from the store after nationalization. He and our trusty cook held the house safe during the siege of Budapest. We spent the siege in our villa on Svábhegy, figuring it would be safer.

I drank in new information about Hungary like a sponge. I wanted to know everything so I would be able to be a part of the new Hungary, to help its development.

In the meantime, life took so much effort: to get a copy of something??? To get a working telephone??? To get the buzzing line and be successful in getting someone you actually called??? To send a fax????? To find a computer???

I used public transportation, which was excellent and walked a lot because everything seemed so close; just a hop, skip and a jump away.

Every lunch and dinner I was invited somewhere, or ate with the Tertáks in their kitchen. They had a small kitchen table with four little seats. Mária put three small cutting boards on the table, which we used as plates. They owned a "before-the-flood" microwave from the Soviet Union. Morning and evening we had cold cuts, cheese, sardines, but what I enjoyed most was: vine ripened and fresh bell peppers, tomatoes, radishes, salad, fruits of all kinds. These were available abundantly in every home. In America everything was available year-round, but brought from so far away, the produce had to be picked while still green, then transported, refrigerated. By the time it reached the table most of its fragrance and taste was gone. It is seldom when we can get fresh, local produce that tastes as sweet and authentic as the ones in Hungary.

I collected a few business connections before I left for my trip at the advice of international organizations. One was Olivine, that built an exemplary waste incinerator. The Company wanted to get established in Hungary. Another was a banker who wanted to bring small investments to small business people that were not usually financed by big banks. And others who wanted to invest in restaurants or had other interests. One wanted to sell dish antennae.

Whenever a business appointment stopped by, Mária acted as my secretary. We had lots of laughs about that when we were not seen by the serious business partners.

One of the business partners and his wife became my Hungarian office from then on, according to our agreement: Dr. István and Edit Barótfi. István was Professor at the Agricultural University in Gödöllő, a suburb of Budapest. He had just assembled and edited the first Environmental Handbook that was going to be published in Hungary and was looking for advertisers. Tom Dutcher, Chief Engineer at Olivine became one of my first clients by buying an ad in the book.

I also had to visit Pécs to discuss a possible sister-city relationship with Seattle. Of course, I contacted Éva Mikes and her husband, Zoltán Trombitás, who lived in Pécs. Éva worked as a lawyer and he was a medical student. They were among the first founding members of FIDESZ. By now they added a sweet little son, Kristóf, to their family.

They expected me at the railroad station and took me to their charming little apartment in an entirely new neighborhood. So many things have happened since they left Seattle. Of course, we corresponded, but when we could talk in person! There were not enough hours in the day!

Together with Éva I went to City Hall. The local elections had not taken place yet, so we talked to the Mayor of Pécs who was still from the old regime. The first time we met, inviting them to become sister cities with Seattle, the representatives of the city were almost flabbergasted as they couldn't figure out what it would mean to establish sister cities with an American city. It was during the time of the Velvet Revolution of the Regime Change and nobody was certain yet how everything would evolve.

"Would it mean Americans coming here?"

"Yes, and Hungarians going to Seattle," I answered.

They looked puzzled. They could not fathom how the city could afford that. Nevertheless, we parted with an agreement that we would look into it and continue talking about it.

While I spent time in Pécs with my dear friends I met several of the founding members of FIDESZ at their apartment. They took me up to the TV tower from where the view was beautiful at sunset. I was interviewed by the local newspaper and the radio. The owner of the radio station gave me his brand-new book named Death Polka. It talked about the oldest daughters of each German national Hungarian citizen that lived in the region. They were taken by the Soviet Army to Siberia, to work in mines. He interviewed the ones who finally returned after years of suffering.

I was so excited about the news, events, happenings, I could hardly wait to tell my family when I arrived home. I just wanted to help, to give my native country my all.

59

Before I left, I gave a letter to Dr. János Zlinszky to pass on to the Prime Minister, József Antall and the Minister of Finance, Ferenc Rabár, about whom János reminded me that he used to be at our teenage parties and played the piano very well.

The first free government's idea at the time was to simply apologize to all people whose assets were nationalized. This was suggested by the Blue Ribbon Commission of European VIPs, among them Hungarian victims of the act.

Dear Mr. Prime Minister!

Despite all the happiness and joy emanating from the newly acquired freedom of Hungary on account of which I congratulate all you hard working people, architects of the Velvet Revolution.

Finally, Hungary has a freely elected Government! Rehabilitations are in process. Two-thirds of the members of Parliament presently serving their term were inmates of Communist prisons. Now they are cleared and thanked for their suffering on behalf of their country. I heard this myself from Iván Darvas, one of the representatives who was in prison. He talked about it when I visited one of the Parliament's sessions.

Nothing has been done so far for the compensation of the respective families involved with manufacturing and commerce who were nationalized. Their assets, livelihood, freedom and lives were ruined, and they were persecuted by those Communists who were forced onto the people despite their votes.

Their suffering was only augmented by sometimes being thought of in the West as "bloodsucking exploiters.'"

The present government wants to introduce a democracy built on the right to own property.

Can this be done while the rights of the former owners are trampled upon? While it is not recognized that everyone has the right to their own that was taken illegally?

This is independent from the inability of Hungary to pay back all the damage. I would suggest the following for your consideration:

THE MOST IMPORTANT IS FOR THE HUNGARIAN GOVERNMENT TO ACKNOWLEDGE: TAKING PEOPLE'S PROPERTY WAS ILLEGAL AT THE TIME, THEN RECOGNIZE THAT <u>FOR THE TIME BEING</u> THERE IS NO MONEY TO RIGHT NATIONALIZATION'S WRONGS. ASK FOR THE FORMER OWNERS' HELP, UNDERSTANDING, PATIENCE AND WORK TOGETHER WITH THEM ON THE SOLUTION.

The country will only win if it asks for and accepts the help of the former owners. We have the original recipes, the manufacturing process, knowledge of the Western markets, as well as marketing, but above all the good will to help our native country.

<u>What good can come from the Government as a 'fence' selling to foreigners, the 'nationalized' assets, stolen by its illegal predecessor? What will the message be to the new owners? Why send the wrong message to those who could and are ready to help?</u>

Then I proceeded to tell our family's story in the letter, including the latest development, the results of my efforts in Hungary and concluded with:

If the Government does not have the money for compensation, how is it going to help to squander the assets of the country?

I am continuing to work for the good of the Hungarian people. To those who need it. But I would like to have justice against those who are misusing the system to their own profit. There is no peace without justice.

Those without conscience will sue and get their money back anyway if not one way, then another.

I trust in you Mr. Prime Minister, in your good will and your sense of justice. We are praying for the success of your grueling work! If I can help in any way, please, let me know.

The letter was delivered, and I hoped it helped.

Summary of research about possibilities with
Molnár & Moser, family homes and apartment houses in Hungary.
(Report written to the Family)

June 21, 1990

Introduction

To characterize the present situation in Hungary: Bandi Orosz, John's childhood friend was called back from retirement in England by Barclay Bank, in London. He was put in charge of doing a joint venture with Ikarus, THE Hungarian state bus manufacturer and Lehel, THE appliance manufacturer in Hungary, both on the imminent verge of bankruptcy. He has been traveling between London and Budapest for the past nine months, spending quite a lot of time in Hungary, yet he has accomplished nothing so far.

You have to look at the following achievements in this light. My stay in Hungary was 19 days.

Background

As we all know Molnár and Moser was nationalized on January 12, 1949. Our father, Dr. Louis Bartha-Kovács, was not even allowed to take his briefcase home. István Boros, our dedicated employee, who to this day lives in our former house, Magyar utca 26, brought it home as his own. The nationalization was so illegal that the law according to which it was nationalized only came into effect in June, six months after nationalization.

I received proof of this from our trusted employee Kata Tóth, who gave me her work record book according to which she became an employee of the State only on June 8th. On May 1st they still marched under the banner: "Employees of Molnár & Moser." Subsequently all our stores operating under different names: Neruda, Irgang, Stessel, Fried were also nationalized, meaning stolen.

The Geigy factory's DDT patent, along with the already delivered ingredients, were simply taken (stolen) by the State (not even nationalized).

Entire value of the inventory in 1949 forints 8 ½ million Forints (USA $850,000 in 1949). I received this information along with the inventory from our employees. We never received a copy of it at the time. In the inventory there were 6,500 kg (14,000 lbs.) of perfume oils and over a million empty bottles.

The houses, including the two family homes, were also nationalized.

The State Company, "Illatszerbolt," took over management of all drugstores and has been using our blue color, which was introduced by our grandfather István Bartha when he opened the new flagship store in Petőfi Sándor u. 11 in the mid 1930s.

Present Status

The present company's name "Azur," comes from M&M's blue color. Azur managed about 200 stores in the past. It was split into three shareholding companies. One has 13 stores and was pinpointed as the one most resembling our former stores. It has 200 employees. The only store they own of our former stores is Neruda. They have the right to export, but no business and no product to export. They do not manufacture anything.

Another company is Azur Union Ltd. with 66 stores, among them our flagship store at Petőfi Sándor utca 11.

A third Azur is the company's original headquarters before the split.

At the moment, the right to rent a certain location can be worth more than the inventory itself. The houses are still State property, however rent for office and business space is deregulated.

Stores:

Petőfi Sándor u. 11., the flagship store, the largest, best located store at the time of nationalization, was made into a self-service drugstore-household store combination (at the demand of the customers as claimed by Azur). Compared to that store, a K-mart is a Nordstrom. We owned this part of the house, therefore there is a possibility of claiming property rights. Azur is a mere tenant.

Váci u. 23. no longer exists as a store. We also owned the house, which is beautifully renovated. It has retail stores in it. If we could get the house back, we may be able to get one of the stores back. This one is in the most strategic location: Váci u. is a walking street right now. Estée Lauder is located almost opposite, in the former Kosztelitz parfumerie.

Váci u. 45. We owned the store and house. Kalkó Zsuzsi, the former manager's daughter, still lives there. We had a jubilant reunion. The house is beautifully renovated, and was not offered yet to tenants who live in it. There is a possibility for a store, but there is no drugstore in the building anymore.

Kossuth Lajos u. 17. and Apponyi tér 5. Stores no longer exist in these locations.

Szt. István krt. 5. probably exists. I had no time to see it, but this can be verified. That was a rental.

Olasz fasor (now Szilágyi Erzsébet fasor) still exists, as far as I know.

The Margitsziget (Margaret Island) store does not exist, but to rent space in good hotels may be possible, though extremely expensive. However, to sell merchandise to existing boutiques is feasible.

I was not able to find any store in Szív u., a branch managed and owned 49% by Mr. Füzy, a former employee.

Stores under other names:

Neruda: beautifully renovated (according to present Hungarian standards). During a big fire in 1958 the herbarium burned down, and the gallery cannot be used. In the back there is a self-service store. Neruda is Azur's most lucrative store and the only one in Budapest under the name "Drogéria" (drugstore). We owned the house and the house next door. The houses were not renovated yet. I don't know if they have been offered to tenants, but our lawyer Dr. István Retteghy is looking into everything.

Stessel, Irgang and Fried no longer exist. These were rentals to the best of my knowledge.

All stores in Hungary are in a despicable shape. No interesting merchandise is offered.

Azur's money investor into the three new shareholding companies is the West German Company Henkel, manufacturer of Persil, Fa, etc.

You all have Azur's fact sheet. At my question of who the three private investors are, Azur replied that they were the three directors of the three Azurs. (This is "robbery in broad daylight" called "átmentés" (saving over) in the Hungary of today. Spontaneous privatization was allowed for a short time, but the State is heavily after these kinds of manipulations.

All this happened, when the Communists decided to become "reform Communists" because they had noticed that if they want to keep the power, they need money, so they simply "acquired it" while they had the say-so. All surrounding countries were giving back nationalized properties to their former owners and profiting by it, except for Hungary.

Negotiations

The following are reported more in logical than in sequential order:

I have talked with the President of the Reprivatization Agency, Mr. István Tömpe. He was mad and said: "they should simply again be nationalized." That of course, depends a lot on the new laws that will be legislated.

Tömpe believes in giving former owners first options. The new State will be based on private property, therefore this has to be respected, even though no one has the money to give any reparation (kártalanítás). The entire country is bankrupt.

Tömpe sent out our correspondence to the Ministry of Industry and Commerce and a strong recommendation to help our cause. He thought our proposition was excellent.

After asking for recommendations and investigating several, I hired for Molnár & Moser a lawyer, Dr. István Retteghy. He was highly recommended by Dr. János Zlinszky, our dear and respected friend, one of six members of the Constitutional (Supreme) Court of Hungary. János said he would trust Dr. István Retteghy with his own family business. I was very much impressed by him.

The consensus of busier lawyers was that they would never represent us, they would send their apprentices to act, while they would busy themselves with being Members of Parliament and catering to the Soros Foundation, or other such concern. This lawyer however, is on the rise, is working on American cases and is willing to be our watchdog by keeping a close eye on what is happening and notifying us when and how to act in any given moment, whenever he sees it fit. This is of extreme importance because laws change daily. One law may be in effect for only a few days and if one acts, one wins. A day later might be too late. A busier lawyer would never alert us.

Retteghy had been in the USA before. He has four children and has to work hard to keep them going. By the way, he was so busy that we could barely find time to meet, but he still made it. (You can imagine about the others.) Yet, he does not charge an arm and a leg. He asked for $50/hr for consulting, but he said he would charge much less on an ongoing basis and only after he had achieved something. I gave him $200 for all he did up until then, including four meetings. One was when he came with me to the second Azur meeting.

I described all the meetings with Azur to the family, which I recorded in the previous chapter.

Summary

Retteghy thinks and so do I:

- There is a market for M&M products.
- Name recognition is there, but not too terribly much.
- Marketing is the key word.
- Target: all those neglected by Azur, at least two-thirds of Hungary's population. If you go into the store today, you will find expensive French perfumes (one-half a month's salary) or such crude products that are good only to keep body and soul together. We always catered for the middle, those who were looking for "good products at an affordable price."

- Possibility: find a company, and Retteghy is looking for one, that would manufacture the goods for us and do the manufacturing under our license, or joint venture with them. (This is what "Vánca" baking powder did.)
- The marketing and exporting know-how had to come from us.
- These products need permits to be sold.

Additional Information

In the meantime, the laws of possession and re-privatization will materialize, and we will know if we are going to get back anything at all, and if so, how much. There are many possibilities, all unforeseen. The country cannot pay anything right now, but one possibility is to get recognition of our right to compensation, then receiving some compensation in trickles over the years.

Another possibility is stock in the existing company, in the value of the amount nationalized (as will be done in East Germany).

As I mentioned above, laws change daily, and they have to be used while in effect. A new one might come any minute, which cancels the previous one. Everything is very liquid at the moment.

To start a company the "Vánca" way, as described above, has its advantages. No license needed if a foreigner owns less than half of a company (though it is possible to get a license within 120 days), which could be bought out later. However, this would need much hard cash in the true "venture" capital sense. I am talking about going around the law, as is customary in Hungary. This means doing what is "not-not-allowed" to do. This is much more efficient most of the time than following "what is allowed to do." (A reminder of the previous 40 years of Communism).

I then advised the family that I had instructed Dr. Retteghy to try to get back our two family homes: Lóránt út 15. and Magyar utca 26. I gave a detailed analysis of the apartment houses: the two in Kossuth Lajos utca 10 and 12, Váci utca 23 and 45, Ráday utca 46, Szondi utca 12 (in place of that is the Hotel Béke now), Pálffy tér 1(now Bem József tér) and Lónyay utca 27. I forgot the house number for that one, but when I walked through the door I knew: this was built by my grandfather. It looked exactly like the inside of the Magyar utca house, built by the same architect.

A curious story about how well my grandfather built everything so solidly nothing could ruin them. István Boros told me that the Communists wanted to drill holes for flagpole holders into the granite foundation of Magyar utca 26. It took them three days and lots of cursing to do it. Yet, when the flag poles were placed into the holes, the walls simply ejected them.

In conclusion: Retteghy is working on our application for our two family homes, as well as finding a small manufacturer for our goods. Caola is going bankrupt and, therefore, is not a candidate.

We may have to start legal proceedings against Caola immediately for name usage, or wait until we establish our own firm. Right now, our advantage of their crime is that they keep name recognition going at their expense. We also will have to go through legal proceedings in order to get compensation on account of ruining our name with merchandise that would have never satisfied our standards; furthermore for illegally using our name, trade mark, and imitating our recipe while claiming it to be the original.

What we do is not bad, but good for both the Hungarian people and the economy. They desperately need know-how, technology, machines, packaging, exporting, and marketing know-how, but most are too proud to even accept that fact. The easiest way would be to show them. Much money is needed, but much can be made by the right combination of persons. One is not enough.

There were so many questions after I sent the report. Who in the family is willing to go? Who can negotiate and deal "around the law" the Hungarian way? Who can set up export to and market in Eastern and Western Europe? Who is willing to? At what price? Who will put money into this venture? Be willing to stay away from the rest of the family and accept many, many hardships, maybe even failure for no fault of his/her own?

We had to count among the disadvantages lost income and stature, status in our position in North America. Another consideration must be that Hungary's environmental conditions are so terrible, they may cause serious health problems, and health care is despicable. For example, there is not one American style adjustable hospital bed in all of Hungary. There are eight telephones for 100 people. Almost all cars are Eastern bloc manufactured, no exhaust controls, seat belts practically non-existent and they drive dangerously under terrible traffic conditions. Dirt and smog everywhere.

60

Hungary's exciting news turned our lives upside down – literally.

We immersed ourselves into Hungarian business, law, trade, possibilities. Every minute John was not at work he was helping me. Our nights turned into days. Nine hours' difference between our two worlds resulted in sometimes staying up all night.

As soon as John came home, we ate dinner, then sat down in front of the TV around 7:00 p.m. and in no time at all we fell asleep. We woke up around 11:00 p.m. (8:00 a.m. in Hungary). We started calling our contacts or tried faxing. Sometimes it took us all night to send ONE fax. Not everyone even had access to a fax machine. For example, our lawyer did not have one. I had to send the fax to Ádám Terták, Mária and Elemér's son who then got in contact with Dr. Retteghy and read him the fax, or took it to him in person, or by courier (or maybe even by carrier pigeon).

A joke went around in Hungary about the phone service. Hungarians claimed that the entire country was waiting for something. Some people waited for a phone to be installed in their home or office, the lucky ones waited on their own phone for a line; any sound indicating connection. Many did not have a separate line but shared one with a neighbor. They could not talk at the same time. Naturally, for our calls everything went through international operators who contacted a Hungarian operator, who tried to reach the requested number. Every call had to be repeated, going through the same process several times before one could even hope for the right person actually answering.

Rare were the offices that had a copy machine. There was no email. Computers were almost non-existent in offices.

Our clients multiplied as more and more people became interested in doing business with Hungary.

We started giving talks about the topic: "Cultures in transition. Translating ways of thinking" when we had realized that even two English-speaking people could not understand each other, if one of them happened to be Hungarian, or a person from any other recently liberated country, the other American.

American: "What you need are middlemen."

Hungarian: "No, no we want to get rid of the middlemen."

The American meant "distributors," which did not exist in Communist countries because the state-owned factories talked straight with the state-owned businesses and sent them the goods if they were available. No middlemen needed.

The Hungarian meant the "black marketeer."

They obviously hit a wall! Even if they spoke the same language and used the same words, the concepts behind the words were different in two fundamentally different social and political structures.

Many books have been written on how to progress from capitalism into socialism, but none on how to do it in reverse. That book had to be written with the blood and sweat of the peoples of Central Europe. They were playing the leads in the drama, but there was no script.

How does this transition between cultures effect people and their thinking?

What is it like to be plunged into a market economy after 40 years of planned economy? The same as if suddenly we would start living in a planned economy.

Most important for business:

LAW! Unless you work for a multinational company and have an office in Hungary, the first thing is: hire a lawyer. At the International Seminar of the Washington Bar Association a lawyer told about her experiences. She was almost arrested when she tried to take a deposition.

In America (except for Louisiana and Quebec) we have Case Law while in Europe Codified Law is used. While in the USA you present evidence through the deposition before the trial, in Europe surprise at the end of the trial is accepted. You do not put your cards on the table before the trial.

To this was added that almost all laws on the books had to be literally changed because there was a peaceful regime change without a Revolution in 1990.

Some of the concepts were truly different in the two regimes.

FREEDOM

In a planned economy everything is paid for, from the cradle to the grave. However, who will decide what is paid for? Naturally the one who pays - the Government. What kind of clothes, housing, education - will be decided by the almighty plan. Total lack of financial worry results in total lack of choice.

No choice - no responsibility. In a market economy one makes choices and accepts the responsibility for them.

For the same reason marketing and advertising do not exist in the planned-economy sense. In an economy where you receive rewards in case of success and possible prison in case of failure, people do not want to have the responsibility for anything, or let others know what they can or cannot deliver. They simply are afraid of being blamed for the result of their advertised skills.

The freedom of CHOICE makes all the difference.

TIME

In the USA time is of the essence. Ho Chi Minh said at the time when Americans bombed Vietnam: "We have won this war." "How can you say that?" the editor of La Prensa asked. "Because Americans are in a hurry. We have time… We'll fight until we win."

When a cycle lasts longer than a lifetime the meaning of time changes. Life went on, even under a 150-year occupation of Hungary by the Ottoman Empire. People were born, married, and died. Yet, their desire for freedom never faded and their hope was handed down through the generations.

MONEY

When we first landed in America, we saw a refrigerator in a shop, advertised as: "Great value." How can a "thing" be of value? To us value was spiritual, a concept: peace, joy, friendship. But, an object - value?

What becomes of the value of saving, when hyperinflation results in using your life's savings (the price of a house and adjacent workshop) for toilet paper? This happened twice in the lifetime of our grandparents.

FEMINISM

It is a totally different concept in the newly liberated countries than in the U.S. While most women here fight for the right to work, the ones in planned economies fight for the right to stay home.

Both fight for the right to choose a lifestyle, but for the exact opposite reasons.

Understanding brings changes in attitudes and lasting solid relationships based on common human values.

People were used to three-way economy for 40 years; the only way to do business at the time. During the day people were at their workplace with access to telephones. They pretended to work, saving their energies for after work. The pay was so low, people considered the company pretended to pay them. During the day when the phone rang the one who answered explained that the work could not be done because it was not in the five-year-plan. However, he/she would be able to do it privately, after work. That was the second economy. People did good work and received good pay. The third way was bribes/tips, especially in the service economy. Nothing happened until you realized you had to give a tip to start the person to move.

Habits are hard to break, but understanding is entering into the picture.

Hungarians are highly educated people. Even though the country is small, percentage-wise we have the most Nobel prize-winners (17) in the world, except for the island-country Dominica, which has one, but is tiny. Hungarians are fast learners.

The first year I went back to Hungary, none of the businesses were open during the weekend after Saturday at noon. Not even in the walking street, where foreign tourists flooded the region – buying nothing – as nothing was available.

Next year, ALL the shops on the walking street were open during the weekends taking care of the souvenir-hunter tourists. People learned fast and implemented their new-found knowledge.

Often awkwardly, Hungarians were trying to conform to the West, to its customs. Unfortunately, they also adopted things they should rather skip, like debt, consumerism, etc.

People used to the Government as the "good father," handing out free education, free health care, etc. have to discover that taxes and social security have something to do with all those "free" things.

As a result, in Europe the social security payments are very high so as to be able to pay for all these "free" services.

Do you think we have bureaucracy here? According to a member of Parliament in Hungary: "Multiply that by 15 to imagine what our bureaucracy is like."

We had to figure out how to deal with that "lack of logical thinking" that besets everyone who becomes a bureaucrat.

My husband John was much more used to them than I was. He taught me a good deal about how to fight back.

1. Answer every question on a form, even if you have to say: "I don't know." The first thing the bureaucrats notice is if there is an unanswered question.
2. Go with the flow! Do not ask a logical question, just satisfy their desire for another signed paper, for a birth certificate, for more fees, for a translation of a bilingual document into one of its languages. After all, bureaucrats think they are not there to serve the people, but to rule

over them and make every procedure the most difficult possible. That makes their work and themselves more important.

3. Be always nice and kind to them, even if they are in a bad mood.
4. In Hungary you can discuss something over the phone, but then you have to send a hard copy by snail mail. And put a rubber stamp on it. That is actually the most important. Without a stamp "nothing doing."

BEWARE! Often people say they do not speak English because they consider "speaking" only if perfect. So, watch what you are saying in front of "non-English speakers."

Bragging-PR-Marketing is out, unless you are interfacing with a liberal. People are modest about their achievements. Often, they say they are not good at something in which they truly excel.

When the regime change occurred in 1990 clothing in Hungary was much more formal for official occasions, or when visiting an office. Err on the side of conservatism.

Do not toast with water!!! It means "you should drown!" Beer was also out until recently. Beer toasts were taboo because the Austrians toasted with beer after the execution of Hungarians who led the 1848 Revolt against the Habsburgs. This taboo was lifted after 150 years had passed. By now even water became acceptable on account of the well-meaning tourists.

Be friendly. LISTEN to your clients, your customers, the people! Do not try to give advice before you are totally familiar with circumstances. I would say six months of living in a country will change your mind about a lot of advice you would want to give in the first months.

61

On November 13th, Elizabeth Alexandra Szablya was born to son Jancsi and Marcey in San José, California. At the time he was Operations Manager of the Clint Center at San José College that included a 3,000- and a 2,000-capacity auditorium. Of course, we had to go to see them.

What a beautiful baby girl! We could not help but love her and admire her big blue eyes and sweet little face. Gennie, the big sister was old enough to diaper her little sister, which she seemed always ready to do.

A few months after that, daughter Rita and Karl's second child, Karl Aaron, arrived and I was off to Richland to help her into motherhood for the second time. These two cousins, Elizabeth and Aaron remained close to each other despite the geographic distance. As always, we had a great time with Rita, playing with baby Karl Aaron Pool. His father and grandfather were called Karl as well. When the baby became two years old, he went to his mother, pointed at himself and said: "Aaron, Aaron," he did not want to get mixed up with all the other Karls. So that is how we called him from then on.

Soon it was time to get ready to go to Hungary again. This time I went with John and daughter Sandy, who wanted to establish an import business from Hungary.

We stopped in Frankfurt, where we stayed with Alec and Sophie, cousins as well as Sandy's confirmation sponsors. We were there for the Corpus Christi procession, with rose petals all over the road wherever the procession went. Sandy was delighted as she had never seen one like it.

John wanted to get back into Hungary for the first time after our escape as we had left – by train. So, we boarded the Liszt Ferenc express in Vienna. It got more and more exciting as we approached the border. For John, the first time back and for Sandy the first time in Hungary. We remembered our crossing the border 35 years previously with three of our seven children: a two-year-old, a four-year-old and a 10-day-old baby. We were arrested twice before we managed to reach freedom.

Presently the day was beautiful, and we eagerly awaited to step across the border again. Suddenly two uniformed customs officers appeared at the door, properly equipped with submachine guns. John became tense. He started sweating as he handed his passport to the guards. As soon as they noticed the color of our passports, they were no longer interested:

"Ah, Americans!" With that they saluted and left, they had not even bothered to open our blue passports. As soon as they were out of sight, John's drops of sweat turned into tears. We were back – for the first time together – in our native land. All three of us hugged and silently enjoyed the familiar landscape, tears rolling down our cheeks.

We pointed out to Sandy the Red Cross building in Győr where we were arrested for the second time during our escape in 1956. Of course, we knew which building, but from a moving train, it was hard for her to follow all the other memories we had along the way. Then we arrived in Budapest, at the Western Railroad Station, an old-fashioned European station with a big crowd milling around, offers of porters, cries in Hungarian and other languages.

Sandy's suitcase was nowhere to be found. We asked the station's employees to please, let us know as soon as it reappeared. We stayed with the Tertáks. John saw Mária for the first time since we had left Hungary. We all cried, laughed, started to speak all at once, and toasted with wine from Ábrahámhegy at Lake Balaton. Mária produced the best of everything she knew we liked.

John and I were going to sleep on the sofa that used to belong to us in a long-forgotten time. It was extra-long, designed by Feripapa especially for John's six-foot, five-inch frame. Sandy settled into the maid's room, sharing it with the freezer and other overflows from the apartment.

Every day we called the railroad station. Sandy's suitcase was nowhere to be found. She started wearing my clothes, which of course were baggy on her, but she was so young and beautiful, no one seemed to notice.

Finally, on the 10th day we decided to go to the station and see for ourselves before notifying the insurance company. We found out that the suitcase has been sitting there, right in the middle of their warehouse. Its label disappeared and no one had the bright idea to ask us if this was what we were trying to find. At least she had her clothes before she was ready to take the train back to Frankfurt, then the plane, and on to Seattle.

The first Sunday there was John's 49th high school reunion in St. Matthias/ Coronation Church, up in the Royal Castle. Since time immemorial this day was reserved for the class reunion for all graduated classes of the Ferenc József Royal Catholic High School. The sun poured in through the magnificent church's stained-glass windows. John recalled the days when he was altar server there, which was also their parish church, many-many years before. He was even Master of Ceremonies during an entire Holy Week celebration, which at the time was much longer than today and was entirely in Latin. The priests of the church were his good friends in his teenage years. He often discussed theological questions with them. At the end of Mass, we always sang the Hungarian Anthem and the song "Boldogasszony Anyánk" to Our Lady, the Queen of Hungary. As we were singing under the multi-colored "Hungarian Gothic" style pillars and ceiling John's tears ran down his cheeks. Sandy was singing with us; she knew the words, even though she was our second child born in Canada, seven years after we had left Hungary.

After Mass, all the classmates with their family members went to a nearby pub. Each class had their own table. In that restaurant I found one of my favorites from childhood: huge, crispy, salted crescent rolls, sprinkled with caraway seed. It was a real treat with the delicious beer. Tibor Soproni was the man who held the class together, kept the list, sent it out to all, and corresponded with the classmates that had left Hungary. We visited the school right by the church, the classrooms where they had studied, and the stories went on and on into the late afternoon.

It was amazing to see how much older the classmates looked who had stayed in Hungary and suffered all those years of difficult times. What they considered "big successes," like being able to get an apartment to rent for one of their children when they got married. It is hard to believe for Americans, but the right to rent an apartment (if you could find one) cost a lot of money. They used all the savings of the entire extended family and sold heirlooms; they used all their connections and went out on a limb to achieve this, their life's great success. Others were totally unable to do that and lived together with their married children, then grandchildren, then maybe even married grandchildren.

We went to the St. Stephen Basilica. In the majestic building we took Sandy to the St. Joseph statue modeled after her grandfather, John's father. The statue was created by the famous sculptor Pál Pátzay (1896-1979). Then we visited the little side-chapel, where St. Stephen's, our first king's right hand, still intact after more than 1,000 years, was displayed in an ornate holder.

While Sandy was in Hungary, we had many opportunities to meet with people who wanted to export. Beautiful ceramics were shown to Sandy. When she asked about transportation, it turned out they did not even think about insurance. So, Sandy asked: "What if they get broken?"

"We will just replace them," the lady answered, being used to state enterprises, where the insurance company would have been a state enterprise too, so it would not have made a difference from which pocket the money came.

Then Sandy had to go ahead and explain why goods must be insured. The owners of the piece were responsible to get it to their clients in good shape and it would be the owner of the Hungarian company who would have to pay for damage en-route, unless otherwise agreed. One way or another, goods had to be insured. Now, that was a new concept for the lady, but she understood.

In Pécs Éva Mikes had a whole show of entrepreneurs in one room to show Sandy their wares. I was most impressed when we went to a shoe factory in Pécs that was bought by Germans. Lo and behold, Sandy had no problems negotiating with them in German. Her German just came back – as a matter of fact. She did not even think twice, just started talking. We were so proud of her and happy that our insistence on sending them to German schools during our stay in Braunschweig paid off.

While in Pécs, we worked with Éva Mikes to bring about the Consulate in Seattle and to establish the Seattle-Pécs Sister City Association. On June 30, 1991 the Soviets were leaving Hungary. To make the transition easier, the Minister of Foreign Affairs, Dr. Géza Jeszenszky and the Soviet Ambassador Abramovich, gave talks at the Club of the Intelligencia (Értelmiségiek Klubja) a few days before. We attended the talks and were quite impressed by the Soviet Ambassador, who spoke entirely in Hungarian. He mastered the language and even joked. When Our Foreign Minister mentioned that our involvement with the Russians started with the First World War, he smiled and reminded the Minister that it actually happened in 1849, when the Tsar helped crush the Hungarian Revolution of 1848. He graciously took the blame for that too.

After the meeting John and I cornered the Foreign Minister and told him: "We want to have a Consulate in Seattle." He did not say "No," he said: "But, we don't have any money." So, we offered him a bargain: "How about an Honorary Consulate?" "Now, we can definitely talk about that." The foundation was laid. Of course, first what we had to encourage and push through was having Honorary Consulates at all for countries that used to be behind the Iron Curtain.

Diplomats of Western countries could not travel in the Soviet Bloc, only with written permission of the Communist government. Therefore, Honorary Consulates would definitely not be trusted; both sides would have considered them as spies in their own country. This meant that first the concept had to be reestablished between the West and the East.

Hungary had never had a Consulate, career or honorary, on the West Coast of the United States. All had to be worked out between the two Departments of the countries' Foreign Affairs, namely the Department of

State in the USA and the Ministry of Foreign Affairs in Hungary. Our job was to push from both sides.

Naturally, Hungary had to establish first a career Consulate General in Los Angeles. We would belong under their authority. Then we could talk about honorary consulates.

We started by talking to everybody we met connected to the Hungarian or the USA Government. Being in Hungary now we took advantage of Zoli Trombitás és Éva Mikes' wide acquaintances in the Hungarian government. Zoli by that time (1991), was the youngest Member of the Hungarian Parliament, which made him the Secretary who took the notes at all the meetings. He could easily get us into the Parliament, along with his wife Éva, who knew practically everyone.

With awe we walked into the Parliament for the first time. After going through security checks, we entered the wide white marble staircase with the red carpet that led all the way up to the top floor. We stepped carefully onto the spotless carpet and went up slowly, holding each other's hands, savoring every minute. We never thought we would be able to return to Hungary, let alone to enter the Parliament!

We watched the session from the Visitors' Galery. Zoli sat right by the President and took notes. Iván Darvas, one of the MPs (a former excellent actor), stood up and started his talk by reminding the others: "The majority of us can say if we have one thing in common it is probably that we had tried out the hospitality of the former regime's prison cells."

We met several members of Parliament, among them Balázs Horváth, Tamás Deutsch, and several members of FIDESZ.

The first time we met Viktor Orbán was on the day the Soviets left. We happened to be still in Pécs. He gave a talk at FIDESZ headquarters across from the Theater in Pécs. After the talk we went inside and toasted with champagne to the joyous occasion. After that we went out to Széchényi tér. The churches were going to ring their bells for an hour in celebration. Unfortunately, the bells were all electric and their motors could not stand more than 10 minutes. Not wanting to give up, the city erected a simple wooden bell tower and people rang the bell one after the other. John and I rang the bell for 15 minutes out of the 60. I knew how to ring bells because when I was a teenager we used to ring the bell at the church in Balatonaliga every day in the evening. John was way too tall to do it, but I showed him the trick. You cannot let the bell swing all the way. You must start the next pull before the swing ends. Otherwise, it would sound like a bell for an emergency alarm.

We visited Péter Fáth, whom I encountered in New York, at his office where he was representing the American Chamber of Commerce in Budapest (AmCham) as its Executive Director. Of course, we became members of the Chamber and discussed cooperation between the AmCham and Seattle. The Fáth Family owned the largest and most well-known lingerie-hosiery store in Budapest, right in the middle of the city. They had twin boys – Peter and Paul – with whom we used to dance as teenagers. This Péter was the son of Péter the dancer. Their store was right across from the Church of the Franciscans, in the middle of downtown. That too was nationalized. Péter's grandmother was a Rothschild girl, as was her sister Klára Rothschild. At the time of their nationalization owners were immediately arrested just in case authorities wanted to ask questions. Time magazine, later, wrote about Klára Rothschild's business, an haute couture salon that was kept open in Budapest, as proof that there were still businesses under Communism. Time magazine failed to mention the price of the deal.

The Aranyszarvas (Golden Stag) restaurant in Budapest was a memory we later often recalled. It was walking distance from the Tertáks. The restaurant's specialty were all kinds of game-dishes: pheasants, deer, elks, rabbits. One evening we went with Sandy and set outside in the moonlight, the gypsy playing his violin right into her ear. Her eyes were radiant, as were ours, singing our favorite "Ahogy én szeretlek, nem szeret úgy senki..." (Nobody loves you the way I do...), looking at the lit-up Citadel on top of Mount St. Gellért that glowed in silver, lit by the moonlight.

We went to Ábrahámhegy, where John's parents owned a summer house and where they had been living since our wedding in 1951, until they followed us to Canada in 1960. When John's parents died, we decided that the best thing to do is leave it to their godson, the Tertáks's son, Elemér. By that time, we had already paid inheritance taxes on the house once, when John's parents "inherited" it from him after we had escaped, and we never ever thought we would even be able to see the house again.

And now we were back and could not stop telling tales to Sandy about our happy days there when we were young. We tried to go with her to Paphegytető, a small mountain/hill, the place where John asked me again if I please, would be his wife, three months after we had officially married. This does not even sound possible, would it not have been in 1951, when we got married in 49 hours, when I was 16, in order to be saved from the Communist deportation of the "Capitalists" from Budapest.

No matter how much we tried we could not get back onto the top of the mountain, it was so overgrown with bushes. We struggled as close as we could and told her our story while trying to find the way.

An old man came out from one of the last peasant houses of Ábrahámhegy and recognized John as the little boy who used to come to see them and play with their son. Naturally, he immediately offered us some of his homegrown wine. The fading sunshine cast its last rays over the vineyard covered hills. We approached the small cemetery where we found the grave of Aunt Vera (néni), Feripapa's second wife, and looked at other tombstones with familiar names. Sandy's beautiful young figure moved through the little graveyard like a butterfly flying from grave to grave.

There was a chapel now closer to the house with a beautifully carved Calvary leading to it. The "strand" (beach), the public lakeshore was nice and sandy. The little stream running into the lake right in the middle of the "strand" was the source of some of the sand.

Many things changed, but nature was still the same. I am sure the fireflies blinked just as they used to when our Jancsi was a baby and we sang to him the Hungarian firefly song that started with his name. The firefly's name in Hungarian is Jánosbogárka "little John fly" that according to the song "blinks and twinkles."

That year marked our 40th wedding anniversary. Mária Terták invited everyone who was present at our original, first wedding and was still alive: the Tertáks, Katus Taky, widow of Feri Taky, our dear friend for generations, whose idea was that we should get married, and the three of us. Mihály Czenner, the notary who married us was a friend of both the Szablya and the Terták families. He put on the same notary ribbon in which he married us, but this time with the original Hungarian Coat of Arms including the Holy Crown. We went through the entire ceremony again before the delicious dinner party.

After Hungary, we waved good-bye to Sandy and spent an unforgettable week in Rome with my former editor at *Our Family Magazine*, a Catholic magazine in Canada, Father Lalonde. His next assignment was to live in the Vatican and translate English and French documents for his Order.

He invited us and took us around like a true native after his years spent in the Eternal City.

He waited for us at the train station and from there we went straight to the Papal Audition, which happened only once during our stay – that afternoon. Pope John Paul II, with whom we had so much in common and about whom I have written so much, addressed the crowd in several languages. He was well known for this gift.

After the audition we got settled with the Sisters in a Convent, right at the Wall of Vatican City.

Fr. Lalonde introduced us to the Villa Borghese, which we missed when we were in Rome for the first time with the children. Every piece in that museum was a particularly beautiful treasure of art. Rather small, but still a jewel of museums.

One day he suggested we should go to McDonalds.

"To McDonalds?" our jaws dropped. "What do you mean, McDonalds? In the middle of Rome?"

He just smiled impishly. When we arrived we found out why. This McDonald was totally Italianized. It was a European looking restaurant with little fountains, serving lovely salads at little tables and a true Italian ambience paired with Italian tastes.

We learned other interesting things. Did you know why the stairs are not one, not two, but one and a half step long in most places in Rome? They were designed to go up on them riding horses! Now that must have been very convenient at one time, not so much any more.

We usually ate at the convent in the evenings, but once Father took us to the monastery, where he lived, and on other nights to restaurants around the city.

We found it really interesting to observe Father when he talked Italian. His hands were moving around, just like the hands of all Italians when they spoke. He was talking with an Italian-American lady on the bus. Whenever they switched to English both of them put their hands down and spoke only with words. Switching to Italian their hands went to work again.

Everything beautiful has to end one day and we were on our way home.

On August 3rd we had a happy Family Reunion for our 40th wedding anniversary with all 26 members of the family present.

62

While we were trying to establish the Hungarian Consulate in Seattle – of course we had to fight first for having honorary consulates again for the newly liberated countries – Iván Novák visited us. He was the Commercial Delegate from Hungary in Chicago. He and I visited many local plants and businesses that were already doing business with Hungary. For some employees at said companies this came as a surprise. Seattle is so far away from Hungary; they did not have immediate contact with the Hungarian companies. Their British branches took care of Hungarian business. They welcomed us, nevertheless. On Iván's second visit he handed me a business card with my name on it, reading: President of the Pacific NW Hungarian-American Chamber of Commerce. He told me we had to have a Chamber first while waiting for the Consulate because that was immediately possible. Of course, that is what was important for him and for us it meant we had a foot in the door for the Consulate. Prior to that, Éva Voisin also asked me to start a Chamber when she had established the Hungarian Chamber in San Francisco, based on the image of the French Chamber. Her husband was French and Éva attended the Sorbonne in Paris. She was a lawyer.

We finally met with each other at the big conference Iván Novák organized in Chicago for all the Hungarian Chambers in the USA. It proved to be an excellent meeting. The speakers were: Lajos Tolnay, the President of the Hungarian Chamber of Commerce in Hungary, Tibor Nemes, the New York Commercial Delegate, Tibor Zselinszky his Deputy, István Vadászy, the new Commercial Delegate in L.A., and István Major, State Secretary at the Ministry for International Commerce.

Lajos Schmidt, an excellent lawyer of Hungarian descent in Chicago, invited us all to his club for a luncheon the next day. Great networking time for all! This is where I first met Edith Lauer, the founder of the Hungarian American Coalition (HAC), an umbrella organization for Hungarian organizations in the USA. She was a delight! We immediately decided to work together from then on. She recruited me to become a Corporate Member representing the Pacific NW Hungarian-American Chamber in the HAC. I readily agreed. We were making plans for her coming to the West Coast to introduce Hungarians to the HAC.

Next, we flew home to Seattle along with Lajos Tolnay, Tibor Nemes, István Major and István Vadászy. The Consulate General in Los Angeles finally became a reality in 1992. István Vadászy, the Commercial Delegate, was just settling in. During the flight some of our guests came over to where we were sitting and talked to us. We had a good time, joking. Two hours into the flight they decided they should move back to their seats as our arrival was imminent. We laughed and enlightened them that we are only midway; we had two more hours ahead of us. They could not believe the distances! Europeans, who are used to traveling to several countries in a few hours, cannot imagine that the cities rated "next door" by Americans, are few hours driving distance.

As we were approaching Seattle and its myriads of lights emerged from the dark they were surprised: "But this is a large city!" "Not any larger than Budapest!" I laughed. Greater Seattle had two million inhabitants, just like the capital of Hungary. Our guests were not everyday people, but ones well versed in international commerce and diplomacy!

As a proof of their importance 120 people showed up for the breakfast where they gave their presentations. That was our highly successful first meeting of our Pacific NW Hungarian-American Chamber. Many of those present became members. The excellent speakers were streaming from Hungary that first year. A representative of Boeing was also a member. Having seen the excellent speakers, he said I should charge much more for membership.

Bruce Chapman, the President of the Discovery Institute, and several of his friends, including Washington's previous governor, John Spellman, Slade Gorton, a Senator from Washington State at the time, Paul Schell, Mayor of Seattle, and the representative from Boeing, formed a support group: "Friends of the Hungarian Consulate" and started promoting the idea to have an Honorary Consulate in Seattle. This was a great help in getting the Honorary Consulate approved by the State Department, the Minister of Foreign Affairs in Hungary, first the place, then the person. Senator Slade Gorton, managed to push the approval through the State Department in two weeks. Nevertheless, from our first words with the Hungarian Foreign Minister Géza Jeszenszky, until the opening of the Consulate it took two and a half years to achieve our goal. The Consulate was officially opened by Ambassador Pál Tar in Seattle for Washington, Oregon and Idaho, on September 13, 1993.

Many important events happened before that. Naturally, the Ambassador had to come to see us if the place and the person were the ones he would choose. I knew he was a classmate of József Antall, the Prime Minister. This meant he must have been the classmate of György O'sváth with whom we grew up together. His sister was my best friend. As soon as he stepped off the plane, I asked him about György. Of course, he was a classmate. Not just that but they used to be in the same boy scout troop, as was the present Prime Minister. I told him a story about György's adventure, while at the boy scouts: One year I spent time with my mother in Mátraháza at a hotel. The scout troop was camped on Gallya Tető which was a tall mountain, towering above Mátraháza. György came to visit us and wanted to stay longer than the troop. The troop went ahead, and he lingered with us. Finally, it started to darken, and he decided to leave. He ran all the way to their camp – and then collapsed.

"That was you?" The Ambassador laughed. "He passed a few of the troops as he was running. I told him he did not have to do that, he should just come with us, but we could not slow him down." That basically cemented my candidacy for the consulate.

He was completely satisfied with what he saw. He approved our home for the Consulate. We had great conversations and a well-attended reception for him with the Hungarian community, as well as the international community of Seattle, members of the Consular Corps and the dignitaries. My father also happened to be here. They understood each other with the Ambassador very well. We took the Ambassador around town. He was sold.

Another important fact also helped me to become the Consul. When I returned from Discover Hungary in 1990, I wrote a newsletter to my clients and for distribution among the prospective investors and business people about how to do business in Hungary. Seeing how well it was received I decided to continue issuing the newsletter called *Hungary International.* I published, edited, and mostly also wrote this newsletter (1990-1993). At that time whatever news we received from official Hungarian organizations and chambers were written in such atrocious English, we always asked them to send the Hungarian version as well, so we should be able to understand it. For example, there was no predicate (verb) in the sentence. It took a while for translators to discover that they need to translate the meaning and not the words as they proceed. Hungarians love long sentences and pepper it with a lot of legal language, quoting the law as often as possible. That made the translators' work extremely difficult, I do not blame them for making the mistakes.

I received my news "straight from the horse's mouth." The grateful Commercial Delegates around the country, led by Ferenc Furulyás in Washington DC thanked me every time they saw me. Ferenc said they had neither the English nor the budget to do it.

I held as my greatest success the time when we explained the new labor law. In one of the Hungarian ministries a clerk told me that the first time he truly understood this law was when he read it in English in my newsletter.

In the meantime, I acquired two associate editors: Erin M. Huntington and Mike J. Benvegnu. I had a wonderful intern too, Sonja Gayem, who was doing her masters degree at Seattle University.

We distributed 5,000 copies of *Hungary International*. AmCham was distributing them in Hungary. In exchange we received their newsletter. We went around in the USA with my husband John and held lectures about opportunities in Hungary in chambers, service clubs, libraries, universities. We continued with the talks after I became Honorary Consul and during the opening of the Consulate I formally handed over the Presidency of the Chamber to David Hughes, who was Commercial Attaché at the U.S. Embassy in Hungary 1989-1991. He founded the American Chamber of Commerce in Hungary in his living room in 1989 because there was no other way yet to do it. He was sent to Budapest in a hurry to greet President Bush at the American Embassy. He wrote many touching short stories about his stay in Hungary and loved Hungary so much he often had tears in his eyes when he spoke about the transition he experienced in Hungary. The Chamber was in good hands.

Ambassador Pál Tar came to open the Honorary Consulate on September 13, 1993, then went on to San Francisco and opened the Honorary Consulate there, with Éva Voisin as the Honorary Consul. We call each other twin consuls because it was within 24 hours that now the West Coast of America had two Honorary Hungarian Consulates, headed by women.

We had a separate celebration with the Hungarian Community, the HAAW, then with the World Affairs Council downtown. Éva Mikes came from Pécs, and the Consul General from Los Angeles, András Márton. The Ambassador handed me the bronze sign for the Consulate with the Hungarian Coat of Arms, but he whispered: "I am going to keep holding it because it is heavy." I was truly thankful for him holding it after I had felt its weight. This sign took its place right beside our home's entrance door; a sign that this now was also the Honorary Consulate of Hungary. The evening ended with an excellent Hungarian dinner at the home of William Ruckelshaus, the first Head of the EPA (Environmental Protection Agency), acting Director of the FBI then Deputy Attorney General. He was away in Washington DC, but Bruce Chapman, former Secretary of State in Washington, and Director of the Discovery Institute in Seattle, who organized the "Friends of the Hungarian Consulate" acted as host. The dinner was cooked by a dear couple, who became our very good friends,

Alex and Christine Boldizsár. The food was delicious. We sat outside, in front of us was Lake Washington. An unforgettable day ended in the moonlight.

There was great interest in Hungary. Good speakers and visiting businesspeople streamed to the entire USA, now also to Seattle. Our goal was to put Seattle on the map of Hungary and Hungary on the map of Seattle. We had succeeded, at least the foundation was laid.

The first years of the Consulate were wonderful and extremely busy. The newly liberated Hungary also meant that those who used to be career consuls now faced a 40-year gap about their own country's true history. We had to help them out and give them advice as often as they had to enlighten us about consular duties. For example, on an October 23rd, when one of them had to give a talk, he turned to me for history of the Uprising in 1956. I sent him the 20th Century program's tape with Walter Cronkite who documented the entire Uprising in 25 minutes. Now all my research and the *Hungary Remembered* project paid off; my supply could satisfy their demands.

What is an Honorary Consul?

In the Middle Ages, when people were shipwrecked, or otherwise arrived into a faraway land, where they had no acquaintances, they were helpless. Therefore, governments had decided to ask respected persons, already citizens of these lands, yet natives of their respective countries, to represent their country in their new homeland.

Hon. Consuls are like "little Ambassadors" as we were told, when we received our mandate. Honorary consuls are granted the title "The Honorable" in order to make them peers of judges and one-star generals. This is important because that is how authorities must respect them and return their calls, when they are trying to help others.

Duties of the Honorary Consul include promoting trade, tourism, and cultural relations between the two countries. He or she represents (in our case) Hungary, starting with the invitation to lunch with the Governor and ending with collect calls from jail.

Honorary Consuls usually do not issue visas or passports but have all the forms and help answer questions. They are authorized to notarize photos, signatures, as well as all documents; powers of attorney, contracts, translations, which then must be accepted by Hungarian authorities. Our signatures and the languages we are authorized to translate are registered at the Ministry of Foreign Affairs. People who want confirmation of that, can call the Ministry of Foreign Affairs. These rules and regulations can be altered by the Ministry of Foreign Affairs, if they satisfy the agreement about honorary consulates in the Vienna Convention of 1963.

Once a year we gather in Washington D.C. where we get our new instructions for that year. Every 3, 4, or 5 years there is a World Conference of Hungarian Honorary Consuls in Budapest, where we get the latest instructions with members of the Government for three days.

Honorary Consuls do not get paid and their expenses are not reimbursed, not even their airplane tickets, or hotels. The Honorary Consuls all have university education; they include lawyers, business people, medical doctors, university professors.

Fees are decided by the Ministry of Foreign Affairs and we must account for the money once a year. We can use the fees charged to offset our expenses, but if there would ever be something left, that would have to be sent to the Consulate General under which we belong.

The difference between Honorary Consuls and Career Consuls is that Career Consuls are paid, they have more privileges, and every 3, 4, or 5 years they are moved to a different country or to their home country for a while. They are the ones issuing visas and passports, although mostly they must send them to Hungary for approval. They are citizens of their home country and mostly they have degrees from a university or college related to International Affairs, Diplomacy, or Foreign Trade. They take their respective countries' Civil Service Exams.

Honorary Consuls, contrary to popular belief, do not have as much immunity as do Career Consuls. Honorary Consuls have immunity while exercising their consular duties. Their filing cabinets and documents have immunity, and they can park in places designated for consuls, as well as at the airport for a certain time when picking up or delivering diplomatic personnel or official foreign visitors.

In the first years Hungary was getting acquainted with capitalism and very often we were asked questions about that too.

Hungarians escaped to many countries all over the world both from the Nazi and the Communist regimes. Now they wanted to renew their contacts with their native lands, re-establish their citizenship. We had to deal with many documents in different languages. Some Hungarians went to South America first before coming to the USA, some to Israel, citizens of the former Austro-Hungarian Monarchy may have come from the countries surrounding Hungary that – at the time – used to be Hungary. Several of us were court interpreters and all of us – at the time – spoke Hungarian well. The language of our joint meetings was Hungarian. We were all people who had been working hard for Hungary in the past.

All of this slowly changed as new honorary consuls were named who received their titles for investing in Hungary or doing business with Hungary. They were of a different kind of supporters of the nation, but our meetings ended up throughout the years speaking totally in English in the USA. In Hungary, at World Conferences of Honorary Consuls there was synchronous interpretation into at least five languages.

63

Back to the home front. Our only child left at home after graduation was Niki, with two university degrees at 20 (One in Liberal Arts Matteo Ricci Program and one in Business.) She moved into her own apartment and worked full time at Nordstrom Financial Headquarters.

One day she had great news. She and four of her colleagues were being transferred to Denver, Colorado because Nordstrom had so many stores now, including the East Coast and Alaska, it was decided that Finance should be on Central Time to accommodate customers. Niki flew to Denver on the Nordstrom Family's private plane. With her colleagues they enjoyed a great meal with silver cutlery and damask serviettes. They felt proud and happy to be chosen to set up the new Financial Center.

While she was still at the University, Niki decided to become an Evangelical Christian. She started attending services at Overlake Christian Church, a true mega-church. There she met Don McKay, a handsome man, whose hair had turned gray despite his young age. He was quite taken by Niki, even though Niki thought he was just a friend from church.

Niki spent a year in Denver. When it was time for her to return to Seattle, Don flew over to help her drive back her Mazda she bought in Denver. Pretty soon the date was set for their wedding: April 24, 1992.

Our home continued to be the "Szablya Hotel" for all visitors from Hungary. On the day of Niki's bridal shower party László Regéczy-Nagy, former prison-mate and Head of the Office of Árpád Göncz, President of Hungary, and our dear friends Márika and Elemér Terták were all staying with us. Naturally, they had to come with us to the shower.

My father came to the wedding with Mrs. Susan Kovac, as they were inseparable. They were both widowed. She was also his secretary and my father helped raise her daughter, Susie, and her twin boys Peter and Paul. We all liked her very much. She was a Hungarian from Slovakia, who had left her homeland in 1968, at the time of the Czechoslovak try for freedom.

The rehearsal dinner, organized by the groom's mother Ginny, took place at a restaurant owned by one of Don's cousins. Don surprised Niki by singing a beautiful love song to her.

We had so much fun preparing for the wedding! All of our family came, as did the Julsons, Mel and Virginia, from Vancouver, B.C. They came to all our family weddings. Mel, as always, took excellent photos during and after the wedding. He took an unbelievable photo of Niki as she was listening to the story of the family crucifix that John handed to her with the date of their wedding added to the list.

The lovely ceremony took place at Overlake Christian Church, the reception at our parish church at St. Madeleine Sophie in Bellevue.

In 1992 we arrived in Hungary again, this year with five children and four with their spouses. Ilike came alone. By then she was divorced.

Niki and Don spent a week with us in Hungary on their honeymoon, then a week in Scotland, from where Don's family originated.

Son Steve took a video of the whole trip which he put on YouTube with 71 other family videos. Tremendous work! I know Steve enjoyed every minute of it!

Naturally, we showed the children our old homes. We started out on Castle Hill, where John grew up. Tárnok utca 2 was the first place he showed the children as this was close to the tourist sights, the St. Matthias (Coronation) Church and the Royal Palace, housing the National Galery, the Fishermen's Bastille and colorful folk-art stores. Right from the Fishermen's Bastille we could see John's old school, the Ferenc József Királyi Katolikus Gimnázium (Franz Joseph Royal Catholic High School), which he described to them in thorough detail, including student-adventures. As a youngster, he just ran down the stairs at the Fishermen's Bastille and there he was. His eyes glowed with love for his school while talking about it, by living those days anew.

This year was the 50th anniversary of John's high school graduation. A special celebration took place at a pub after the usual every-year-anniversary Mass at St. Matthias Church. Walking down to the pub John showed our children Várfok u. 2. He lived there the first decade of his life. The house was a show-house for Feripapa's (Ferenc Szablya Frischauf) interior and exterior design business. He was also an accomplished painter. Tintimama, Ernestine Lohwag, his wife, was a famous portrait painter. She painted royals, and aristocrats and of course her beloved nephew, very often. John's mother was a sculptor. The only person not an artist was John's father. However, after retirement he dedicated his life promoting art as the President of the Society for Art in Industry.

Both Feripapa and John's father and their wives lived in this house together with the only son between the four of them: my dear husband John. Can you imagine growing up in a beautiful show-house, surrounded by artists, being the only child in the house? Luckily, the maids were his allies and covered for him, for all his mischiefs. For example, one day he and his best friend Thomas decided to play "procession." They fastened a burning candle at the end of a broomstick and wandered around the house, not even noticing the black stripe this created on the ceiling as they proceeded. Feripapa did not blame them in the end because he could not figure out how in the world they could have achieved this feat.

John pointed at the windows, explaining who lived in which room. He was so excited to show his old home to the next generation and tell them about his adventures..

Then we went over to the Pest side. Now it was my turn to remember. Our old home, where I was born and lived until the age of 19, was Magyar utca 26, the house built by my Grandfather in 1931. We showed the children not only the house, but also the park in front of it, where at the time of the Uprising in 1956 several people were buried. I remember one young girl's grave that struck me especially at the time. She was 15 when she died a hero's death.

Right across from the house was not only the park, but also the Károlyi Palace, which became the Petőfi Literary Museum. Right behind the Museum building, in the back of the Park classic concerts were played several days a week in the summer, while I was growing up. The acoustics were best if we went out our back door onto the gallery above the inside yard, where the ancient city wall still stood.

The Egyetemi templom (University Church) was one block away. Niki and Don urged us to hurry and go there. They must have felt they had to be there just then. Indeed, when we arrived there, John suddenly remembered it was the 70th anniversary of his parents' wedding exactly at 12 noon, when we stepped into the church. Niki and Don wore their rings, which they had received from us at the time of their engagement.

This was the actual church of the University and the Seminary. Most of the fifth-year students in the Seminary were already priests. They and the professors said over 50 Masses every day. Basically, it was easy for us to go to Communion every morning on our way to school, as every five minutes a new Mass started at one of the side altars.

As a child I was allowed once to play on the church's organ because we knew the priest, Rev. Frigyes Teller, who was the organist and choir director. He sat beside me and produced all kinds of special effects the organ was capable of emitting, while I played. I was fascinated.

Close to the church I pointed out a store, which used to be one of our drugstores under the name "Irgang." The main store was at Petőfi Sándor u. 11. Now it was named "Cameo" and it did not much resemble our elegant store of old. Váci u. 23 was our second store that opened, which was the shopping street. It was now turned into a walking street.

One of our stores under the name "Neruda" was the *only* store still called "Drogéria." My grandfather bought this store from the original owners "Neruda Nándor and Sons," but kept the name. It was a true old fashioned, antique looking drugstore. A 100-acre land where herbs were grown belonged with the store that specialized in all kinds of herbs.

Last we went to the home we had left in 1956, on Bécsi út. Our neighbor, Juci, who became Louis' godmother during the Uprising, laughed and cried for joy to see him and us again. She still lived in the same place.

From there we went to see St. Margit Hospital, where Louis was born during the Revolution. It was an emotional day to say the least.

Our first big party was at Gundel restaurant, that Ronald Lauder and George Láng bought and totally remodeled to bring back its original beauty. This was the day when the restaurant re-opened and a reception was held for the Gundel family members. John's grandmother was Mária Gundel, sister of János Gundel, who started the original Gundel restaurant in Budapest. After George Láng's lecture Ronald Lauder took around our group to show us not only the restaurant and banquet rooms, but the former family residence which was made into private dining rooms for parties and the famous wine cellar. The tables were set with the original Zsolnay porcelain. Throughout the restaurant the Hungarian impressionist paintings, which were family heirlooms, decorated the walls. They were still there, but they were taken ("nationalized") by the Communists and never returned to their original owners. During the party, the György Lakatos Gypsy band was playing. The "primás" (first violin and conductor of the band) was playing on a Guarnerius violin. Guarnerius was one of the three best violin makers in Stradivarius' days. According to the new laws former owners did not get back their properties, but George Láng and Ronald Lauder had the decency to pass some money to the family as well. When he was young, George Láng learned a few dishes from Károly Gundel himself, the last owner of the restaurant. Unfortunately, he was no longer alive at the time of this great re-opening, but children, grandchildren, and spouses, along with great-grandchildren and cousins filled the entire establishment. Károly Gundel himself had 13 children, 11 of whom lived to be adults and continued to keep up the family numbers.

The Parliament, arguably the most beautiful one in the world, was completed in 1902. Its architect, the famous Hungarian Imre Steindl, never saw it finished, but even when he was no longer strong enough to stand, he was directing the construction from his wheelchair. The neo-gothic building's walls glittered in the sun with their golden hues on the lace-like structure inside. The murals depicted Hungary's history. To go up on those stairs where so many of our famous ancestors trod! To put our feet on the red carpet in the middle of the snow-white marble stairs again, now with our children!

We even had a chance to sit in the Galery while the meeting of the House took place. Among the representatives we saw was the then truly young Viktor Orbán, Head of FIDESZ, meaning Young Democrats Association. No one over 35 could become a member. This is how they wanted to make sure none of them had any political role in the Nazi or the Communist system. Zoltán Trombitás, Éva Mikes' husband was also on the floor representing FIDESZ.

We, who never even dreamed to be able to return to our native land, were sitting in the Gallery, watching the new laws being made. As it was a "Velvet Revolution" without bloodshed, all the Communist laws were still in effect and they had to be changed one by one. The representatives had their work cut out for them! The representatives claimed there were one million that needed changing.

One of our evenings we went to the Busuló Juhász, (The Sad Shepherd) restaurant on the side of St. Gellért Hill, where John's parents, as well as we, got engaged. Excellent gypsy music was playing. With tears in our eyes we sang each other our favorite romantic songs, while outside the stars were watching our happiness.

Our first trip out of town was to the exact place where we crossed the border. We rented three cars to accommodate the entire brood.

Our first stop was at the Forestry University of Sopron. This was the part of the Sopron university that stayed in Hungary. We helped settle the other half, who escaped and for which we interpreted and translated while they became affiliated with the University of British Columbia 1957 to 1963. The two halves of the University finally accepted each other and were on friendly terms. We went to the President's office. He gave us a detailed map and outlined the way where we walked on December 8th, the day of our escape from Sopron all the way to the border.

We started in pouring rain, which turned the trail into a muddy disaster for our entire hike. This time we drove to Lehár Ferenc utca 4, the house from where we left on December 8, 1956, where we had to stay for two days while our host arranged our trip with the guides at the border and walked back from there.

When we got to the house a lady came out. She recognized us from the time when we stayed there for two days. They too had similar visitors at the time who intended to leave the country. She immediately invited us in and brought lovely, fresh cherries. She was so excited to relive those days with us.

It was raining as we started out to the Austrian border. John explained everything in detail to our children. Ilike was the only one who could remember it all from the children who were present in 1992. We walked and walked in the endless rain treading mud. In 1956 the sun finally greeted us just as we started our walk, after two days of rain. Following the old man, our host, we watched for his signals we agreed on. For example, if he took off his hat and wiped his forehead, it meant to slow down, if he played with his cane, we could go ahead. We started out in 1956 with both older children (ages two and four) walking. Louis in the basket was carried by John. After about two miles Jancsi got tired. We gave him some sleeping pills and put him in John's knapsack. Ilike was ahead of us with a couple, friends who also wanted to leave Hungary. Later we found out from her that she kept having nightmares about a couple, a fat blonde lady and a man who were kidnapping her. She was about 16 years old when she told us that and we could enlighten her who the couple was. They had no intention to kidnap her! The route was almost 10 miles long to the border. When we reached Fertőrákos, we stopped at the guide's home, where I nursed the baby. The guide went down to the guards at the border and found out when and where the changing of the guards took place. This meant that all the personnel had to be at that place at the time. Then, it was possible to cross the border at the farthest place from there for 15 minutes.

"We started out in the dark" – this was John telling the story to our children – "it was a great night for our escape. There was no moon, only the stars gave us their twinkling lights. We were walking on top of a terraced vineyard with a barbed wire fence. Suddenly, there was a hole in the wall, just one brick missing, and your mother started to slide slowly down into the vineyard below. The wine stalks would have spiked her, leading to an almost certain death. 'Watch your step!' I whispered to her. I could not bend down because then Jancsi would have fallen from the knapsack. Thank God, the barbed wire fence got caught in her coat. By then the guide noticed it too and pulled her up."

"I felt I was sliding, but I could not stop myself!" I added. "We followed the edge of the lake in total mud, just like it was today. I carried a knapsack, with just six diapers and a few medicines, the most important things. I was still very weak from giving birth and fell twice. I wanted to throw away my coat because I felt so warm in the freezing weather. My mind advised me differently and I kept it on. I hurried as fast as my legs would carry me and the guides held me on both sides."

"Two men joined us from seemingly nowhere" – it was now John's turn to continue – "and took the baby in the basket from me. They carried the baby all the way and then disappeared, just as they came. We never saw them again. Two angels provided by God to help us on our way. The guides pointed to some trees in the distance and said the border was very close to them. They pointed at some lights in the distance, indicating that was Austria. We were so afraid we would be caught again. We had already seen the lights of Austria during our previous escape."

"John was ahead of me, I kept asking the guides where the other members of my family were," I said excitedly because by then we started to relive it all.

"I was ahead with the two boys. We finally felt the soft sand of the 'no-man's-land' under our feet. Then I was in Austria. Those minutes or two seemed like ages before Anyu too was reaching the raked sand. Then suddenly she was in my arms."

"Ilike ran to us, embraced our knees and cried with us."

Louis, the one who was in the basket in '56 wanted to go down to the exact spot, where we crossed the border, but a few of us could not continue to walk because of the mud. My shoes were shot by then, I had to throw them out, but the men followed them, as did his wife Kate. Son Steve was videotaping it all, so now we have the exact emotional event on YouTube. Louis and his father stood in a great embrace, crying. When they came back Louis and Kate embraced me: "Thank you for giving us freedom!"

The children all thanked us once again for bringing them to safety. "I am so glad we made it okay," said John, while patting Louis' back.

64

Next stop Lake Balaton. Our little convoy arrived in Ábrahámhegy, where John showed them all the sights and places where he spent his summers. We went to the beach with its sandy shore, but we also visited the neighbors' and their neighbors' wine cellars. We descended into the dark, cool cellar with big barrels on both sides. The moss on the wall held several coins. If the moss could hold a coin, it was just the right amount of moss needed for optimum wine. Of course, all neighbors offered us "tastes" of their own wine. Both Steve and Kristy tried the "lopó" (stealer, a glass tool to get wine out of the barrel by sucking on it) with success. Of course, some of the children's generation – although all married – have never experienced what happens if drinking in a cellar – when the outside air hits you so does the amount you "tasted." Some of the giggling younger generation took long afternoon naps after this adventure. On one of our evenings, we had the opportunity to eat "bogrács gulyás." The famous Hungarian "goulache" (as called in the USA) cooked in a kettle over a campfire. That is how it tastes best.

For another dinner we went to a restaurant in Révfülöp a place only six kilometers away (about four miles), where a panoramic view of the Lake Balaton and surroundings opened in front of our eyes. Before 1956 we used to walk or bike to Révfülöp, as well as to Badacsony Tomaj, which was about four kilometers (two miles) in the other direction. Of course, we took our children to Badacsony, a mountain famous for its great wines. Our children's favorite "lángos," the equivalent of "elephant ears" in America, tastes the best with garlic and sour cream, but you can put on it whatever you fancy.

From Badacsony we took a boat across to visit Mária and Elemér Terták in their cottage on the Lake. Their grandchildren were there with them and their mother Csaszi, Adam's wife. John told the children he and his parents used to row across the lake to the Tertáks when he was a child.

On our way to our next stop, Pécs where we spent our honeymoon, we drove to Tihany. Here Lake Balaton is the deepest: 30 feet. On this peninsula stands an old baroque church in all its splendor. On the way up the mountain a lovely field of lavender beckoned. Vendors offered their wares everywhere. Artists tempted us with their delightful ceramics.

We crossed the Balaton by ferry and continued our way on the Somogy side towards Pécs. On an old house we discovered a stork nest with baby storks; typical on Hungarian village chimneys.

In Pécs we were greeted by our old friends Éva Mikes and Zoli Trombitás. Zsuzsa Sarok, a journalist friend and her husband, a Professor of Medicine at the Janus Pannonius University in Pécs, housed some of our children. We lived in Zoli's parents' home as they were still in Seattle. Zoli's brother Karcsi brought us fresh warm crescent rolls and hardcrusted buns every morning for our breakfast.

We showed our children the cathedral, the Bishop's Palace and the catacombs. An interesting statue of Franz Liszt looked down on the square from a balcony. Next came the downtown parish church, which used to be a Muslim Mosque during the Turkish occupation, but was later changed into a Catholic church. The inside is a very interesting study in styles, as the building adapted to different religions.

Across from the church was the Nádor Hotel, where John and I spent our honeymoon. Naturally we had to visit Éva at her office in City Hall. She was now the Vice-Mayor of Pécs.

Turning into the walking street past City Hall, we were soon at the Theater. Across the street John pointed out his grandparents' home, where his mother grew up. His grandfather, Alexander Huszár later became a Supreme Court Judge 1914-1929, which meant a move to the capital city.

A curiosity in Pécs is the Wall of Padlocks, where newly married couples put their own lock with the other hundreds.

Our next stop was in the Hungarian Great Plains, in Cegléd. Little Grandmother's house was no longer there. My aunt and her family were moved into an apartment, when the government decided to demolish their home (already nationalized anyway) and built an apartment house in its place. Their house was on Kossuth Ferenc utca, one of the main streets leading from the railroad station to the Main Square with the Catholic and Protestant churches. The other main street, running parallel to Kossuth F. Street was Rákóczi út. A little train taking people to their vineyards ran right in front of my grandparent's old house.

The memories came flying back as we followed the street to Main Square. Kitty-corner to the church the old stationery store was still there. When I was little, Laky néni, the owner of the stationary store, used to tell me I had the same soft voice as my father used to have when he came in to buy something.

We went into the church with the children. The painted statues of saints and the murals mirrored all such churches from the last century. Beside the church was the big Protestant church. On the other side of the church was the Guild House, built by my grandfather when he was the President of the Guild. I remember the picture in the newspaper when the building was inaugurated. My grandfather received a Medal from the Governor for his promotion of culture in his town. In this great house there was a movie, theater performances, and other events. We used to go to every new performance with my little grandmother.

My grandfather had a leather goods store. They also made handcrafted leather goods. His store was on Rákóczi út. That too was nationalized, but he was "allowed to work" in his own store as an employee of the State.

My grandfather had an employee, Pista, whom I had known since he was staying with them from age 14, as Grandfather's apprentice. He became the boss after the store was taken, but he loved my grandfather and treated him as his own father. The store was moved to a side street, but it was still there. I was told Pista was the manager. I hope he bought the store when it was re-privatized. We had many good times with Pista. I was 7-10 years old, when he was 14-17, so I was allowed to bicycle with him to the confectioner's store where we both had ice cream cones, while he kept me up to date on the happenings in town.

In front of the churches, on the Main Square, is where the Sunday Market and two lesser weekday markets took place. I loved those markets. From five in the morning, we could hear the carriages rattle in front of our window. I was so excited. I could not wait to see the attractions. There was a toy I loved. On a little stick, at the end of a string, was a little bird. There was a whistle hidden inside the bird. So, if you swished the stick through the air, the birdie whistled. It was called "farán-fütyülős rigó" the bottom-whistling nightingale. Then the lovely hand-crafted honey-cake hearts with a little mirror in the middle, or other figurines made from the same cake, decorated with icing. They were not for snacking, but for giving them to your sweetheart to be remembered by her. Whenever we went to the market, we always bought aprons. I enjoyed choosing from the many different colors and patterns. Oh, there was so much to see and admire!

Going towards the railroad station we passed my father's high school and Gubodi Garden, where my grandparents first noticed each other, while promenading with their friends on a Sunday afternoon. Right beside it was my beloved swimming pool.

The Kossuth Museum grew into a real treasure since my father's high school professor, József Sárkány, founded it after WWII. Lajos Kossuth, Hungary's great national hero of the Revolution of 1848, loved Cegléd. Ferenc Kossuth, after whom the street was named, was his father. After the Revolution was crushed Kossuth went into exile. He came to tour the USA and was one of the very few people who was given a chance to speak to the Joint Session of Congress. Out of the first four people to do so, two were Hungarian. Albert Apponyi, Hungarian Prime Minister after WWI, was the other Hungarian. The other two foreigners were Lafayette and Sir Winston Churchill.

Not far from Cegléd is the town of Szolnok on the Tisza river. Kati Fábry, (Mrs. Benedek) my second cousin, who was originally from Szolnok joined us there and told us about all the family connections. My Bartha grandfather's father was János Bartha. He had a sawmill on the river. He was an excellent businessman. He had 14 children. Their mother and seven of the children died from smallpox. The remaining children were brought up by him and his mother-in-law. One of the children was my grandfather, another Kati's grandmother. By the time János Bartha died, my grandfather too had become a highly successful businessman, owning a factory and a chain of drugstores. He built his father a mausoleum in the form of a small chapel in the corner of the cemetery. Kati had been taking care of all the family graves because she was able and willing to do it. She led us down to the cellar to show us the marble plaques that marked the graves of my grandmother, and Dr. István Bartha Jr., their son, who had died at 23 from multiple illnesses. His PhD was laid on his coffin, he had passed away just before receiving it. In the beautiful little chapel, we said a prayer for those who rested there.

In 1992, it so happened that an Alaskan volcano erupted. What did that have to do with us? We got a phone call from a young Hungarian couple at the airport. They were stuck in Seattle because no planes were flying into Alaska. All of Anchorage was covered in ash. Naturally, we gathered them up from the airport and took them to our home. We alerted our son Steve, who lived close by. He had a mini-van. We all piled in and had a great guided tour of Seattle. We stopped at a grocery store to load up on food, then went to a Godfather's pizza. All typical American experiences of the day.

The stranded couple? Drs. Viktor Orbán and Anikó Lévai, both lawyers, a lovely 28-year-old couple were the ones who became our guests that night. We first met Viktor in Pécs, on the day the Soviets were leaving Hungary, at the FIDESZ headquarters, when we toasted their good-bye with champagne. They received our contact number from mutual FIDESZ friends. We instantly recognized our soul brother and sister in them. In the evening we even showed them a tape of *Hungary Remembered*, our project for the 30th anniversary of the Hungarian Uprising in 1956.

When in Hungary, they invited us to their home in Haris köz 4, where Anikó cooked an extraordinary meal for us. This was after the birth of one of their children. We met with them annually from then on. When Viktor gave a talk to AmCham, the American Hungarian Chamber of Commerce in Budapest, I wrote an article about him in my newsletter for American business people, entitled: "Will he be our next Prime Minister?" His talk in perfect English was excellent. Well, it was not the very next election, but he did become Prime Minister for the first time at age 35.

65

Our first consular get-together at the Hungarian Embassy in Washington DC, took place in December of 1993. Our Prime Minister, József Antall, has been sick with lymphoma for a couple of years. He died during the time of our conference.

Ilike staged a big party in Columbia, MD for us during our stay. We had invited the Ambassador and the Honorary Consuls and many of Ilike's friends and had a great time. However, before the Ambassador proceeded to the party, he stopped to talk with John and me. He whispered to us that our PM is having his last hours. Before he died he had a long talk with Viktor Orbán and passed on his legacy to him. By morning he had died. The nation's reaction was tremendous and overwhelming. He lay in state at the Parliament. The entire country wanted to pay tribute to him. People, like ocean waves, overflowed the Parliament to have a last look at our first freely elected PM. Péter Boros took over his remaining time before his mandate expired.

József Antall predicted that the next election will bring the opposition into power because no matter what he or any prime minister could do in that first term, it will not be right. It will be the first attempt to lead a country back from Communism into Capitalism.

He was right. The Socialist Party, the Reform Communists, won the second free election, with Gyula Horn as the Prime Minister. We were in Hungary at the time with the Tertáks and could not figure out what got into the people.

We Honorary Consuls knew that Ambassadors were supposed to resign when the government changed. We offered our resignations to Géza Jeszenszky, the Minister of Foreign Affairs, but he asked us to stay in place. The Government has finally established a consular corps they could trust. We understood, along with the fact that we were serving the Hungarian people. We all stayed.

Our Hungary tour with children/grandchildren was repeated many times in the coming years. By now every one of our children and grandchildren have been to Hungary at least once. János was the only one of the children who spent a month in Hungary without our participation. However, we wrote everything down for him to take the appropriate tours. He also spent time in Pécs to consult with the theater under the guidance of Dr. Elizabeth Schillinger, a dear friend, who was also a consultant with the City of Pécs. Of course, the Trombitás-Mikes family was extremely important and fun during his stay.

In August 1993 we had an extended family reunion in Winnipeg, celebrating my father's 87th birthday, where all the families from Toronto and Seattle (or anywhere in between) showed up. There were 53 of us. My father was still practicing and making house calls as an M.D. even at his age. We strongly tried to persuade him to retire, but he insisted he wanted to practice because if he stopped being a doctor, he would be nothing.

It was good to be in his house again. The house my mother chose, and they all loved; the furniture and carpets we cherished throughout the years. I never lived in this house, only for short vacations, but somehow it was still "home" in Canada. The big screened-in porch where one could sit in the evenings when the temperature was bearable, the lovely garden around it, the big dining room table by the kitchen and the living room with its big sofas, the scene of many parties with Hungarians as well as with Canadian doctors. A few of us lived in the house in the two bedrooms upstairs, but an entire floor of a nearby hotel was rented by the family. At the first luncheon we started out with one table, then as people arrived, the waiters kept adding small tables, and adding small tables, and adding small tables. In the end there were 35 of us having lunch together.

The hotel manager was a fast learner. The next day they had a big room for us to have our meals together. We had a wonderful time speaking, joking, laughing, getting acquainted with new family members. The youngest one was Andrew, my sister Elizabeth's grandson, her daughter Edith's baby, only a few weeks old.

August 3rd was the big celebration, which started with Mass at St. Anthony's Hungarian Church. My father was a magnanimous benefactor of the church. The new altar, made of Italian marble, was bought by him in memory of my mother. The parish priest gave a heartfelt homily, appreciating all the work Father has done for the community. He gave my father a special Blessing from the Pope beautifully framed. The liturgy was planned by my sister Elizabeth, who was a teacher in a Catholic School in Toronto and routinely did such planning. The Prayers of the Faithful was read by the 12 grandchildren.

After Mass, a tasty Hungarian dinner was served in the Parish Hall. Marie thanked the participants who came in great numbers. I reminisced about the time when we were little. Of course, I could remember times that not even my sisters could recall.

463

Son Steve created a tremendous slide presentation about our family's life.

One of our grandchildren, Adam (five years old), Steve and Kristy's son, grabbed the mike and jumped around, singing his heart out, doing a great job!

We spent most of our time at my father's house with him, but the young people tried to see all the sights in Winnipeg. We talked about old times. Father liked to talk with my husband, who was the only person by then in the whole wide world, who still called him by his childhood nickname "Nyika" or "Nyiki." John was only 10 years younger than my mother, therefore the closest to my father's age in the entire family. He was also acquainted with Father's friends, who used to dance with my mother. He worked together with them as engineers in the Ganz Factory before our escape. Ferenc Taky, who brought us together with John, was one of my father's very best friends, as well as ours. Father and John always found a lot to talk about. My mother was only 36 when we married, therefore it was decided we were going to call our in-laws by their first name.

~

Finally, on September 13th the Honorary Hungarian Consulate opened in Seattle. That meant I had now all the duties described in previous chapters, which made our lives much busier. Thank God John had retired from Ebasco in 1991, so now we were both diving into our new duties together.

We arranged for him a huge retirement party, attended by family, friends and even one of his brilliant graduate students from UBC, who came from Eastern Canada, Bryan Smith with his wife, Cathy.

When we went to our annual consular meetings in Washington DC, we always visited Ilike, who lived in Columbia, Maryland, which was right between Baltimore Maryland and Washington DC. We usually stayed with her. As we stepped out of the airplane, she introduced us to Chuck Dann, her fiancé. We knew already about Chuck, but their engagement was the big news. Chuck was a brilliant man, a lawyer. He could not have any children, so he and his parents were overjoyed to have two teenagers who now had two grandparents living close by.

In May of 1994 we were back to celebrate their wedding. May 14th was the date. They were beautiful in their wedding attire, as were all the family members. It was held in the garden of the African American Museum, recently opened. They were married by a family friend, Luther Starnes, a Methodist Minister, who had an interesting profession under Governor Schaefer. The Governor attended religious services at Luther's church. They knew and trusted each other. I think it should be made compulsory in every state to have such a "Special Secretary." This was his proper title. He called himself "Secretary of Hard Luck." He had free entrance to all the state government's departments. People who had unsolved problems with any government department could write to him and he took care of the problems. That was especially important for people who did not have any other means to help themselves, like poor people, old people, people in jail.

A fantastic party followed to celebrate Ilike and Chuck's new life together. Anna, 17, was Maid of Honor and Alex, 13, was the ringbearer.

Ilike and Chuck then left for their honeymoon to St. John, a U.S. Virgin Island in the Caribbean, and we took care of the children and their home while they were gone. They had a lovely house in Columbia, a planned community established by one of Ilike's former employers Jim Rouse. The city consisted of "villages," where all the facilities, like grocery stores, pharmacy, bank, sport opportunities, schools were located. Ilike lived in the end unit of a row of townhouses, which meant they had more light and view of the surrounding natural beauty. A little stream flowed down in the valley behind their home. A sloping hillside with big trees and a trail led down to it. Another garden was in the front. A terrace in the back, a porch in the front finished the beauty and comfort of the home. Columbia Mall was close and was a fun place to visit with or without the children. During winters it featured a several-stories-tall Christmas tree made from poinsettias. Anna introduced us to the yummy Auntie Ann's pretzels at the mall.

I enjoyed Chuck's beige leather armchair and ottoman every morning when I had to wake up Alex every 15 minutes to get him to school on time.

On October 8, 1994, Niki's first child, our 13th grandchild, John William McKay, was born. He looked so perfect! From the first minute on he fell in love with his Grandfather John. John enjoyed a grandchild not only near, but Niki brought him over three times a week to be with us. We spoke Hungarian to him all the time when he was at our home. Soon, when he was about seven or eight months old, when his mother was turning onto the freeway ramp leading to our house, he exclaimed: "Papa? Papa?" meaning "are we going to Papa's?" Then the overjoyed smile at Papa's constant attention showed us John's love for his grandfather. During the summer months we went to the swimming pool with him and Niki. He enjoyed floating in his device with us in the radiant sun.

On John's first birthday, Niki and Don announced they were expecting again. Niki was trying to avoid me in the week before because she knew I would see it on her new-mother-radiant-face that she was pregnant.

The night when Michelle Claire Dominique was born, her brother John stayed with us. I took a photo of him and his "Papa" watching TV together. In one hand his bottle, the other in a bowl of popcorn. He had a gorgeous smile on his face, indicating he was in Seventh Heaven. Just like his grandfather.

His adoration never stopped. In the first years of his life, as soon as he saw me, he said: "Papa? Papa?" meaning "If you are here, where is Papa?"

We went with Niki and the kids to Bellevue Square Mall often. Whenever Papa appeared, or John had noticed him, he flew as fast as his little feet would carry him, to embrace his idol.

When he was three years old and they were having dinner at our house, I happened to sit down beside him at the table. He apologetically looked at me: "Please, don't sit here, I am keeping this place for my 'Best Friend'!" meaning of course, Papa. From then on, they called each other "Best Friend."

In the meantime, I tried, once again, to get my original scout story "Troop 56" published. A couple of years ago *Highlights* magazine's book publishing arm, Boyds Mills Press that just started a young adult line, decided to undertake the publishing. Kent Brown, the owner of the Publishing Company had a classmate who had escaped from Hungary in 1956. He remembered how his friend always looked up at airplanes that can bring you to freedom. However, my original book was the story of five scouts, 17 years old, while Kent wanted to publish it from one point of view and 14-year-old boys. I realized, although I had knowledge of six languages, I could not talk "childrenese" in English. I was never a child in English. I started learning it when I was 12 and I did not speak English with my children. That is when I found my co-author, Peggy King Anderson, an award-winning children's writer, at the Christian Writers Conference. At first, she was hesitant when I asked her, but I gave her the manuscript for our lunch period. She came back after lunch and accepted. She fell in love with Stephen, who became the main character. She did a marvelous job! She became a Hungarian while changing the manuscript, she studied the Uprising, she felt with us. She got so angry that the free world did not help, she stopped and shook her daughter, and friends "Why didn't we do something?"

It was finally ready for 1996, the 40th anniversary of the Hungarian Uprising of 1956. We submitted the book in the contests of both the Washington Press Association and the National Federation of Press Women and received First Prizes statewide and nationally.

The Hungarian American Coalition had an early Board meeting in November, where we had a several-day-long conference on Human Rights as regards to Hungarian minorities in the surrounding countries. One of the participants was Bishop László Tőkés who started the Uprising against Ceausescu in 1989. I had the honor of sitting beside him during one of the dinners.

We launched my book, *The Fall of the Red Star*, at the banquet of that conference. The publisher gave us 200 free books to distribute among the attendants. I signed them all before the dinner started. The keynote speaker was Kati Marton, the well-known author. Her parents were also there, Endre and Ilona Marton, who were the AP and UPI correspondents in Hungary during the Uprising in 1956. They received later in the USA the reward for reporting under extreme conditions. Endre became a professor at Georgetown University. Ilona taught French at a high school. In Endre's book *Under Forbidden Skies* he gave a true account of their experiences. We have met them several years previously and enjoyed our friendship with them.

The book launch was a surprise for all the guests. To represent Kent Brown, the publisher, he sent Tom White who gave a delightful talk and I spoke as well. Kati Marton was lovely when she congratulated me. Unfortunately, neither my husband John, nor Peggy King Anderson could be there at the launch. They could not make the trip to Washington at that time.

While we had the Mikulás dinner at the Embassy as a rule, the Hungarian American Coalition did not want to ask the brand-new Ambassador for the space. We had our banquet at the German Embassy, where I went with Ilike. If she could, she always came to these fun dinners. This time she helped put the books on all the chairs!

The publisher did his absolute best to promote the book and so did we and Peggy. John and I were traveling all over the United States to visit schools, associations, clubs, meetings and lectured everywhere. We sold 1,200 books that first year just the two of us. We paid for our own expenses, but we were put up with friends, so had little else to spend money on than our airplane tickets.

We gave our most fruitful talk at the Columbia Tower Club, in Seattle's tallest building. The Club of those who traveled around the globe invited us at the proposal of George Brain, the Dean who, along with his wife Harriet, helped my sister and family escape from Ethiopia. Not only did all the Club members buy books, but one of them, the Head of PEMCO, ordered 500 books with the company's imprint as donors to the Seattle Schools.

Our publisher did so much for us! There was another book launch in Seattle, where Kent Brown was here in person and both Peggy and I enjoyed it together with our husbands. We had not planned it this way, but Peggy broke her ankle and still had her soft cast on. I fell and hurt my ankle, so I too had a soft cast. We wore identical Hungarian tops and black skirts (that we planned). We even looked alike. That is how we entered the room with huge smiles. Peggy had five children, I had seven. We were both Catholic mothers. No wonder we understood each other so well and had a great collaboration on the book. People used to ask us how we wrote together. We used to laugh and tell them that one of us wrote the vowels, the other the consonants.

One of the big events the publisher organized for us was an entire hour on CSPAN-2, the book channel. It was videotaped at Tillicum Middle School. Peggy, John and I gave our usual talk to an actual class. (https://youtu.be/gIer44inQeY)

Peggy and I were begging the publisher to come out with the paperback edition, so children can buy their own copies. Before he gave in, he wanted us to show we will be able to sell at least 1,000 copies. Both my daughter, Ilike, and I, bought 500 copies each and we had the 1,000. Ilike distributed it to scouts and schools in Maryland. We gave away many, but also sold many. People who came to the Consulate usually bought at least a copy. Of course, John and I also continued to give talks and sell the books at these events.

The publisher, Kent Brown, sent a few samples of the book to the Hungarian Ministry of Education, to Dr. Judith Kádár-Fülöp, who was at the time President of the International Reading Association in Hungary. She was ecstatic. "This is what we need right now!"

In the summer, when I was in Hungary, we went together to several publishers in Hungary and talked about possibilities. Judith invited me to the annual meeting of the Hungarian Reading Association in the Széchenyi Library on Castle Hill. She already had English speakers read the book. It was an unbelievable experience. The teachers and child psychologists practically begged me to translate the book.

"I should translate it? But I have not lived in Hungary for 34 years!"

"It does not matter! We will edit it! We need this book so much. We have to teach the history of the Hungarian Uprising against the Soviets in 1956 and we do not know anything about it! During the past 40 years we either were not told anything about it, or we were told lies. This would be excellent for the schools!"

I agreed. So, I went ahead and translated the book into Hungarian, which the Holnap Kiadó published among the books recommended for schools. Remember, the original book was written in English, then published in Hungarian for the first time by the Hungarian-American Scouts for the 30th anniversary of the Uprising, 1986. At that time, I translated it into

Hungarian. Then it was rewritten, according to Boyds Mills Press' wishes with Peggy. Now I translated into Hungarian – again.

Dr. Judith Kádár-Fülöp was organizing the publishing of the book. I never heard of them during the year. Finally, before I left for Hungary that summer, I called her and asked about the book. She said: "Well, everything will be as we had discussed it." "What is it we discussed?" She answered: "The book will get published by the time you get here."

We had a fabulous book launch at the English bookstore, Dr. Eszter Milkovich, the publisher of the book, organized the fantastic party. Many of my former classmates showed up. I talked in both English and Hungarian, switching from one language to another, not repeating, but "continuing" what I had said so it should be interesting even to those who understood both languages.

At the Budapest Book Week I had special hours for signing. Obviously, John and I alerted all our friends, relatives, classmates. I did not have a free moment while I was sitting there.

The book just came out in time for the Frankfurt World's Fair of Books in 1999, when Hungary was the honored guest. It was exhibited there in both languages. Four of us Hungarian writers had a panel discussion about the Uprising. I had a trilingual flyer printed especially for the Fair, in English, Hungarian and German.

Famous Hungarian author, the doyenne of Hungarian writers, Magda Szabó, was also at the Frankfurt Fair. We had met before at the Budapest Book Week, when we were signing books together at the Holnap Kiadó's tent in June. I gave her a copy of *The Fall of the Red Star* in English in Frankfurt because by that time I ran out of the Hungarian version. Next time we met she said she read the entire book (in English) on the plane from Frankfurt to Budapest. She could not put it down. She said I should keep writing; I should use my God-given talent.

For 10 years the book was never out of print in America and neither is it now. When the publisher gave us the rights back, I immediately republished it on amazon.com and kindle. It is now available worldwide.

The Hungarian version was recently republished in Hungary by Holnap Kiadó, again as a book recommended for schools.

The International School in Hungary is teaching my book in English.

I was invited to talk to the class reading it. One of the little boys told me after my talk: "This was the best class we ever had." My friend, Hungarian-American Piroska Nagy, their teacher, herself a remarkable author and photographer, invited me.

Every one of my visits to Hungary was exceptional and unique. We always worked so hard that time just flew by. A cavalcade of business meetings, consular affairs, family and friends, enjoying being alive and back in Hungary again…We made the most of it.

66

The first ever World Conference of Honorary Hungarian Consuls was held in Budapest in 1996. At first, we received an invitation asking for a registration fee. We wrote letters immediately to the Ministry of Foreign Affairs regarding our disappointment at the idea that we should pay for them telling us what we should do for them for free. We had to pay the cost for our plane tickets and hotel bills anyway. Luckily, the Ministry immediately understood and waived the registration fees.

The World Conference consisted of three days of serious work. Ministers and their deputies talked about the most important and latest developments, laws, rules, and regulations. There were 102 Hungarian Honorary Consuls around the world and 99 of us showed up. John and I lived at the Tertáks, just as several other consuls who stayed with friends, to cut costs. That meant we had to get up with the birds to get to the hotel in time for the lectures and seminars, even though we had to stay out late for the dinners.

An unforgettable experience! We were shown everything promotable abroad, tourist opportunities, trade possibilities, cultural events, exchanges between universities. Consuls were networking all day. We met for the first time, János Fenjvesy, Honorary Consul in Caracas, whose informative and witty Christmas letters we have been receiving for a while through our friend Erika Hawkins in Trinidad. János, as Honorary Consul, was the only representative of Hungary in all of Venezuela. There was no Embassy. The closest Embassy was in Colombia. Venezuela's passport and visa applications had to go through Colombia. He begged the Ministry to let them send these applications straight to Hungary because it would get there so much faster than going first to Colombia. In South America, the mail was unimaginably slow, if it even got to its destination.

After the Conference, Prime Minister Gyula Horn, received word that Mrs. Clinton, who was returning from Kosovo, was going to stop in Hungary. He decided to throw a party for her at the Vadász Terem (Hunter Hall), the Parliament's formal dining room. He needed people whom he could invite at a moment's notice. The Honorary Consul from Texas, USA Retired Colonel Solymossy, was an Advisor to the U.S. Forces in Pápa, Hungary and in connection with the war in Kosovo. He and Edith Lauer, Chair of the Hungarian-American Coalition's Board, remembered the Hungarian Honorary Consuls from the U.S. who might still be in Budapest. Luckily, I was one of them. John and I received an invitation for the dinner with Mrs. Clinton. All together there were 64 people at the buffet dinner. When I talked with Hilary Clinton, I reminded her of our first meeting in Tucson, AZ. We talked about our books.

Hungarian goose liver is a delicacy that defies description. We urged her to try it, but she was not inclined to do so. She tasted other Hungarian foods and liked them. The cuisine was extraordinary in that dining room. We were indeed lucky with John because we had many occasions to eat there, visit the Parliament for work to assist our native land in these exciting transitory times.

This year we celebrated our 45th wedding anniversary. The Tertáks again invited Mihály Czenner who performed our civil wedding, and he repeated the ceremony. When we came home, we repeated the celebration with Mass joined by our entire family. Our oldest granddaughter, Anna, Ilike's daughter, spoke during Mass and retold the story of our escape, coached by her father, Barry. She did an outstanding job.

We had lunch with our grandchildren only, then dinner with only our children. We all had an extra special time!

Our children presented us with a delightful present. A big white album filled with photos and memories. Each of the children had to write down their favorite memory of us, just one, while growing up. We had a chance to write one too.

I wrote my letter to my one and only love forever, my husband:

Through your love God made me whole. As a 16-year-old I looked at life with curious awe, yet with the reality of our experiences. I put my hand in yours and I knew I wanted it to be forever. My life was full of desires, of yearnings for something indescribable, for something beyond me. On our honeymoon we were walking down one day from the Tettye in Pécs. We reached the edge of the mountain, a small stone fence, a viewpoint. That moment the noon bells started ringing all over the landscape and we stood there – no longer two people, but one. There and then I realized: my desires and yearnings were fulfilled. Through your love God gave me a glimpse of His love – in Him we were one.

John wrote:

I have many, and I mean many, fond memories with Anyu. Probably my most favorite occurred in Ábrahámhegy on a beautiful, sunny Sunday, after Mass, on the 2nd of September, 1951. For more than a month Anyu was torn: should she finalize our marriage or not. She asked me several times not to bring up the issue. On that day, the two of us went up to the top of Paphegytető. I lifted up Anyu on top of a boulder. The view of Balaton was magnificent. I became restless and could not hold it back: I asked "Would you marry me for good?" Tears began to run down her cheeks. I helped her down, but could not resist to ask: "At least, do I have a chance?" With a mischievous smile and a twinkle in her beautiful brown eyes, in a fashion only true Hungarian high society women could flirt, she looked at me and said: "I think so." The rest is history.

That same year Rita received her degree in Environmental Science from WSU in Richland. She was the last of our children to graduate because she insisted on getting married instead. John was so happy about this last graduation in our family, he put on his gown and sat with the professors. He handed the diploma to his daughter and as a good European – he kissed her hand. I do not think this ever happened in the history of the university. It was a great feeling to see John and Rita together on stage. They were both beaming with happiness. Rita's husband and two children were jubilant.

Hungary celebrated 1,100 years of statehood that same year. Being the Honorary Consul I had to organize the great event in Seattle. Our dear friend Béla Siki, a world-renowned Hungarian-born pianist and Head of the Piano Department at the University of Washington, agreed to play a concert for this event. This was incredibly special. Previously he sent graduate students if we asked. Of course, this was an occasion to behold! Professor Bob Harmon again hosted us at Seattle University. He did not deem their own piano good enough for such a great artist and rented a Steinway for the evening for $700 and paid for it himself. This became another unforgettable evening. Béla Siki was moved to tears. I saw him tremble from emotion arising in him during the standing ovation, when I went up on stage to give him a Certificate of Appreciation on behalf of the Consulate.

The summer of 1997 saw us back in Trinidad again. Our godson Philip Julien married Angelique, originally from The Netherlands. John and I just had to be there. We stayed for three weeks as guests of the Juliens, this time in a hotel. The wedding was at their estate, where Pat and Ken now lived. They built everything according to their plans, in a lovely location. The wedding took place in the nearby Catholic Church. The event surpassed everyone's imagination. It was well organized, and everything overflowed with abundance and happiness.

After the wedding we spent time in Erika and Don Hawkins' Tobago house. We were there by ourselves, in the beautiful surroundings. A housekeeper came every day. When we went to church Marie Thérèse Rétout, my journalist friend, introduced me after Mass as the columnist they have been reading for many years. It was nice to be in this "home" again. The beaches were just as enticing as they used to be, the flowers bursting with abundance and life was beautiful.

After Trinidad we went to Hungary, where finally the compensation came to an end at the satisfaction of nobody, except those who became rich during the privatization. While the newly liberated surrounding countries gave back nationalized property to their owners, Hungary decided against that. I believe it was a grave mistake. The country itself was in a bad shape economically because all the factories were misused and not maintained during the past 40 years. How do I know that? I have been through many of them with clients I accompanied from the USA, who were interested in buying or investing, starting something new. Many of the factories manufactured products that no one, only the Soviet Union, bought from them. Right then, not even the former Soviet Union was willing to take the merchandise because they could get much better products from anywhere in the world. Why did they manufacture those products? Everyone had to be employed. Therefore, it did not matter whether they manufactured worthless shoes or machine parts, they were employed, and everyone worked because that was enforced.

In the case of one of the factories, the city trying to sell it to foreigners, said: "We just cannot give it back to the former owners. They would ruin the factory because they don't have the professional knowledge." Those former owners not only had the knowledge, but also the family secret recipes. They could have made superior products and brought in the same kind of money for development, even from foreign investors, but the company would have remained in Hungarian possession.

Instead they brought a law that made a mockery of "compensation." I have the official "Magyar Közlöny," the official Government paper publishing all the new laws and regulations. However, I will give it to you in a nutshell because, as most laws, it is long and incomprehensible to people not familiar

474

with the legal language. This is how it appeared in my newsletter, *Hungary International*, Volume 2. No. 5 (a copy of each issue can be found in the Széchenyi Library in Budapest). The new law about compensation for former property owners and their heirs. The resolution was passed on April 25, 1991, 189 members voted for it and 108 against with 11 abstentions.

The new law affirms the right to private property and provides a nominal compensation for former owners of land, factories, stores, and houses. All those whose property was "nationalized," more accurately confiscated, after June 8, 1949, are eligible for compensation...

...The damages will be estimated according to tables exclusively on square footage, regardless of where the property was located. Compare the square footage of a luxury apartment on Fifth Ave. in New York and a house in a village in Iowa. Same square footage – same compensation. And the amount? 10HUF (the equivalent of which at the time was 6 ½ cents in U.S. dollars) per square foot.

In the case of businesses the number of employees will be taken into consideration when determining value.

The amount of compensation will also be based on certain averages. Furnishings and other valuables present at the time of nationalization are already included in this amount. (Compare a kitchen table to a Louis XIV antique desk – all included in the following prices):

Portion of damage*	Compensation
0-200,000HUF	100%
200,001-300,000HUF	50%
300,001-500,000HUF	30%
500,001 + HUF	10%

*Damages up to 200,000HUF will be compensated in full. For amounts in excess of this amount, the above table will be used. Example: Damages of 1,500,000 will receive only 40,000HUF, meaning five times less than the one whose damage was only 200,000 HUF.

The limit for any individual will be 5,000,000HUF. Heirs of the individual would get a portion of that (this was not announced ahead of time, but this is how the wording was applied).

For example, our summer home, with this kind of square footage price was appreciated at 12,000,000HUF at the time. My mother owned several apartment houses, our winter home, and the businesses were in her name.

All she received was 5,000,000 divided by three for the three girls. We did not even get that much because by the time we received it, the compensation vouchers were not worth much. Speculators bought up these vouchers and bought businesses, shares, stocks during the privatization. What was left? We were able to sell our vouchers at 60-70%. Some were not even that lucky. They could sell them for 30% of their value only.

That is what I meant by finally the compensation was "finished" for us in 1997. As an outcome John and I bought two return tickets to Istanbul to visit our dear old friends Linda Robinson and Jim Geary, whom we first met in Trinidad. Jim was Irish, teaching at the UWI for six years. Linda was American. While in Turkey we bought a leather coat at the Grand Bazaar and later a pair of shoes back in Hungary. That was the amount we had received as "compensation" for the several million dollars worth of assets that were nationalized in 1949. That would be the equivalent of billions today. Recently we were told that our summer home was for sale for over a billion HUF.

But, let's talk about the happy events in Istanbul. Linda and Jim lived in an apartment that looked down on the Golden Horn, the Bosphorus and the Marmor Sea. It was located just across from the Topkapi, the Blue Mosque and the Hagia Sophia. Just to sit on their balcony was a dream!

We stayed with them the entire time. They also took us to any place we wanted to go and fed us at Turkish eateries which were excellent, without exception. The figs were so sweet and delicious!

Naturally, we went over to see all the beautiful sights we could see from the window, but this time we went inside and admired the spectacular beauty of these ancient and glamorous buildings, ornate with gold, ceramics, patterns and artwork.

The Grand Bazaar was fascinating. Gold and silver jewelry formed small hills. The jewels were available for only the price of gold that went into them. The goldsmith's work did not make any difference in the price.

"What nationality are you?" the merchants asked while they treated us to tea.

"Hungarian? Ah, but they are good friends of ours. Arany, szőnyeg, bőrkabát! (Gold, carpet, leather coat!)" I doubt there was any language in which they could not enumerate their most favored merchandise. We bought a beautiful ceramic plate and the above-mentioned leather coat.

Anyway, the Turks nowadays think of Hungarians as great friends. True, they shop in Turkey a lot. The Turks think creatively. They believe the Turkish occupation of Hungary was liberating for the Hungarians, protecting us from the Western nations.

True that some of the Hungarians who rebelled against the Habsburgs escaped to Turkey. One of them was Ferenc Rákóczy in the 1700s. He was a Hungarian prince. When he arrived in Rodosto (Greek name) Tekirdag in Turkish, he built a palace. He also built a fountain in front of the palace. According to muslim belief if a person builds a fountain that believers can use for ablution before prayers that person will go straight to heaven. He was well beloved by the people there.

Jim and Linda took us there to see the palace, which is now a Museum.

Before we left for Turkey Géza Jeszenszky, the Foreign Minister who made me Honorary Consul, told us that we just had to meet the Honorary Consul of Hungary in Tekirdag. He was so unique and kind! He even learned Hungarian. We called him before we went to Turkey. Someone answered in splendid, but for us un-understandable Turkish. We tried English. Answer in Turkish. We tried Hungarian. Answer in Turkish. French? German? Nothing seemed to work.

We called again. Same result.

Finally, we called him from Turkey and had a great conversation in Hungarian. It turned out he was out of town and his father came over to watch his home. His father answered the phone. He spoke only Turkish.

The Consul could not have been nicer. He invited all four of us and told us many stories. The Hungarian Consul General in Istanbul was his good friend. They struck up a friendship while they volunteered together to renew the palace of Ferenc Rákóczy II. Month after month they worked together and simply by talking with each other he learned Hungarian. He proudly showed us around the Rákóczy Museum. At the door, a Turk was selling souvenirs on behalf of the Museum. We thought he was Hungarian as he spoke as the Hungarians at that time in Hungary did, using slang words. We asked and he said he was Turkish. He just learned Hungarian from all the Hungarian visitors to the Museum. The Hungarian language is so difficult, it was out of our experience to hear these two Turks speak it so well.

Honorary Consul Erdogan Erken then took us to see the Turkish-Hungarian Friendship Park to symbolize our friendship, where on one side of the Park stood the statue of Ferenc Rákóczy II, on the other the side, the statue of a famous Turkish poet.

We loved being in Istanbul and talking with Linda all day, while Jim took care of his engineering business. Linda made it her goal to know Istanbul inside out. She certainly knew every little nook and cranny. We just had to make a choice – and off we went. We even ventured into Asia for a moment. We boarded the ferry and stepped onto the soil of another continent. It was exhilarating!

When we finally returned to Hungary, we received the news: on September 4th our 15th grandchild, Shivana Ilona Zilda Ramdin, was born to Sandy and Navaal. We were so excited to hear from Niki, our youngest daughter: "She is so beautiful!" She was like a little doll. She remained that way. She was always petite, light as a butterfly, gracious, sweet. She is just as beautiful today. She graduated from university in 2020.

67

1998 was a magical year. We were there at the time of the elections and our long-time friend, Viktor Orbán, was elected Prime Minister. Just as I predicted in my newsletter after I had heard him talk in English to the American Chamber of Commerce in Hungary. At the time of the election he was 35 years old. FIDESZ knew they were doing well, but it came almost as a surprise that they actually received the majority of the votes and could form a government. Elizabeth Schillinger was the Head of PR and she took us fast into a room, then got Viktor and brought him there so we could talk to him. It truly was a euphoric experience.

He and the PM of the United Kingdom, Tony Blair, were both young and big soccer enthusiasts. The two of them understood each other very well. In those days Viktor was not just a spectator, he also played soccer, just for fun, but he wanted to remain in practice.

The next World Conference of Hungarian Honorary Consuls was called in 1999. The sunset from the Parliament was unforgettable. We stood by the window talking with Viktor. The Young Democrats made it! While they were still "young." The upper age limit was 35 to be a member. Now they had to change the age limit because the founders, who were now the ruling party leaders passed the magic number of years. They could have older representatives, running in the name of FIDESZ, like János Horváth, who finally became the doyen of the Hungarian Parliament. He was still representing FIDESZ when he was in his 90s.

The Orbáns moved from their apartment into the PM's residence on Svábhegy. We visited them there. It was still the residence left over from the Communist times, nothing special 60s architecture. The President of the country lived in a similar residence close-by.

Dr. Anikó Lévai, Dr. Viktor Orbán's wife, was a professor teaching Financial Law at the University in Gödöllő. She drove her own small car. She behaved and dressed so normally, without any big ceremony, no one would have thought she was anybody important, unless they recognized her. She was just as natural and sweet as always. She was an excellent cook and a great mother. In our Christmas letter in 1997 we had a photo of our trip to Istanbul. She said she wished they would be as happy when they will have been married 45 years as we looked in that photo, at the time we had our 15th grandchild.

In 1998 our daughter Rita came with us to Hungary. We took her around to all the usual places. One place where none of the other children had been was Pannonhalma. A 1,000-year-old Benedictine Archabbey with a school that was not nationalized during the Communist times. It was one of the schools kept open for all the world to see: there was religious freedom in the country. The Catholic schools that remained open all warned the students before admitting them: they will probably not be able to enter any university. But for those to whom it was already practically impossible to do so because of their descent, having been born into families that were not workers or peasants, it did not make any difference. They would not be admitted to university anyway. These outcasts of Communist society knew the education they would receive at the Benedictine school will be excellent. The Archabbey, a beautiful medieval building was founded in 996.

By the time we reached Sopron, son Steve joined us. He was on a business trip in Italy and hopped over to meet with us. We visited the border, of course, and this time we stayed with our dear friends Dr. Margit Bánó, her husband András Tamási and son, Márton (Marci) Tamási. She was an exchange professor at the University of Washington for a year. During that year we became particularly good friends. We let them borrow one of our cars for the year. They bought a beautiful old peasant house in Hegykő, close to Sopron, where Margit was teaching. We stayed with them. Across from them there was a pub. Son Steve went over for a drink with András. When he returned he was bursting with pride. People in the pub kept buying him beer because they were so impressed by his Hungarian – even though he was born in Canada – they wanted to celebrate him.

Sopron became part of the "golden triangle" the Western part of Hungary that prospered from foreign investments and from the closeness of Austria. Sopron was overflowing with beauty parlors and dentist offices. The Austrians came across the border to use their services, which were much cheaper than at home.

While in Hungary John was invited to speak at the Electrotechnical Museum, by Professor Tivadar Horváth. He was happy to give a talk again in Hungarian, in Hungary about his beloved energy and electric power. The audience was very appreciative.

When we were back home again, the Consular Corps of Washington was in an uproar. At the inauguration of the Governor the Consul General of China came up from San Francisco. He caused a scandal by refusing to sit at the same table with the Director General of Taiwan. While Taiwan was the fourth largest trading partner with Washington State, the Chinese did not even have a representation in Seattle at the time. Nevertheless, this Consul General took the time to visit all the career consuls in town, explaining to them that it was impossible to have her in the Consular Corps of WA. They could not be included. They were actually not included in the Consular Corps, only in the Consular Corps of WA, which was a private club of the consuls. The Dean of the Consuls at the time happened to be from Russia and he would not want to disagree with his Chinese counterpart. We negotiated with him, and the career consuls with the Chinese Consul General in San Francisco, trying to make them understand what a private club is and how it differs from the Consular Corps. Even the State Department representative in San Francisco came up and affirmed that the Consular Corps is a list, not a club.

Steve Siebert, the Honorary Consul of The Netherlands and well-known international lawyer came up with the solution we needed. My husband, John, and I took part in the legal battle. He was a great help. He had a minor in international law when he did his PhD in Economics. He wrote one letter, and I wrote another to our friend, the Russian Consul General, the Dean of the Consular Corps (the longest serving career consul in town). My letter was about understanding him as I grew up in the Marxist school system, but we must understand what a private club is. This is a different system. He was too scared.

Steve's clever solution was renaming the Consular Corps of WA to Consular Association of WA and we voted to include other persons related to international affairs beside the consuls. Representatives of the City of Seattle, of the State Government, commercial representatives, retired U.S. diplomats and TECO (Taiwan Economic and Cultural Office) were welcome to join. We changed the bylaws and established an Executive Board of the Association. Stephen was the first President, and I became the Secretary. The Dean of the Consular Corps was an ex officio member of the Executive.

~

I stopped publishing *Hungary International* after I became the Honorary Consul. By then English publications coming from Hungary improved to the level Americans could understand.

Now I had another newsletter to write for the Consuls. I took notes and wrote stories about consular news, as well as synopses of the talks given by that month's speaker. The newsletter went out once a month along with the invitation to the next meeting.

Consular life in the city was busy and fascinating. Our programs were outstanding, helpful to all of us consuls, especially the honorary ones. In Seattle, most consuls were honorary. Very few countries had career consuls and there were several countries that switched to having just honorary consuls instead throughout the years.

We needed our monthly meetings for networking and discussing ways to solve our many problems, like our national getting lost and never found in the forbidding mountains, suicides, deaths of homeless nationals, deaths of nationals whose relatives we needed to find, knowing only their remarried mother's maiden name, telling a five-year-old of his mother's death, settling estates and transferring them, how to transport pets to a foreign country? How to take ashes home? How to take dead loved ones home in a coffin? Visiting people in jail, how to deal with immigration at the airport who would not let some tourists into the country and wanted to deport them.

We became familiar with what we can do in catastrophic emergency situations and were shown the headquarters in the County. Everything was at least double secure. There was one question to which there was no answer: "What if electricity and all its supporting systems go?"

Almost every day there was a reception, an event, a celebration of one National Day or another. When I first became the Consul, Seattle had 37 consuls of various nationalities in town, but by now, 27 years later, this increased to 43. Washington State derives a large part of its income from international business, import-export. Seattle-Tacoma Port was the second largest on the West Coast because the crossing of the Pacific was 24 hours faster, than from California.

Every year we were invited to a Navy ship, or aircraft carrier, where the Captain had a reception for us. One year was especially memorable because while the party was going on in the radiant Pacific sunset, surprise parachutists were jumping right into the midst of the party on the aircraft carrier.

Rita and her family were with us for that party. Their eyes radiated the pleasure they felt. The next day we celebrated their daughter Krystal's seventh birthday with a brunch at the Space Needle.

In 1999 husband John had two knee replacements: one in January, another one in July. He was an exemplary patient. He enjoyed watching the video of the surgery and tried to interest everyone in it. He obeyed all the instructions. After surgery, a machine was constantly moving his knee. The machine was readjusted as his knee was getting better. He was made to walk right away, and the third day he came home with a walker. He continued to do physical therapy with a nurse, then on his own. In a few months he was proudly showing off how he could squat all the way down and stand back up without even holding on to anything.

While he could not come to church yet, I brought him Communion. We sat down in our favorite place by the window, looking out onto Lake Washington and the Olympic Mountains as I was handing him the host: "The Body of Christ!" There were just the three of us there in total unity as Jesus entered our hearts.

Indeed, this was our dream house! We did not want to move from there until we had to move to the cemetery. And yet...Niki organized all the local children and grandchildren to come to the house and get our garden in shape. They all worked tirelessly, while John and I watched them from the inside with Michelle, who was only a year and a half. She was glued to the window and cheered on the others. We were standing at the big dining room windows that had full length glass walls on both sides. In the back was a large patio with a beautiful rock garden and roses. This lovely shady patio was the eyewitness of many family and consular parties. Guests used to overflow on both sides of the house. The Washington Press Association, the Seattle Free Lances and the Seattle-Pécs Sister Cities as well as the World Without War Council all had many of their parties in our home.

Inside our house was like a Museum of Hungarian impressionists. Works of Mednyánszky, Barabás, Koszta, Körösfői-Krisch, Elek Lux, István Simkó, Ernestine Lohwag, Frieda Konstantin, Ferenc Szablya-Firschauf, Gyula Rudnay were all names you could find in Hungarian museums. These treasures were brought to us by John's parents in 1960. John used to show them in a guided tour to our guests. Hungarian visitors were in awe.

Sándor and Gaby Lezsák were our guests in the "Szablya Hotel" when he gave the March 15th talk at the Hungarian Association's National Day celebration in Seattle in 1999. Sándor Lezsák continued Tibor Tollas's work and legacy.

We recalled with them the happy days we spent as their guests in Lakitelek, at the Népfőiskola they founded. At that time József Antall was still the Prime Minister. In the evening we all gathered on a huge field and listened to his excellent talk. Among others who followed his talk was Imre Sinkovits, the famous actor. He was the one who recited the patriotic poems at the Statue of Sándor Petőfi at the beginning of the 1956 Uprising.

During the day we had plenty of opportunities to mingle with these well-known and other political and cultural heroes. Tibor Tollas was still alive and took part in the three-day event. We stayed in a small hotel, our room next door to Tibor's. In the afternoon we went down to the Tisza, which was just "blooming." The entire river looked like a field of yellow wildflowers as we were swimming among them. Actually, they were mayflies dancing their mating dance on the river, the last act of their lives. Once you have seen this, you will always remember it's delight.

The Népfőiskola (People's College) was founded by Sándor Lezsák to have conferences, seminars, courses for ordinary people, from all walks of life who wanted to deepen their knowledge in a certain topic about Hungary, culture, art, folk art, folklore and at the same time it became an archive for deposits of all works Hungarian. I sent them my works too in English as well as in Hungarian.

The Népfőiskola is thriving under Lezsák's leadership. Sándor is presently an MP and the VP of the Parliament.

At a later year, after Tibor Tollas's death, I was at a meeting in Hungary that Sándor Lezsák called. He invited all the hostesses at whose homes Tibor Tollas stayed while traveling, holding together the Hungarians of the world. It was called a meeting of the "Silver Orchidéés" because it was Tibor's custom to reward each of his hostesses with a silver orchidéé broche.

Thank God, Sándor and Gaby still work tirelessly for all Hungarian causes with a thriving Népfőiskola in Lakitelek – where so many events had their start.

Album

1990 – 1999

*Flyer for Szablya
Consultants, Inc,
1990.*

*FIDESZ ad that says
"Please Vote," 1990.*

FIDESZ leaders talk to celebrating crowd in Pécs – Day Soviets left Hungary, June 30, 1991.

FIDESZ leadership Victor Orbán, Éva Mikes, Tamás Deutsch, Zoltán Trombitás, 1991.

Hungarian visitor, Nino de Blasio from Pécs, interviewed in Szablya's hotel kitchen, 1991.

Author with József Antall, then PM of Hungary, 1991.

The Seattle-Pécs Sister Cities Association 30 years ago, 1993.

Dr. Victor Orban, current PM of Hungary, and wife Dr. Anikó Lévai with Szablyas Seattle, 1992.

*Governor Clinton with
Helen M. Szablya
at NFPW reception,
Little Rock, Arkanzas,
cca 1992.*

*Family reunion with all three Bartha-Kovács daughters
and their families at my father's in Winnipeg, 1993.*

Opening of Consulate, September 13, 1993.

Singing with the gypsies, in Budapest, Búsúló Juhász restaurant, where both John's parents and we celebrated our engagements. The song was: "No one loves you the way I do...," 1992.

At Ilike and Chuck's wedding, with Ambassador Pál Tar and wife Anne Marie, 1994.

Helen and John toasting in Maryland, cca 1996.

Mrs. Clinton in Hungarian Parliament with Szablyas July 8, 1996.

Balaton lunch with Tertáks, 1996.

Hungarian Ambassador to USA, Dr. Géza Jeszenszky, and Edit, his wife, cca 1998.

Karaoke at son Steve's. Apu's favorite, cca 1998.

At Frankfurt International Book Fair. Panel discussion about the year 1956, 1999.

Our dream house in Bellevue 1984-1999.

Bellevue house Christmas Night.

68

At the strong advice of our children we started looking for a condominium and made the difficult decision to sell our dreamhouse. We wanted to spend our old days sitting by our window, looking at our view, loving each other. But it was getting too difficult to even take down the garbage container to the sidewalk on our steep driveway.

However, we knew God would lead us to the perfect condo! We put up our house for sale. Month passed after month – no buyer. I was secretly half-hoping we would have to stay. Poor John who just had the second knee-replacement that year moved with a lot of pain looking at new places where we would live. Sometimes, he would want to give up and just take something that looked half acceptable, but I did not give up.

The six months expired, and we did not continue with the real estate agency but tried to sell it on our own. We asked a friend at Microsoft and he put it in their newsletter. Miracles never cease! A young couple, both working for Microsoft, showed up. They loved the house and bought it. By that time, the year 2,000 had rolled around.

And, just in the nick of time we found our condo. Often, I went alone to preview the condos to make it easier on John.

At first, I did not know what to think about this condo and told John maybe he should not even look at it. He was just after one of his surgeries. He must have sensed something because he said. "Let's go!" The condo's decoration was all light, including the ceramic tiles and the fireplace. "Let's put in an offer!" John said. On the second viewing it looked much better to me. John immediately pointed out all the advantages. Listening to him I had to agree. He looked at the window: "See, we can see a big sky! Remember, we decided if it was not as beautiful a view as ours, at least it should have a big sky to admire the colors of the NW skyscape."

We moved in April. Although we could not stay in our dream house in Somerset forever, at least this was the home where we spent the longest time together. Almost the same time as in Pullman, but from Pullman we were away for two years during our sabbaticals.

Our new condo was in Kirkland, the suburb just next to Bellevue. Our new home was over 1,900 square feet, almost the same size as our house at 2,200. The view was not the same, but it had a small forest, behind which one could see Kirkland Parkplace Mall's lit up building. The lights looked like Christmas lights, but they were on year-round. A beautiful sunset was ours to see every evening. The condo was on the first floor, the first one left of the elevator and there were no stairs at all in the garage, or in the hallway. The place was fairly new, just right for us in every way. The master bedroom had its own bathroom with a jacuzzi tub and a walk-in shower. The bathroom walls consisted of mirrors all around. The nice big living room had plenty of space for our big dining room table on one end and a fireplace on the other. A modern kitchen opened on the other side to a family room, which became my office and the Consulate. I loved my office right by the kitchen. It made cooking and working simultaneously a breeze. We had a big table in the office too and bookcases in every free square inch of every room. Another bedroom and the den became John's office and the home of our 13 filing cabinets. One of his walls, right above his desk were full of his diplomas, Professional Engineering (P.E.) certificates from five states and two Canadian provinces, fellow certificates from IEEE (USA) and IEE(UK) and more.

Mostly engineers are accused of being technocrats, but John was a true polyhistor. He had a degree in Mechanical Engineering with an Electrical Option, one in Economics, one in Education majoring in Philosophy and Psychology, a Phd in Economics minoring in International Law. His thesis was: "The Importance of Art in Industry." Then to top it off he and his psychology professor knowing they may have to do physical labor under Communist rule because of their descent, enrolled in a certificate course of lathing. They pretended to have had only high school education. They graduated from that too. So now they could claim to be bona fide workers would the need arise, and actually do the job.

Our new neighbors turned out to be delightful. The condo had 12 units, which made it possible to have occasional parties at Christmas time and during the summer a barbeque in the small back yard. We sang Christmas carols and exchanged "white elephant" gifts at Christmas. Even the Board meetings were enjoyable with such fun-loving people. The post office was right across the driveway from us, shopping was walking distance. We went down with John to have coffee at Kirkland Parkplace and loved browsing through the books at the bookstore. The moviehouse had all the new movies and many restaurants beckoned from downtown Kirkland. The marina in the middle of downtown was a favorite walking place with my dear John. He enjoyed looking at the luxurious yachts and the antique wooden boats in perfect navigable shape. A little park adjoined the marina, where in the summer we could listen to concerts. Someone remarked that our Kirkland had the same feel as the famous Sausalito in San Francisco. An "Anthony's Home Port" restaurant was just by the marina. We loved to sit in the bar, meaning the upper floor, and enjoy the view from there while having dinner. Needless to say, these rare occasions did not happen daily, as we did not have enough money for that, but our walks did.

In 2000 we made it to Hungary again for several meetings of METESZ, Federation of Hungarian Scientists Conference. This time grandson Steve, 19 years old, accompanied us. He was lucky because he had a chance to see not only Hungary, the usual tour, but also Transylvania. A new company of teachers organized "village tourism" to Transylvania and wanted publicity in the United States. They offered to take a few American-Hungarians for a good price to sample the excellent tour. Lucy and Tibor Fueresz also joined us. We had the comfort of an air-conditioned minibus. Transylvania has a special place in the hearts of Hungarians as before WWI it had been a part of Hungary for a thousand years. At that time at the Peace Treaty of Trianon Hungary lost 71% of its territory and half of its population.

We crossed the border at Ártánd. The first two nights we slept in Tordaszentlászló (Savadisla), the next six we spent in Zetelaka (Zetea), in homes of Hungarian hosts. Everywhere we were expected with "pálinka" (Hungarian for homemade brandy) and "kürtös kalács" (pastry horn) a Transylvanian delicacy. The dough in strips is rolled onto a form and baked that way. It can be made sweet, or salty, mostly with nuts. Inside it is empty, so it resembles a horn. Hence its name. Every meal was home made, we slept in the hosts' house, while during the day we visited the sights and browsed among the folkart marvels galore.

The beauty of Transylvania awed us. The tall mountains, dense forests, mysterious lakes, ravines, the Szekler gates (székely kapu) tall delicately wood-carved gates, and the people! We saw fortress churches of both Szekler and Saxon origin. These 160 registered buildings are amazing! The churches are surrounded by a fortress. Many attacks came from the East: Turks, Tartars, and they had to be stopped, the towns had to be protected. In the fortress every one of the families had a separate place, where they had to store food enough for their families for an entire month. When they took out something to keep the stock fresh it had to be replaced immediately. When the city was in danger, the population moved into the fortress for protection and to defend the city.

Nagyvárad (Oradea) Királyhágó (Bucea, a mountain passage), Bánffyhunyad (Huedin) were on the first day's itinerary as we approached Tordaszentlászó, our night stop. At Bánffyhunyad we were surprised by a Hungarian TV crew. They were en route to Csíksomlyó, the famous Marian pilgrimage place and on their way, they interviewed people heading there. They promptly took the opportunity to interview our little group. The church at Bánffyhunyad's pillars, walls, railings were decorated, every square inch of them with the local Kalotaszeg region folk art embroideries, one more beautiful than the other. The 17th century paneled ceiling was a wonder in itself! We visited Kolozsvár (Cluj), the Torda (Tordu) Gorge and Salt Mine. We went as far as we could into the Gorge, but after a while John and I stopped and let the others go further. It was too difficult to move ahead for us. The salt mine was deep. We could look down into it, but our grandson decided to run all the way down, then back up again. He ran the 740 some feet (225 meters) down and up in no time at all! As a 19-year-old young man he needed to let some energy off! The other four of us could not even think of trying it! Our guide Zoltán Török was a history teacher. His explanations about history and the current political situation spoke to our hearts. He used to tell us old folks: "Well, let us stroll, stroll," when we were complaining, he switched to: "Let us mosey, mosey along!" We had lots of fun with him and with our excellent driver Attila Bellon. At Korond we couldn't resist the handmade ceramics, watching one of the old women painting the intricate designs on the vases, pitchers, plates. We just had to buy some.

On the Saturday before Pentecost we took part in the 434th annual, famous pilgrimage to Csíksomlyó (Şumuleu). Unfortunately, John and I were not up to the one and a half hour walk from the car to the Mass. Even though this was a short walk compared to that of all the Transylvanian parishioners who walked all the way from their parishes under their flags or crosses, some of them for two entire weeks. These groups were called "Keresztaljak" (People under the cross). In the villages they crossed, people welcomed and housed them. Several groups walked through our village, where the two of us watched the entire awesome ceremony on TV. Steve, our grandson, walked representing our whole family. That year more than 200,000 people attended the Mass. Many of the pilgrims wore their folk costumes. Representatives of the Hungarian and the Romanian Government usually came to these occasions. The green grass on the surrounding hills served as pews, where people sang the age-old Hungarian hymns to the Virgin Mary, the Hungarian National Anthem as well as the Székely (Szekler) Anthem (The székely are Hungarian people who live in Eastern Transylvania). The altar was set up under a shelter, the Mass lasted for almost two hours. The loudspeakers announced the various cities where groups came from, including our little group from the United States. Even while watching the Mass on TV we joined the songs and totally immersed ourselves in the great unity among all Hungarians of the world.

We visited Szováta (Sovata) and Gyilkos lakes (Lacu roşu) and finally we could take a swim in Lake St. Anna. Its gentle water caressed our travel-weary bodies. The others were too polluted for swimming and were being cleaned. The surrounding mountains embraced the emerald blue of the lake.

The second time we visited Kolozsvár we went to the famous Házsongárd Cemetery, where we saw the graves of famous Hungarians. Two hundred of the mausoleums and graves in that cemetery were declared historical monuments. Its greenery was designed to caress the soul.

We stopped in Arad, where we paid a visit to the memorial of the 13 martyrs of the 1848 Revolution, executed there after the Revolution was crushed by the Austrian-Russian coalition.

We stopped in and visited 45 localities in 12 days, among them Segesvár (Sighişoara), Gyulafehérvár (Alba Iulia) and Brassó (Braşov), we heard the story of Frankenstein and other myths and mysteries of Transylvania, too many to describe them all in details, but the memories will always be with us. This trip was made more memorable for us because we could be with our grandson Steve, for an extended time and get to know him as an adult, a young man.

Driving back into Hungary we spent the night in Mako, then continued our way through Szeged and stopped at the National Historical Monument in Ópusztaszer, where Árpád Feszty's famous circle-mural of the Hungarians entering Hungary in 896 is displayed. To preserve this exquisite painting-statue-multimedia it was disassembled in Budapest during WWII. It was rebuilt in Ópusztaszer. Well worth stopping to enjoy its beauty.

～

John and I attended the Hungary 2000 meeting at the Hungarian Parliament. Hungarians working for Hungary in the diaspora around the world were invited to plan the next century for Hungary and Hungarians. We met with many old friends, among them Éva Szörényi, the famous Hungarian actress and freedom fighter who helped save my lecture in Pasadena. She lived for Hungary. The Maltese Knights made her a Lady of their organization. She was honored and decorated by the free Hungarian government. She gave a one woman show in celebration of her return to Hungary.

In the USA, she brought up three scouts, was leader of her sons' scout troop, the soul of Hungarian theater life in Los Angeles, while also visiting other cities in the USA, Canada and the diaspora.

We sat side-by-side with Dr. János and Mária Zlinszky, as well as György O'sváth, whom I had mentioned before. We grew up together and in 2000 they both had leading roles in the new free Hungary. Naturally all the members of the Government were there. To our great surprise we ran into HRH Otto von Habsburg, the last Heir to the Hungarian throne. He was as friendly and casual as any of the participants in the meeting. He explained to us with a great smile on his face that in the Hungarian Royal Parliament the noblemen's Bocskai jackets were black for the Protestants and colorful for the Catholics. We were pleased because we had just ordered one for John (nobody would have a size available for his measurements) in a merlot silk brocade. Otto was crowned at age four to be the crown prince, when his father Károly V. became king in 1916. After WWI, the family was exiled to Portugal. Otto married and had seven children. His wife, also a Habsburg Princess, was a student at the same Sacré Coeur school I attended, only in Austria. When we arrived in Pressbaum there was great excitement about one of her children being born. We had a baby at the same time too. Otto was a member of the European Parliament, an excellent economist, who even in his 90s gave talks about software! If all Habsburgs would have been like him, there would have never been an uprising against them in Hungary. He was actually offered to become President of the Hungarian Republic, but he did not run. However, he assisted Hungary in whatever he could. I heard he had the idea for the Pan-European picnic in 1989 at the Iron Curtain border, where the two foreign ministers of Austria and Hungary cut the barbed wire and let the East German tourists escape to West Germany. That act culminated in the breaking down of the Berlin Wall later in the year.

When book-week rolled around in Budapest I was signing books at the tent of Holnap Publishers. Magda Szabó was again there. She was the next author to sign books. Imre Kertész, who later received the Nobel prize, was among the signers. He gave John and me a signed copy of his latest book. Many of my classmates and friends showed up to buy books, which were sold in English and in Hungarian at the book-week.

~

We barely arrived home from Hungary when the IEEE Summer Power Meeting took place in Seattle again. We were on the planning committee in 1984 and in 1992 as well. We were taking full part in the planning and organizing committee again. Our committee received rooms in the Westin hotel, giving us 24 hours a day to assist all the members and their families coming from around the world. The busy Westin was a circular tower-skyscraper hotel in the middle of downtown Seattle, with gorgeous views in all directions. Every room looked out on Seattle's magnificent seascapes and landscapes. There were several bars set up by companies, associations, and utilities. Excellent cocktails, made by engineers! The best! They erred on the "right side," the way they liked them! Son Steve and Kristy were among the helpers too, as by this time Steve was a member of IEEE. At the same kind of event, in 1984 we were asked to give a keynote address to the attendees about our escape from Hungary. Louis, our then baby and the youngest Hungarian refugee, by 1984 an engineer and a member of IEEE was there with Kate, his wife, and their three children, about the same age as ours at the time of our escape. We brought them up on stage and introduced them. Their baby was carried in the same basket and wore the same clothes Louis did at the time of our escape. Louis joined the talk by confessing, he was considering during our talk, whether he would be able to leave everything behind, right this moment, take his three children and escape! He decided he could not do it. He thanked us profusely for bringing them to freedom. All our children were doing this many times, especially on our "Freedom Day" December 8th.

That year we went again to the "Sopron Homecoming Ball" in Vancouver, B.C. We were asked by the former students to open the ball because we happened to be the only faculty couple present. Of course, we were more than happy to oblige.

Our oldest granddaughter, Anna Meiners, had been living in Los Angeles ever since she graduated and auditioned as an actress many places. She also worked as a waitress, as is customary for would-be-actresses. One day someone ran in breathlessly and told her. "Run to the next corner, Jay Leno, the Host of The Late Show is auditioning there." She ran and was accepted. She was on the Jay Leno show with her act. She was imitating a woman, who was testifying anonymously, in a distorted voice, which she did with her own voice. It was a hilarious performance. We were all so happy for her. She also did stand-up and worked in the Sunday Company at The Groundlings.

Later at a Brazilian restaurant where she worked, she happened to meet a young Brazilian man who was studying to become an architect. And that is how it all started…

69

50 YEARS! Our anniversary celebrations happened in five places. One of them was in Hungary again. This time we had a Mass said by our age-old priest friend, Miki Gáspár in the same church where we married and repeated our wedding vows.

This time many of the family members participated. Ilike and her best friend Nora Chester, our granddaughters Anna (Ilike's daughter) and Gennie (János' daughter) came to celebrate with us and tour Hungary. Mária Terták's son Ádám was there with his daughter Niki and Józsi Schmaltz, my godson with his wife Zsuzsa, and their daughter Esther. Those two daughters were classmates and good friends. Our granddaughters had great fun with them, being about the same age.

We visited our escape route again. The change was indescribable! We surely would not have recognized it if we just saw the photo! There was a lovely park and a small guardhouse in the middle of the park, where workers, who crossed the border from one country to work in the other could show their papers. That is all that was left from the horrible Iron Curtain! Anna took our picture as "we were looking back one last time to Hungary," which is on the back cover of the first volume of this book: *My Only Choice: Hungary 1942-1956.*

There is a picture in the Museum of Fine Arts in Budapest by Pál Szinnyei-Merse: "The Nightingale" depicting a nude turning her back towards the viewer, watching the bird up in the sky, lying in a field of red poppies. We came across just one such field of red poppies. The girls ran into the field and were picking poppies, while we took their pictures in the radiant sunshine under the blue skies.

The apartment where we had met with John was now a Postal Museum, so we could show our little group the exact place and balcony, where we spent our first hours together.

We had some alone days with Gennie before everyone else arrived. One day we went shopping with her, had lunch at Gerbeaud confectioners, we took her to the Opera, had champagne during the intermission and had a great dinner. I told her this was a young girl's "dream day" that she was able to live today. At least in my days it was.

The celebrations continued once we returned. We had a huge party in Kennewick, in Eastern Washington, in daughter Rita and Karl's home. The family went every year to Sequim, crabbing. They always caught enough crabs to have a huge party and then give some to family members or friends who came to visit them. They usually camped at the National Park and were busy cleaning all the crabs and fish they caught. More and more of their friends joined, some of the family members among them.

We had the big barbeque dinner in the brilliant color orgy of the Eastern Washington slow summer sunset.

Ilike organized one for us when we were in Baltimore for the winter consular meeting.

One of the parties was in the evening at Steve and Kristy's house in Bellevue, which was simply perfect for a huge gathering. There was plenty to do for the children. Kristy used to run a day care center in the house. They had a lot of play equipment in a big yard with lovely fir trees in the back. Barbequed salmon was one of their specialties. John and I dressed in our green and gold Trinidad shirt and stole. In the backyard we "held court" for all the toasts and questions addressed to us. One of our dear friends, David Hughes, asked us: "What is your secret for a long and happy marriage?" John answered immediately: "Commitment on both parts and a lot of sex." You should have heard the laughter! That set the mood for the party, which went on and on.

On October 12th all parties culminated in a Mass celebrated by a priest friend, Father Steve Szeman, at Holy Family Catholic Church. John gave me a huge bouquet of pink roses. We wore our festive Hungarian clothes.

Our children decided to have Henkel Trocken champagne for our anniversary which was known to be our favorite since our sabbatical in Braunschweig. It was not available in Washington State, but it was in Denver Colorado, where Louis and his family lived at the time. He went ahead and ordered a case. Now, how can he get it over to Washington? Of course, the mail was not supposed to take it across state borders. But it was okay to ship a case of cooking oil. By some magic act, the case of champagne was transformed into a case of cooking oil and mailed as such to Niki's house. She was not home, when the parcel arrived, so her neighbor signed for it. "What in the world are you going to do with this much oil?" her neighbor greeted her on arrival. Niki laughed and told her the story.

Right after Mass, while still in the hall of the church we opened a bottle and toasted with the delightful champagne.

After that we went to a restaurant right by the Marina in Kirkland, where we reserved a hall for our family reunion. The toasts and fun went on right into the night. I love it when our children "roast" us. They tell all kinds of memories and funny things which happened while they were growing up, and "characterize" us in such a delightful way, my tears are running down my cheeks from laughter!

Naturally, the "Flaming Szablyas" had to do their performance. Our adult children enjoyed harmonizing just as much as they did when they were children. They are so tuned in to each other, they need only a few minutes to practice, if that, when they get together.

On October 24th Rohan Ramdin, Sandy and Navaal's second child, a boy, was born. At first Sandy wanted only her own little family to be there and Kristy, Steve's wife, who was a doula. A doula is there at births to coach the mother and father with the birth. Kristy was really good at that.

Then suddenly we got a phone call: "Come, Sandy wants you to come and be here too." We came, but there was a big congestion on the bridge, so by the time we arrived Rohan was just born, we missed it by a minute or two, but he was still not washed, only loved by the entire family. I took a photo of Shivana cuddling him in her arms with a big smile. I love that picture!

Shivana was as light as a butterfly and as well behaved as a lady. Rohan, on the other hand, was a big boy, behaving like a boy. One day when he was a few months old, but not a year old yet, he was feeding himself with his hands, messing up his face royally. Shivana looked at him and told us: "You must forgive him. We still have to teach him manners."

So much fun to enjoy grandchildren! Someone said: "If I would have known grandchildren were so much fun, I would have had them first!"

Now we had all the opportunity to enjoy grandchildren. The ones in the Seattle area used to come over to our house in Kirkland and "sleep over." We had a pull-out sofa, which made a queen size bed. The adult child, usually Sandy, who accompanied the grandchildren, and two more children could sleep on the sofa. On the cushions removed from the sofa was good for another space. We had a loveseat, which was too short for a bed, but that is where John always wanted to sleep until he was almost ten years old. The rest slept on the floor on inflatable mattresses, sleeping bags, whatever they could find. There was always lots of laughter, almost impossible to make them go to sleep.

Our big table was our usual gathering place. Luckily, we had our old kitchen table in the office for the overflow.

The next year Gennie managed to come to Hungary three times while she was in Löwen as an exchange student from the University of British Columbia in her junior year. She traveled all over Europe during her stay and also visited our friends Linda Robinson and Jim Geary in Istanbul.

Maria Szablya was a junior in high school and went as a Rotarian exchange student to Chile for a year.

Several of John's friends were members of the Hungarian Academy of Sciences (MTA, Magyar Tudományos Akadémia). He was nominated and accepted to become an "Outside Member" (meaning he lived abroad) of this very prestigious Institution.

Glorious sunshine accompanied us on May 16, 2002, as we entered the Hungarian Academy of Sciences, where we were greeted by Dr. István Nagy and the organizers. Members of the Academy, relatives, friends ,and our classmates filled up the sunlit hall.

"Energy – Society and the Individual," was the title of John's inaugural address as a Member of the Academy. It was geared to the general public. The talk was 14 pages with many illustrations of the history of energy. I am going to summarize it.

According to Plato, slavery was necessary in order to enable a few people to freely engage in intellectual activities, the "luxury of the mind." It is impossible to think that today someone would dare to voice such an idea!

Cheap and easily accessible energy is just the basis for our physical well-being. More importantly, it makes our spiritual well-being possible. We can say without exaggeration that energy became the most important "basic substance" of our society.

Abundantly available energy not only alleviated physical labor in the last 100 years, but it also practically replaced it. More important were the unbelievable possibilities of development for the human spirit and the access it provided for the masses to cultural activities.

Around 1880 the work of three people changed our civilization and culture tremendously. Nicholaus Otto invented the internal combustion engine in 1876; Edison started operation of the Holiburn Viaduct Station power plant in London in January of 1881 and the Pearl Street Station in New York in September of the same year; while Benz mounted an internal combustion engine onto wheels in 1885. With that, the world has changed.[1] Old philosophies became unusable, and new societal development has been trying out one method after another, and will continue to do so in the future. Some have worked - others have not. That will continue in the future. But we can determine one thing: never have we had so many artists working on this earth as nowadays; books published today manyfold outnumber publications of 100 years ago; and today more people are going to concerts in one day than in an entire decade during Napoleon's times.

The "luxury of the mind" is ours. And for these activities we do not need Plato's slaves because we have steam-turbine-slaves.

SOCIAL STABILITY

Norbert Wiener, Professor at MIT, who established the science and coined the word "cybernetics," was already saying in the 1960s that society's entropy naturally increases and with that its disorderliness. I am afraid that he will be right, although I hope he will not. How can this be helped?

Figure 9 shows the per capita energy consumption of various countries related to their gross national product (GNP). Both scales are logarithmic, meaning that the difference between the beginning and the end of the coordinate axes is a thousand-fold.

It is immediately noticeable that various countries are located in an approximate linear configuration along the double line. Therefore, we can say that there is a strong relationship between the per capita gross national product (that is "well-being") and energy consumption. More energy consumption means better well-being.

It is interesting to observe that countries on the bottom of the figure are politically not very stable, are prone to interior revolting, while countries on the top of the figure are politically stable. It seems that access to energy stabilizes a society.

Have many thought about the fact that Karl Marx died before the "energy revolution" (Figure 10)? At the time of his death electric energy had been in existence for only one and a half years in London and accessible only for the rich.

---

1 Edison's activities are the most important of the three because energy became transportable using a pair of wires to the location of utilization, in an odorless, tasteless, and essentially safe way.

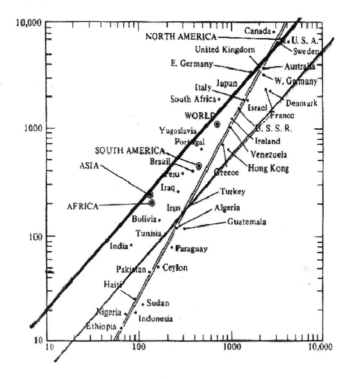

Figure 9

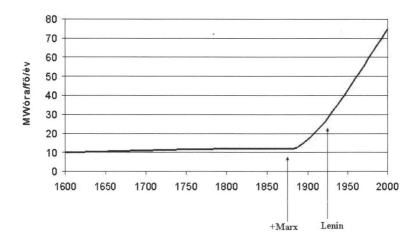

Figure 10

> The dates of the death of Marx and "Lenin's equation" are shown on the curve of energy consumption.
>
> However, the curve of energy consumption was already on the rise when Lenin declared: "Socialism is nationalization of the means of production plus electrification of the entire country."[2]
>
> Marxism was already almost obsolete at the time of Marx's death, and it is not possible to build a modern society based on it in the 21st century. The reason is that in the years around the end of Marx' life, opportunities that had never before existed opened up for humanity.

Then comes the discussion about the various forms of energy and when coal and oil will totally run out, even if the world would entirely be filled with oil, with only a thin layer of soil.

The importance of energy for the development and survival of humanity is of extreme importance. We should not be afraid of the unknown. He gave many examples. Here are two interesting ones:

> Why was the electric chair introduced as the means of execution in the USA? Because Edison, who developed the 110 Volt direct current system, and manufactured it through General Electric, wanted to turn the public against Westinghouse's high voltage alternating current. If he had been successful in thwarting the high voltage electric energy transmission, then "today we would be watching television by candlelight."
>
> The British Parliament wanted to pass a law to close down John Murdock's gas lines in London, at public pressure. So John Murdock invited the Members of Parliament and their spouses to the gas factory for a great feast. During dinner he cut a big hole in one of the gas containers with a pick, then proceeded to ignite the escaping gas. Locked gates stopped the panicky escape. As the MPs and their wives realized that nothing went wrong, they quietly went back to finish dinner and enjoy the lavish entertainment. Nothing came of the law. Can we imagine life today without gas heating?

Again, as always during his lifetime John showered me and his family with thanks and gave us credit for our help with the preparations, he referred to our joint lecture at the IEEE-Eurocon Conference in Amsterdam in 1974 and

---

2 Known as the "Lenin Equation" in the form: (Socialism) = (Nationalization of the means of production) + (Electrification of the country)

for translating his talk into English. He thanked our children for critiquing, data and editing, as well as our friend Dr. István Barótfi for valuable data contributed.

He gave his talk again at the University of Washington the following fall, where it was equally well received.

The success was tremendous! The audience especially liked that they could understand the entire lecture, despite the scientific content, no matter what their profession happened to be.

70

Can you believe this photo was taken in Columbia, Maryland in December of 2001? It was our usual Consular Day in Washington DC and I packed snow boots and a winter coat. I had to borrow sandals from Ilike, who hosted us again. That photo taken by her dominated our Christmas letter!

Ilike and Chuck had been living in a townhouse, which they transformed into a dream during the years while they lived there. The lovely little stream and the old trees, the forest-like setting, Columbia's special design and ambience was perfect.

No wonder we were surprised when they wanted to sell it and buy an old mansion in Ellicott City, up on the mountain. Understanding their decision came after we learned to appreciate its charm. Their magic worked again, and the house returned to its traditional glory through their efforts. The garden was an earthly paradise under their hands. The neighbors were lovely, and the two of them fit right into the crowd, as they always did.

In 2003 Ilike had her 50th birthday party! It was a party to end all parties! I love the photo where Ilike is dancing with Apu! It hangs right here by my desk where I can always see it, as is the picture where Chuck and Ilike are lifting their glasses for a toast. Chuck was laughing as he told us: "I gave Helen an unlimited budget for her party…and she surpassed it!" He was so proud and laughed heartily as he said that.

Oh, how much fun we had! The liquor was flowing, we danced, their friend Jamie brought those funny lights we could twirl, the food was to die for, as always at their parties! For her party they had a tent built around the porch and infrared heaters kept it warm in January! It was awesome and unforgettable!

The previous year we received a fabulous gift from our children for Christmas. John traveled Alaska very often because of his projects at work, sometimes more than once a week. His stays were usually short – not worth it for me to go with him. He regarded Alaska as unbelievably unique and beautiful! Of course, he wanted to show all the exciting places where he went, but that was too expensive, unless you had work to do there.

Kristy and Steve had a vacation-condo, which offered an Alaskan trip for that year. Kristy told the other children and they added their money to the price. We received the cruise for Alaska from our children for Christmas.

We enjoyed the "Carnival Spirit" cruise June 18-25, 2003. Our ship left from Vancouver, British Columbia in Canada, which is a mere two and one-half hours' drive North of Seattle. Our tour was the seven-day Northbound Glacier Route. Cruising through the Inside Passage our first stop was Ketchikan, then Juneau with the Mendenhall Glacier, Skagway. Cruising the Lynn Canal our next stop was Sitka, then through the Prince William Sound with an evening cruise to view College Fjord, arriving in Seward.

It was our first cruise. Even with exaggeration we could not possibly call our crossing the Atlantic in January of 1957 in a bitter winter storm, while working on 500 immigrant visas a "cruise."

Everything was new to us. We received a credit card, which was our identifier as well. On the ship we could not use money, or other credit cards, only this card we were given. We found out that this little card let the crew know whether we are on board or not. We went to several excursions everywhere we stopped: The crew wanted to know we made it back safely. The ship had several restaurants in case someone wanted an alternative to the dining room, where all the meals and the midnight buffet were served. There were gift shops and bars and a casino with many gambling machines. Some of the passengers seemed to have just one thing in mind: to gamble. Day and night, as soon as the ship left port and reached international waters, the casino opened, and its enthusiasts could not have cared less where they were or what they missed seeing.

Every evening there was a great variety show, while drinks and food were served.

Our children got us a room with a balcony, which gave us ample opportunities to gaze at the beauty of the unending wilderness and natural wildlife. The loudspeakers announced every time a whale, a seal, an eagle, or any other wildlife could be seen in the water or on the shore.

We brought summer clothes with us, but the wind was chilling on the balcony and the deck. We had to buy a sweater in the shop. Inexperienced as we were with cruises, we did not think of bringing evening attire with us. We were surprised when we saw the others dressing up to the hilt.

Whenever the ship stopped, we took advantage of the excursions offered. Ketchikan got its name from the Tlingit Indian word: "Kichnzaan" meaning Salmon Creek. In the 1930s Ketchikan had 11 canneries producing two million cases of salmon a year. To this day salmon is their livelihood, although at one time copper and gold mines lured miners to town. Many of the homes were built on pillars over Ketchikan creek. Bordello Row Walk brings back the memory of the women available to entertain the miners, long since retired. We were treated to a great lumberjack show: log rolling and other fantastic contests testing their abilities.

Juneau, John's favorite Alaskan city, gives the impression of a lovely fairy-town with its old buildings in an Old Western atmosphere, pubs, and restaurants. Despite being the capital city of Alaska since 1906, Juneau is not big. It must be magical to be one of its 30,000 inhabitants as we learned from one of Jancsi's classmates, Charles Rohrbacher, his wife Paula, and nine-year-old son Miguel. Their daughter Phoebe was at work. Charles painted beautiful icons and worked for the Archdiocese of Juneau.

The Mendenhall Glacier close by is of course a must. The ice looks blue because the ice in the Glacier swallows all colors, except the blue. The beauty of Alaska is unique, majestic, and frightening.

How can you describe the stark beauty of infinite water, forests, mountains, and ice, while knowing that the area is empty, except for the small towns here and there? Alaskans carry dawn sleeping bags in their cars. Their clothing is made of natural materials, the same the animals use, as only those can protect you from Alaska's climate. You simply must understand and constantly be aware that you are alone...alone...nobody will know where you are unless you plan your trip and leave the plan with someone. Not even then can you take it for granted someone will succeed in finding you.

John enthusiastically showed me whatever he could and wished he could show me more, like Petersburg, where the rain almost never stops. When the sun comes out, a holiday is unofficially declared. Everyone leaves work and enjoys the sunshine. The delightful tiny shrimps are a gourmet's feast. But the ship did not go there. Or the Arctic region, the pipeline, the workers' quarters in the oil fields, the tiny bush-planes that meant transportation between the northern-most places. He embraced them all in his heart when traveling for work to these remote places.

Our next stop was in Skagway! Few people make their home in this little town year-round, but during the summer it is an inviting tourist stop. Some shops even advertise in their shop-windows: "We live here all year round." Many of its streets go straight up the hill on stairs built from big rocks and stones. That is the "street"! No other way to get to the house in the second or third row. All furniture, appliances, everything must be carried on these "streets" to the home. Though very romantic, I certainly would not like to live there. The Yukon-White Pass Railway trip out of Skagway was a fantastic experience in beautiful sunlight.

Sitka situated on the outer side of the Alaska panhandle on Baranof Island, has been continuously inhabited for the past 8,000 years. At that time Mt. Edgecumbe erupted and spewed more than 20 feet of ash over the Sitka Sound. The Tlingit Indians gave it the name, "Shee-Atika," meaning "people on the other side of the Shee," which was contracted by the people into Sitka. Much later in 1804 Sitka became a Russian settlement and the Russian capital of Alaska, until 1867, when the United States bought Alaska from the Russians in the "Alaska Purchase" (for $7.2 million, called at that time Seward's folly).

The original Tlingit and Russian relics of the city's past are treasured everywhere. The Sitka National Historical Park nicknamed "Totem Park" is filled with totem poles, a fortress and a beautiful Russian bishops' house that is a museum now. It contains 100,000 artifacts from the Tlingit and Russian cultures.

An energetic dancing group "The New Archangel Dancers" performs Russian dances. The group started out being all male. Then men were less and less interested in dancing, so the women took over and they did the men's parts of the dances as well as the women's parts. These delightful women in men's folk clothes did the demanding dance steps with great grace and energy!

During WWII, The USA brought in 20,000 troops to build a Naval Air Station and Coastal fortifications. The ruins can still be seen on the surrounding islands. After the war, the city shrunk back to 9,000 residents, but is slowly growing.

Our tour guide, herself a mother, told us that children go right into the water when it gets up to 55 degrees Fahrenheit and though they get purple lips and tremble, you just cannot chase them out. Talking about relativity!!!

Our tour ended in Seward. We were taken to Anchorage from there by car. We stayed in Anchorage for another four days. We drove 500 miles to explore the region. We tried to see Mt. McKinley from Talkeetna, but it was overcast. On the way back we visited the Alaska Transportation Museum, seven acres packed with the most interesting machines. The Kenai peninsula was next. We detoured to a fascinating town, Whittier, reachable only through a road/railroad tunnel, driving on railroad tracks for two and one-half miles. We were given instructions about possible signals and had to wait for when there were no trains scheduled for us to enter safely. Whittier consists of a 19-story condominium building, where all the inhabitants live and that's all; the rest are some restaurants, a wharf and the railroad terminal (not even a decent depot).

Alaska had an almost unknown history in WWII, having fortifications on a chain of small islands. Whittier was one of the important headquarters. Officers and their families lived in those condominiums. There was another large building, now abandoned. Apparently there was a movie house, swimming pool, all kinds of entertainment there during WWII. Now, it was mostly retired people and some who worked in Whittier. We bought a book there, which I thoroughly enjoyed reading. It was written by a widow, who decided to go and live wherever she would put her finger down on the map with closed eyes. It was Whittier, AK! So she decided to explore the possibilities and bought one of the condos. She stuck it out! Even though she described one of her days with a 55-mile-per-hour wind when she was trying to get back to her building from her car on what felt like an ice-skating rink. She tried and tried, but could not straighten up. She finally noticed her neighbors indicating with sign language to come back to the building on all fours. She made it! Very proud of herself, naturally! And, thankful to her neighbors!

The scenery, as everywhere, was out-of-this-world.

We enjoyed every minute of the Midnight Sun which barely reached the horizon, then rose again to its full splendor. This deprived us of seeing the true Northern Lights, except for the time when we saw two suns and realized it was a form of Northern Lights and then we saw some of the colors too.

The radiance and the size of the flowers in Alaska was totally unexpected for me. The 24-hour sunshine made flowers grow everywhere in the wild, but especially in gardens and, on every lamp post in town flower arrangements glowed in all the colors imaginable. We saw a lady go around in an electric cart with an elongated watering can as she supplied the baskets with the necessary water.

From Anchorage we flew back home, totally exhausted.

⚊⚊

The next glorious World Conference of Hungarian Honorary Consuls took place again in 2003. This time granddaughter Mary came with us. While she was mingling with consuls from everywhere in the world, she got enough invitations from them she could have taken a trip around the world visiting them. Many of the consuls brought with them children, grandchildren who formed little parties and went together to discover the nightlife of Budapest. The comparatively young Consul of Utah joined them to have some "adult" supervision and off they went!

President Ferenc Mádl and his delightful wife, Dalma, had a usual reception for the consuls. As you can see from our photo, we had a great time. I was chatting for quite a while with Dalmi. We discovered mutual friends. I was lucky. The crowd has not discovered yet who she was.

During the Conference all the Honorary Consuls who had already served for 10 years or longer received a "PRO AUXILIUM CIVIUM HUNGARORUM" (for helping the Hungarian citizens) medal.

A day cruise on the Danube took us to Szentendre the paradise of folk art and artists in general. Every time we went to Hungary, we tried to see this little town with its Greek Orthodox Church, open as a Museum, and Margit Kovács's Museum. She was a creator of artistic ceramics in the true rustic tradition. Feripapa, John's Uncle, was one of her professors, also the Director of the School for Applied Arts. He defended her against other professors from spoiling her original innate talent. The Museum was the house in which she used to live with her mother.

The year was not finished yet. When we arrived home, we had a grand celebration in a park: son Jancsi's daughter Gennie and son Jancsi both graduated from university.

Nadine, Louis' daughter graduated from university in Denver and Maria Steve's daughter graduated from high school in Bellevue.

Steve, Louis' son who was a "computer genius" when he was three years old, started work right out of high school at a computer company and by the time he was 23, he was able to buy himself a house.

I don't want you to think that it was always milk and honey for us. We had our share of illnesses and worries, just like any other family, but I prefer to concentrate on the good news. Besides, with a family this large there is always good news to take the edge off the bad news.

71

August 22, 2004. The happiest day of our lives! A rare occasion when you receive the grace to know when it happens. A beautiful day in Bellevue in Steve and Kristy's home and backyard, where John and I celebrated our 70th and 80th birthdays. Our children and grandchildren gave us this greatest of presents. ALL of them gathered on that day, even if one of them, Mary, Louis's daughter had to fly back to university three hours into the party, but not before we took a great family photo. Gennie, Jancsi's daughter did not think she could possibly make it for one day from New York, but Kristy simply sent her a ticket and said: "You will be here!"

John's desire was fulfilled. As if he knew…

For his 80th birthday he wished for the entire family of 34 to be present. Even our oldest granddaughter Anna Meiners's fiancé, Fred Pompermayer Morini, made it.

A professional photographer took photos during the entire party, but the family photo became our trademark, our forever photo without the next generation.

The party was Szablya (by birth or marriage) family only. The tall trees in the background are the green belt behind Steve and Kristy's large backyard, excellent for parties. The photographer asked families to dress all their members in the same color to be easily recognized in the big photo.

Joyfull cavalcade of voices in every room, two-year-old Rohan running around in his little red shorts and white shirt, his father, Navaal, in his cricket whites, 28-year-old Anna, as the oldest grandchild, Aaron and Elizabeth, the same age teenagers fooling around while eating Cocoa Puffs, all grandchildren's favorites, while the photographer was trying to take a picture of all of them feeding on their beloved cereal.

The adults were more into champagne and other delicious food. Navaal was barbequing fish with the help of the other like-aged sons and sons-in-law.

Then came the "roasts," which I love. Children were taking turns telling stories about us, the funnier the better. This time they made a point in thanking us for bringing them to freedom and for being the "best parents" (no bias here), Niki joking about her being the spoiled one, as the youngest.

Karaoke followed in the basement with the lovely singing voices of our children and grandchildren. Of course, the Flaming Szablyas came up with their barbershop quartet, and the roasting went on and on. Ilike explained how all this singing started when we went up to Vancouver for my father-in-law's funeral who loved singing harmony. The original three: Ilike, Jancsi and Louis, had to sing it again, here at the party – on popular demand. Ilike also told the story of Starlit Stairway, when all the Szablyas were singing together, except Niki because she was still a baby. Ilike then told the story of Summer Palace's little street urchins in the play "Under the Gaslight" (Steve and Sandy eight and six years old) who shamed the big actor's barbershop quartet with their imitation's quality. The next year Rita joined them, and they became an act of their own.

We were roaring with laughter as Louis was telling us about Apu buying a pair of underwear for $5. When he got to the cashier, he found out they cost $10. He was astonished and asked: "But, it says a pair of pants. Here is one and here is the other. A pair of pants."

Rita told stories about our camping adventures at Lake Coeur d'Alene. Mrs. Caine used to come with us at times. She knew that region inside out. She told the two little girls, Sandy and Rita her stories. Showed them a place where there was a fire. Oh, the girls were scared. They held each other tight and trembled. So, she told them: "Oh, but you don't need to be afraid because if the fire or anything else like that shows up and sees me, it says 'Sorry, just kidding' and runs away." The girls felt relieved. Now they were safe. They trusted Mrs. Caine and believed everything she told them.

For us that was the family vacation. John worked on weekends and we went out to the lake, when it belonged only to us, namely on weekdays. So Rita, when first confronted with the idea of Karl's parents taking a six-week vacation every year, said to Karl: "You are kidding? Right? Professors had a vacation in the summer?" She went on with the roasting and our tears were rolling from laughter.

More karaoke. Now the parents, John and I, had to take a turn. We sang some of our favorites and got a standing ovation from our children, when we sang "Tea for two and two for tea, me for you and you for me alone, we will raise a family, three boys for you and four girls for me. Can't you see how happy we will be?" They wanted an encore. One of them was "Will you still need me, will you still feed me when I'm 64?"

The boys were playing soccer outside, others were on the pinball machine right beside the karaoke singers. And champagne everywhere, in the special glasses Ilike and Chuck had ordered for this occasion. On the side in gold: In Celebration John – June 25, 1924, Helen – September 6, 1934, the last line: 2004.

And the little children running around! Granddaughter Elizabeth was singing karaoke while Shivana came close. She grabbed Shivana holding a microphone and danced her around in her arms, while they both tried to continue singing. Rohan, two years old, was adding his voice now and then to contribute to the cacophony.

Mary sang beautifully with the karaoke machine. She was preparing to become a music teacher. She had to leave, just after she finished singing. The rest stayed for a long time, enjoying family togetherness, on this, the happiest day of our lives.

John and I went to the American Translators Association Conference in Toronto in 2004. Toronto of course meant another huge celebration with family for our birthdays. My sisters, Marie and Elizabeth made a beautiful collage of original photographs from both our childhoods and our married lives. It hangs in my bedroom with all the signatures of the Toronto family. Canadian Thanksgiving is in October. It was totally unbelievable, but Elizabeth's son, Pali had a party outside and we swam in his swimming pool in Toronto at Thanksgiving!

While in Toronto we went to the Opera. After the performance John was unable to walk back to the parking lot, so Marie's daughter, Maria, drove up to the theater to pick him up.

After our return home our doctors were trying to find out what was wrong with him. Finally, one of the nurses remarked that he might be anemic and that may cause his shortness of breath.

In January he was diagnosed with two kinds of acute leukemia. He was given two weeks to live.

I remember my feet turning into lead and numb as I was walking around the grocery store, while he was getting a transfusion. Denial was taking over my entire body. "It just can't be! He is so alive! He cannot die! There is no life without him!"

Dr. Tonya Wahl, an excellent doctor and a charming woman, who had just returned from maternity leave, became our oncologist. How did we know all that? Daughter Sandy was a pharmaceutical rep before Rohan's birth, and she asked her former colleagues. They all claimed she was excellent and up to date on the latest methods.

We went into the hospital with John to undergo chemo treatment. Dr. Tonya Wahl came in and we asked her if we could bring in champagne. She wondered why. Sandy and I said: "To celebrate life!" We toasted and were prepared to start treatment.

Instead of starting treatment Dr. Tonya Wahl came in again and told us that the five doctors with whom she worked in one office were talking about John's case and the six of them unanimously decided he should not undergo chemo because of his age. They would not agree to torture him. Tonya said if we wanted to try to treat the untreatable, we would have to go to another M.D. We were glad we could go home and receive the treatment of blood transfusions and Prednisone 100 mg per day.

January 19th we went out with just our seven children, as a good-bye dinner and dance. Of course, we always had to dance. It was our life: "We will forever be dancing!" was a very appropriate card I bought for John for our anniversary one year. We had a marvelous time and danced our heart out. The pianist could not believe that John was going to die. He wished us to come back again next year at this time.

Son Jancsi brought along his teddy bear to the dinner, the Hungarian one that John's parents brought out with them from Hungary, dressed in the clothes my mother-in-law made for him, a small bag with a tiny passport inside. John had a teddy bear like this too when he was young. We took a photo of father and son with Teddy. We tried to spoil John in every possible way. Of course, all the girls danced with him too. It was a beautiful farewell.

After three months of the two weeks predicted, Tonya said she would no longer predict anything. He outlived any prediction. At one point the decision was made to stop the transfusions. And – miracle of miracles! His platelet count went up on its own. All the prayers for him around the world helped! We just continued the treatment. His platelet count was kept up with transfusions, but because it was low, even the smallest injury could have ended in bleeding to death. He had to be protected against any infection because his immune system was down on account of the steroids.

This could have been a "Hell of a Year," but instead it became "Heaven on Earth." For 10 months we floated on the love and prayers of our family: children and grandchildren. Ilike continuously shuttling between Baltimore and Seattle for eight months, which she had to stop finally in August because all the vacation she had left were 10 days and she saved those for helping me after the funeral. Rita and Louis moved in with us for a while, one after another. Niki, Sandy and Steve, our local children, as well as their spouses and children spoiled us constantly. Jancsi and Marcey moved to Philadelphia, but Jancsi was still here til June because Elizabeth, their daughter, was graduating from 8th grade. I will never forget as he left, Apu and Jancsi were walking out of the garage and Jancsi said: "Let me put my head on your heart, I loved doing that so much!" He did it, while walking arms around each others' shoulders, sobbing.

In February John wrote a letter to our children. At the time there was a movie: "The Magnificent Seven" that is why he addressed the letter to the Magnificent Fourteen, adding the spouses to the original seven.

Dear Magnificent Fourteen,

The last few weeks were unbelievable. The love, care, and support Anyu and I received from every member of the Family was a thrilling experience. We knew that you love us and care about us yet, the amount and intensity of your love and care was beyond anything we could imagine.

Thank you for being such wonderful individuals. Thank you for bringing up children who showered us with the same outpouring love that radiates from you. Each individual in its own right. Each filled with love, and ability to love. To tell them about my life and seeing them listen to it, mesmerized, was a lifetime experience. Please make video recordings of Anyu reminiscing within the next six months.

All I can say "Dear Lord! Thank you for letting me have these thirty people as my Family. Thank you for their outpouring and passionate love. I knew they love and care about me, but you allowed me to have an experience beyond. Thank you... Thank you... Thank you...

I pray you have the same experience all your lives as we do.

Finally, I ask you to:

1. Keep the Christmas Eve tradition alive at Anyu's residence (it means very much to her).

2. Take her out to a nice place on her Birthdays and have a fun time.

I should ask you to take good care of Anyu, help her, be with her when she needs you. But this is unnecessary. You already decided this in your Hearts.

I love you,

Apukátok

2005-02-06

And came the answers:
We promise.
We will.
And from Sandy and family, who wanted me at that time to end up living with them:

> *Édes Apuci és Anyuci!*
>
> *We, too, have felt so blessed to have you in our lives. You can be assured that the Christmas tradition will continue at Nagymama's residence, wherever that may be – and hopefully, soon, we will have to walk only a few steps to celebrate Christmas in her home, with us! And we will celebrate her birthday, rest assured, with dinner, festivities, and in our case, mass. Thank you, Apu és Anyu, for being so magnificent yourselves these past few weeks. You are wonderful.*
>
> *Sok, sok puszi, Szandi, Navaal, Shivana és Rohan*

Ilike wrote after a weekend spent here with us:

> *I am so happy today because we were all able to be together and share good times together and love Apu together. There is no greater gift than love, and Anyu and Apu have bestowed upon all of us the ultimate lessons of that gift. Thanks to all of you who are there each day to support Anyu and Apu in this last adventure they share together in this life. Lots of love to you all!*

After the last sleepover with all the local grandchildren Sandy, their usual "chaperone" wrote:

> *Yesterday night, when I got up I suddenly noticed the moon. It was magnificent – like the Eucharist – the Eucharist! I thought about God waiting for you and sending the moon to me as a sign that He is ready to take you into His loving arms – our Heavenly Apu's arms. And just now, just this moment, I saw a bald eagle soaring high into the heavens. What signs! What glorious signs that my Apuci will be with us always, praying for us, praying with us, leaving this Earth and being with us in a new way. Anyu has said that right now, you both are floating on love from everyone. When you're ready, let that love float you up to Heaven. We will know you're still with us, in the legacy you left behind – your love, your love, your love.*

As an increasing number of friends and relatives realized our situation, the emails kept coming to appreciate what John's life meant to them. I will quote a few that meant the world to us:

From Kinga who stayed with us during the 1976/77 school year:

> I would like to share how deeply you influenced my life: You planted the seed of faith in my heart, by taking me to church every Sunday, by making me part of the chorus, although I must admit my voice was (and still is) far from nice to listen to. I still keep the New Testament that I received from you before I left. You taught me that it is never an inconvenience to visit friends and people in need, by taking me to visit elderly and needy people. You taught me to share and be part of a big family, and many times I long for that. I still keep many vivid memories of the house, holidays spent there, everybody sitting around Ilike, all of us looking at her daughter Anna…Helen taking the Holy Communion to people who could not come to church. I keep the memories of John showing us the first snowfall one night and calming us during the thunderstorms and teaching us to count the distance between lightning and the house. These memories you gave to me, they come with me, and are part of who I am today. You can claim you made a difference in many people's lives, and mine is one of them.

From Gary Knight, a friend of son Steve and of the entire family, who wooed three of our daughters one after the other, and became a professor, the Head of International Business at Florida State University:

> I know of no one who has made more of a difference in the world than you John. You are such a great man, an inspiration to so many. (How many economists could escape communist oppressors and transform themselves into renowned electrical engineers while raising seven kids?) I have modeled my life after the example of various people, and you are chief among them. This is really true: a professor with deep interests in the world, trying to make it a better place, by influencing young people and trying to do the right thing, with a deep interest and respect for the best of what humanity has produced. I am describing both of us.

I was so glad John could read these letters, coming before his death. He answered Gary:

Your letter brought tears to our eyes. To know that our lives affected someone's like yours is the greatest recognition life can give. And to know that our ideas are, and will be, transmitted to future generations, is a "bonus maximus." Thank you for your letter.

From Bill Dearing (WSU Electrical Engineering Class of 1978). He took the Energy Management and Planning Class in 1977.

> I looked at the topics we covered in class, and it is amazing how relevant all the energy related policy and technical issues remain today, almost 30 years later. While predictions about running out of oil, gas, and uranium always seem to push forward to some unknown date, the search for real alternatives remains a relevant topic as we lurch from one 'energy crisis' to another...I very much enjoyed your class and exploring and speculating about the future...my career in public power has focused much more on these power planning issues than solving complex circuit designs...I would like to thank you for your contributions to my career and to WSU in general. I will always remember your kindness, stories of Hungary, and insights you shared with us that could only be obtained having lived through those experiences.

From Vancouver, B.C.:

> Maybe you don't even remember me, one of the many Sopron students, but I vividly remember you as your figure always towered above the crowd. I ask for God's blessings and help, praying for you and your family. I wish God should give you strength and trust in Him for the struggles of the difficult days. Our miners' greeting is very appropriate now: 'Good luck!' With loving empathy Laci Magasi, your fourth year Sopron/Vancouver student.

And, from the other end of the spectrum from Holt Ruffin, the President of the World Without War Council with whom we had been working so much for the freedom of the captive nations:

> I found myself thinking back twenty years, when I first met you and Helen dancing rock and roll at a party...of a superb event you hosted at your home in Bellevue – filled to overflowing – for Humberto Belli of Nicaragua's La Prensa (a newspaper which, to my amazement, you already

527

knew about); of a stream of other interesting evenings and people at
your house – from impressive Hungarian writers and activists to local
treasures…you and Helen giving a superb dramatic reading at the UW
bookstore…from your book about your escape from Hungary. Interesting
as these events were, they left me feeling touched by something deeper,
the "Szablya values": devotion to family; defense of the principles of
freedom and democracy worldwide; the importance of faith and church;
and – as if this were not enough! – your wonderfully affirmative view of
life, its possibilities, richness, and not least, its comic aspects.

The most important and meaningful present came from his student group
who had the tenth anniversary of their graduation at our house. Jake and
Ann Hardy, and Steve and Merryl Muchlinski organized and founded a
Dr. John F. and Helen M. Szablya Power Engineering Scholarship Fund at
WSU. The plaque was handed over to Rita (Szablya) and Karl Pool, the only
people who could be present from the family. They lived in the Tri-Cities
and could easily drive over for the event. Then through tele-conference we
too could take part in this outstanding event. Rita gave a lovely talk.

John was able to talk to and with the former students. Laughter and tears
mingled during the unforgettable celebration. The Dean Anjan Bose gave
a talk, and all John's colleagues came to pay their tribute. The first one to
say a few words was Dr. Ed Schweitzer, a former student and neighbor, who
was now the second largest employer in Pullman after WSU. He founded a
factory which is doing great business globally. Ed wrote a note to us:

> Congratulations to both of you for your Washington State University
> honor. You have made a big difference in hundreds or thousands of lives…
> including mine. Thank you for all the personal attention…dinners, Rico's,
> counseling at WSU…And thanks for just being great friends.

John's thank you note to the students:

> *Thank you so much for this fantastic plaque, but even more for what
> stands behind the words that speak so much about those who wrote
> them. I know you will follow in my footsteps and someday today's
> young engineers will quote you, like you quote me today. Therefore,
> there will always be people who will know that the day has 24 hours,
> but – there is always the night. But all kidding aside, I wish you with
> all my heart that you too should receive as much joy and recognition*

in your old age as you are giving me, and you should know what it means to know that you have not lived in vain. THANK YOU!

Even then he was joking and expressing his love as always.

Back in February we received a phone call from my sisters. I told them we were just discussing funeral arrangements for John. They answered that it is a good time because we are discussing funeral arrangements for our Father. He died in St. Joseph Nursing Home where he had been living for almost 10 years. He was 98 years old. I could not risk going to his celebration of life, not knowing when John was going to leave me. I wrote a letter to him. Jancsi and Louis went to represent the family.

My dear Dad, you know how much I would love to be there to say good-bye to you until we meet again. And yet, I know you are more with us now than you have ever been before. Now, you are always with us.

I want to thank you for always being there for us when we needed you; for being the wonderful provider that you have been. For always thinking of us first, for making sure we had all we needed.

I am asking my son, Louis to deliver this message to you because he was named after you and he will continue to bear your name.

Remember the days we spent at your Young Street apartment? Louis was just a baby then. You worked so hard! Even though we tried to be with you as much as we could, sometimes we would not even see you for three days at a time. We knew you were home some time during the night because your bed was slept in, but we had no idea when. We stayed up until the last TV show was over and we woke early because Louis wanted to eat, yet you were already gone by the time we woke up.

You knew you wanted to become a doctor when you were just 3 years old and you fulfilled your dream. You worked until you were 87 years old. You remained a doctor all your life always helping people – curing them was your goal.

I remember how defeated you would feel when one of your patients would die. Obviously, you knew it was inevitable and yet… you did not want to give up.

You were always so dedicated to your patients that you would not even notice the weather; you just did your job regardless. And it was not just the weather you wouldn't notice.

You went out in the middle of the 50-day siege of Budapest and helped the wounded soldiers regardless of who they were, Hungarians, Germans, Soviets, all received your care, You were also there for the many neighbors who needed your help.

While the battle lines surrounded our house for six weeks, you performed surgeries with the only tool that you had – a razor blade.

You carried away an unexploded shell in your bare hands to get it out of our reach. You were not afraid when it came to protecting us, in fact you were brave.

I am very grateful for the very special time we had together at the Mayo Clinic. For ten days we talked about the times when we were still in Hungary and you were already here in Winnipeg. You told me what it was like to start alone in a new country, without the support of your family. You did not speak the language and you were studying for your doctor certification exams. I remember you writing us that you would never be able to pass the exam on the first try. Yet, you did it, at 42 years old and having only barely spoken any English a year earlier.

I want to thank you once again, for giving my sisters and me life.

I want to thank you for supporting us with your love and all that we needed while growing up, even though you were far away from us.

I want to thank you, for having been such a wonderful doctor to your patients, for understanding their needs and putting them always before yours.

I want to thank you for placing our wishes before yours, for always wanting to help your children, grandchildren and great-grandchildren.

I want to thank you for what you have been to us while you were alive and what you will be to us from now on.

I know that you will continue to shower us with your love and intercede for us in Heaven – until we meet again.

John and my last big public appearance was in July. Governor Christine Gregoire and her husband Mike invited the consuls for a dinner at the Mansion. John was feeling quite well and was able to come with me. Governor Gregoire arranged for us to be able to drive up right to the house to make it easier on John.

A beautiful evening and a marvelous time for all of us!

Conversations with Father Bob (Camuso), a Catholic radio program invited John and me to talk about what it was like to live with John's condition, knowing he would soon leave us and how we prayed. He was a charming host and put us both at ease. We talked similarly about our prayer habits and what we were thinking about death, especially when John was expecting it any day. After all, we have lived together for 54 years, since I was 16. We both had a special relationship with God. I felt God's answers in my heart whenever I asked a question, John said he felt like he was living with God. He used to have talks with him coming from school when he was younger. We prayed together, read the Bible together, discussed it. "Death is a part of life," John said. "When the time comes, and God calls, we leave. We are old, so it will not seem like a long time before Helen will join me. In the meantime, I will hold her in my arms forever, as promised." At one point during the interview Fr. Bob was so impressed by John he jokingly asked if John wanted to take over his program. We had a good laugh, but of course that was not on the air.

In August John wrote to the Electrical Engineering Department at UW. He wrote an address for a festive occasion – "Engineers: Robots or Humans." – and recommended that I should deliver it because he was no longer strong enough. He also sent an essay on the difference of Islam and Christianity to a Jesuit friend, Fr. John Foster. He just went on and on, working, even trying to sell waste management equipment for Hungary.

Then, one day he stood up from the computer and said: "I am not doing the emails anymore."

72

We continued living and hoping, but the days between transfusions became less and less as we approached the inevitable. Hospice proved to be a wonderful experience. They came to help us with so many things. Nurses came to check on John, they brought all his medicines for free, they made sure we had all our power of attorneys, End of Life Directives and Will in place. They gave us literature about what to expect at the end of life. This was in the spring.

However, after a few months they simply decided John did not show any signs of dying, so they will interrupt their visits until we really needed them.

They came back in September and continued their excellent work.

John loved to plan, manage, and design things and was great at PR. He took it upon himself, to plan his funeral, to have his obituary written, the announcements. He wanted the "Flaming Szablyas" to sing at his funeral. As the "Flaming Szablyas" did not want to end up in puddles of tears, which would make singing obsolete anyway, we decided they had to record it. Niki took us to a real studio at her church. John came with us and had the time of his life listening to the songs he loved so much.

Sandy chose a lovely vase to be used as our urn. John wanted to be cremated. He heard so many of the Transylvanian tales about people waking up in their graves, he wanted to make sure he was dead. I decided I was going to keep the urn until I died and then the grandkids will roll around the urn with both our ashes in it to make us one in death as we have been one in life. After that John wanted us to be buried in the earth. His ashes are still here in my living room.

Our children thanked us for not only teaching them how to live, but now also how to die.

Granddaughter Anna and Fred married in a civil ceremony in Baltimore, but the big celebration was going to be in 2006 on June 25th, John's birthday. Anna came with her mother and we went shopping for bridal gowns to give Nagypapa a taste of what she will look like as a bride.

In the meantime, we received a notification from the Embassy that I received the Presidential Order of Merit, but it was for both our lives and what we did for Hungary. András Simon, the Ambassador insisted he wanted to come to Seattle and personally give us the Order of Merit. This should have been given in the Parliament by the Prime Minister, but there was absolutely no hope for that. The Ambassador called. We were negotiating about how to proceed. He said he could come in two weeks. I told him even yesterday would have been too late. So finally, he agreed to let the Consul General from Los Angeles, Ferenc Bösenbacher, come with our good friend, the Commercial attaché Ödön Király. We invited a few close friends, leaders of the Hungarian community and of course, our family. The event, although small, was catered at our home. John just had enough strength to stand up with our grandson Jancsi standing behind him – holding him.

He was so happy that he was able to survive my birthday and our wedding anniversary, and now even this wonderful celebration, his tears were freely running down his face.

Five days later he died.

It is very hard for me to cry. I have not cried while John was still with us, even though he did and my tears were welling up, but only inside. Then after he had breathed his last, I told him I accompanied him to the gates of Heaven, but I have to stay until he comes to pick me up. I encouraged him to do it any minute he wants me. Then I was sobbing, and sobbing, and sobbing. It just broke out of me, like a waterfall.

While I was standing beside him sobbing, I felt his whole being enter into me. He gave all his knowledge, his talents and love, and I knew what I needed to do. I was going to continue everything as we have been doing all our lives.

Niki was with us. Actually, she called me and said: "NOW! Come!" Thank God she noticed it. That morning the "death rattle" started the horrible breathing that seems like he is in agony. The hospice nurse told me they do not feel anything, it just sounds awful, but it may last several days. Thank God it didn't.

Kristy was first to arrive followed immediately by Sandy, who lit many little candles in every one of the family members' names on the big dining room table.

Sandy said first: "May he rest in peace," when we all stood around the bed. She arranged everything with the funeral directors, and she organized the memorial according to John's plans. We followed his desires.

At the offertory, during Mass, the 16 grandkids brought up a pink rose each and put them into a vase that was at the altar. I brought up a red rose. We also carried up symbols of his life, like a toy train, John and his "best friend's" favorite hobby. Our family crucifix stood right by the urn.

According to John's wishes we all wore happy, colorful outfits, I wore my embroidered Hungarian jacket I used for many of my consular appearances.

Father Steve, who said our 50th anniversary Mass, was the celebrant. On behalf of the family, Steve's wife Kristy volunteered to speak:

All I'll have to do is look around. You'll always be here.

I will see you in the shape of my husband's head, in his strong shoulders and handsome silhouette. I will know you are here by the gentleness of his touch and the kindness in his voice. You will be here when he opens the car door for me or kisses my hand. You will be here when he speaks true words and stands up for what he believes. I will know you are here when we stand in church and he confirms his belief in God. You are here when I see his successes, when I see how intelligent he is and when the spark of the engineer in him shines through. I will know you are here by his devotion to his family and by his steadfast integrity. You are in him and will always be here.

I will know you are here by my son's eclectic love of music and by the pleasure he finds in old movies. I will know you are here when his interest and curiosity abound. I will know you are here when he laughs at Victor Borge or Young Frankenstein. I'll know you are here when I look, in awe, at the good person he has become because of you. I will see you in the shadow on the ground, when my son, once, in such need of your guidance, stands a tall, fine, man in the sun. I will know you are here, you run deep in his veins.

I will see you in the sunlight of my daughter's hair. I will know you are here because of her love of culture, her wanderlust, her desire to see the world and know about its people and ways. I will see you in her every time she is confident and sure of her convictions. I will know you are here when she speaks to others about the price of freedom and her desire for peace. I will know you are here by her generosity of time and resolve to help others. I will know you are here when she insists on tradition and when she is corny and sentimental. I will know you are here when she sees a breathtaking sunset and calls me to watch it with her. I will know you are here, her heart holds your spirit.

I will see you in the laughter of my family. I will hear you in songs, and feel you when I dance. I will know you stand by when I am strong when I need to be and I know you are here, in the loving goodness you sowed in each of us. I will know you walk by my side each time I hear a whisper in the wind and know the right thing to do. I know you are here because I will always feel your love.

Go peacefully to God, I have no worry; I know you will always be here.

The big church Holy Family in Kirkland was overflowing. Several people came from Vancouver, B.C. and of course all the family was there. Friends, colleagues, and their families. Ron Masnik, the President of the Consular Association of WA spontaneously stood up and said good-bye to his friend. Bandi Jákóy from the Sopron group sang one of the Sopron songs in Hungarian, just at the spur of the moment.

Maybe it looked strange to some, but I was standing in the door, with a beaming smile, repeating: "thank you for coming." The family was happy we managed to satisfy John's desire, and we had such a wonderful proof of people's love for him.

After everyone had left, all I could just repeat over and over and over was "Thank you! Thank you! Thank you!" I thanked God, John, Csaba, our dear friend, for preparing me in this wondrous way and each and every one of my family members for making our lives so beautiful and meaningful even in these last months! I felt that everything went just perfectly, including the timing. It was the right moment for him to go and for us to let him go to enjoy his well-deserved perpetual presence of God. There was joy in my heart for him and for all of us, knowing when I will get to that point he will be there with outstretched arms. And until then – he will hold me in his arms – forever. He promised, and he has been doing it ever since.

73

The celebration of life was over. The children brought me home.

"Are you going to be OK on your own?" they worried. I assured them I will be just fine.

I was 71 years old, and for the very first time in my life I was completely alone – at least physically. I had a photo on my desk of John with his eyes on the sleeping Shivana in his lap. When I came home, I first saw John's desk. He had a slightly different version of that same photo, but a shock ran right through me: he looked up at me with his eyes wide open. I felt his smile caress me: "Here is looking at you!" He was with me.

As daughter Sandy told me once: "You will be able to do anything you want..."then her voice trailed as she continued: "except the thing that you would most want to do..."

I decided at John's death bed as I felt him move into my whole being, on that memorable day, October 29, 2005, I would continue to do everything as we have been doing together. The decision was strong. Life-determining.

A few days later I wrote John a letter, remembering one of his last nights:

One night John woke up. I wrote down this experience as a letter to him:

"Gyere! Menjünk!" "Come. Let us go! Nothing hurts."

"O.K." I said cautiously, "Let us go! But where?"

You were sitting naked on the bed, no longer even able to stand, but full of enthusiasm and ready to leave.

You were ready. Ready to go and meet your Creator. I was willing to go with you, but I knew you could not take me on this trip, no matter how much we wanted to stay together. But we did stay together – forever. You promised you would hold me in your arms. And you have been holding me ever since – just like always.

Remember, when we talked about what would happen if our oldest, our little Ilike, would die, when she was but 13. She had a knee surgery and we were afraid it would be cancer. You said we would thank God for the gift of her, for the beautiful years he had given us with her.

So that is what we did in the last, beautiful 10 months of your life together, while we floated on the love and prayers of our children.

Thank you for teaching me how to live. And thank you for teaching me, through our shared, lived experience, how to die. Even our children thanked us for teaching them how to die through our examples.

I continued our life. You continued to be with me and I continued to give thanks to God for the beautiful 54 years, spent together, for the way you engulfed me in your love, the fragile 16 year old and made everything easy, despite all the difficulties. Solace and companionship, friendship and love, sexual and spiritual, was always there.

We kept asking in wonder, how we deserved all that God has given us. I guess, it is not a matter of deserving. Maybe it is a matter of thanking God for all we receive and thereby realizing all His blessings.

Weighing on me now was the consulate, our translation business, the consulting with Hungary minus a person who did half the job. He was helping with whatever he could, until that devastating day, when he left the computer for the last time, deciding he would no longer do the emails.

I threw myself into work. While I was working, I constantly listened to classical music, coming from our speakers on one side and our Bose radio on the other, sounding like a true surround-sound. I floated on our favorite music, while working and working and working...

I went down to the Marina frequently, where we used to take our walks. At the end of the planks, I stopped and looked out onto the lake and the sky. And I felt John's arms around me, his being surrounding me, his kisses on my mouth ignited fire within. When I opened my eyes the beauty of the setting sun colored the horizon a bewitching pink-orange-green-blue washed by the waves of the water. I just had to close my eyes and he was there again.

The children were marvelous! The neighbors gave me their love and help. Friends and the church community were all by my side.

On that first night, when I was sitting at the table, not even thinking about food, Linda from upstairs brought me a plate of sandwiches. We opened cans of beer and sat together, having dinner. Linda was an evangelical Christian, while her husband Ahmed was Muslim. They were the kindest people, so much in love with each other, they were the only other couple, who as soon as the elevator door closed, started kissing. Just like John and I. Ahmed used to come and sit with John while I went to Mass. He said to sit with a sick friend is just like going to church. Linda was a teacher, a nurse, and a professional clown. What a combination! Our next-door neighbors Mabel and Frank, Gwen at the end of the hallway, the Taylors and Roberta at the other end... We started calling each other occasionally when one of us wanted to go out for dinner, and if it clicked, we took off to the Crab Cracker, John's and my favorite restaurant in these last months.

Life went on despite my 200% workload. Or maybe because of it?

Anna's church wedding was planned for June 25, 2006. Ilike came over to Seattle to help me choose a grandmother-of-the-bride evening gown.

How we all wished John could have been there in person! We had so much fun finding clothes for several of us. John used to be an expert on ladies' clothes. His mother, who brought him up to be praised by her daughter-in-law, took him to fashion shows, where she was always invited and explained ladies' preferences for her son.

The entire close family was present at the wedding, and many members of our extended families from Toronto, my sisters' children, and grandchildren, from Pullman and Washington DC Barry's family and from Brazil Fred's entire family. Many friends in Los Angeles, and Helen and Chuck's friends from Baltimore.

The wedding was held in Los Angeles, where Anna and Fred lived. Anna planned it, and Barry, her Father, designed and orchestrated the wedding ceremony, which was held in the exquisite Chapel of Pepperdine University in Malibu. The sun shone through the Chapel's colored glass wall adding to the ambience and festivity.

The celebration started Friday night, as the guests arrived in the hotel's bar, where South American music was played while we cheered and mixed with the new friends from all over, but especially Brazil, Frederico's homeland. We were lodged in the same hotel. The family had ample opportunity to mix and have fun. I met Fred's family for the first time. We found out his mother and I were the same age, except she was the mother of the groom, while I was the grandmother of the bride. We could not understand each other, but we certainly tried with hands and words and smiles. Graziella, her oldest daughter, was a dentist. She spoke English very well. She translated wherever she could, as did Fred. Walkyria, his artist sister, did not speak much English, but she was so kind and sweet!

Children and grandchildren milled around, emerged from the crowd, then disappeared again. Everyone was happy and tipsy, laughing and talking about the wedding.

Saturday the partying continued, bachelor and bachelorette parties were going on along with the rehearsal dinner in the same happy atmosphere.

Then came Sunday. Anna was a beautiful bride and Fred a handsome bridegroom. The bride's Father Barry lived in a relationship with Peter, whose Mother was reading from the Old Testament, as was her son, Ilike and Barry, Anna's parents read the Beatitudes from the New Testament to include our family's motto: "Blessed are the pure of heart for they shall see God." We all said the Our Father together, everyone in their own tongue. I started the family readings and I read again at the end. The blessings of relatives went around the room. Our family crucifix was right on the Altar, which I brought up when we entered the Chapel, as was the Torah, brought up by Peter's Mother.

The priest and Barry worked out a beautiful liturgy, unique to the couple.

Coming out from church we took an extended family photo of each side of the family. The one included in this book was taken from our side of the family. The call went out: "All members of the Szablya Family by birth or marriage, as well as Helen's sisters' families!" It took a few minutes to get us all together. Anna was our first grandchild to get married, also the first of all our collective Bartha-Kovács grandchildren, so everyone wanted to take part in the event.

After the ceremony, the party moved over to Geoffrey's, a restaurant with a 260-degree view of the Ocean. The sun was vibrating with happiness just as the young couple.

Despite the sun, the dancing went on full blast, and continued all night after the toasts. I was not the only one who danced blisters onto her feet! Sons and grandchildren did not let me sit. They knew how I enjoyed dancing.

The sun slowly sank below the horizon. California's gorgeous colors blended in the sunset wherever we looked. But the dancing went on and on...

2006 was also the 50th anniversary of the Hungarian Uprising. In Hungary, the events did not turn out as expected, but in Seattle, being the Honorary Consul I had a chance to work myself into oblivion.

The Seattle Hungarian Community (HAAW, Seattle-Pécs Sister Cities) together with the Consulate organized 10 events in 12 days to commemorate our glorious four days of freedom, the first nail in Communism's coffin.

Our first event was on October 12th, which would have been John's and my 55th wedding anniversary. The celebration took place at the Kirkland Parkplace Bookstore, with Hungarian food, dancing, singing, a violinist and a book presentation of *The Fall of the Red Star* with Peggy King Anderson, my co-author.

The bookstore was filled to the brim with celebrants. We sold 48 books that night. Peggy's husband was still there and enjoyed the success with us. Unfortunately, he too followed my John to Heaven not long afterwards.

After the book presentation daughter Sandy and I went to my home, drank champagne and ate Hungarian home-made sausage with it, consoling each other. The one we wanted most to be with us was there in spirit only.

The events then cascaded, one after the other. It was hard when you were either part or the head of the organizing.

The second event was a folk music concert by the Carpathian Folk Quartet and a "táncház" folk dancing to the music, at the Mercer Island Congregational Church, on Friday, October 13th.

Zoltán Kodály's Missa Brevis was presented as a concert on October 15th at St. James Cathedral, by Opus 7, one of the resident choirs of the Cathedral that would be singing it at our big celebration as well. Zoltán Kodály is a famous Hungarian composer, world-renowned for collecting Hungarian folk-songs, his method of teaching music and his compositions.

A "Kopjafa" unveiling took place at City Hall on October 19th. A "kopjafa" is a Hungarian version of the totem pole with all symbols having a meaning to them. The carving was done by a former Sopron student, accomplished forest engineering researcher László Józsa, whose hobby was wood carving. He carved it especially for this occasion. It remained at City Hall on display for a long time, presented by the Seattle-Pécs Sister City Association.

Movies and a Forum about 1956 with a panel of eyewitnesses were presented on Friday, October 20th at the Mercer Island Congregational Church. Hungarian newcomers, working at Microsoft, many of them from Transylvania, or just other recent immigrants, were seeing and hearing the 1956 events for the first time. They have mostly not been born yet at the time and Communists did not teach anything about 1956, or gave them false information, if anything. Here they saw the actual movies made during the Uprising and heard those speak who were there at the time.

We have been working on the grandest event with my good friend, Mária Kramar all year, with Archbishop Alexander Brunett, Auxiliary Bishop Joseph Tyson and John Adams, the Organist of St. James Cathedral, as well as with the wonderful Dr. Corinna Laughlin, the Director of Liturgy at St. James. The Hungarian Protestant Bishop Sándor Szabó came from Los Angeles. He gave a second sermon in Hungarian after Communion.

On the program a beautiful design was created of all the Hungarian saints and Our Lady of Hungary by Masa Feszty. The liturgy was in both English and Hungarian. On the program the parts said in English, appeared in Hungarian and vice versa. The Prelude included Boldogasszony Anyánk, the song to Mary, Queen and Forever Protector of Hungary, continuing with the Te Deum.

Auxiliary Bishop of Seattle Joseph J. Tyson was the Presider as Archbishop Brunett had to be in Montana that day. Bishop Tyson's family came from Europe. So, the Archbishop joked with him about knowing all those languages anyway. The Bishop then talked about his origins in his sermon, but apologized for speaking no Hungarian, only German and Croatian, although his origins were from near Odessa, where many Germans lived since Catherine the Great's time, until the Soviet times, which had finished them off. He was a lovely man, enjoying every minute of his presence at our gathering. He ended his sermon with:

> "No, I am not Hungarian, but I know that those cracks in our Berlin Wall started forming in Hungary with the 1956 Uprising and that same Wall completely melted away in 1989 because Hungary allowed her land to be used as a transit path for East Germans to come West. Hungarians as a people were the first to stand in front of tanks in the name of freedom and it is that freedom that sends us straight to the scriptures....
>
> "No, I am not Hungarian. But in 1956 we were all Hungarians and today we are all Hungarians in our love of freedom. For this we say, "'God Bless Hungary' 'Isten áldd meg a Magyart!' Peace be with you!"

The Hungarians supplied the readers Dr. Zoltán and Maria Kramár, six of us were Eucharistic Ministers, the Master of Ceremony was Zoltán Ábrahám. The Opus 7 choir sang Zoltán Kodály's Missa Brevis. At Communion time Kodály's Ave Maria resounded in the church. Hungarians, their families, and friends, along with the VIPs totally filled St. James Cathedral. The readings were especially chosen for the occasion: from the Maccabees and Revelations. The Gospel was by St. John about Jesus's message of Love.

After Communion, the Hungarian Bishop Sándor Szabó said the second sermon in Hungarian. We sang the Hungarian and the Transylvanian Anthem to finish the beautiful celebration.

Hungarian events just cannot be held without food. After Mass we shepherded everyone over to St. James Parish Hall, where a delicious lunch, prepared by Mária and Miklós Németh and Sándor Boldizsár, our master chef, was awaiting the joyous crowd.

My talk included Victor Orbán's message to all Hungarians for the 50th anniversary of the Uprising. It was followed by Rob McKenna, Attorney General of Washington, and a good friend. He talked about the freedom we fought for and that was finally achieved after so many years. Governor Christine Gregoire sent us a Proclamation declaring October 23, 2006 "Hungarian Freedom Fighter's Day." The Mayor of Redmond Rosemary M. Ives and the Mayor of Issaquah Ava Frisinger sent us Proclamations as well, honoring our anniversary. Then Keith Orton, the Director of International Affairs for Seattle, who had been working with the sister cities, spoke in place of the Mayor. Next was Miguel Velasquez, VP of the Consular Association, greeting us on our national holiday with a big smile and love.

As a surprise I presented a medal to Mária Kramár: "Hero of the Revolution." I was given the opportunity from the Embassy to apply for medals to hand it to the well-deserving, who took part in the Uprising. Mária not only helped Pál Maléter at the Killián Barracks by working with an ambulance to carry the wounded and the dead away from the building and bringing the freedom fighters whatever was necessary. She continued to help after she had escaped and returned to the country several times working for British Intelligence. I was so happy to be able to be the one to decorate her. I had two more of these to hand to their recipients, but they were not present at this time, so they had to wait to receive theirs at a later time. Mária beamed!

Our folk dancing groups gave performances to everyone's delight. The gathering continued until late into the afternoon, but it did not mark the end of our celebrations.

Next in line was a concert by world-renowned Hungarian pianist Endre Hegedűs on October 22nd. He played Chopin, Bartók and Liszt at Benaroya Hall, Seattle's beautiful, modern concert hall adorned with Chihuly glass pieces of art, some of them two stories high. A surprise came in the last number when one of Seattle's own artists, Judy Cohen joined him. They played "Les Preludes" symphonic poem for four hands by Liszt.

We had a full house and standing ovations for this extraordinary artist and his surprise guest.

We had several interviews with various Hungarians that appeared in *The Seattle Times*, in the *European Weekly*, in the *Progress*, in many newsletters and church bulletins, in PR announcements and Calendars of Seattle and Tacoma as well as other surrounding smaller towns' newspapers. I wrote an Opinion article for *The Seattle Times* "America's 'innocent ignorance'." This definition was first coined by Nobel-prize-winning author Pearl S. Buck. She also added: "if there was such a thing." I gave many examples of this, one of them being the Hungarian Uprising in 1956, when ignorance of history and international affairs in America determined the fate of the world. Then came examples of 2006 politics: Iraq and Darfur, where blood, just like on the streets of Budapest, wrote history. Americans realizing their leadership role try to help, but "innocent ignorance" stands in the way, when we listen only to the evidence we want to hear, when we do not agree with elections that do not go "our way" when we ignore rights of others to think differently, when we do not understand cultural differences. We know nothing about those we want to help and attempt to help them in a way that they can only resent. Historical events are important because if we don't learn from the past, we will be forced to relive it. Extreme right and extreme left are equally horrific. The only system worthy of humans is democracy. The greatest weakness of democracy is that it can be voted out of existence. "Innocent ignorance" can kill us. All those who have democracy must realize the choices they have, and make the right ones, or they will have to suffer the consequences.

The Hungarian American Coalition published 56 Hungarian refugees' stories in English and Hungarian under the title "56 Stories." Our story was included in two versions. One by me and one by daughter Helen (Ilike) who was four years old at the time. At the book launch in Washington, DC at the Kossuth (Hungarian) House Ilike read our stories.

On October 23rd the actual 50th anniversary, we had an "Academic Conference on 1956" hosted by the University of Washington about the Revolution of 1956, about Hungary's past, and its future in the European Union. The Conference was held in the Walker Ames Room in Kane Hall at the University of Washington and was open to the public. Speakers included Professor Péter Dobay from Pécs, Dr. Csaba Hegyváry the noted psychiatrist originally from Hungary, László Józsa from Vancouver, B.C. member of the Sopron Forestry group and wood carver of the "Kopjafa," Honorary Consul Helen Szablya and former foreign service officer David Hughes. The organizers at the university were counting on about 50 people, but the hall was filled to the brim. All 160 seats were taken.

This presentation was repeated at the University of Washington in the Husky Union Building, from a different angle next day Tuesday, October 24th at a Teachers' Conference as a Master Teacher Workshop: "Revolts and Revolutions: Central and Eastern Europe in the 20th Century."

One of our good friends and member of the Hungarian Community, Susie (Zsuzsa) Ördögh Zimsen, was a member of the Olympic swimming team in 1956 in Melbourne. The water-polo gold medal was won by the Hungarians, after blood colored the pool during the Soviet-Hungarian water-polo match. Susie's good friend was the injured person. A Hungarian-Australian Dezső Dobor was preparing a documentary based on the team members' stories, as well as a coffee table book of photos. He interviewed Susie in California for 40 minutes, while she was visiting one of her five children there.

Naturally, we had big celebrations in all the towns where Hungarians lived in the USA and Canada as well as in all other parts of the world. We, the survivors were old, but still young enough to enjoy the celebrations and make sure our descendants would remember...

Our children, along with the children of the Adamovich's, decided they would celebrate together at the annual Sopron Homecoming Ball at Canadian Thanksgiving, which is in October. The Sopron Forestry University was going to celebrate next year because that would be their 50th ball.

We, 27 of the possible 34 family members, all came to the Ball in 2006. What a happy reunion for all who could make it! Several of the grandchildren made it for the first time. Son Jancsi danced with his daughters, Louis with his daughters and grandsons with their mothers as "debutantes" were supposed to do. Naturally, the grandsons just had to dance with their grandmother too.

Dancing, singing the usual Sopron songs, drinking, laughing, then dancing again, picking up news from all the friends, many of whom shared our long-ago past!

74

2007. The Sopron Forestry University's members were celebrating the 50th anniversary of their first school year in the New World. This time the two, the part that stayed at home in Hungary and the one that emigrated to Canada, celebrated together. And I wanted to be a part of it.

So off I went to Vancouver, B.C. to be one of the speakers in the afternoon session of the big day: June 14, 2007. The Forestry Building had an Open House with memorabilia from the "good old Sopron days" with photos of each graduating class and their adventures in Abbotsford, Powell River, Vancouver and Victoria, as well as in the "bush" the Canadian virgin forests that waited for their expertise to be mapped, researched, maintained and so much more.

The morning events took place at the Main Mall Outdoor Amphitheatre Forest Sciences Center with federal, provincial and University VIPs appreciating the Sopron Forestry University's many achievements. Among them were Jack N. Saddler, Professor and Dean of the Faculty of Forestry, UBC. And his counterpart from Hungary, Dr. Sándor Faragó, Rector (President) of the University of West Hungary (Sopron), The Ambassador of Hungary to Canada, His Excellency Dr. Pál Vastagh, Miklós Grátzer, UBC-Sopron Alumnus, former Student Body President at the time of the affiliation of the Sopron University with UBC. This meant he was one of the negotiators who traveled with Dean Kálmán Roller to all the discussions, and took part in the agreements with UBC and the authorities. He was one of those to whom I presented the Hero of the Revolution Medal for the 50th anniversary of the Uprising in Seattle.

My talk in the afternoon was presented during the Alumni Recognition Event. It was so well received! I recalled all our mutual memories. I started by telling them: although they respected me as a person from a different generation, a professor's wife with three children, I was actually younger than many of them, being only 22 at the time. I told them how we forged the papers ourselves to send us to Sopron University to take over the place of a professor who had left the country. We managed to escape with the help of those forged documents, only to find the university in Austria and the Canadian Ambassador asking us to join them. All the way we laughed through our shared fun times, how the students used to call Louis "the singing basket" when he cried and how they were swinging him back and forth to quiet him. I showed the video of Miklós and Márta Kovács's wedding, where the parish priest handed us the Latin version of a prayer to translate into Hungarian, whispering: "The Bishop insists on saying this prayer. So, please, do your best." I don't think many realized what actually happened, when John recited a beautiful prayer, which almost matched the Latin one. He only had a few minutes to go over the text. He got lots of praise for it. The dogwood story that almost got us all into trouble on March 15th. Dogwood being a protected tree, it was against the law to pick even one little flower of it. Let alone decorate the entire hall with those beautiful flowers. That was also the day when Dean Roller announced we were stateless now, as the Hungarian Government decided all Hungarian refugees would lose their Hungarian citizenship.

Some of the more sobering surprises at our arrival: students had to pay tuition and they had to work for that tuition in summer jobs. And what kind of jobs! Working in a virgin forest was not even comparable to working in a Hungarian park-like forest. The jobs were dangerous.

Also, as in all democratic countries, so too in Canada, elections were held regularly. The Government changed from Liberal to Conservative. Joseph Diefenbaker became Prime Minister. He did not want to take on the responsibility that the Liberals accepted, namely, to sponsor the university.

I told the audience about our great chance to meet with the Roller children and grandchildren at our daughter's home in Maryland, two years before today's big celebration.

My late husband John, who, along with Dean Roller, their father and grandfather respectively, was at all the negotiations as interpreter. As such, he could testify as an eyewitness to their father's wisdom, diplomacy and peaceful constitution, without which we would have never been able to survive. When tempers flared, he managed to remain calm. He and Dean Andrews (on the part of UBC) fought tooth and nail and would not let the Government back out of the deal. Not only did the University survive, but it went onto achieve wondrous success in Forestry and in the end, it even managed to get back together with its original Alma Mater, and today we were there to celebrate that 50 years ago Sopron University became affiliated with the University of British Columbia.

My talk ended here, but I would like to add a few causes to celebrate the Sopron University's achievements.

In 1986 Dean Roller's book *Sopron Chronicle* was published for the 30th anniversary of the Hungarian Uprising. June 2, 1999, Dean Roller received an Honorary Doctorate from the University of British Columbia for his achievements, the unprecedented migration from a university from one continent to another, and chronicling it in this book. The same book was published in Hungarian in Hungary first in 1996, then republished with more information added in 2000, "...mi is voltunk egyszer az Akadémián." For his life's work Dean Roller was decorated by the Hungarian Government in 2002. Finally, he also received the Honorary Doctorate of the Sopron University's Hungarian branch.

Dean Roller was proud to have received the appreciation of his work from Otto Habsburg, our last Heir to the throne of Hungary.

The Sopron Alumni had tremendous achievements, especially if you realize they were working in a language they did not know at their arrival. Thirty-three percent of graduates went on to get a postgraduate degree. Compare that to the five- to six-percent average for the Canadian students. Many became professors, distinguished professors and even a dean.

They mapped British Columbia. They contributed to research in Forestry, in the Paper and Wood Industry. One of them became a medical doctor, another a hotel manager and another a film producer and professor at the University of Washington, working with Walt Disney and PBS. They all are proud and happy Canadians. 90% of them still live in Canada.

UBC's Forestry Building has a beautiful "Székely kapu" donated by the Sopron alumni, carved by László Józsa. For the 50th anniversary László carved a Hungarian "Kopjafa" with great symbolic meaning. Everyone received a Key to Symbolism: starting from the bottom: five rings each representing a decade. Earth with Equator, indicating where we presently reside. Dogwood and Bastion (B.C.'s provincial flower), home and stability. Tulip, the female symbol of students, staff and Alumnae. Moustache, the male symbol in Hungarian folk art. Microscopic structure, roots, wood, wood chemistry, R & D. Trees, the forests of B.C., Canada and the World, the foresters' profession. Pinecone, a seed, a new beginning, the "fruit" of education.

The next year, on May 31, 2008, our oldest granddaughter Anna gave birth to her firstborn, our oldest great-granddaughter, Ava Dora Morini.

We have to take a four-generation photo! Off I went to Los Angeles, where my daughter Ilike, the happy grandmother, was already there helping Anna, introducing her to motherhood, just like I introduced her.

Anna and Fred's place was too small to stay with them, so I was lucky to have wonderful friends who put me up for the night. I flew in and out within 24 hours. And we took the photo! Boy, was it difficult! Little Ava was not in the mood to cooperate. She was already showing her determined character at this early age. If she did not want something, then that was it. She did not do it. We tried over and over to make her smile, but at least just to stop crying. We fed her so much to be happy, she finally threw up. But she was resisting all our efforts. In the end we had to be satisfied with a photo on which she stopped crying for a moment. She looked pretty sad in the picture, but all four generations were finally on it. In my Christmas letter I had a smiling photo of her in addition to that first infamous one. Now as I am writing this, she is 12 years old and helping to take a photo of her little sister Ella, who is two.

That same summer was another Hungarian Honorary Consuls' World Conference. This time I had two grandchildren and the fiancé of one with me who received royal treatment from a dear friend Dr. Katalin Keresztesi of "jump rope fame." Remember the Hungarian jump roper team who won the world championship in Olympia, Washington? She was the accompanying Professor from the University of Physical Education in Budapest (Testnevelési Főiskola). Jancsi, son János' son, and Brianna Prentis-Crane, were engaged to be married. They were joined by Krystal Pool (daughter Rita's daughter). They participated in all events of the Conference and thoroughly enjoyed every minute, adding a side trip to Lake Balaton just on their own.

The Vajdahunyad Castle in Városliget is the exact replica of the original Vajdahunyad Castle in Transylvania. It was built for the Exhibition organized for Hungary's Millennial in 1896. On this warm summer evening it bathed in festive lights. The hostess was the Minister of Foreign Affairs, Kinga Göncz, former President Árpád Göncz's daughter. Grandson Jancsi got extremely excited when he heard that the Japanese Honorary Consul of Hungary at the Conference was Mr. Suzuki himself. He established a factory in Hungary. He was one of the keynote speakers at the Conference. I became friends with his interpreter. We met at the delicious buffet dinner. Jancsi could not have been more excited to speak to *him*. It turned out splendidly. I never saw two people communicate as happily as those two, none of whom spoke the other's language. They had no problem discussing how wonderful the Suzuki motorbike was. The best. Their smiles spoke a language of their own. Of course, the interpreter was helpful, but they managed to convey these thoughts to each other before she had even opened her mouth. We had a marvelous time. After the evening events the young people had their own excursions to the nightlife of Budapest. Especially nice of Katalin's son, Bence, to take them around. He was much, about 20 years older than these three. Next day Katalin told me she got up at 6:00 a.m. and there was no sign of them yet. Bence gave them a thorough lesson of what it is like being a Hungarian and staying up all night having fun.

The President of Hungary, László Sólyom had a reception for the Conference as well. Our Christmas letter included a photo with him and the four of us.

As soon as we arrived home the Seattle-Pécs Sister Cities Association started to prepare for two glorious events in Pécs's history. The first was the 1,000th anniversary of the Bishopric and the foundation of the cathedral in 2009. The Archbishop of Seattle, Alexander Brunett himself, was coming with our committee to the grand celebration of several days. This year was dedicated to the Church. Archbishop Brunett was a kind, jovial, good-humored man, willing to go along with many trials and tribulations. The first was that we picked him up at the airport, transferred him to a minibus and along with the committee drove straight down to Pécs, an approximately three hours' drive, to arrive straight to a huge concert, organized for the arriving 45 bishops from all over the world. By the time the evening was finished, we were famished. We found a pizzeria that was still open. We were so hungry the Archbishop was able to eat a whole pizza by himself.

The Archbishop was staying at the Bishop's Palace in the heat that vacillated close to the 100-degree Fahrenheit mark, give or take a degree or two – without air conditioning. The poor organist of Seattle's St. James Cathedral, Joseph Adams, who came with us to give a concert, suffered likewise in the guesthouse. The committee, who was not invited to sleep there, had a great time at the air-conditioned hotel. We felt so sorry for those two poor people. But then, you cannot offend the Bishop by not accepting his invitation. The Archbishop's window looked onto the square where the concert took place and where an extremely loud rock-opera was performed next evening. Even opening his window did not produce any relief.

Sunday Mass was celebrated on the same huge square where the concert took place. St. Stephen's right hand was brought down from Budapest in its artistic reliquary resembling a small church. The 45 bishops concelebrated Mass on the big day. The Primate of Hungary Cardinal Erdő was the Presider. I was expecting to have to do a lot of interpreting for the Archbishop, but lo and behold, they immediately greeted each other in Italian and Latin. They had no problems communicating whatsoever. On the last day of his stay Archbishop Brunett went all by himself to meet with Cardinal Erdő. I arranged for him to stay in the Hilton on Castle Hill from where he could walk over to Cardinal Erdő's place. The Hilton graciously agreed to host the Archbishop free of charge and gave him the best room with a gorgeous view of the entire city. He later confided in me that this was the best room and night of his stay.

Joseph Adams played a well-attended organ concert in the Cathedral and invited Szabolcs Szamosi the organist of the Cathedral to come and play in Seattle, which soon became a reality.

Professor Peter Dobay was again a great help during our stay in Pécs. He organized a side trip to Siklós, an old castle turned museum and after that we were feasting on the wines of Villány, a famous wine-growing region, with delicious Hungarian food. Archbishop Brunett loved the sightseeing tour. Villány is so close to the border with Croatia that we were told the cannons could be heard during the Kosovo war and once a stray bomber threw down a few bombs onto a Hungarian village. Luckily, no one was hurt, therefore it did not become an international catastrophe.

Pécs was in full preparation for the next year 2010, when it was chosen to be one of the 10 Cultural Capitals of the EU. We got a chance to see some of these previews. For example, Zsolnay Park, which included the old mansion of the Zsolnay family, totally renovated, as well as their Mausoleum, surrounded by a beautiful park. The factory also had a shop open for tourists to buy their exquisite pieces at a discounted price. In front of the Cathedral excavation of the catacombs was extended. A glass roof was planned strong enough to be able to withstand even truck traffic. A new library was being built that would house both the university's and the city's libraries.

Seattle-Pécs arranged another excursion for 2010, when Pécs was the Cultural Capital of the EU. The library was finished. Mária Kramár was the President of the Sister Cities Association. She did a great job together with our favorite woodcarver, László Józsa, who carved a festive kopjafa for the occasion. Salmon were swimming jól all through the totem-pole-like kopjafa. It symbolized the Hungarians who had escaped in 1956, but kept returning to their native land, just as the salmon always returned to the place of their birth when it was time to deposit their offspring there. Both Mária and László gave an extraordinary talk at the opening of the library presenting Seattle's gift to the City of Pécs.

In return, the Chief Librarian of the city's and the university's joint library, came to visit Seattle. Dr. Ágnes Dárdai Fischer stayed with the Kramárs. I was designated to be the interpreter. We went through all possible libraries in Seattle, the University of Washington library, the modern downtown Seattle City Library, designed according to the latest library concepts and occupying an entire city block, the King County Library System. She loved the new concepts she could take home with her to apply at their library.

Every year the Seattle-Pécs Sister City Association hosted two students from Pécs to get them acquainted with America. They stayed for 10 days and were shown everything Seattle had to offer: the Boeing factory's Everett plant, Microsoft, the Aquarium, the Art Museum, Pike Place Market and were given a barbeque party at the end of their stay. That party was always hosted by the excellent cooks, the Boldizsárs.

75

It was an ordinary February afternoon when my phone rang:

"Navaal collapsed," I heard Sandy's voice. "He was playing ping-pong with his two MD friends. They are working on him and calling an ambulance."

"Keep me posted, let me know in which hospital we can visit him," I said. He had had a heart attack before, when he was 39 years old, but it left no trace. He ate healthy, he worked out, he was in great shape.

Time passed and I prayed for him. I don't know why I said: "May he rest in peace..." I did not intend to say that.

Then the phone rang and Sandy said in Hungarian: "Navaal died."

I asked: "Should I come now, or later?"

"Later," she said. "Ben (a neighbor and best friend of Navaal's) is taking me to him. Prepare to stay for some days."

I felt devastated. They were so happy, so much in love, they had two beautiful children seven and 11 years old. Navaal wanted me to move in with them for my old days, which were on their way. And now he died, not I. At our age, Navaal's mother (same age as I was, 75) and I, would have been happy to die for him, instead of him. We kept repeating that. But he was gone.

Grandson Jancsi and his fiancé, Brianna, came over right away to Sandy's house to meet the children when they were coming home from school. The entire family as one wanted to support Sandy, help Sandy, do whatever they could.

When she reached Navaal his body was still warm. That is how she said good-bye to him. She was happy they had a beautiful morning together. When he left, she stood by the window, waived to him, and threw him kisses with both her hands. That was the last time she saw him alive. He had such a massive heart attack that the two doctor-friends present and the arriving medics could not revive him, no matter how much they tried.

Zilda, Navaal's mother, was crying very hard. She was inconsolable. Veeron, Navaal's brother with whom Zilda lived, and his family all came down from Vancouver, B.C. right away and stayed until the funeral. His other brother, Anil and his family, came from Trinidad. Some came from England, Canada, other parts of the USA. The Trinidadian relatives all wanted to view the body before cremation.

The celebration of Navaal's life took place at Sandy's parish church, Assumption, in Seattle. Father Oliver organized a beautiful Mass and spoke lovingly about Navaal and his family. Anil was the one who took Navaal's ashes into the church at the start of Mass. Navaal loved playing cricket. All the members of his team came in their white cricket uniforms and with their cricket bats held up like swords, his friends formed a long arch of glory for Navaal, who for years was their Captain.

Vipul, Navaal's close friend, organized a gathering in the evening at Murphy's Irish Pub, which he owned, inviting everyone who was in town. Every member of our family was present from all over the United States: Baltimore, New York, Philadelphia, Houston, Denver, Los Angeles.

We reminisced together about Navaal, about the good old days when he was alive.

Sandy continued to stay home with the children as long as she could. They joined a group of parents and children called "Safe Crossings" that supported those who lost a parent. This group helped them tremendously to find their way in life again under their extremely different circumstances.

Her friends from church delivered dinner to her house every night to help her survive. Navaal and Sandy loved to garden. They had beautiful tomatoes, lettuce, all kinds of vegetables. One day she was overheard by one of the parishioners, when she was crying: "Who will plant the tomatoes?" Then the parishioners grabbed shovels and other garden tools and did all the spring work for her in one afternoon.

There was an awful lot of bureaucratic office work to accomplish after Navaal's death. Sandy took it all in her hands as executor of Navaal's will and fought for her kids to get as much as possible from the different insurance companies. She managed to invest 100% in the 529 plans just before the deadline. This ensured four years' tuition for the children at a university in Washington State.

She planned for years on remodeling the house. I advised her to do it now, while she had the money to do it. She put in a new bathroom downstairs and renewed the kitchen, put in a dishwasher, remodeled the upstairs bathroom, put in new windows and lighting on the main floor. Shivana's room got a lovely French door leading to the backyard where they loved to barbecue.

⟜

Ilike and Chuck went to Paris to celebrate their 15th anniversary. They enjoyed every minute of their stay in the rented apartment. They walked all over Paris, enjoying not only the unique sites, but all the bohemian life around them, the little bistros, cafés, the wine, the Seine, the Left Bank, walking, breathing in the dream that was Paris.

Then, after they came home our beautiful strong, healthy 56-year-old daughter phoned us. She had cancer. A very different kind of cancer. The doctors could not figure out what it was. Something covered everything in the X-ray. They suspected appendix-cancer, then ovarian? Then, it turned out to be cancer on the entire lining of her stomach "peritoneal carcinomatosis!" The doctors told her if this would have happened three to four years before, they would have sent her home to die. However, now there was a new kind of treatment. It turned out the doctor who performed that surgery five minutes from where they lived, was their friend. He gave Ilike and Chuck a 70% chance of survival. They were overwhelmed with joy. She was going to try it.

She wanted me to go to Los Angeles and meet her there so we could take another four-generation photo. I told her I had a good feeling about this. She will survive.

"Why not me?" was all I could think of. I told God I would be happy to take her place. I was already old…

We met in Los Angeles for a few unforgettable days. Ilike and I stayed in a boutique hotel, meaning a small hotel, including lovely specialties – like a boutique.

We had wonderful times together with Anna and family. We invited them over to the swimming pool, which Ava loved. Ilike's son Alex and Kim joined us too.

On Thursday, Nov 12, 2009 at 8:52 a.m., Chuck, her husband, wrote:

> Hi. Just heard from the operating room. Mom/Helen is doing well, and the surgeon is starting to remove the tumor cells from her abdomen. No estimate as to when she will be finished. The next call will be at 2:30 pm. I will send another e-mail after this call. Chuck

Chuck kept up the updates every few hours. The surgery lasted 11 hours.

We found out only later that when her abdomen was opened two liters of fresh blood spurted out. If she would not have been in the operating room, she would have died by the time they would have gotten her there.

Where did the blood come from? The cancer was all over the inside of her abdomen. The ovarian duct sucked it all in like a vacuum and formed a tumor there. That tumor exploded at the same moment her abdomen was cut open. It was a miracle she did not bleed to death. They proceeded to take out her womb, her ovaries, her appendix, her gallbladder, her spleen and 10% of her liver. Then a 107.5-degree hot chemo bath was applied for 90 minutes inside her abdomen. The cut went from her breastbone to her pubic bone.

Immediately after surgery she was unrecognizable from all that was altered in her body; from all what she went through.

The next day she was sitting in an armchair and drinking fluids. She would get chemo for the next 10 months starting in January. At that time she was looking at five years possible survival. The hope was that by then science will find other remedies.

She went home after 10 days. Anna was with her the next 10 days, then I came over for another 10. On the 12th day she went shopping with Anna for Ava, her granddaughter. She went to the beauty parlor, to the movies, in the same house where they lived. Of course, she was extremely tired after each excursion, but she wanted to go. She had a long deep sleep after each.

On the 19th of December she and Chuck flew to Los Angeles to share their granddaughter's first Christmas. It was pretty miserable because she caught a cold on the plane, but they were there.

That happened 11 years ago. God was extremely good to us. Not long after her surgery she was on a TV show with her wonderful doctor. In this they explained together the procedure and how to recognize this dangerous condition.

After that, Helen served on the inaugural committee for what is now the annual "Heat It to Beat It!" walk. The walk raises more than $150,000 each year for research and education. The first walk, she was there at the start, but was so weak, she could not yet walk the entire stretch. The walk was virtual this year because of COVID-19.

Ilike found out she had BRAC 2, an inherited cancer gene. All her brothers and sisters got tests and the girls who tested positive decided to have a hysterectomy and a double mastectomy to pre-empt their chance of getting cancer.

Again, as always, we experienced the power of prayer.

76

Nadine's Masters graduation from the Johns Hopkins University SAIS International School started a whole avalanche of graduations: master's degrees, bachelor's degrees, high school graduations all over the family. You probably do not want to hear the whole list, but several engagements, marriages came one after the other. The grandchildren were just at the right age for these events.

On February 22, 2011, Jancsi and Brianna's first child, János Szablya the 5th, was born. We call him by his middle name, Miles, because it would be confusing to do it otherwise. He was our second great-grandchild. On our Christmas letter we had a photo in which all the János Szablyas were displayed. Three in real life and two only in photos.

That was the year when Ambassador György Szapáry came to present a medal to Mark Pigott, owner of PACCAR, a local company. PACCAR established several plants in Hungary. We had lunch the next day with Mark Pigott, the Ambassador and Fr. Stephen V. Sundborg S.J., the President of Seattle University, owned by the Jesuits. The lunch was in the President's private dining room. Mark Pigott and his family have been donating large amounts to the University. It was in Pigott Auditorium, if you can recall, where we presented *Hungary Remembered* for the 30th anniversary of the 1956 Uprising.

In the evening we met with the Hungarian Community. Before the meeting, while talking in private I asked the Ambassador if I could finally become an "Honorary Consul General," as all of the Hungarian Honorary Consuls already had the title. He was curious as to why. I told him, jokingly, but with a serious face: "Because I will get twice the salary." He looked surprised and joked back: "Two times '0' is still zero."

At the meeting he announced to the Hungarian community that I was promoted to Honorary Consul General. Since then the rules have changed. Now, Honorary Consuls cannot be Consuls General, only the career consuls.

The reception was at Katalin Pearman's house on Mercer Island, who was going to be the next consul. Her husband, Jim, was the Mayor of Mercer

Island. Her home was full of dignitaries: state, county, city, international VIPs, and loving, warm hospitality.

The Ambassador was guest speaker and distributor of awards at the University of Washington's Central European Business Center. The recipients were winners of the reenactment of an EU meeting, each student representing a country.

As usual I went to the July 4th Naturalization Ceremony at the Seattle Center. All consuls were invited, but there were a few of us who always showed up. Jim McDermott, Congressman, was there every year, as was Senator Maria Cantwell, the Governor, the Mayor of Seattle, and the Director of Seattle Center. The Head of Immigration introduced the 500 to 600 would-be new citizens to the judge, who took their oaths and granted them their citizenship.

Every year the organizers of this wonderful event, the Ethnic Heritage Council led by Alma Plancich, gave the "Spirit of Liberty" award to someone who was a naturalized American and did outstanding work in keeping his or her compatriots living their traditions in their new homeland. 2011 was my turn to get the award. Daughter Sandy, grandchildren Maria, Shivana, and Rohan became part of the celebration, all in Hungarian folk costumes. Grandson Adam Szablya, sat with me on the podium. Alma Plancich introduced me, then Congressman Jim McDermott gave the keynote address about me and the "Spirit of Liberty" award. Finally, I gave a grateful talk for selecting me.

Even though it was extremely hot in the July sunshine I made a point in coming to this beautiful celebration every year. It touched me every time, as we too were naturalized. Introduction of the immigrants went by nations in alphabetical order. Those who came from that country stood up to be acknowledged. The youngest and the oldest new citizens were introduced. A Native American Storyteller did an excellent job every year telling an old legend of their tribe. Another played the violin as background music. As the story progressed, the storyteller changed costumes. He became an eagle. The audience was supposed to add to the story when we all had to push up the clouds back into the sky that were threatening to squash the people. Together we could do it.

The ceremony started with the Marine Band playing and ended with the Total Experience Gospel Choir singing "America the Beautiful" in their unique way.

Left to right: Adam Szablya grandson, Hon. Consul of Hungary, Helen M. Szablya, and Congressman Jim McDermott, handing the Spirit of Liberty award to Helen.

Our then Consul General in Los Angeles, Amb. Balázs Bokor, decided to include me in his book *56 Hungarians in the West*. Every word of his interview was spot-on.

That year in Hungary I met my new friend, Dr. Zsuzsa Hantó. We have been working together ever since. When we used to go to Hungary with John to make it easier for our friends, we simply sat down at the Déryné Confectioners, across the street from the Church of Krisztinaváros and scheduled a new person for every hour. I kept up that habit after John's passing, as it was easy and enjoyable. A lovely lady from Australia, who provided the Hungarian radio station there, Lilli Szanyiszló, whom I met at my classmate and good friend, Muci Barta's home, talked me into meeting with another interviewer, Attila Kovács and with Dr. Zsuzsa Hantó.

Zsuzsa sat down across from me and smiled. Immediately we started to talk about our favorite topic: Hungary's freedom and the truth about Hungary's history; the sins and victims of Communism. She started as a professor of sociology and history. She herself was a victim of Communism. Her entire life was subverted by it. One of her students asked her about what a "kulak" was. She answered the question: "It was a peasant who had more than the allotted amount of land, was resisting getting into the co-operative, therefore was considered an enemy of the people."

That is how she ended up researching the *Banished Families* (English title of her book) about all those honest, good people who were deported into "internal exile" and "relieved" of all their possessions.

I suggested that she come to the USA, to the West Coast, we will arrange her tour. When she learned I married at 16 to escape deportation, she asked me to write a chapter for her upcoming book: *Haramiák és Emberek* (Monsters and People). The story of our marriage was the only chapter in which someone wrote about escaping that fate.

We parted on this note, with lots of enthusiasm to start our work.

Steve and Kristy, who have been working extensively in Africa at first to build a hospital, then with the help of the Jesuits, Steve became co-founder of the "Professionals Without Borders" after having worked with "Engineers Without Borders." Ultimately this enterprise turned into "Kilowatts for Humanity". In 2011 they went to Zambia where they visited the school, which by the people's choice was named after Kristy. It became her passion to raise money for the school.

Steve wrote an article for IEEE about the project of supplying small units of power to villages that previously had none. One way to accomplish that was to put a water wheel into a river, which generated the energy to be turned into electricity. Through that the Internet was now available for these villages, they could charge cell phones, send money, bank with their phones, enhancing the economy of the small settlements. Steve received the "Spirit of Community Award" for his work as the Head of Maintenance at Seattle University for managing to reach 100% carbon-neutral operation at the university. He was also chosen to be a member of the Jesuit Honor Society Alpha Sigma Nu.

The same year Niki's daughter Michelle, just graduating from high school, received the "Highest Community Service Award" from her high school.

Niki's business again became the "Best audio-visual production company in the NW."

Sandy, having been at home with the children since Navaal's death, decided to go to Seattle University to get a master's degree in psychology, to make a living as a psychotherapist. She started in the fall. Both children were in school and I was there if she could not be home.

It was hard, but she enjoyed it. She no longer wanted to be a pharmaceutical rep because that required a lot of traveling and she could not do that as a single parent.

May 3, 2012, Zsuzsa Hantó arrived for her tour up and down the West Coast to market her book *Banished Families* the English version of her *Kitaszítottak*. The book was the story of those deported by the Communists 1951-1953 into "internal exile" not knowing where they would be taken, ending up in stables, or pigstyes more often than not. In the book she included all those nationalities who were forcefully "exchanged" between countries after 1945, when borders were moved. If their ethnic origin was different from that of the majority in their village they were deported to the country where their mother tongue was spoken. All they could take with them had to fit in their suitcases. The other assets: house, land, furniture, appliances, businesses, farms were confiscated. The book contained a CD with the official list of all those deported from Budapest 1951-1953. People were asked to read the names and correct the grammatical mistakes made by the security police, who often misspelled names. An amazing book – we had to plan an amazing tour.

We organized the trip with Mária Kramár and Judith Kallo, two dear friends. We went together everywhere. Judith was our designated, passionate driver. Of course, the Hungarian American Association of WA (HAAW) and the Seattle Pécs Sister Cities Association (SPSCA) along with their presidents, Zsuzsa Stanfield and Clarissa Szabados-Mish, worked tirelessly on the project and raised money to fund it. Mária invited Zsuzsa Hantó to her house for the duration of her Seattle stay. From here we took Zsuzsa up to Vancouver, B.C. and down to Portland, Oregon.

The road to British Columbia with its many views delighted Zsuzsa. We talked all the way while driving. The Museum of the Native American (called "First Nation" in Canada) Art was a gem. Exceptionally well designed and displayed it became one of the most cherished memories of our trip. The Sopron memorials throughout UBC and the "Székely kapu" (Szekler Gate) carved by László Józsa in front of the Forestry building, then the Totem poles and "long house" of the First Nation along Marine Drive were close to where we used to live in Vancouver, B.C.

Zsuzsa signed many books after the Hungarian Mass at the "Our Lady of Hungary Church." Her talk was later at the Hungarian House.

In Portland, Tünde Balogh, who would become my successor for Portland and the Hungarian community, organized her talk. Professor Lajos Éltető, who was the founder and the soul of the Portland Hungarians, was present, Ágnes Kovács-Forgó, an artist and leader of the Hungarians, with her husband, and many more. Great success accompanied us everywhere. As we traveled together with my dear organizing friends, we had fun evenings with good food and drinks.

We organized several programs in Seattle. May 19th Zsuzsa talked to the HAAW. We organized a lecture at the University of Washington, where Zsuzsa, for the first time, delivered her lecture in English. What a glorious event that was! We were so happy she made it! Of course, champagne toasts followed at my home.

From Seattle she flew to Sacramento and San Francisco, where she had a presentation sponsored by Éva Voisin, my "Honorary Consul-twin" and the Woodland Priory, a Hungarian Benedictine School, with Father Maurus (Béla Németh) in charge. Los Angeles and San Diego came next. In Los Angeles Amb. Balázs Bokor, the Consul General, and Miklós Pereházy, President of the Hungarian House, organized her lecture. It was thanks to Miklós Pereházy's Interex Company that Zsuzsa's books arrived in time and safely.

All my contacts everywhere greeted her with love and great expectations. Success accompanied her everywhere.

Who was Dr. Zsuzsa Hantó? She had two PhDs in Sociology and in History. She was committed to uncovering the sins and the victims of Communism showing how the deportations punished not only the deported, but also the "rich" peasants, the "kulaks" because it was into their homes, barns, hen houses and pigsties where the deported people had to live. The Communists thereby have reached a double goal. Two of their population's "undesirables" were punished by the same law.

Dr. Hantó has written many books and over 100 articles about these topics both in Hungarian and in English. She did an enormous amount of research. She was the Dean of Research at the University in Szolnok, Professor at the University in Debrecen and the Szt. István university in Gödöllő. She was the Leader or Co-leader of 21 national and international projects for the Hungarian Academy of Sciences, the PHARE Program, USAID, the Smithsonian, to mention only a few. With her colleagues she produced an educational movie about agriculture after Socialism in Hungary in Hungarian and in English. She was now traveling around with her recent book *Banished Families,* which was warmly recommended by excellent reviews. The books were available right after the lecture.

In my Consular Column in the HIREK I wrote:

> Dr. Zsuzsa Hantó's book in English: *Banished Families* shows in a unique and easily readable form, that which today's youth – considering freedom a matter of fact – can not even imagine. The more important it is to read it and imagine the feeling. Close your eyes and imagine that the action films' most threatening monsters appear in front of you, shake you up from your sleep and let you know that right now, or maybe within 24 hours they will come to get you. You can take what you can carry. Whatever will remain in your home in the next 24 hours will belong to the family that

will get your home. Imagine what you will take. After a little while, when you decide what to take, think about who will come with you. Because it is possible that you will throw away even what you carry, in order to pick up, or support that person when they cannot keep up. This book has true stories, those of our relatives, friends, ancestors, described with scientific thoroughness. Each story is different, but to a certain extent they are all the same. And, if we do not want to relive history, then we have to read the story of the old, we have to learn that extreme left and extreme right both brought tragedy to our nation, therefore we have to avoid both in order to keep our freedom which we consider so much a matter of fact.

Dr. Zsuzsa Hantó is with Her Excellency Colleen Bell USA Ambassador to Hungary and Csaba Hende Hungarian Minister of Defense at an occasion of remembrance about Ferenc Koszorús, a well-known saver of the Budapest Hungarian Jewry. The event was organized by Zsuzsa.

Album

2000 – 2020

We both have Bocskais
Hungarian costumes,
cca 2000.

Re-visiting the border where we crossed in 1956, with daughter Ilike, and
granddaughters Anna and Gennie, 2001.

MTA member diploma. Apu Dr. John F. Szablya, 2002.

A MAGYAR
TUDOMÁNYOS AKADÉMIA
168. közgyűlése
megállapítja, hogy

Szablya János
akit
a villamos gépek és hálózatok
terén kifejtett munkássága
elismeréséül
KÜLSŐ TAGGÁ
választott,
az akadémiai tagságából eredő,
az akadémia alapszabályaiban
megfogalmazott jogokkal
és kötelezettségekkel
rendelkezik

Budapest, 2001. május 7.

FŐTITKÁR

ELNÖK

Ilike's 50th birthday dancing with her father, 2003.

Best friends, grandfather John Szablya and grandson John McKay enjoying their beloved train store. in Kirkland, WA. 2002.

John and I with Dr. Mihály Czenner who married us on June 12,1951, and recreated the ceremony in 2001.

Our 50th wedding anniversary in son Steve and wife Kristy's backyard, Seattle, 2001.

Our 50th wedding anniversay in Hungary with daughter Ilike and grandchildren Anna and Gennie, 2001.

President of Hungary Ferenc Mádl, with Helen, John, and granddaughter Mary Szablya. World Conference of Honorary Consuls, 2003.

Madeleine Albright book signing at Microsoft, 2003.

Family photo taken at our 80th and 70th birthday celebration. All direct descendants and spouses, 2004.

Apu, son Janos and Teddy, January 11, 2005.

Dinner at Governor Christine Gregoire's mansion with Consular Corps. Chris and Mike with Helen and John. Last official event John attended, July 19, 2005.

Jake Hardy and Steve Muchlinsky handing the plaque of the WSU Szablya Scholarship Fund they established to honor their beloved professor, John, 2005.

We receive the Hungarian Presidential order of Merit five days before John's death, 2005.

Taiwan Economic and Cultural Office (TECO) reception with Director General and his wife, 2006 or 2007.

Anna Meiners, oldest granddaughter, and Fred Pompermeyer Morini's wedding. All family showed up, June 25, 2006.

The Julien family. Pat, Ken, Steve, Philip, Angelique, Kaylan, Nathaniel, 2010.

Family reunion with Mungs in California, 2011.

Dr. Zsuzsa Hanto, center, talks to audience. Vancouver, BC, 2012.

Istvan Seregely, the excellent film producer who made all the YouTube videos on our tours of Hungary, cca 2013.

Ambassador of Hungary to USA George Szapáry's visit in Seattle, with Helen Hon. Consul General of Hungary, cca 2014.

Son Steve with waterwheel on river in Africa. KWHs for Humanity, 2013.

All grandchildren by birth order, 2014.

The most remarkable sunset showing us God's and our spouses John and Navaal's presence while talking about them at my 80th birthday in daughter Alex's backyard, 2014.

In Search of Meaning, Seattle University. Helen signing books, 2015.

Book week. Kairosz publisher's tent with classmate Aratóné, Erika Schmidt, 2016.

*Cegléd signing books
with translator
Attila Jeney, 2016.*

Daughter Rita Pool's family at granddaughter Krystal and Dr. John Bass's wedding. Aaron Pool grandson and wife Amy, April 25, 2015.

Consular Christmas party with Lt. Governor Brad and Linda Owen, Seattle, 2016.

My Only Choice: Hungary
1942 - 1956 *was published
in Hungarian, 2016.*

With Judith Kallo and Mária Kramár, partners in organizing many events, cca 2017.

Steve Hawking and Niki with her kids. Niki's company
Blue Danube Productions produced the event for the scientist, 2018.

Niki's family – Niki, John and Michelle McKay, 2019.

77

Every year, since we had left our homeland, we wrote a Xmas letter to our family and best friends to keep in touch. I ask you now, dear Readers to become one of those best friends and get our latest news through our newsletters.

In 2012 my Christmas letter found me bursting with good news:

 *2012*

Blessed Holidays and a happy New Year!

I am bursting with my good news, so I have to tell it to you first. For many years, when telling parts of our lives' story, we were urged to write a book. So I did! My book will be available in about a month's time anywhere in the world where there is amazon.com, also in Kindle form. You will be able to order it in any bookstore, as it will come up under "books in print."

Anne Applebaum, Pulitzer Prize winning author of *Gulag*, most recent book: *Iron Curtain The Crushing of Eastern Eurrope 1944 -1956* wrote this for the cover of my new book, *My Only Choice:* "Helen Szablya's story will shed light on a dramatic era in European history, one which Americans hardly know and will find fascinating to discover."

This is what Hungary was like between 1942 and 1956 as I have lived it. I am not a history professor and was born only in 1934, but with my John, who was 10 years older than me, we remembered many things starting with 1930; as a matter of fact, even before that. I often quote my father-in-law who had read newspapers since 1887. World history played a big role in our lives. I can remember with what excitement I listened to the BBC news and Moscow's broadcast at age nine. We sat biting our nails beside the radio to find out who won the elections in the United States when I was eleven.

If you live in the Seattle area, I will be talking and signing books at the Kirkland Parkplace Bookstore (Kirkland Community Bookstore) on March 10, at 2 PM. The Hungarian American Association of WA will co-sponsor the event with the bookstore and organize a program of music and dancing.

Please, if there is a possibility organize a talk and book signing in your hometown or neighborhood. I am planning a tour of the USA and Canada to travel to the places that invite me. THANK YOU FOR YOUR HELP!

In 2012 Bartók's Blue Beard's Castle was performed by the Seattle Symphony with glass scenery by Chihuly, the great glass artist. I did something I never expected to do in my life: I performed with the Seattle Symphony. I was the Hungarian Narrator in Bluebeard's Castle.

A magnificent performance! The symphonic orchestra was sitting on stage in the background. The glass scenery was in front of them and the singers in full costume. I have never seen a performance like that of the Bluebeard's Castle. A champagne reception followed, where Dale Chihuly, his wife, and Charles Simonyi, who was the donor for the performance, happily toasted those behind the scene. Among others, son Steve and his daughter Maria came to the performance just to listen to me, then they were going to leave. They couldn't. They were mesmerized by the performance.

Two lovely weddings and two engagements in the family completed this marvelous year.

Anyu/Nagymama/Dédmama/Helen/Ili

First marriage of the year, Mary Szablya (Louis' youngest) and Jeff Gleason, in Denver, CO, on July 14, 2012

Second wedding of the year, Alex Meiners (Helen's son) and Kim Bubar, married in Pasadena, CA, September 29, 2012

First engagement of the year, Genevieve Szablya (Janos' oldest) and Amin Tehrani, in New York, on Christmas Day, 2011. Wedding date: February 16, 2013.

Second engagement of the year, Aaron Pool (Rita's son) and Amy Martell, celebrated in Kennewick, WA, on September 15, 2012. Wedding date: August 3, 2013.

2013

Dear Family and Friends,

Blessed Holidays and a Happy New Year! I hope you are well and enjoying life.

Our year was eventful, to say the least. February 16th was the first family wedding of the year when Gennie Szablya (son Janos' daughter) and Amin Tehrani were wed in New York; and the second wedding was on August 3rd when Amy Martell and Aaron Pool (daughter Rita's son) were wed in Kennewick, WA. Both were beautiful, as you can see in the photos.

Also this year, Amy and Aaron graduated from Washington State University (WSU); and John McKay (daughter Niki's son) graduated from high school and started WSU. Daughter Alexandra (aka Sandy) graduated from Seattle University with an MA in clinical psychology and is starting her own practice.

On November 13th great-granddaughter Lucy Bee Szablya (son Janos' granddaughter) was born and joined his brother Janos Szablya V, aka Miles. On November 17th Krystal Pool (Rita's daughter) and John Bass announced their engagement. I meant what I said that this was an eventful year!

On March 10th my most recent book, *My Only Choice: Hungary 1942-1956,* was launched with great success. Twice as many people came to the Seattle book launch and reception than we had anticipated. The bookstore Kirkland Parkplace Bookstore, the Hungarian American Association and the Seattle-Pécs Sister City Association brought excellent food and supplied great publicity. Thanks to everyone for your support!

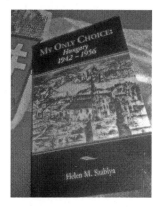

I had many book presentations in Seattle, Ellensburg, Portland, Cleveland, Baltimore and the Hungarian Embassy in Washington, DC. Thanks to everyone who helped!

In September I was in Hungary for the Fifth World Conference of Hungarian Honorary Consuls. I had three book presentations in Hungary fabulously organized by Dr. Zsuzsa Hantó. Her book, *Haramiák és Emberek,* which included the story of our wedding in 1951, was also presented.

I visited the American International School at the invitation of their teacher, Piroska Nagy, because the sixth graders were reading my book, *The Fall of the Red Star.* I was also interviewed three times for radio programs (Kossuth Rádio, Judit Cservenka, and Jeney Attila) as well as one interview with Károly Sziki for the Toronto Hungarian TV.

The best part of the visit was that Dr. Zsuzsa Hantó organized a surprise birthday party for me as I was in Budapest for my 79th birthday. I was also there for my high school (Sophianum) class reunion. A big THANK YOU to everyone who made my stay so fabulous!

Attached I am sending you an ad that I placed in the HIREK, our Seattle Hungarian-American bilingual newsletter featuring all my books and book translations presently available at: www.helenmszablya.com

Visit me on Facebook: www.facebook.com/helen.m.szablya?fref=ts or visit My Only Choice: www.facebook.com/groups/myonlychoice

I wish you all the very best from the bottom of my heart.

Anyu/Nagymama/Dédmama/Helen/Ili

2014

This photo was taken in daughter Alexandra's garden where my 80th birthday celebration was held on August 2nd. The seven children organized the event. All their families and spouses, including 16 grandchildren, three great-grandchildren and two more on the way were there. My actual birthday is September 6th, however, in order to accommodate work and school schedules, summer vacation was the perfect time to get together!

I have already written about the fabulous party organized by my children, the singing, the toasts, the jokes, the many happy memories, so on to next year's Christmas letter.

2015

My Dear Family and Friends, December 15, 2015

We, all the 42 of us Szablyas (by blood or marriage), wish all of you a very merry Christmas and a happy New Year, as well as wonderful all other holidays that fall into this season.

My latest book, *My Only Choice: Hungary 1942-1956* will be published in Hungarian, translated by Attila Jeney, a great literary translator, in the spring in Hungary. I chose to continue writing our story instead of translating the book myself. Even the Hungarian friends encouraged me to continue rather than translate. I am looking forward to the launch.

My youngest and oldest great-grandchildren out of the six. Calvin Tehrani born July 26, 2015, son of Gennie Szablya and Amin Tehrani.

Ava Dora Morini, daughter of Anna Meiners and Fred Pompermeyer Morini, born May 31, 2008, flower girl at Krystal Pool (granddaughter) and Dr. John Bass, Army Captain's wedding.

John and Krystal, the happy couple. Their wedding was in Spokane, WA on April 25, 2015. They now live in Tacoma, very close to Seattle. The last photo is of the happy parents of Krystal: Rita Szablya and Karl Pool. Both their kids and spouses graduated and happily married.

With love,

Anyu/Nagymama/Dédmama/Helen/Ili

2016

Dear Family and Friends!

Most of the direct family gathered in Seattle to commemorate the 60th anniversary of the 1956 Hungarian Uprising against the Soviets. THANK YOU ALL FOR COMING! Such a great joy to be with all of you for this memorable event! On October 22, 2016 we gathered at St. James Cathedral where our family photo was taken. The commemoration began with a Mass at St. James Cathedral in Seattle, continued with a program and reception. The Lt. Governor, Brad Owen and his wife Linda, as well as many consuls representing other countries attended. I introduced the program. My successor, The Honorable Katalin Pearman, who took over from me in three beautiful events on October 2, 13th and 22nd, finished it. This made me – after 23 fruitful years – Hon. Consul General Emerita of Hungary.

Granddaughter, Shivana, standing beside me in the photo, graduated from high school this year and is attending the University of Washington! And, granddaughter, Maria Szablya, (parents Kristy and Steve Szablya) and

Bernie Rivas announced their upcoming marriage to take place in Mexico City on May 13, 2017!

On May 19, 2016, the Hungarian version of my book, *My Only Choice: Hungary 1942-1956 – Vasfüggöny kölnivel...Magyarország 1942-1956* – was launched in Budapest. The book launch took place at the Vigadó, a most distinguished Concert Hall. The Book Launch was opened by Dr. Anikó Lévai, wife of Prime Minister Viktor Orbán, who talked about our long-lived friendship. Almost 200 people came to the launch (standing room only) and the books quickly sold out.

The entire Hungarian program was organized by my great friend, Professor Dr. Zsuzsa Hantó and the excellent translator of my work, and good friend Attila Jeney. It was a wonderful, glorious trip. My friends' love made it so.

I would like to start with a humongous thank you to all my helpers, without whom I could not have accomplished this beautiful adventure. Many of my family members: Michelle, Marcey, Helen and Maria from Toronto all came to make it easy for me.

The second event was at Litea, a well-respected bookstore on Castle Hill, filmed by Duna TV and recorded by Kossuth radio (again, standing room only). During my month-long stay beginning May 16th I was interviewed numerous times by TV, radio and print media. DUNA WORLD aired the presentation.

In spite of pouring rain, the room in Cegléd for the third presentation, opening the local start of the Book Week, was packed. Most significant was that the Cultural Center in which this occurred was built by my grandfather as a gift to the community and is still going strong! The title of the talk: "In America I dreamt of Cegléd!" Thank you my daughter Helen/Ilike, for doing a great job posting everything immediately on Facebook and taking many photos!

On June 9, I had the opportunity to speak in the Budapest Parliament at the 65th anniversary conference of the Communist Deportations. The conference was organized by Dr. Zsuzsa Hantó and Mária Törley. This conference gave voice to the survivors of deportations themselves and I addressed how it was possible for some to escape these horrible deportations.

Seattle-Pécs are sister cities, so the next event took place in Pécs, where the Mayor, Dr. Zsolt Páva, (also an old friend), handed me a special flag of the Uprising, with the hole in the middle, to popularize the 60th anniversary of the Hungarian Revolution abroad.

On the last day, June 10, I was featured at Budapest Book Week on Vörösmarthy tér. The allotted time for my book-signing was 5-6PM, but at 6:30PM people were still standing in line to buy their books and have them signed! According to the publisher, Kairosz, "Vasfüggöny kölnivel" was their firm's best-selling book at the 2016 Book Week!

I lived to see older people appreciating reading the truth about our past, and younger people learning what the past was like – which was not at all taught by the communists – they only propagated lies.

What a glorious way to end my career as Hon. Consul General of Hungary, after 23 years of spiritually very rewarding work. I love helping people!

NOW! I am continuing to write the book about our adventures after having stepped across the border, and into Freedom! In Hungary people told me they cannot wait, I should immediately start sending what I have and Attila is eager to start translating it.

THANK YOU ALL FOR YOUR WONDERFUL HELP AND FOR EVERYTHING YOU CONTRIBUTED TO THIS GREAT SUCCESS AND HAPPINESS!

Anyu/Nagymama/Dédmama/Helen/Ili

2017

Big event of the year! Granddaughter Maria Szablya and Bernie Rivas were married on May 13th with 27 of 43 family members, including parents Steve and Kristy, celebrated with them in Mexico City.

The Los Angeles Consulate General of Hungary and The United Hungarian House organized a lovely event featuring the Hungarian version of my book: *Vasfüggöny Kölnivel... Magyarország 1942-1956*, while promoting its original, English version:

My Only Choice: Hungary 1942-1956. Thank you to Tamás Széles Consul General of Hungary, Miklós Pereházy, President of the Hungarian house and his excellent helper Csilla Székely for a flawless evening. Thank you to Helen and Chuck, their children, and grandchildren in L.A. who helped make my trip such a joy and success.

The Morini Family: oldest grandchild Anna, Fred and great granddaughter Ava are expecting a new arrival any day! Fred is an amazing photographer as you can see. Before I sent my letter, Ella Grace was born on December 7th.

The Tehrani Family: granddaughter Gennie, Amin and big brother Calvin expect their second in May.

I could write volumes about the many activities of my wonderful, growing family, all of whom I love dearly...but I will stop with these highlights!

I wish you all the very best with all my love,

Anyu/Nagymama/Dédmama/Helen/Ili

2018

Dear Family and Friends,

Happy Holidays and may God bless you abundantly!

As is my custom, I would like to bring you up to date on our latest news:

Edith Billie Meiners, August 5, 2018 · Darius Ward Tehrani, April 4, 2018 · Ella Grace Morini, Dec.7, 2017

These three are the newest great-grandchildren! The 10th is expected to arrive in February to parents Maria & Bernie.

Although I was unable to attend, both of the Hungarian versions of my books, *The Fall of the Red Star* and *My Only Choice: Hungary 1942-1956* were released in second runs with huge success!

In the meantime, I am writing the continuation of my life's story – what it was like to experience life as a refugee and an immigrant – and the culture shock that all immigrants experience.

Niki's two children, John and Michelle McKay, both graduated from WSU in 2018. John majored in Mechanical Engineering and is now commissioned as a Naval Officer and stationed in Norfolk, VA. Michelle majored in Psychology with the goal of becoming a mediator. I was delighted to be a part of their celebrations.

Niki (Szablya) McKay, was the first person inducted into the Hall of Influencers by Northwest Magazine. Blue Danube Productions, her production company has already won "Best of the Northwest" every year for the past 12 years.

A lovely surprise, Louis is working at Grant County PUD and Steve Szablya at Schweitzer Engineering Labs in Pullman – both have new jobs in Eastern Washington – it enabled me to visit Pullman for the first time in 20 years and have a book signing!

In June, I visited my Los Angeles family and we celebrated together at Alex and Kim's new home in Burbank with a great barbeque. We had a wonderful time! All of daughter Helen's family was there together. I left it for last because one week later Chuck, Helen's wonderful husband, beloved by all of us, died from a massive stroke at age 71.

From July to October, Helen traveled to all the cities where they had lived and loved together. Hundreds of people took part in seven separate events.

Wishing you all a wonderful and prosperous 2019 with lots of love!

Anyu/Nagymama/Dédmama/Helen/Ili and Family

2019

Dear Family and Friends, Kedves Család és Barátaink,

The happy newlyweds Alexandra Szablya and Vince McDonough August 14, 2019

Welcoming our two new darling step-grandchildren Barry and Darryln McDonough, pictured with Alex's two children Shivana and Rohan Ramdin.

Great-grandchild number 10: Audrey Maria Rivas born February 17, 2019, Parents: Maria Szablya and Bernardo Rivas, Maria is our son Steve and Kristy's daughter, first time grandparents.

The Hungarian version of my book *The Fall of the Red Star* had a second edition in Hungary recommended for schools.

The Hungarian version of *My Only Choice: Hungary 1942-1956* also had its second edition/ third printing this summer launched with a very successful program organized by my friend Dr. Zsuzsanna Hantó, excellent Hungarian historian/sociologist and Attila Jeney, the outstanding translator of the book. Maria Winters, a hero of 1956 and MP in Hungary also gave a talk at the launch.

We wish all of you Happy Holidays and a healthy and successful New Year! Love, Peace and Joy all around!

Anyu/Nagymama/Dédmama/Helen/Ili

2020

Dear Family and Friends,

We wish you all a merry Christmas, a happy New Year, and Happy Holidays! We thank God for being alive.

Son János and Lys Hornsby tied the knot on May 5, 2020. The COVID events of the year dictated to have a very private, small wedding. Party to follow in a time more appropriate for parties. They are both retired. Both have adult children, János has four grandchildren, whom Lys loves to spoil along with János. They live in Covington, WA, between Seattle and Tacoma.

Shivana Ramdin, our 15th grandchild

graduated from the University of Washington with a degree in Communications and is looking for a job. Rohan, her brother, our 16th and youngest grandchild graduated from Roosevelt High School and was admitted to the University of WA. During COVID time he has been busy making excellent Tik Tok videos and music, which he writes and performs as well.

Niki's company Blue Danube Productions and her team started a new software company called Galoo, LLC. Their product galoo-Spaces brings the physical space to the virtual world. Using bioptic scanned, real-world venues transferred to the online world with livestreaming and total social engagement support within the virtual venue – something that currently doesn't exist as an all-in-one solution. The more people who are seeing this incredible software, the more ideas come for how it can be used. I am so proud of her for creating a new path during this pandemic year.

The pandemic, as horrible it was, through its lockdown gave me enough time to finish the second volume of my autobiography. It will be published in Hungary in the spring and in the USA for October 23rd, the 65th anniversary of the Hungarian Uprising in 1956. Attila Jeney, the excellent translator simultaneously translated the book into Hungarian, while I was writing it. *From Refugee to Consul: An American Adventure* will be the title in English.

My family and I wish you all a much better 2021 with lots of love,

Anyu/Nagymama/Dédmama/Helen/Ili

78

As I no longer needed my second bedroom, which was my consular office, I moved to the apartment next door with just one bedroom. For writing it was just perfect. I could no longer accommodate my big table in my new place.

My Christmas present to my Family that year was the following letter:

My Dear Family, Children, Grandchildren, Spouses and Great-grandchildren, Sisters and their Families,

This Christmas I would like to do something innovative. I would like to give you something I created. And what do you think it is that I would do? Cook? Bake? Sew? Embroider? Knit? Crochet? Keep reading and you will find out!

Please, accept my gift to you with the love I wrote it. I am sending this to you with all my best wishes for Christmas and the New Year!

Thank you for loving me and for being YOU!

A FAREWELL TO THE "BIG TABLE"
A Memory and a Legacy

I looked out the window to see as the new owners took it to their car. Carefully, oh so carefully. They loved it and that was a good feeling that someone will cherish our "big table".

Our first apartment had a small kitchen table in Hungary. We ate at that table in two shifts. First our two children, then the parents. Only two could sit at the table.

After our escape from Hungary, we had a table, where, by then, all five of us could sit.

As our family grew, so did our tables.

By the time there were nine of us, we had the "big table." The bodies grew around the old table.

Yet, there was always place for someone's friend, or one of Daddy's students. Pullman was a small town, where Washington State University was located. In Pullman and the neighboring city, Moscow, ID there were all together 24 thousand students at the time, but hardly any had parents in these cities. Friendly professors' homes turned into second homes for these students. Our door was always open until 2 a.m.

And people gathered around the big table. We had many dinners around the good old relic. During Advent the children gathered around, lit the candles on the advent wreath and sang Christmas carols. They sang melody, harmony and counter-point. They made up their own parts.

That table saw many happy birthday parties and family friends.

When we were "only the family" any topic could be brought up at the "big table." Ideas flowed, brainstorming sessions broke out, jokes, fun, all happened around it. Everything was allowed for discussion when we were at the family table.

We always kept the "big table." We brought it with us to Seattle. We still were sitting all around it, whoever happened to be there from the family. There were always more and more of us.

Helen was the first to get married. All the others followed in due time.

Grandchildren came one after another. They too found their places at the family table. Somehow everyone made a place for the next generation.

We feasted our eyes on our growing family. What a beautiful feeling to see the happiness of the next generations.

Then, the grandchildren started to marry. By the time Anna, our oldest grandchild, got married Daddy was no longer physically sitting at the table, but his spirit held all of us in his embrace. His love blessed our "big table".

Along came the great-grandchildren, as the grandchildren started their own families. Whenever they were around, they too found themselves at the "big table."

The tradition continued. Everything could be discussed during our togetherness. We still loved the "big table" and sat around it. It became a concept, a symbol of our love for each other.

And now… the "big table" was gone.

No more family togetherness? No more "anything goes" between us?

My new home was too small for the "big table".

Will everything cease to be as it was?

Then emails started flying between the siblings and their children, copying me and all the others. Texting group conversations. The tone was the same. Just like around the "big table."

The children had their own "big tables" in their own homes by now, but between these big tables the "big table", the original one, turned virtual.

The problem of "anything goes" was solved because the tone, the fun, the jokes, the discussion all spoke THE LANGUAGE OF LOVE.

THANK YOU!

The Honorable Helen M. (Ilona) Szablya is the Honorary Consul General Emerita of Hungary for the States of Washington, Oregon, and Idaho, based in Seattle.

Born and raised in Budapest, Hungary, she is an award-winning author, columnist, translator, lecturer, and former publisher of *Hungary International*, a newsletter for Americans about business in Hungary. She has two university degrees, speaks six languages, and lived in five countries under seven different political systems. The number of her English language publications exceeds 700 articles and five books, many of which have won awards.

Helen was President of the Washington Press Association (WPA) and received its highest award, that of the "Communicator of Achievement." The National Federation of Press Women (NFPW) awarded her with a National First Prize for Editorials and the First Affiliate Presidents Award in 1988. Helen was project director and co-author of *Hungary Remembered*, an oral history drama/lecture series – a project commemorating the 30th anniversary of the Hungarian Uprising of 1956 (with a major grant from the Washington Commission for the Humanities). It was featured on world wide wire services in 42 languages. It won two international awards and the George Washington Honor Medal from the Freedoms Foundation. Helen was an "Inquiring Mind" lecturer for the Washington Commission for the Humanities about freedom related topics.

Her book *The Fall of the Red Star* is about an illegal boy scout troop during the 1956 uprising. It won first prizes from the WPA and the NFPW. The book, translated into Hungarian by Helen, was published by Holnap Kiadó under the title *A vörös csillag lehull*, with a grant from the Hungarian Ministry of National Heritage. The book is a recommended text for schools in Hungary and is used as a textbook in the International school there. Both versions were exhibited at the Frankfurt Book Fair, when Hungary was the honored guest.

Helen is listed with Marquis Who's Who in America and several other biographies.

Helen Szablya and her late husband, John, who was Professor Emeritus of Washington State University, Fellow of the Institute of Electrical and Electronics Engineers (IEEE), Registered Professional Engineer in seven states and two Canadian provinces, outside Member of the Hungarian Academy of Sciences, and author of over 140 technical publications, have been living in the Seattle WA area. The couple has presented many hundreds of lectures on Hungary. They coauthored papers in the areas of energy affecting human culture and on translating/interpreting. The Szablya's have seven children, 16 grandchildren and 10 great-grandchildren. The family was named "Hungarian Family of the Year" by the Hungarian Congress in 1981, in Cleveland, OH.

Five days before John's death the couple received the Order of Merit from the President of the Republic of Hungary for their lives' work, October 2005. In 2011, Helen was awarded the Spirit of Liberty Award from the Ethnic Heritage Council.

Made in the USA
Middletown, DE
01 February 2022